FLIGHT

VOLUME FOUR

Villard • New York

2007 Villard Books Trade Paperback Edition

Published in the United States by Villard Books, an imprint of The Random House Publishing Group, a division of Random House, Inc., New York.

VILLARD and "V" CIRCLED Design are registered trademarks of Random House, Inc.

ISBN 978-0-345-49040-7

Printed in the United States of America

www.villardbooks.com

1 2 3 4 5 6 7 8 9

Illustration on pages 2–3 by Reagan Lodge
Illustration on pages 4–5 by Chris Appelhans

Editor/Art Director: Kazu Kibuishi
Assistant Editors: Kean Soo and Phil Craven
Associate: Alfred Moscala
Our Editor at Villard: Chris Schluep

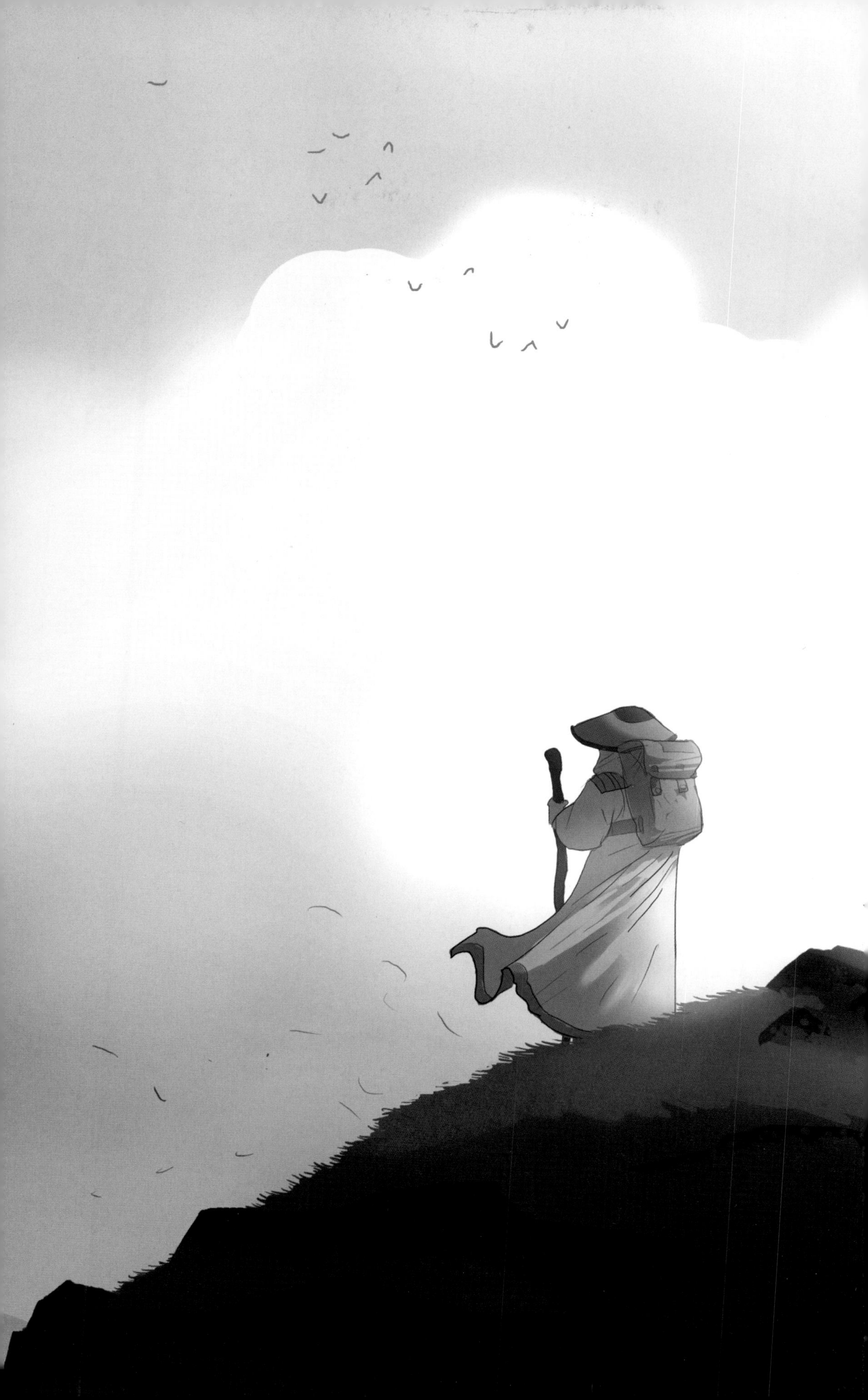

CONTENTS

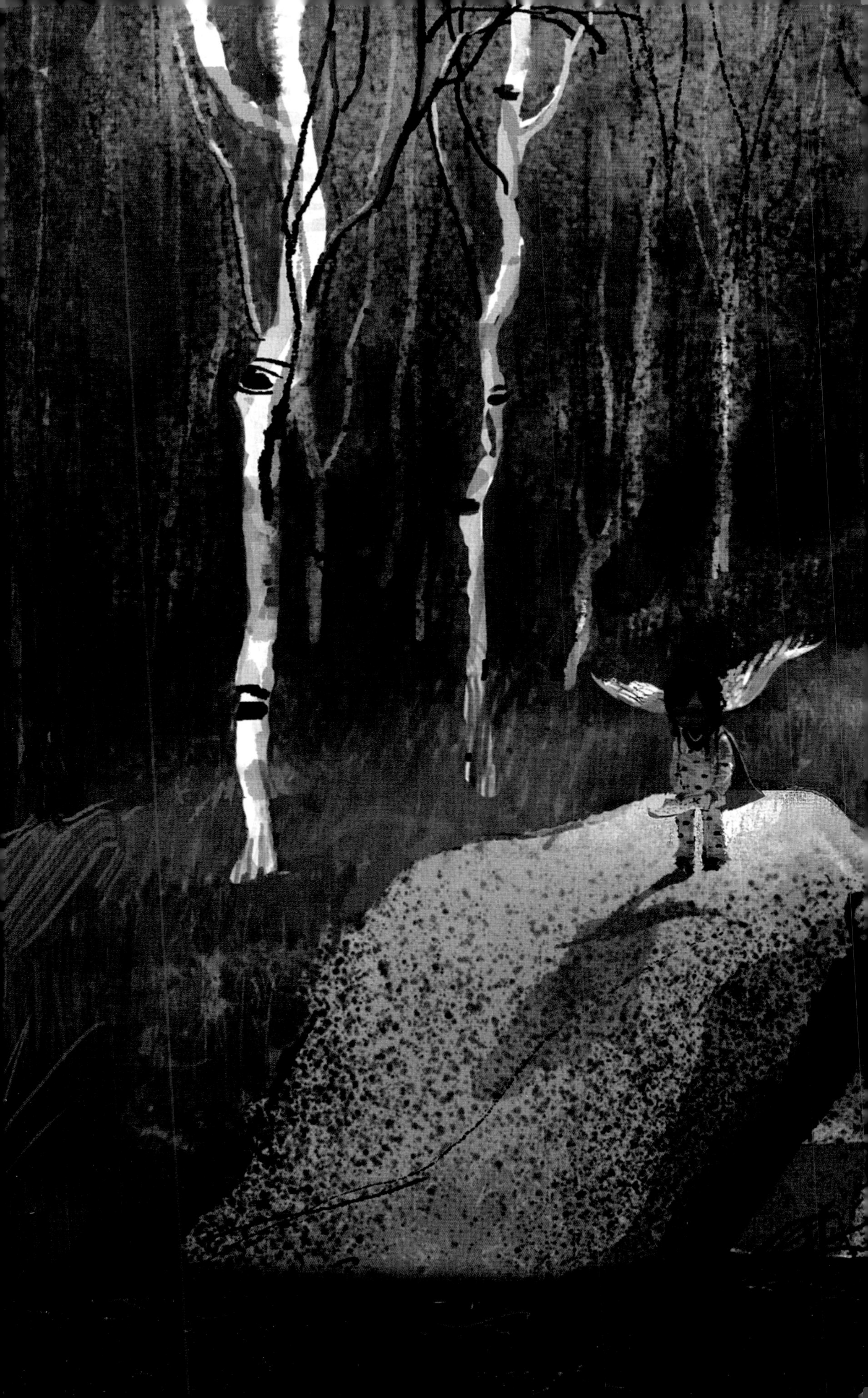

FLIGHT

VOLUME FOUR

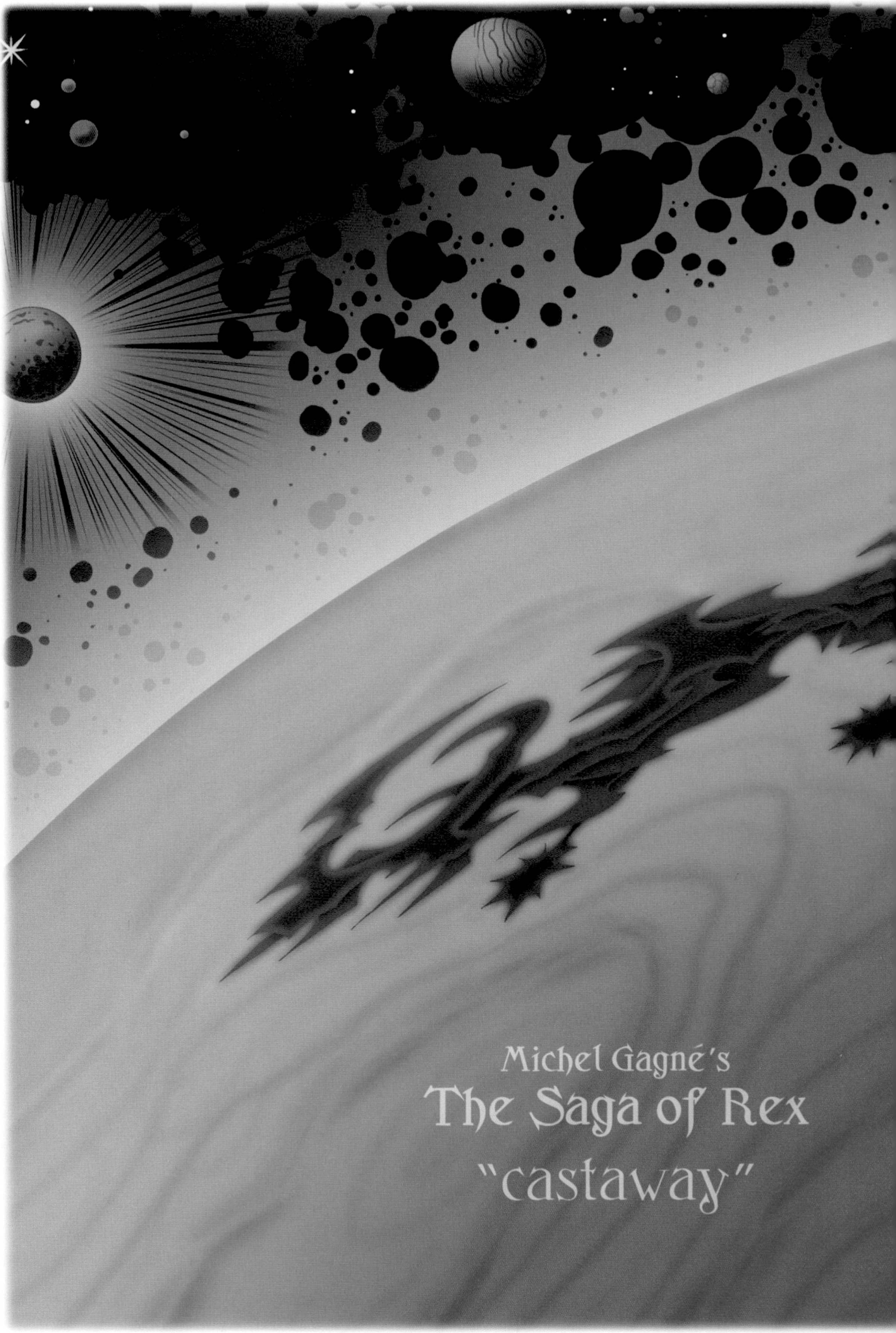
Michel Gagné's
The Saga of Rex
"castaway"

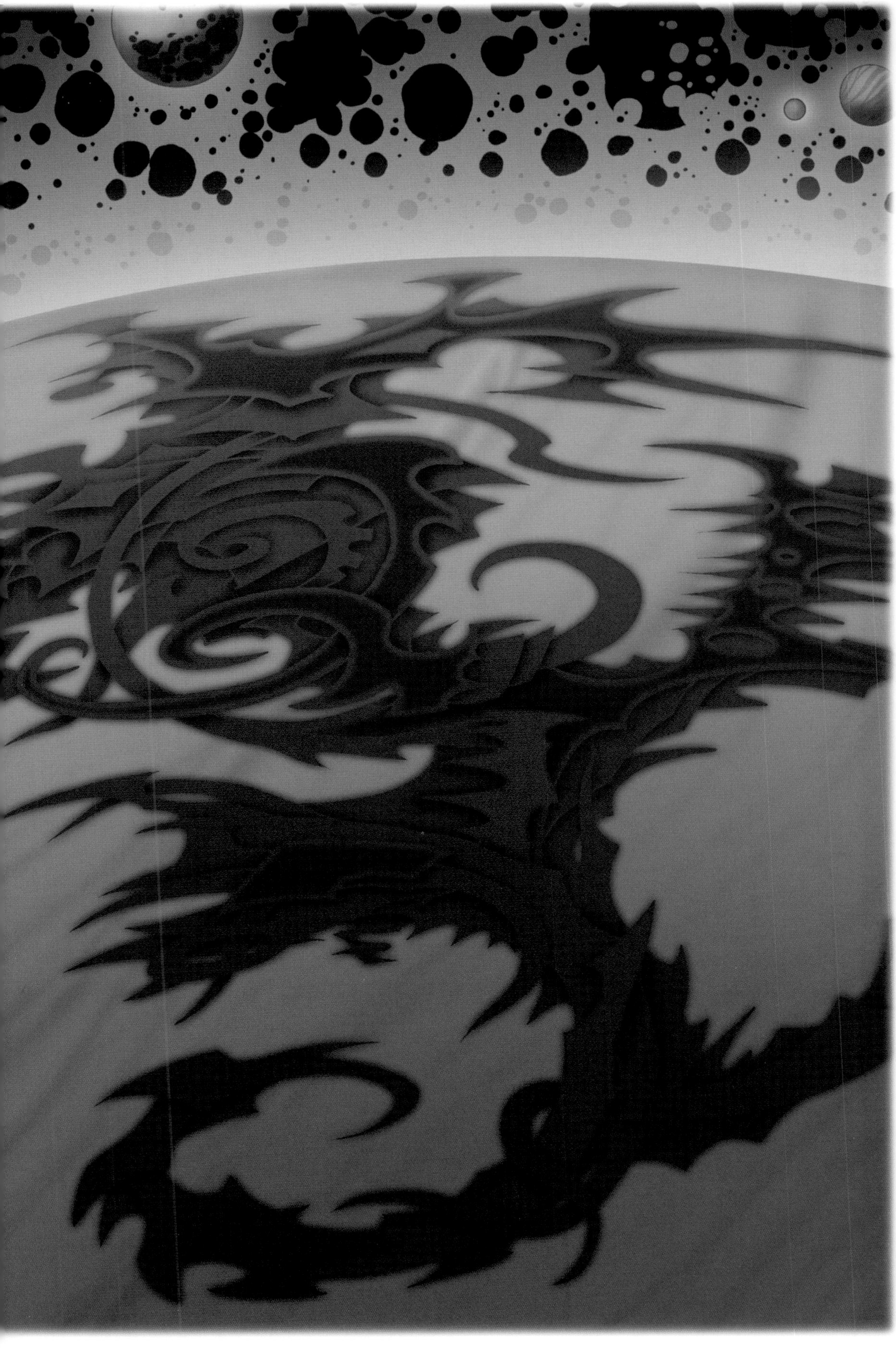

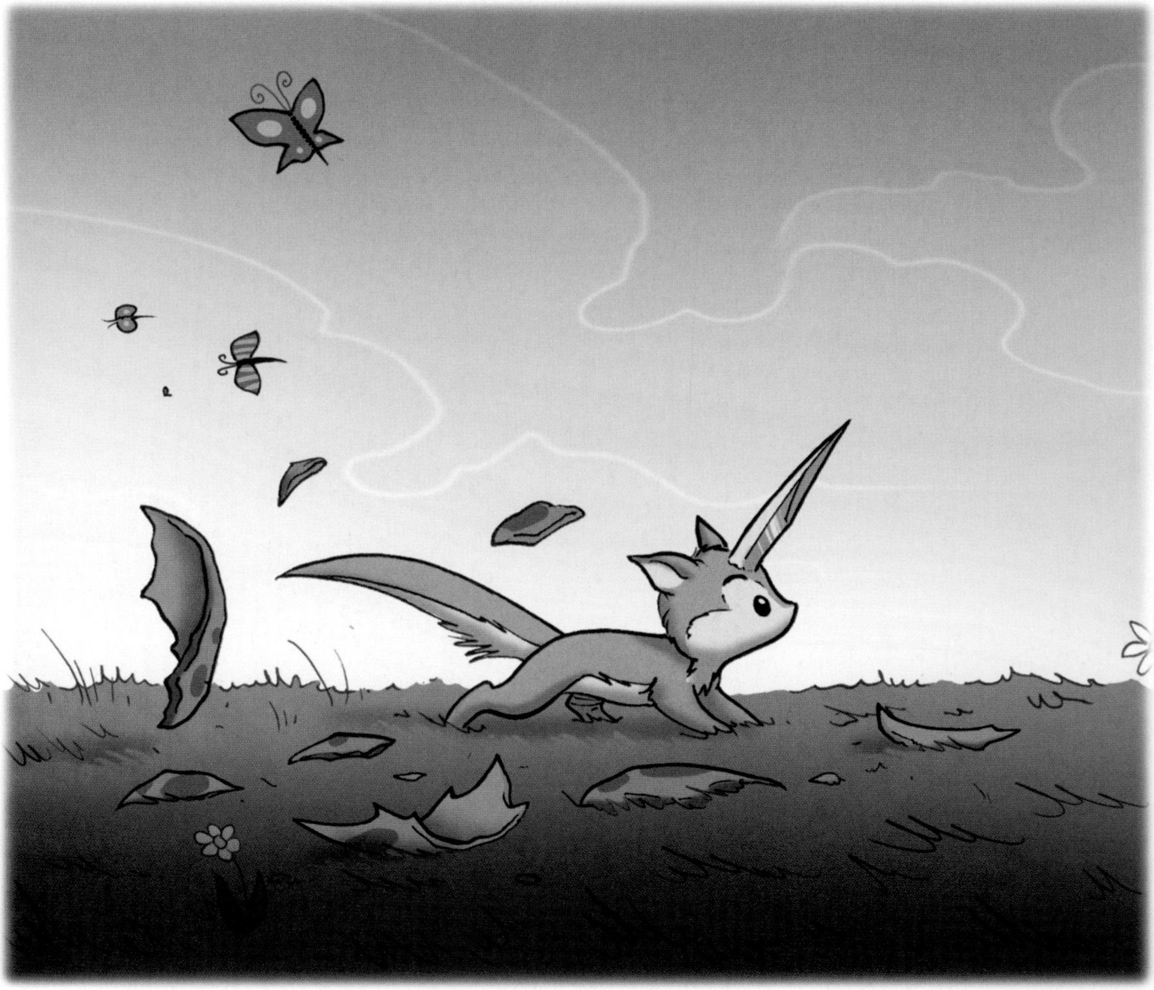

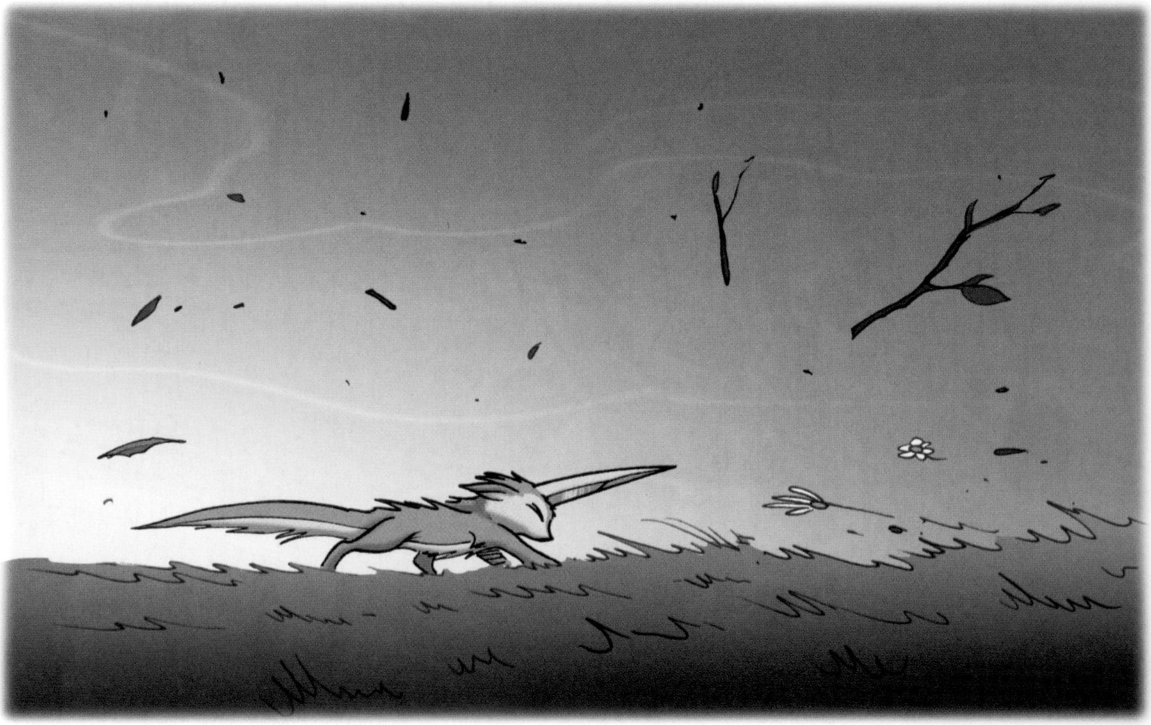

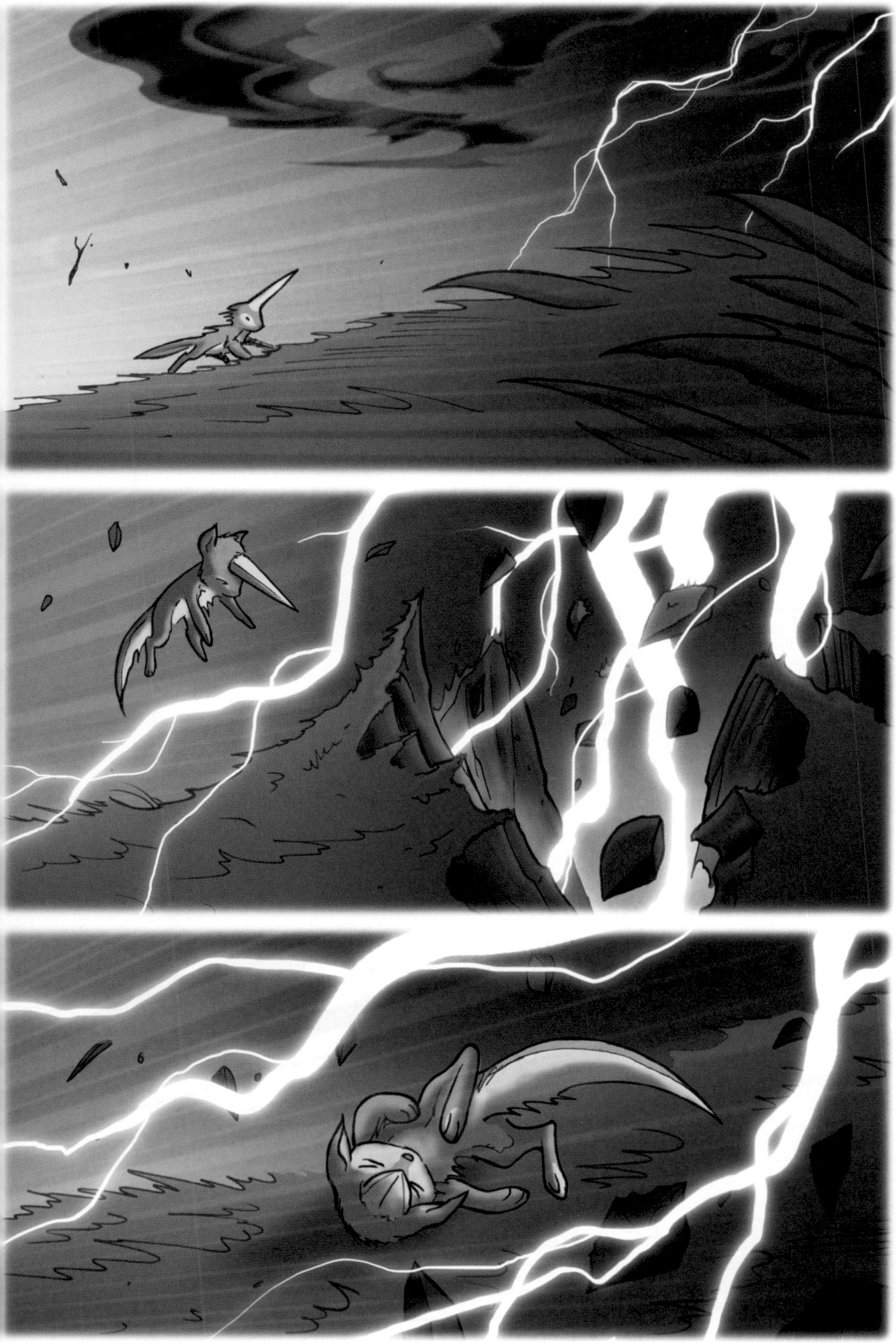

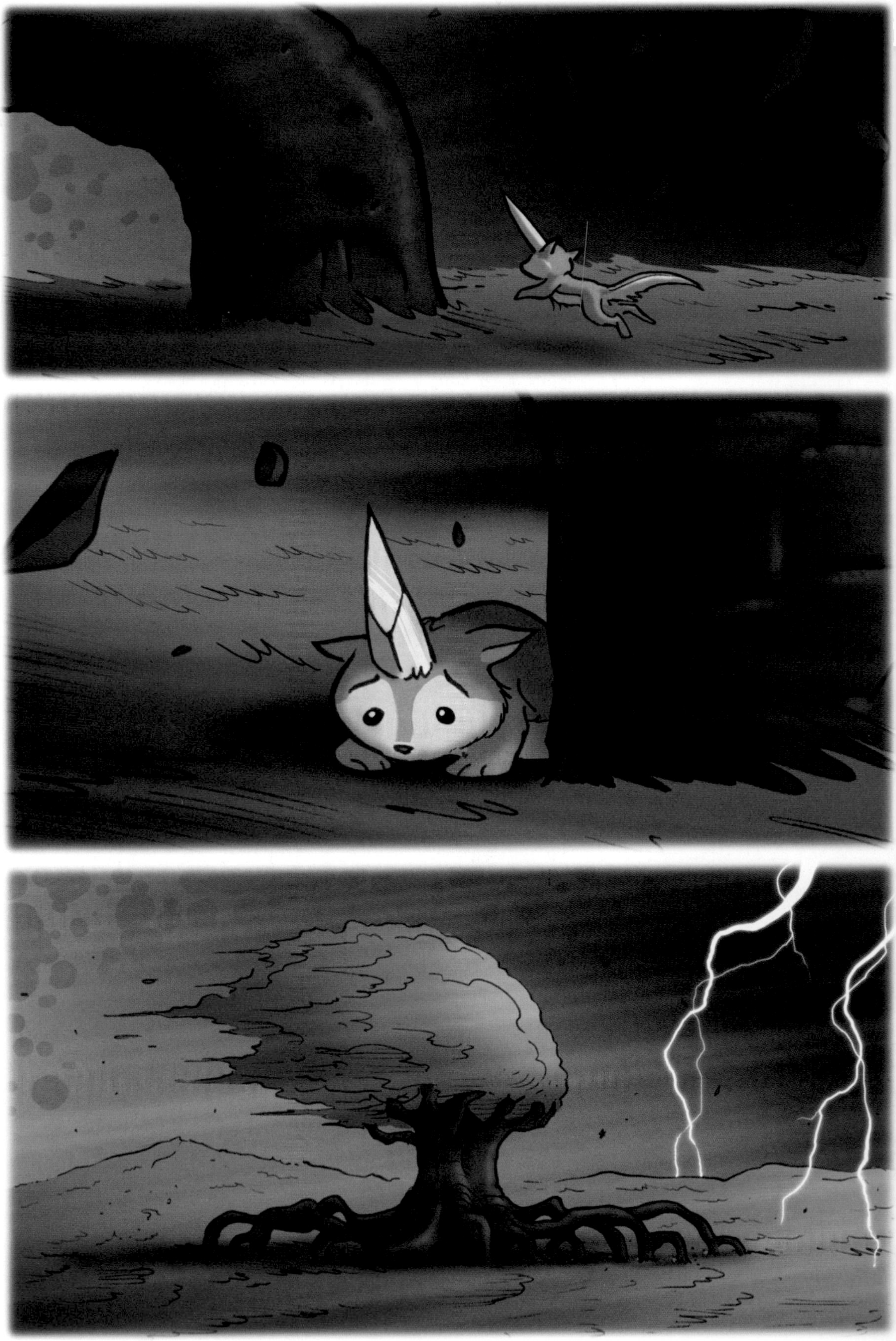

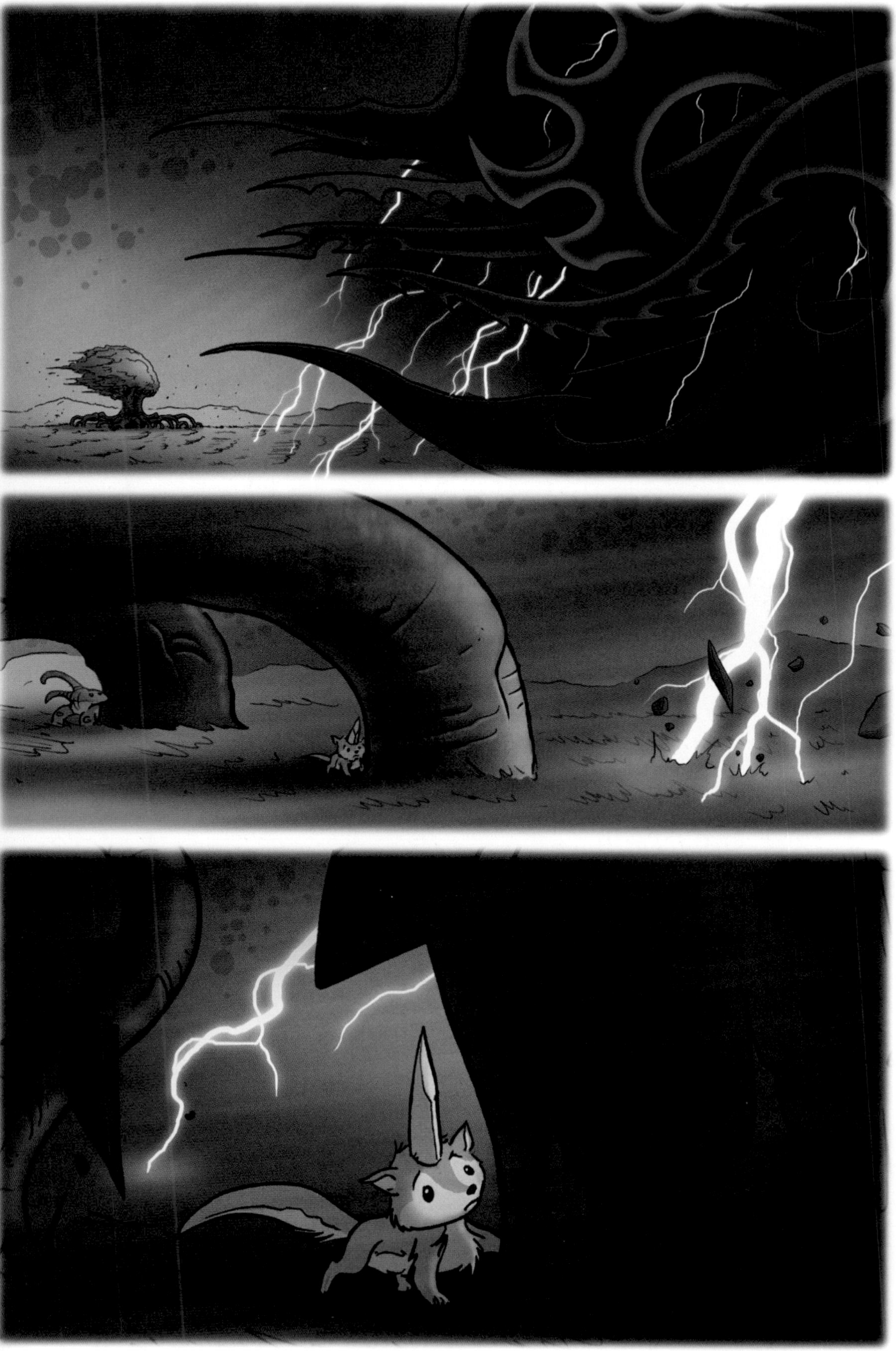

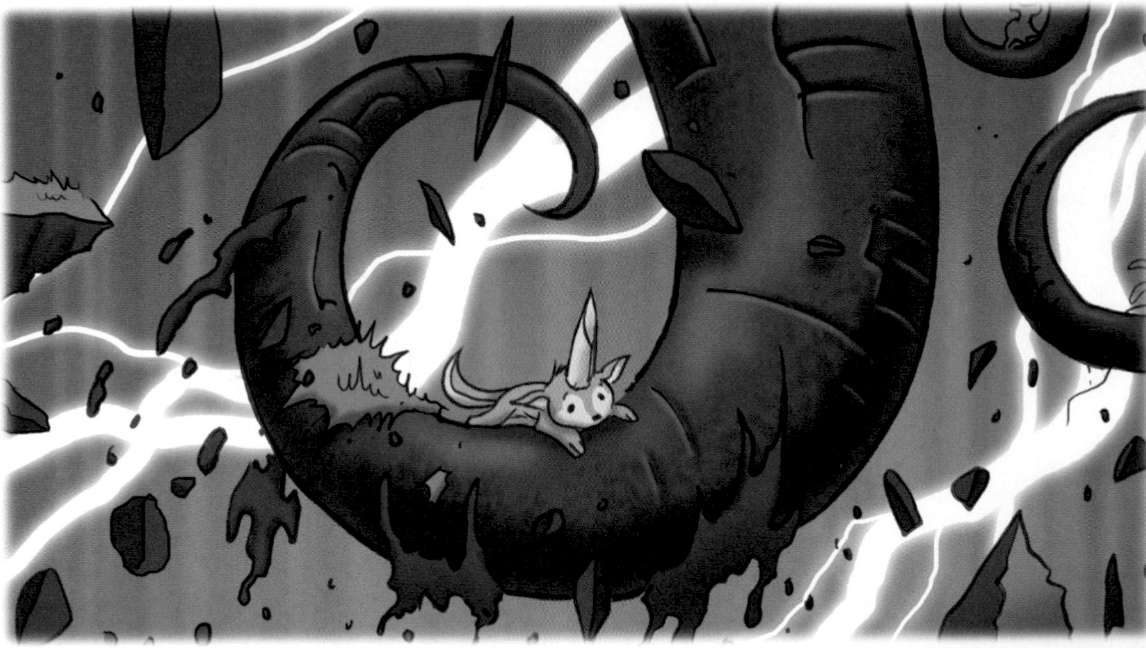

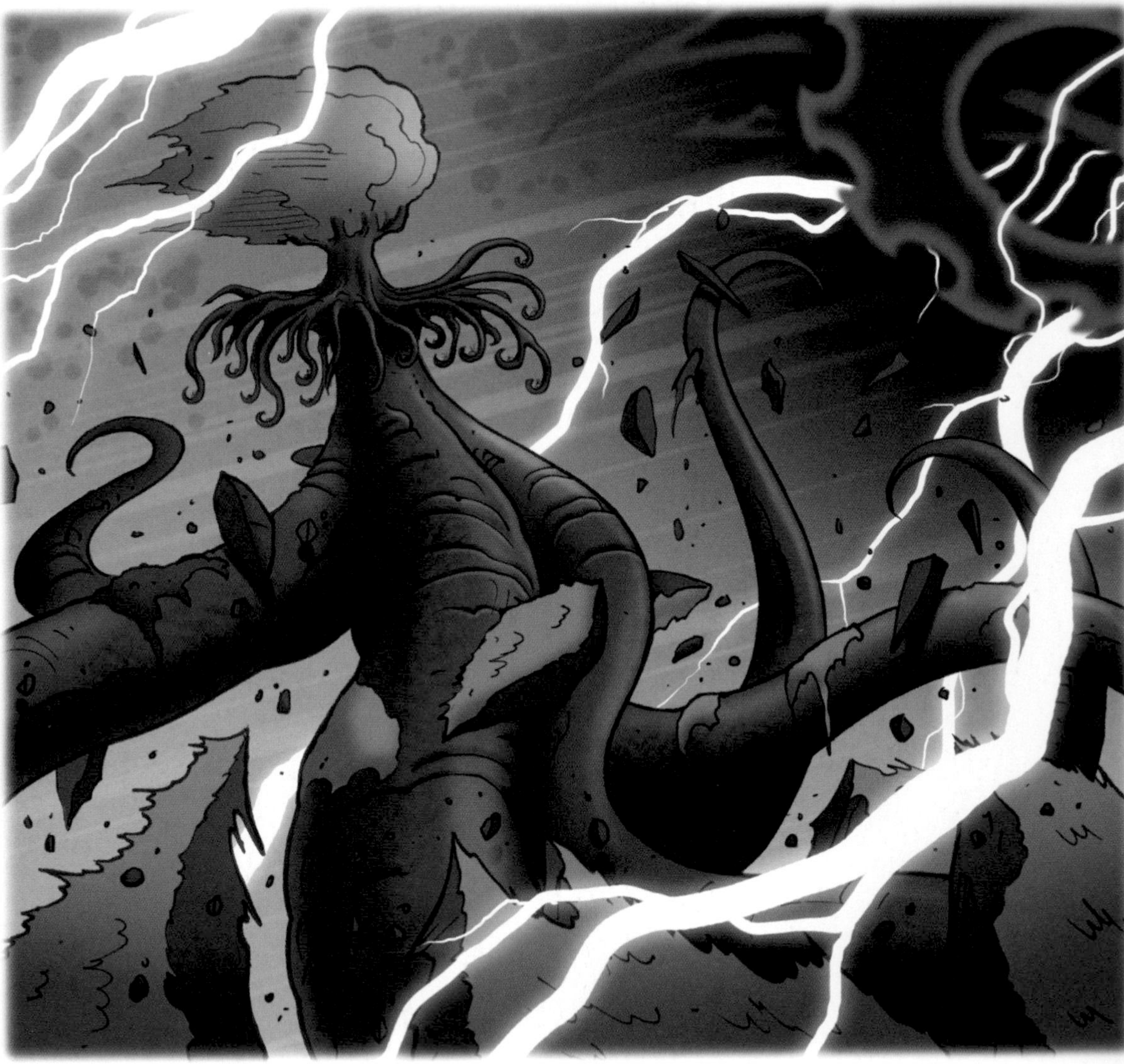

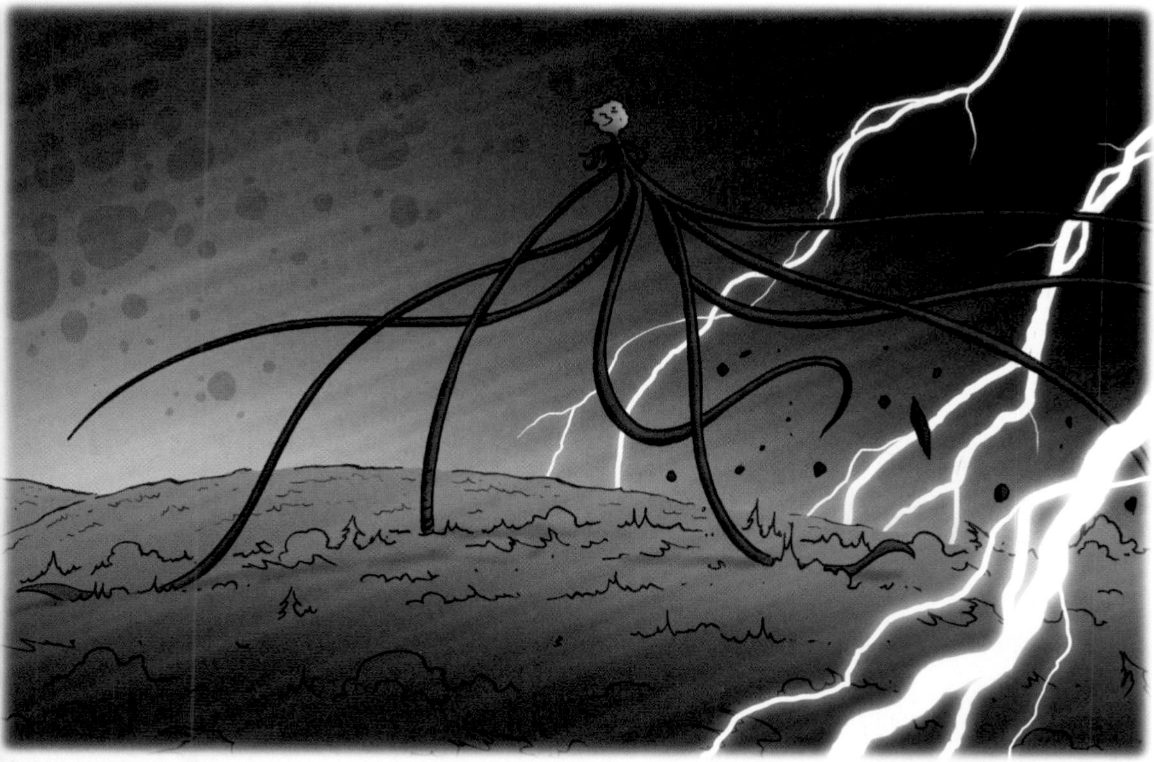

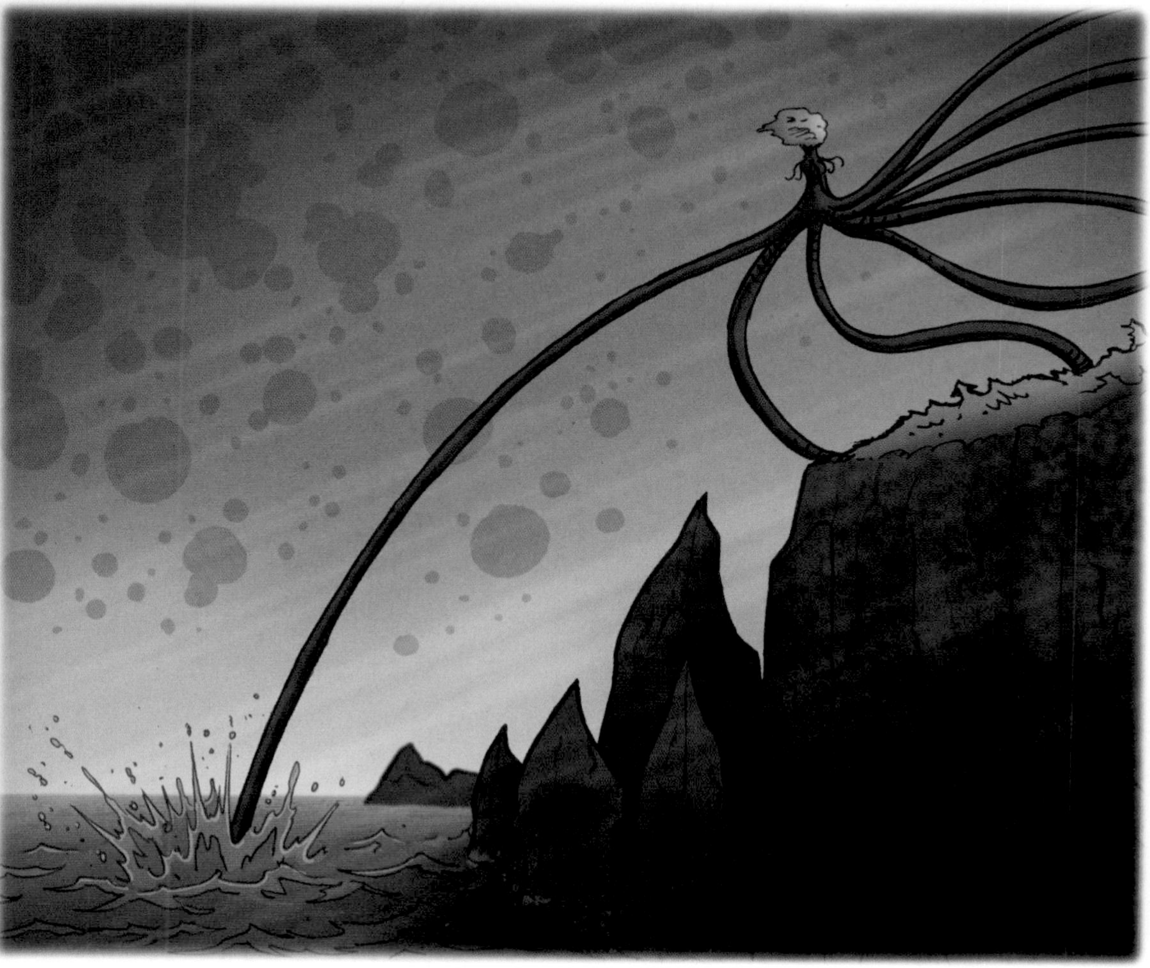

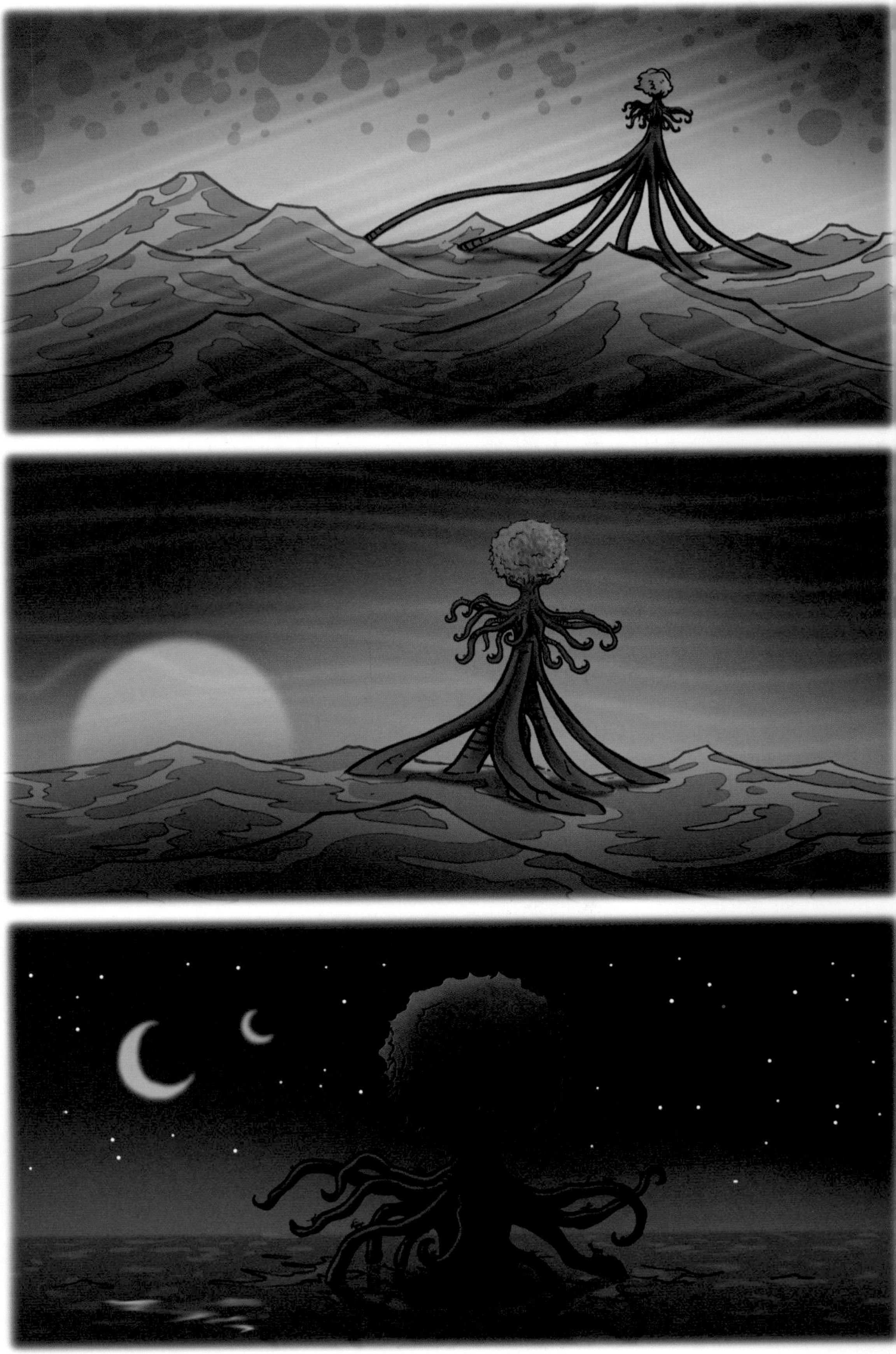

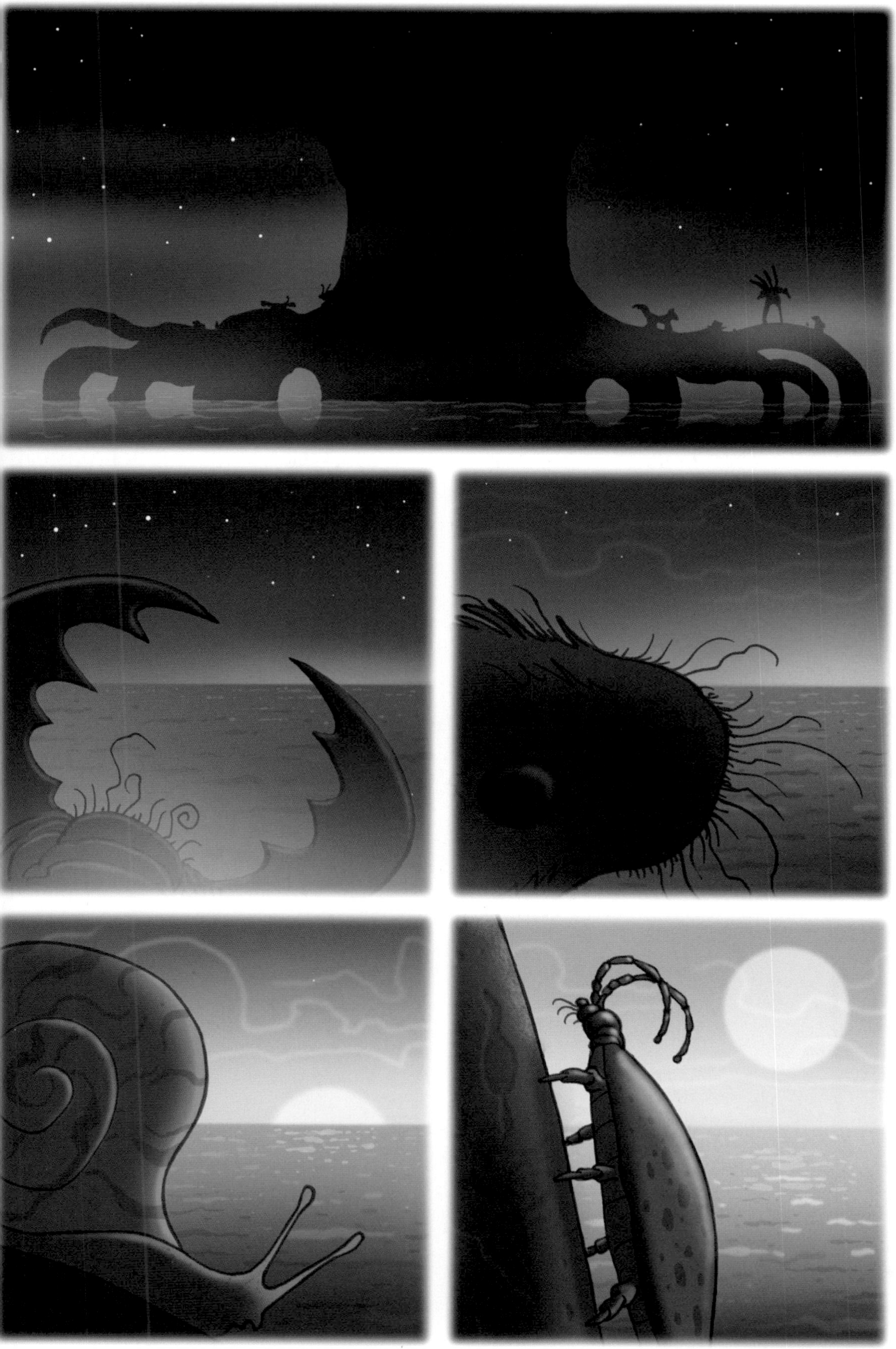

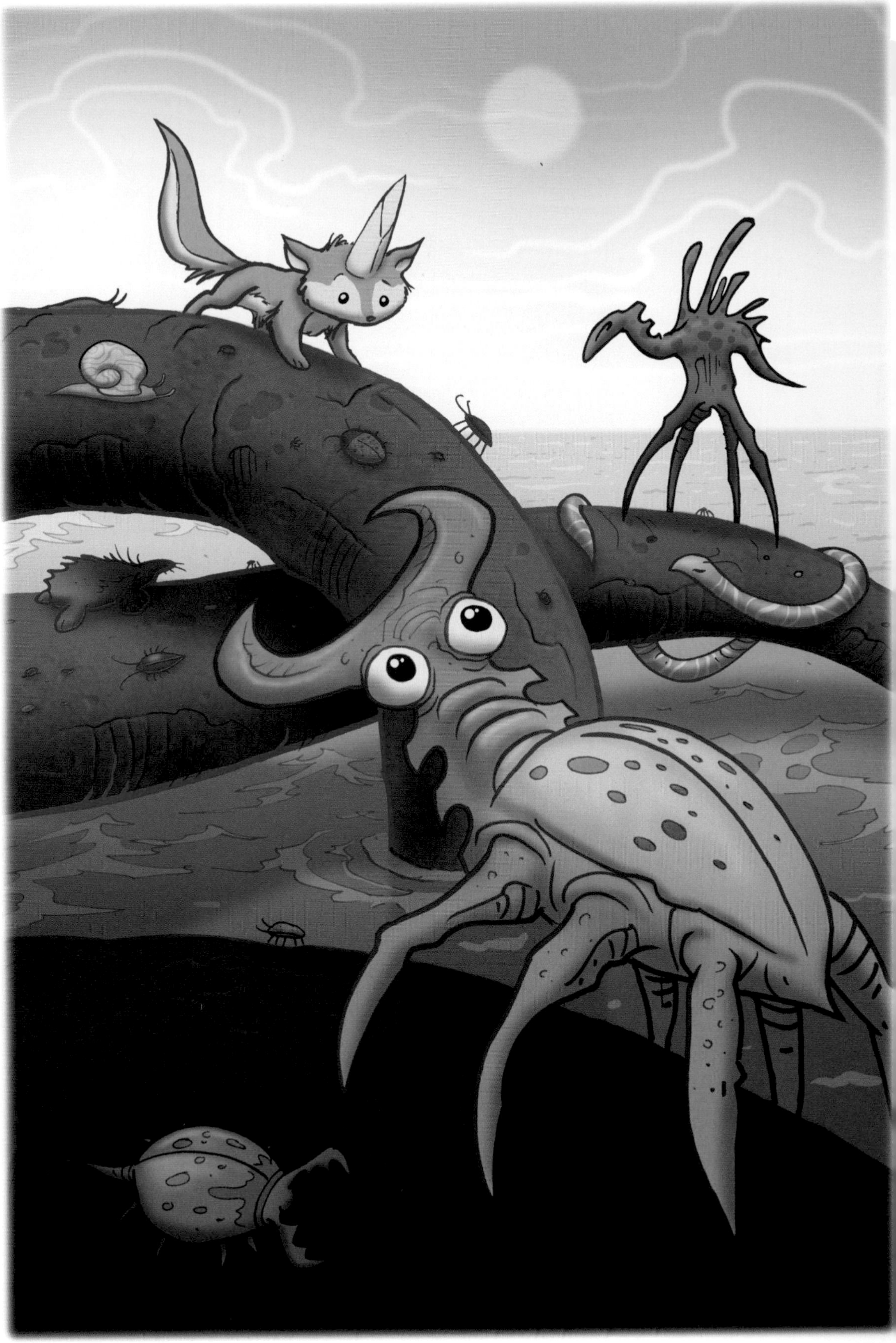

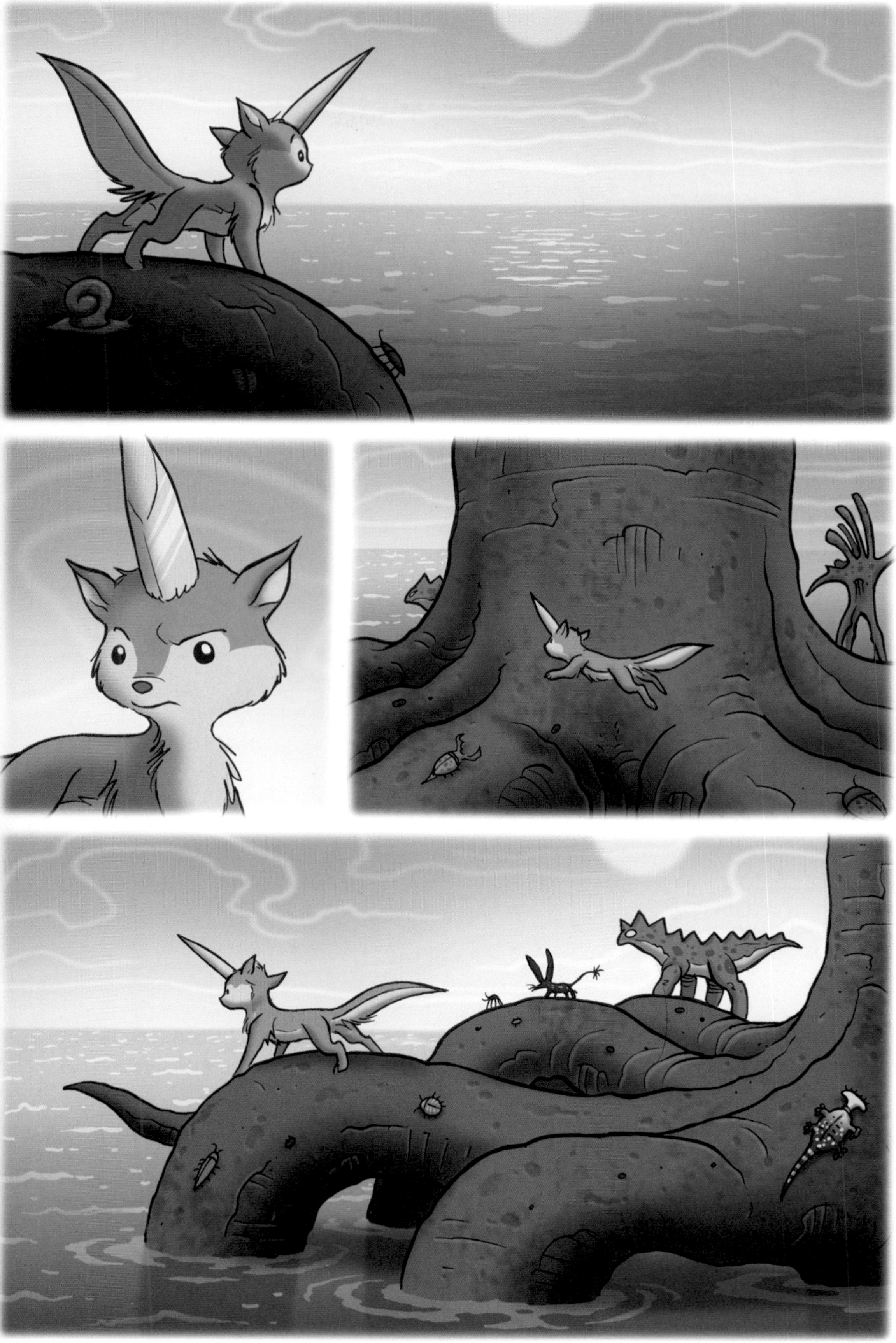

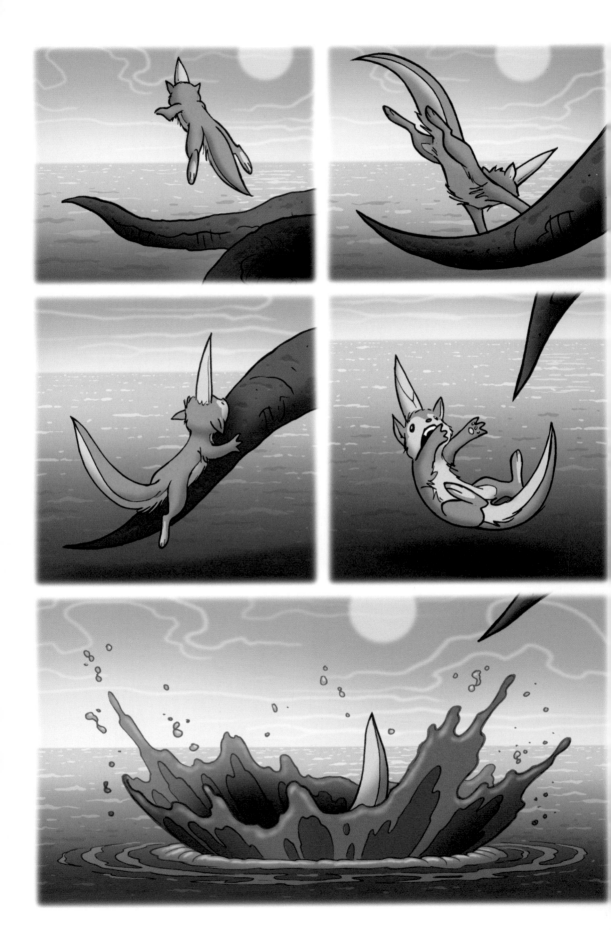

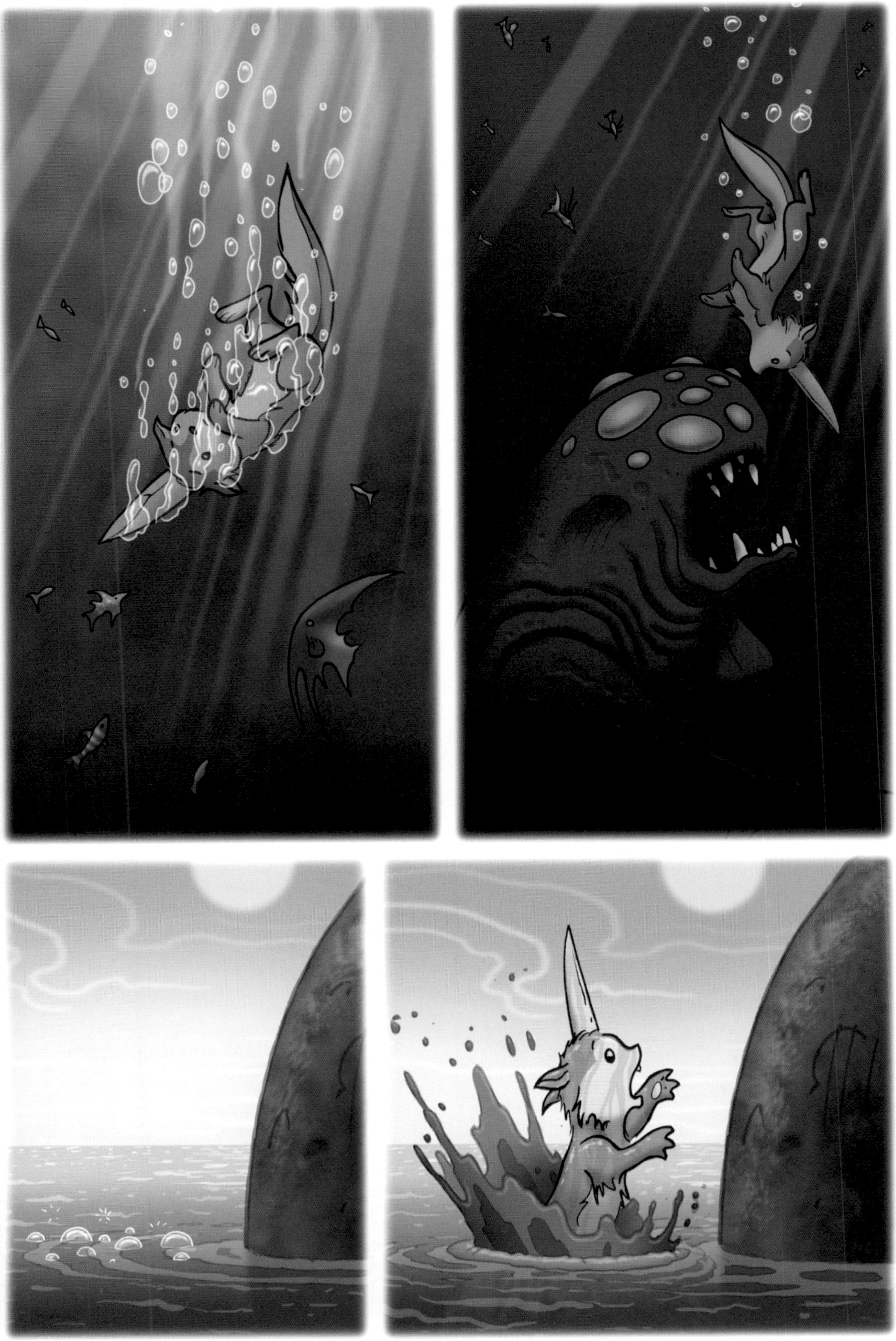

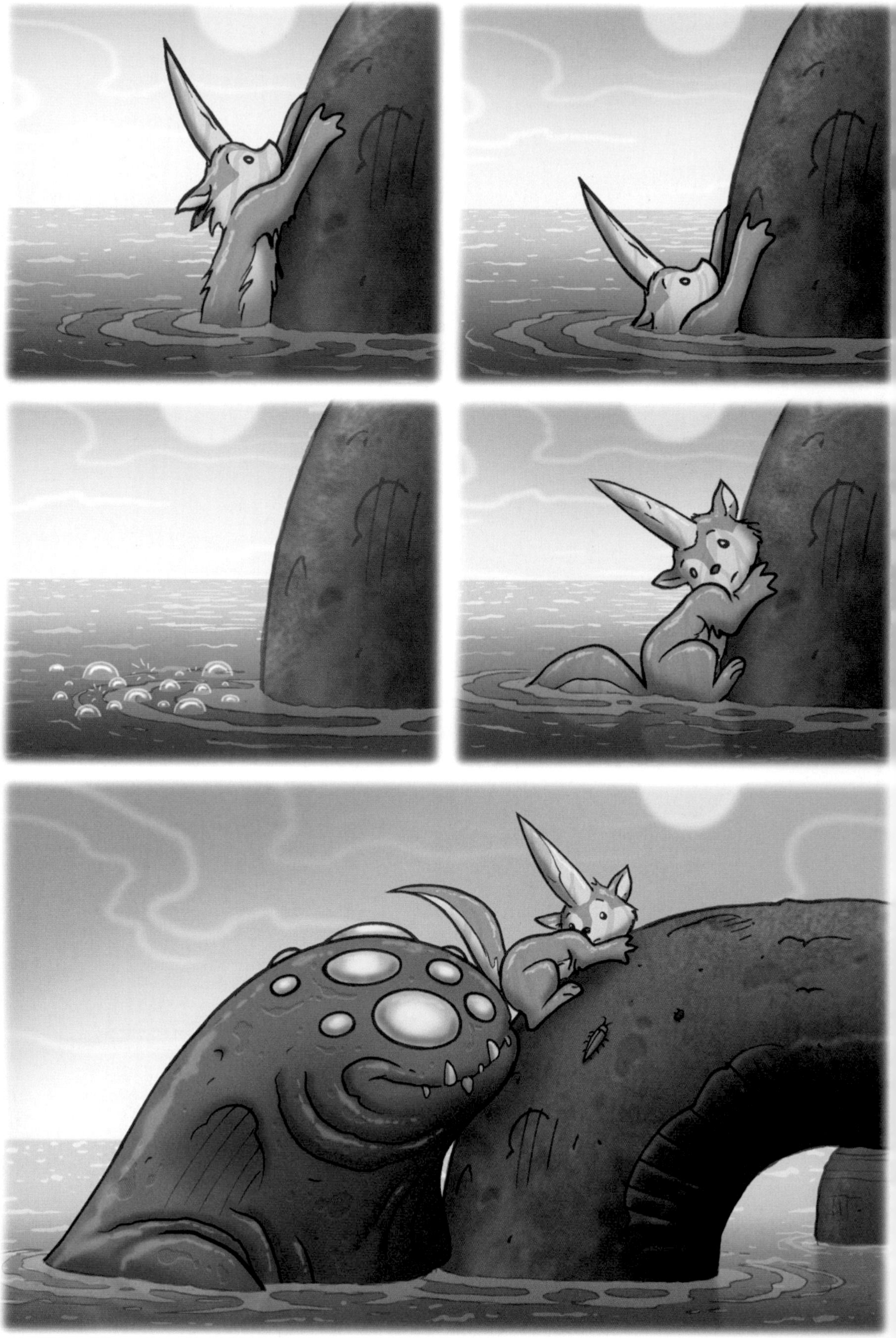

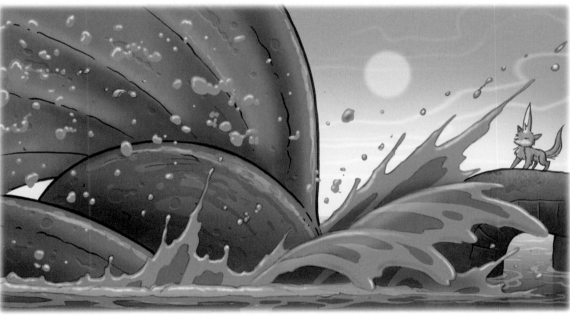

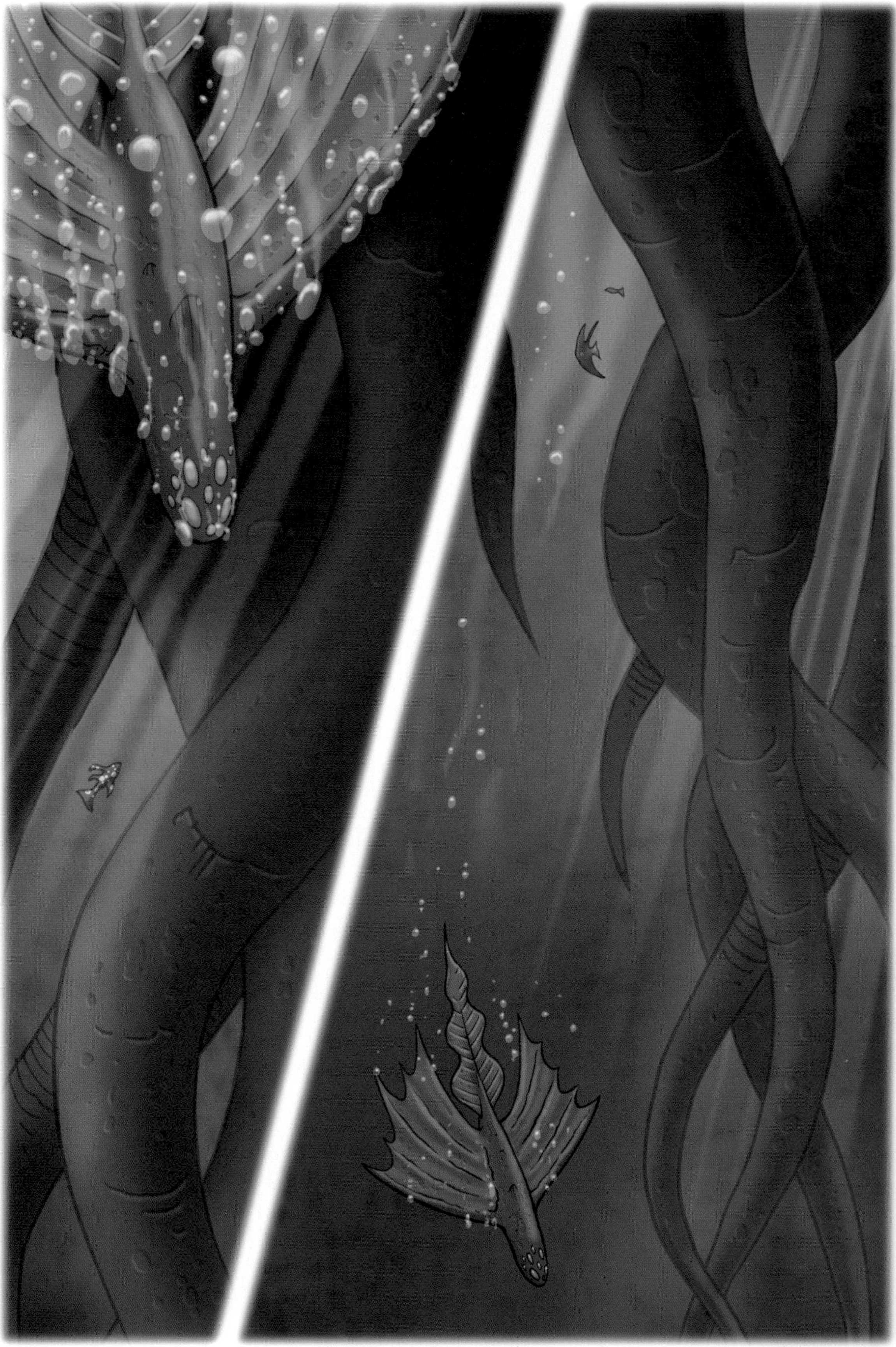

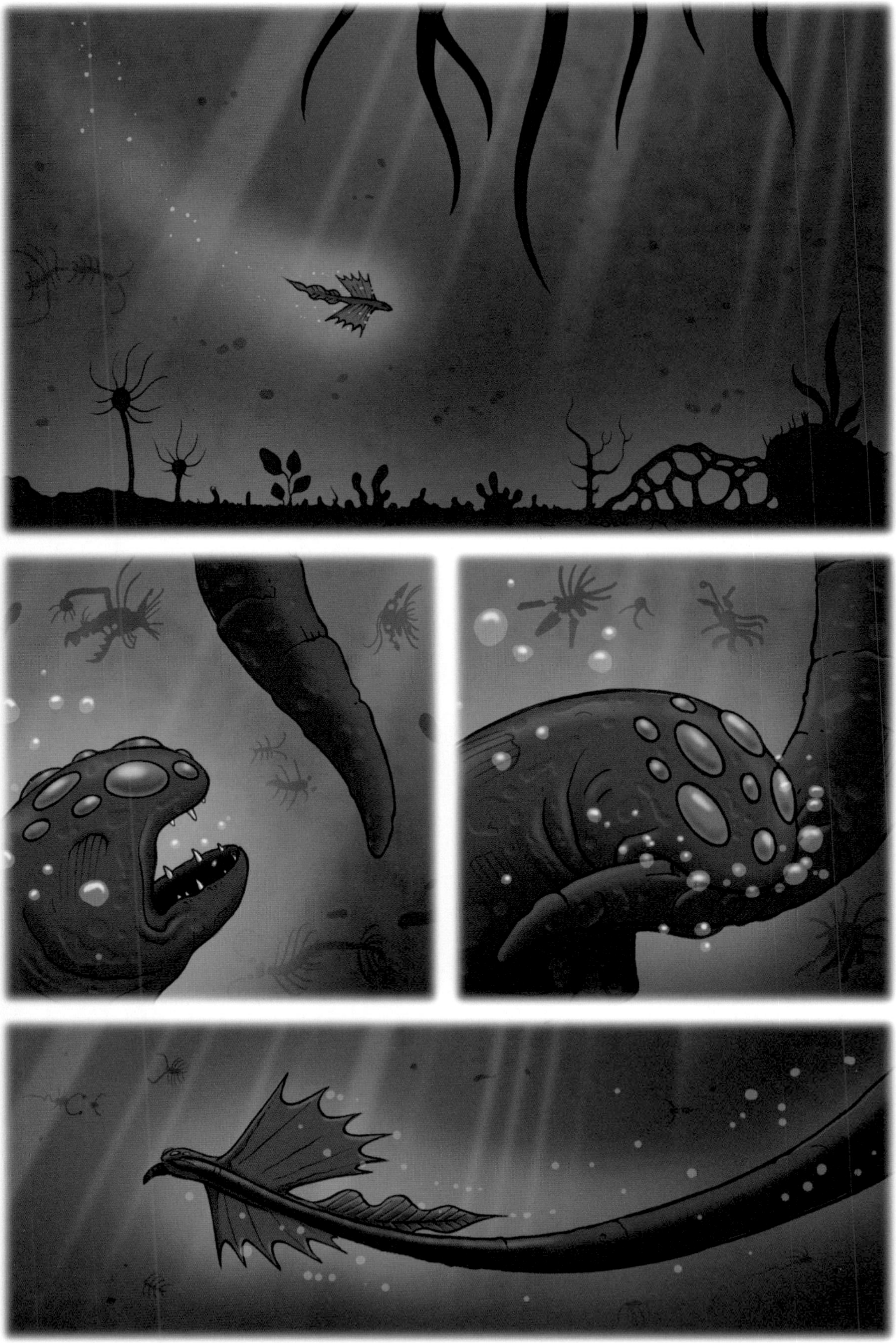

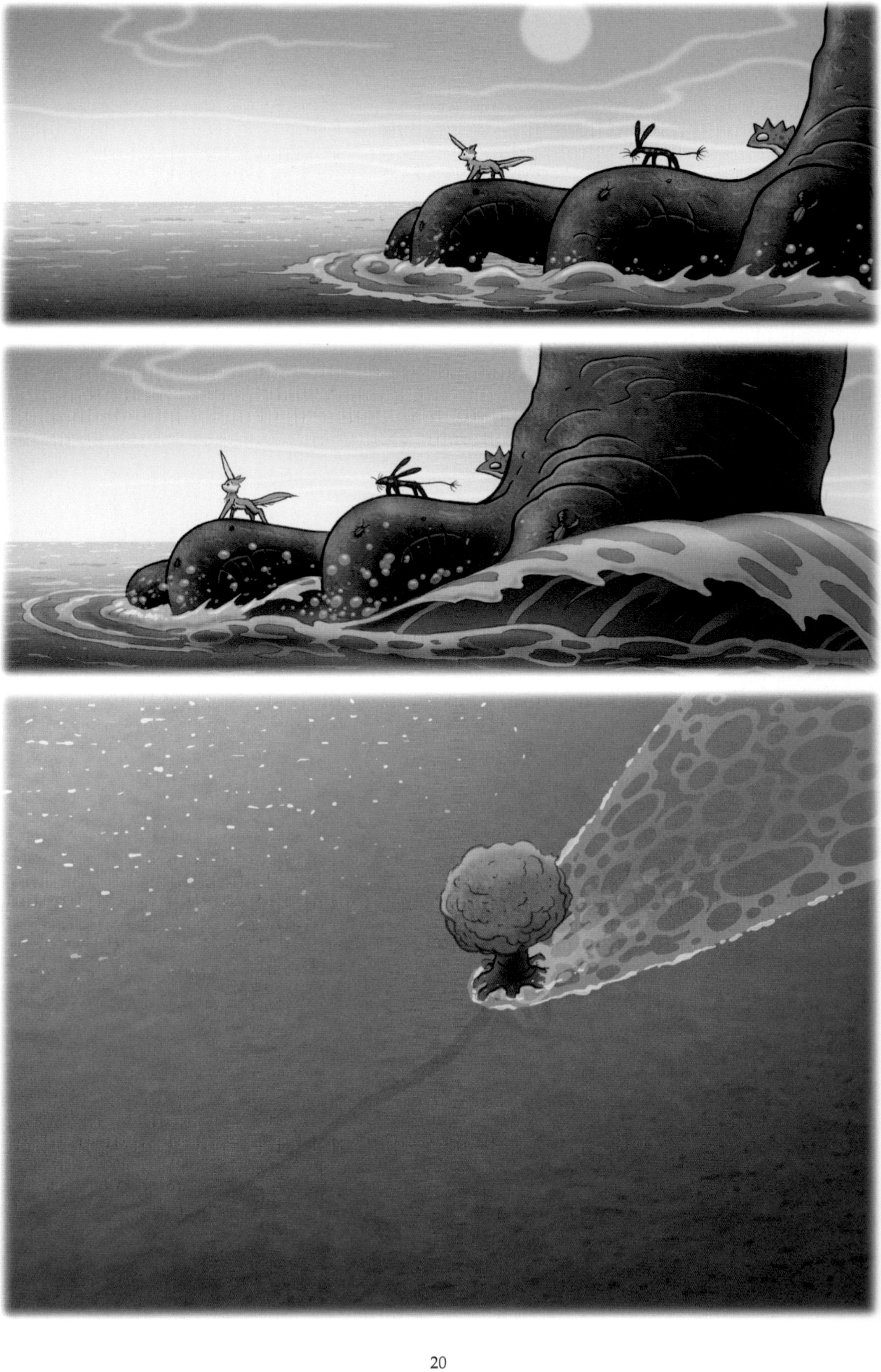

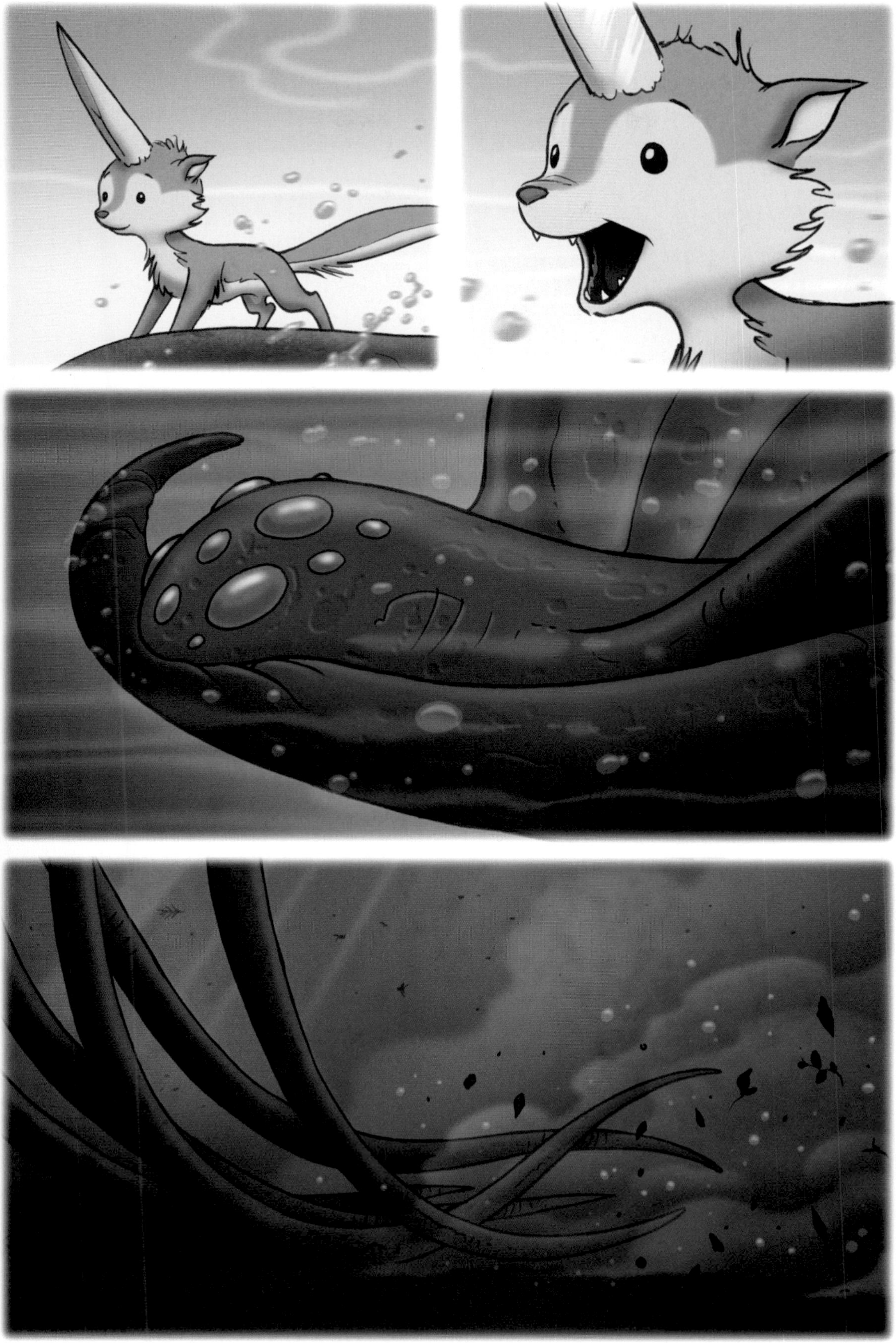

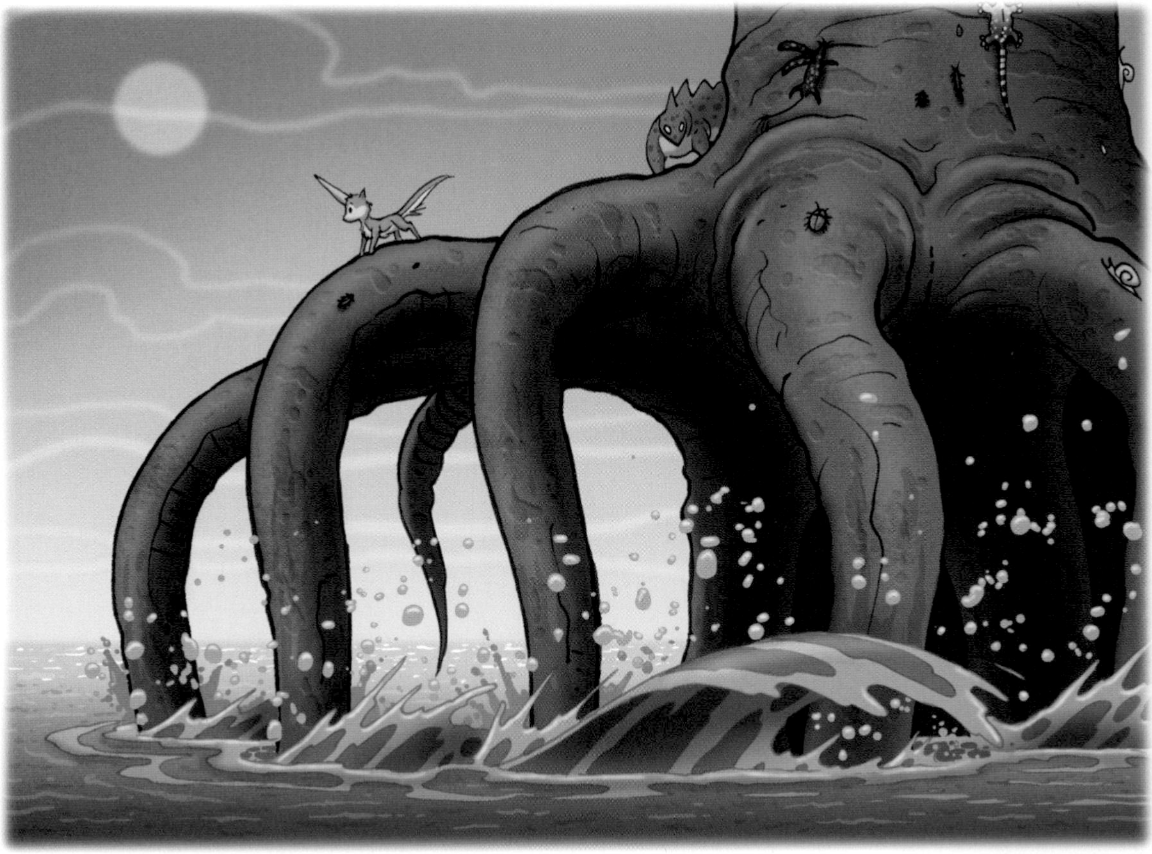

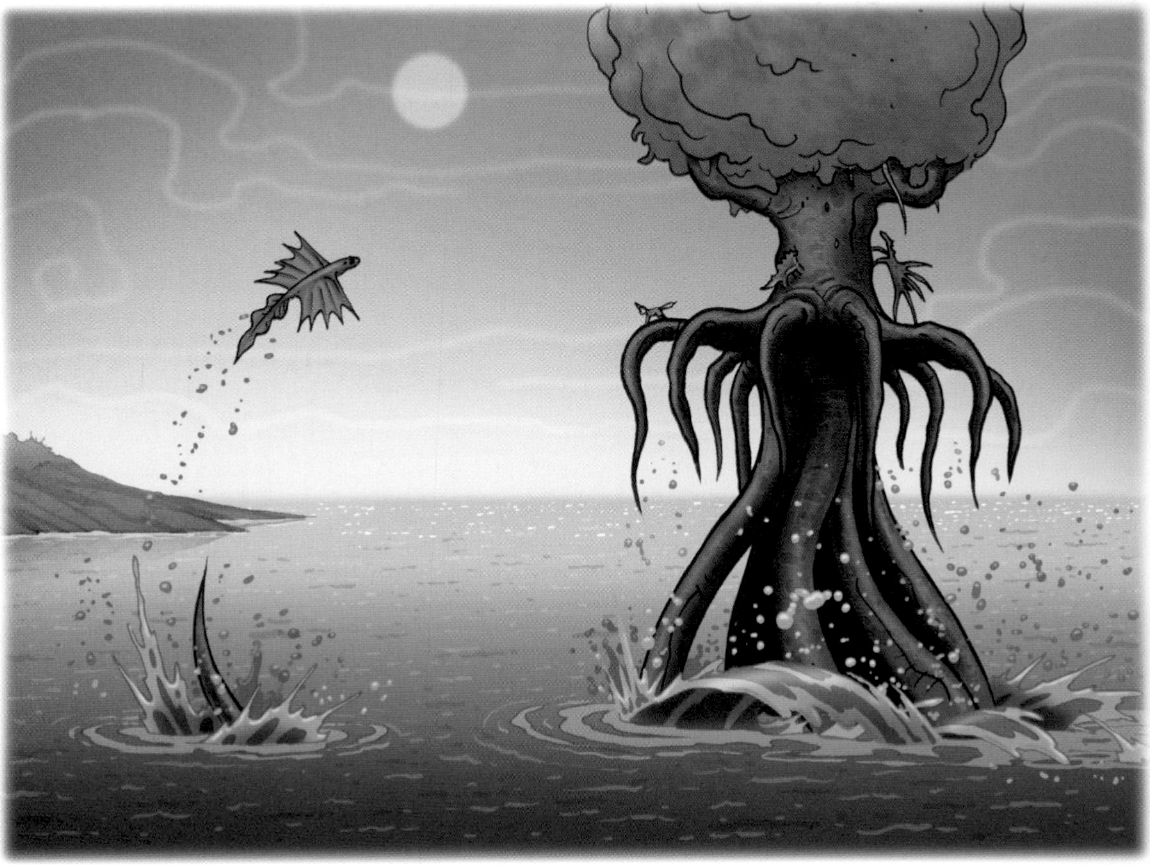

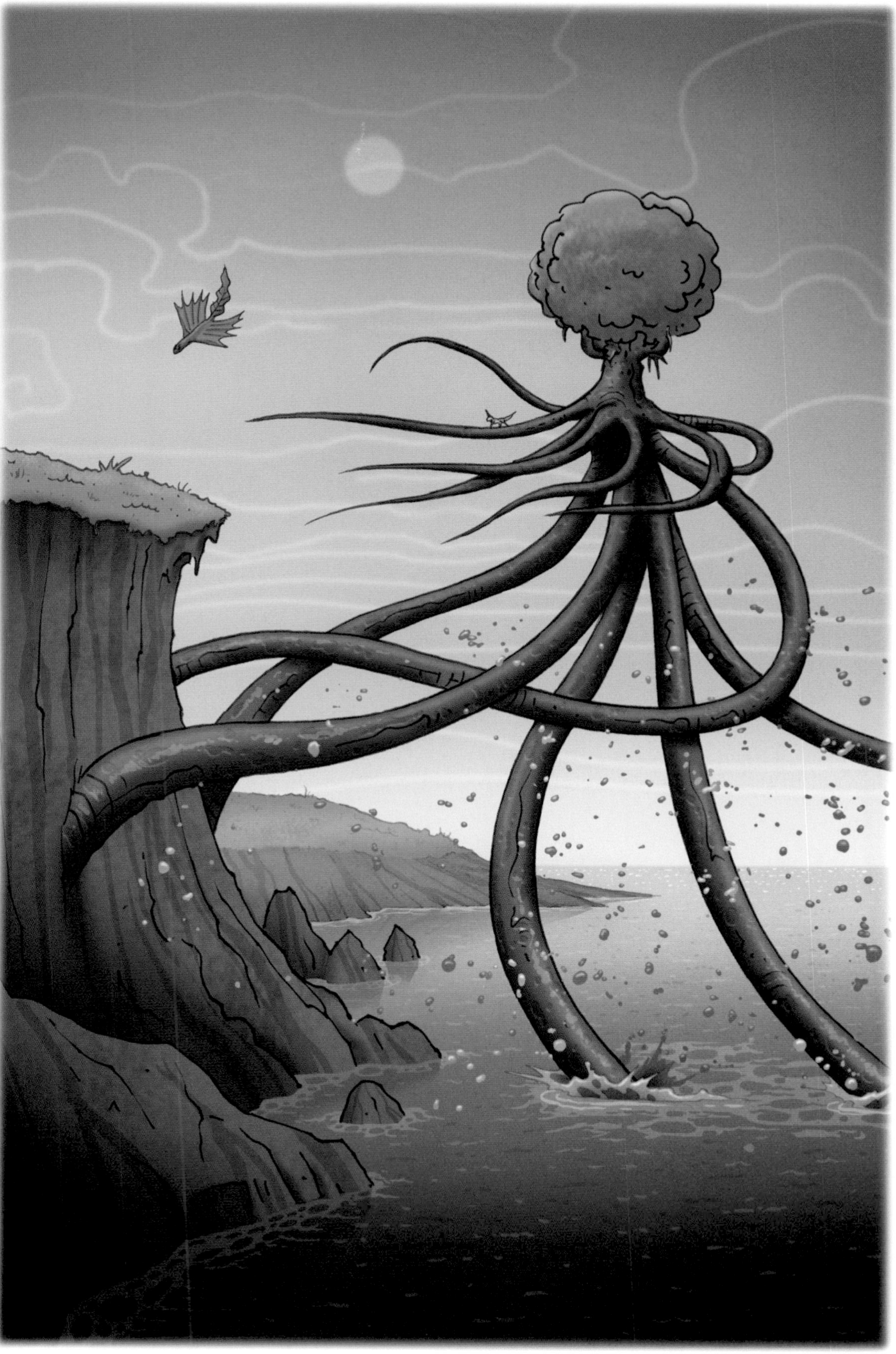

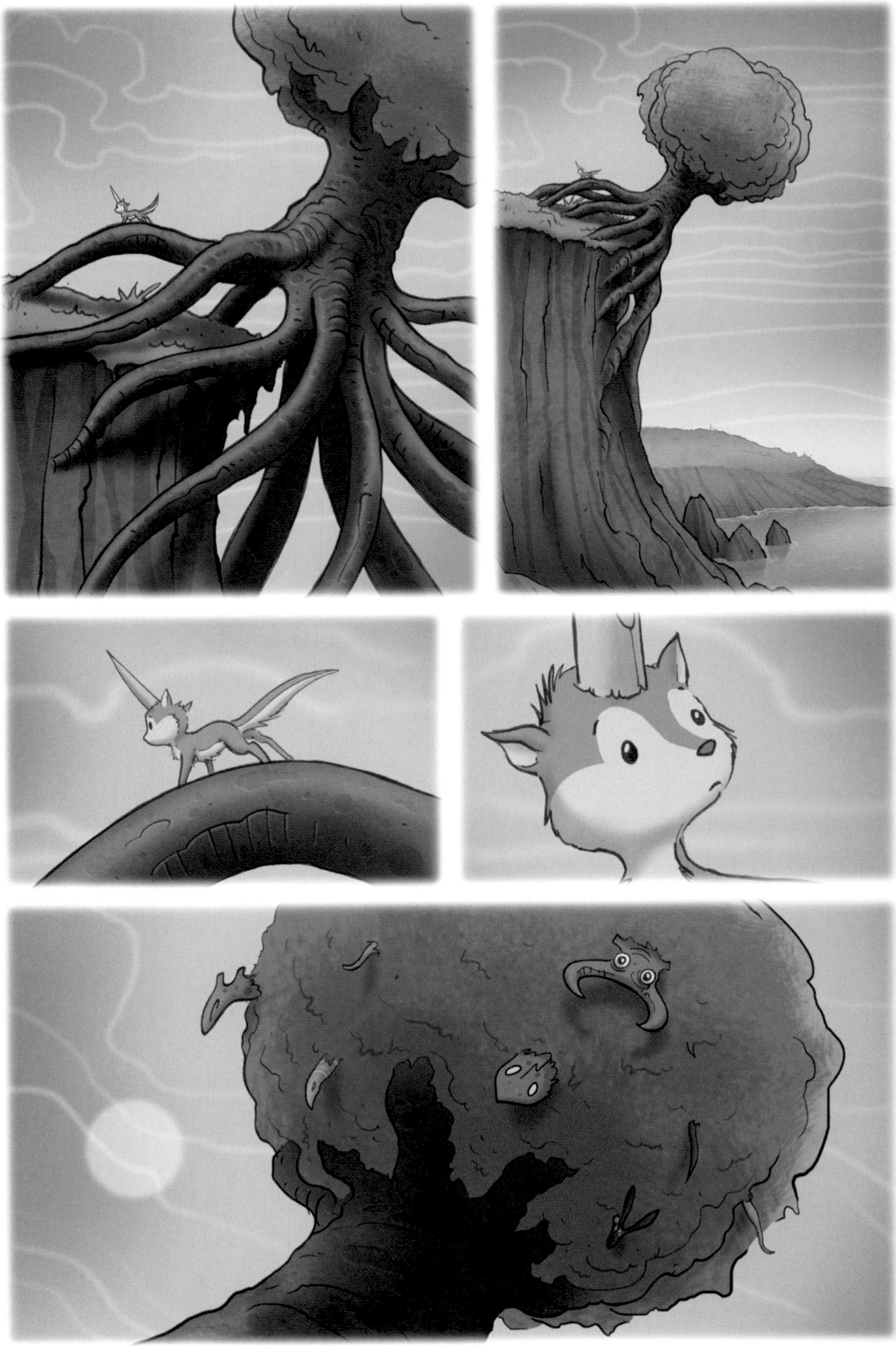

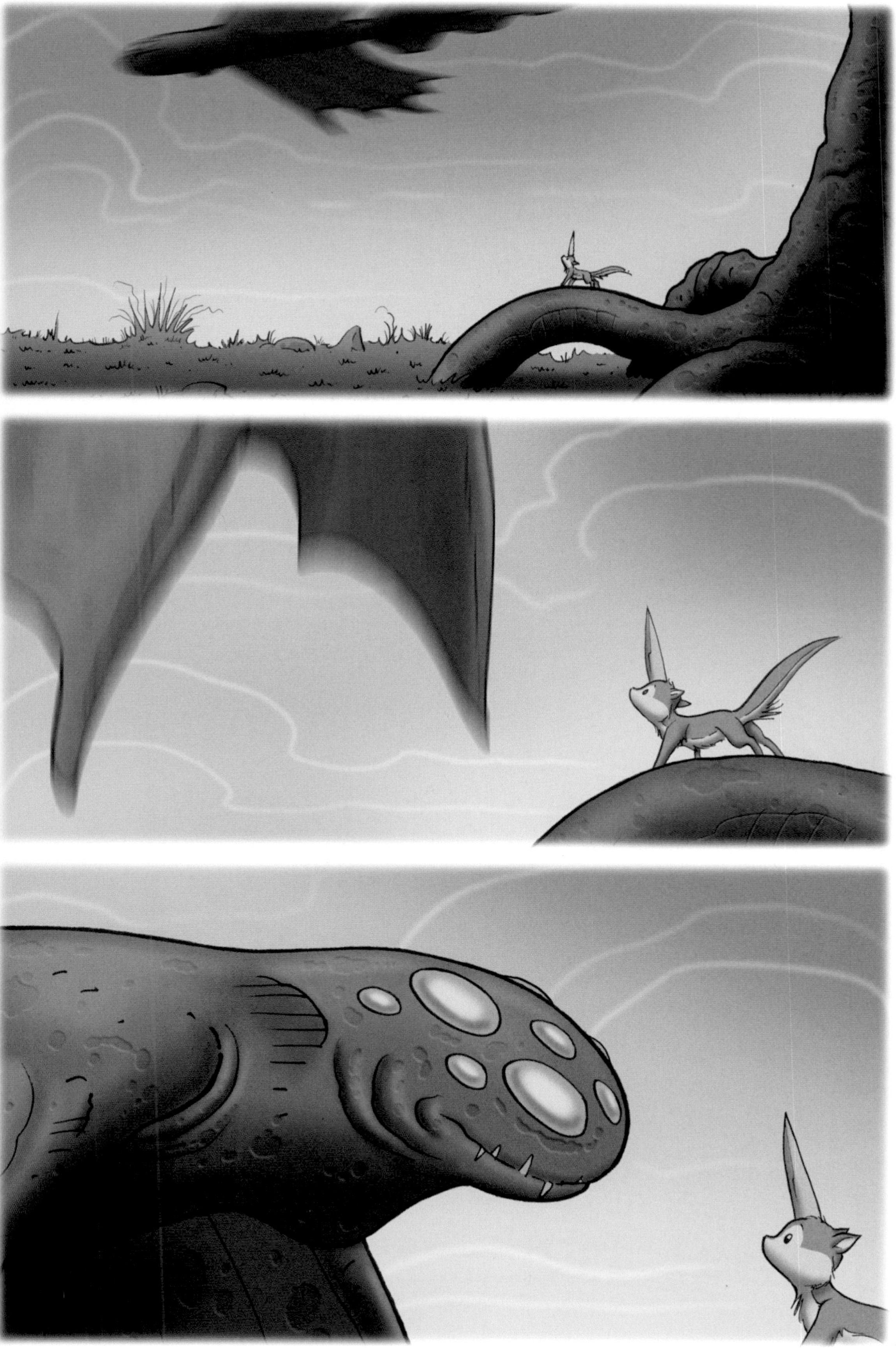

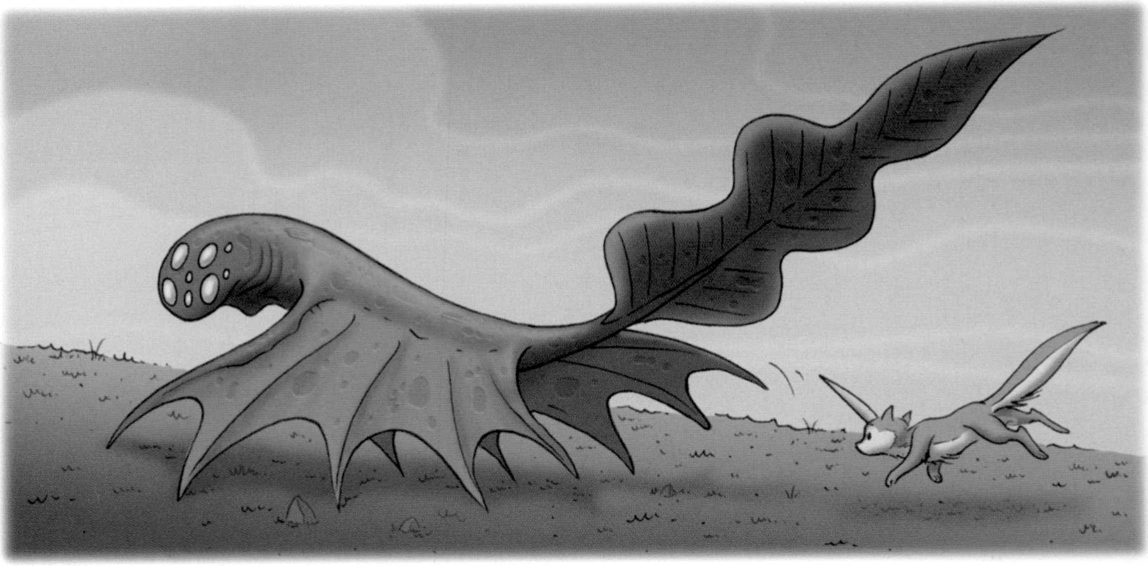

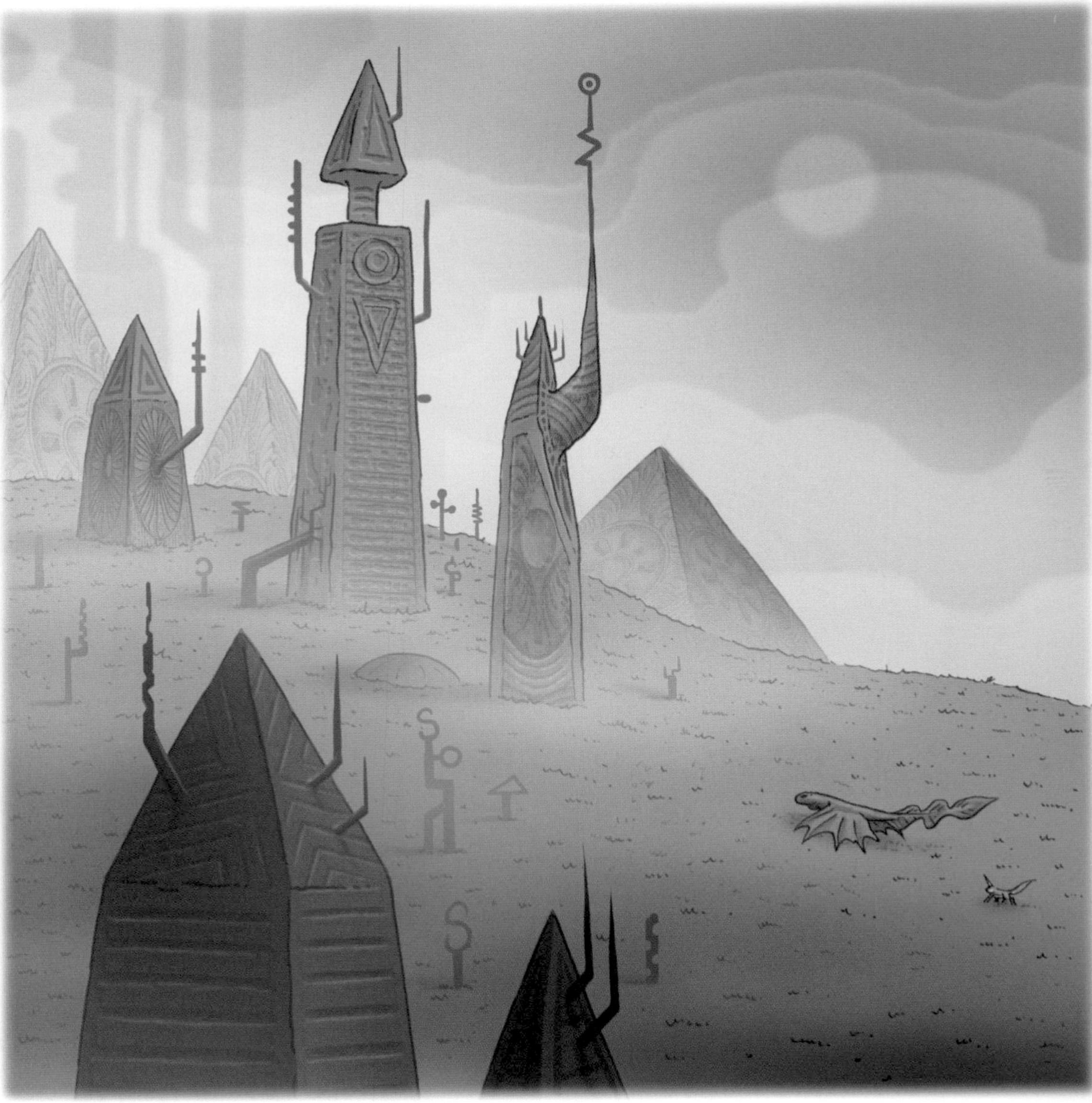

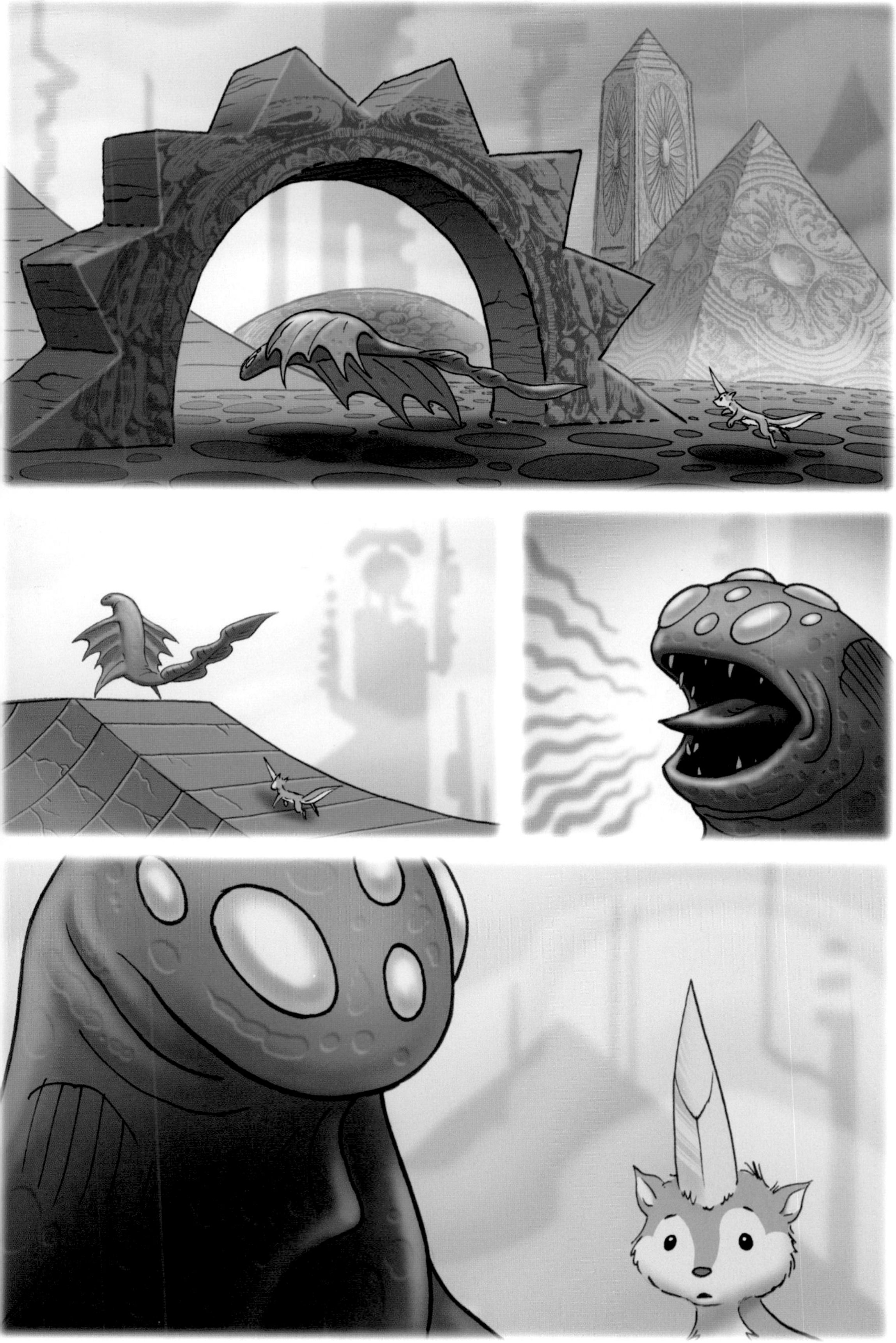

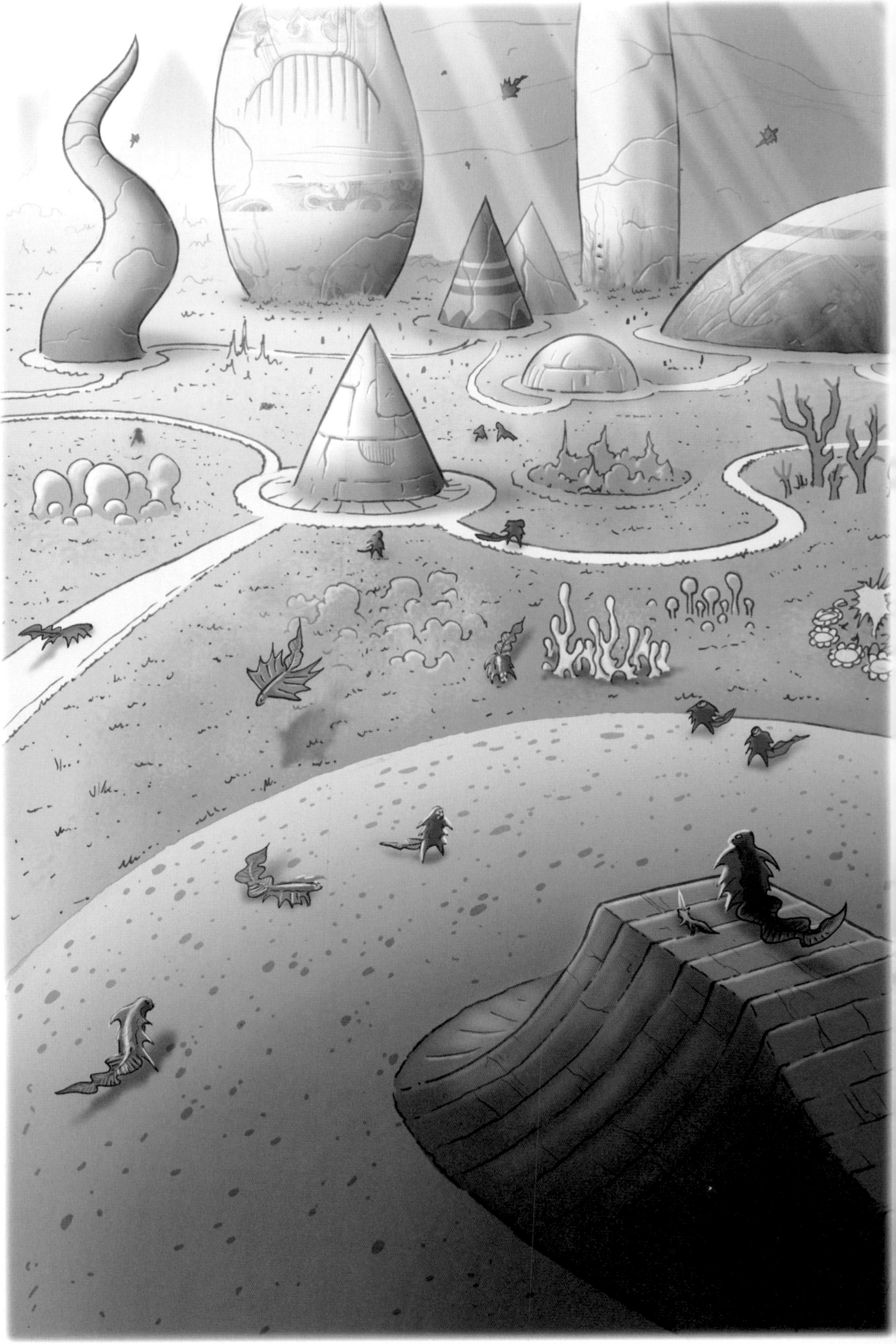

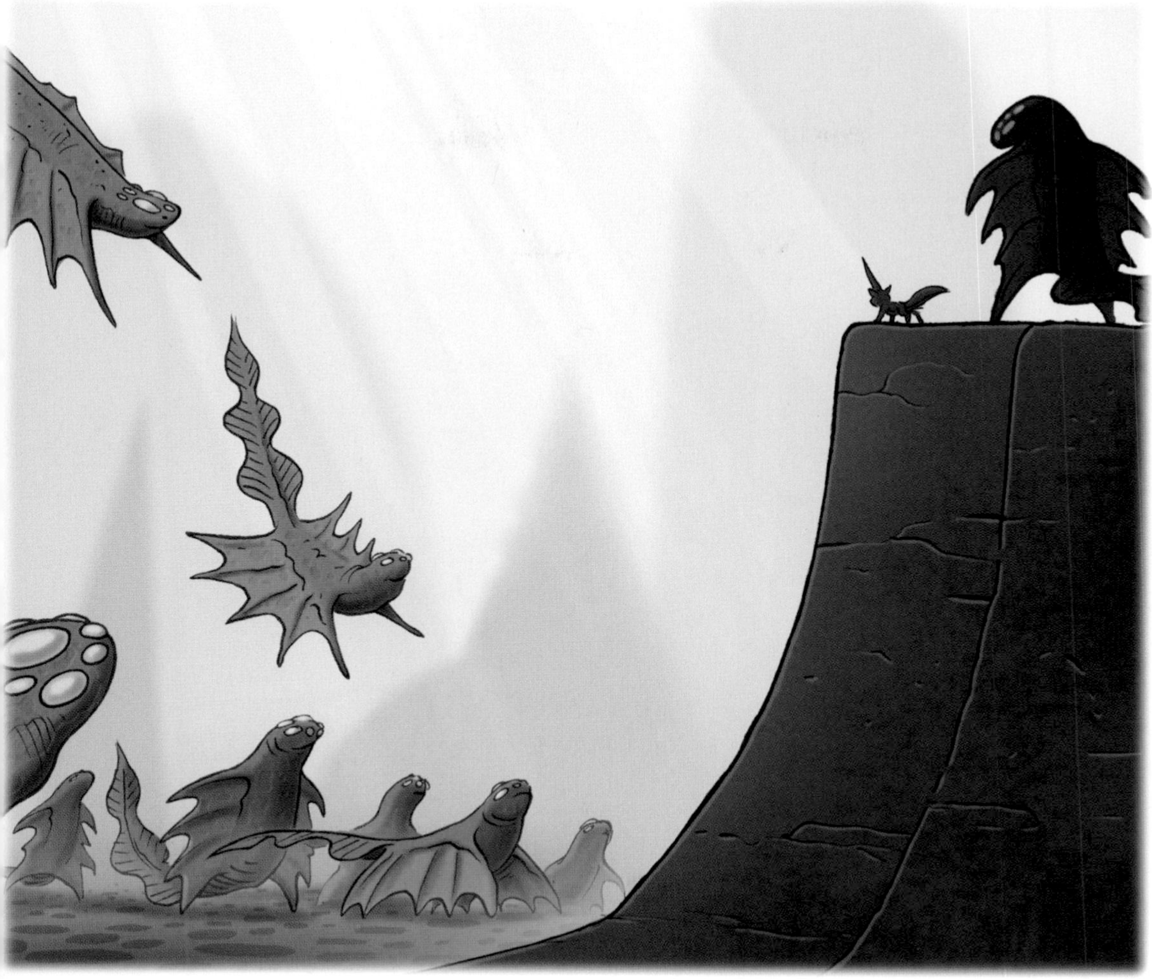

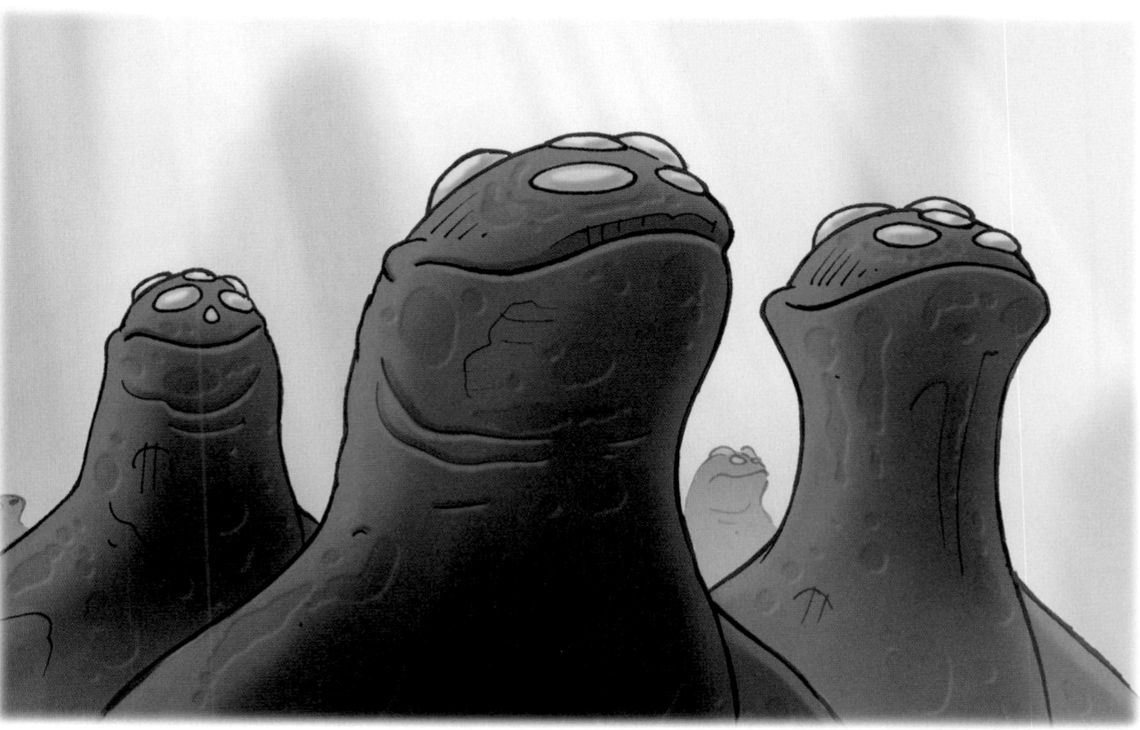

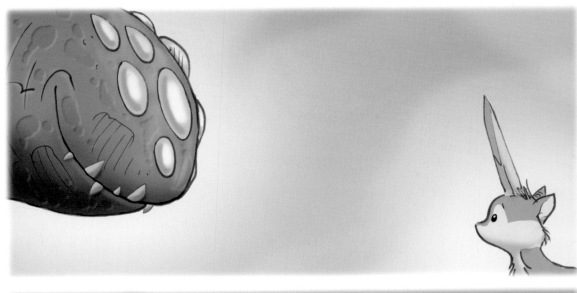

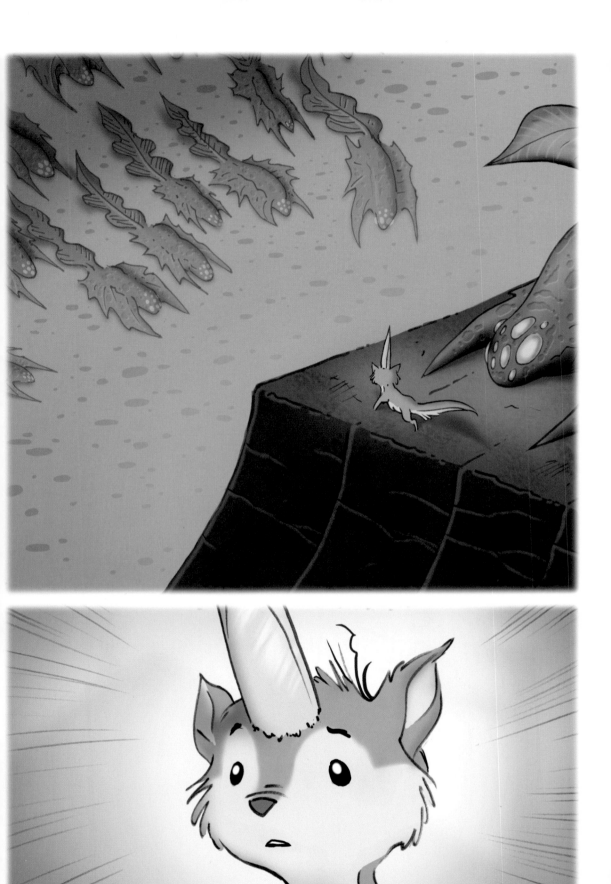

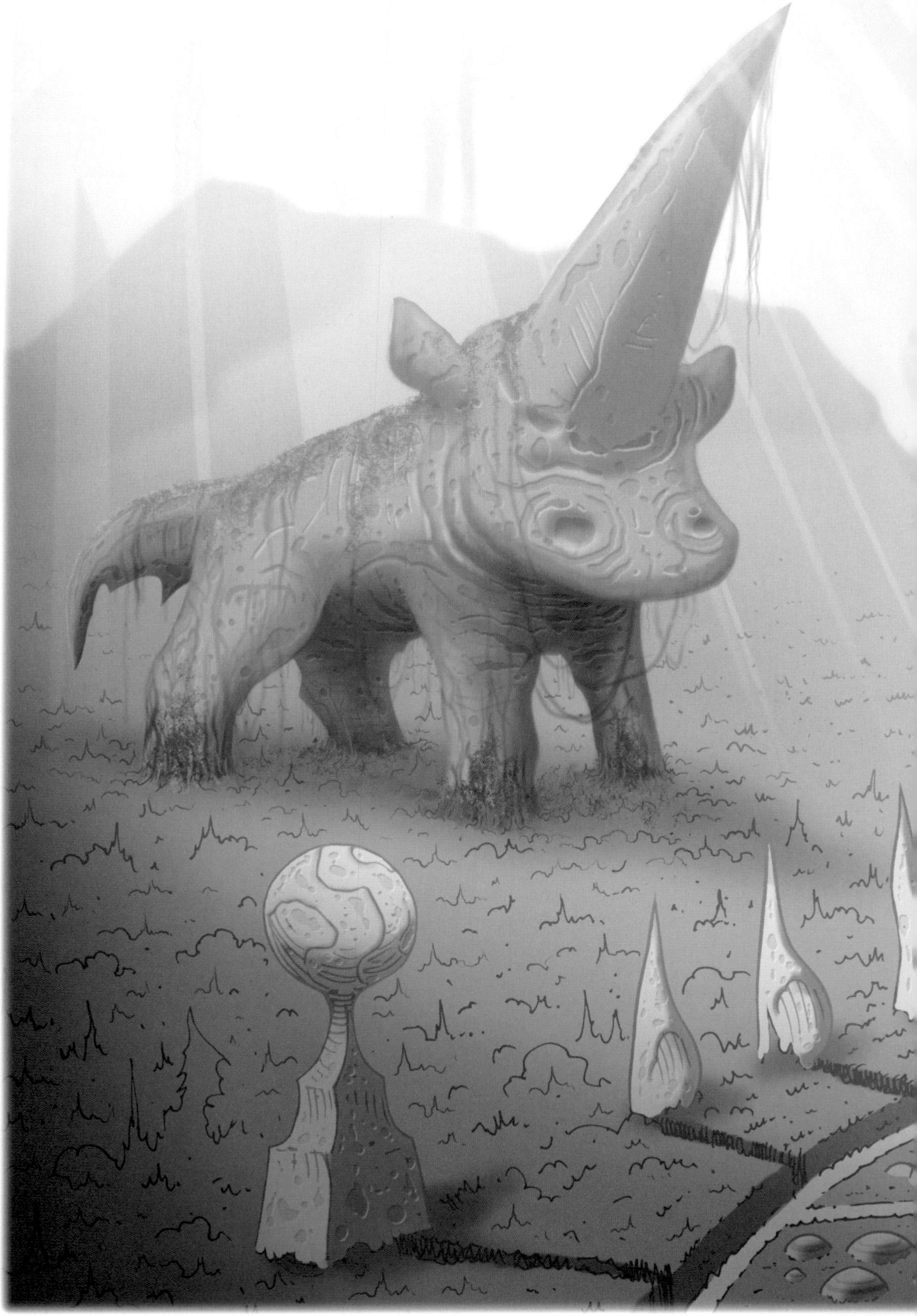

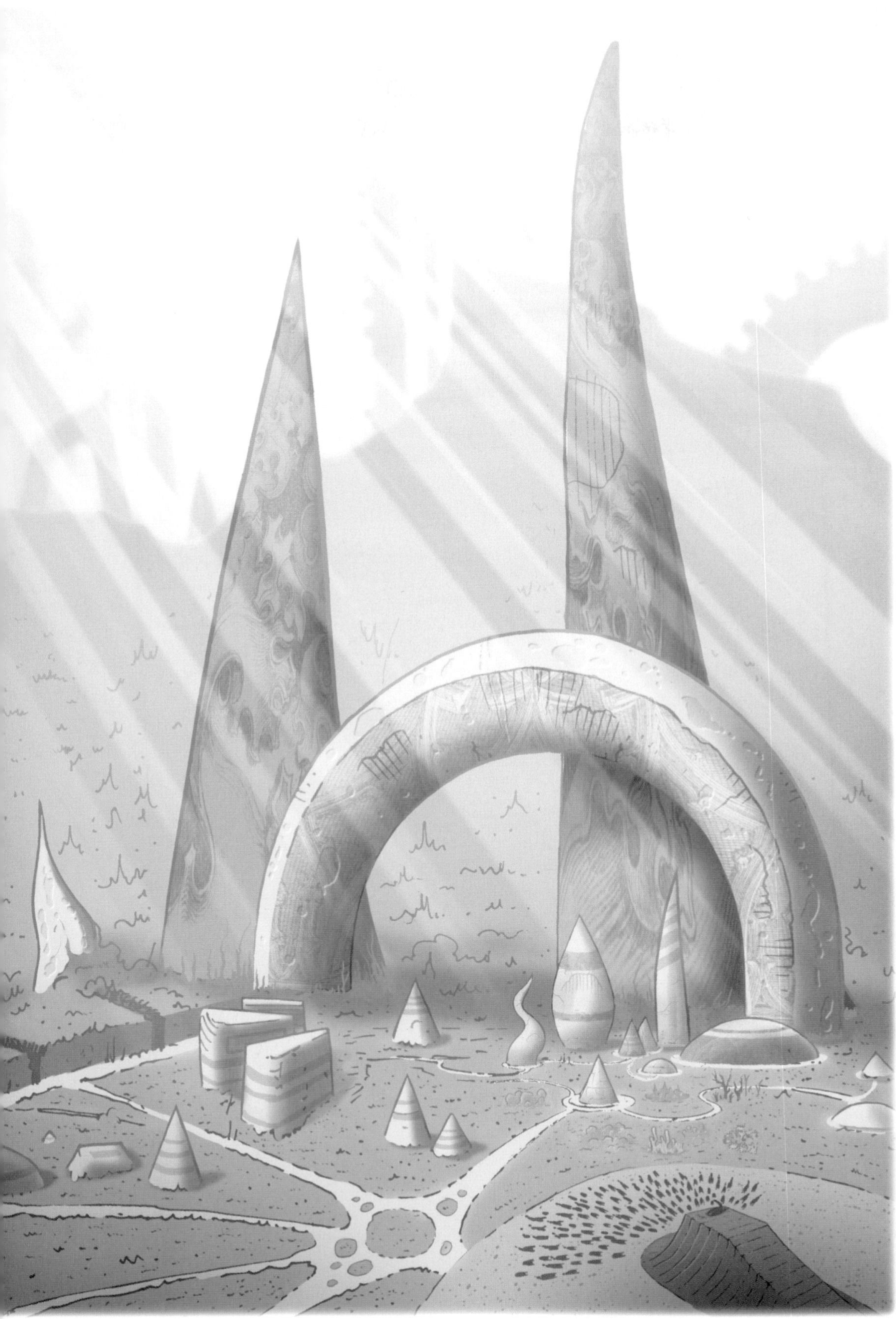

To be continued...

Food from the Sea

by Amy Kim Ganter

할아버지 드림

for grandfather

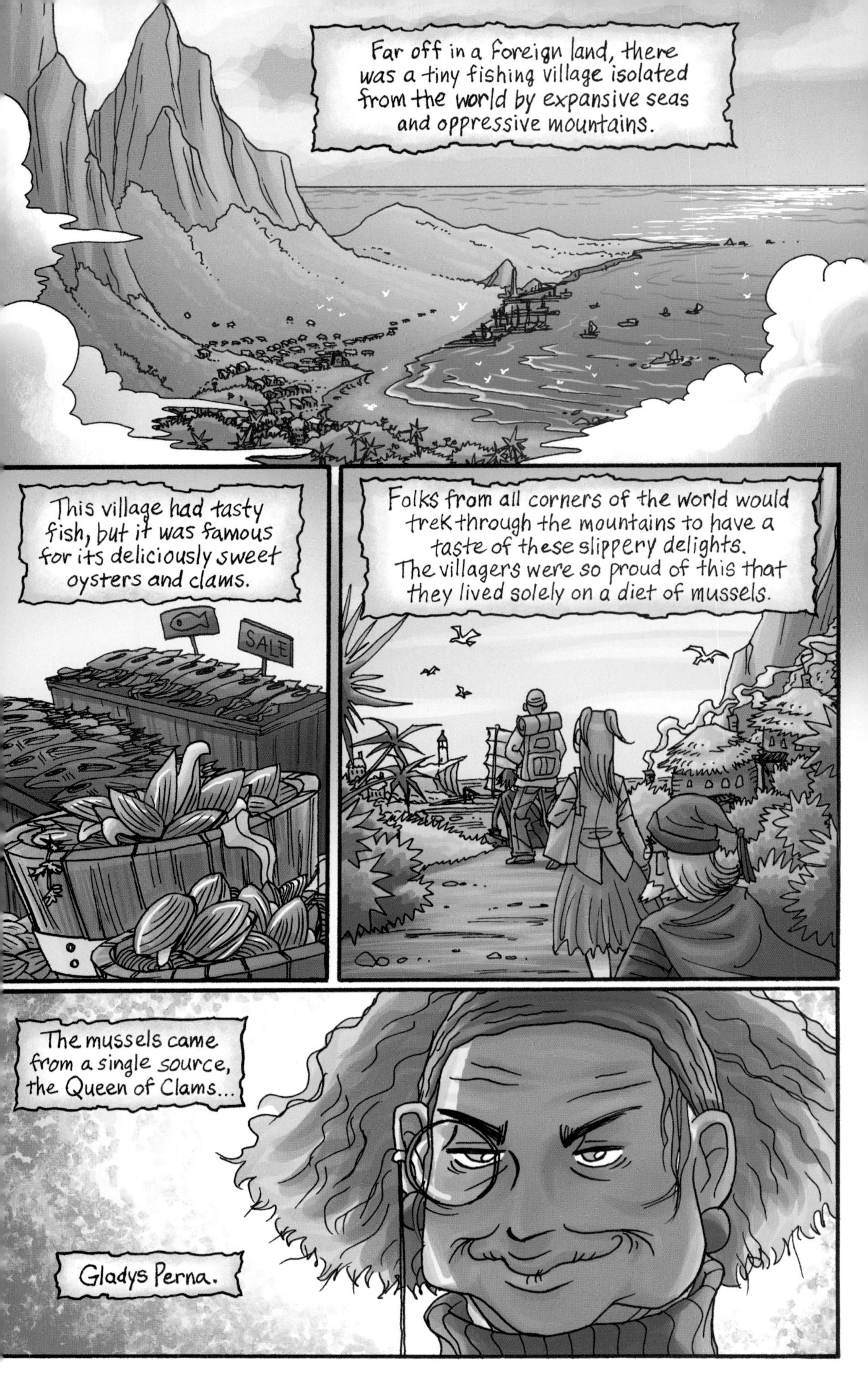
Far off in a foreign land, there was a tiny fishing village isolated from the world by expansive seas and oppressive mountains.
This village had tasty fish, but it was famous for its deliciously sweet oysters and clams.
SALE
Folks from all corners of the world would trek through the mountains to have a taste of these slippery delights. The villagers were so proud of this that they lived solely on a diet of mussels.
The mussels came from a single source, the Queen of Clams...
Gladys Perna.

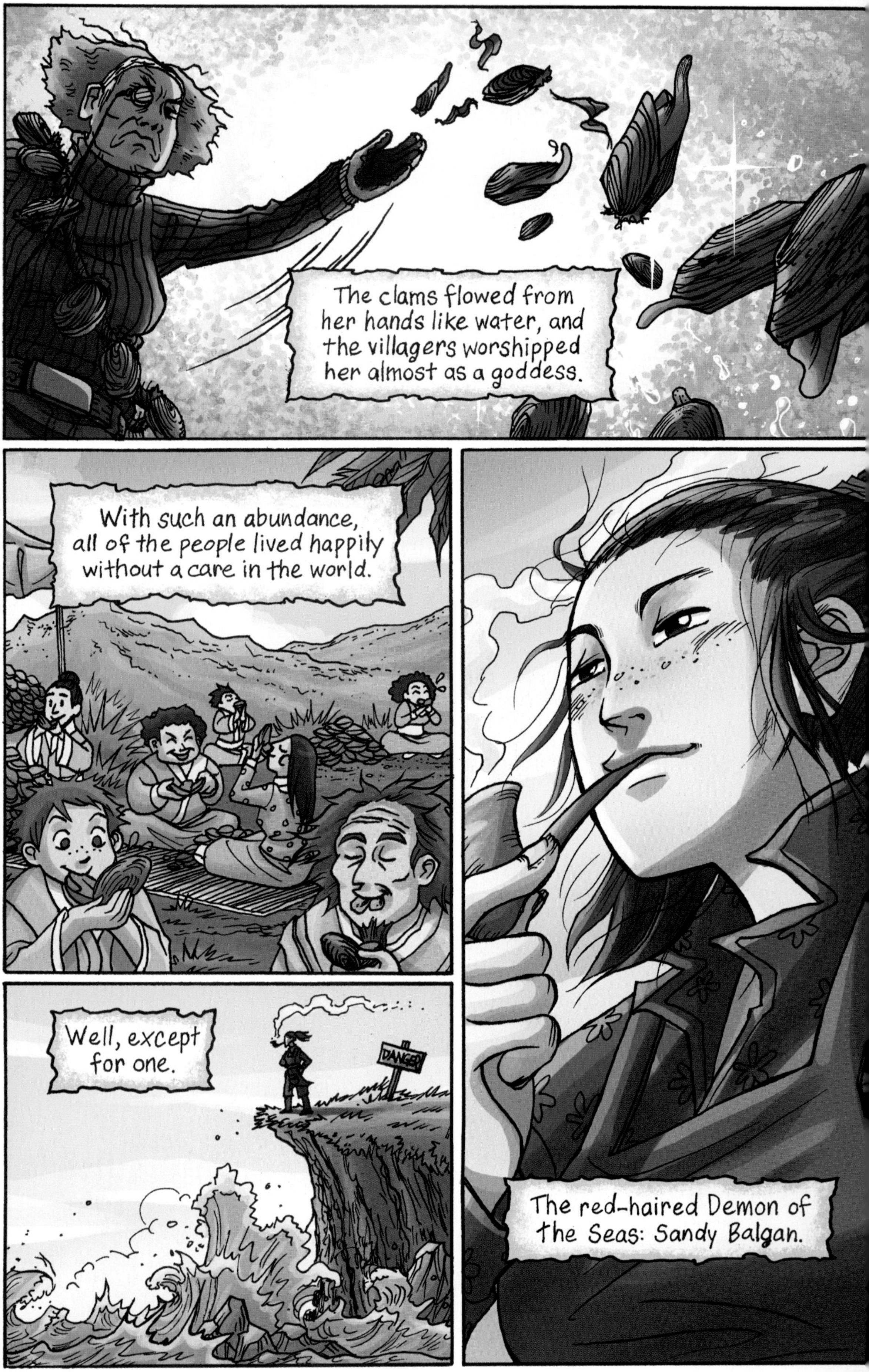
The clams flowed from her hands like water, and the villagers worshipped her almost as a goddess.
With such an abundance, all of the people lived happily without a care in the world.
Well, except for one.
DANGER
The red-haired Demon of the Seas: Sandy Balgan.

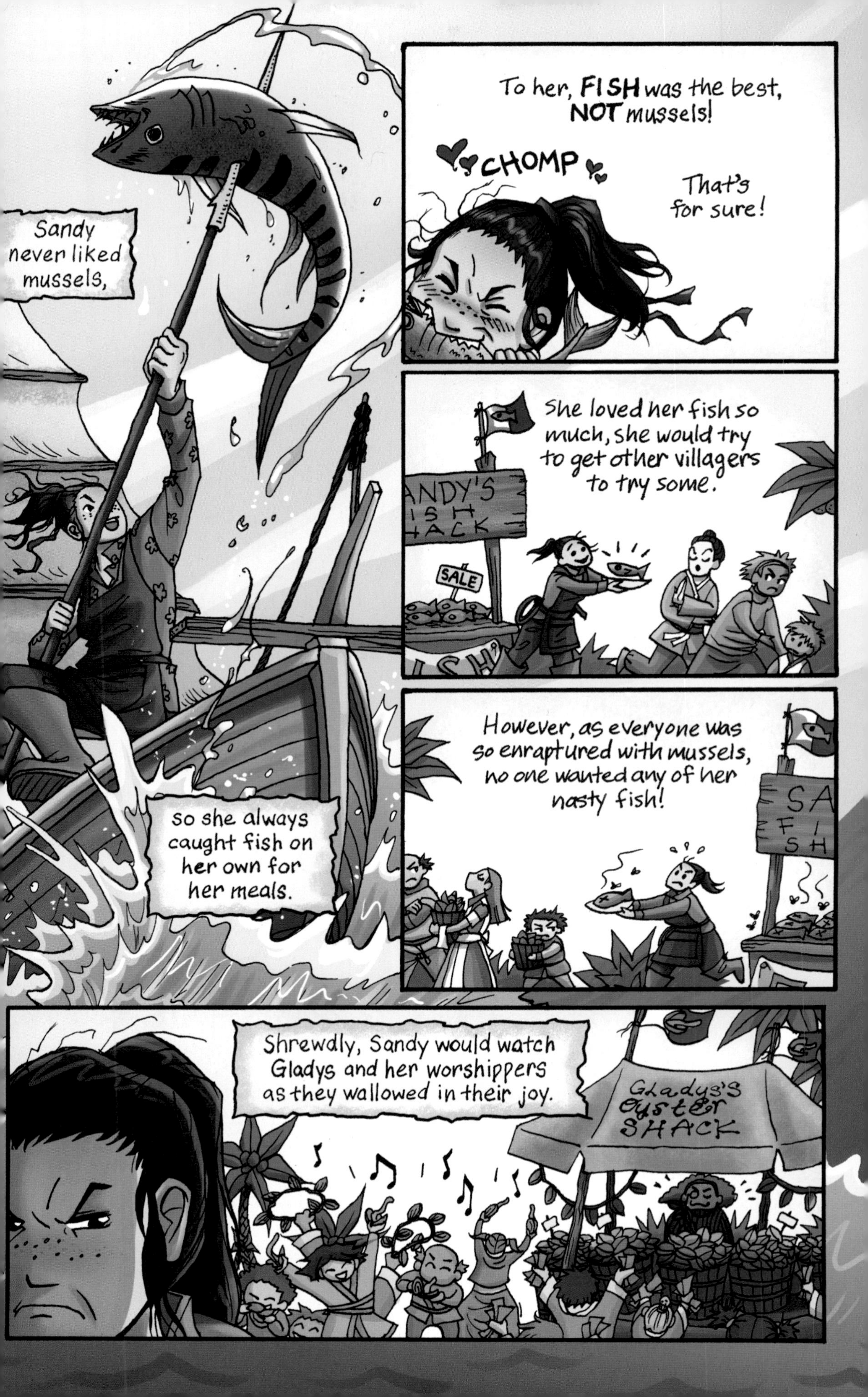
Sandy never liked mussels,
so she always caught fish on her own for her meals.
To her, FISH was the best, NOT mussels!
CHOMP
That's for sure!
She loved her fish so much, she would try to get other villagers to try some.
SANDY'S FISH SHACK
SALE
However, as everyone was so enraptured with mussels, no one wanted any of her nasty fish!
Shrewdly, Sandy would watch Gladys and her worshippers as they wallowed in their joy.
Gladys's Oyster SHACK

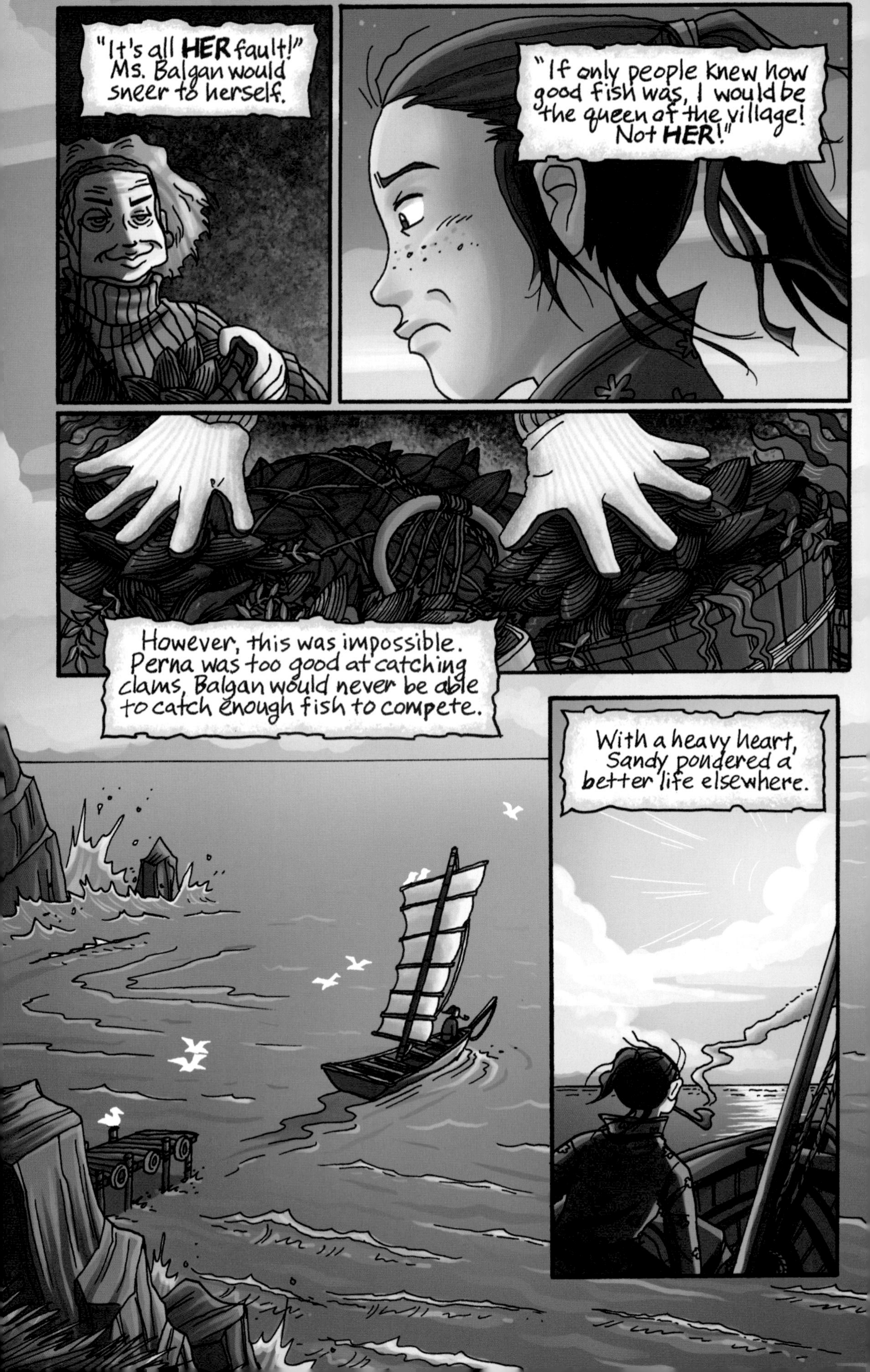
"It's all HER fault!" Ms. Balgan would sneer to herself.
"If only people knew how good fish was, I would be the queen of the village! Not HER!"
However, this was impossible. Perna was too good at catching clams, Balgan would never be able to catch enough fish to compete.
With a heavy heart, Sandy pondered a better life elsewhere.

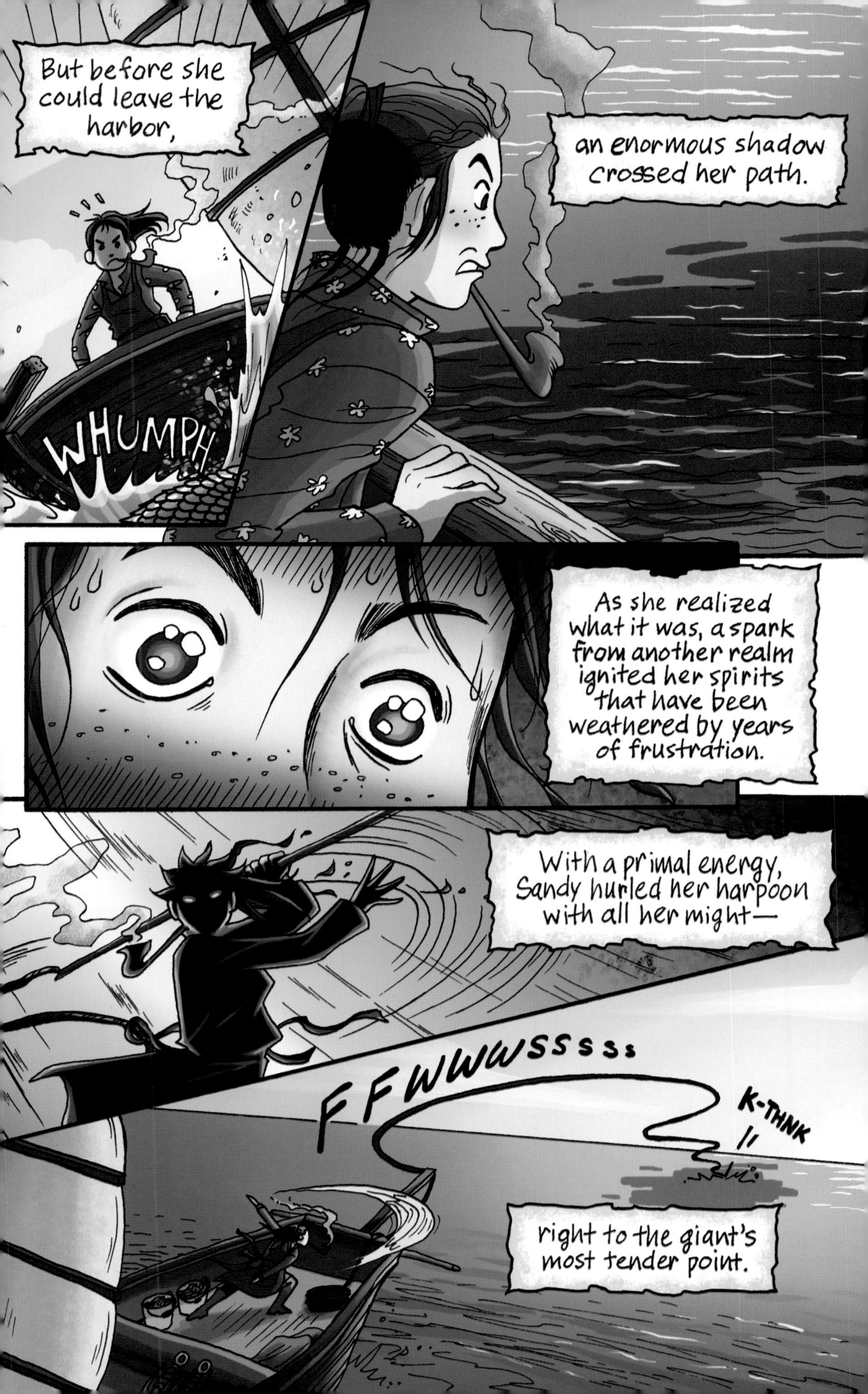
But before she could leave the harbor,
an enormous shadow crossed her path.
WHUMPH
As she realized what it was, a spark from another realm ignited her spirits that have been weathered by years of frustration.
With a primal energy, Sandy hurled her harpoon with all her might—
FFWWWSSSSS
K-THNK
right to the giant's most tender point.

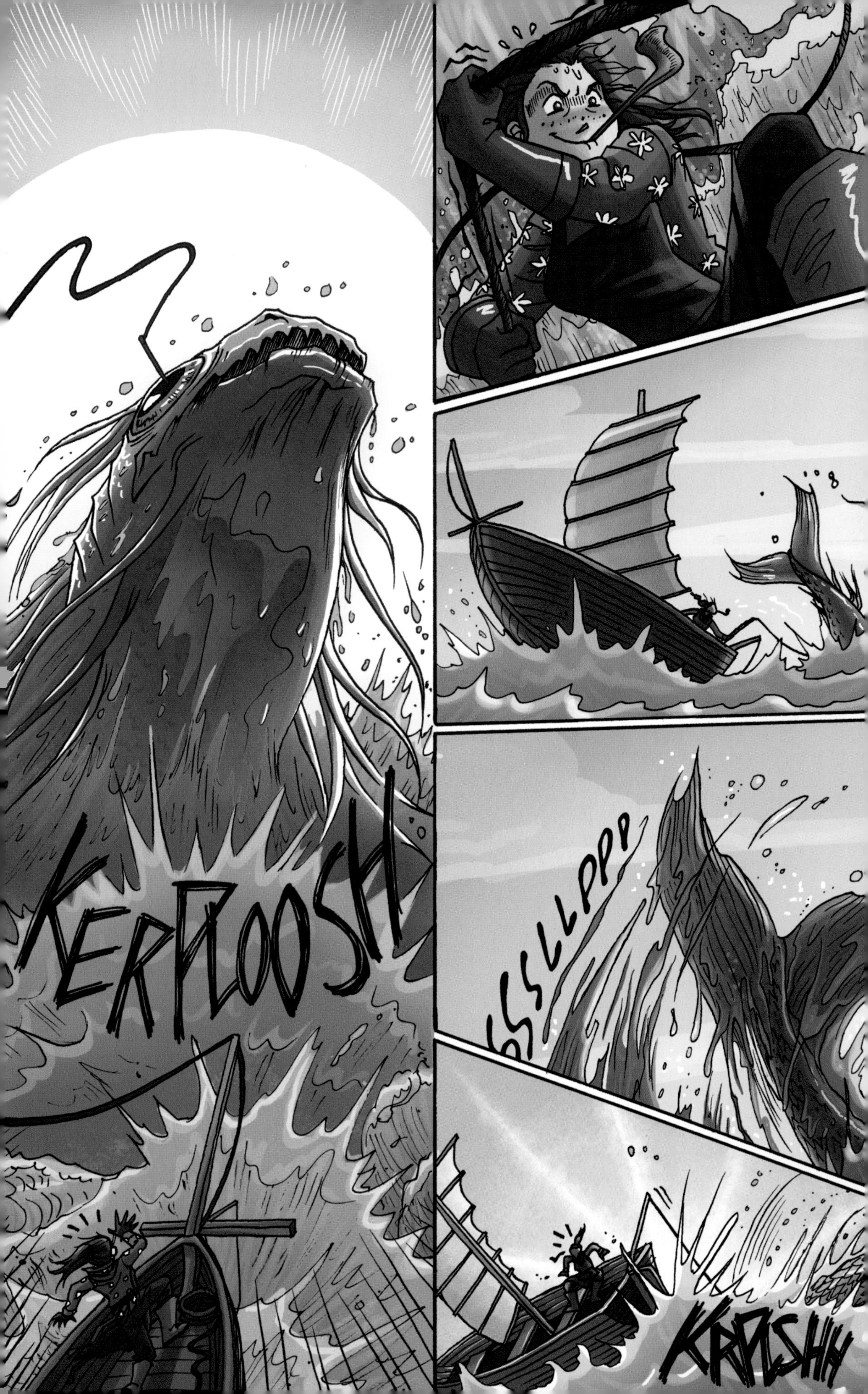
KERPLOOSH
SSLLPPP
KRASHH

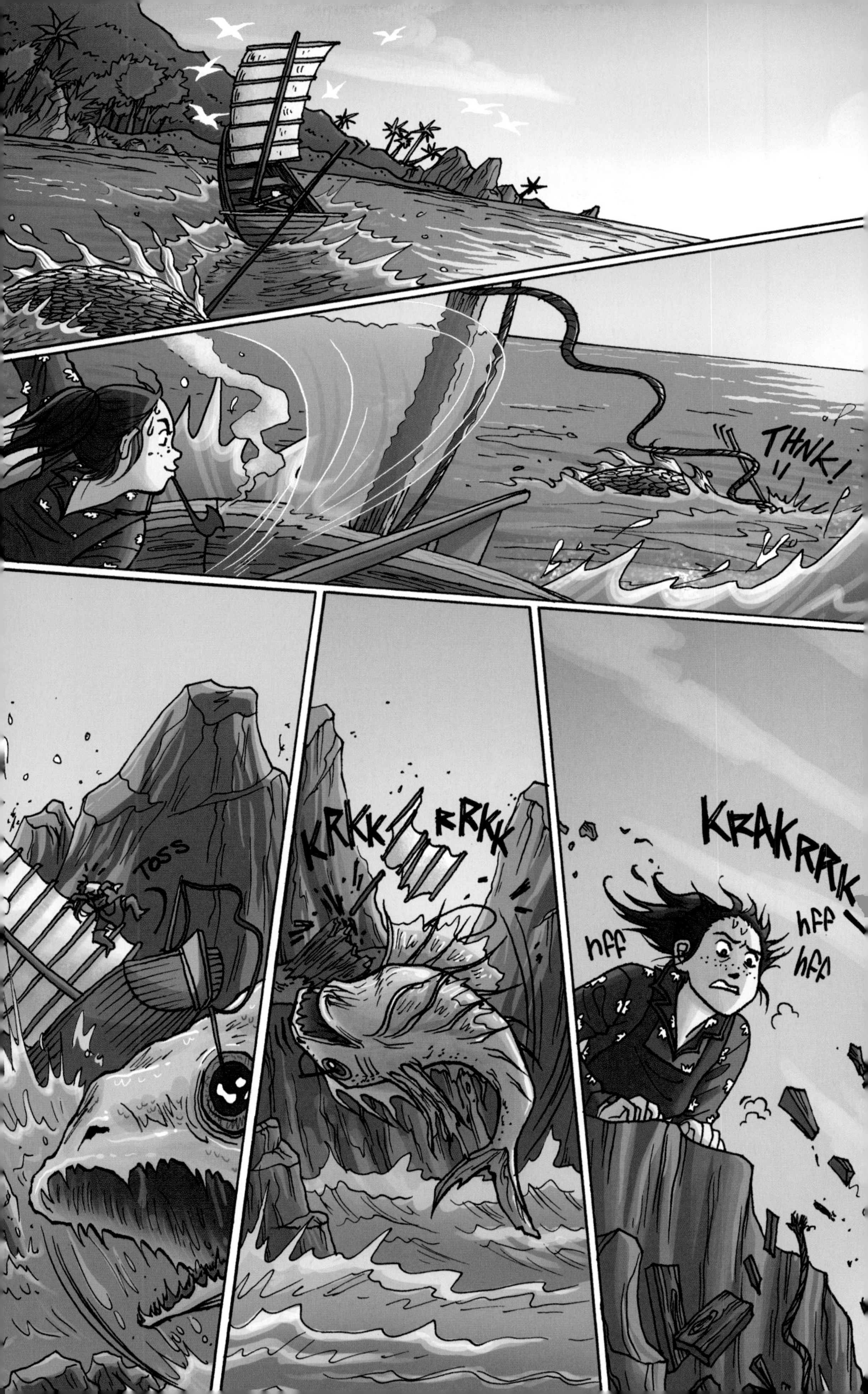
THNK!
TOSS
KRKK
RRKK
KRAKRRRK
hff
hff
hff

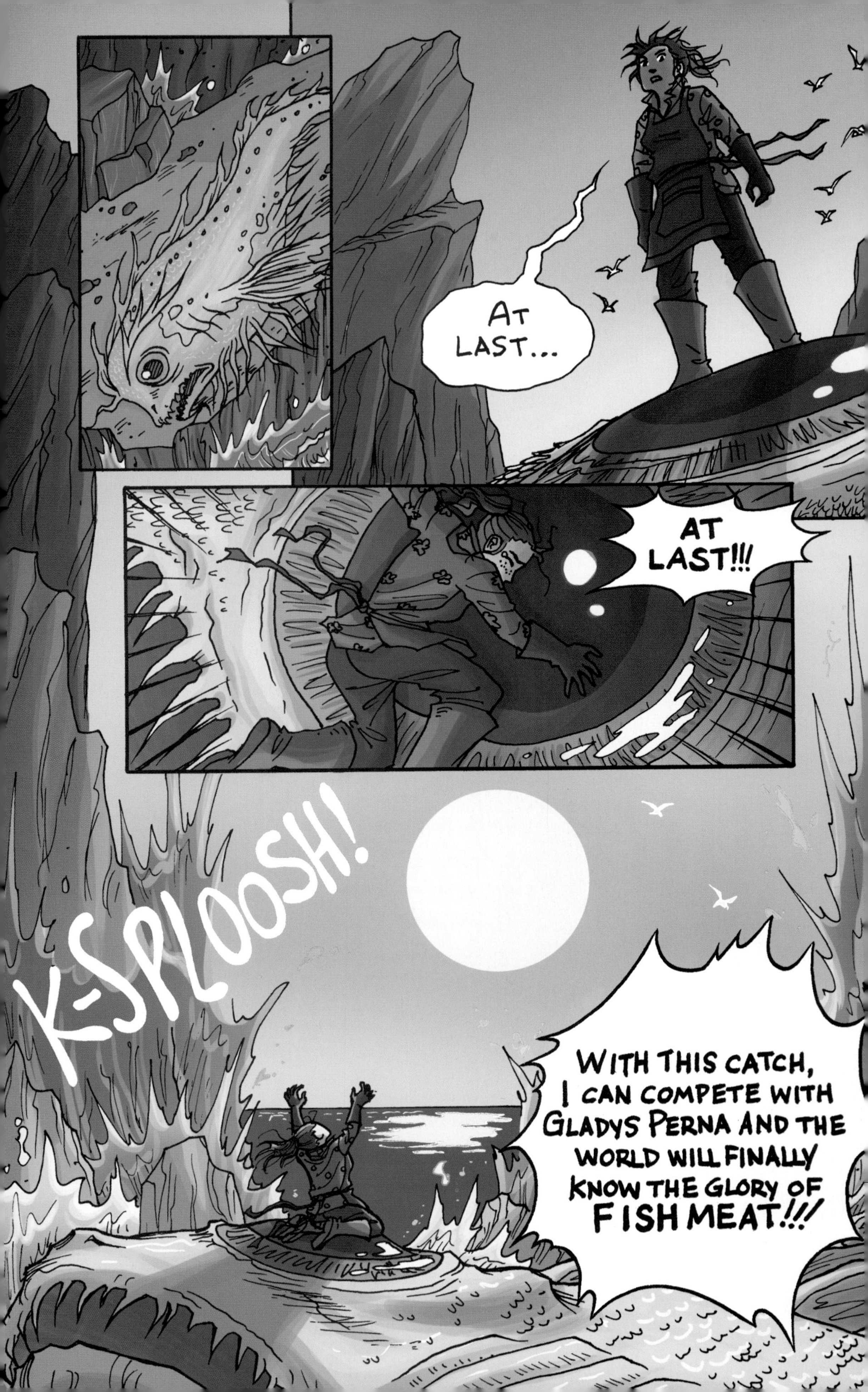
AT LAST...
AT LAST!!!
K-SPLOOSH!
WITH THIS CATCH, I CAN COMPETE WITH GLADYS PERNA AND THE WORLD WILL FINALLY KNOW THE GLORY OF FISH MEAT!!!

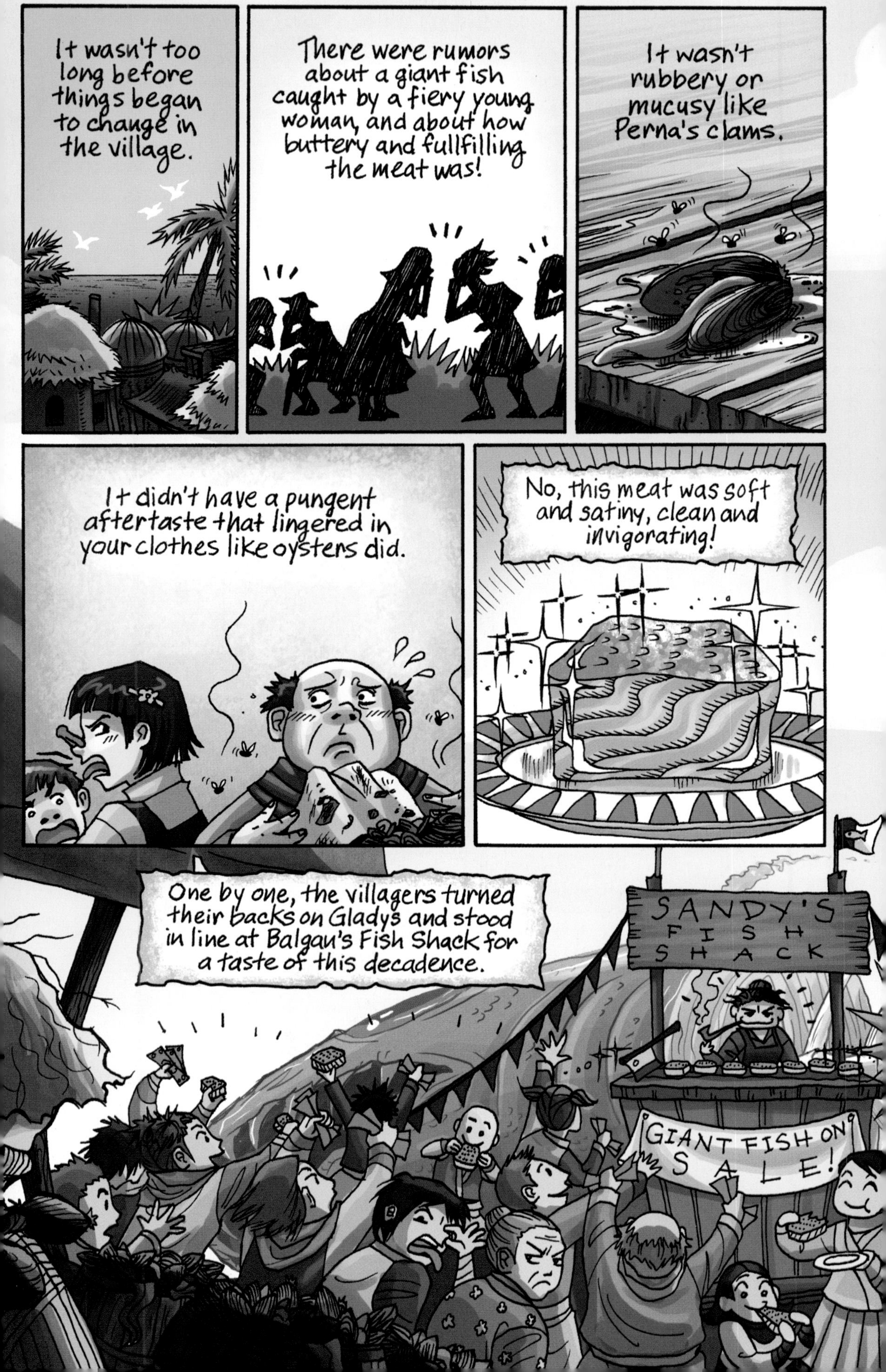

It wasn't too long before things began to change in the village.
There were rumors about a giant fish caught by a fiery young woman, and about how buttery and fullfilling the meat was!
It wasn't rubbery or mucusy like Perna's clams.
It didn't have a pungent aftertaste that lingered in your clothes like oysters did.
No, this meat was soft and satiny, clean and invigorating!
One by one, the villagers turned their backs on Gladys and stood in line at Balgau's Fish Shack for a taste of this decadence.
SANDY'S FISH SHACK
GIANT FISH ON SALE!

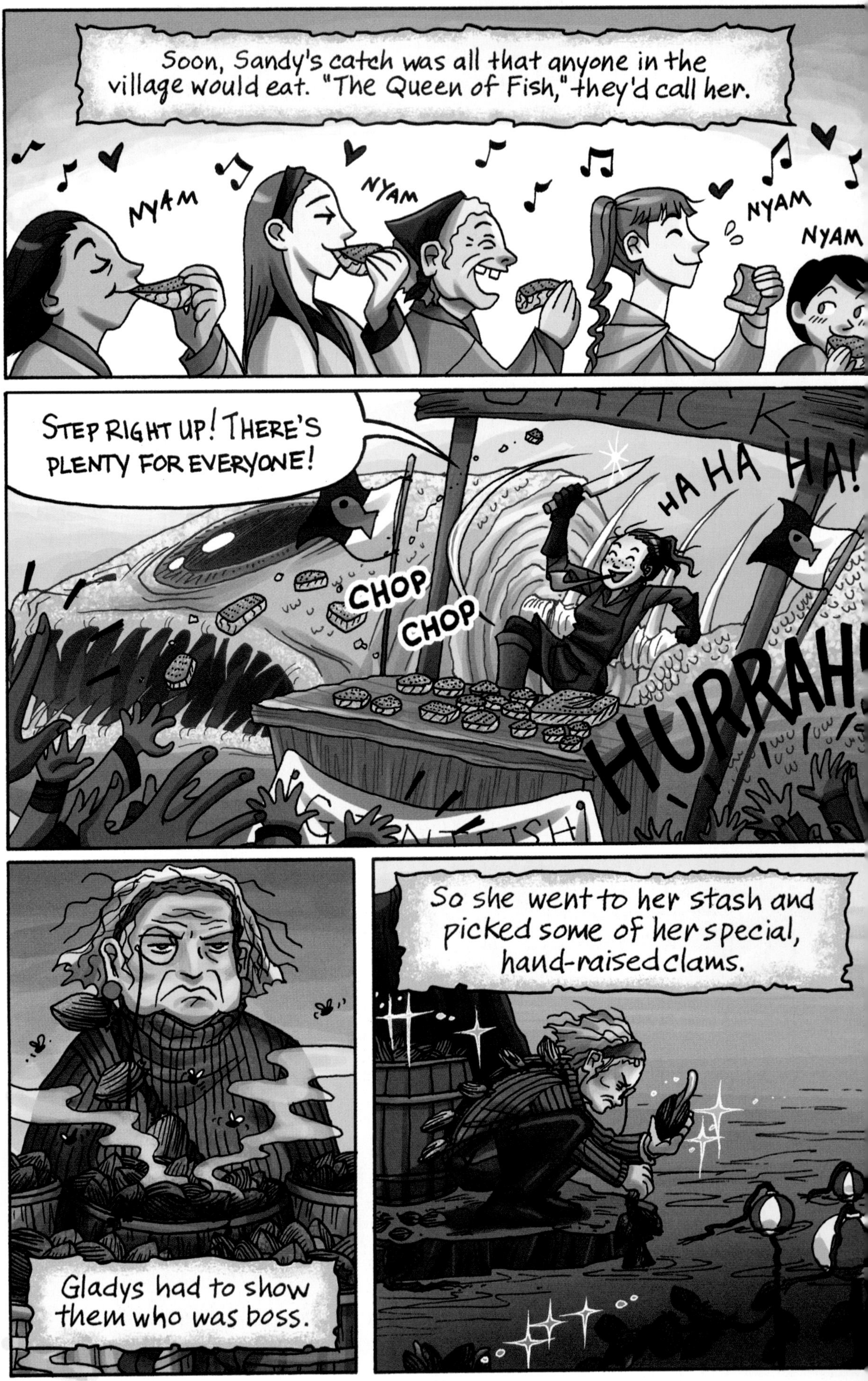
Soon, Sandy's catch was all that anyone in the village would eat. "The Queen of Fish," they'd call her.
NYAM
NYAM
NYAM
NYAM
STEP RIGHT UP! THERE'S PLENTY FOR EVERYONE!
CHOP
CHOP
HA HA HA!
HURRAH!
Gladys had to show them who was boss.
So she went to her stash and picked some of her special, hand-raised clams.

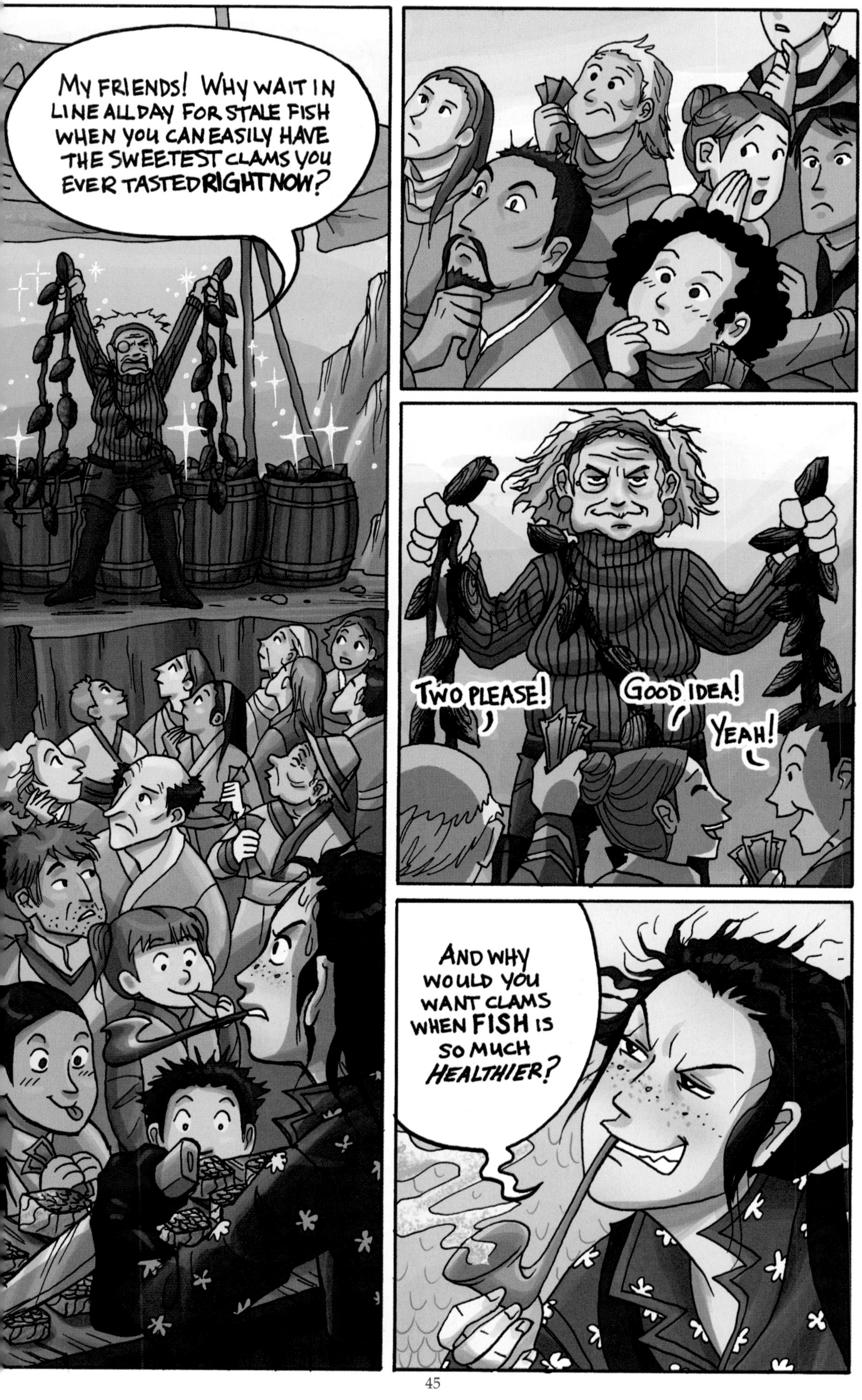
MY FRIENDS! WHY WAIT IN LINE ALL DAY FOR STALE FISH WHEN YOU CAN EASILY HAVE THE SWEETEST CLAMS YOU EVER TASTED **RIGHT NOW**?
TWO PLEASE!
GOOD IDEA!
YEAH!
AND WHY WOULD YOU WANT CLAMS WHEN **FISH** IS SO MUCH *HEALTHIER*?

THUNK!

FISH IS FILLED WITH OIL! CLAMS ARE FILLED WITH NUTRIENTS!

CLAMS TASTE LIKE RUBBER!!

FISH TASTES LIKE PAPER!!!

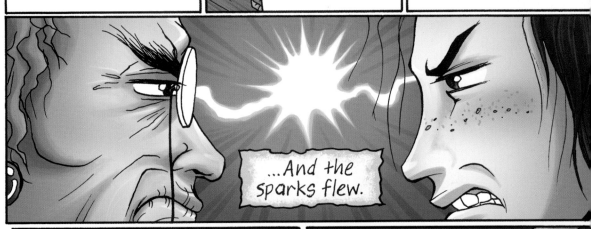

...And the sparks flew.

They became obsessed and never left their shacks.

They spent so much time with their wares, they even began to look like them!

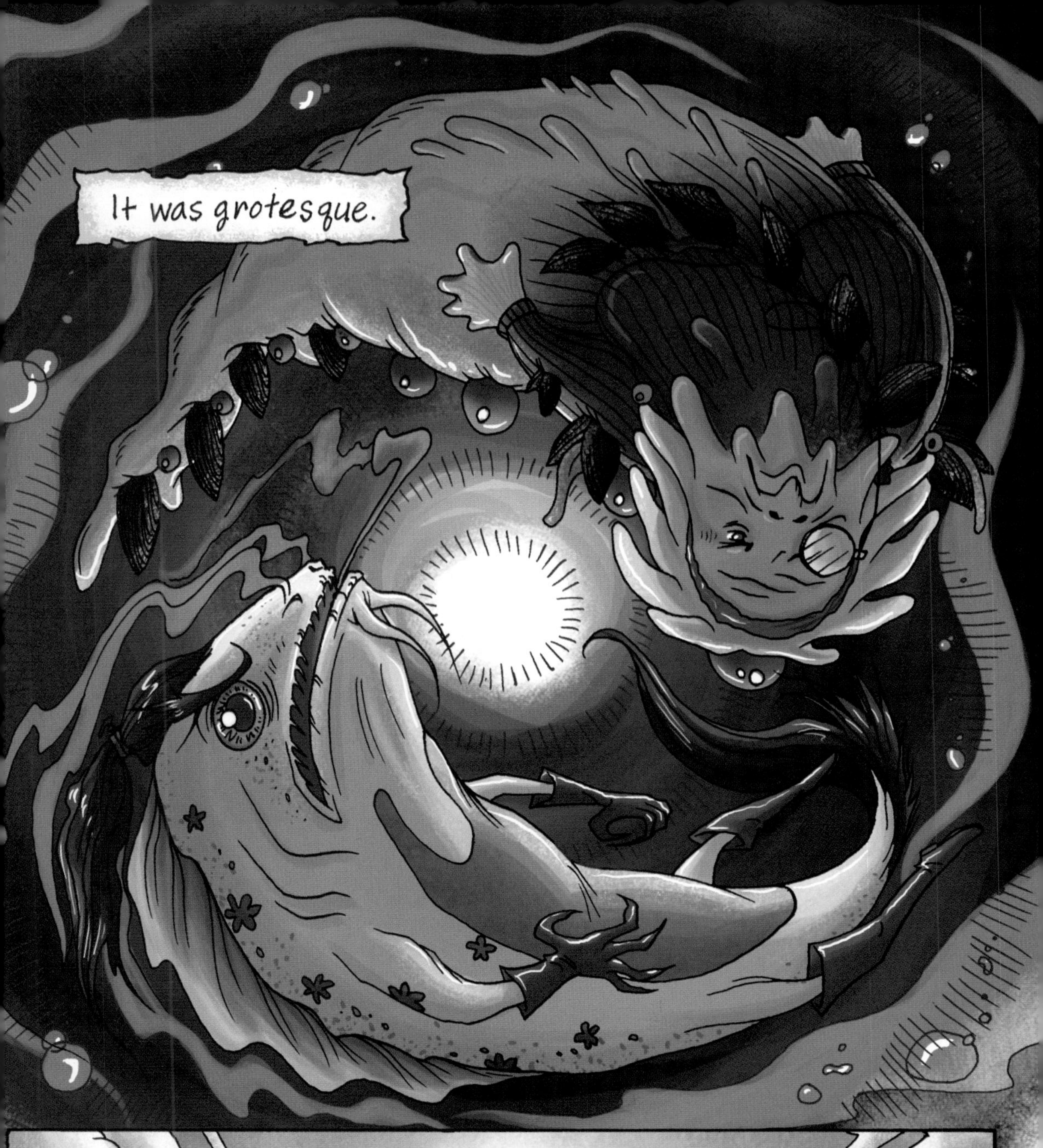
It was grotesque.

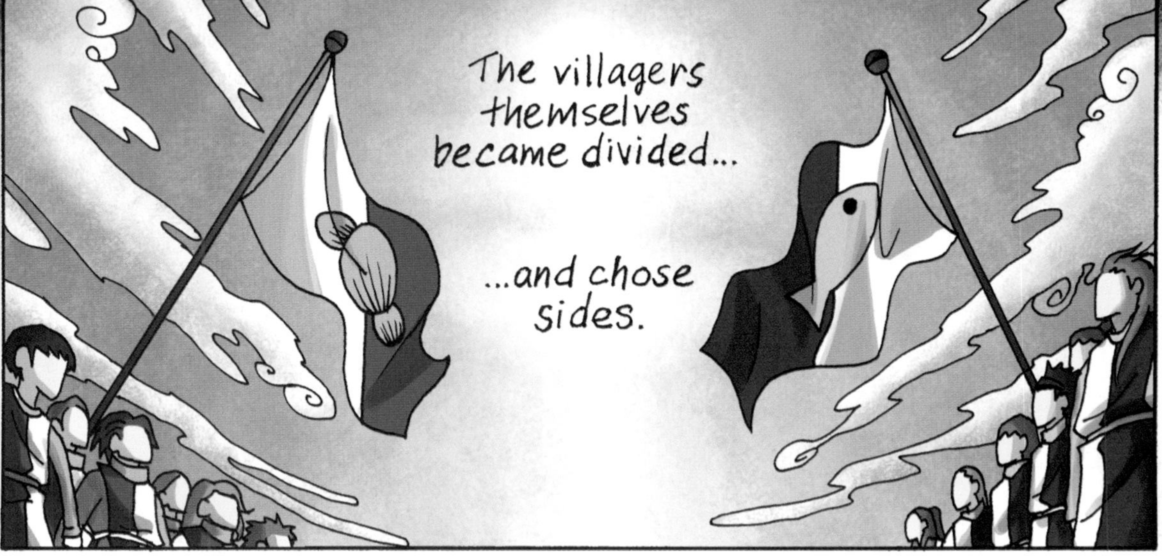
The villagers themselves became divided...
...and chose sides.

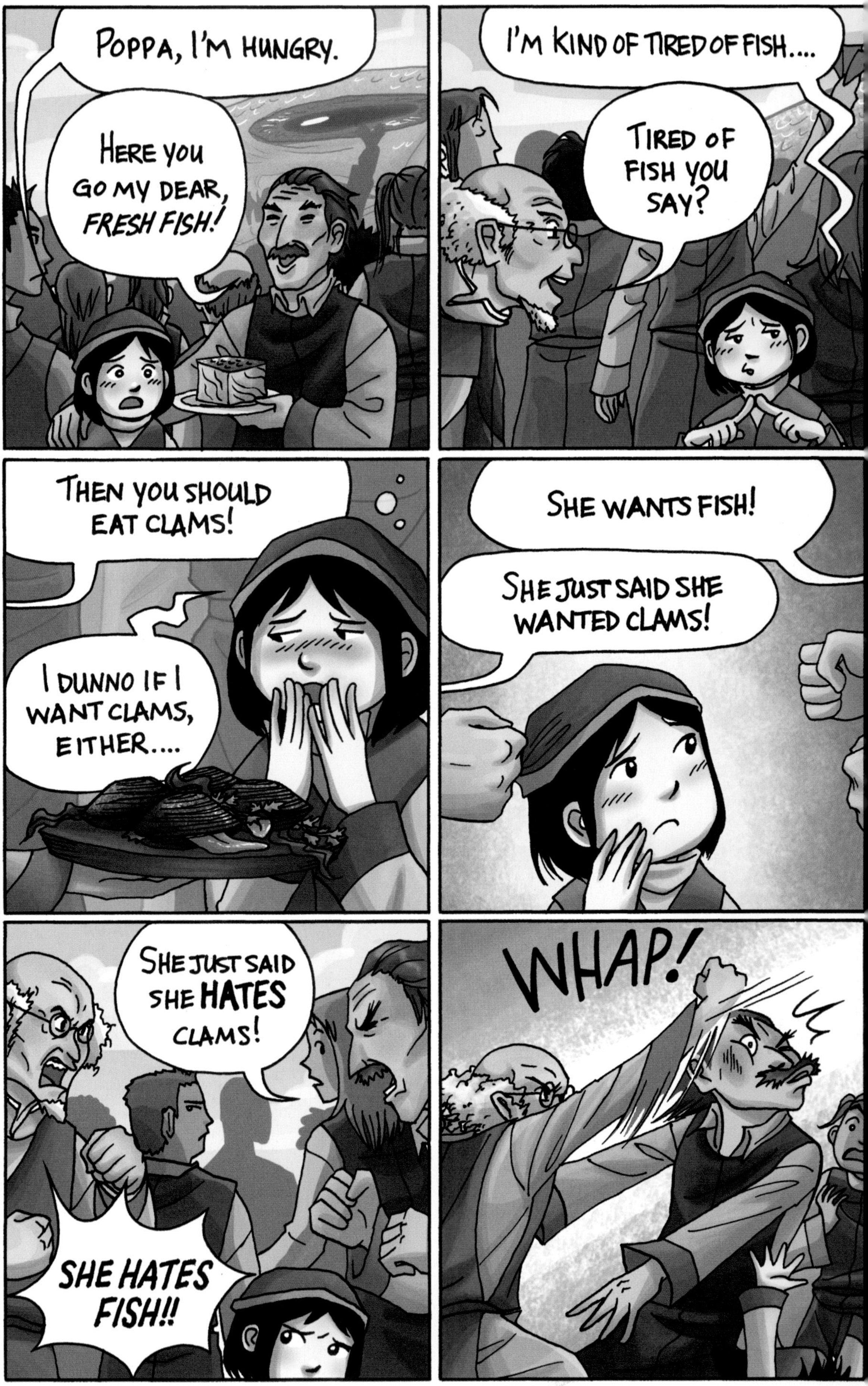
POPPA, I'M HUNGRY.
HERE YOU GO MY DEAR, *FRESH FISH!*
I'M KIND OF TIRED OF FISH....
TIRED OF FISH YOU SAY?
THEN YOU SHOULD EAT CLAMS!
I DUNNO IF I WANT CLAMS, EITHER....
SHE WANTS FISH!
SHE JUST SAID SHE WANTED CLAMS!
SHE JUST SAID SHE **HATES** CLAMS!
SHE HATES FISH!!
WHAP!

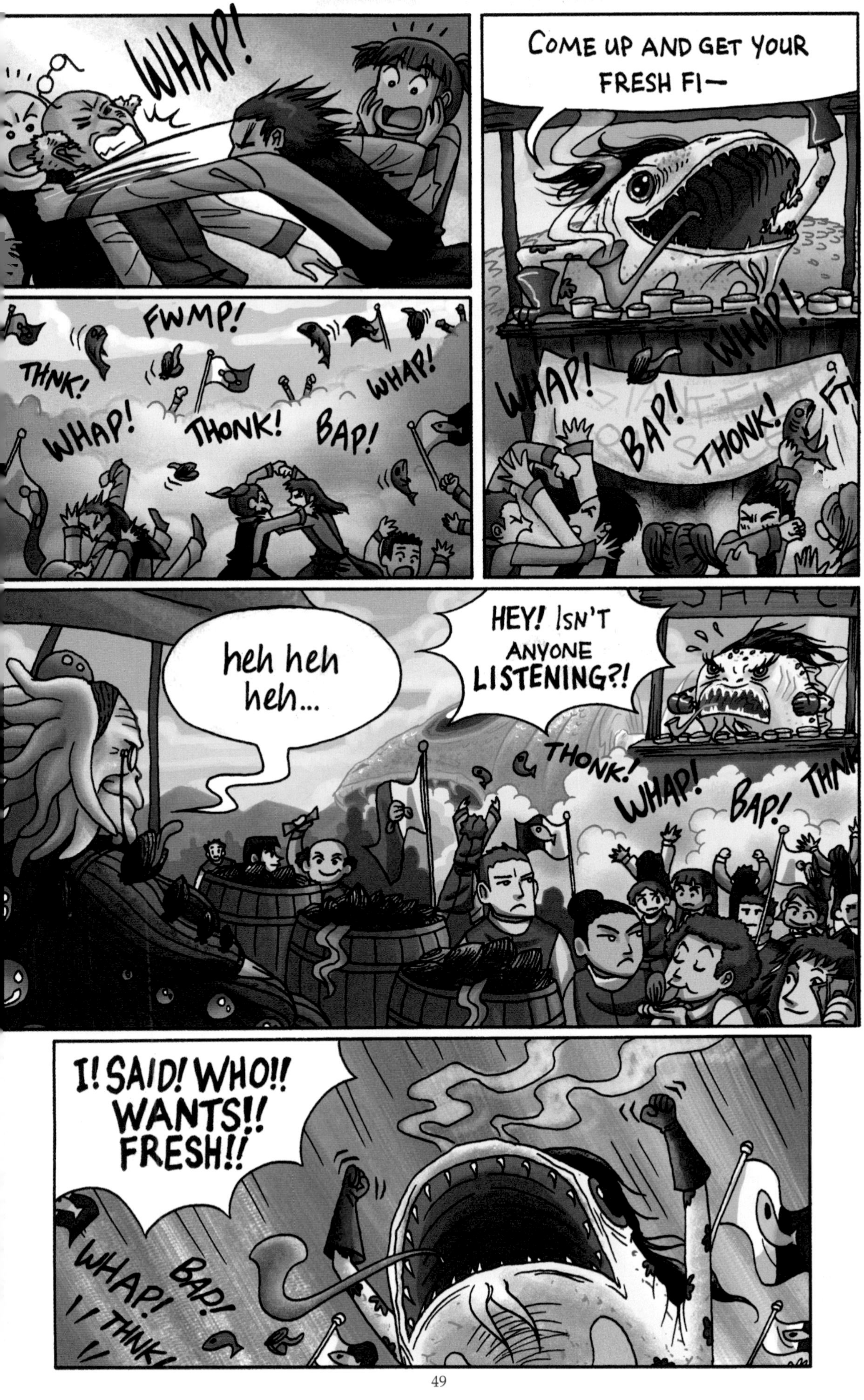
WHAP!
COME UP AND GET YOUR FRESH FI—
WHAP!
BAP!
THONK!
WHAP!
FWMP!
THNK!
WHAP!
THONK!
BAP!
WHAP!
heh heh heh...
HEY! ISN'T ANYONE LISTENING?!
THONK!
WHAP!
BAP!
I! SAID! WHO!! WANTS!! FRESH!!
WHAP!
BAP!
THNK

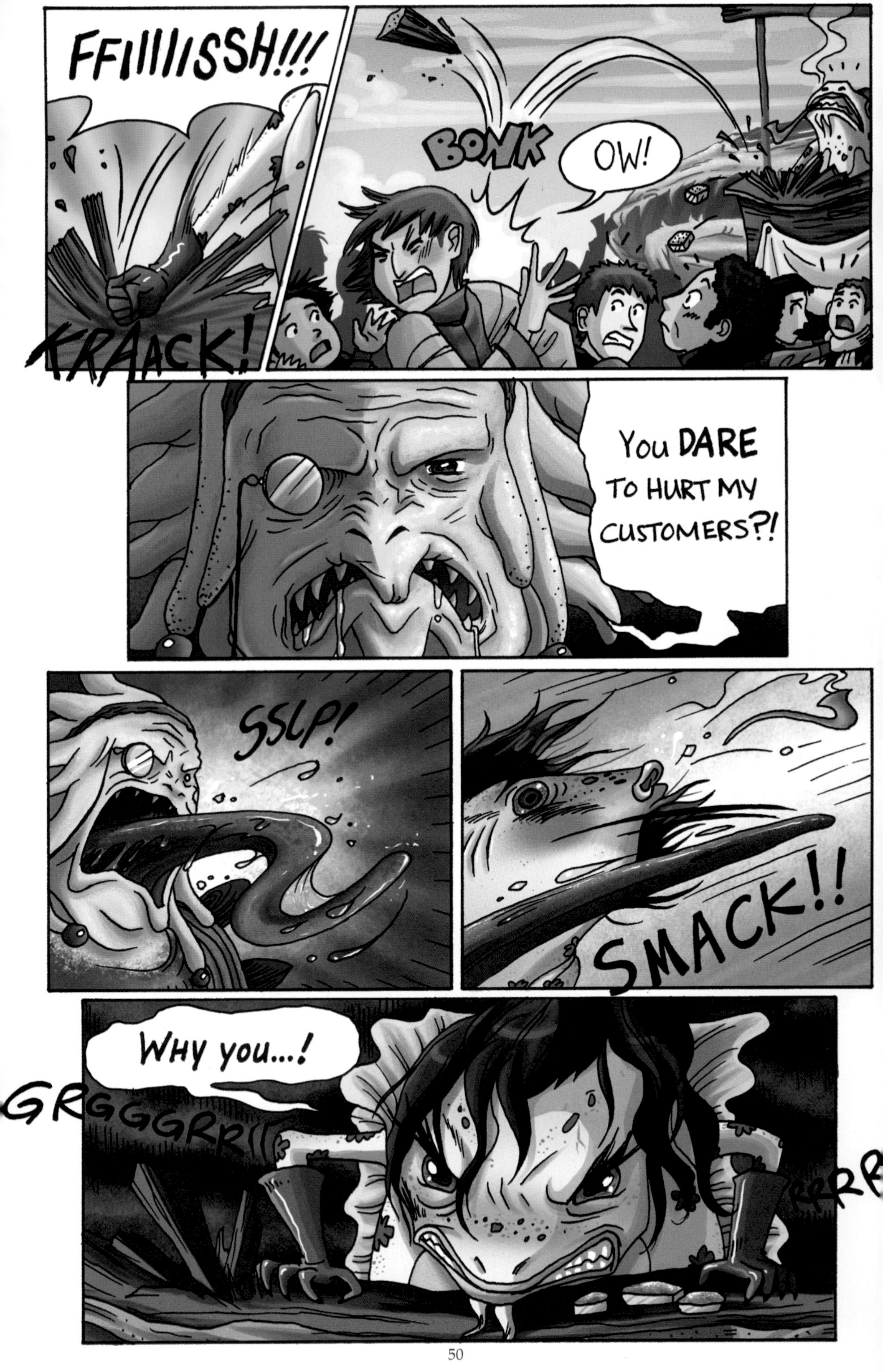
FFIIIIISSH!!!
KRAACK!
BONK
OW!
You DARE TO HURT MY CUSTOMERS?!
SSLP!
SMACK!!
WHY you...!
GRGGGGRR!!
RRRR

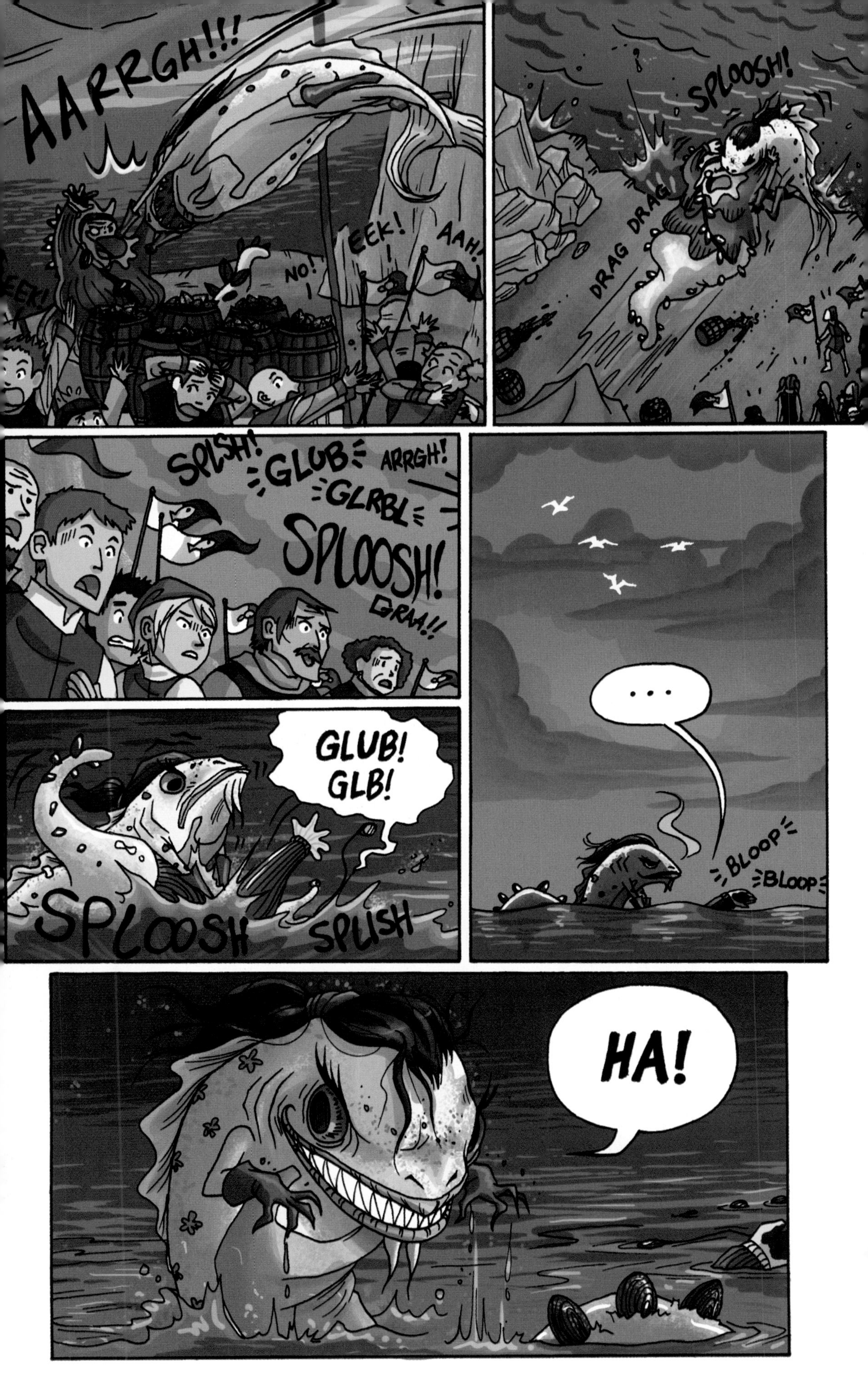
AARRGH!!!
EEK!
NO!
EEK!
AAH!
SPLOOSH!
DRAG DRAG
SPLSH!
GLUB
ARRGH!
GLRBL
SPLOOSH!
GRAA!!
GLUB! GLB!
SPLOOSH
SPLISH
. . .
BLOOP
BLOOP
HA!

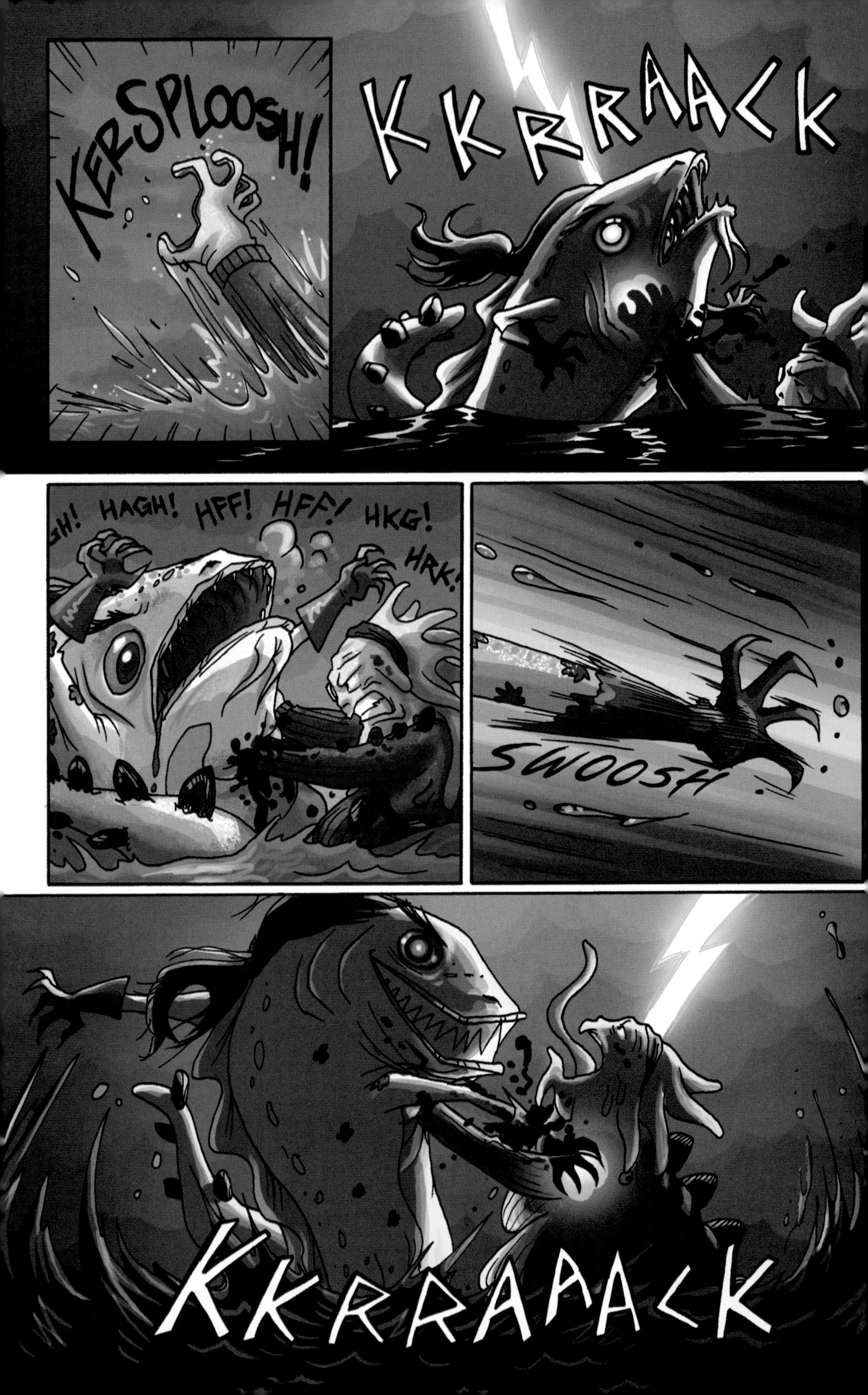
KERSPLOOSH!
KKRRAACK
GH! HAGH! HFF! HFF! HKG!
HRK!
SWOOSH
KKRRAAACK

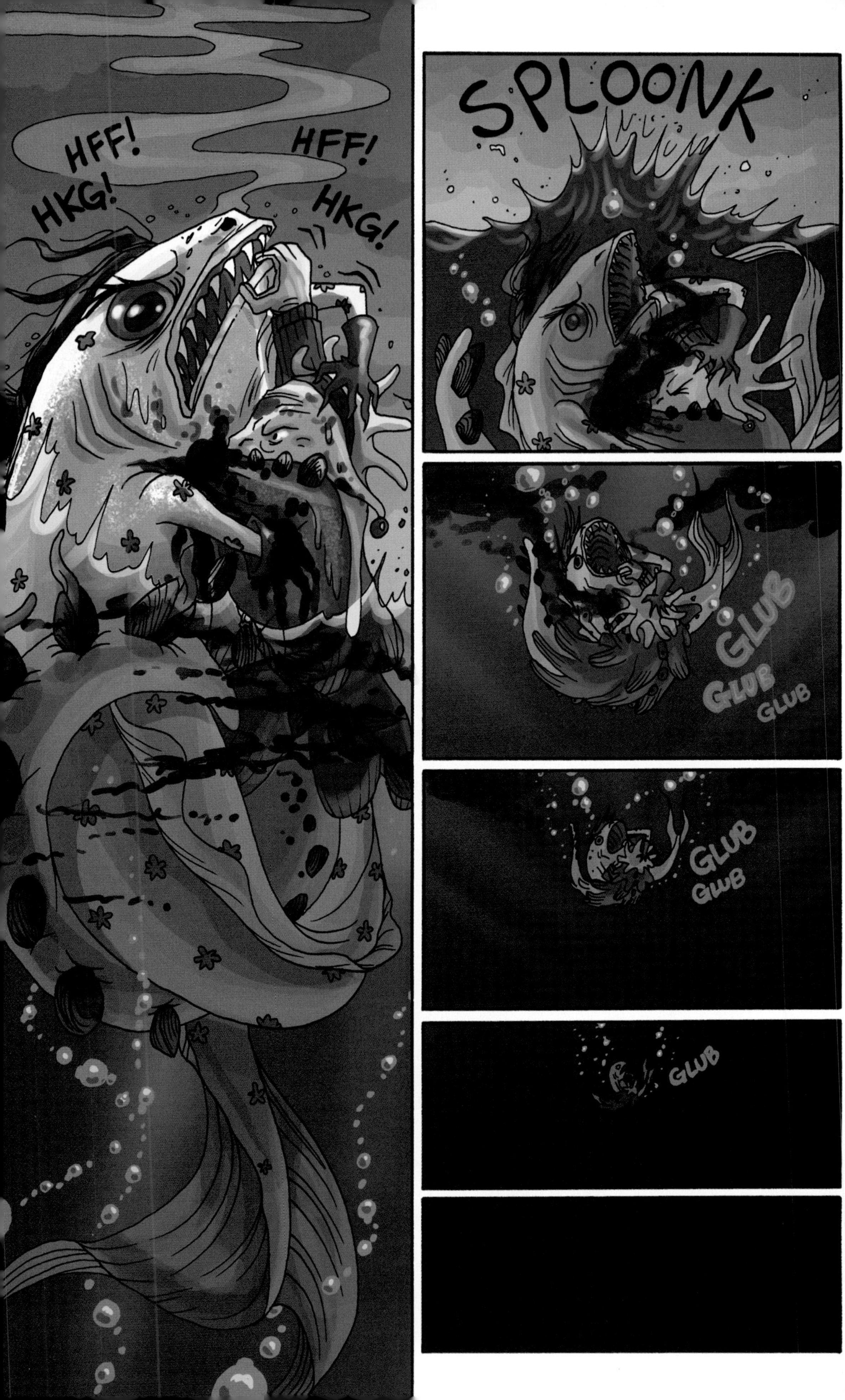
HFF!
HKG!
HFF!
HKG!
SPLOONK
GLUB
GLUB
GLUB
GLUB
GWB
GLUB

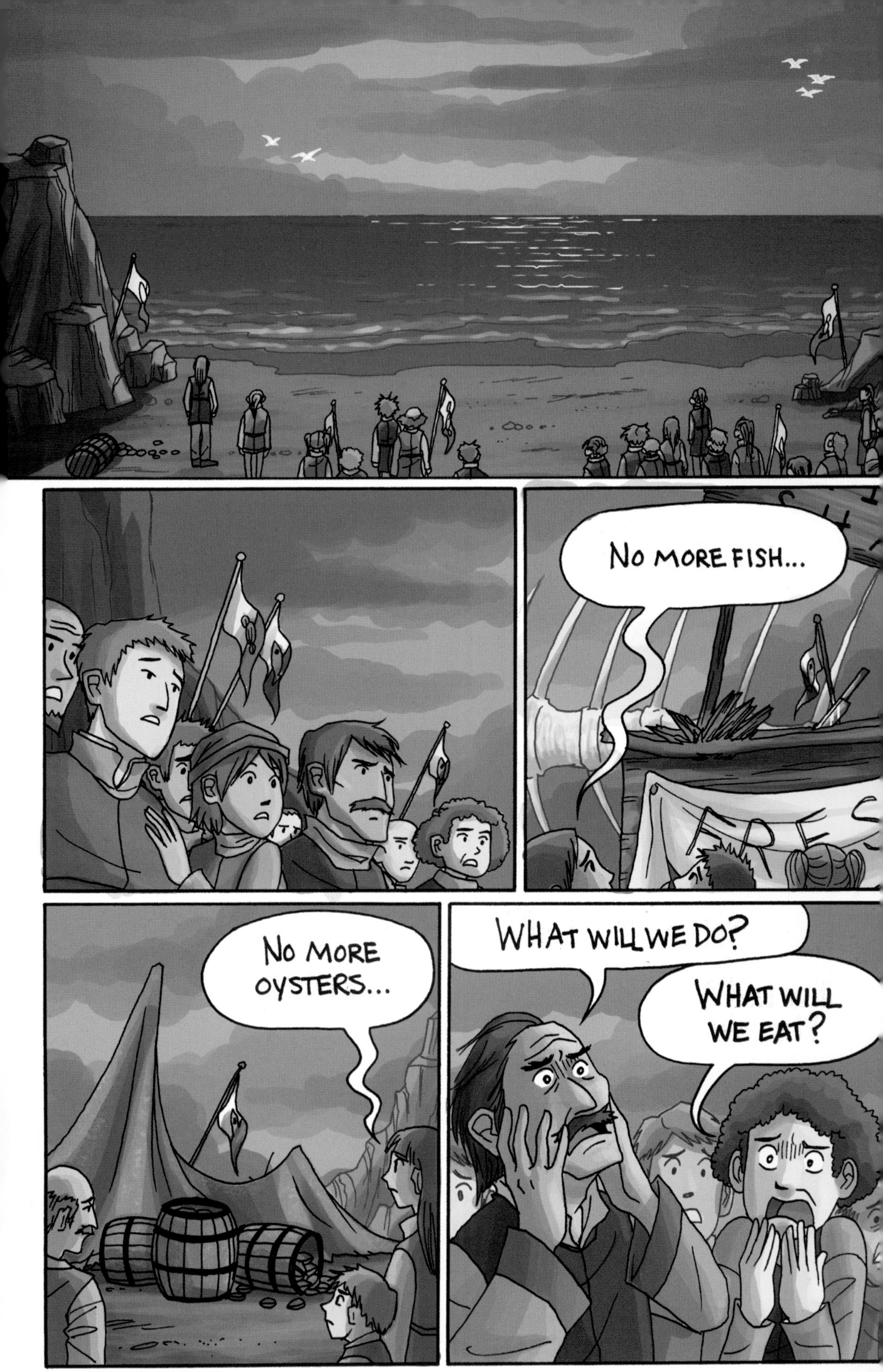
No MORE FISH...
No MORE OYSTERS...
WHAT WILL WE DO?
WHAT WILL WE EAT?

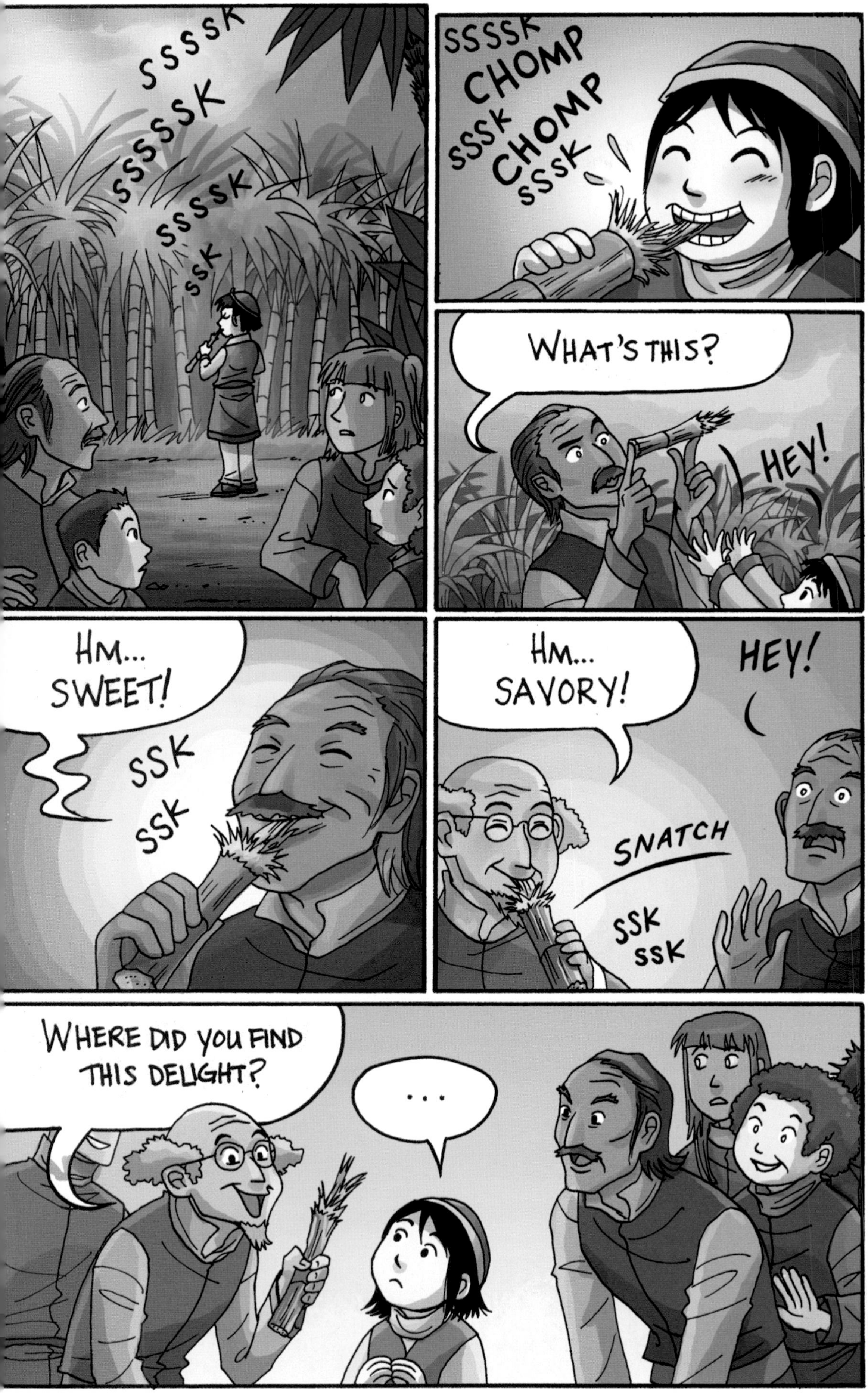
SSSSK
SSSSSK
SSSSSK
SSSSSK
SSK
SSSSK
CHOMP
SSSK
CHOMP
SSSK
WHAT'S THIS?
HEY!
HM... SWEET!
SSK
SSK
HM... SAVORY!
HEY!
SNATCH
SSK
SSK
WHERE DID YOU FIND THIS DELIGHT?
. . .

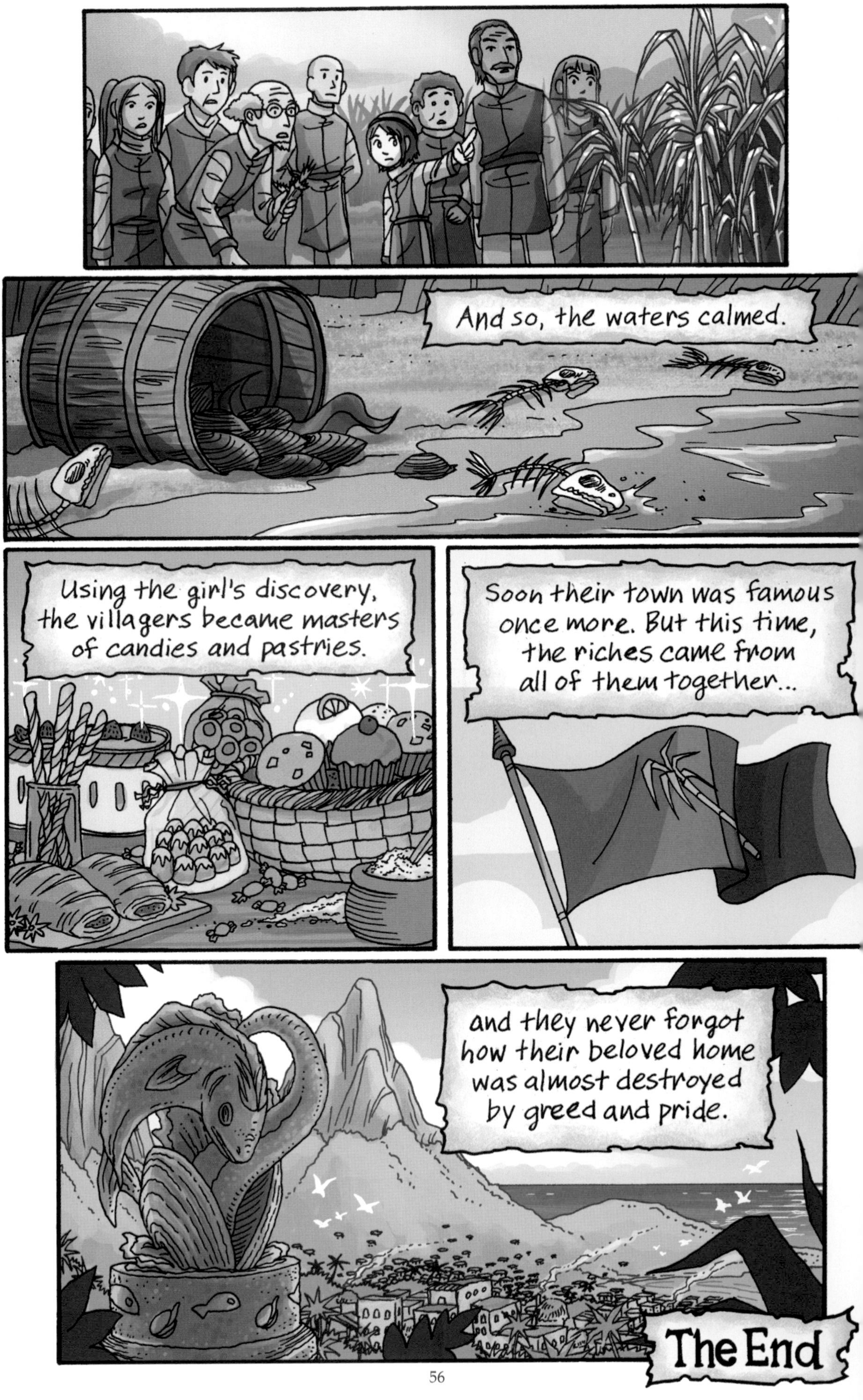
And so, the waters calmed.
Using the girl's discovery, the villagers became masters of candies and pastries.
Soon their town was famous once more. But this time, the riches came from all of them together...
and they never forgot how their beloved home was almost destroyed by greed and pride.
The End

Farewell, Little Karla

by Thomas Herpich

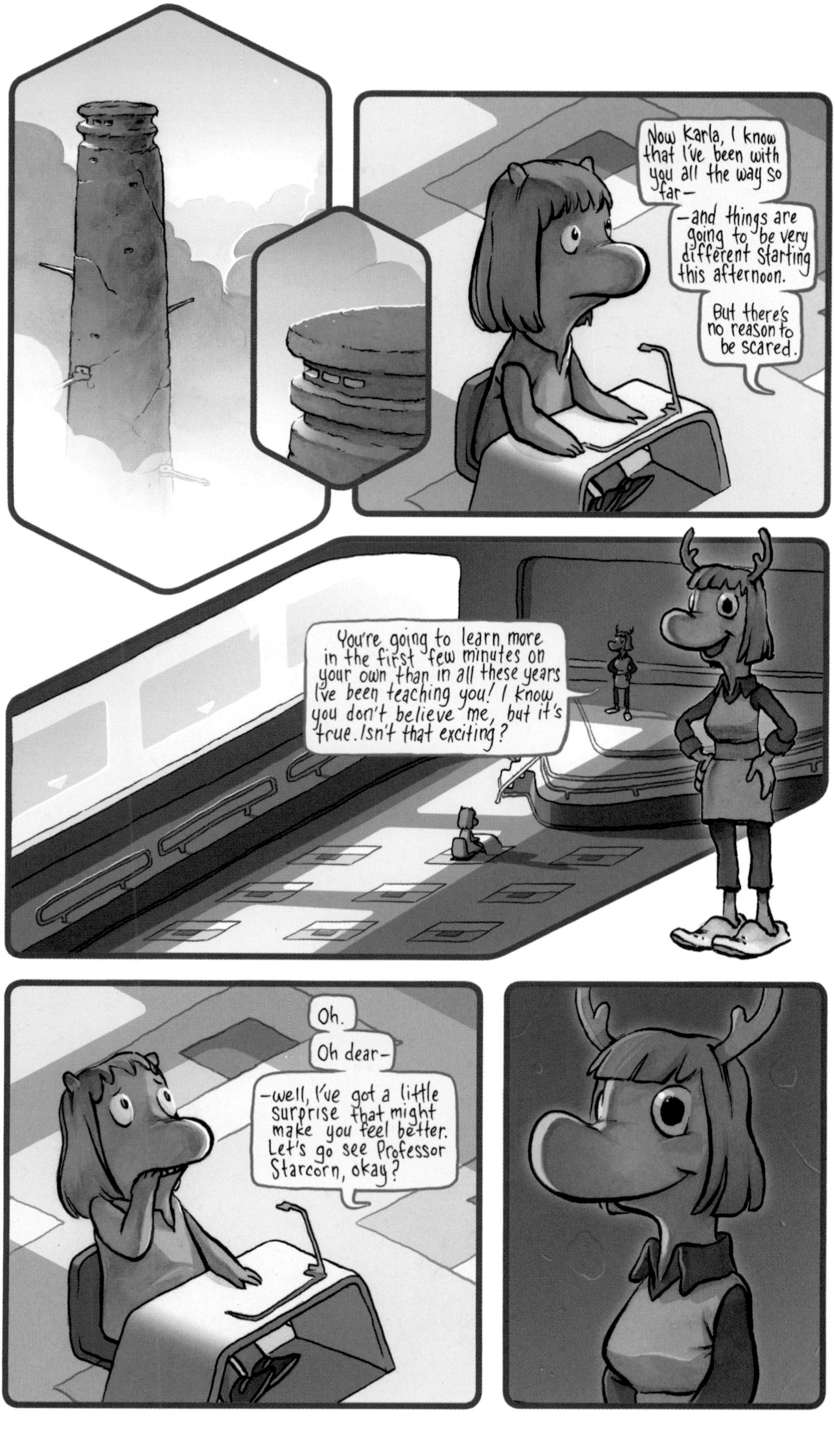

Now Karla, I know that I've been with you all the way so far–
–and things are going to be very different starting this afternoon.
But there's no reason to be scared.
You're going to learn more in the first few minutes on your own than in all these years I've been teaching you! I know you don't believe me, but it's true. Isn't that exciting?
Oh.
Oh dear–
–well, I've got a little surprise that might make you feel better. Let's go see Professor Starcorn, okay?

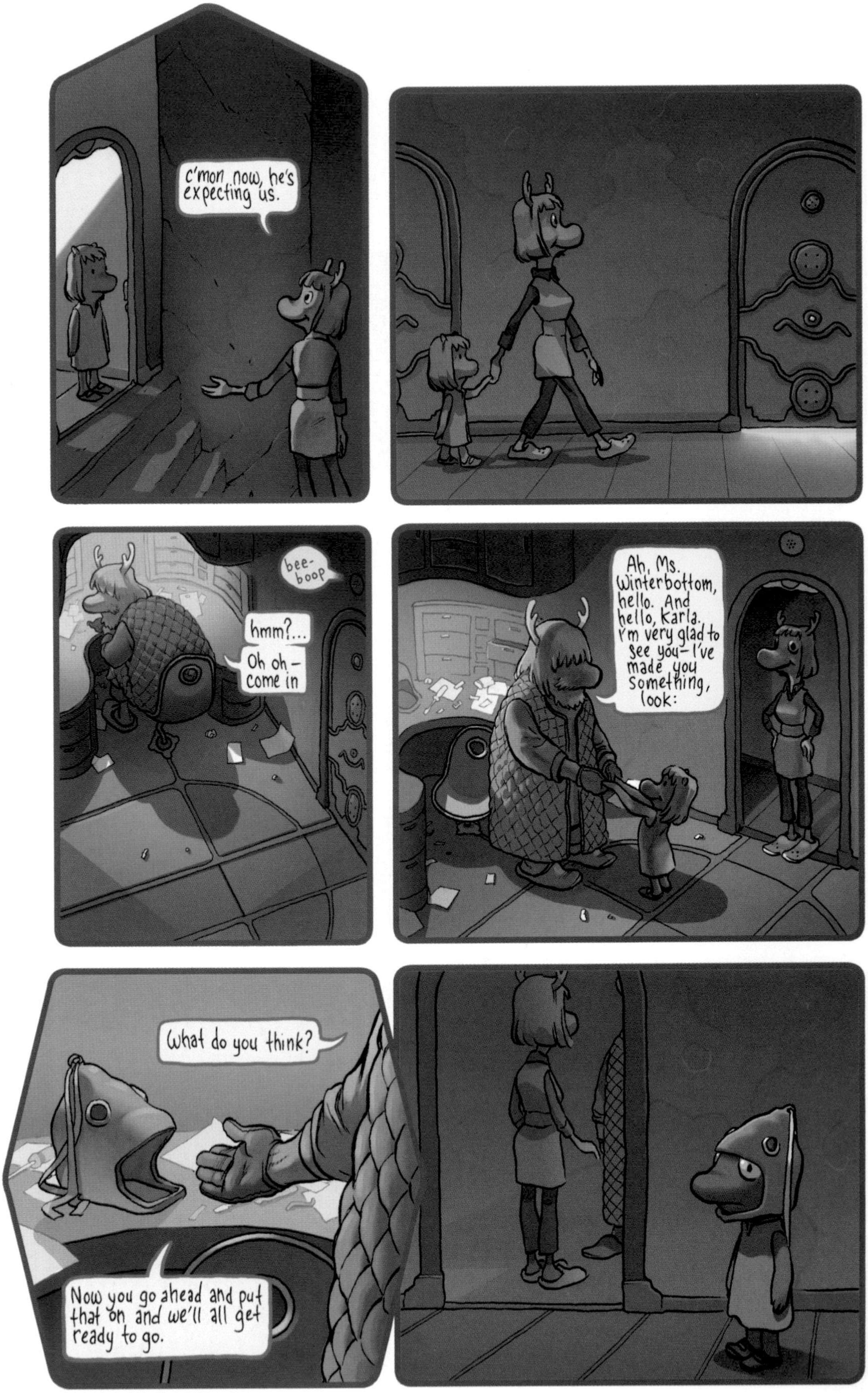
C'mon now, he's expecting us.
bee-boop
hmm?...
Oh oh - come in
Ah, Ms. Winterbottom, hello. And hello, Karla. I'm very glad to see you- I've made you something, look:
What do you think?
Now you go ahead and put that on and we'll all get ready to go.

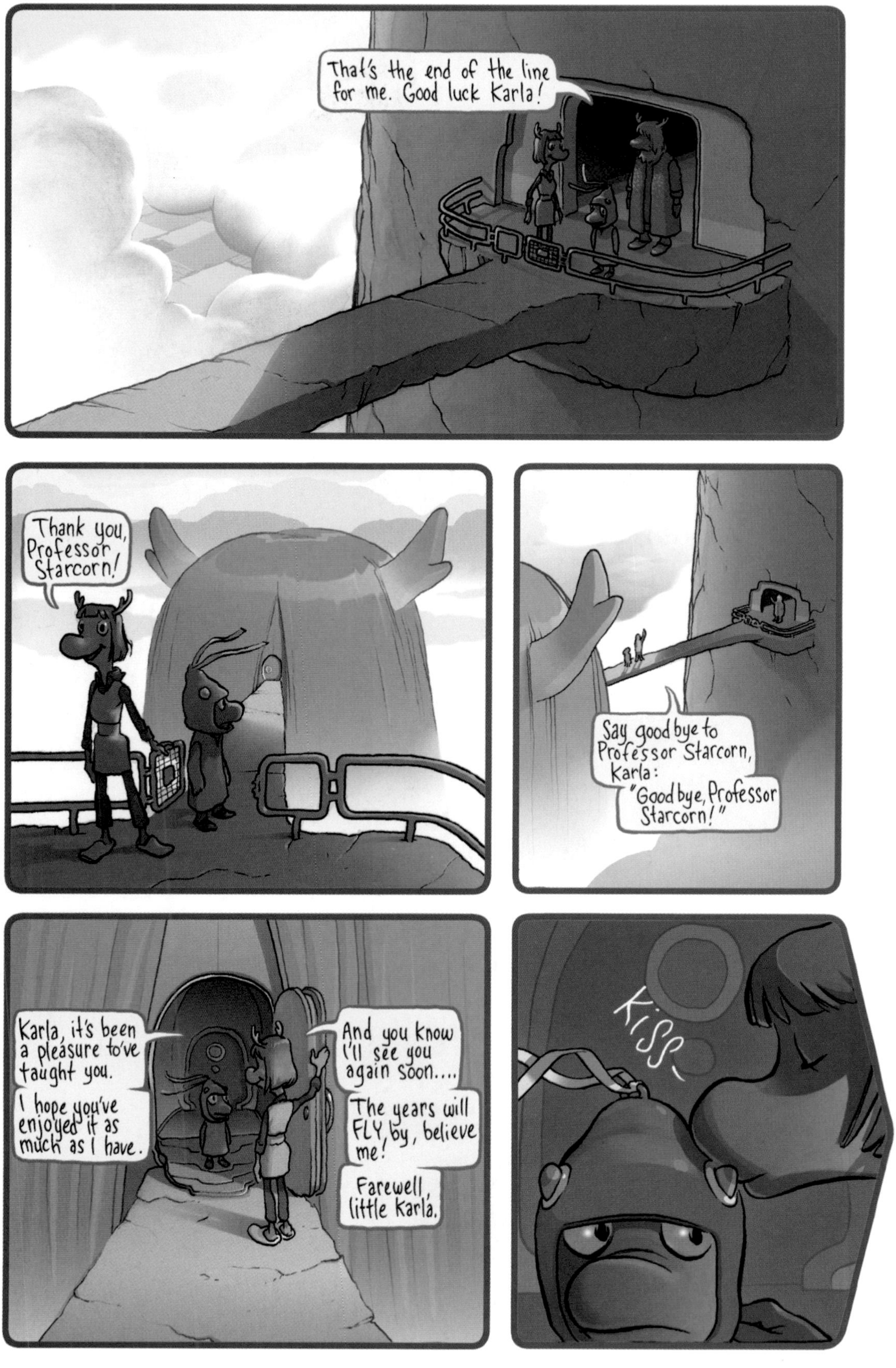
That's the end of the line for me. Good luck Karla!
Thank you, Professor Starcorn!
Say good bye to Professor Starcorn, Karla: "Good bye, Professor Starcorn!"
Karla, it's been a pleasure to've taught you.
I hope you've enjoyed it as much as I have.
And you know I'll see you again soon....
The years will FLY, by, believe me!
Farewell, little Karla.
KISS

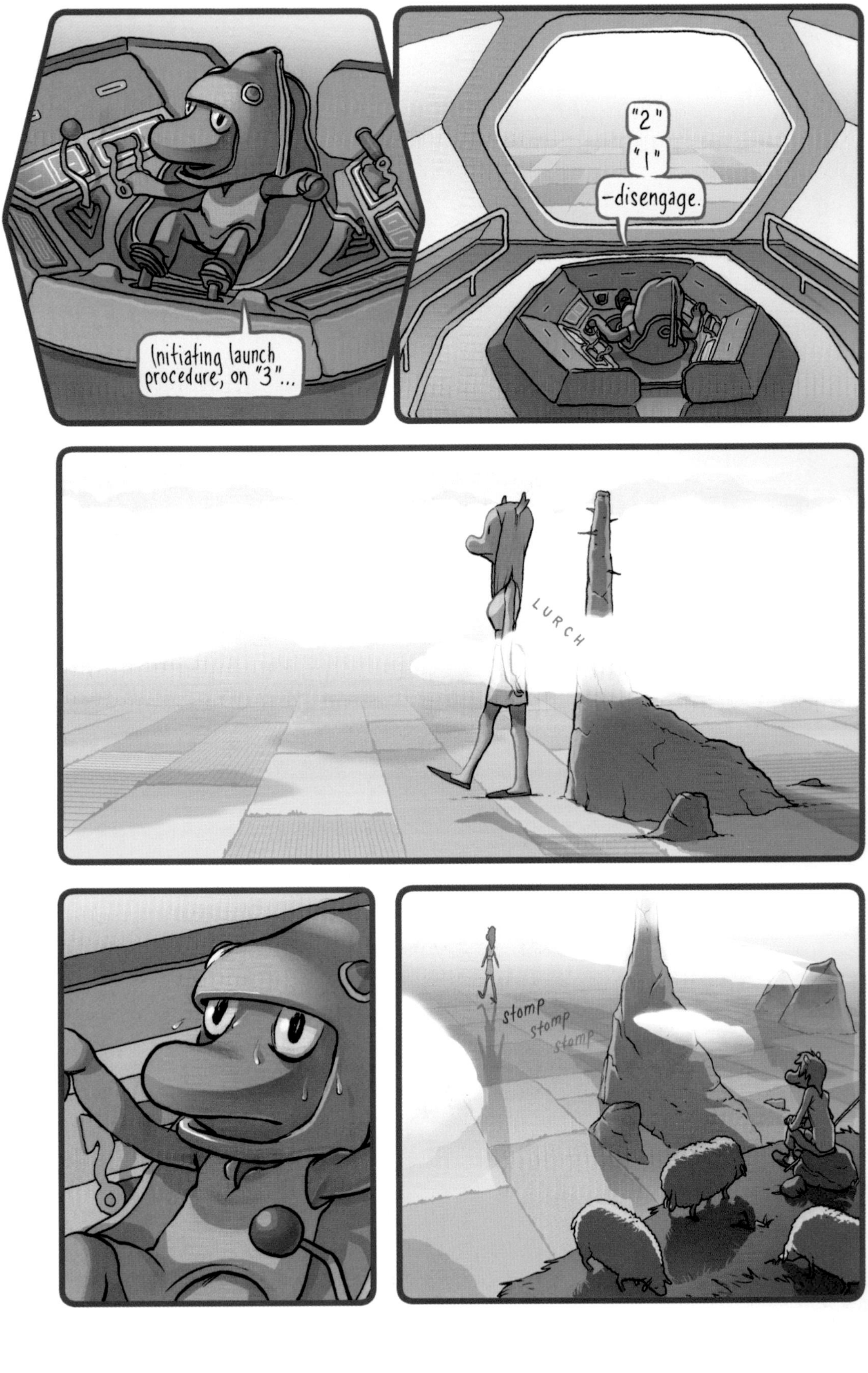
Initiating launch procedure; on "3"...
"2"
"1"
-disengage.
LURCH
stomp
stomp
stomp

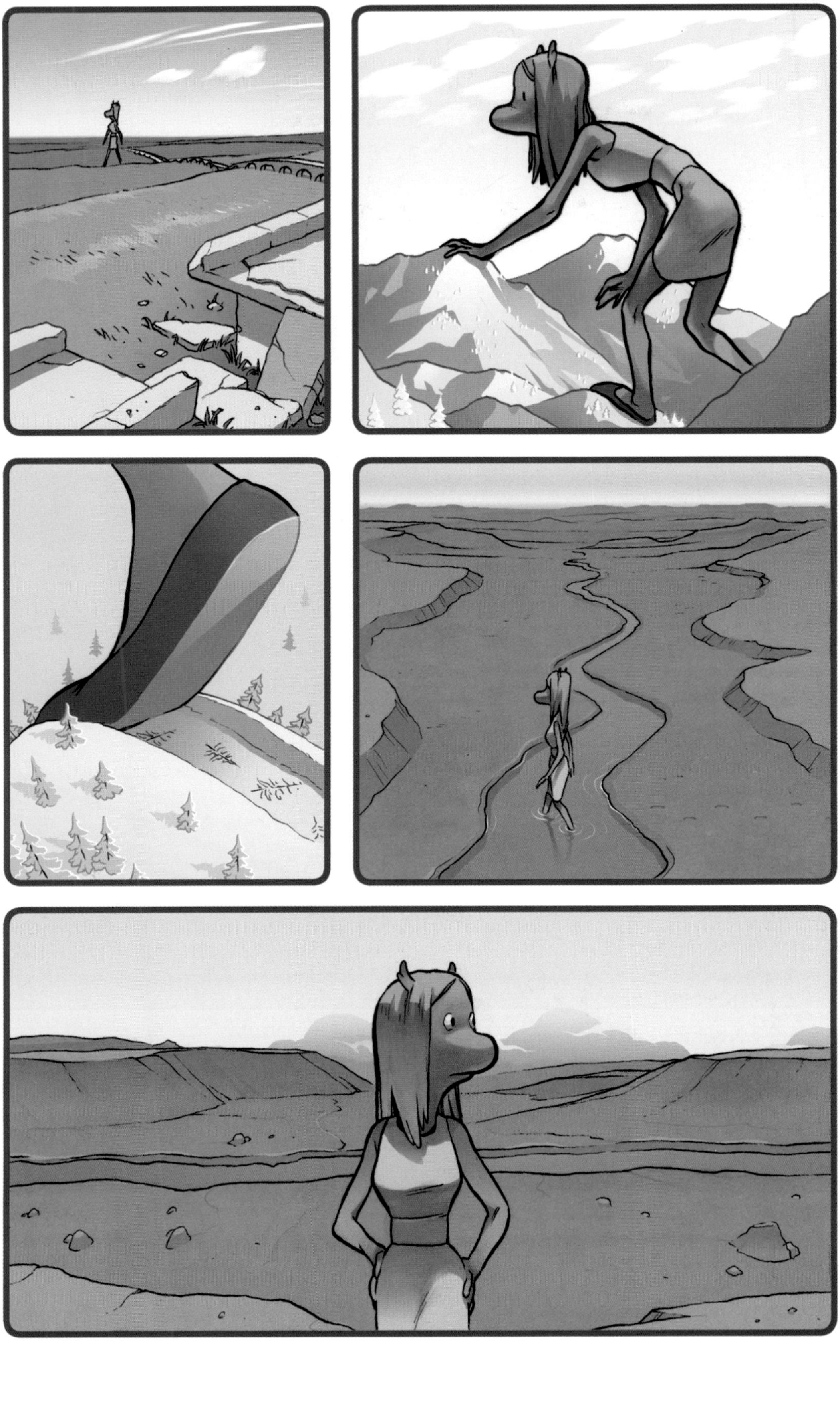

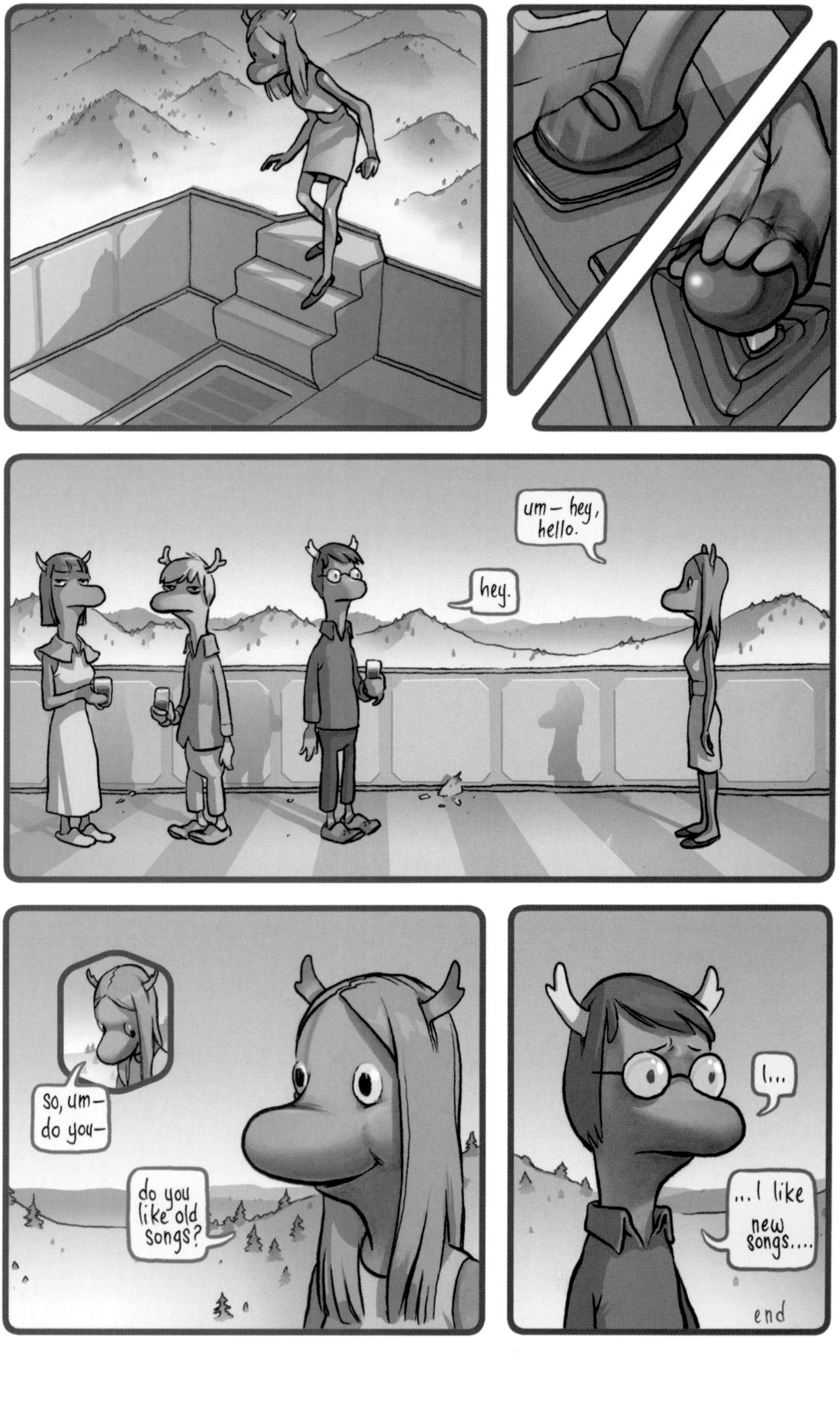
um— hey, hello.
hey.
So, um— do you—
do you like old songs?
I...
...I like new songs....
end

OCTOBER
2006

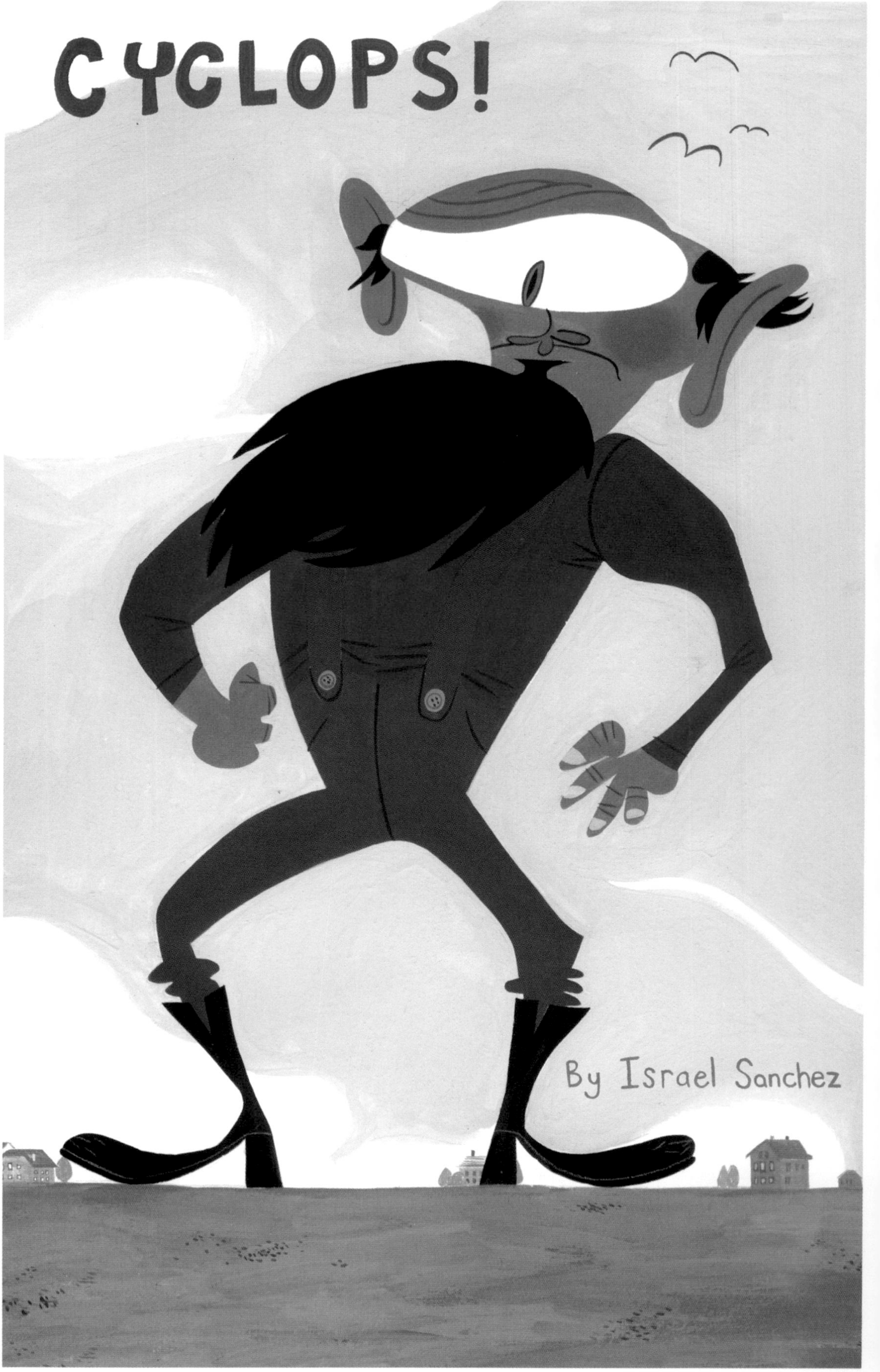
CYCLOPS!
By Israel Sanchez

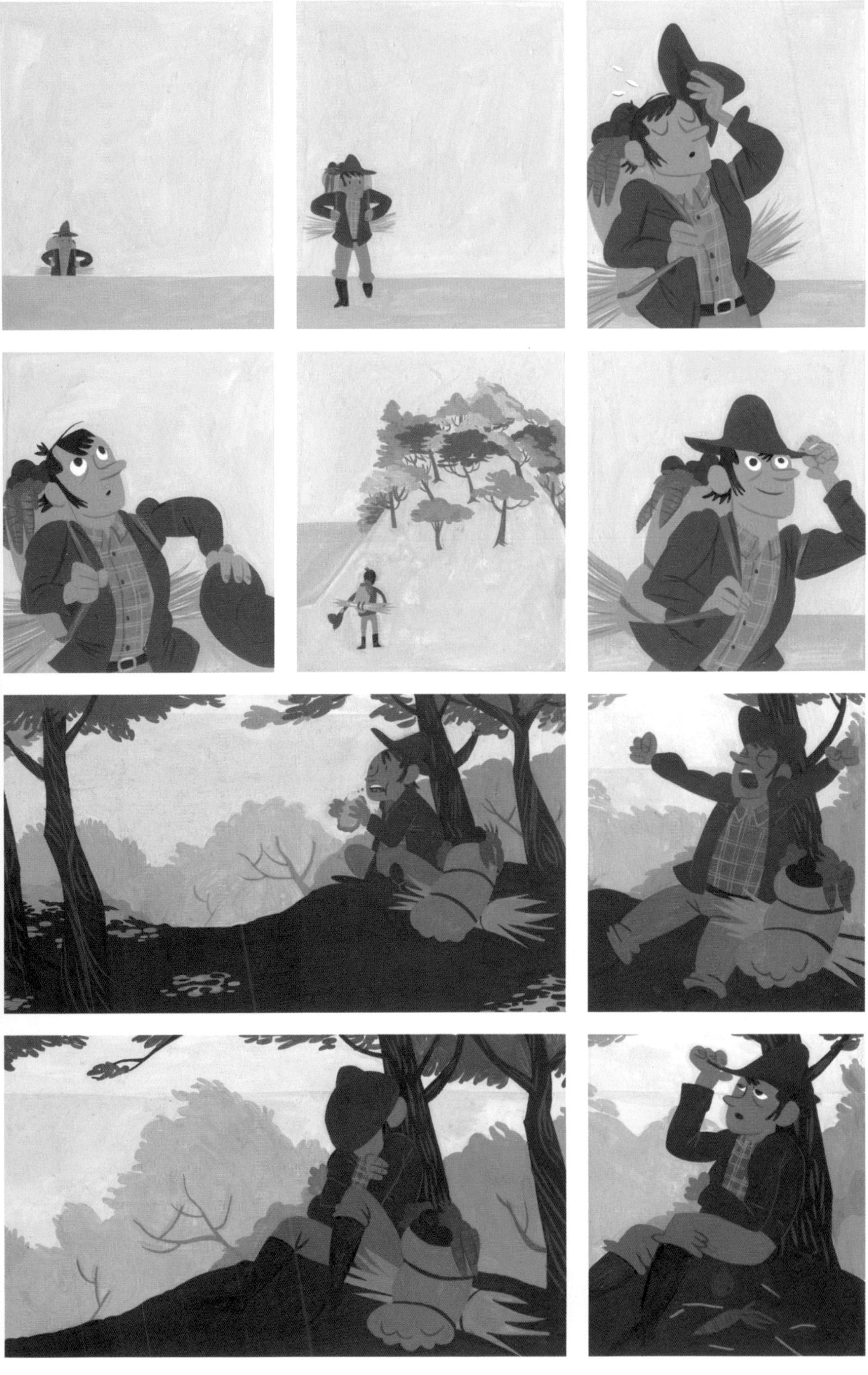

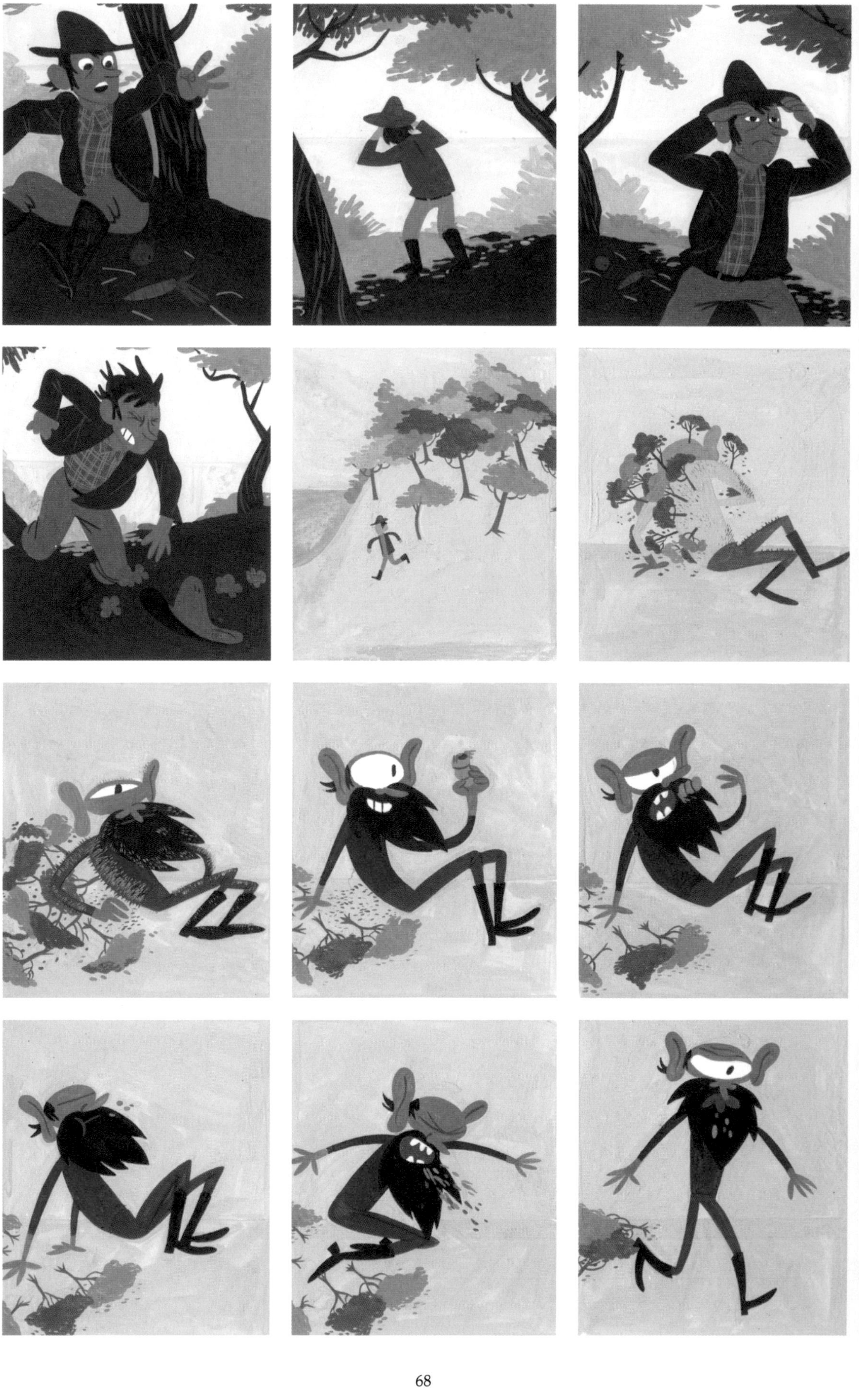

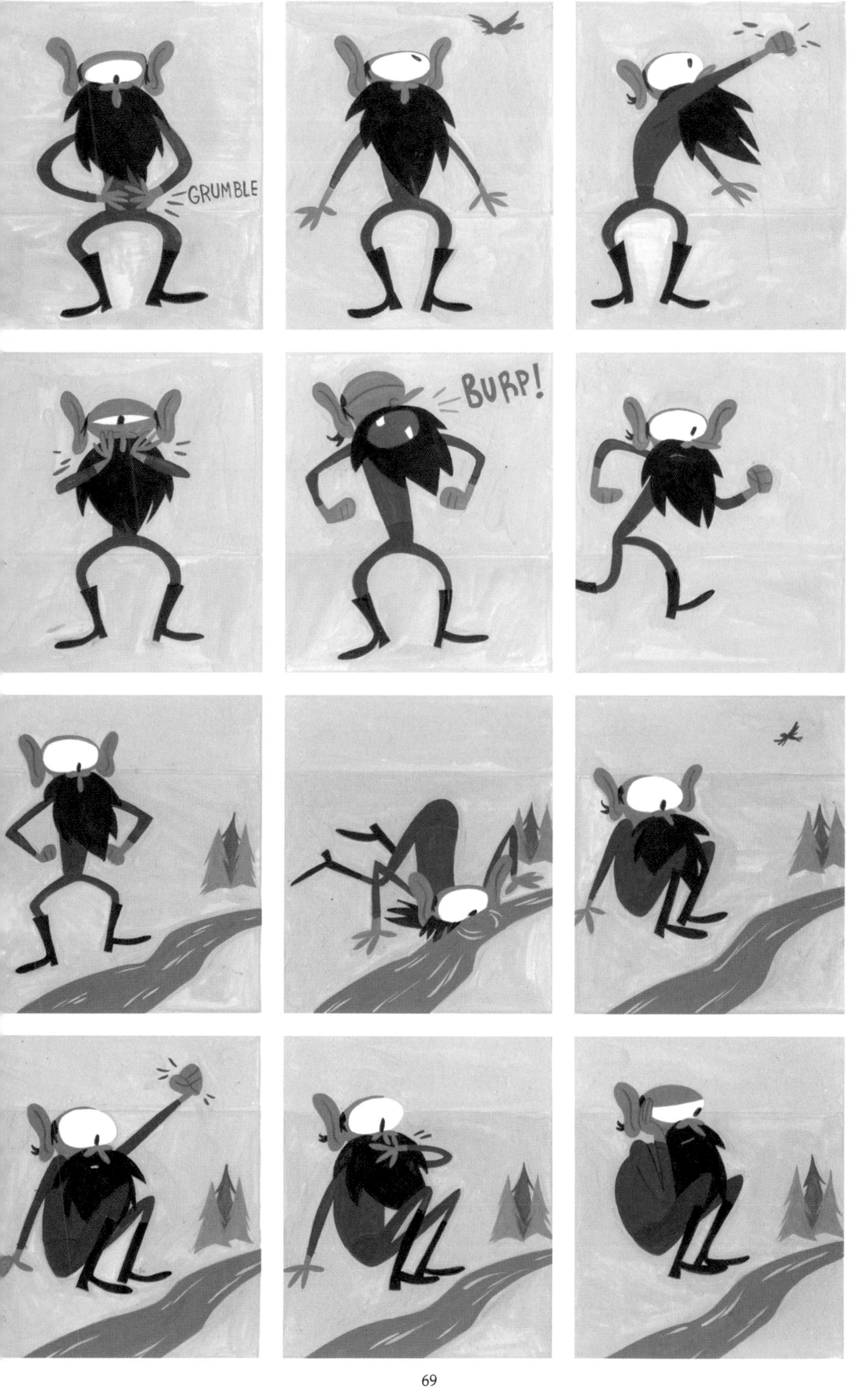
GRUMBLE
BURP!

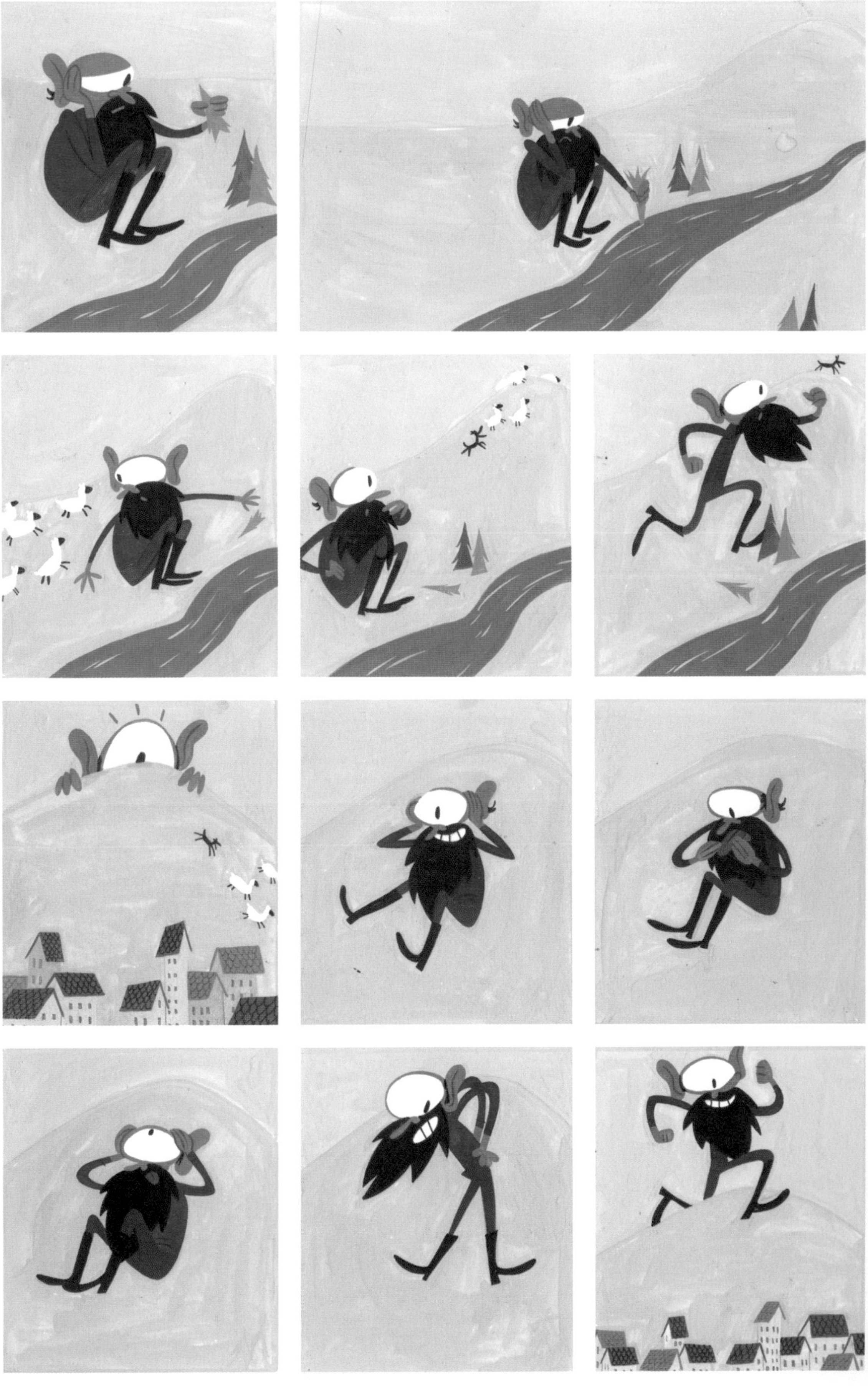

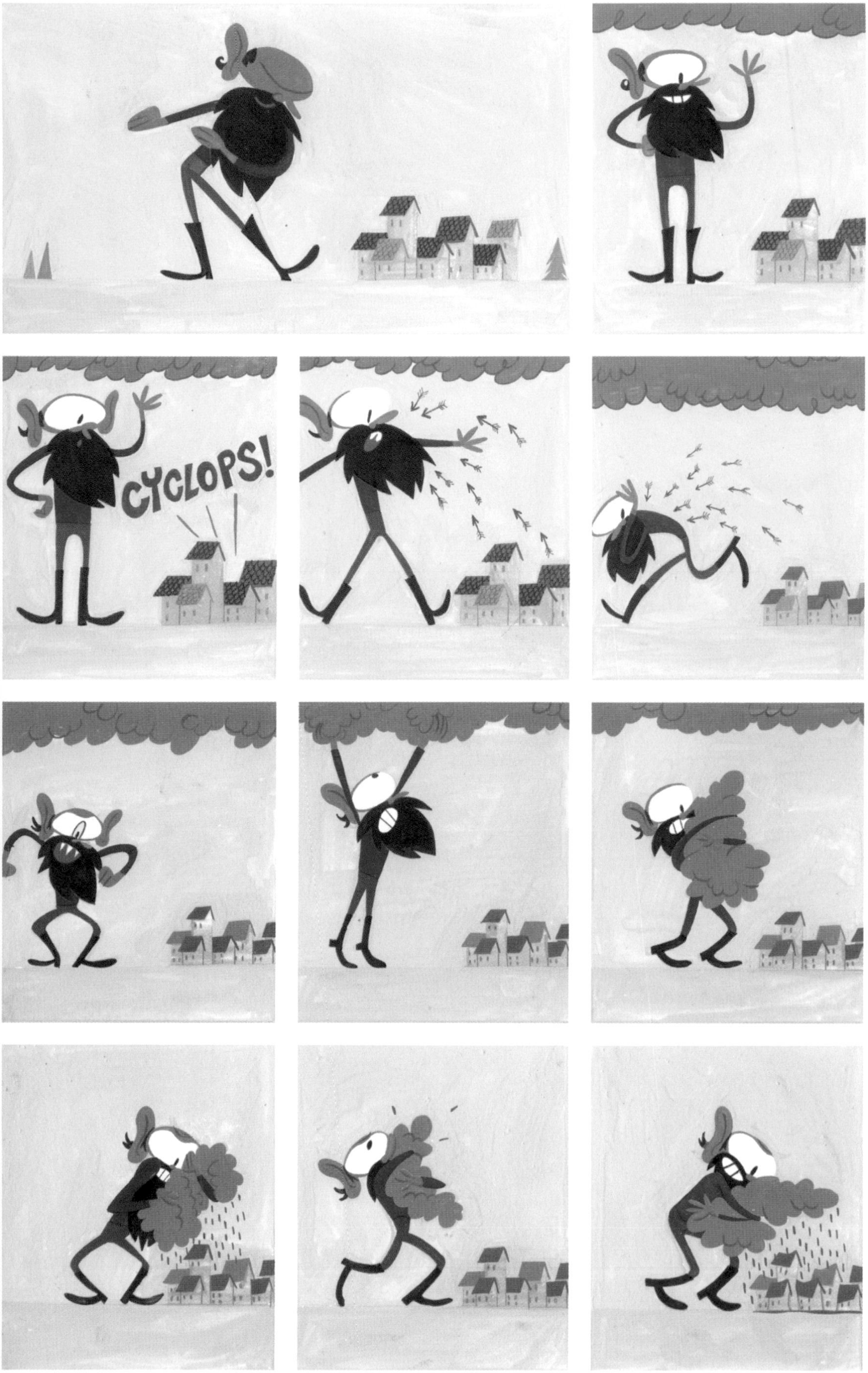
CYCLOPS!

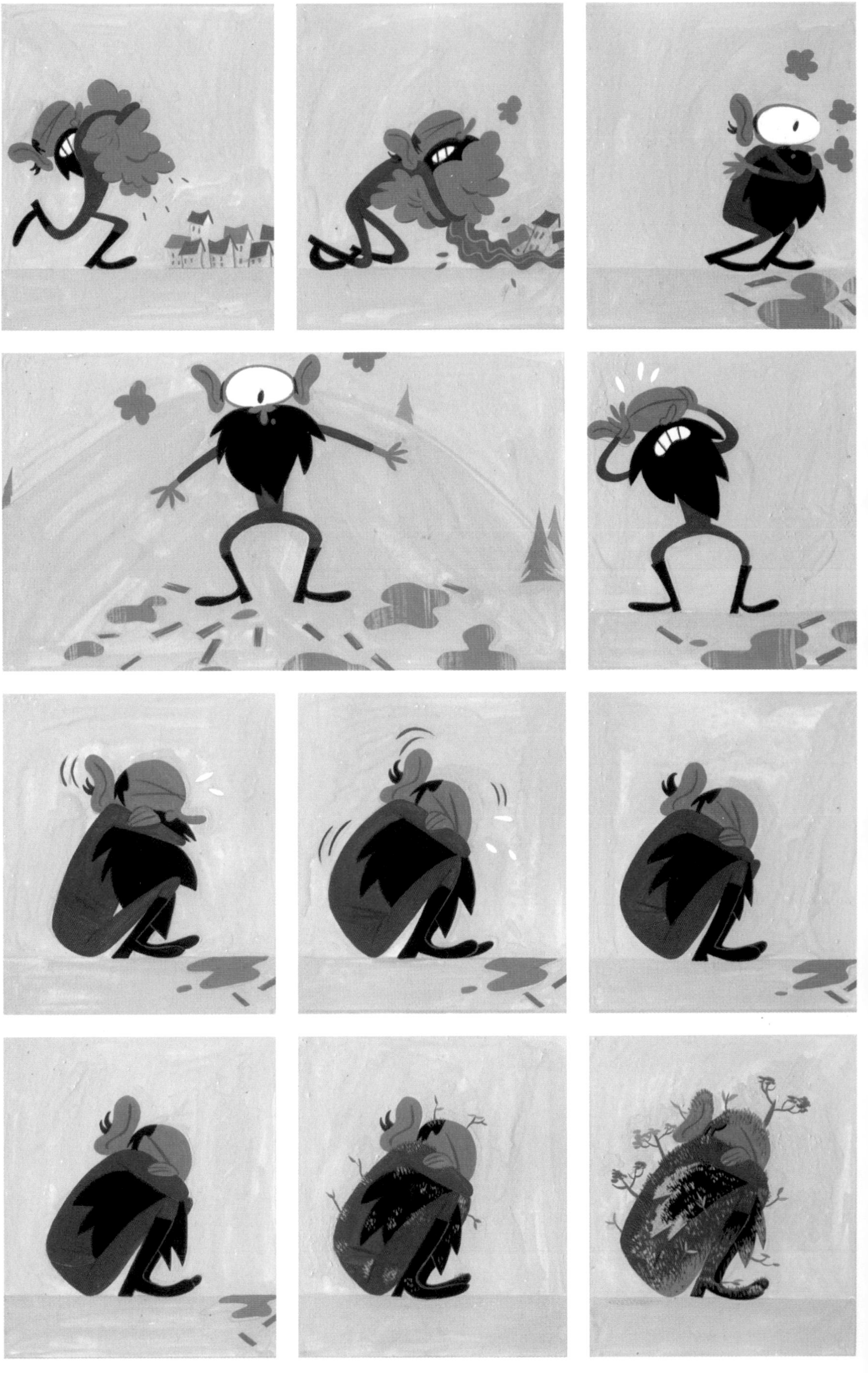

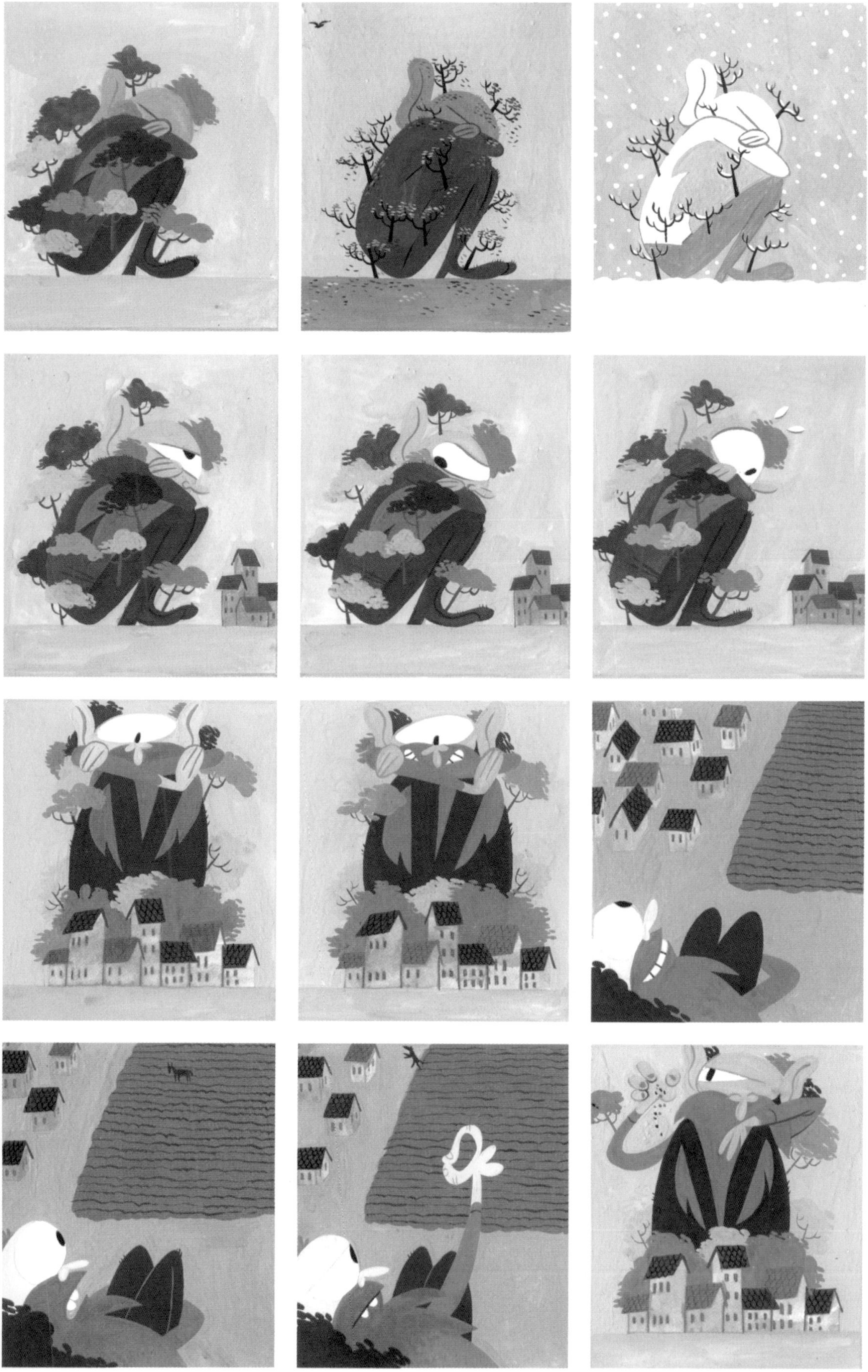

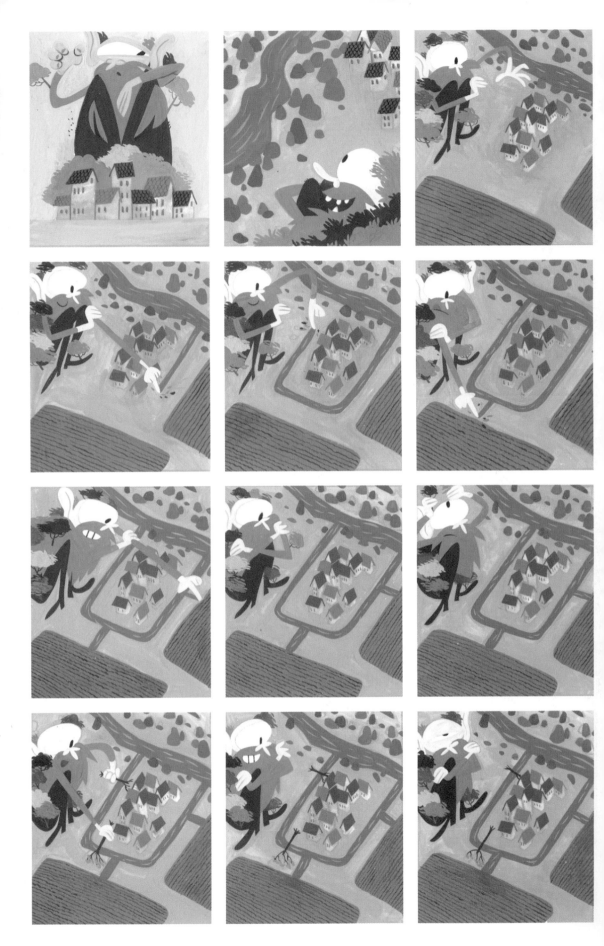

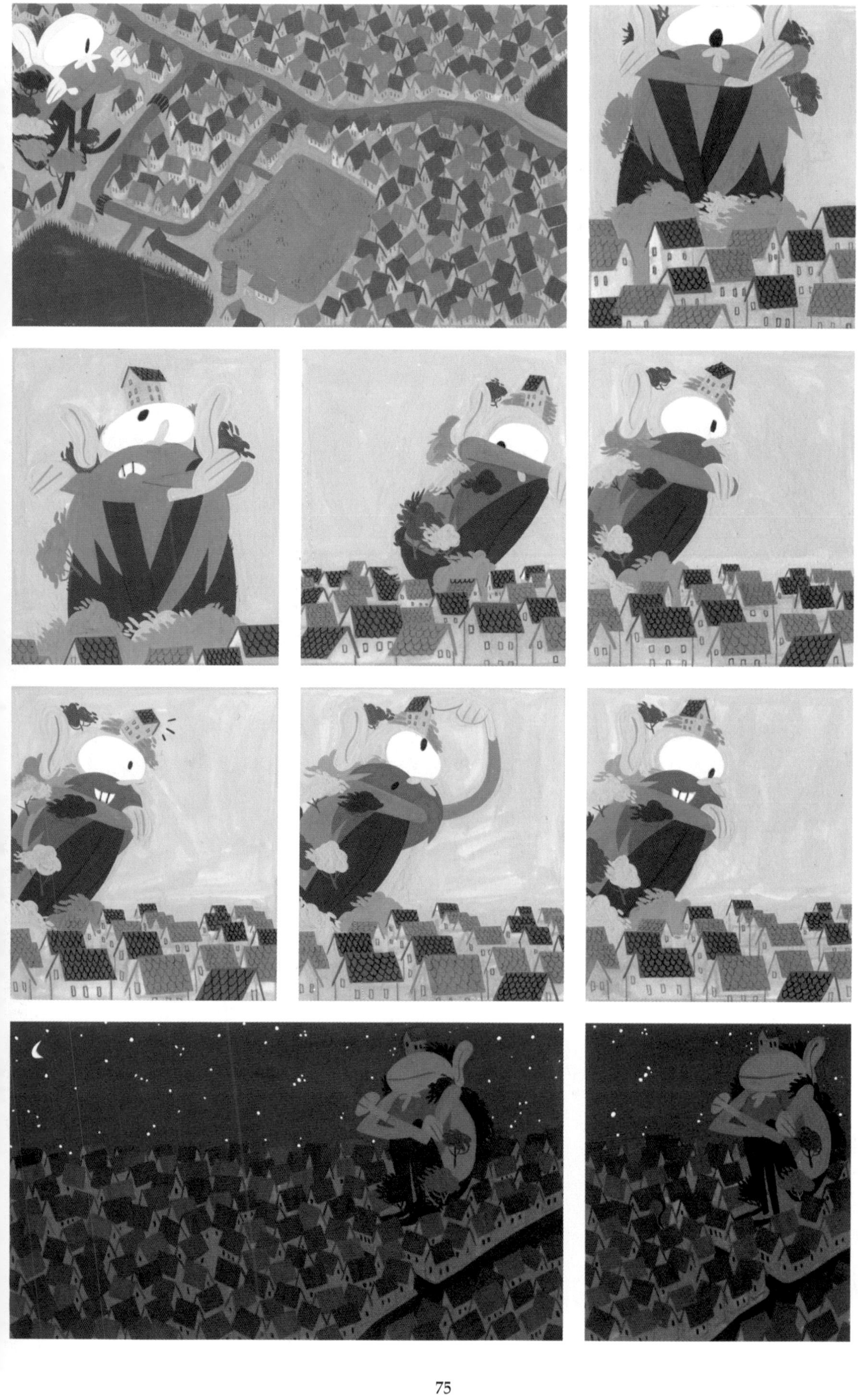

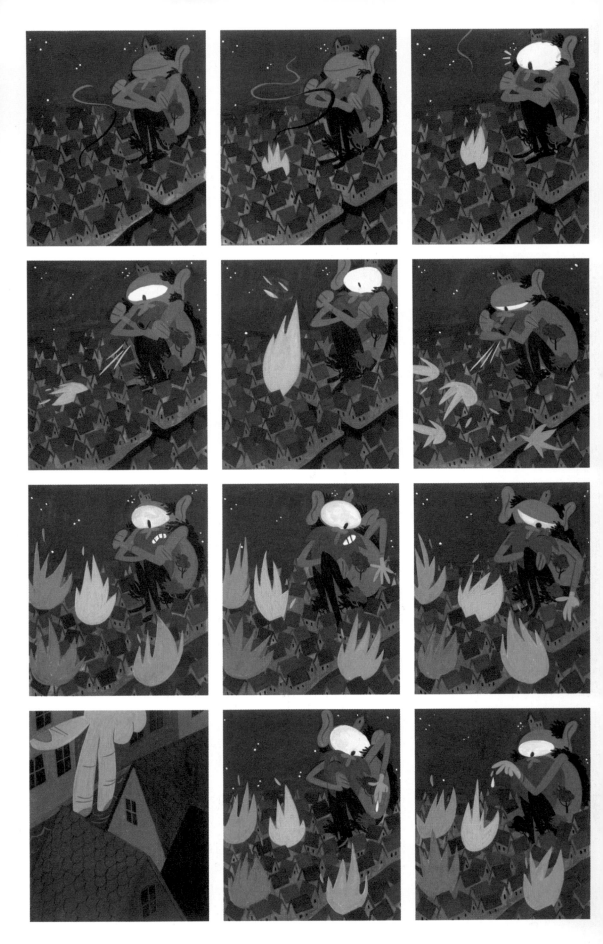

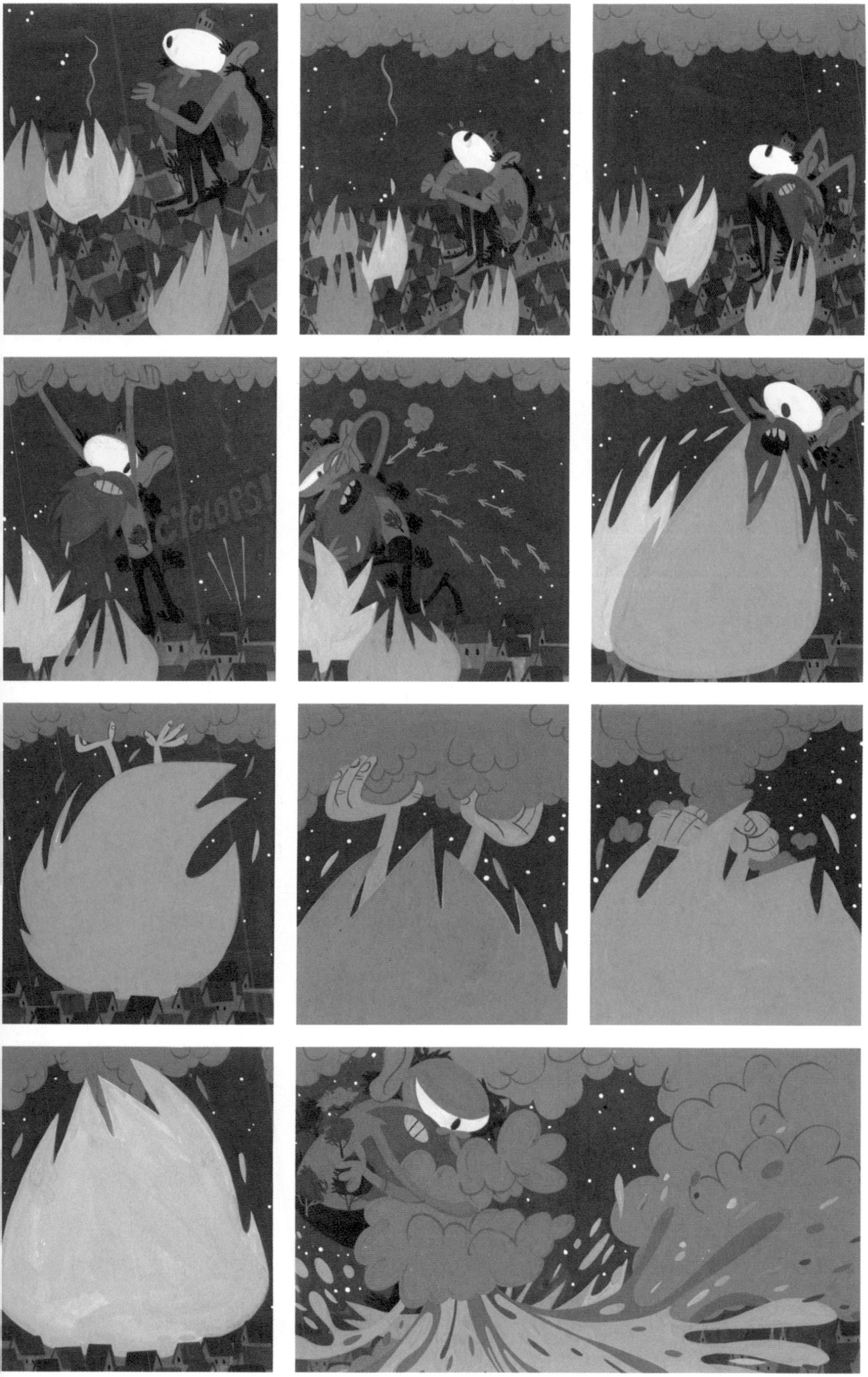
CYCLOPS!

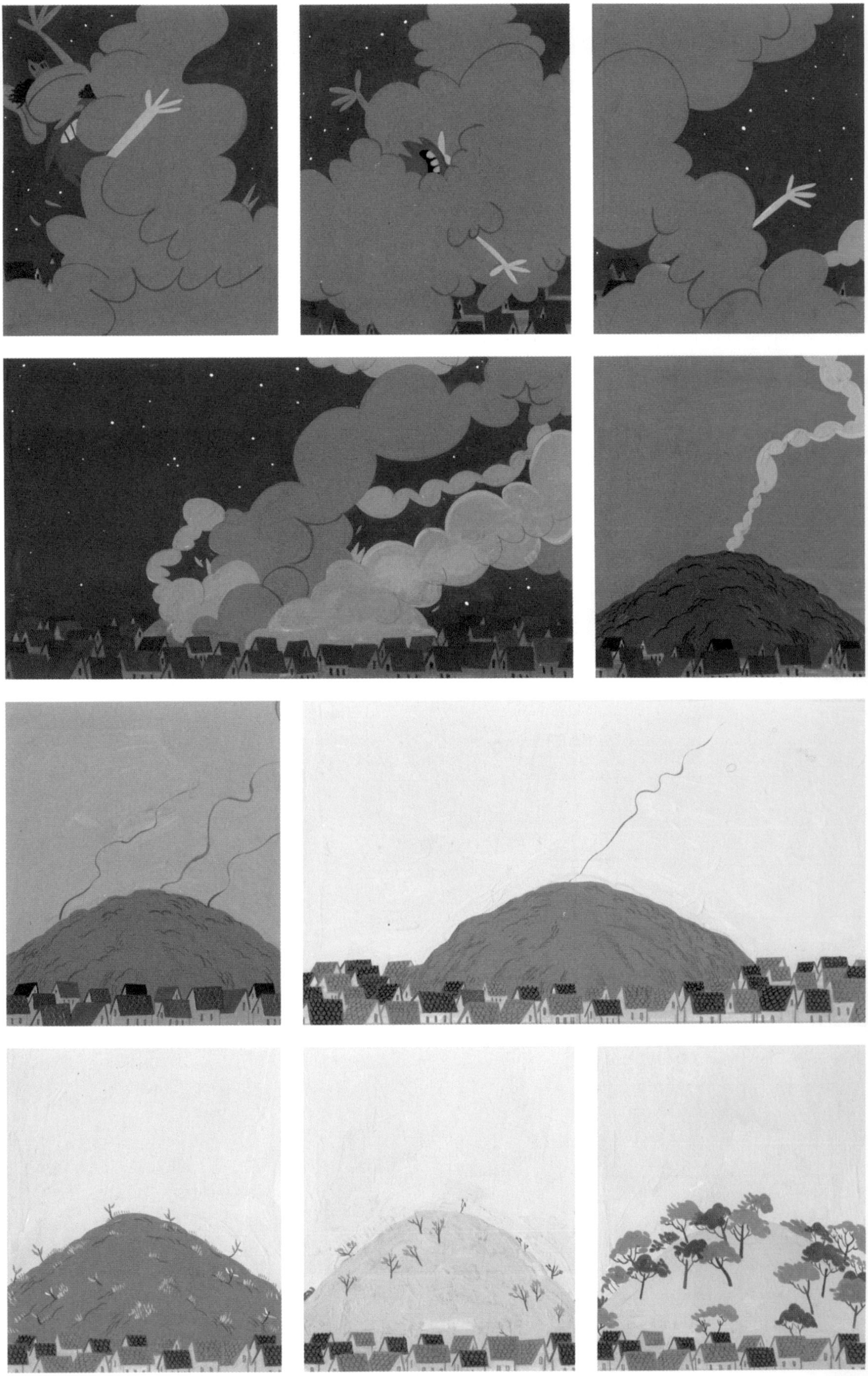

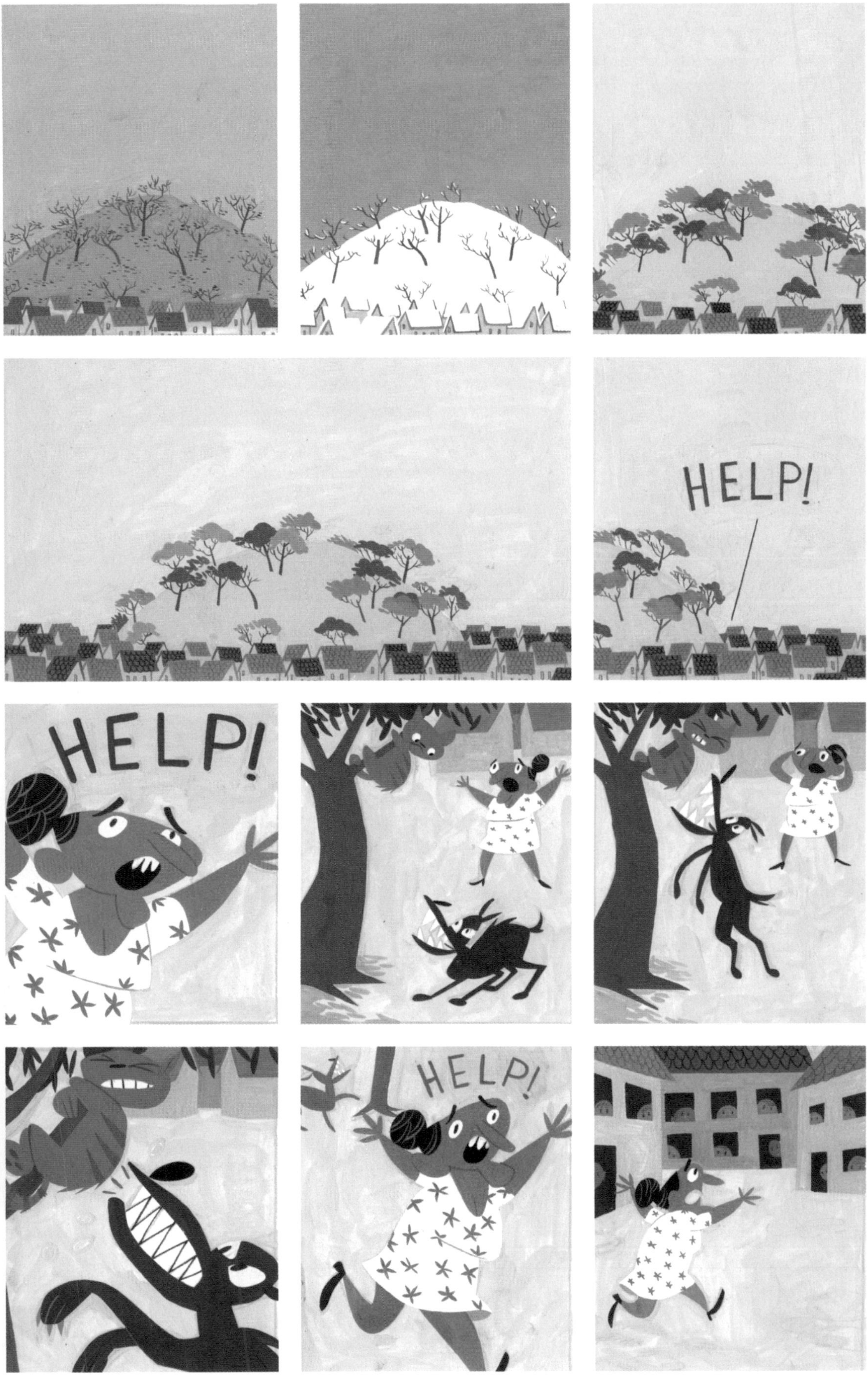
HELP!
HELP!
HELP!

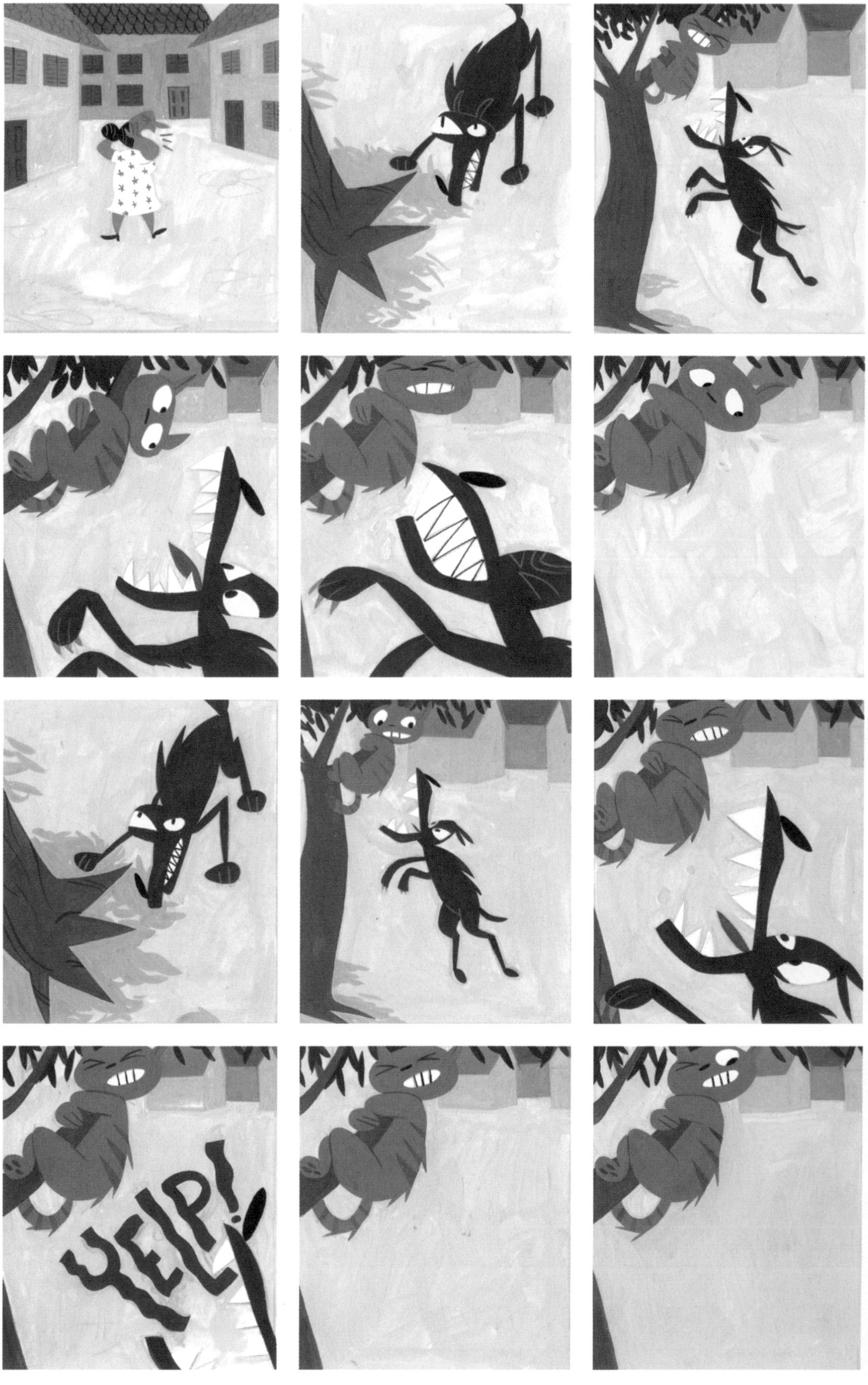
HELP!

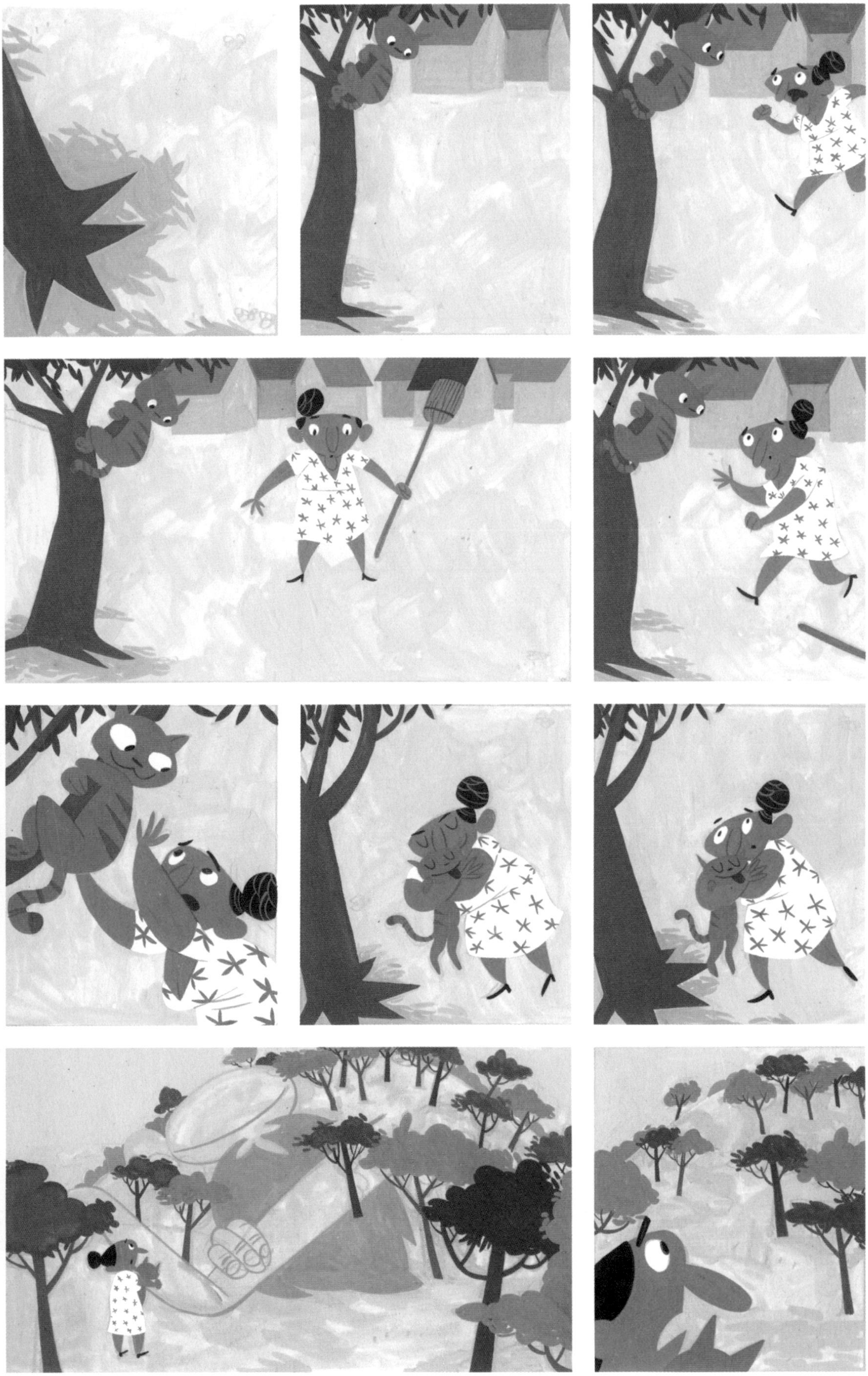

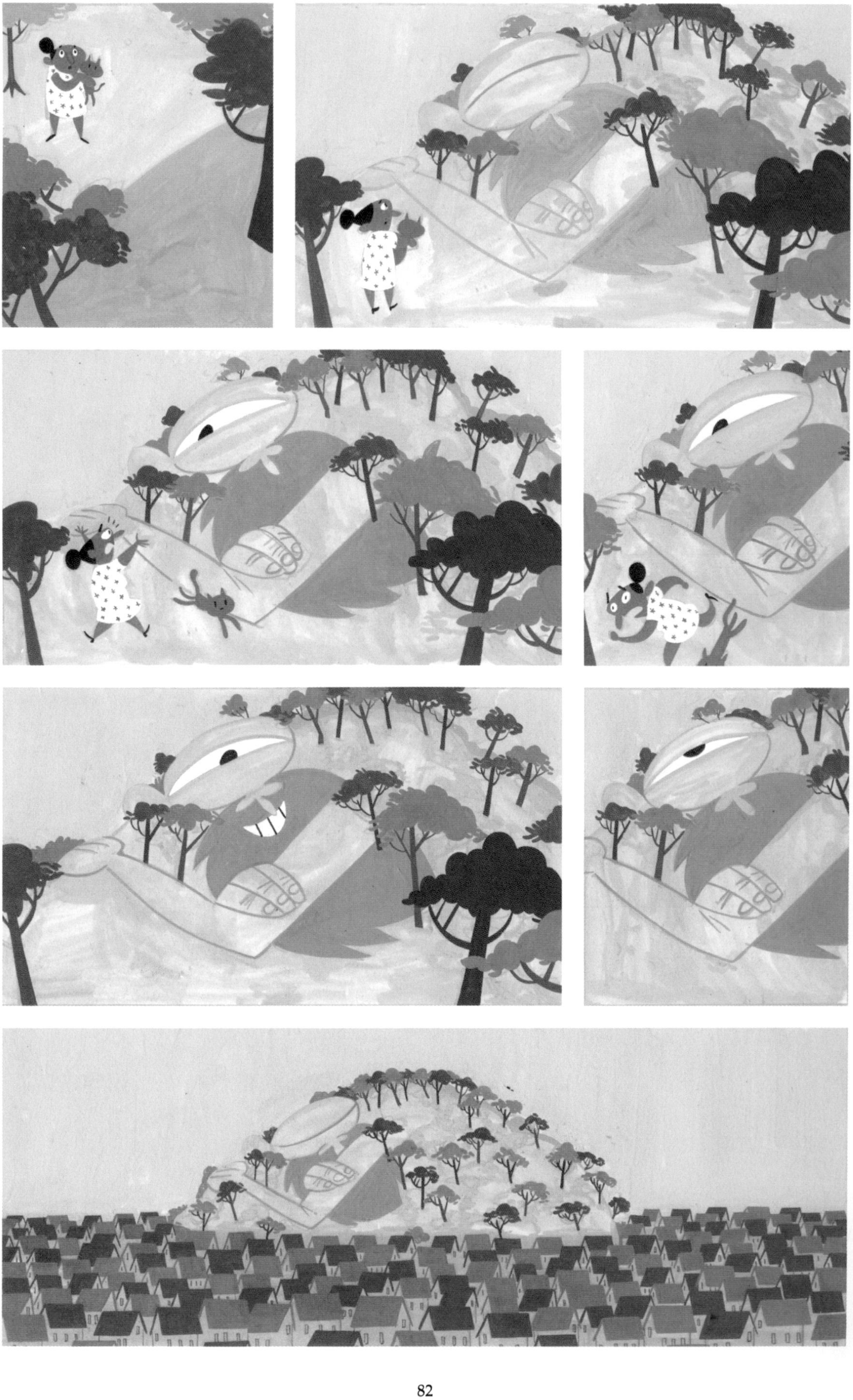

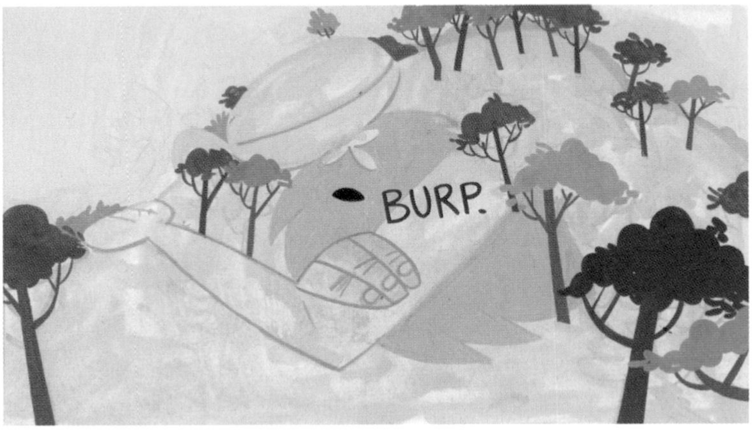
BURP.

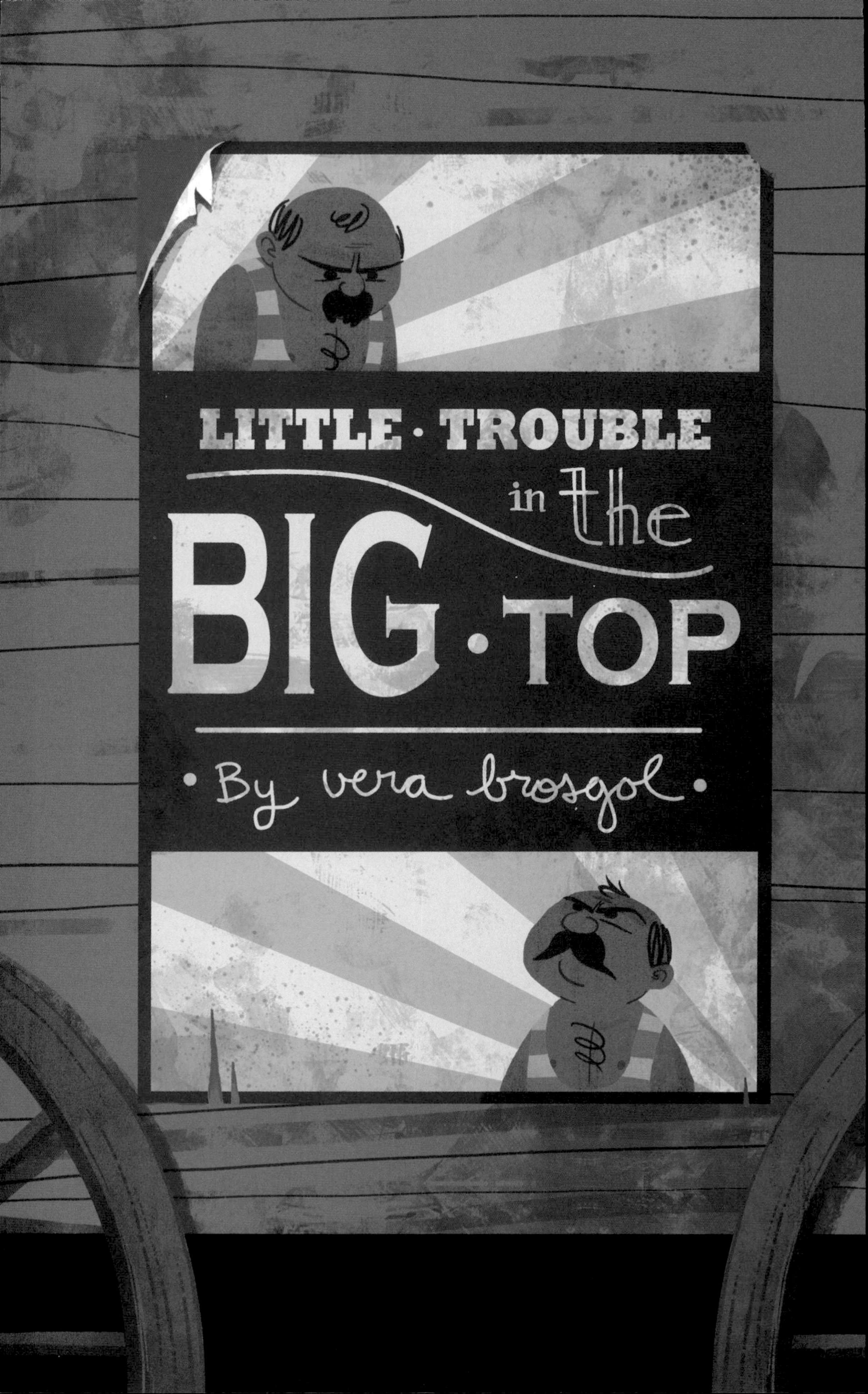
LITTLE · TROUBLE
in the
BIG · TOP
· By vera brosgol ·

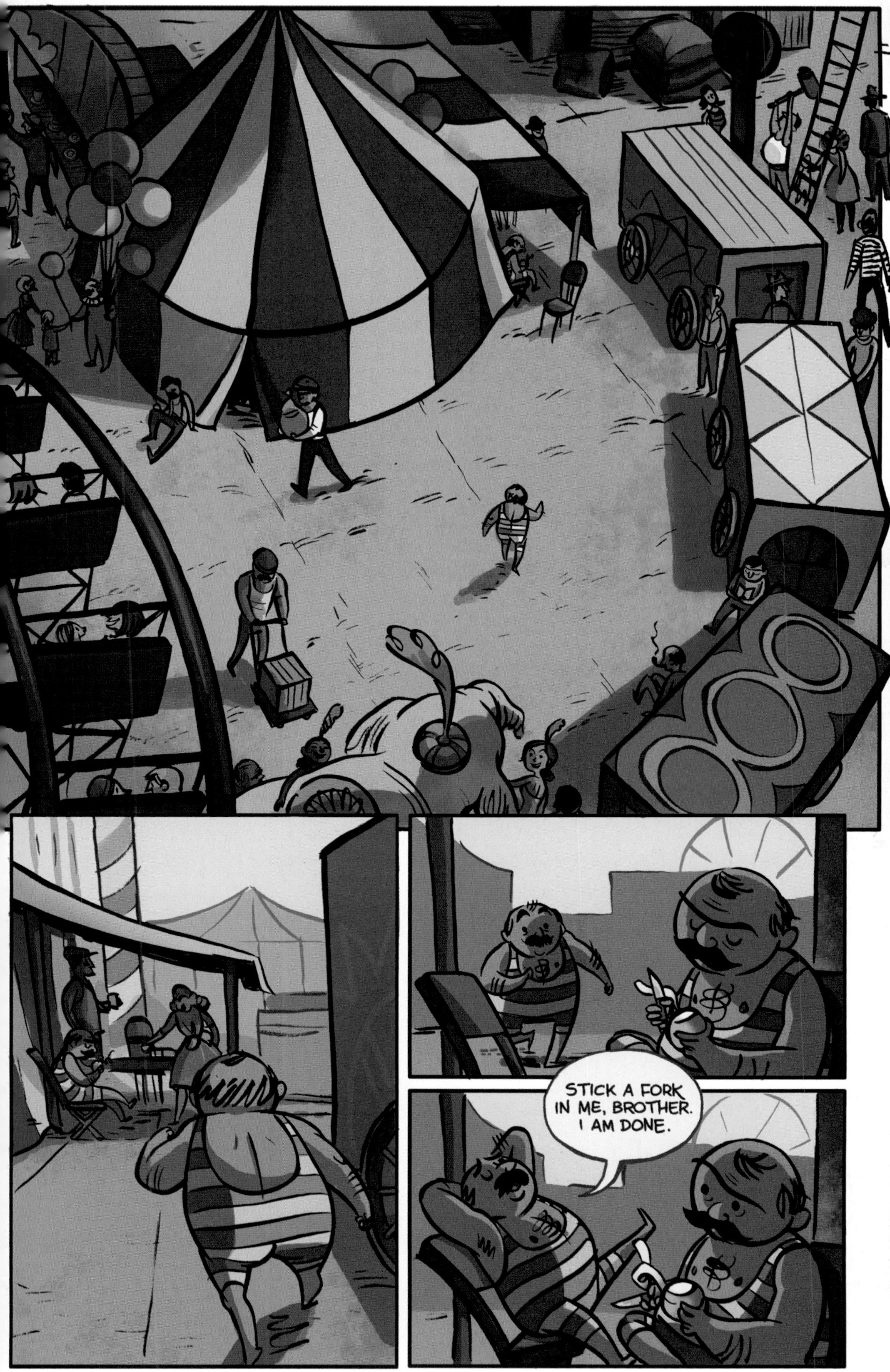
STICK A FORK IN ME, BROTHER. I AM DONE.

MARCO, I HAVE DONE WHAT MOTHER SWORE ON HER DEATHBED NEITHER OF US WOULD EVER DO... I HAVE FOUND MY **BRIDE**.

LET'S GET A LOOK AT HER, THEN.

OVER THIS WAY. SHE JUST STARTED IN THE BIG TOP TODAY!

SHE'S THE NEW TRAPEZE GIRL. I MEAN, OF **COURSE** SHE IS! SHE IS AN ANGEL, FLYING OVER THE HEADS OF FATTER, UGLIER WOMEN, WHO —

ALRIGHT ALREADY, KNOCK IT OFF. LET'S SEE.

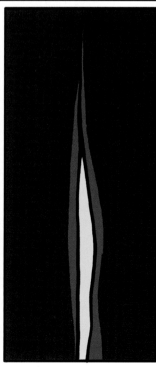

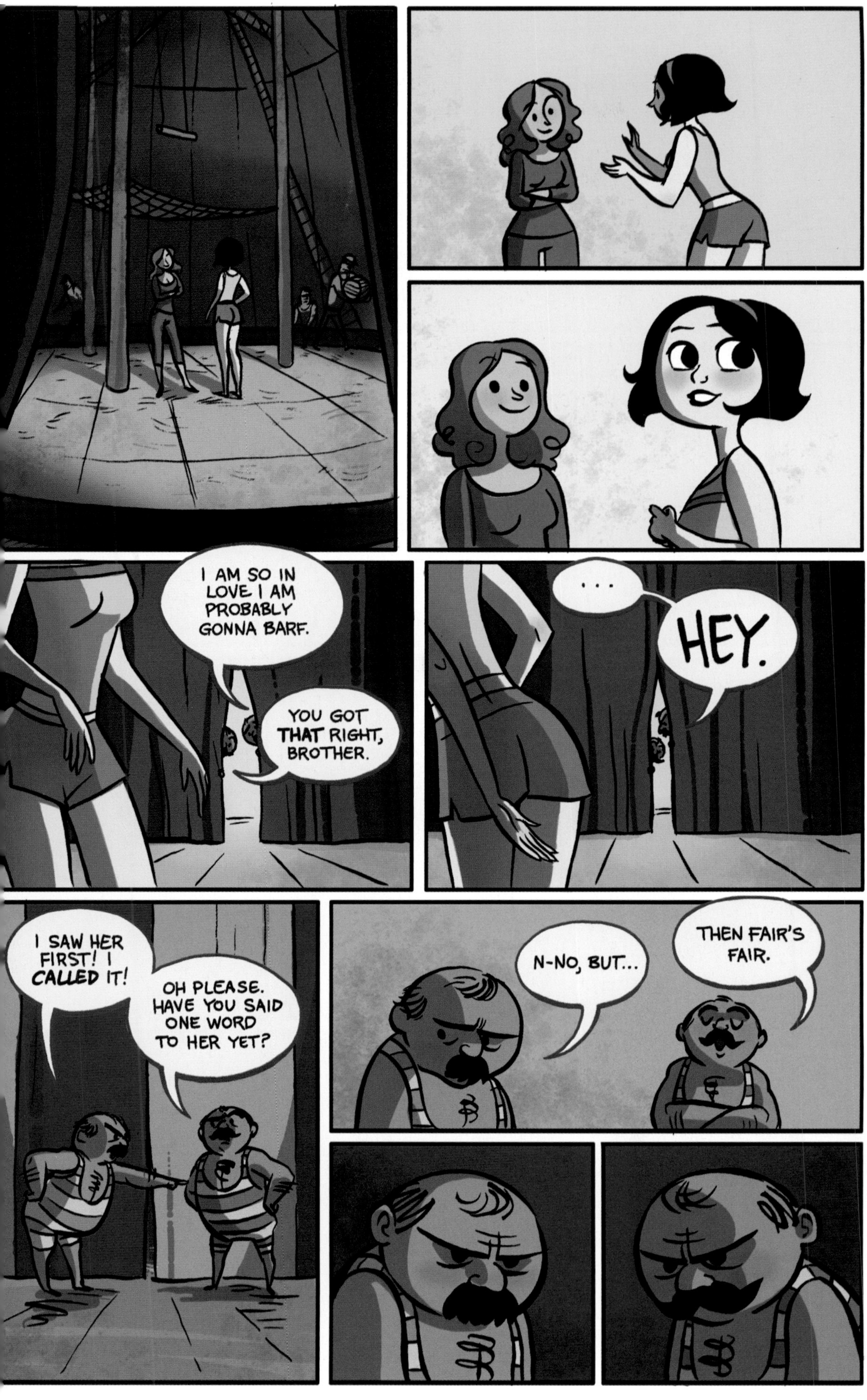
I AM SO IN LOVE I AM PROBABLY GONNA BARF.
YOU GOT **THAT** RIGHT, BROTHER.
. . .
HEY.
I SAW HER FIRST! I ***CALLED*** IT!
OH PLEASE. HAVE YOU SAID ONE WORD TO HER YET?
N-NO, BUT...
THEN FAIR'S FAIR.

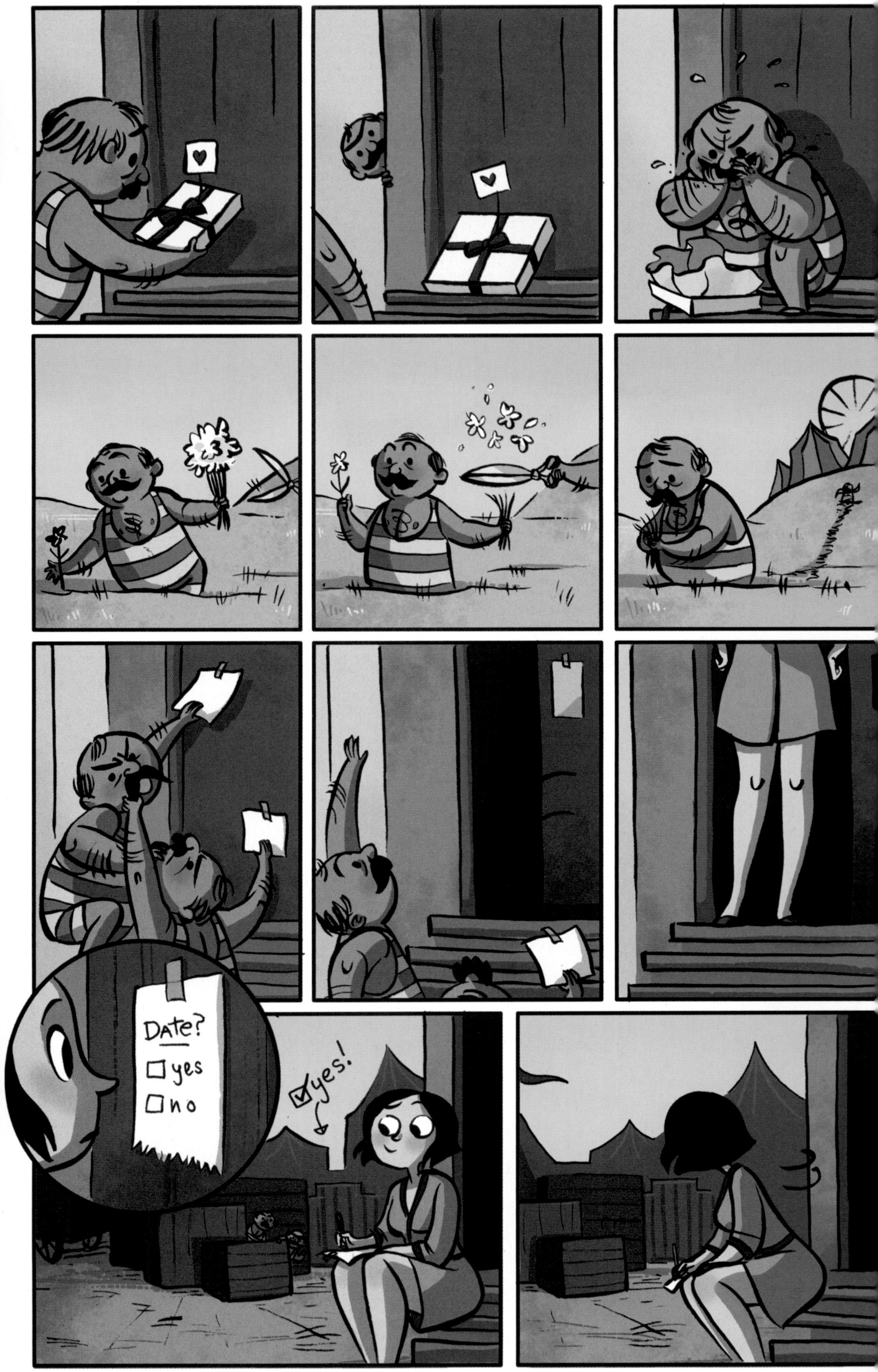
DATE?
☐ yes
☐ no
☑ yes!

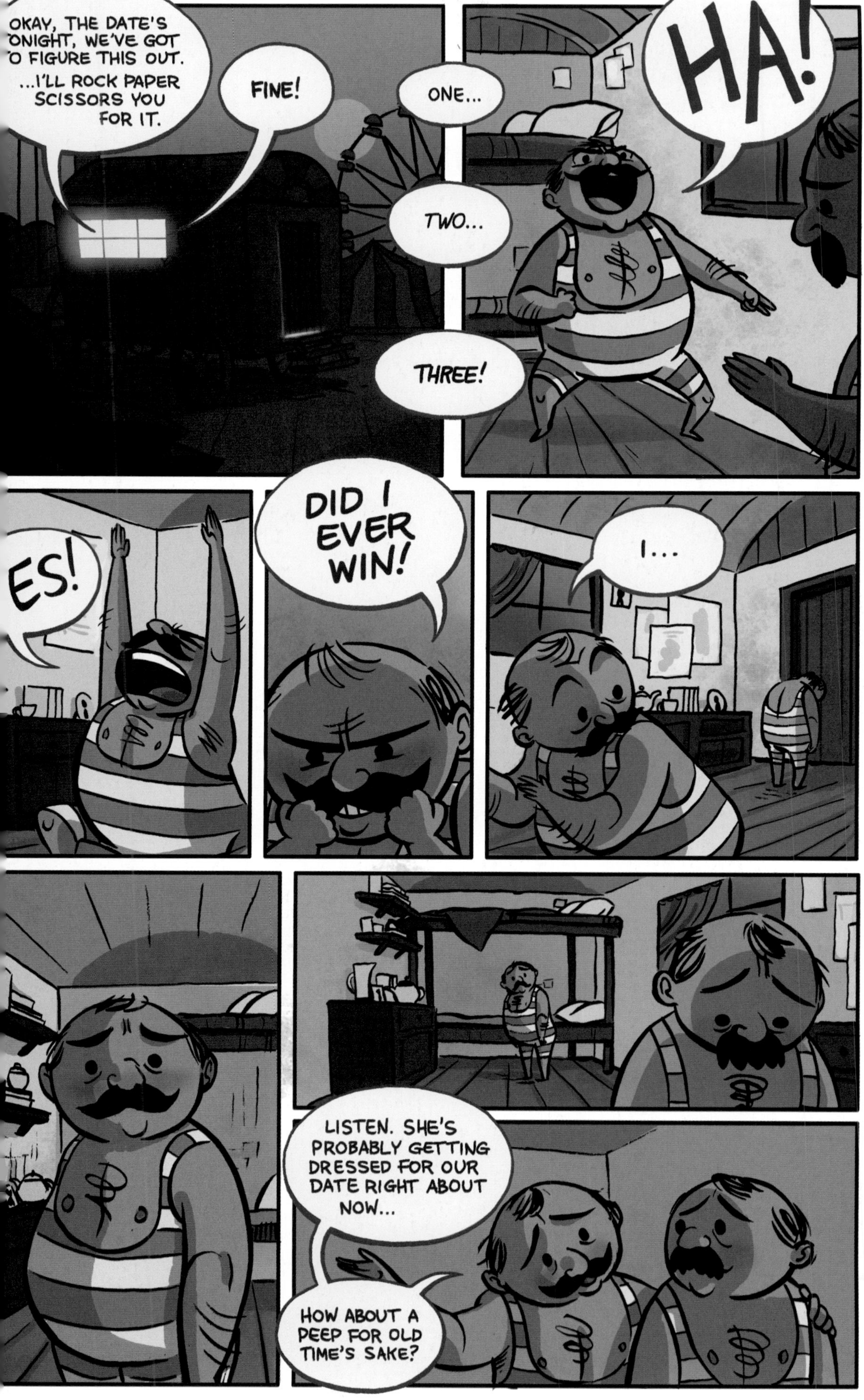
OKAY, THE DATE'S ONIGHT, WE'VE GOT O FIGURE THIS OUT. ...I'LL ROCK PAPER SCISSORS YOU FOR IT.
FINE!
ONE...
TWO...
THREE!
HA!
ES!
DID I EVER WIN!
I...
LISTEN. SHE'S PROBABLY GETTING DRESSED FOR OUR DATE RIGHT ABOUT NOW...
HOW ABOUT A PEEP FOR OLD TIME'S SAKE?

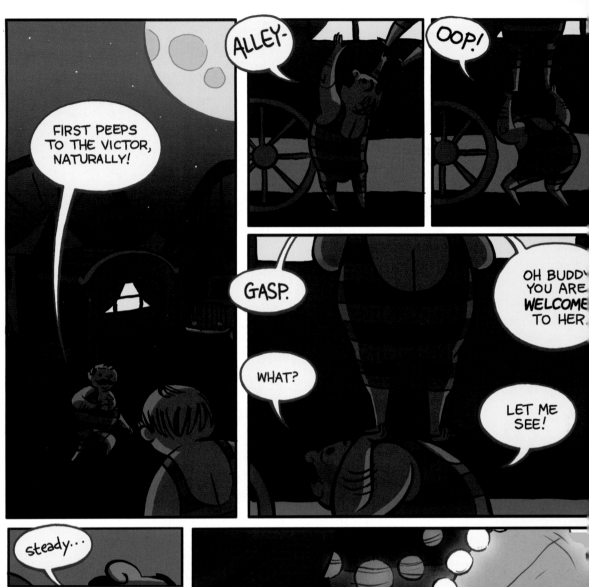

FIRST PEEPS TO THE VICTOR, NATURALLY!

ALLEY-

OOP!

GASP.

WHAT?

OH BUDDY YOU ARE **WELCOME** TO HER.

LET ME SEE!

steady...

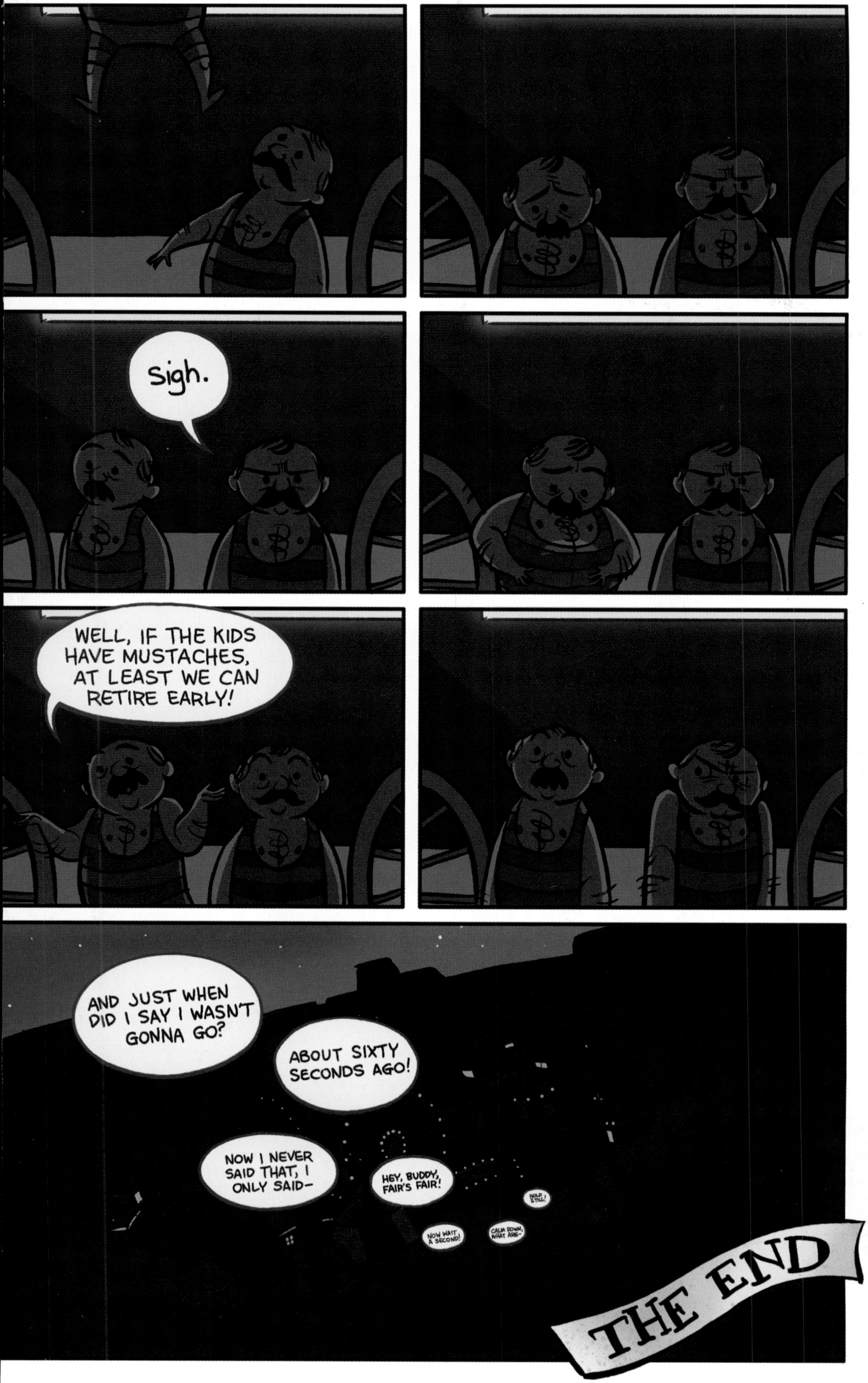
Sigh.
WELL, IF THE KIDS HAVE MUSTACHES, AT LEAST WE CAN RETIRE EARLY!
AND JUST WHEN DID I SAY I WASN'T GONNA GO?
ABOUT SIXTY SECONDS AGO!
NOW I NEVER SAID THAT, I ONLY SAID-
HEY, BUDDY, FAIR'S FAIR!
HOLD STILL!
NOW WAIT A SECOND!
CALM DOWN, WHAT ARE-
THE END

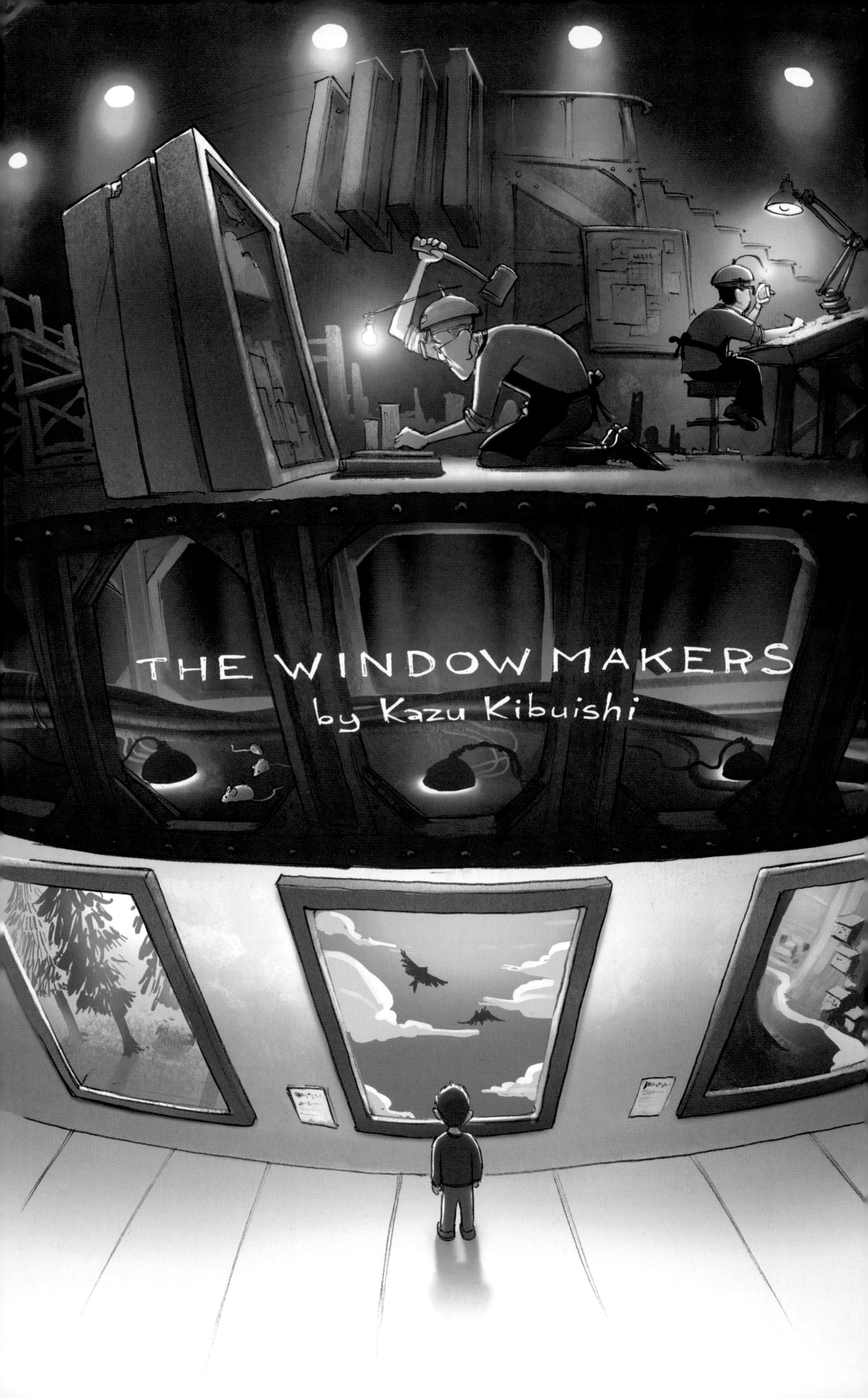
THE WINDOW MAKERS
by Kazu Kibuishi

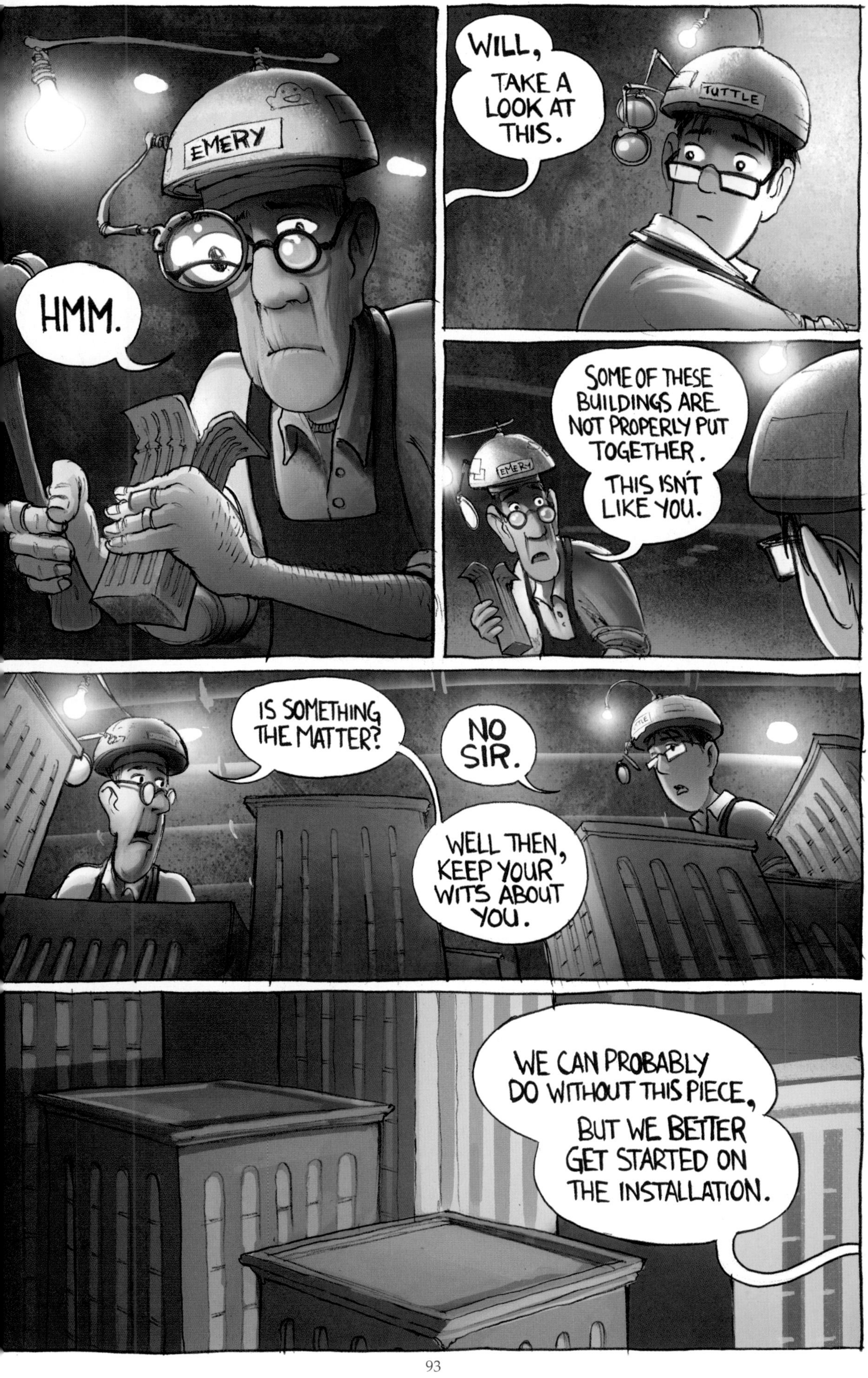
EMERY
HMM.
WILL,
TAKE A LOOK AT THIS.
TUTTLE
SOME OF THESE BUILDINGS ARE NOT PROPERLY PUT TOGETHER.
THIS ISN'T LIKE YOU.
EMERY
IS SOMETHING THE MATTER?
NO SIR.
WELL THEN, KEEP YOUR WITS ABOUT YOU.
WE CAN PROBABLY DO WITHOUT THIS PIECE,
BUT WE BETTER GET STARTED ON THE INSTALLATION.

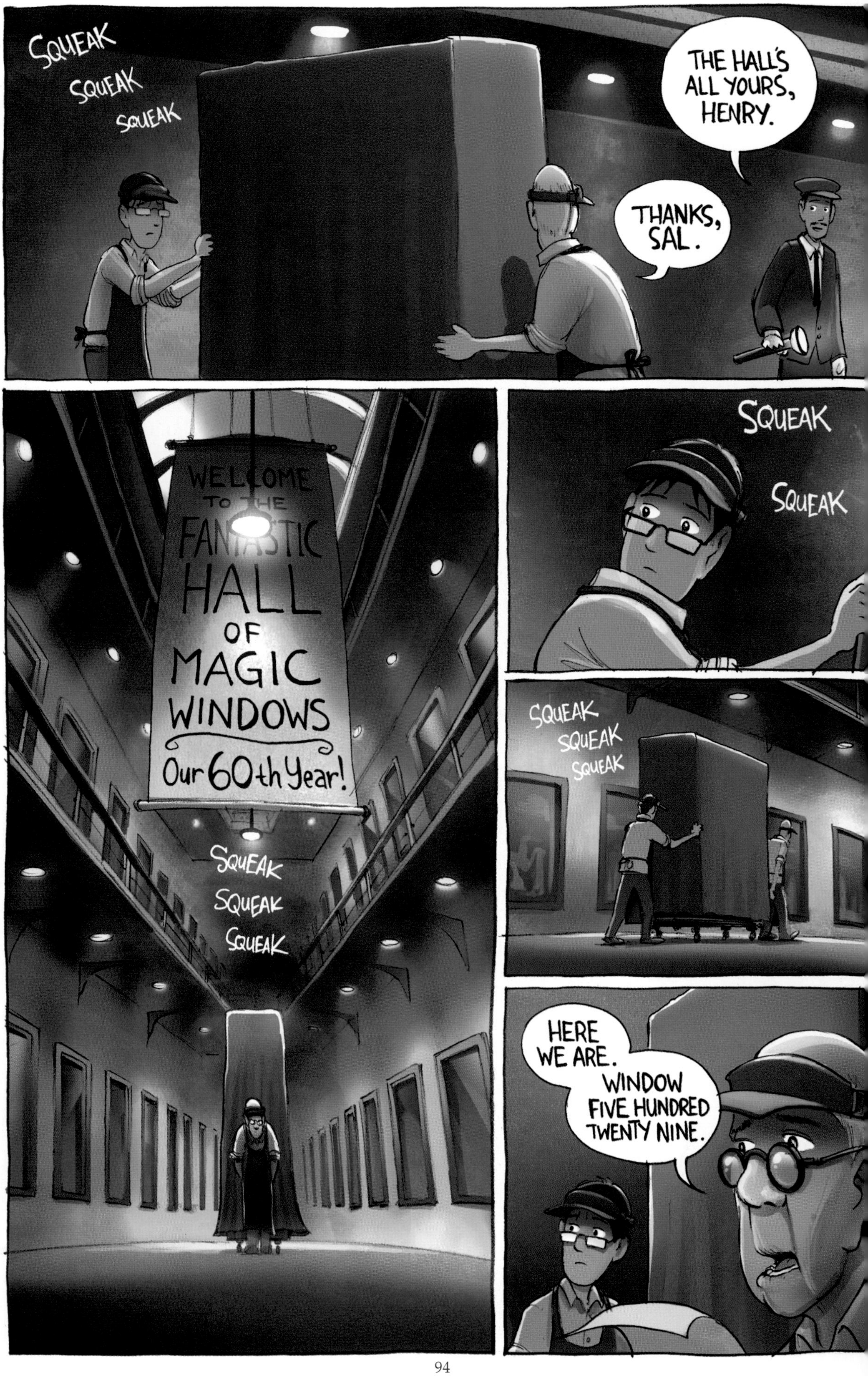
SQUEAK
SQUEAK
SQUEAK
THE HALL'S ALL YOURS, HENRY.
THANKS, SAL.
WELCOME TO THE FANTASTIC HALL OF MAGIC WINDOWS
Our 60th Year!
SQUEAK
SQUEAK
SQUEAK
SQUEAK
SQUEAK
SQUEAK
SQUEAK
SQUEAK
HERE WE ARE.
WINDOW FIVE HUNDRED TWENTY NINE.

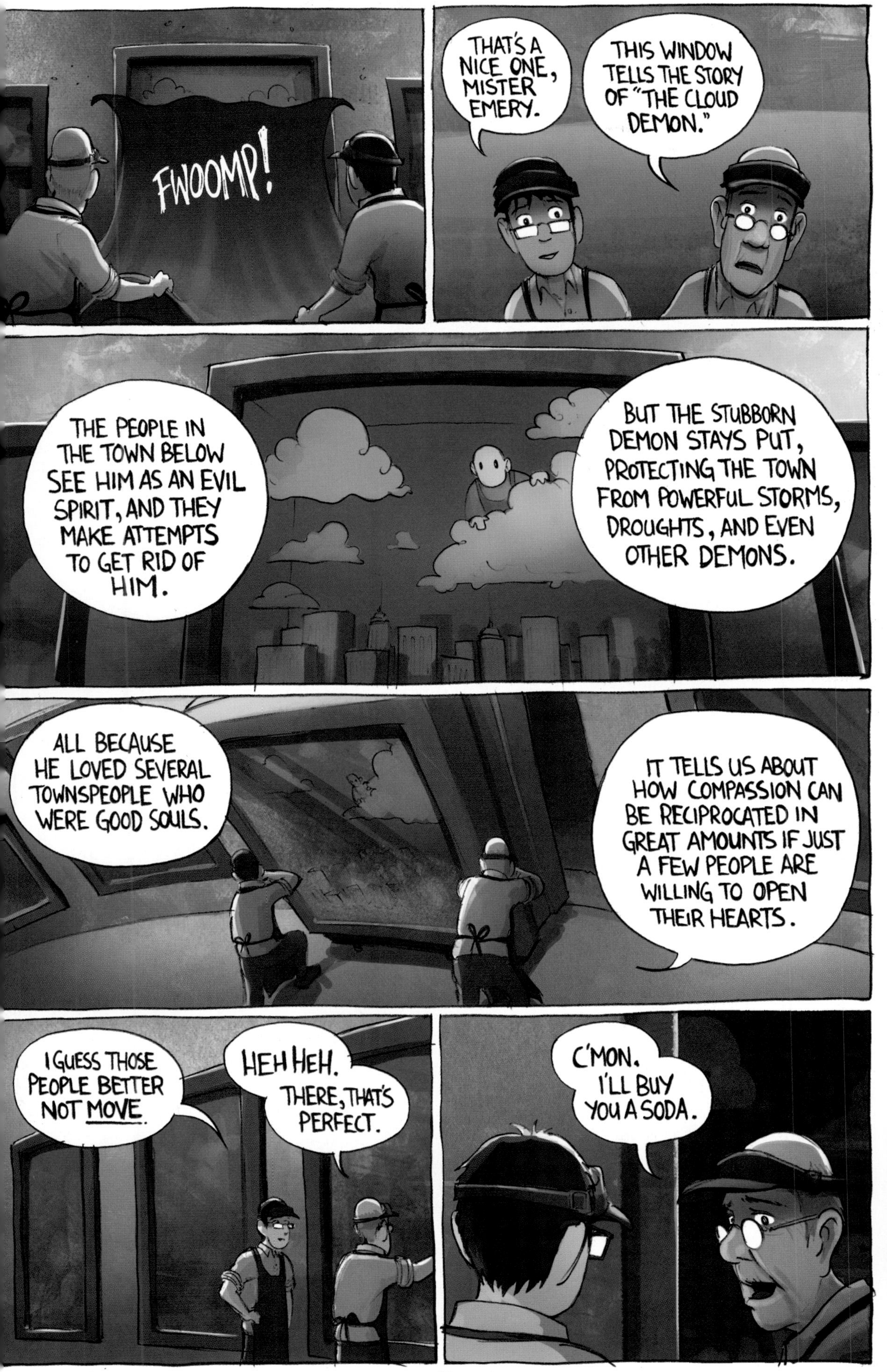
FWOOMP!
THAT'S A NICE ONE, MISTER EMERY.
THIS WINDOW TELLS THE STORY OF "THE CLOUD DEMON."
THE PEOPLE IN THE TOWN BELOW SEE HIM AS AN EVIL SPIRIT, AND THEY MAKE ATTEMPTS TO GET RID OF HIM.
BUT THE STUBBORN DEMON STAYS PUT, PROTECTING THE TOWN FROM POWERFUL STORMS, DROUGHTS, AND EVEN OTHER DEMONS.
ALL BECAUSE HE LOVED SEVERAL TOWNSPEOPLE WHO WERE GOOD SOULS.
IT TELLS US ABOUT HOW COMPASSION CAN BE RECIPROCATED IN GREAT AMOUNTS IF JUST A FEW PEOPLE ARE WILLING TO OPEN THEIR HEARTS.
I GUESS THOSE PEOPLE BETTER NOT MOVE.
HEH HEH.
THERE, THAT'S PERFECT.
C'MON. I'LL BUY YOU A SODA.

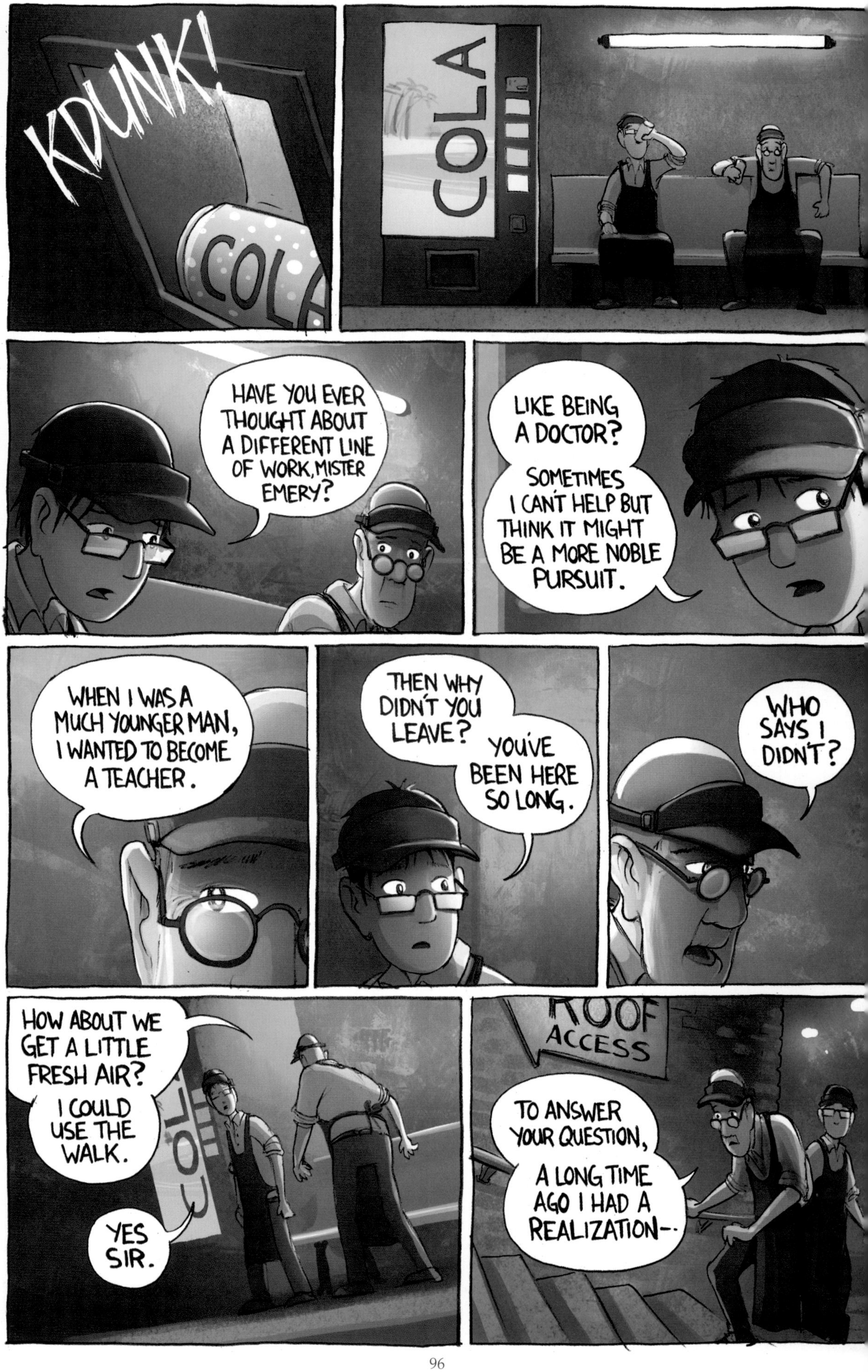
KDUNK!
COLA
COLA
HAVE YOU EVER THOUGHT ABOUT A DIFFERENT LINE OF WORK, MISTER EMERY?
LIKE BEING A DOCTOR?
SOMETIMES I CAN'T HELP BUT THINK IT MIGHT BE A MORE NOBLE PURSUIT.
WHEN I WAS A MUCH YOUNGER MAN, I WANTED TO BECOME A TEACHER.
THEN WHY DIDN'T YOU LEAVE?
YOU'VE BEEN HERE SO LONG.
WHO SAYS I DIDN'T?
HOW ABOUT WE GET A LITTLE FRESH AIR?
I COULD USE THE WALK.
YES SIR.
ROOF ACCESS
TO ANSWER YOUR QUESTION,
A LONG TIME AGO I HAD A REALIZATION--.

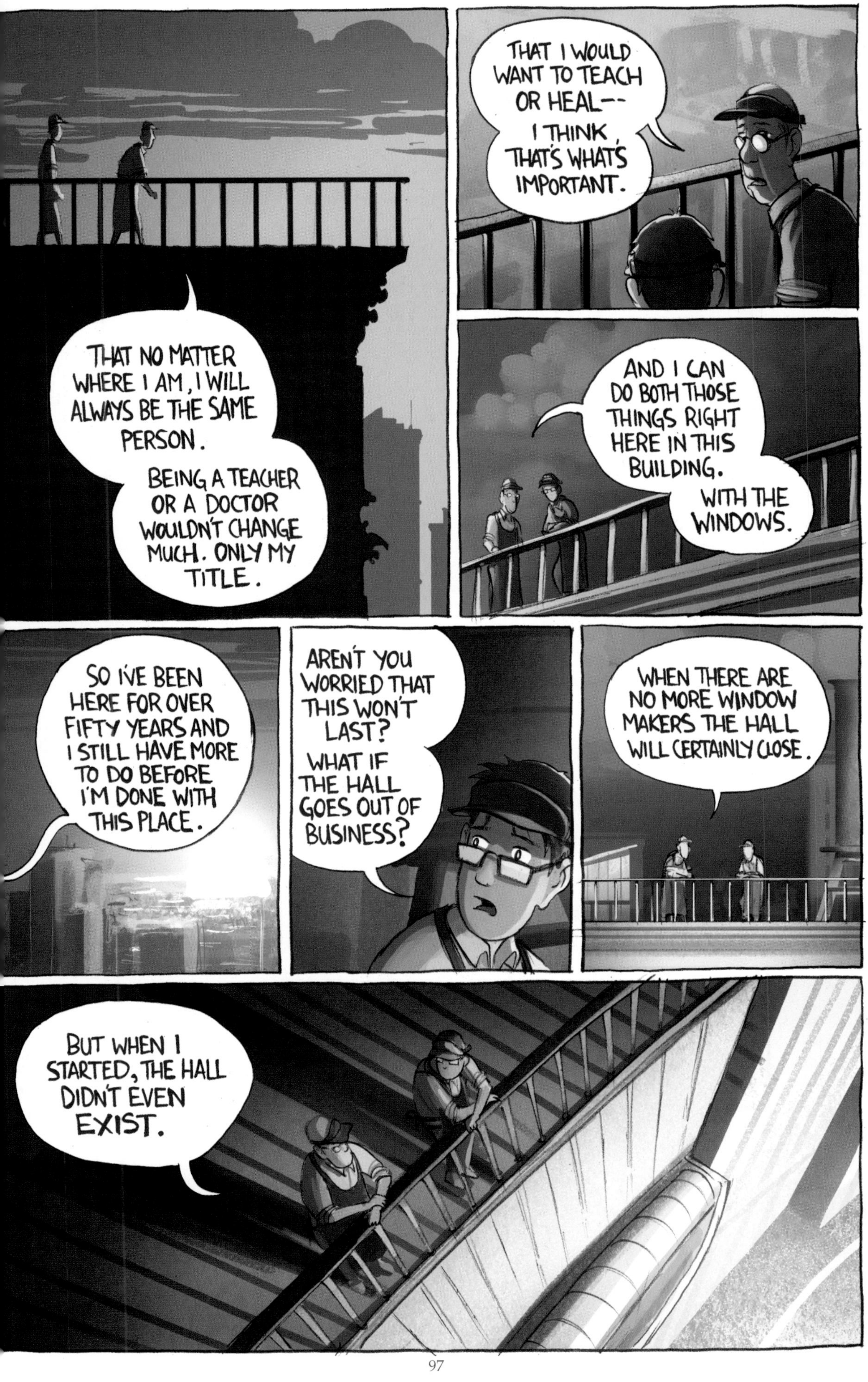
THAT I WOULD WANT TO TEACH OR HEAL-- I THINK, THAT'S WHAT'S IMPORTANT.
THAT NO MATTER WHERE I AM, I WILL ALWAYS BE THE SAME PERSON.
BEING A TEACHER OR A DOCTOR WOULDN'T CHANGE MUCH. ONLY MY TITLE.
AND I CAN DO BOTH THOSE THINGS RIGHT HERE IN THIS BUILDING.
WITH THE WINDOWS.
SO I'VE BEEN HERE FOR OVER FIFTY YEARS AND I STILL HAVE MORE TO DO BEFORE I'M DONE WITH THIS PLACE.
AREN'T YOU WORRIED THAT THIS WON'T LAST?
WHAT IF THE HALL GOES OUT OF BUSINESS?
WHEN THERE ARE NO MORE WINDOW MAKERS THE HALL WILL CERTAINLY CLOSE.
BUT WHEN I STARTED, THE HALL DIDN'T EVEN EXIST.

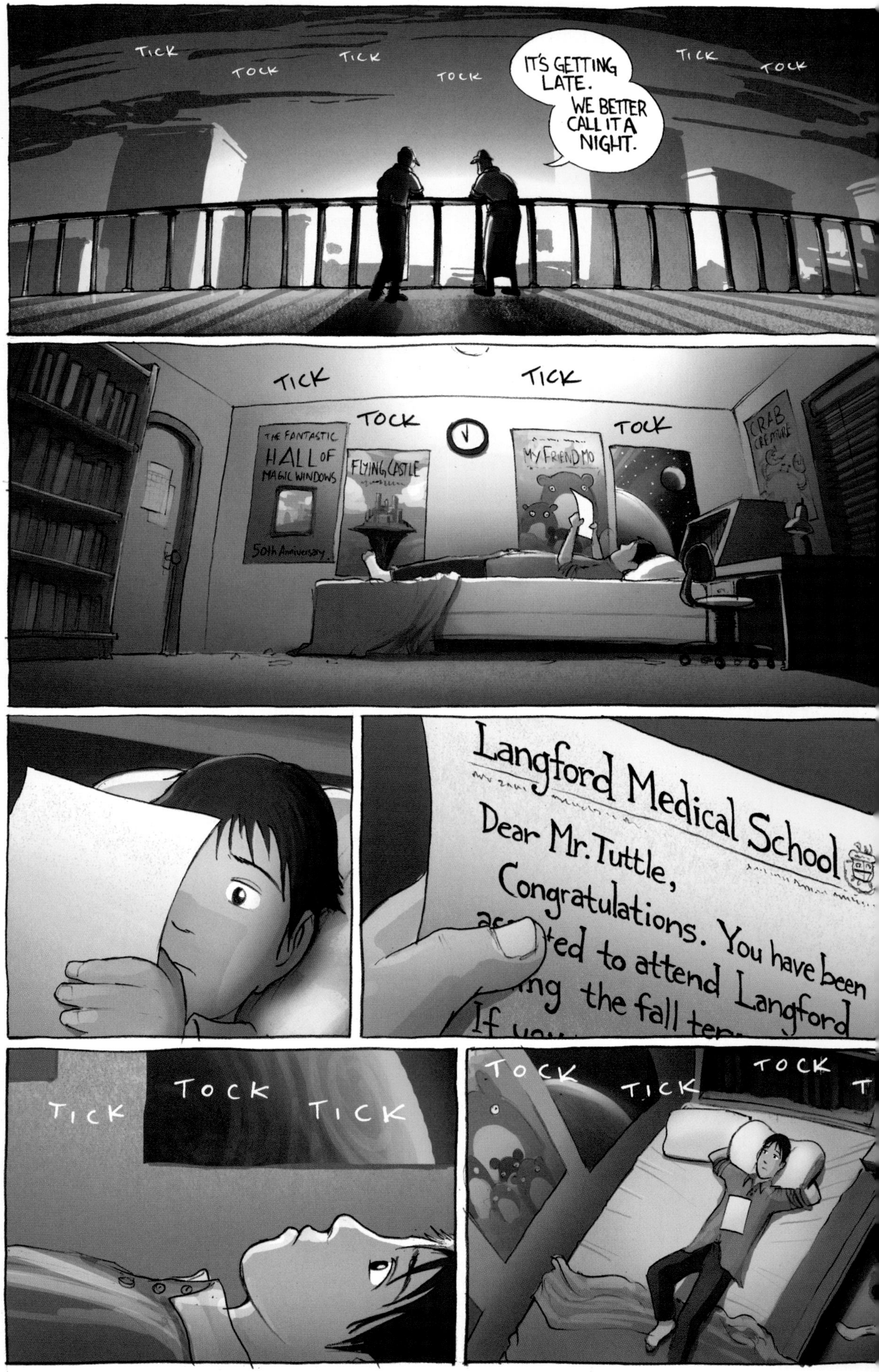
TICK
TOCK
TICK
TOCK
IT'S GETTING LATE.
WE BETTER CALL IT A NIGHT.
TICK
TOCK
TICK
TICK
TOCK
TOCK
THE FANTASTIC HALL OF MAGIC WINDOWS
50th Anniversary
FLYING CASTLE
MY FRIEND MO
CRAB CREATURE
Langford Medical School
Dear Mr. Tuttle,
Congratulations. You have been
ac ted to attend Langford
ing the fall ter
If you
TICK
TOCK
TICK
TOCK
TICK
TOCK

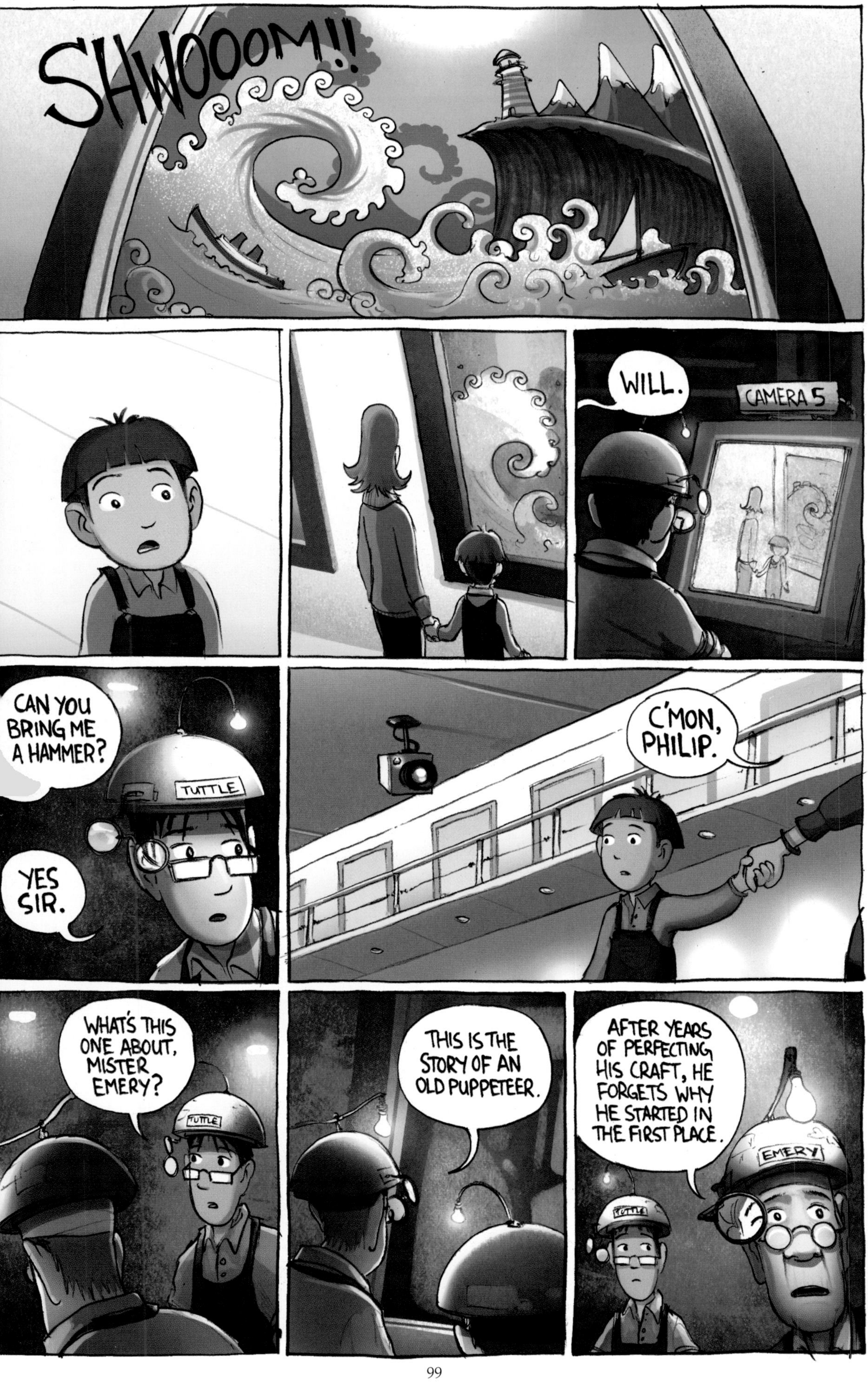
SHWOOOM!!
WILL.
CAMERA 5
CAN YOU BRING ME A HAMMER?
TUTTLE
YES SIR.
C'MON, PHILIP.
WHAT'S THIS ONE ABOUT, MISTER EMERY?
TUTTLE
THIS IS THE STORY OF AN OLD PUPPETEER.
AFTER YEARS OF PERFECTING HIS CRAFT, HE FORGETS WHY HE STARTED IN THE FIRST PLACE.
TUTTLE
EMERY

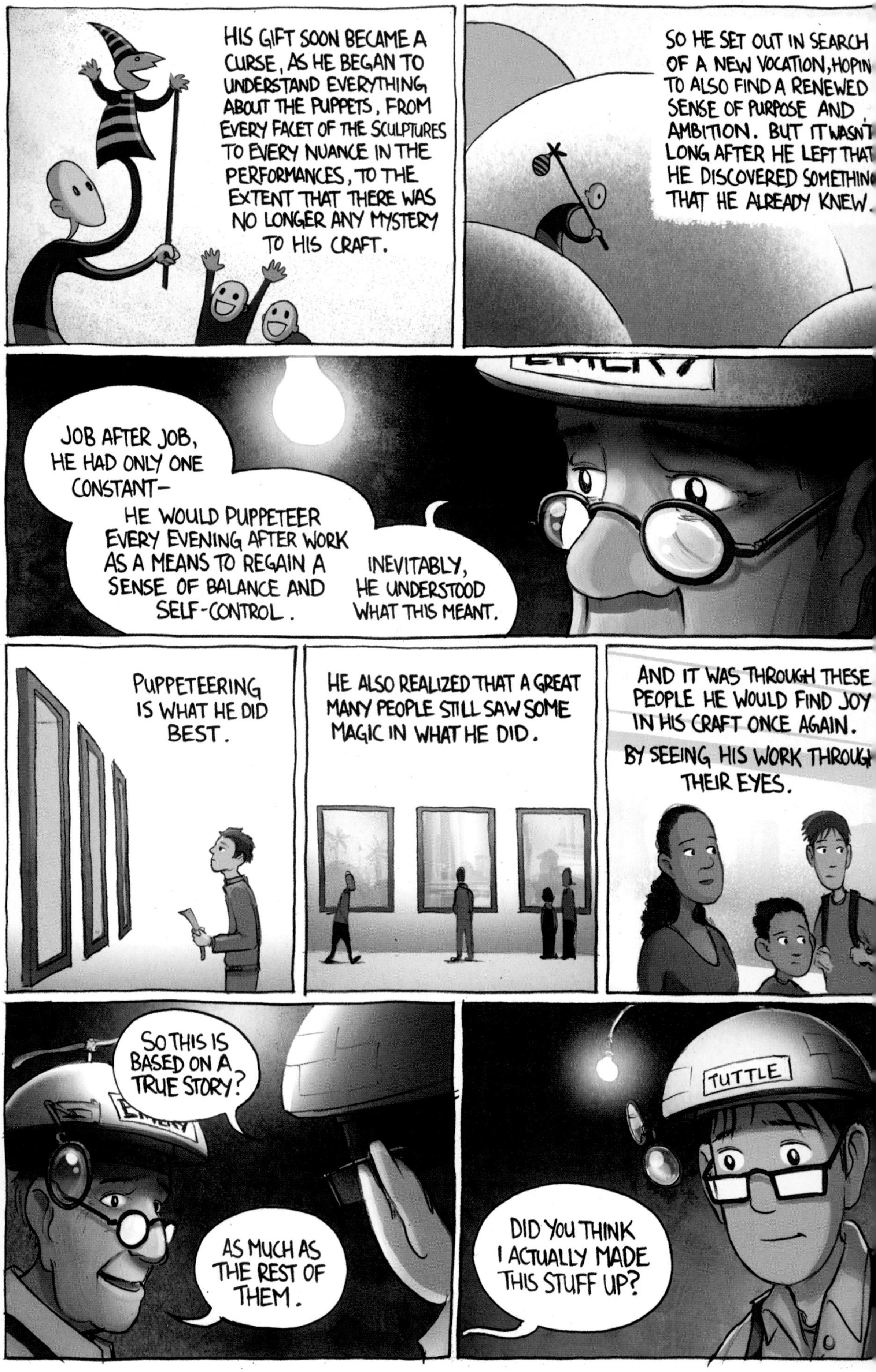
HIS GIFT SOON BECAME A CURSE, AS HE BEGAN TO UNDERSTAND EVERYTHING ABOUT THE PUPPETS, FROM EVERY FACET OF THE SCULPTURES TO EVERY NUANCE IN THE PERFORMANCES, TO THE EXTENT THAT THERE WAS NO LONGER ANY MYSTERY TO HIS CRAFT.
SO HE SET OUT IN SEARCH OF A NEW VOCATION, HOPIN TO ALSO FIND A RENEWED SENSE OF PURPOSE AND AMBITION. BUT IT WASN'T LONG AFTER HE LEFT THAT HE DISCOVERED SOMETHIN THAT HE ALREADY KNEW.
JOB AFTER JOB, HE HAD ONLY ONE CONSTANT—
HE WOULD PUPPETEER EVERY EVENING AFTER WORK AS A MEANS TO REGAIN A SENSE OF BALANCE AND SELF-CONTROL.
INEVITABLY, HE UNDERSTOOD WHAT THIS MEANT.
PUPPETEERING IS WHAT HE DID BEST.
HE ALSO REALIZED THAT A GREAT MANY PEOPLE STILL SAW SOME MAGIC IN WHAT HE DID.
AND IT WAS THROUGH THESE PEOPLE HE WOULD FIND JOY IN HIS CRAFT ONCE AGAIN.
BY SEEING HIS WORK THROUGH THEIR EYES.
SO THIS IS BASED ON A TRUE STORY?
AS MUCH AS THE REST OF THEM.
TUTTLE
DID YOU THINK I ACTUALLY MADE THIS STUFF UP?

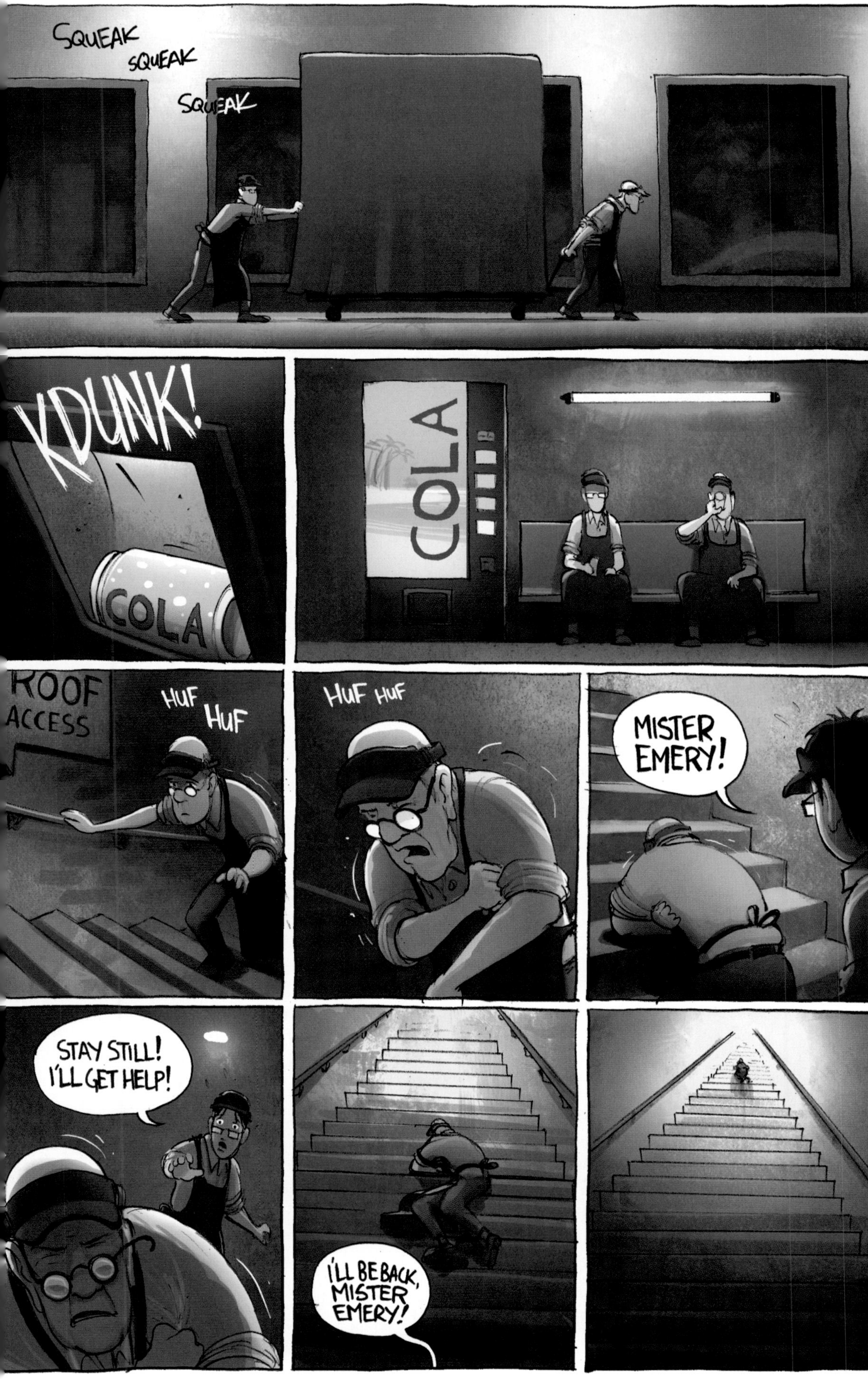
SQUEAK
SQUEAK
SQUEAK
KDUNK!
COLA
COLA
ROOF ACCESS
HUF HUF
HUF HUF
MISTER EMERY!
STAY STILL! I'LL GET HELP!
I'LL BE BACK, MISTER EMERY!

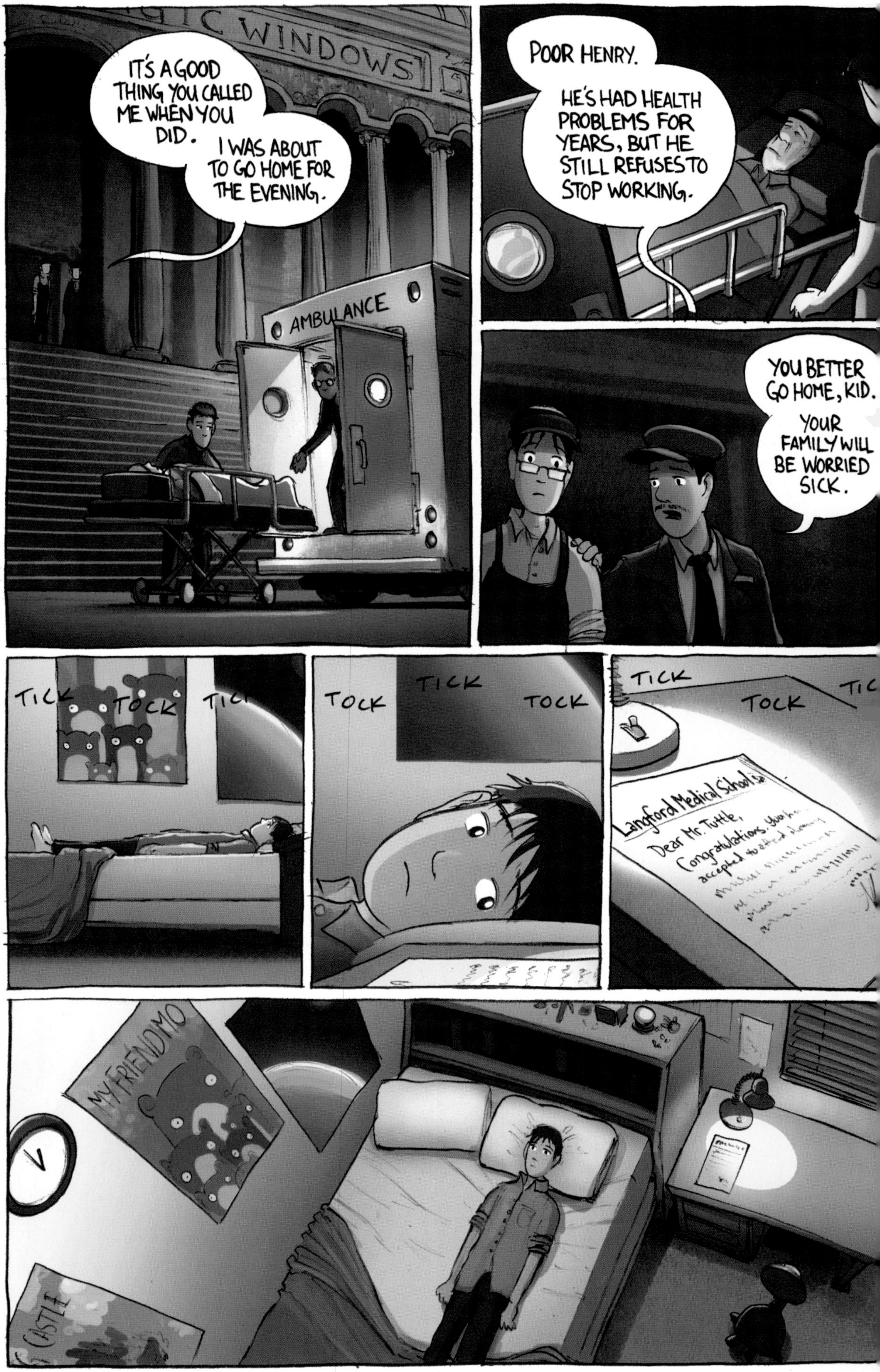

WINDOWS
IT'S A GOOD THING YOU CALLED ME WHEN YOU DID.
I WAS ABOUT TO GO HOME FOR THE EVENING.
AMBULANCE
POOR HENRY.
HE'S HAD HEALTH PROBLEMS FOR YEARS, BUT HE STILL REFUSES TO STOP WORKING.
YOU BETTER GO HOME, KID.
YOUR FAMILY WILL BE WORRIED SICK.
TICK TOCK
TOCK TICK TOCK
TICK TOCK
Langford Medical School
Dear Mr. Tuttle,
Congratulations. You have
accepted to attend
MY FRIEND MO
CASTLE

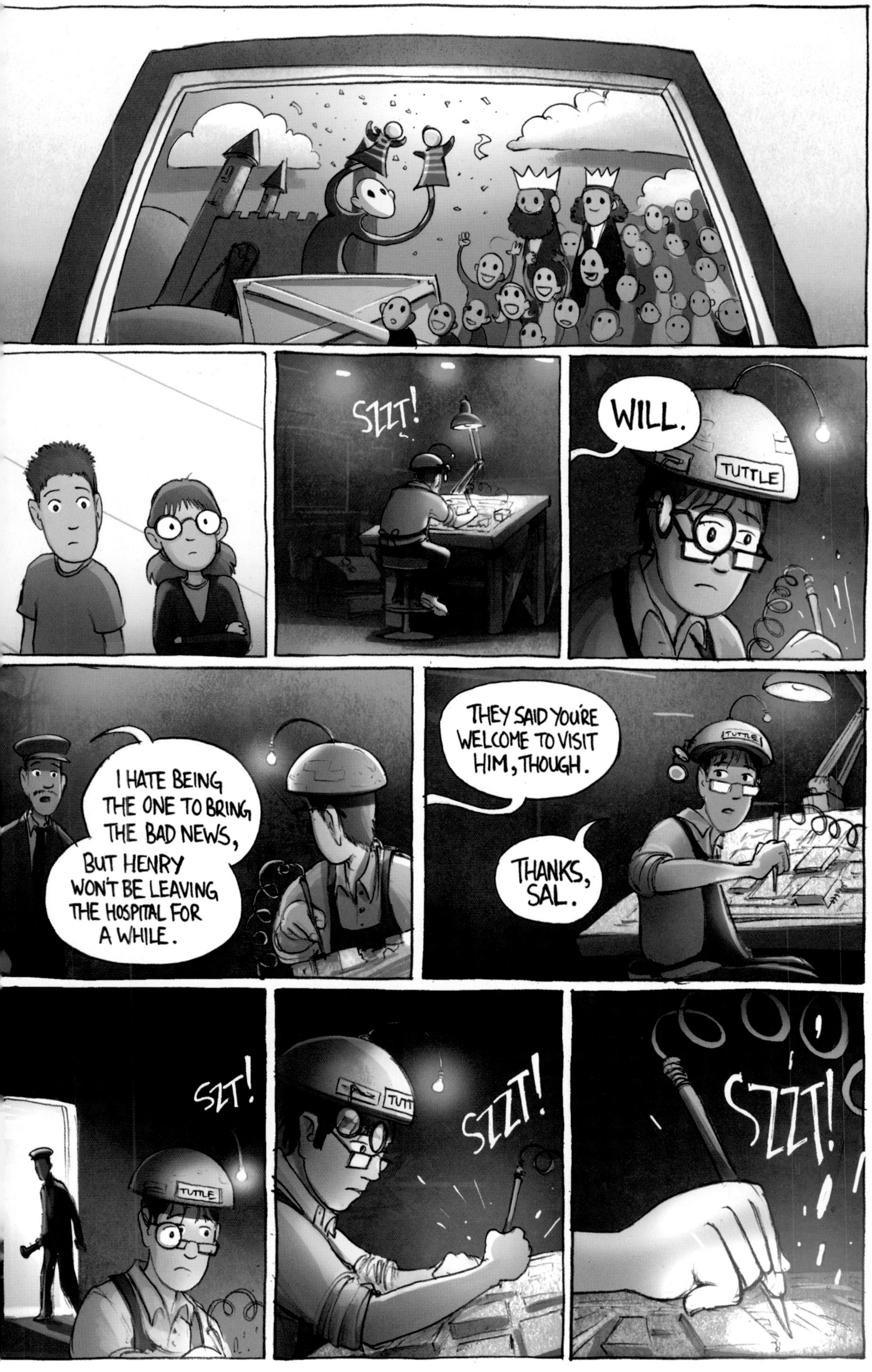
SZZT!
WILL.
TUTTLE
I HATE BEING THE ONE TO BRING THE BAD NEWS,
BUT HENRY WON'T BE LEAVING THE HOSPITAL FOR A WHILE.
THEY SAID YOU'RE WELCOME TO VISIT HIM, THOUGH.
THANKS, SAL.
SZT!
TUTTLE
SZZT!
SZZT!

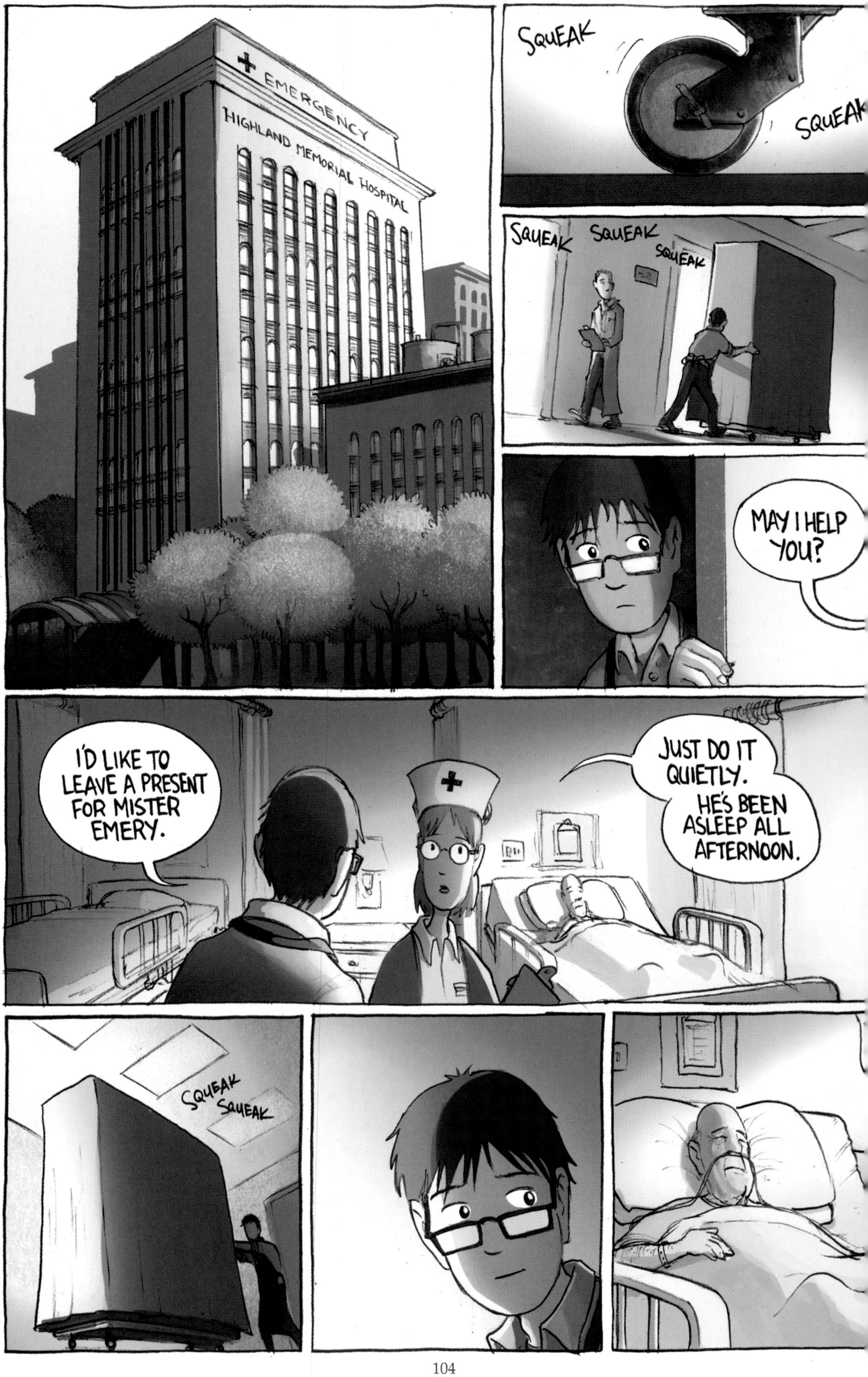
EMERGENCY
HIGHLAND MEMORIAL HOSPITAL
SQUEAK
SQUEAK
SQUEAK
SQUEAK
SQUEAK
MAY I HELP YOU?
I'D LIKE TO LEAVE A PRESENT FOR MISTER EMERY.
JUST DO IT QUIETLY.
HE'S BEEN ASLEEP ALL AFTERNOON.
SQUEAK
SQUEAK

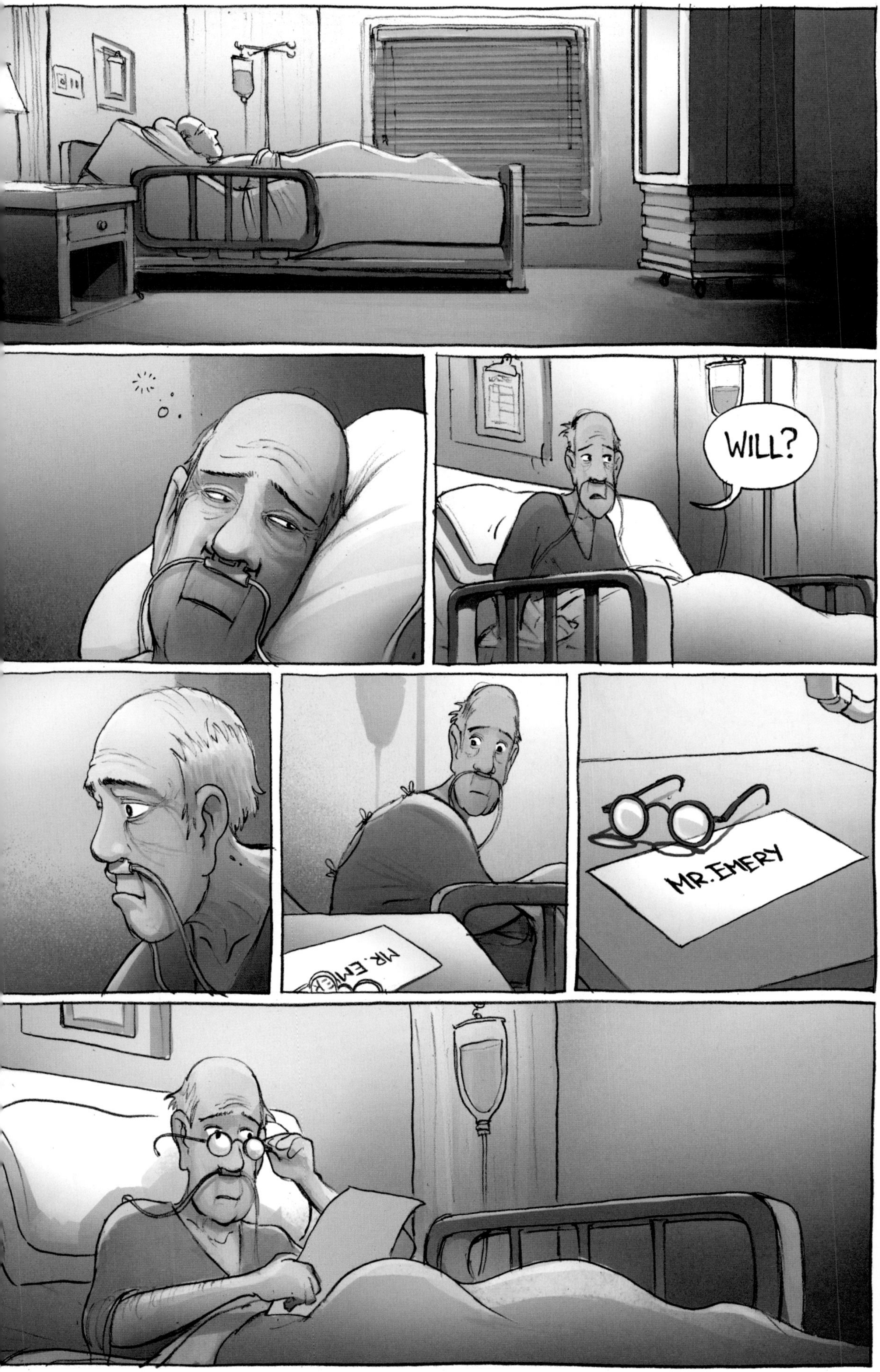
WILL?
MR. EMERY
MR. EMERY

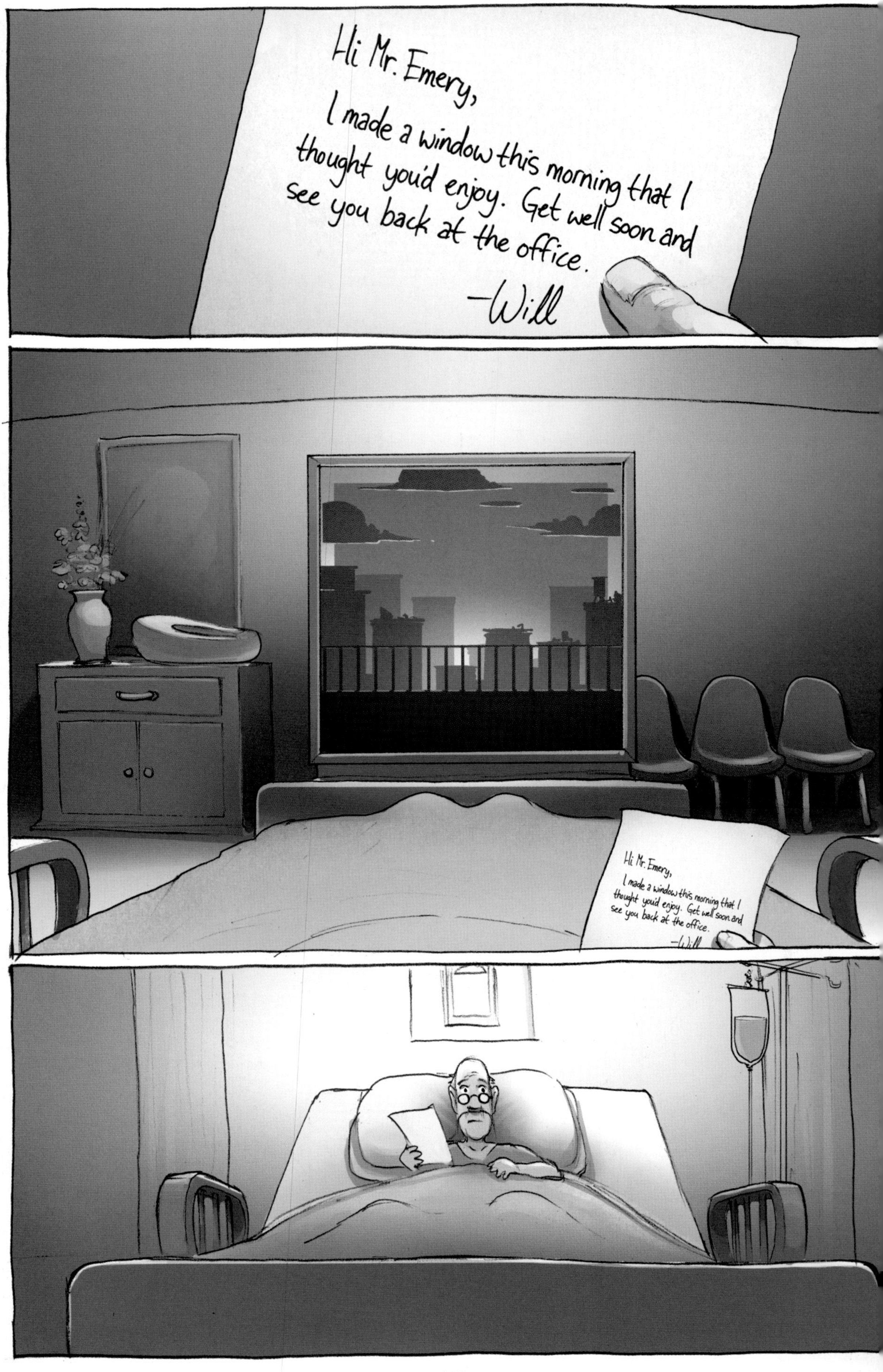

Hi Mr. Emery,
I made a window this morning that I thought you'd enjoy. Get well soon and see you back at the office.
-Will
Hi Mr. Emery,
I made a window this morning that I thought you'd enjoy. Get well soon and see you back at the office.

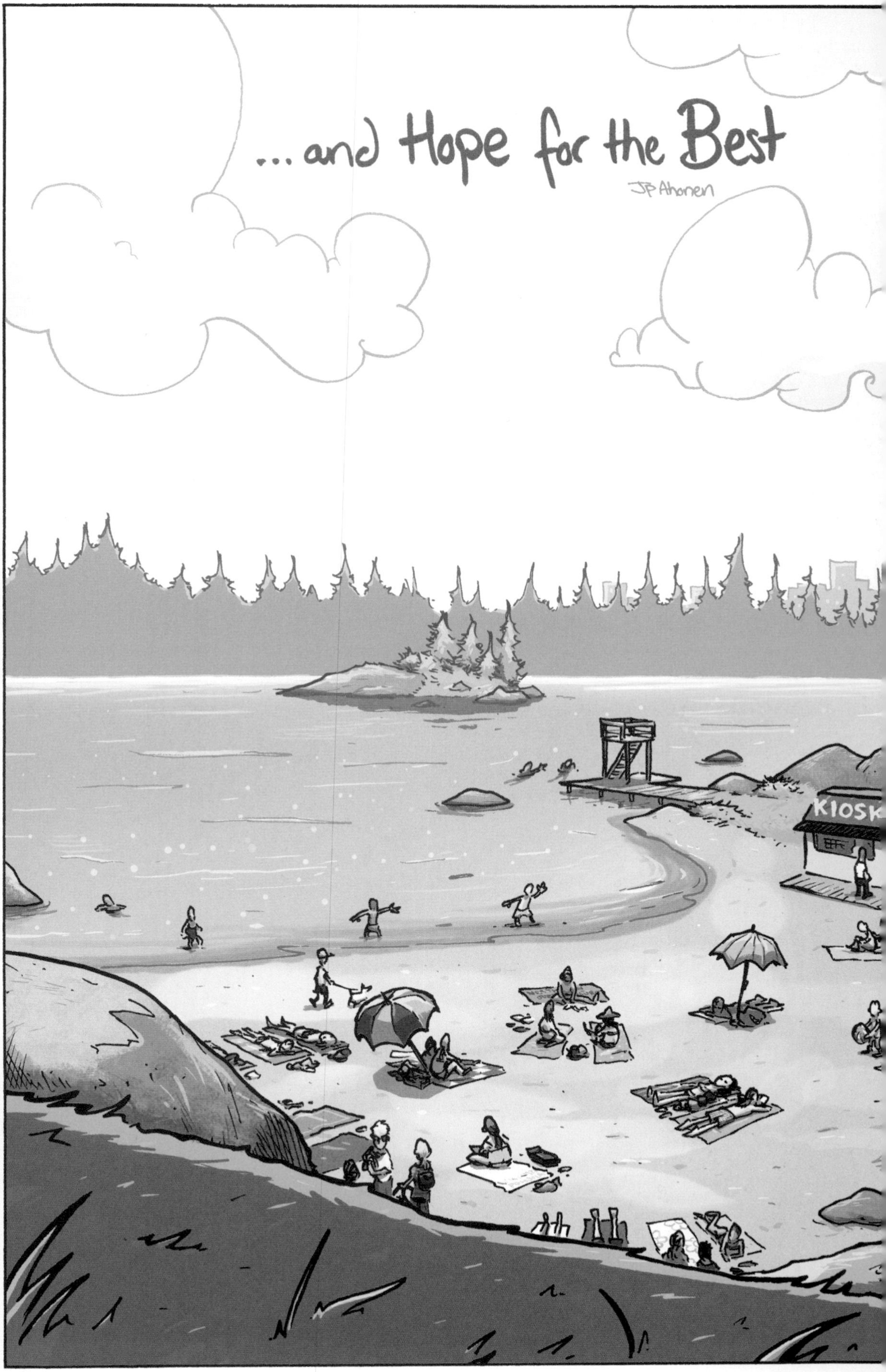
...and Hope for the Best
JP Ahonen
KIOSK

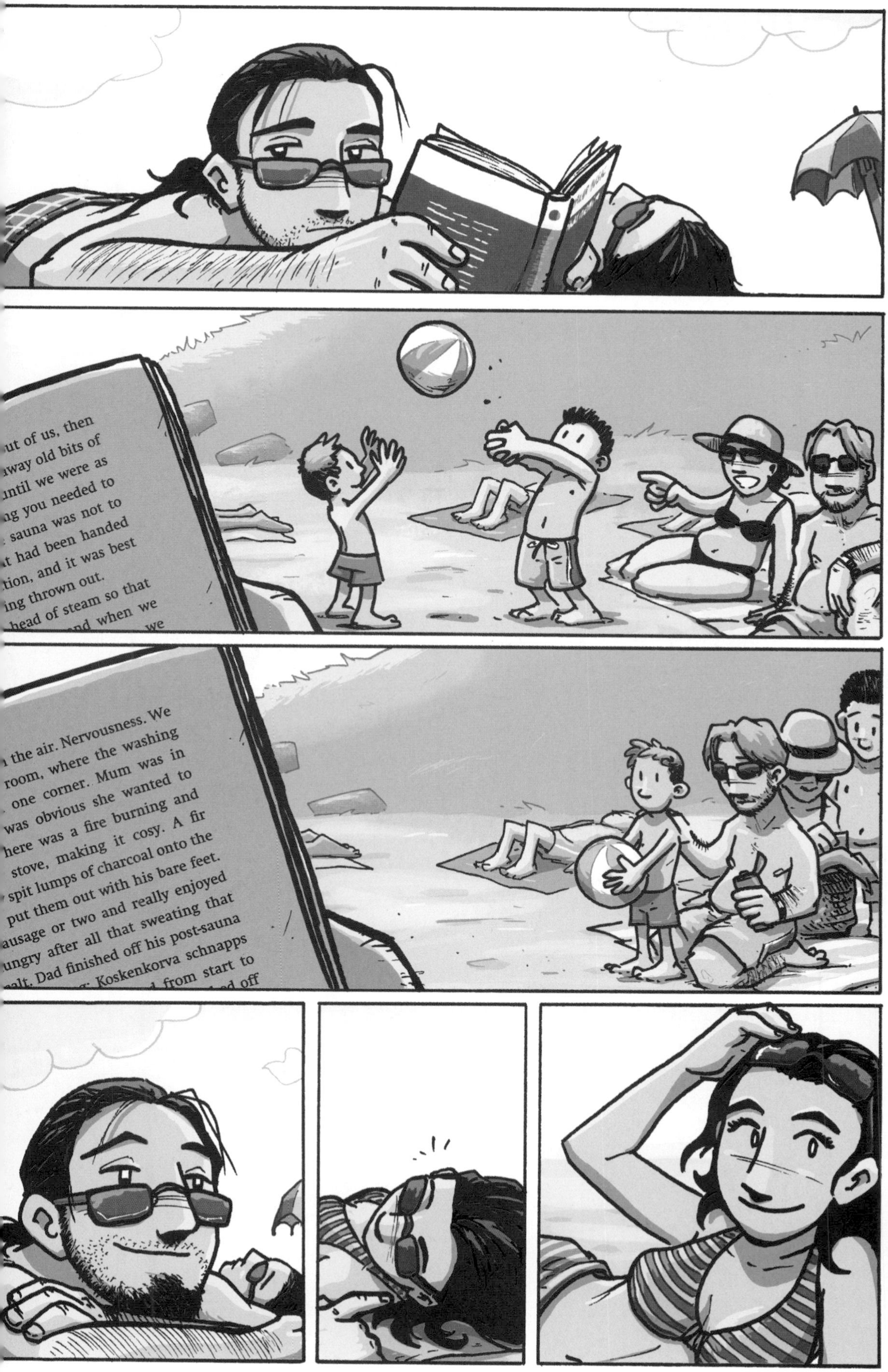
ut of us, then
away old bits of
until we were as
ng you needed to
sauna was not to
t had been handed
tion, and it was best
ing thrown out.
head of steam so that
and when we
we
the air. Nervousness. We
room, where the washing
one corner. Mum was in
was obvious she wanted to
here was a fire burning and
stove, making it cosy. A fir
spit lumps of charcoal onto the
put them out with his bare feet.
ausage or two and really enjoyed
ungry after all that sweating that
Dad finished off his post-sauna
Koskenkorva schnapps
from start to

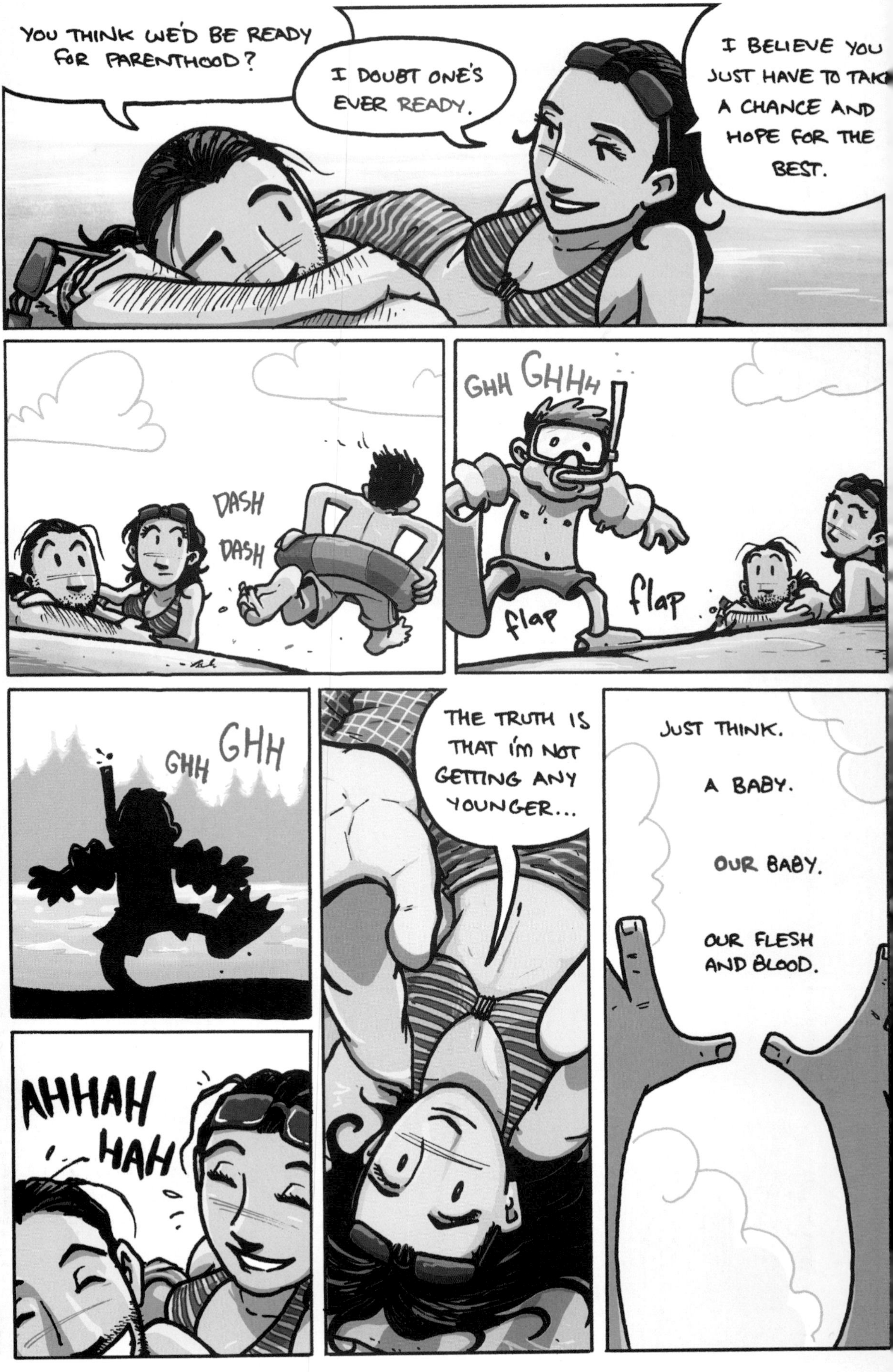
YOU THINK WE'D BE READY FOR PARENTHOOD?
I DOUBT ONE'S EVER READY.
I BELIEVE YOU JUST HAVE TO TAKE A CHANCE AND HOPE FOR THE BEST.
DASH
DASH
GHH GHHH
flap
flap
GHH GHH
AHHAH HAH
THE TRUTH IS THAT I'M NOT GETTING ANY YOUNGER...
JUST THINK.
A BABY.
OUR BABY.
OUR FLESH AND BLOOD.

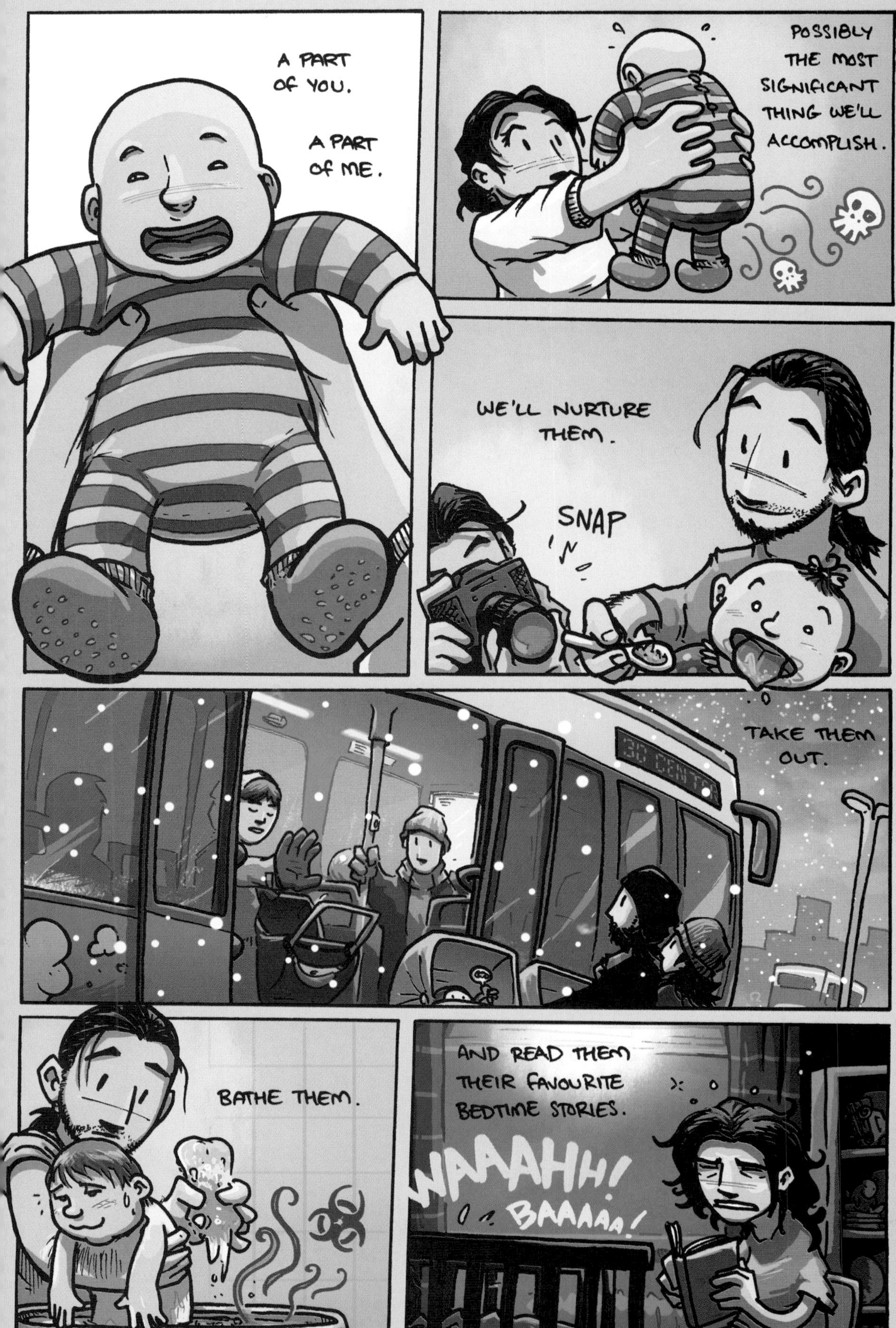
A PART OF YOU.
A PART OF ME.
POSSIBLY THE MOST SIGNIFICANT THING WE'LL ACCOMPLISH.
WE'LL NURTURE THEM.
SNAP
TAKE THEM OUT.
BATHE THEM.
AND READ THEM THEIR FAVOURITE BEDTIME STORIES.
WAAAHH!
BAAAAA!

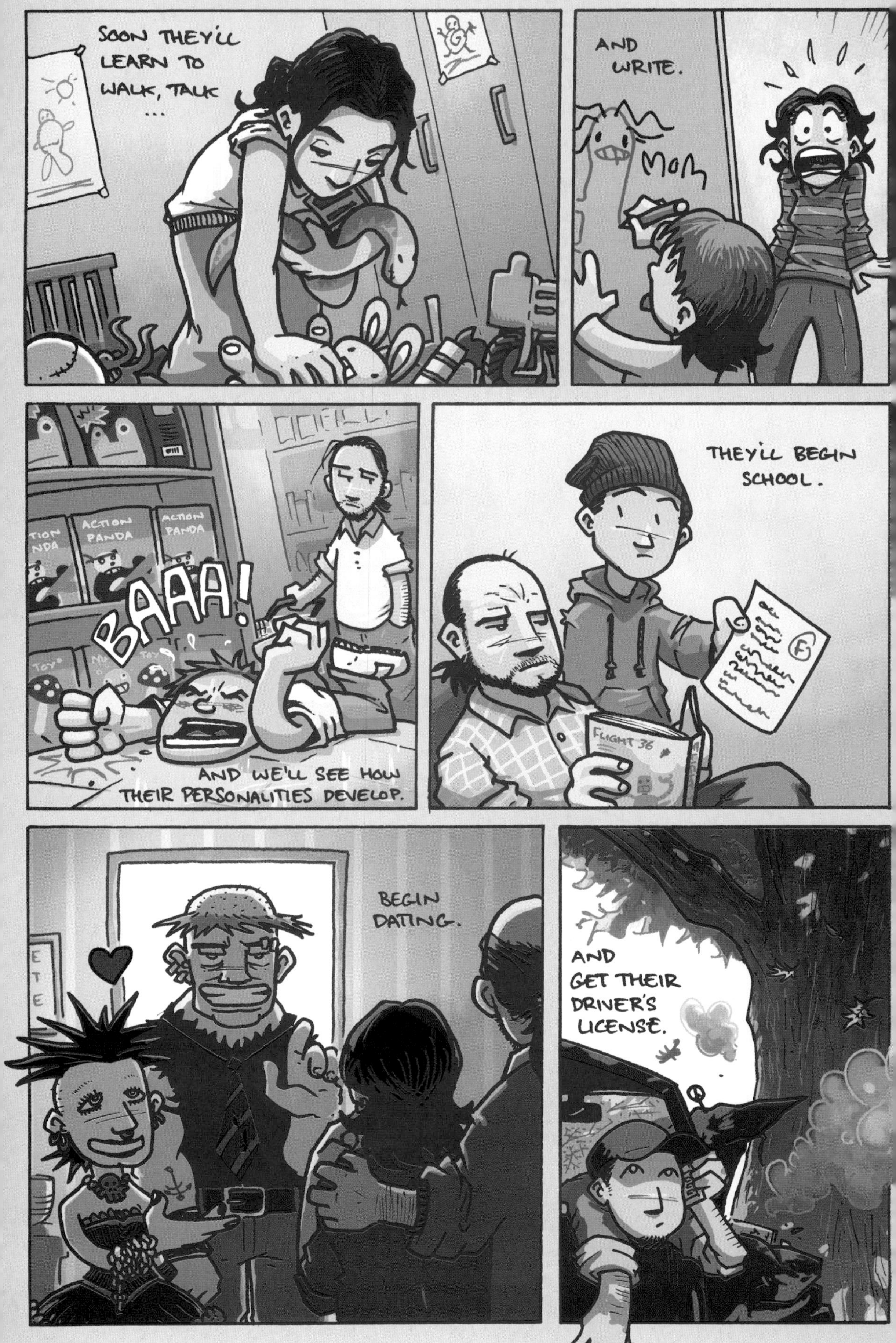

SOON THEY'LL LEARN TO WALK, TALK ...
AND WRITE.
MOM
ACTION PANDA
ACTION PANDA
BAAA!
AND WE'LL SEE HOW THEIR PERSONALITIES DEVELOP.
THEY'LL BEGIN SCHOOL.
F
FLIGHT 36
BEGIN DATING.
AND GET THEIR DRIVER'S LICENSE.

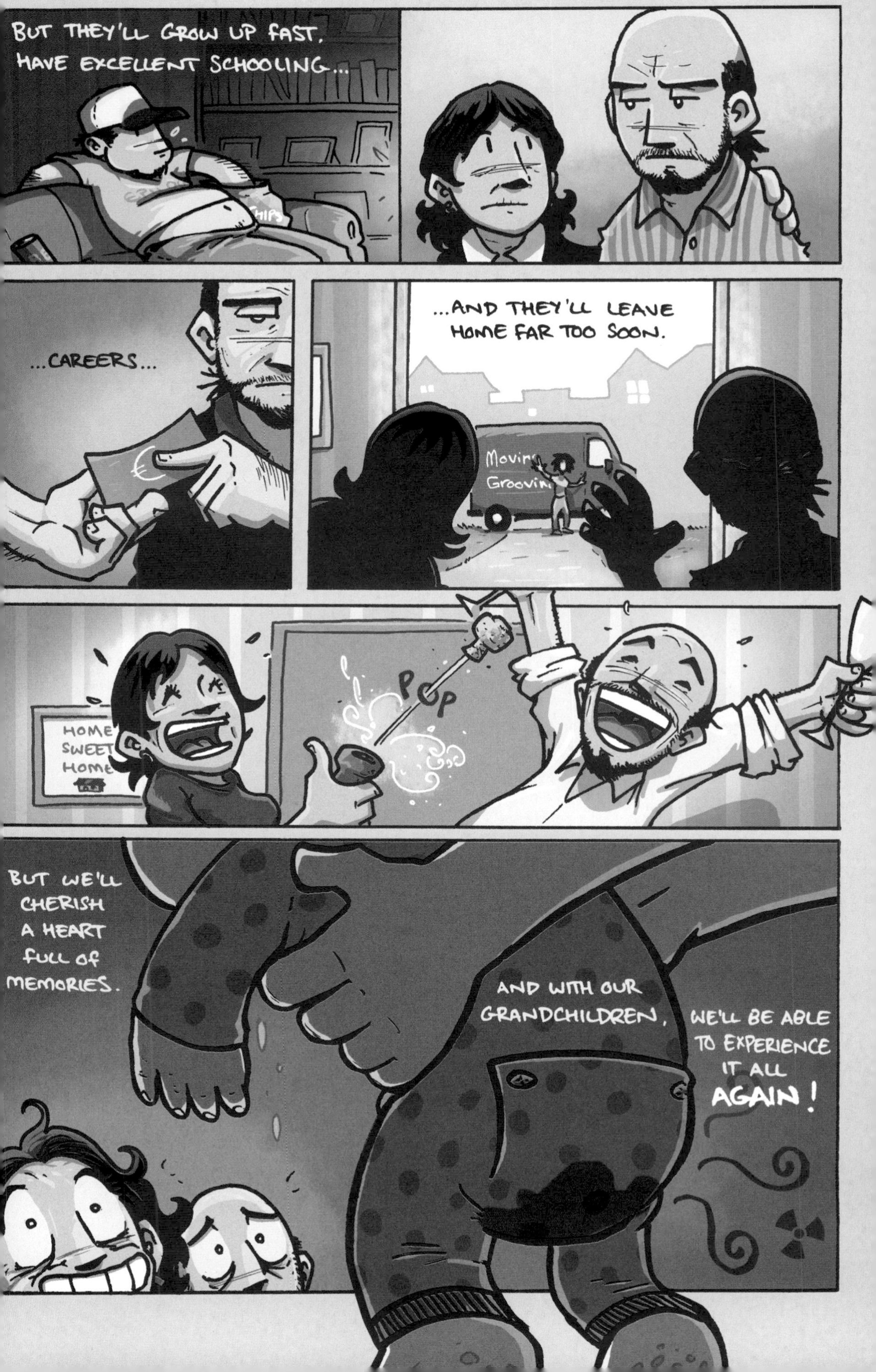
BUT THEY'LL GROW UP FAST, HAVE EXCELLENT SCHOOLING...
CHIPS
...CAREERS...
...AND THEY'LL LEAVE HOME FAR TOO SOON.
POP
HOME SWEET HOME
BUT WE'LL CHERISH A HEART FULL OF MEMORIES.
AND WITH OUR GRANDCHILDREN,
WE'LL BE ABLE TO EXPERIENCE IT ALL AGAIN!

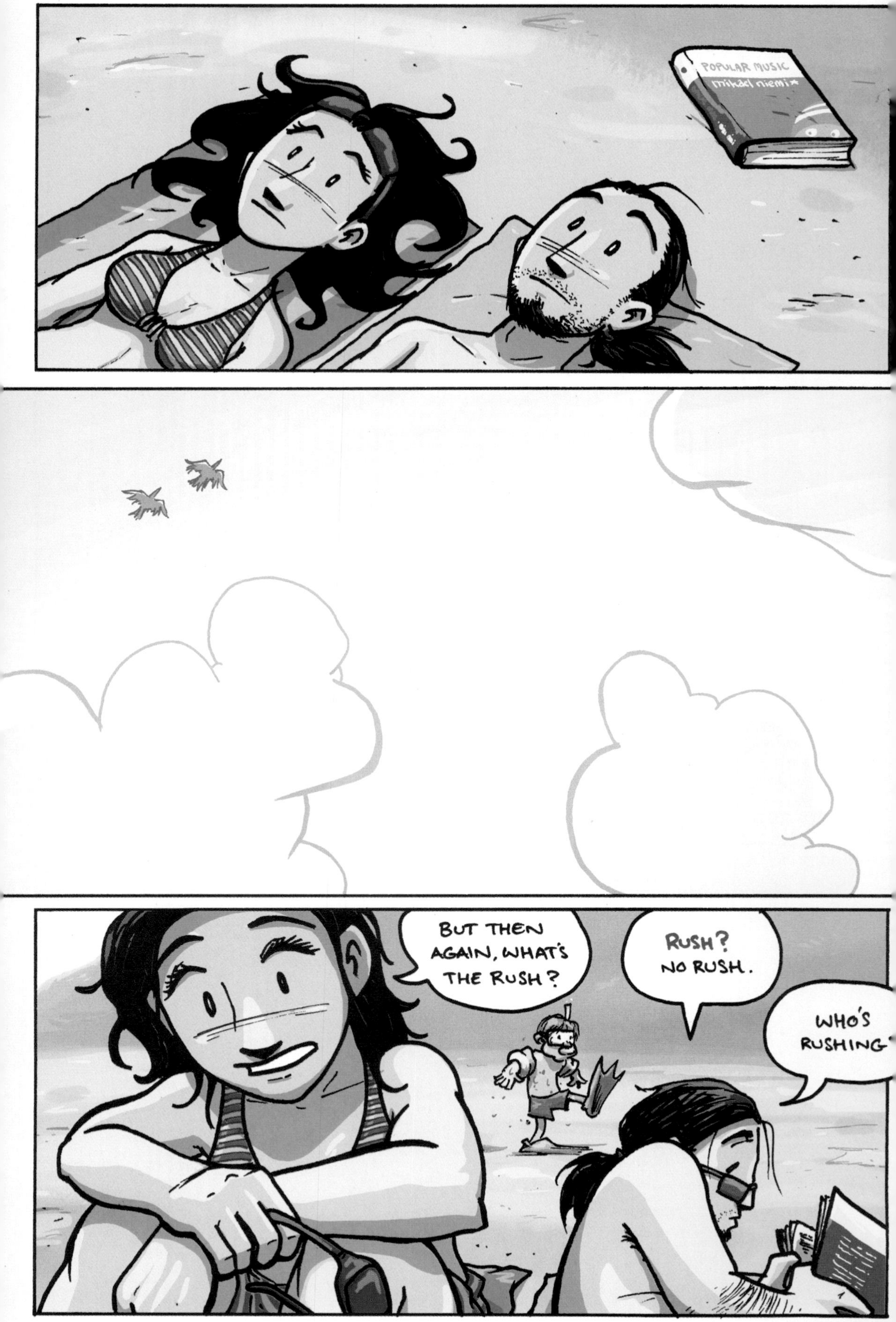
POPULAR MUSIC
mikael niemi
BUT THEN AGAIN, WHAT'S THE RUSH?
RUSH? NO RUSH.
WHO'S RUSHING

Dedicated to
Paula & Jukka Ahonen

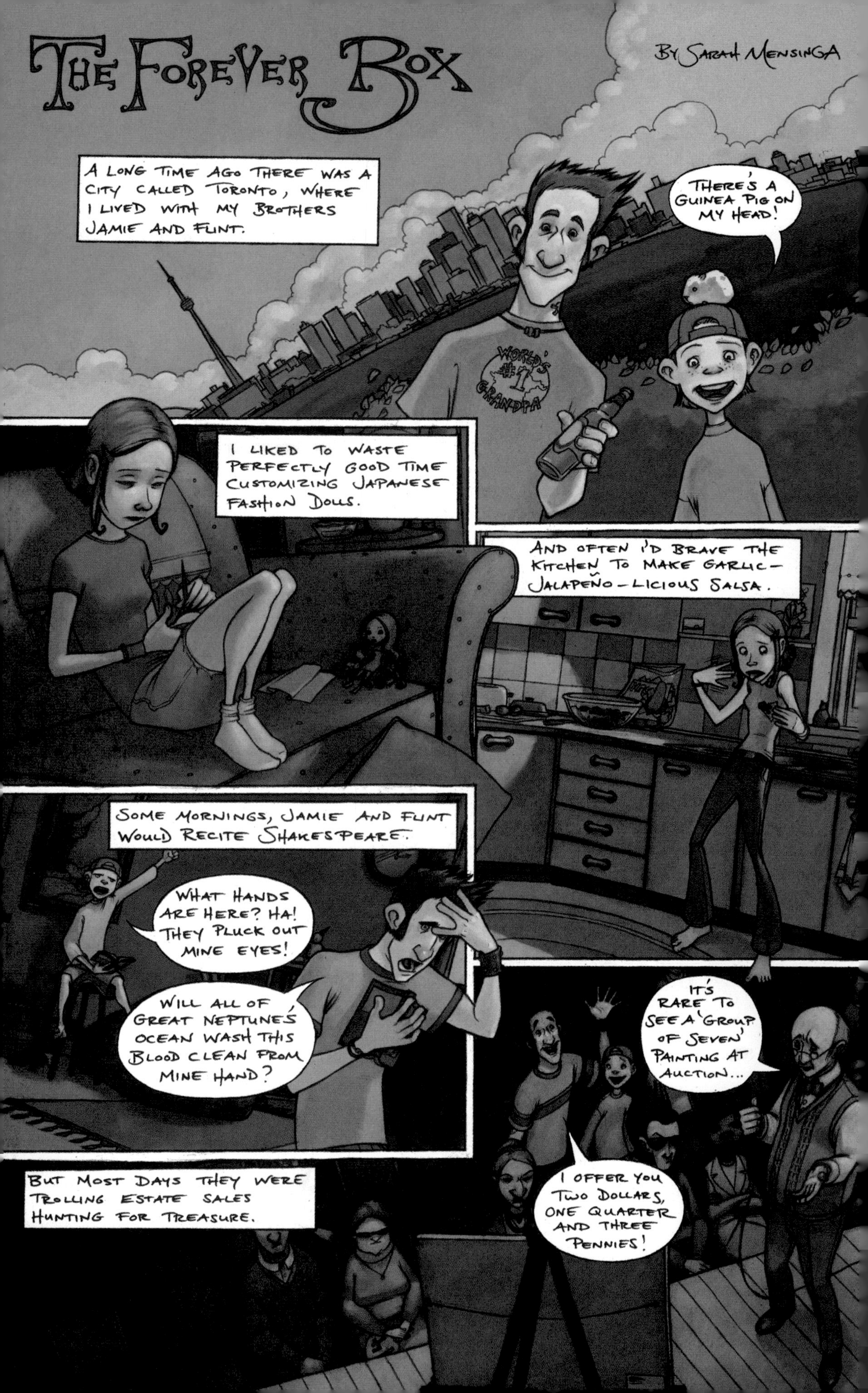
The Forever Box
By Sarah Mensinga
A long time ago there was a city called Toronto, where I lived with my brothers Jamie and Flint.
There's a guinea pig on my head!
World's #1 Grandpa
I liked to waste perfectly good time customizing Japanese fashion dolls.
And often I'd brave the kitchen to make garlic-jalapeño-licious salsa.
Some mornings, Jamie and Flint would recite Shakespeare.
What hands are here? Ha! They pluck out mine eyes!
Will all of great Neptune's ocean wash this blood clean from mine hand?
But most days they were trolling estate sales hunting for treasure.
It's rare to see a 'Group of Seven' painting at auction...
I offer you two dollars, one quarter and three pennies!

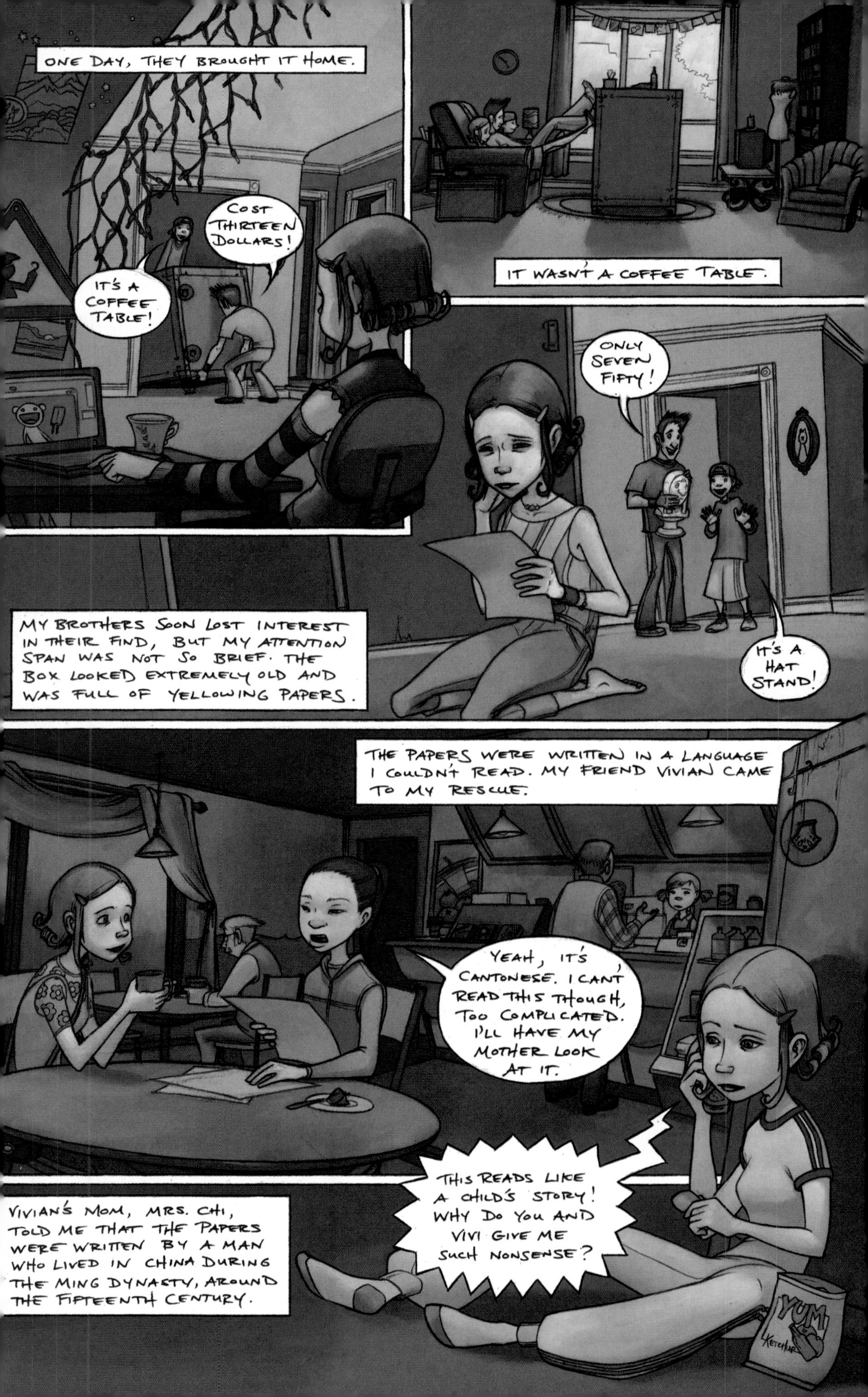
ONE DAY, THEY BROUGHT IT HOME.
IT'S A COFFEE TABLE!
COST THIRTEEN DOLLARS!
IT WASN'T A COFFEE TABLE.
MY BROTHERS SOON LOST INTEREST IN THEIR FIND, BUT MY ATTENTION SPAN WAS NOT SO BRIEF. THE BOX LOOKED EXTREMELY OLD AND WAS FULL OF YELLOWING PAPERS.
ONLY SEVEN FIFTY!
IT'S A HAT STAND!
THE PAPERS WERE WRITTEN IN A LANGUAGE I COULDN'T READ. MY FRIEND VIVIAN CAME TO MY RESCUE.
YEAH, IT'S CANTONESE. I CAN'T READ THIS THOUGH, TOO COMPLICATED. I'LL HAVE MY MOTHER LOOK AT IT.
VIVIAN'S MOM, MRS. CHI, TOLD ME THAT THE PAPERS WERE WRITTEN BY A MAN WHO LIVED IN CHINA DURING THE MING DYNASTY, AROUND THE FIFTEENTH CENTURY.
THIS READS LIKE A CHILD'S STORY! WHY DO YOU AND VIVI GIVE ME SUCH NONSENSE?
YUM
KETCHUP

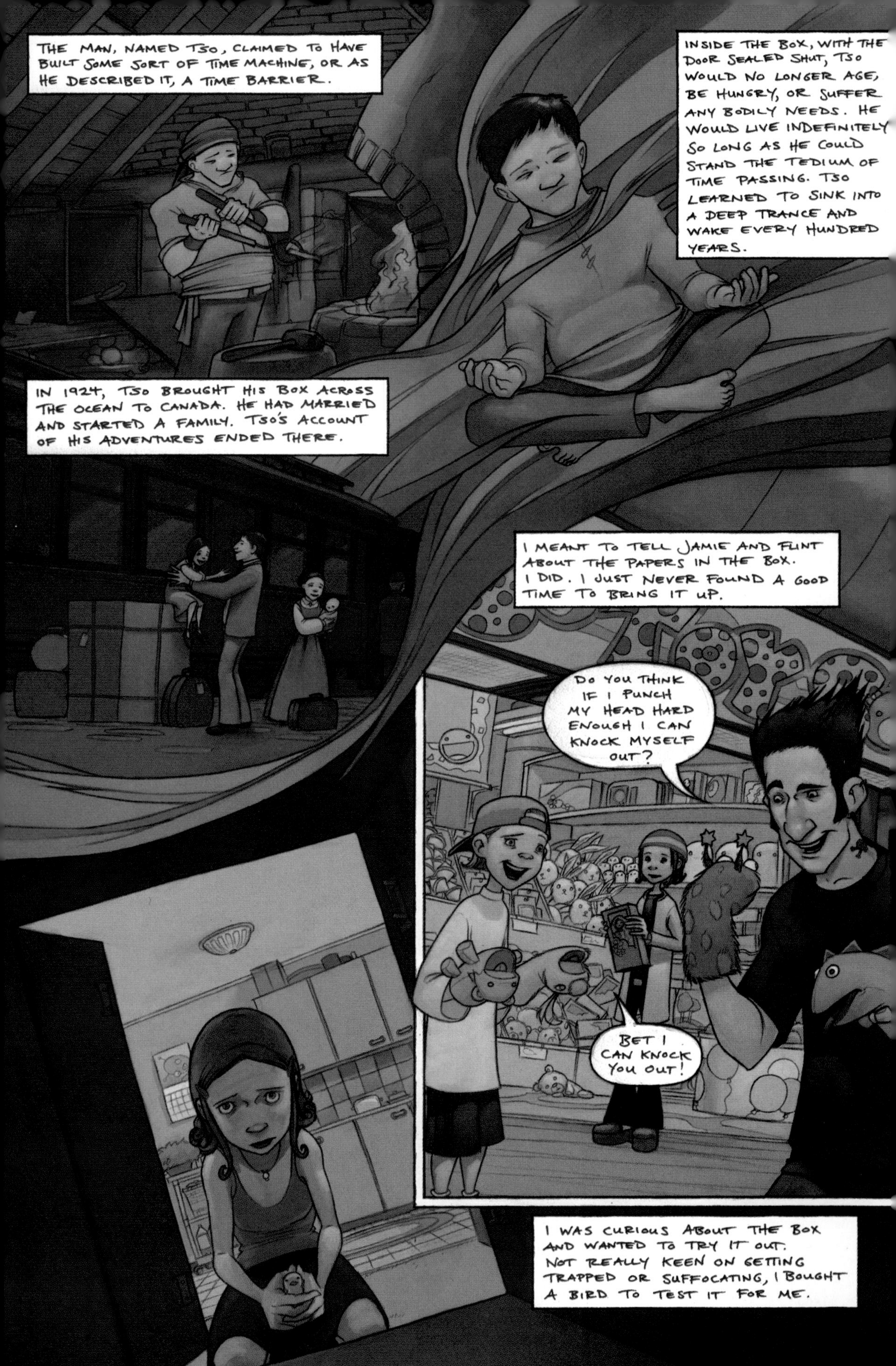
THE MAN, NAMED TSO, CLAIMED TO HAVE BUILT SOME SORT OF TIME MACHINE, OR AS HE DESCRIBED IT, A TIME BARRIER.
INSIDE THE BOX, WITH THE DOOR SEALED SHUT, TSO WOULD NO LONGER AGE, BE HUNGRY, OR SUFFER ANY BODILY NEEDS. HE WOULD LIVE INDEFINITELY SO LONG AS HE COULD STAND THE TEDIUM OF TIME PASSING. TSO LEARNED TO SINK INTO A DEEP TRANCE AND WAKE EVERY HUNDRED YEARS.
IN 1924, TSO BROUGHT HIS BOX ACROSS THE OCEAN TO CANADA. HE HAD MARRIED AND STARTED A FAMILY. TSO'S ACCOUNT OF HIS ADVENTURES ENDED THERE.
I MEANT TO TELL JAMIE AND FLINT ABOUT THE PAPERS IN THE BOX. I DID. I JUST NEVER FOUND A GOOD TIME TO BRING IT UP.
DO YOU THINK IF I PUNCH MY HEAD HARD ENOUGH I CAN KNOCK MYSELF OUT?
BET I CAN KNOCK YOU OUT!
I WAS CURIOUS ABOUT THE BOX AND WANTED TO TRY IT OUT. NOT REALLY KEEN ON GETTING TRAPPED OR SUFFOCATING, I BOUGHT A BIRD TO TEST IT FOR ME.

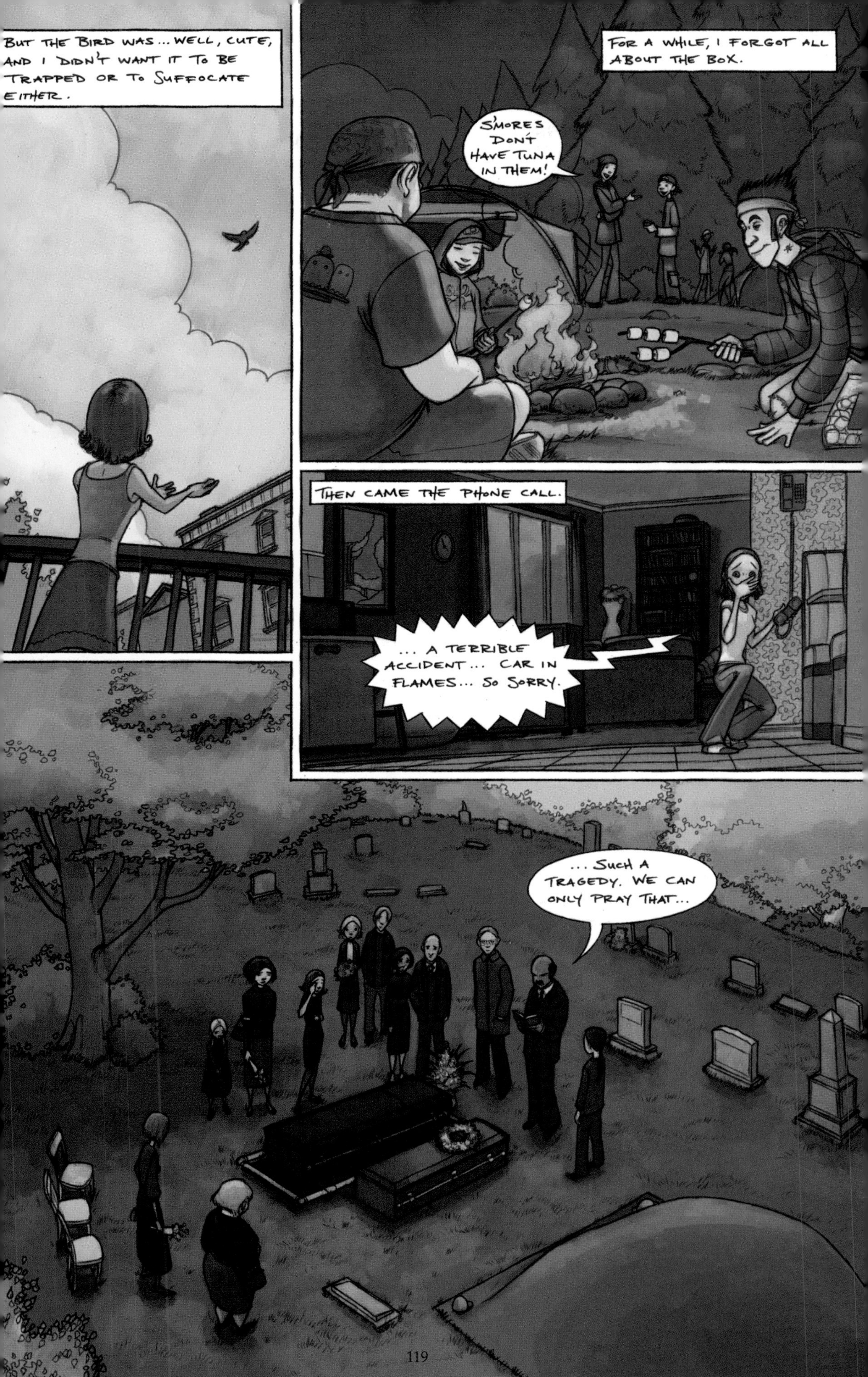
BUT THE BIRD WAS... WELL, CUTE, AND I DIDN'T WANT IT TO BE TRAPPED OR TO SUFFOCATE EITHER.
FOR A WHILE, I FORGOT ALL ABOUT THE BOX.
S'MORES DON'T HAVE TUNA IN THEM!
THEN CAME THE PHONE CALL.
... A TERRIBLE ACCIDENT... CAR IN FLAMES... SO SORRY.
... SUCH A TRAGEDY. WE CAN ONLY PRAY THAT...

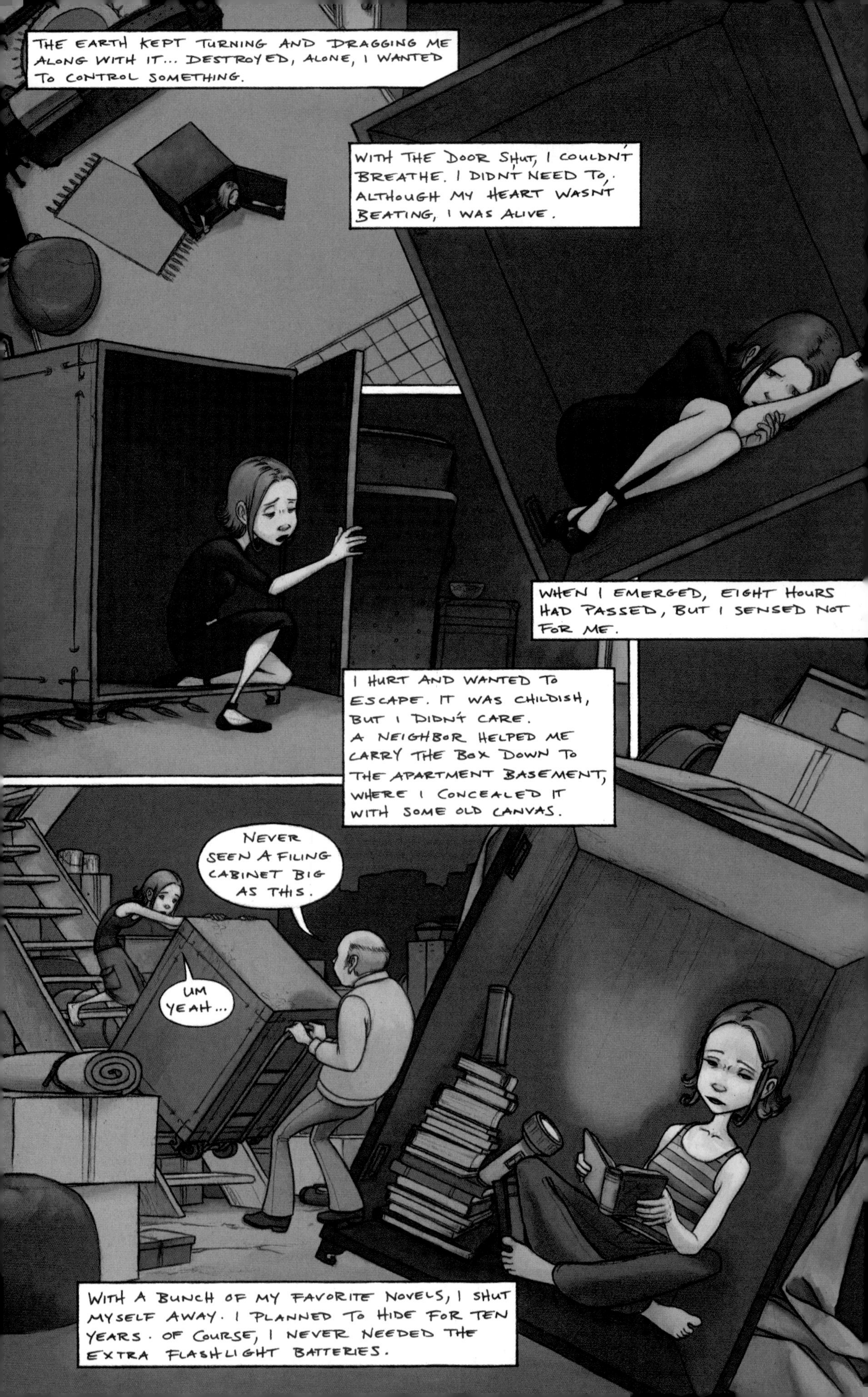
THE EARTH KEPT TURNING AND DRAGGING ME ALONG WITH IT... DESTROYED, ALONE, I WANTED TO CONTROL SOMETHING.
WITH THE DOOR SHUT, I COULDN'T BREATHE. I DIDN'T NEED TO. ALTHOUGH MY HEART WASN'T BEATING, I WAS ALIVE.
WHEN I EMERGED, EIGHT HOURS HAD PASSED, BUT I SENSED NOT FOR ME.
I HURT AND WANTED TO ESCAPE. IT WAS CHILDISH, BUT I DIDN'T CARE. A NEIGHBOR HELPED ME CARRY THE BOX DOWN TO THE APARTMENT BASEMENT, WHERE I CONCEALED IT WITH SOME OLD CANVAS.
NEVER SEEN A FILING CABINET BIG AS THIS.
UM YEAH...
WITH A BUNCH OF MY FAVORITE NOVELS, I SHUT MYSELF AWAY. I PLANNED TO HIDE FOR TEN YEARS. OF COURSE, I NEVER NEEDED THE EXTRA FLASHLIGHT BATTERIES.

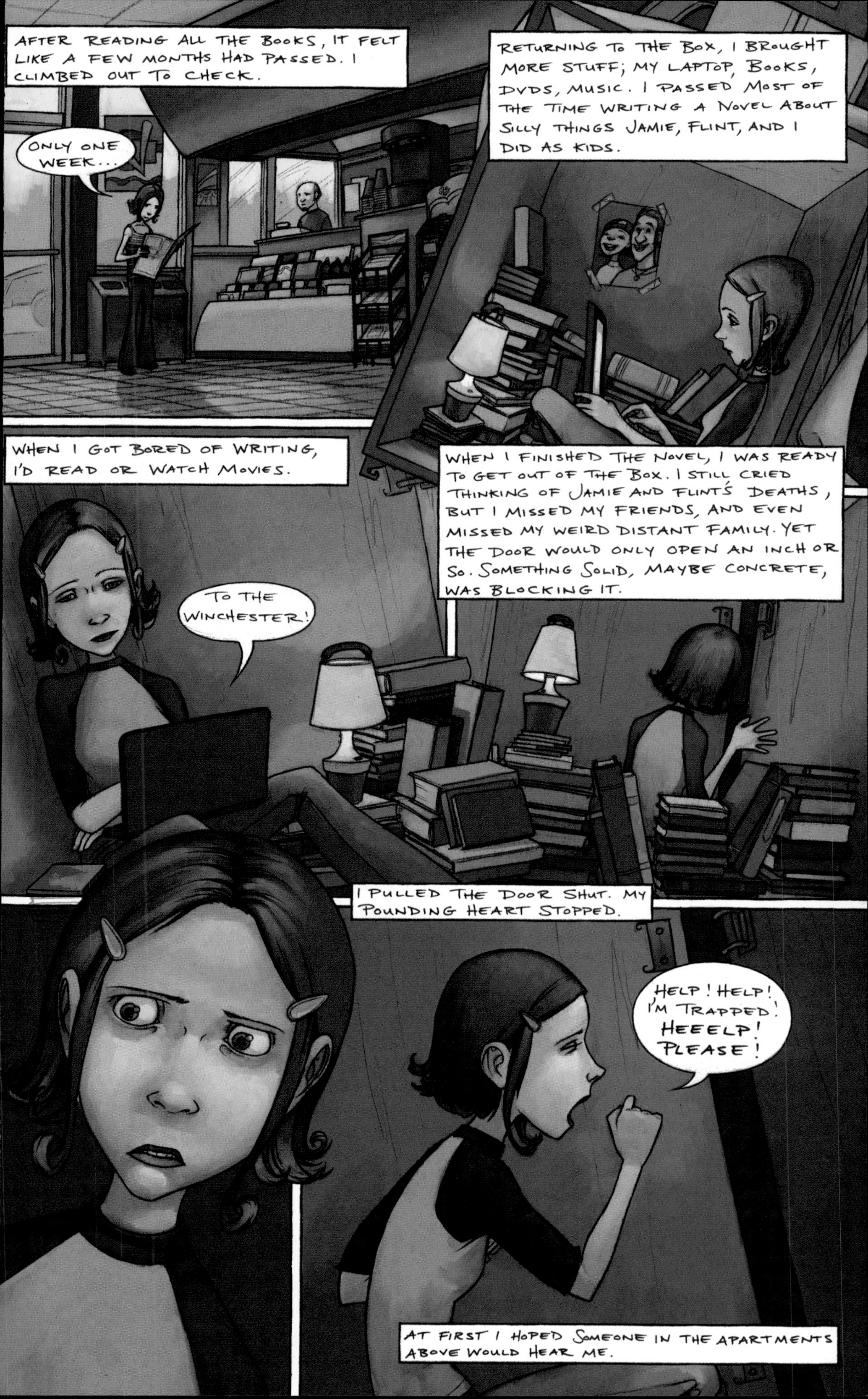
AFTER READING ALL THE BOOKS, IT FELT LIKE A FEW MONTHS HAD PASSED. I CLIMBED OUT TO CHECK.
ONLY ONE WEEK...
RETURNING TO THE BOX, I BROUGHT MORE STUFF; MY LAPTOP, BOOKS, DVDS, MUSIC. I PASSED MOST OF THE TIME WRITING A NOVEL ABOUT SILLY THINGS JAMIE, FLINT, AND I DID AS KIDS.
WHEN I GOT BORED OF WRITING, I'D READ OR WATCH MOVIES.
TO THE WINCHESTER!
WHEN I FINISHED THE NOVEL, I WAS READY TO GET OUT OF THE BOX. I STILL CRIED THINKING OF JAMIE AND FLINT'S DEATHS, BUT I MISSED MY FRIENDS, AND EVEN MISSED MY WEIRD DISTANT FAMILY. YET THE DOOR WOULD ONLY OPEN AN INCH OR SO. SOMETHING SOLID, MAYBE CONCRETE, WAS BLOCKING IT.
I PULLED THE DOOR SHUT. MY POUNDING HEART STOPPED.
HELP! HELP! I'M TRAPPED! HEEELP! PLEASE!
AT FIRST I HOPED SOMEONE IN THE APARTMENTS ABOVE WOULD HEAR ME.

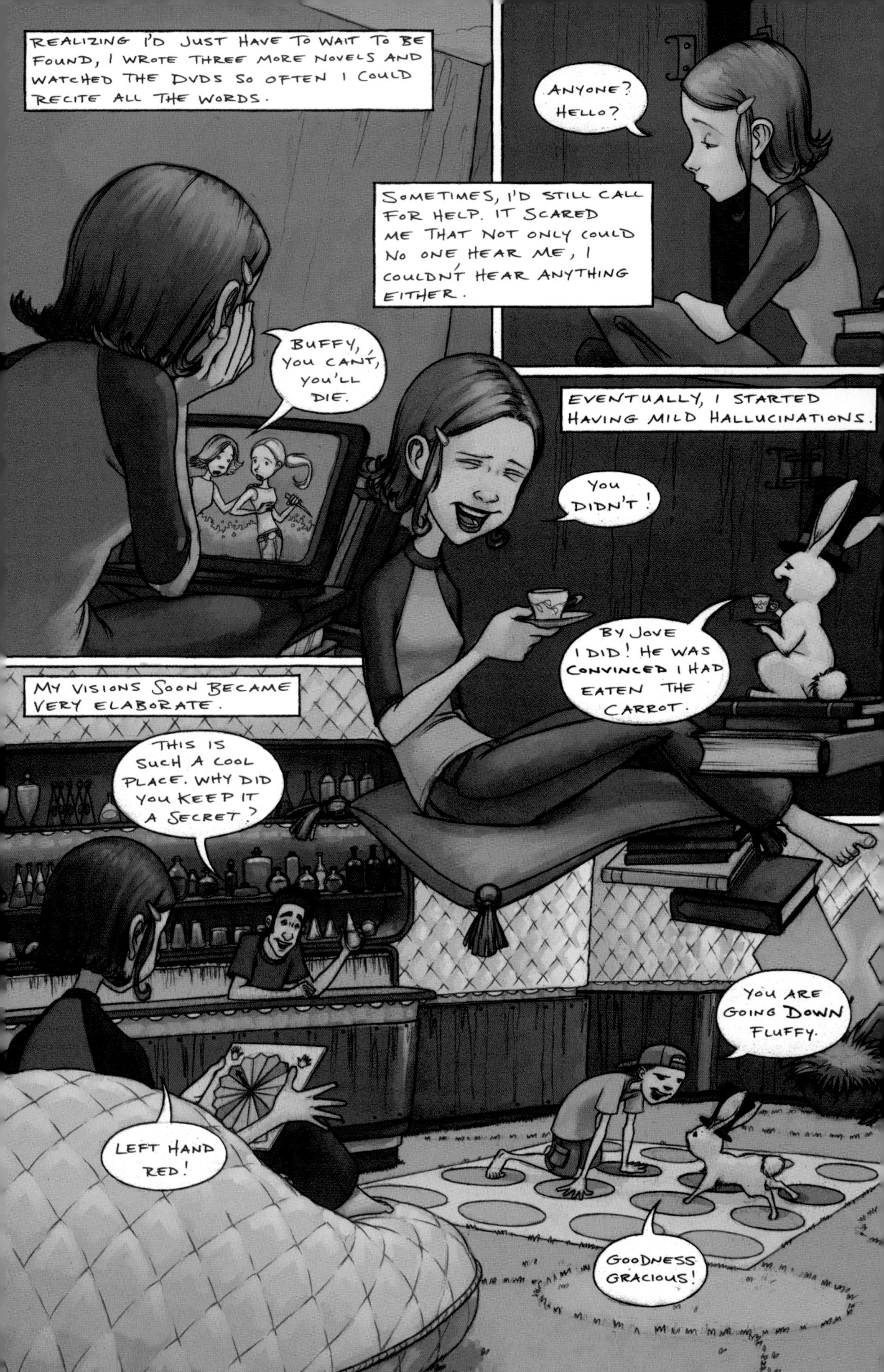
REALIZING I'D JUST HAVE TO WAIT TO BE FOUND, I WROTE THREE MORE NOVELS AND WATCHED THE DVDS SO OFTEN I COULD RECITE ALL THE WORDS.
BUFFY, YOU CAN'T, YOU'LL DIE.
ANYONE? HELLO?
SOMETIMES, I'D STILL CALL FOR HELP. IT SCARED ME THAT NOT ONLY COULD NO ONE HEAR ME, I COULDN'T HEAR ANYTHING EITHER.
EVENTUALLY, I STARTED HAVING MILD HALLUCINATIONS.
YOU DIDN'T!
BY JOVE I DID! HE WAS CONVINCED I HAD EATEN THE CARROT.
MY VISIONS SOON BECAME VERY ELABORATE.
THIS IS SUCH A COOL PLACE. WHY DID YOU KEEP IT A SECRET?
LEFT HAND RED!
YOU ARE GOING DOWN FLUFFY.
GOODNESS GRACIOUS!

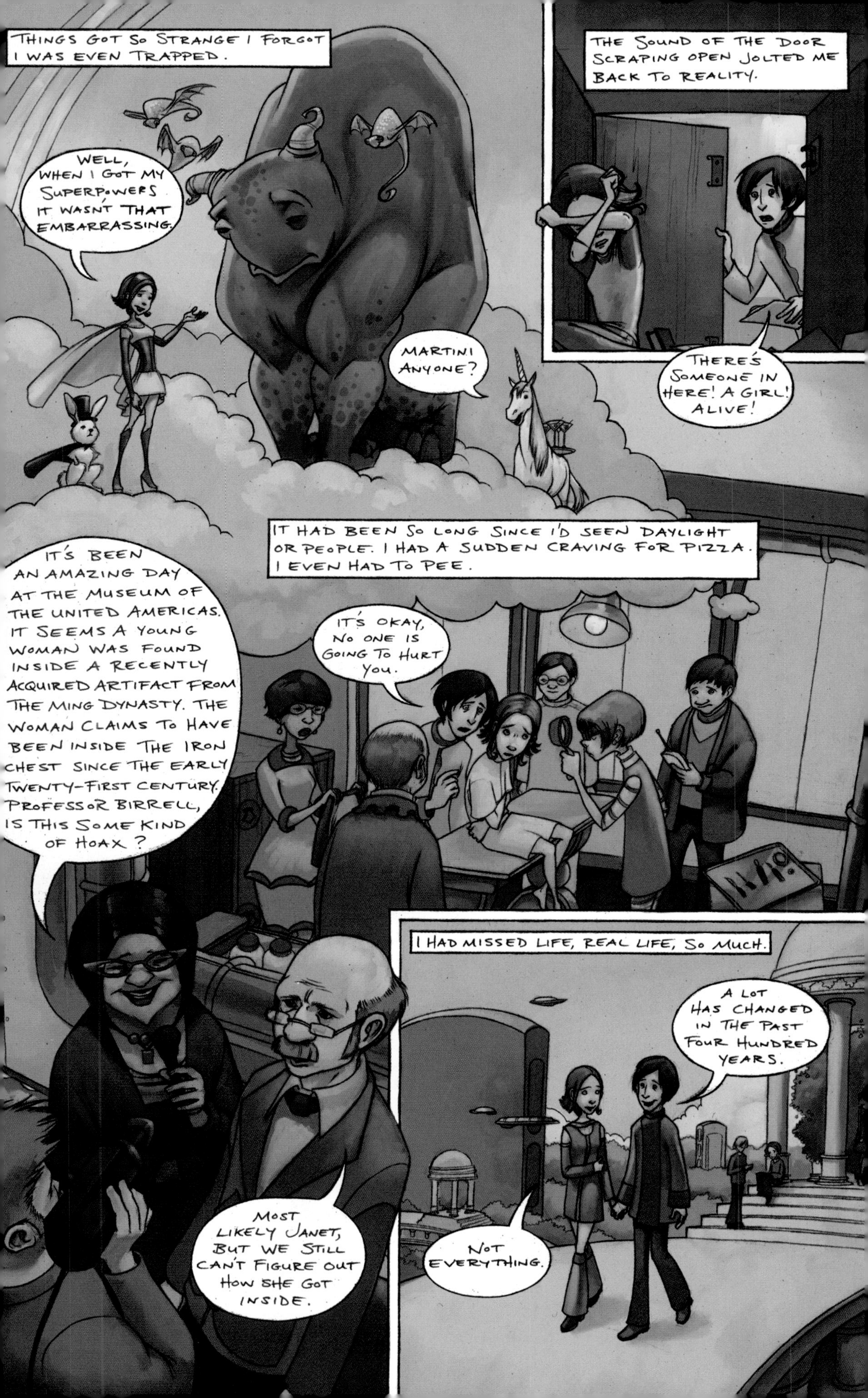

THINGS GOT SO STRANGE I FORGOT I WAS EVEN TRAPPED.
WELL, WHEN I GOT MY SUPERPOWERS IT WASN'T THAT EMBARRASSING.
MARTINI ANYONE?
THE SOUND OF THE DOOR SCRAPING OPEN JOLTED ME BACK TO REALITY.
THERE'S SOMEONE IN HERE! A GIRL! ALIVE!
IT HAD BEEN SO LONG SINCE I'D SEEN DAYLIGHT OR PEOPLE. I HAD A SUDDEN CRAVING FOR PIZZA. I EVEN HAD TO PEE.
IT'S OKAY, NO ONE IS GOING TO HURT YOU.
IT'S BEEN AN AMAZING DAY AT THE MUSEUM OF THE UNITED AMERICAS. IT SEEMS A YOUNG WOMAN WAS FOUND INSIDE A RECENTLY ACQUIRED ARTIFACT FROM THE MING DYNASTY. THE WOMAN CLAIMS TO HAVE BEEN INSIDE THE IRON CHEST SINCE THE EARLY TWENTY-FIRST CENTURY. PROFESSOR BIRRELL, IS THIS SOME KIND OF HOAX?
MOST LIKELY JANET, BUT WE STILL CAN'T FIGURE OUT HOW SHE GOT INSIDE.
I HAD MISSED LIFE, REAL LIFE, SO MUCH.
A LOT HAS CHANGED IN THE PAST FOUR HUNDRED YEARS.
NOT EVERYTHING.

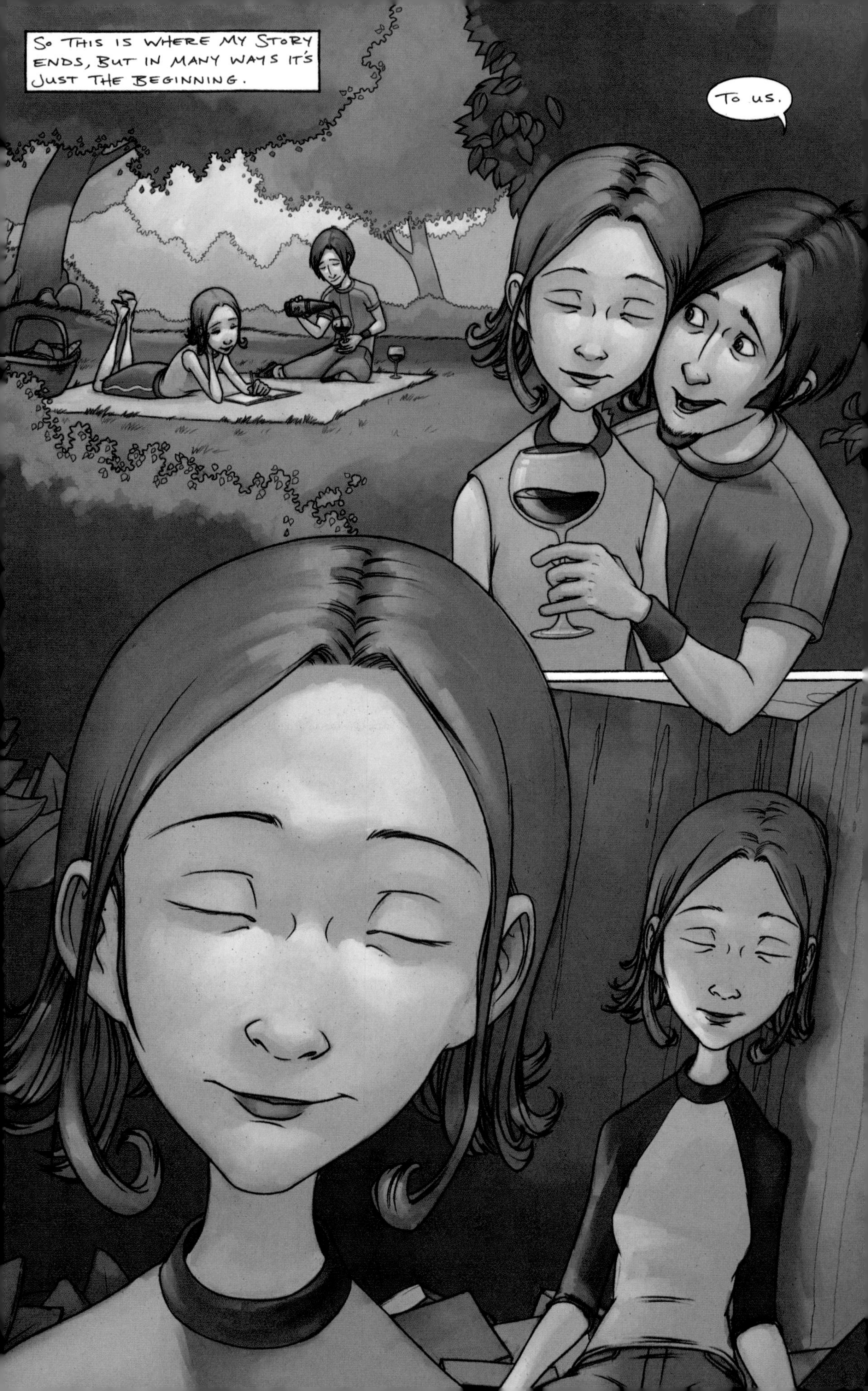
So this is where my story ends, but in many ways it's just the beginning.
To us.

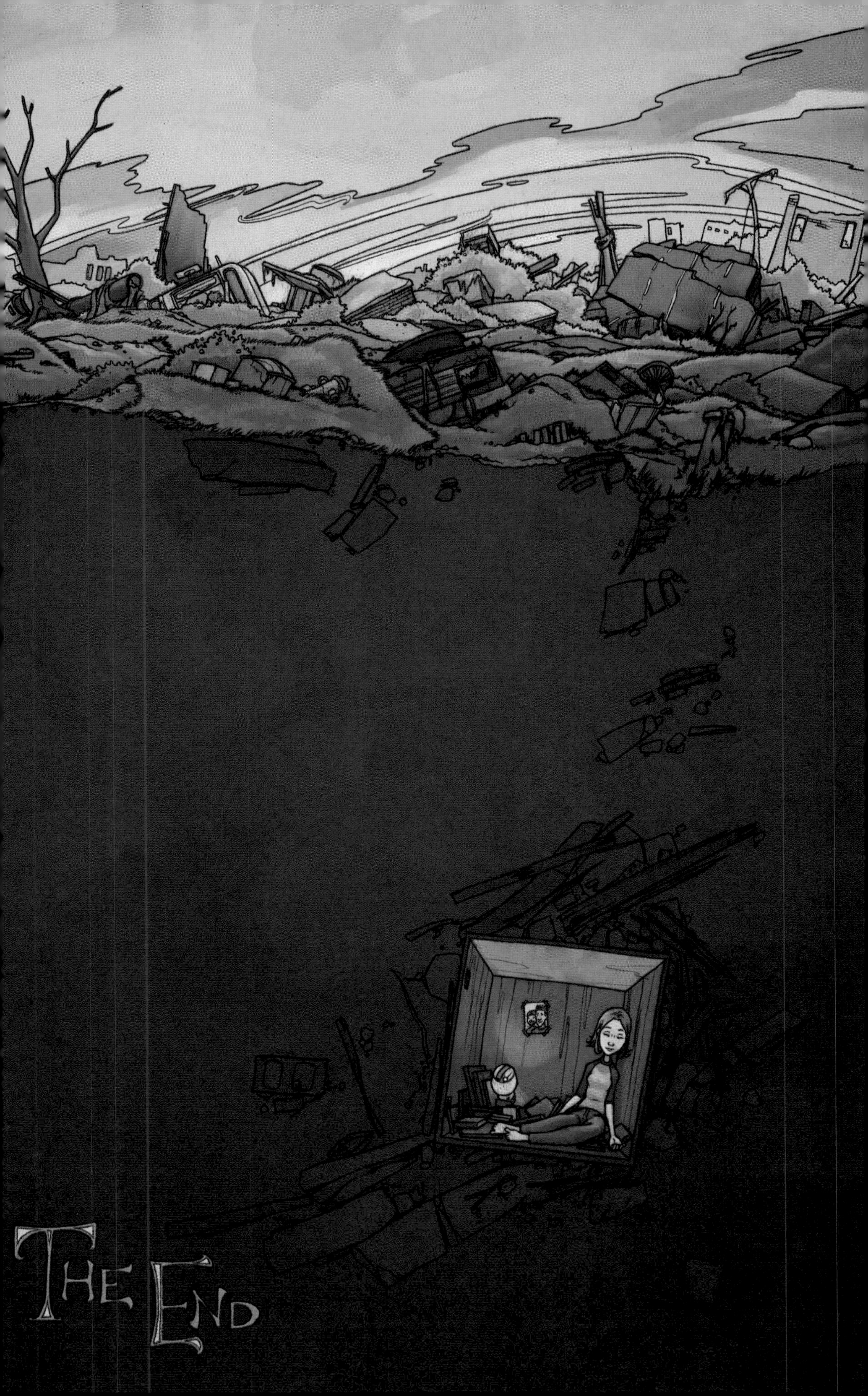
THE END

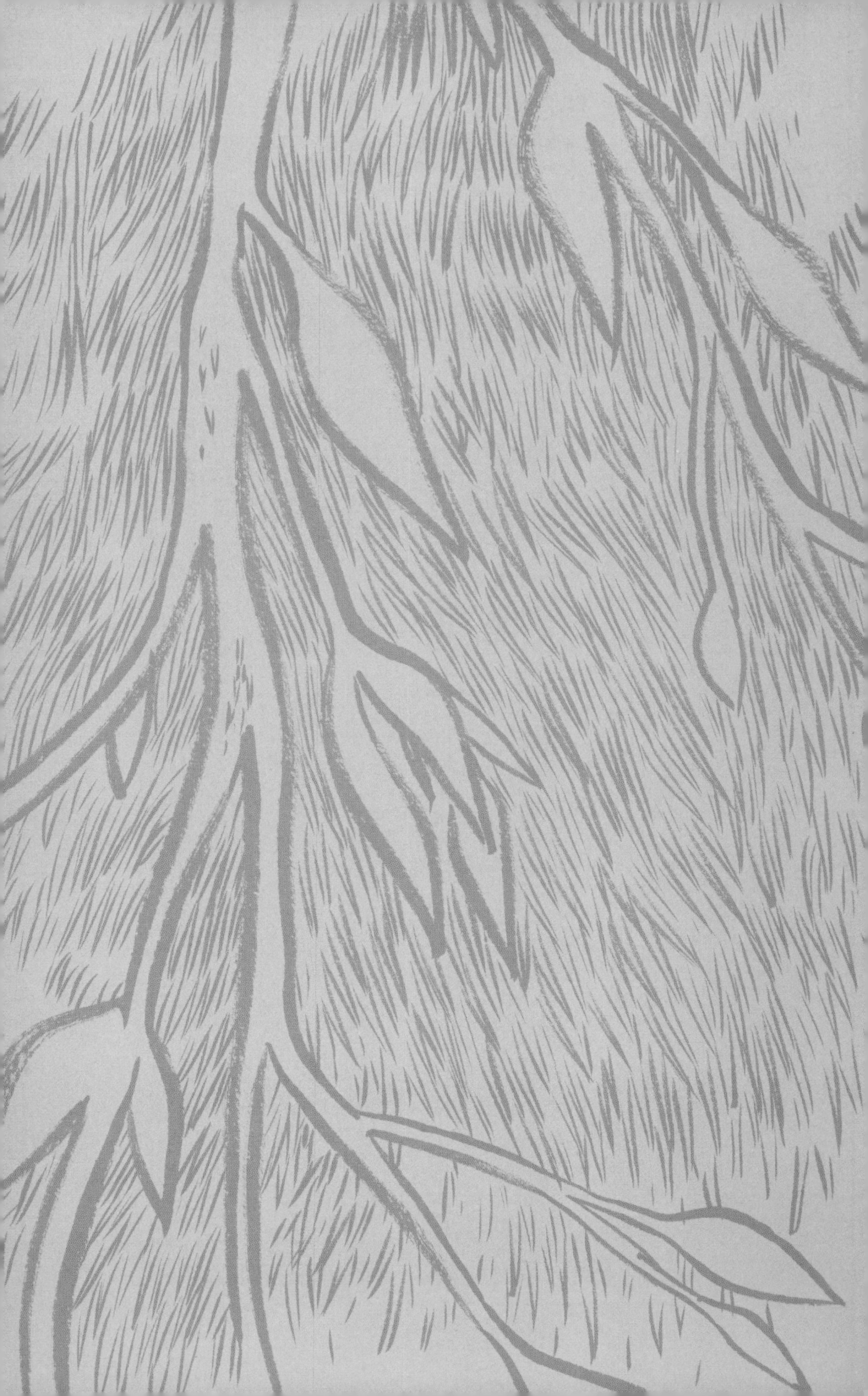

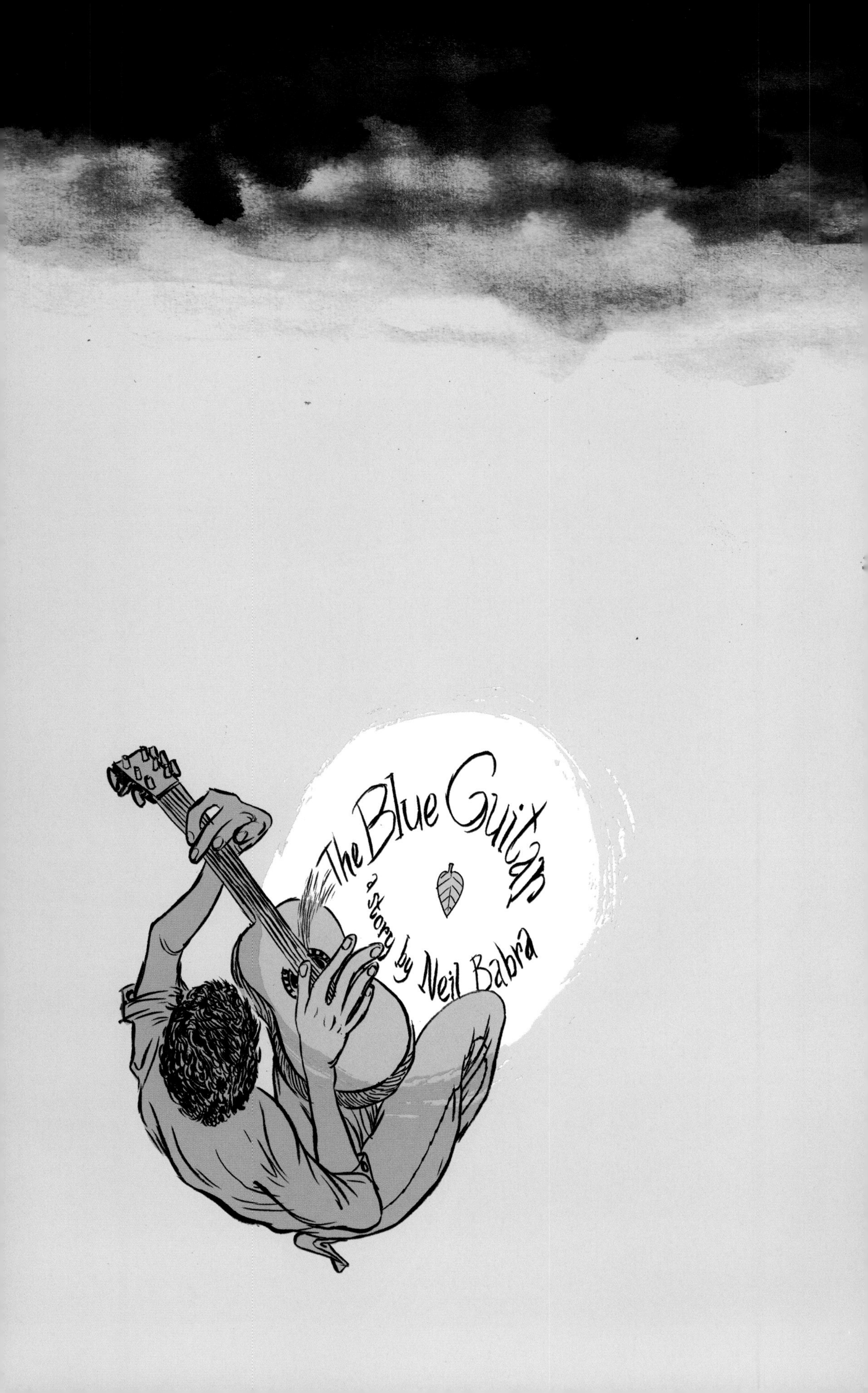
The Blue Guitar
a story by Neil Babra

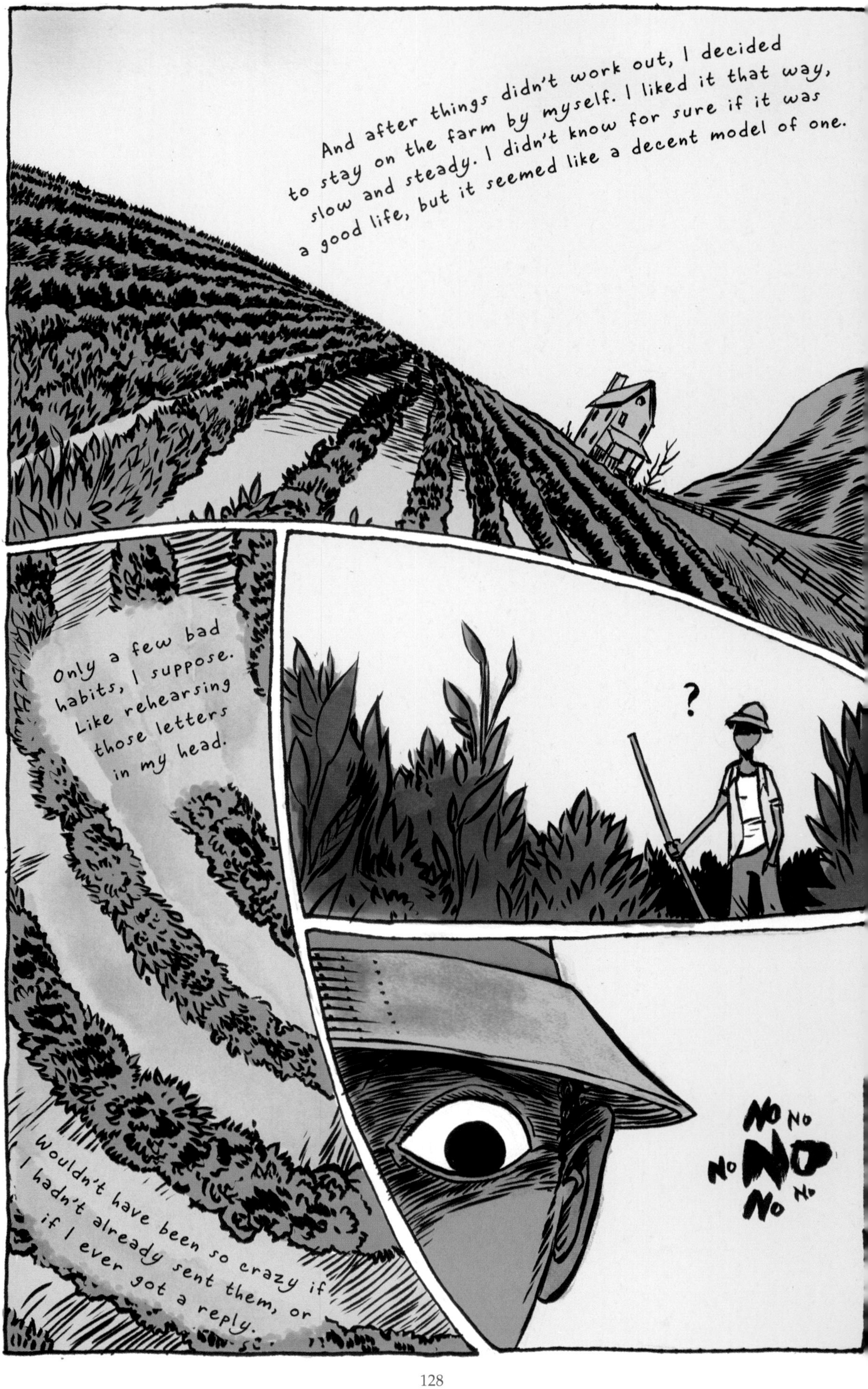

And after things didn't work out, I decided to stay on the farm by myself. I liked it that way, slow and steady. I didn't know for sure if it was a good life, but it seemed like a decent model of one.
Only a few bad habits, I suppose. Like rehearsing those letters in my head.
?
Wouldn't have been so crazy if I hadn't already sent them, or if I ever got a reply.
NO NO NO NO NO NO NO

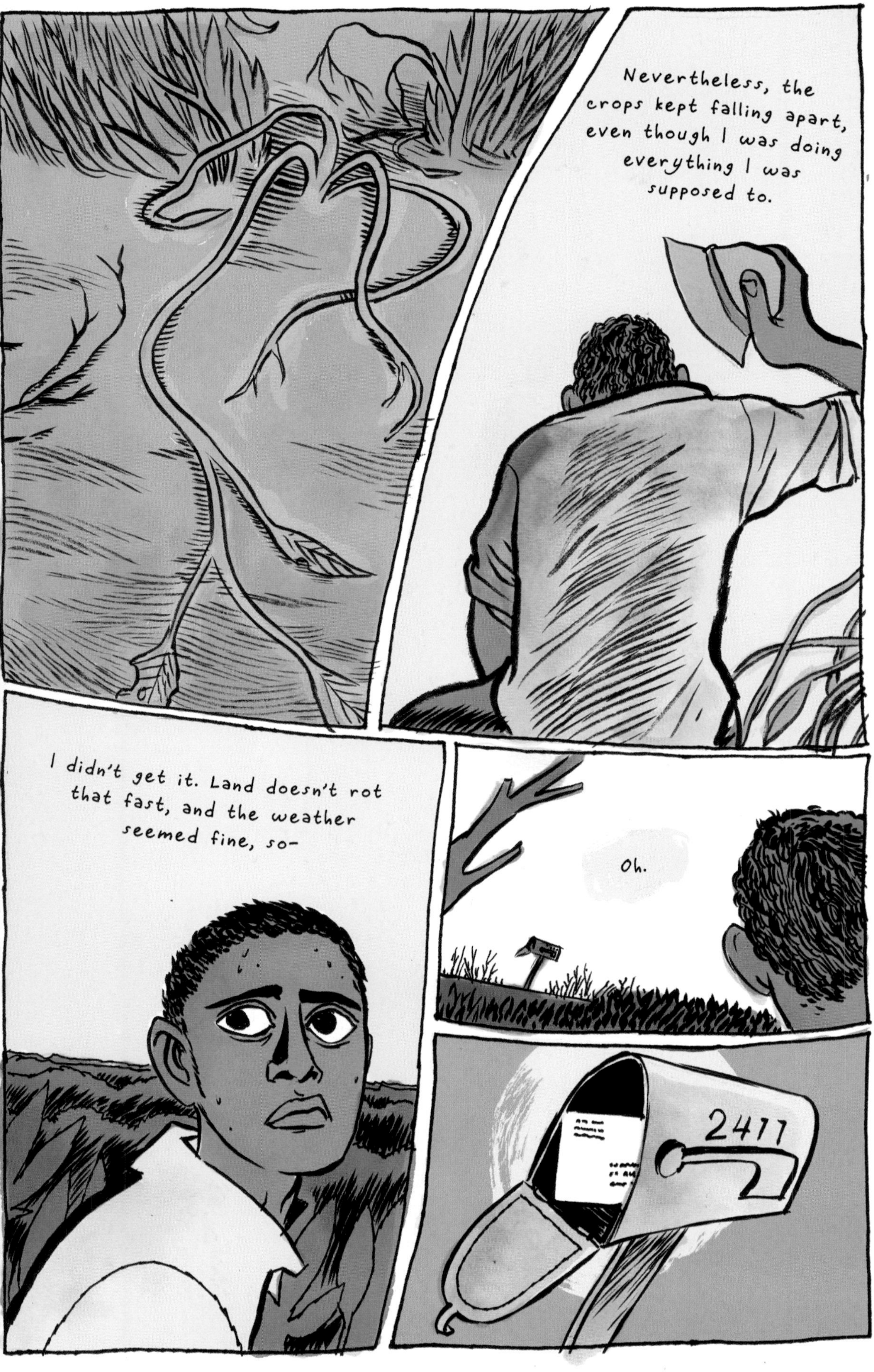

Nevertheless, the crops kept falling apart, even though I was doing everything I was supposed to.
I didn't get it. Land doesn't rot that fast, and the weather seemed fine, so-
Oh.
2411

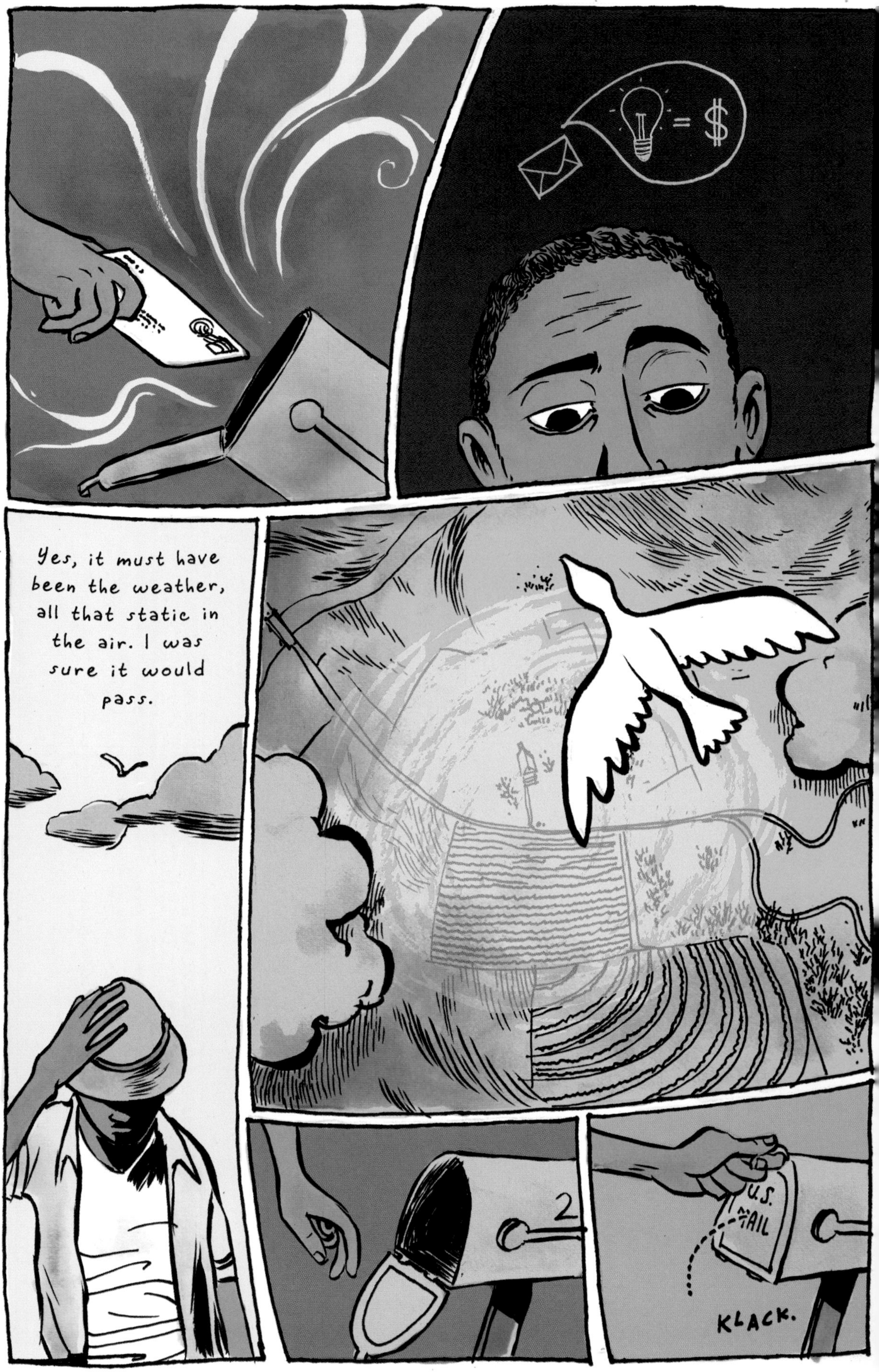
Yes, it must have been the weather, all that static in the air. I was sure it would pass.
2
U.S. MAIL
KLACK.

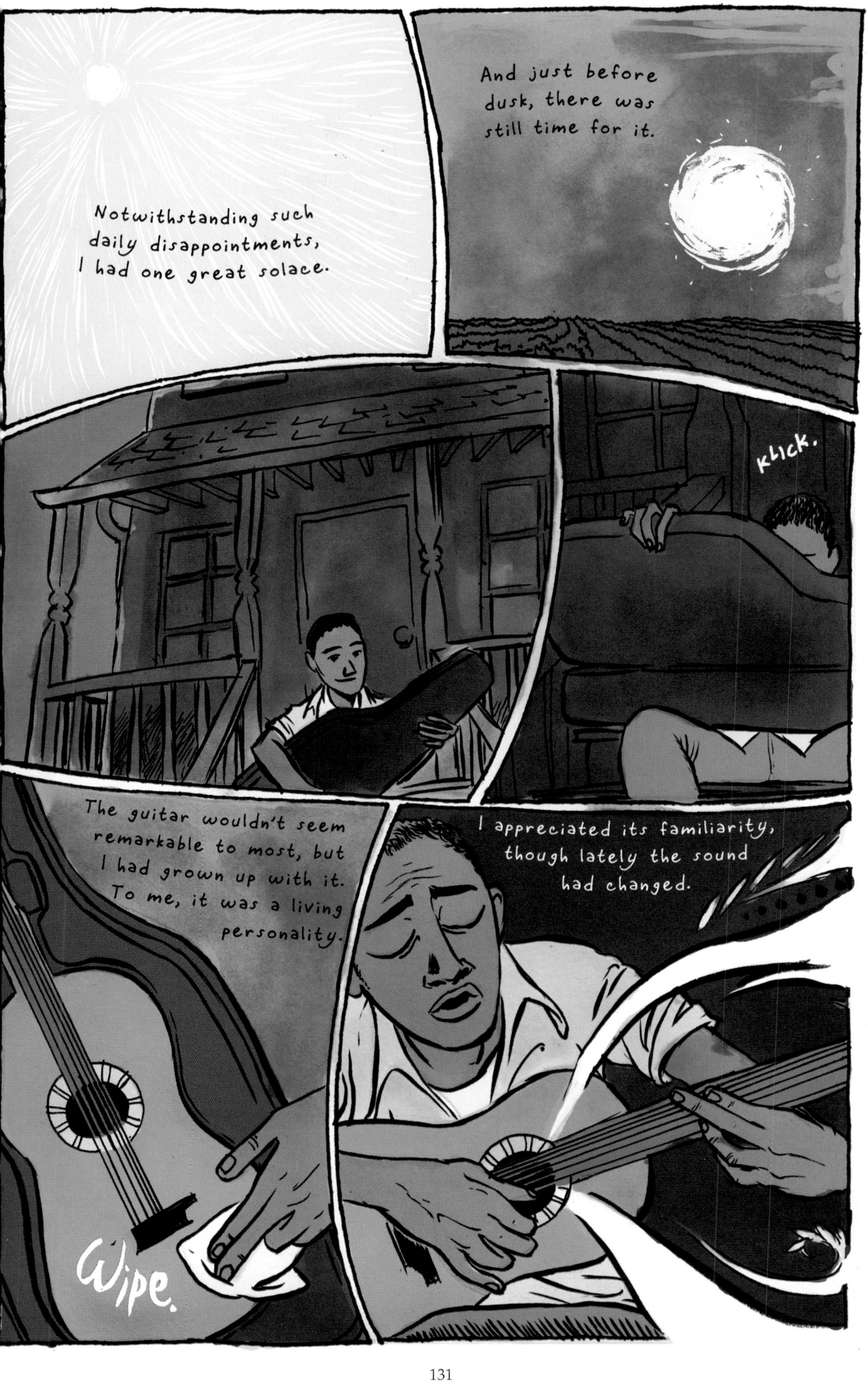

Notwithstanding such daily disappointments, I had one great solace.
And just before dusk, there was still time for it.
Klick.
The guitar wouldn't seem remarkable to most, but I had grown up with it. To me, it was a living personality.
Wipe.
I appreciated its familiarity, though lately the sound had changed.

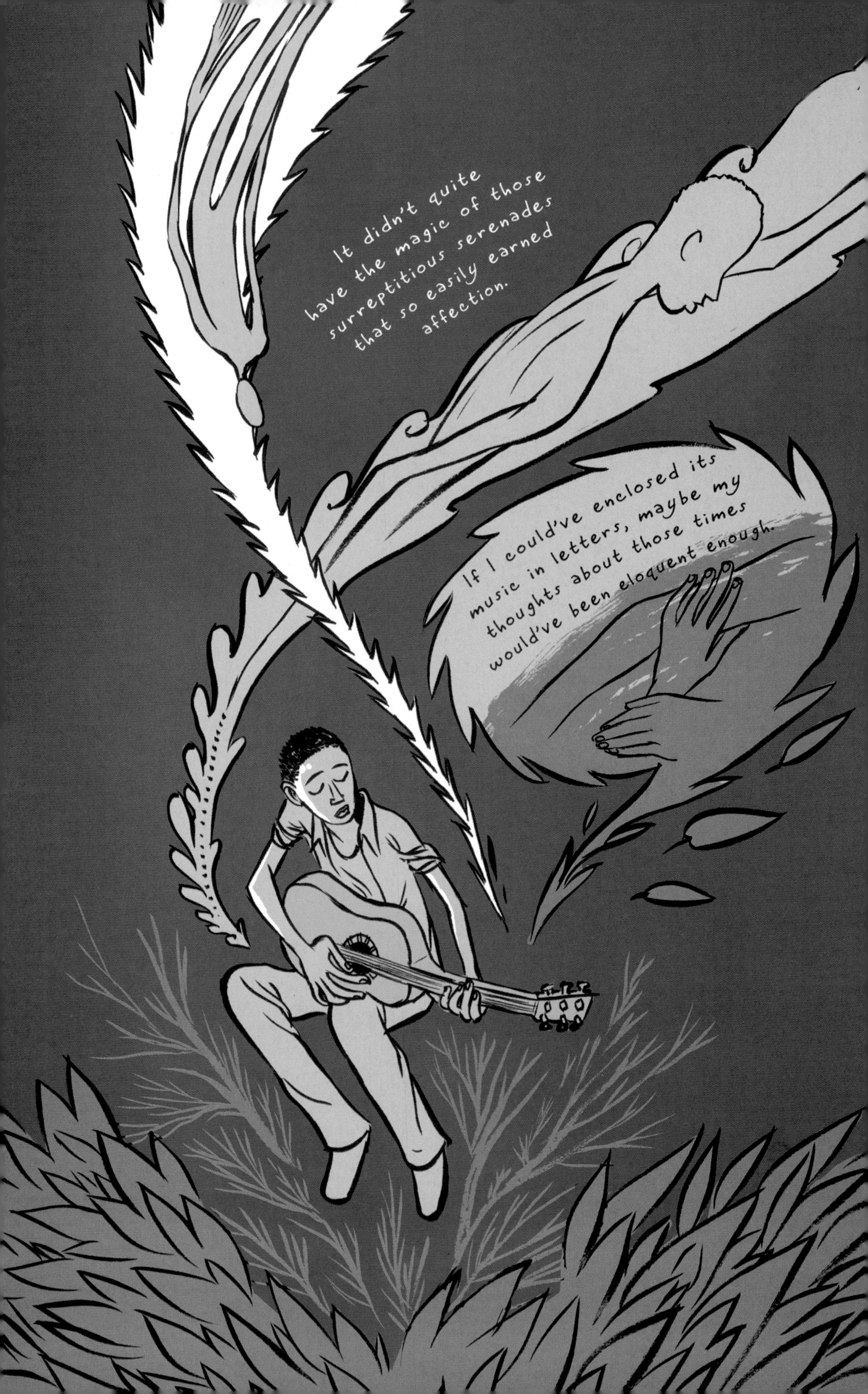
It didn't quite have the magic of those surreptitious serenades that so easily earned affection.
If I could've enclosed its music in letters, maybe my thoughts about those times would've been eloquent enough.

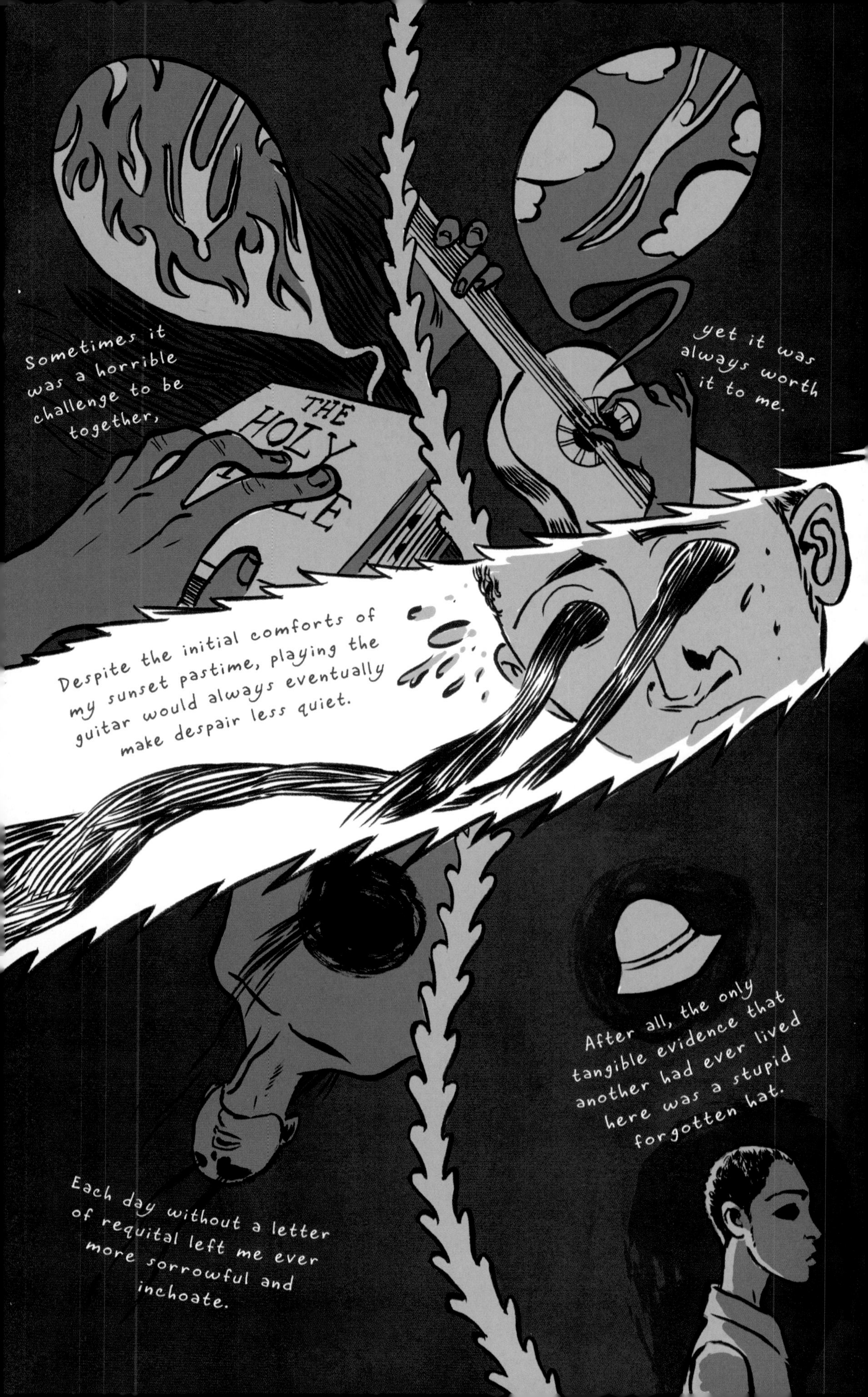

Sometimes it was a horrible challenge to be together,
yet it was always worth it to me.
THE HOLY BIBLE
Despite the initial comforts of my sunset pastime, playing the guitar would always eventually make despair less quiet.
After all, the only tangible evidence that another had ever lived here was a stupid forgotten hat.
Each day without a letter of requital left me ever more sorrowful and inchoate.

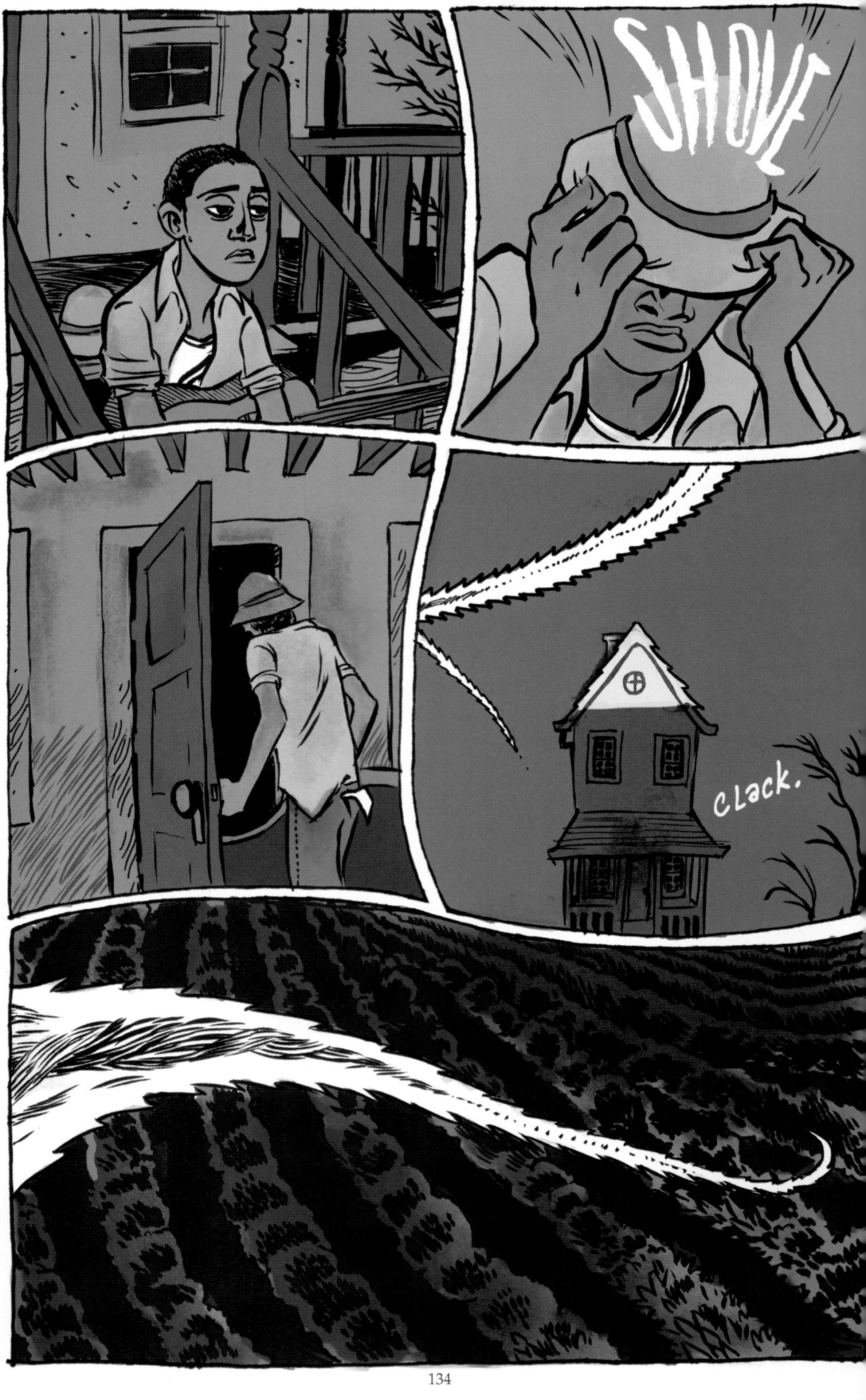
SHOVE
clack.

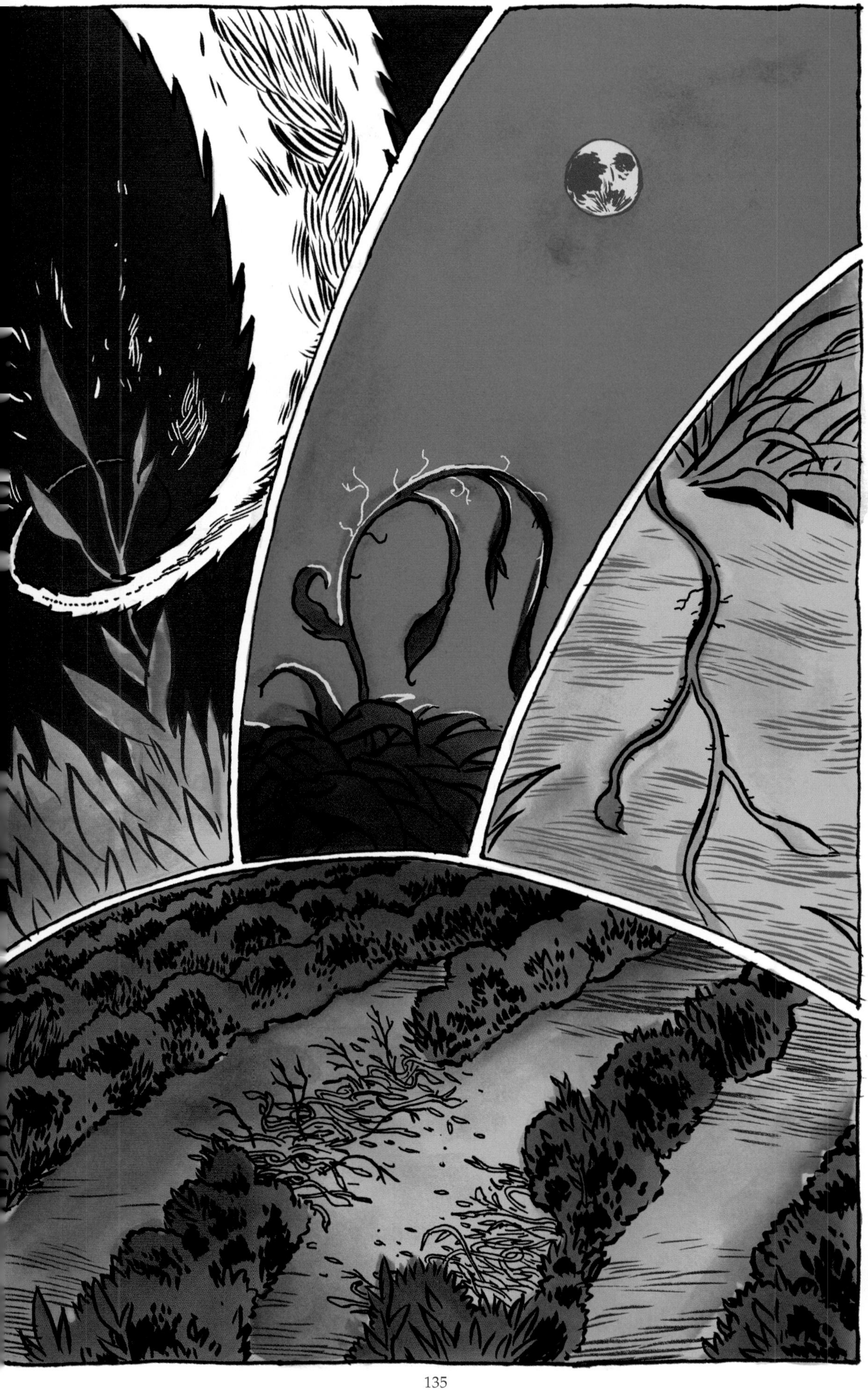

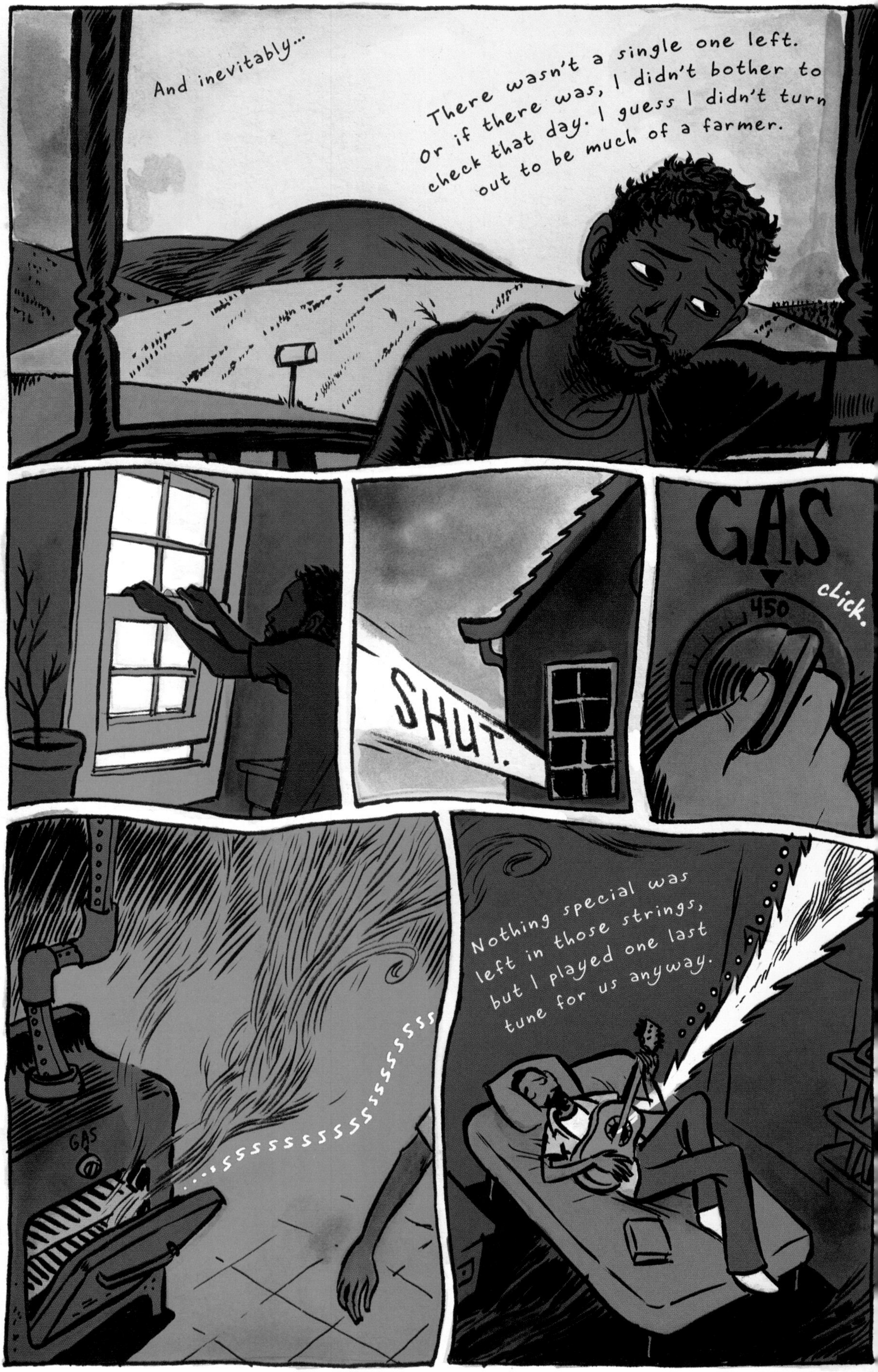
And inevitably...
There wasn't a single one left. Or if there was, I didn't bother to check that day. I guess I didn't turn out to be much of a farmer.
SHUT.
GAS
450
cLick.
GAS
...sssssssssssssssssss
Nothing special was left in those strings, but I played one last tune for us anyway.

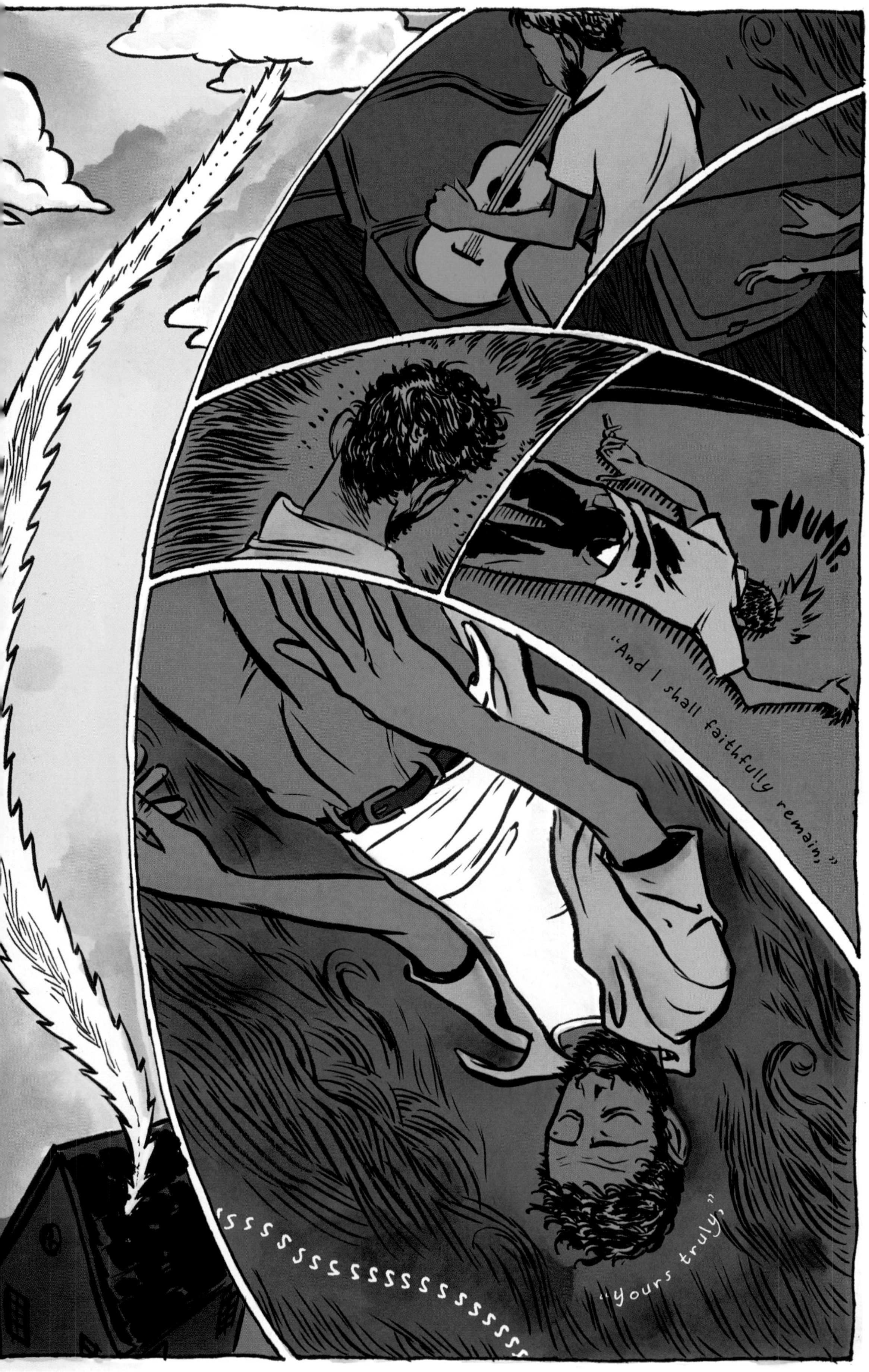
THUMP!
"And I shall faithfully remain,"
"Yours truly,"
SSSSSSSSSSSSSSSSSSSSSS

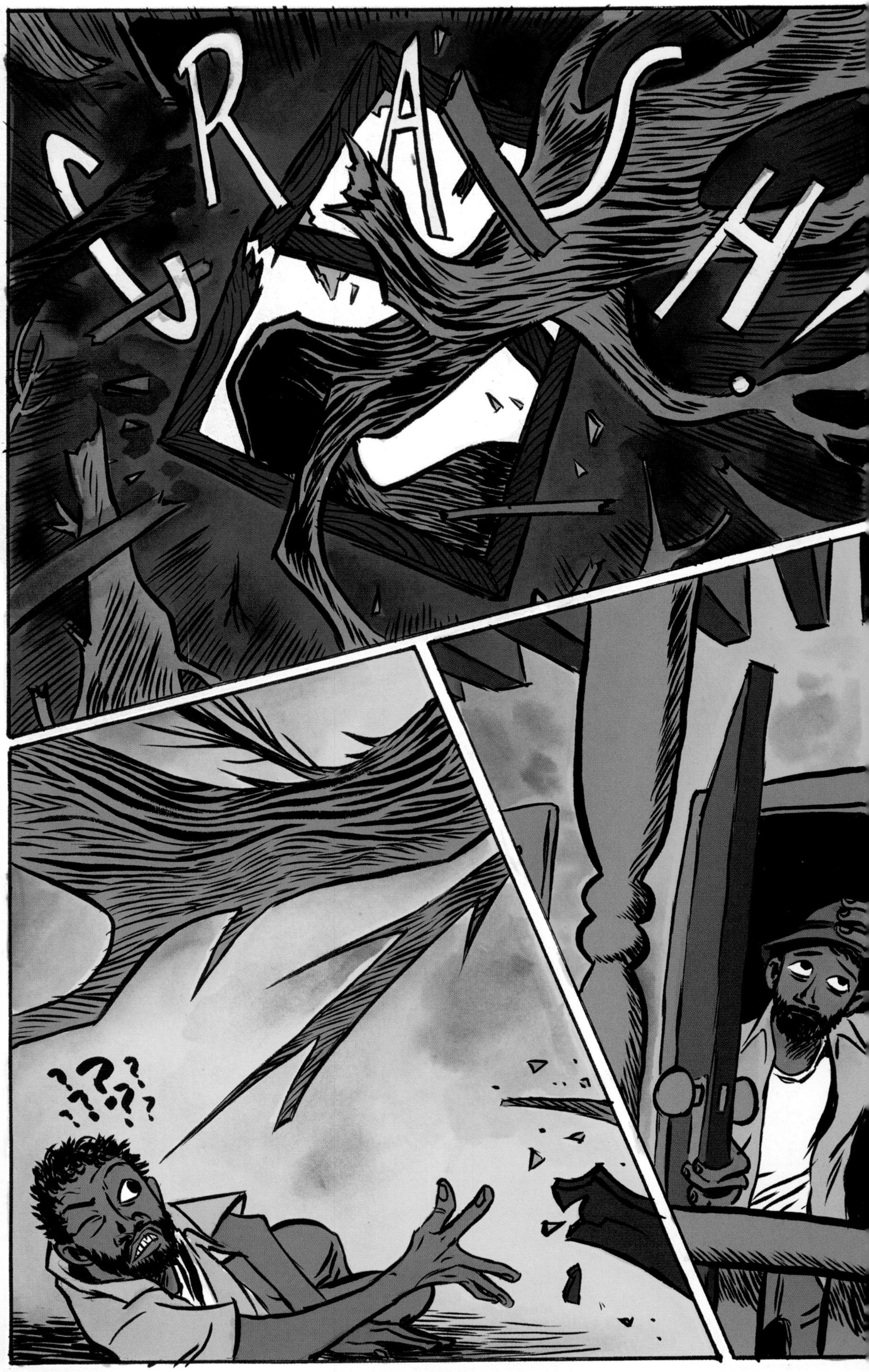
CRASH

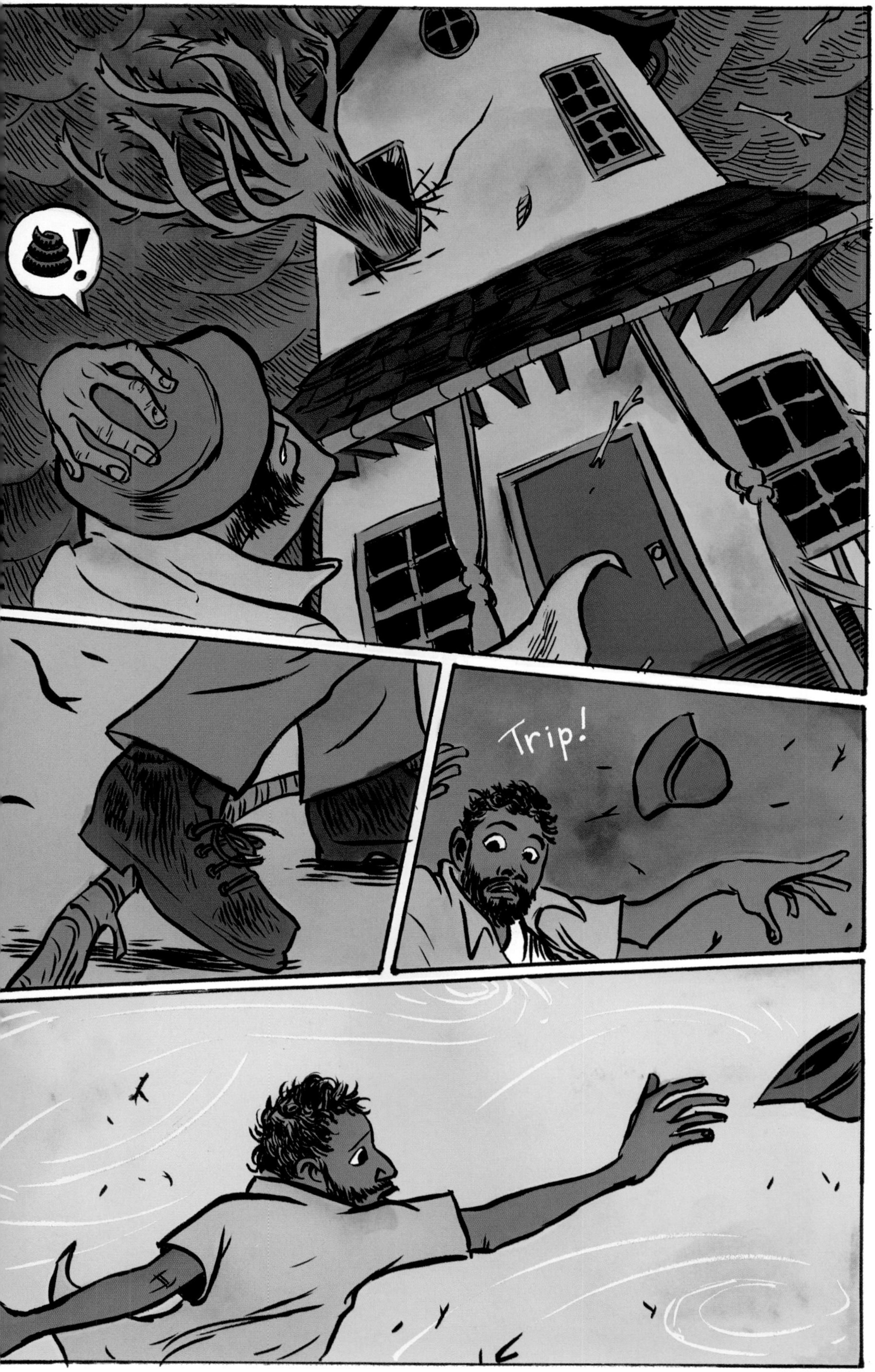
Trip!

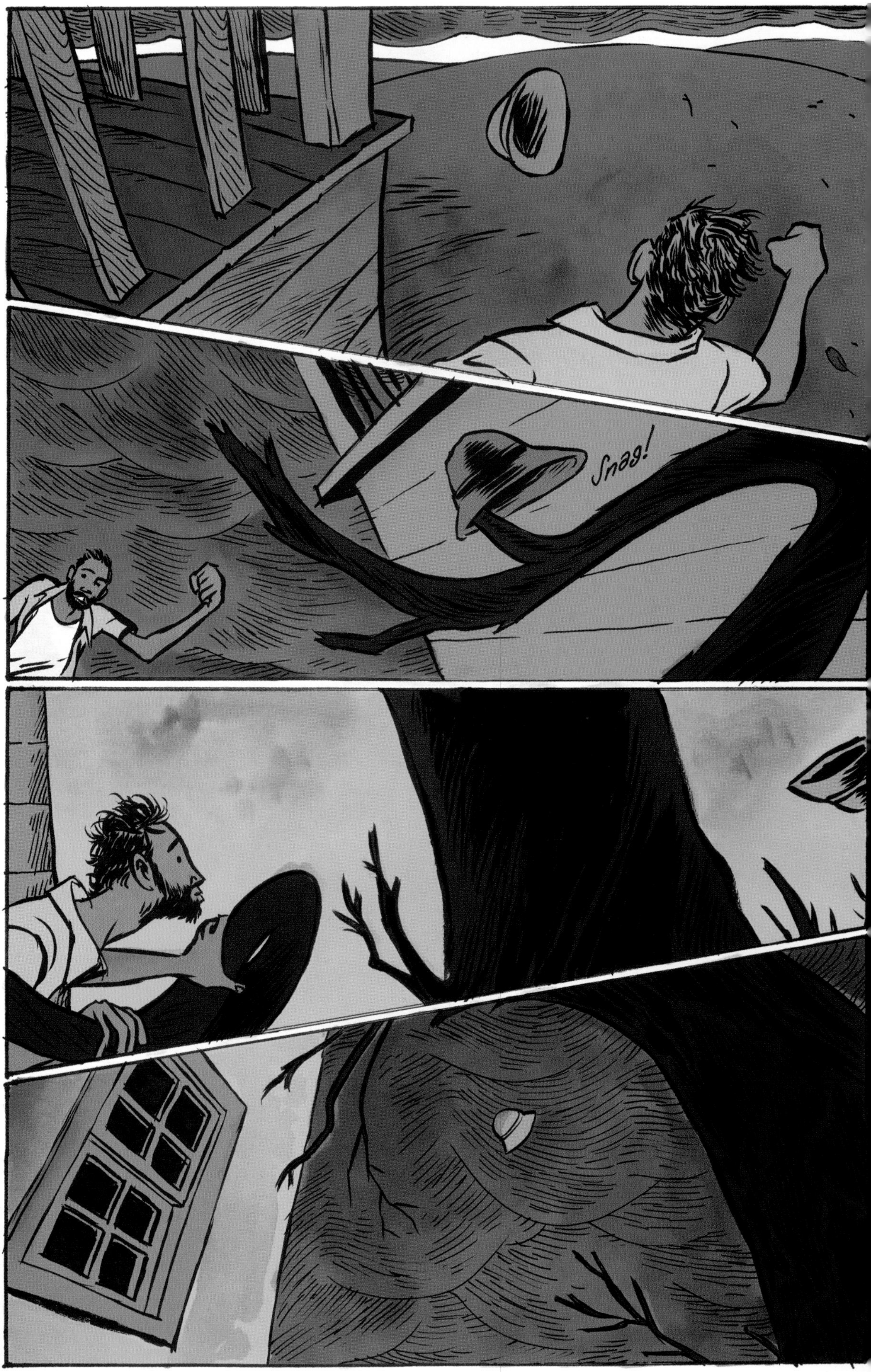
Snag!

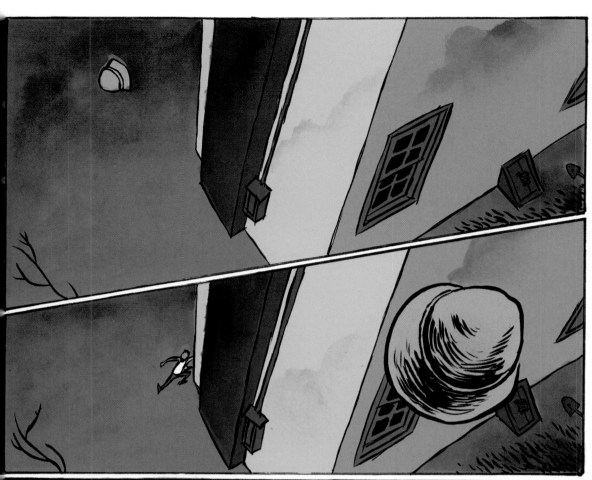

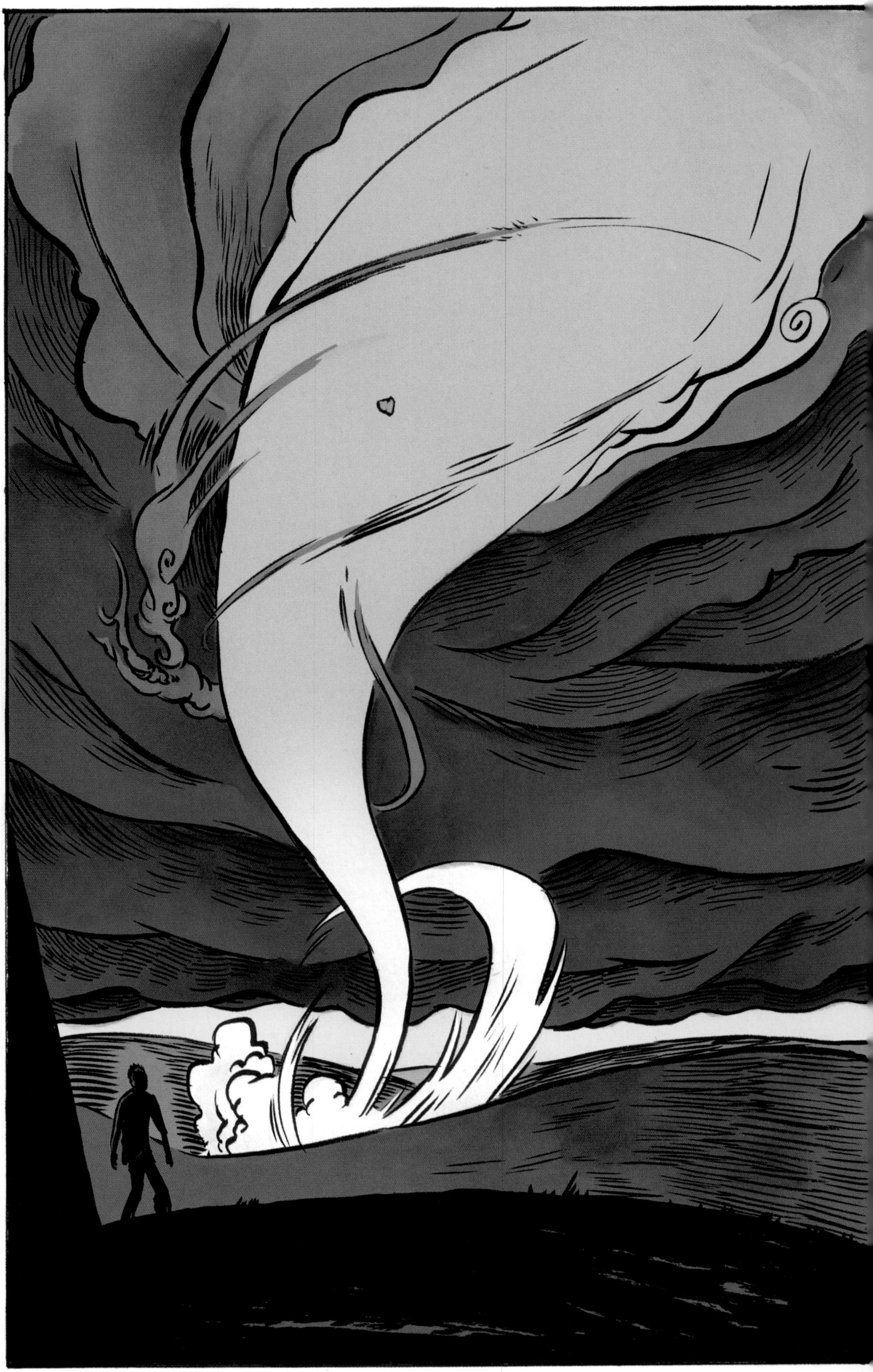

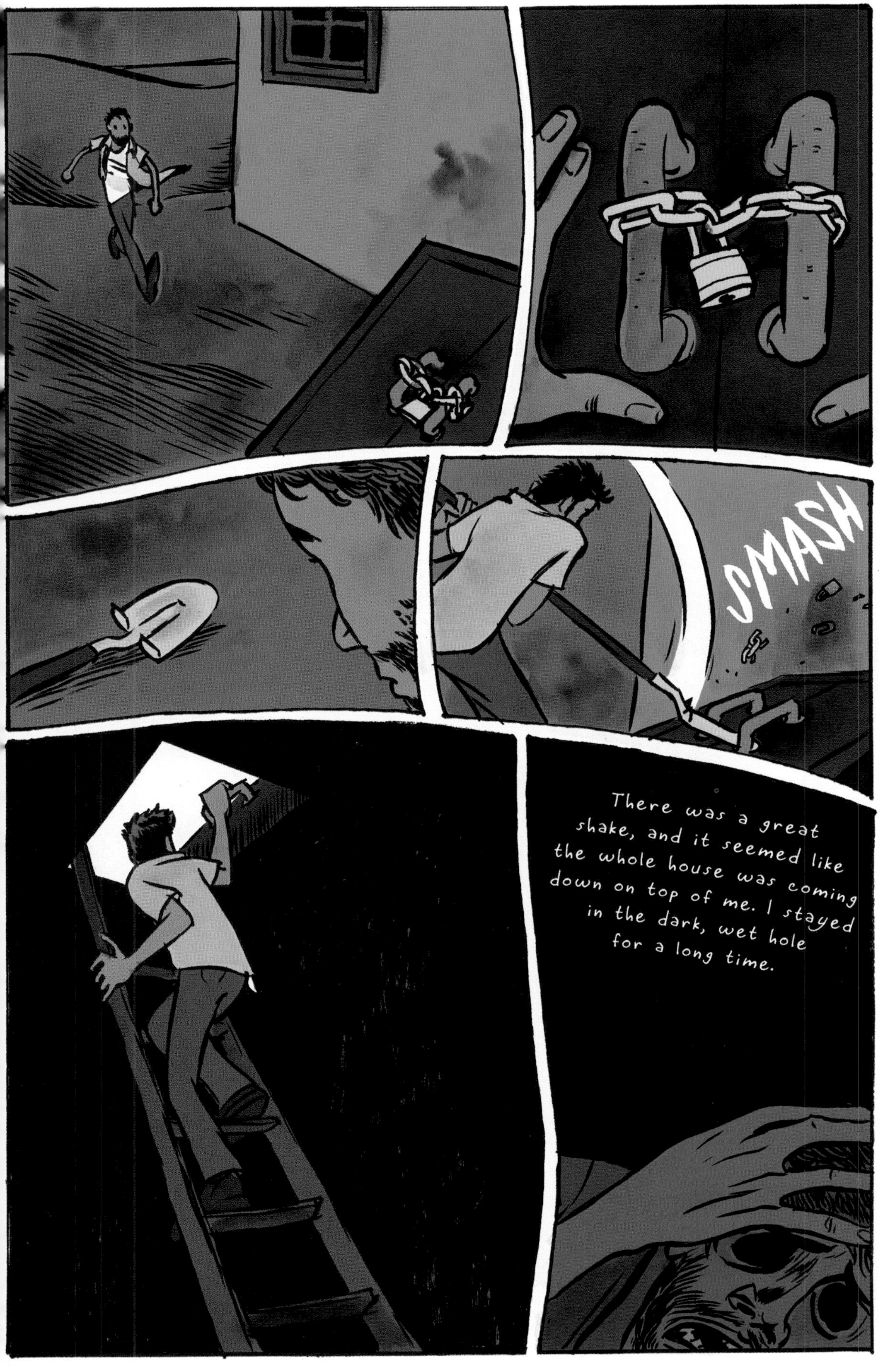
SMASH
There was a great shake, and it seemed like the whole house was coming down on top of me. I stayed in the dark, wet hole for a long time.

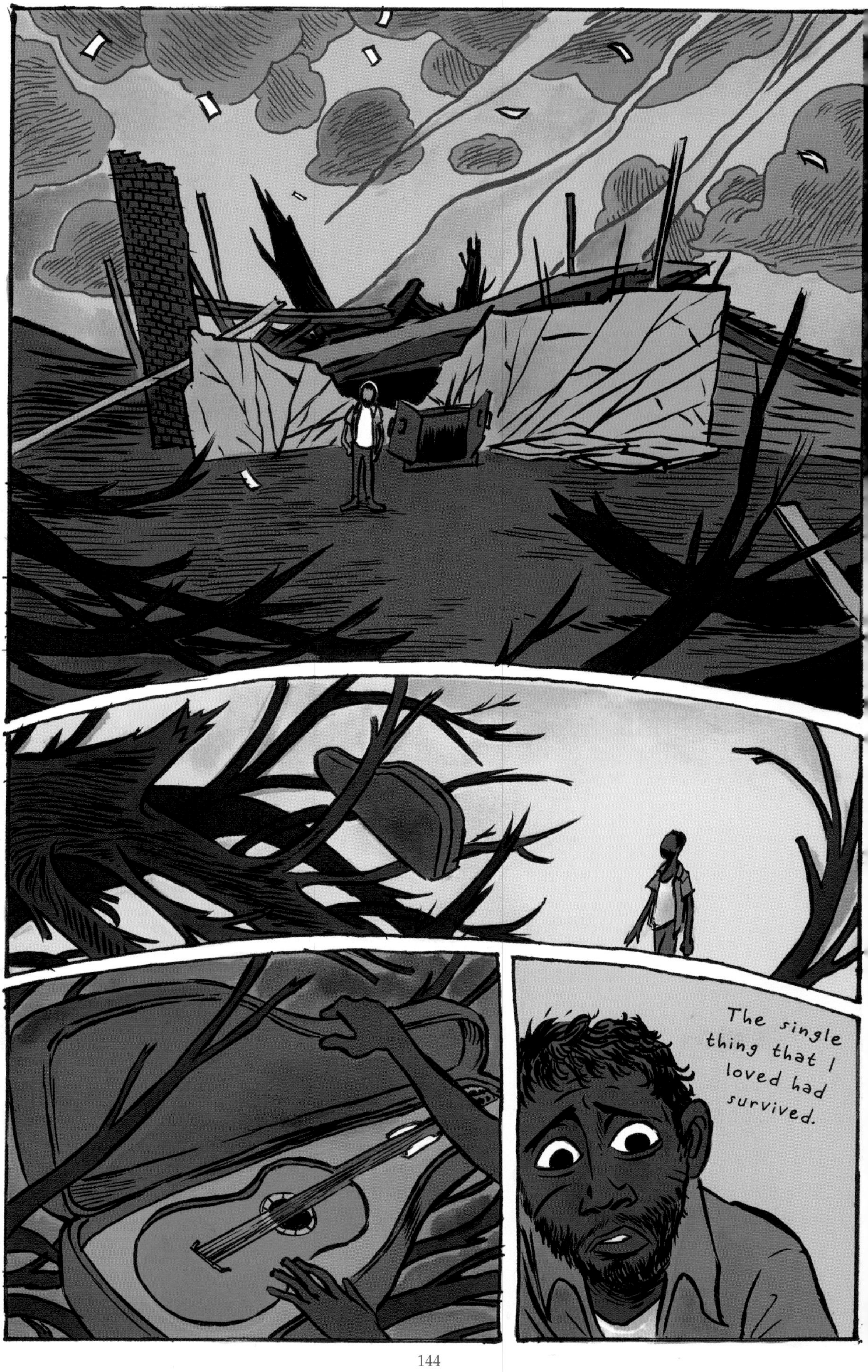
The single thing that I loved had survived.

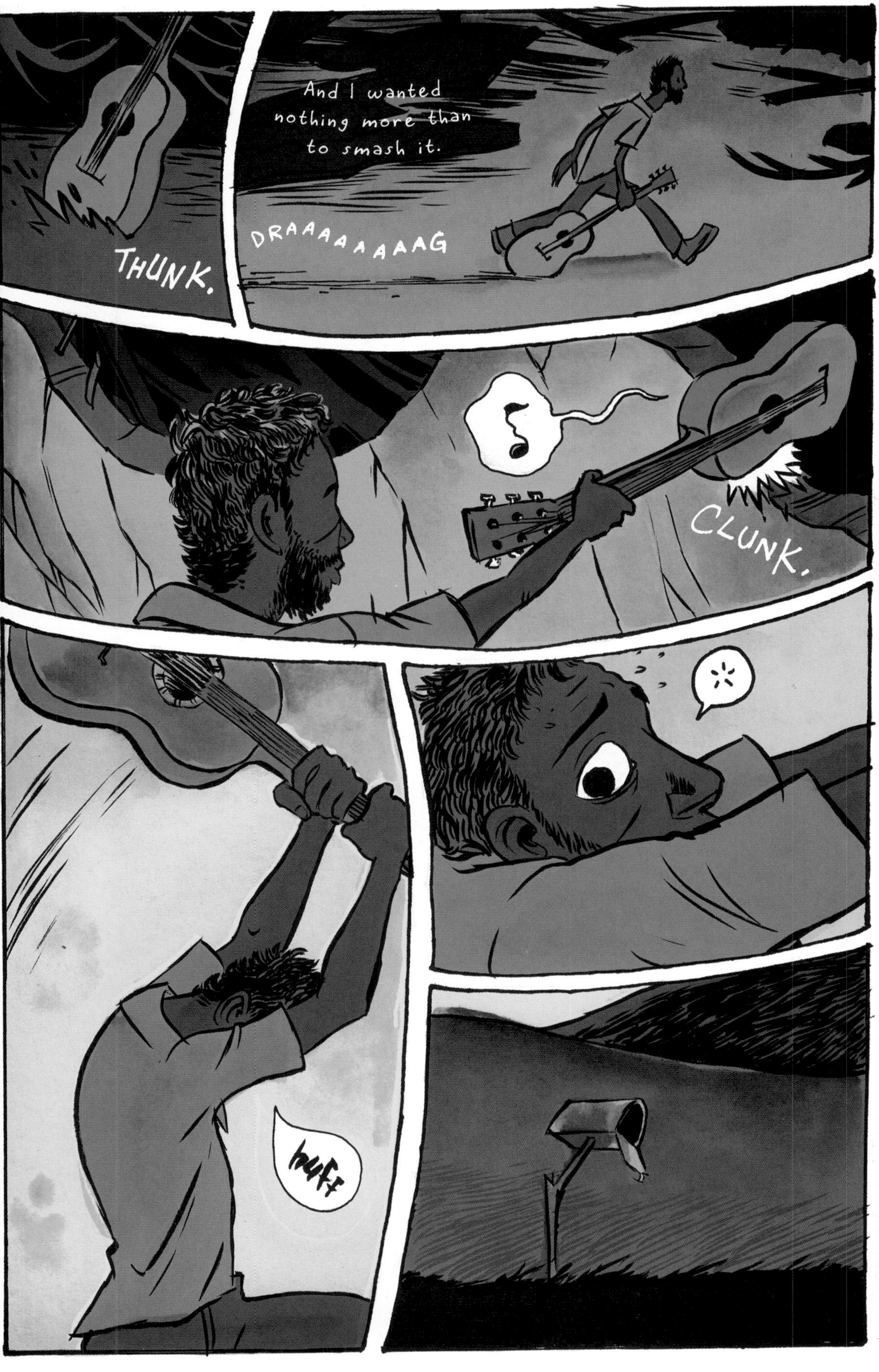
THUNK.
And I wanted nothing more than to smash it.
DRAAAAAAAAAG
CLUNK.
huff

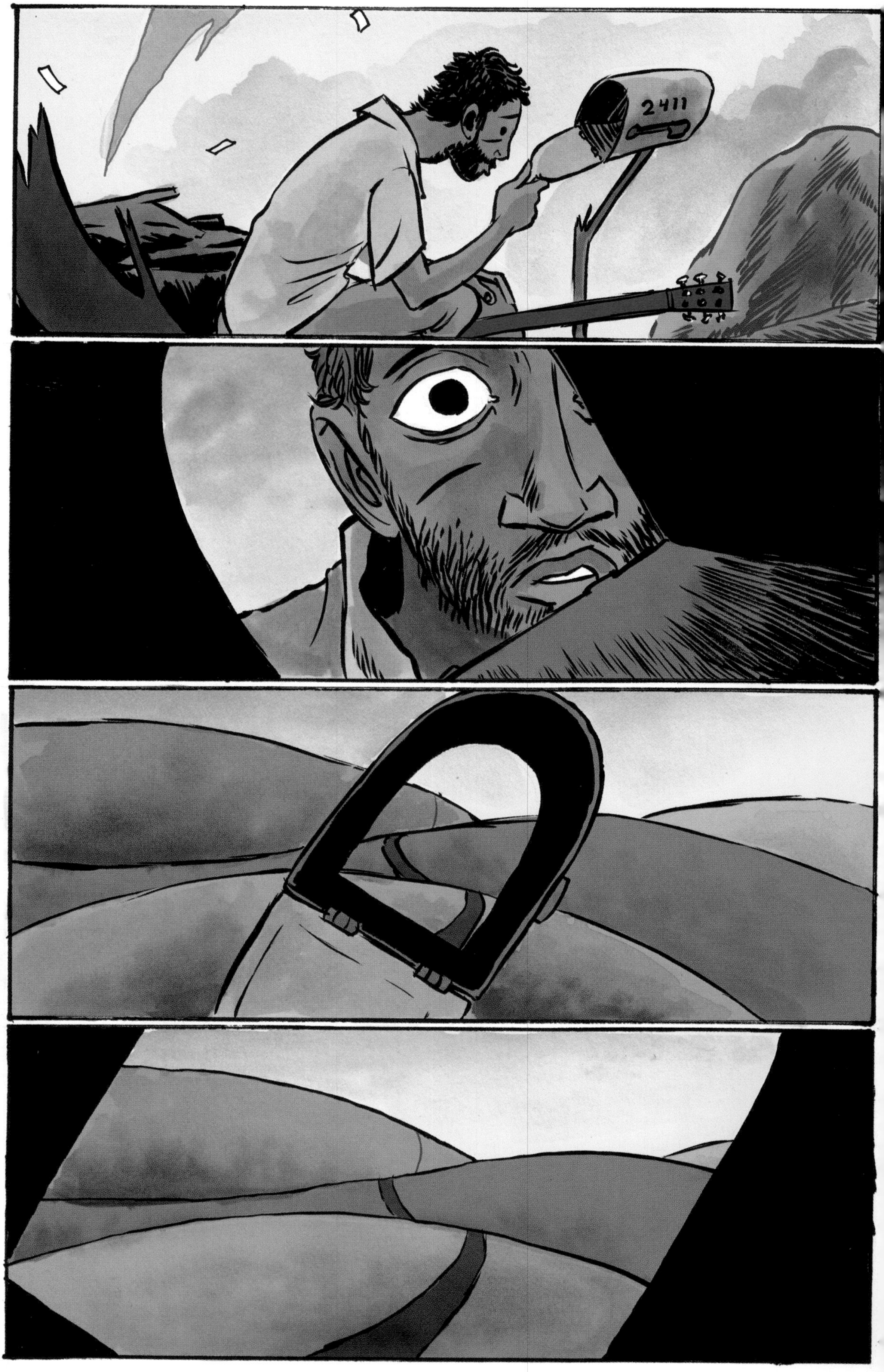
2411

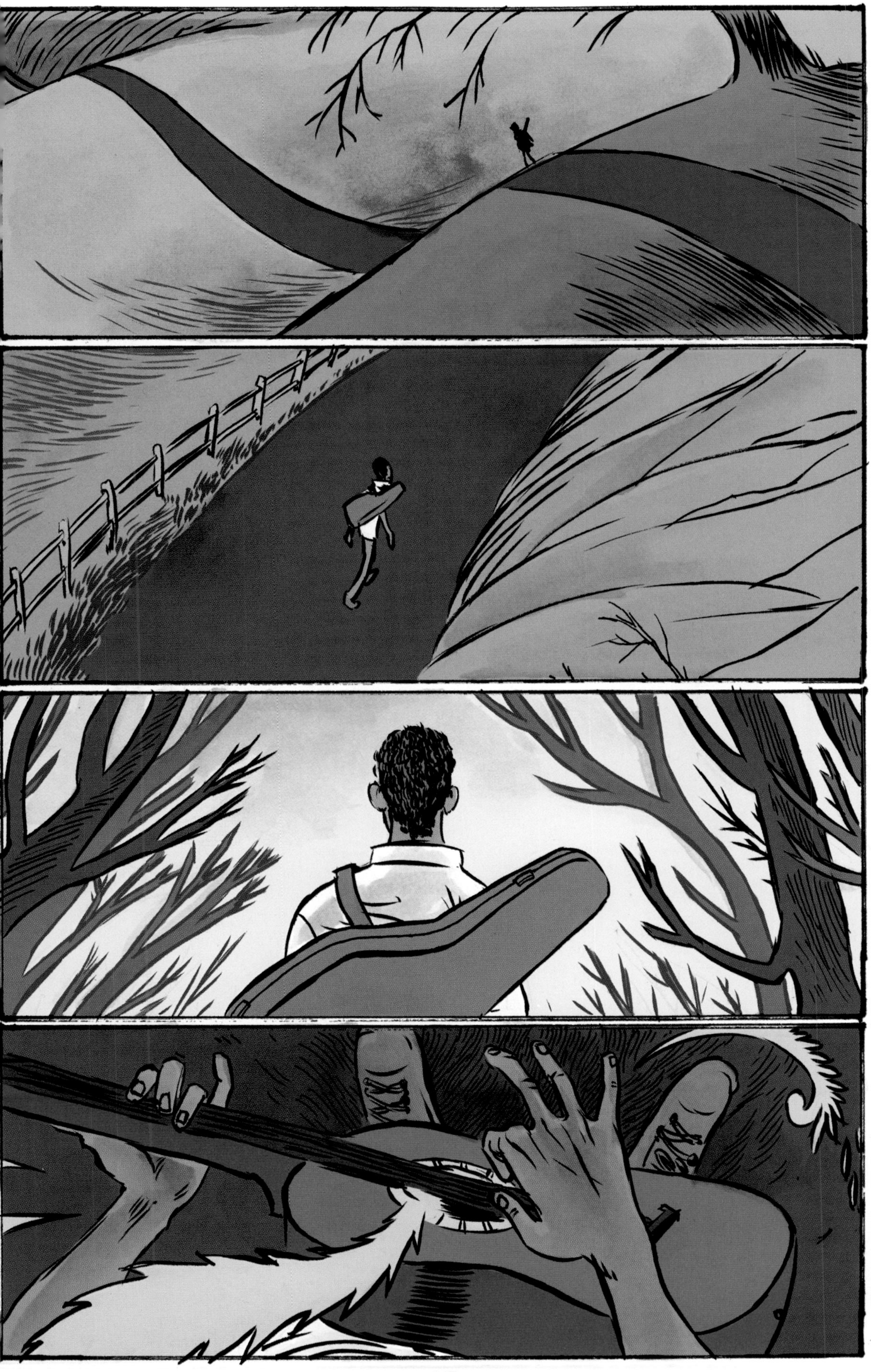

I decided to preserve and
care for the blue guitar,
and in return, it served
me well in the strange
and interesting times
that followed.

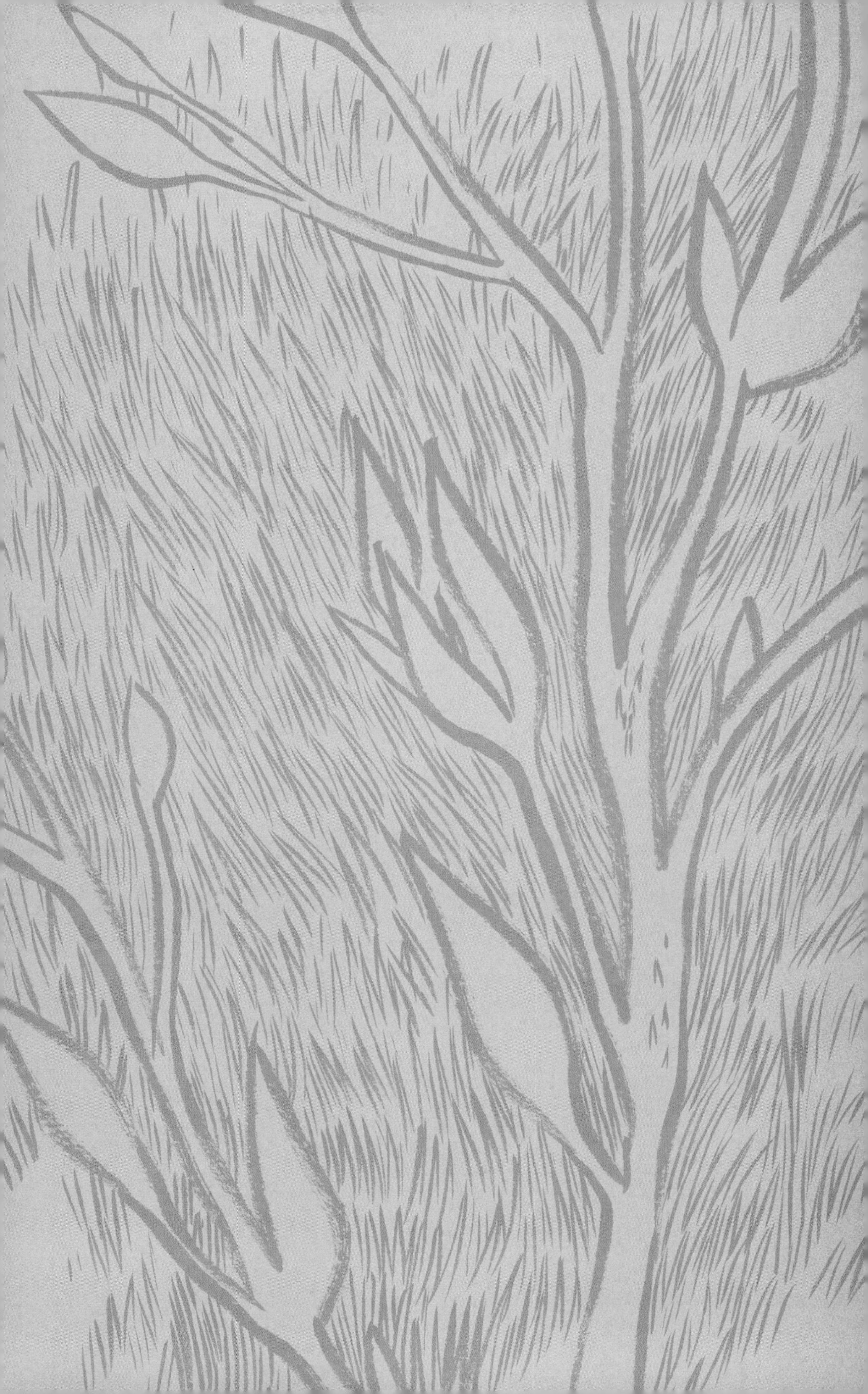

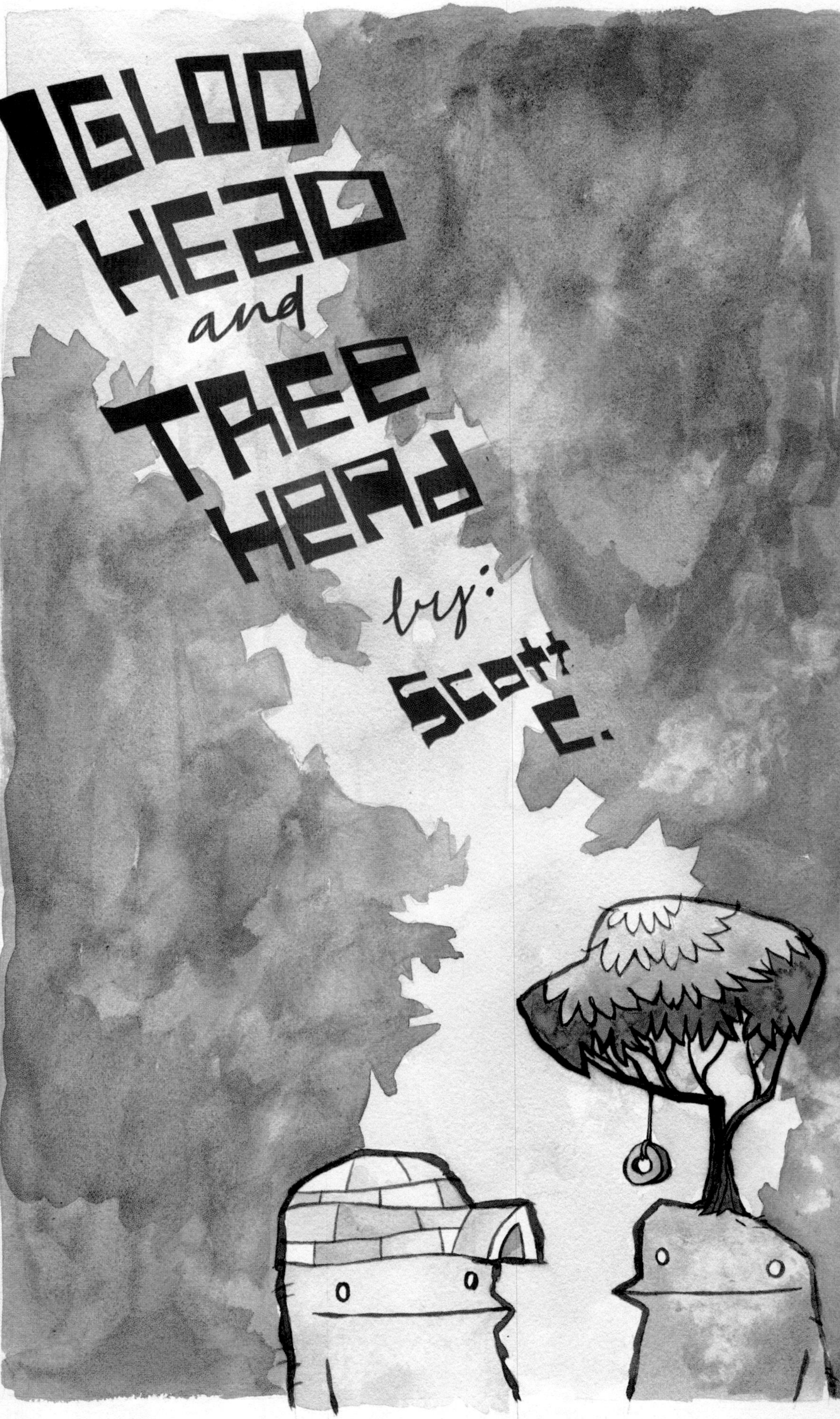
IGLOO HEAD and TREE HEAD
by: Scott C.

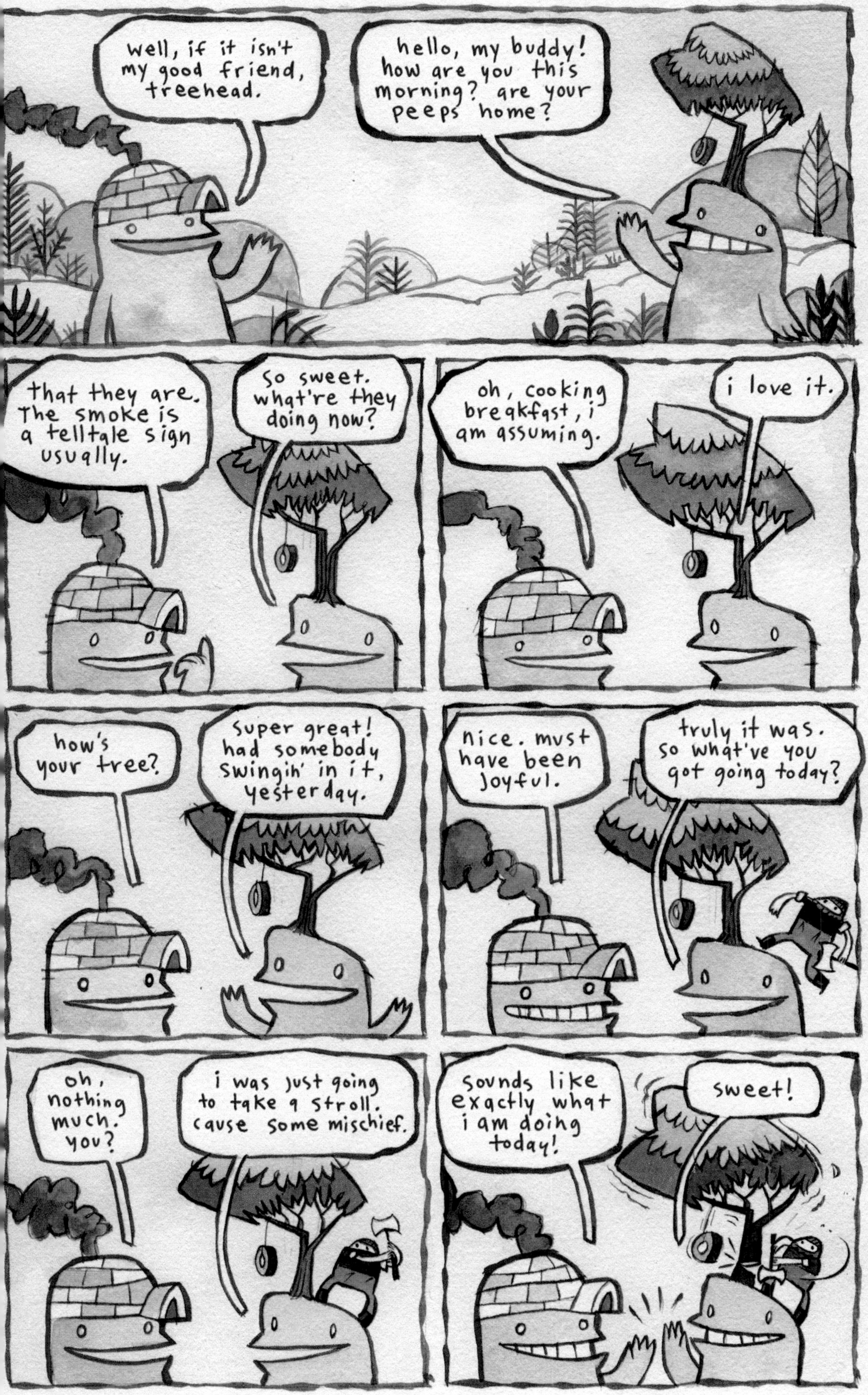

well, if it isn't my good friend, treehead.
hello, my buddy! how are you this morning? are your peeps home?
that they are. The smoke is a telltale sign usually.
So sweet. what're they doing now?
oh, cooking breakfast, i am assuming.
i love it.
how's your tree?
Super great! had somebody swingin' in it, yesterday.
nice. must have been joyful.
truly it was. so what've you got going today?
oh, nothing much. you?
i was just going to take a stroll. cause some mischief.
sounds like exactly what i am doing today!
sweet!

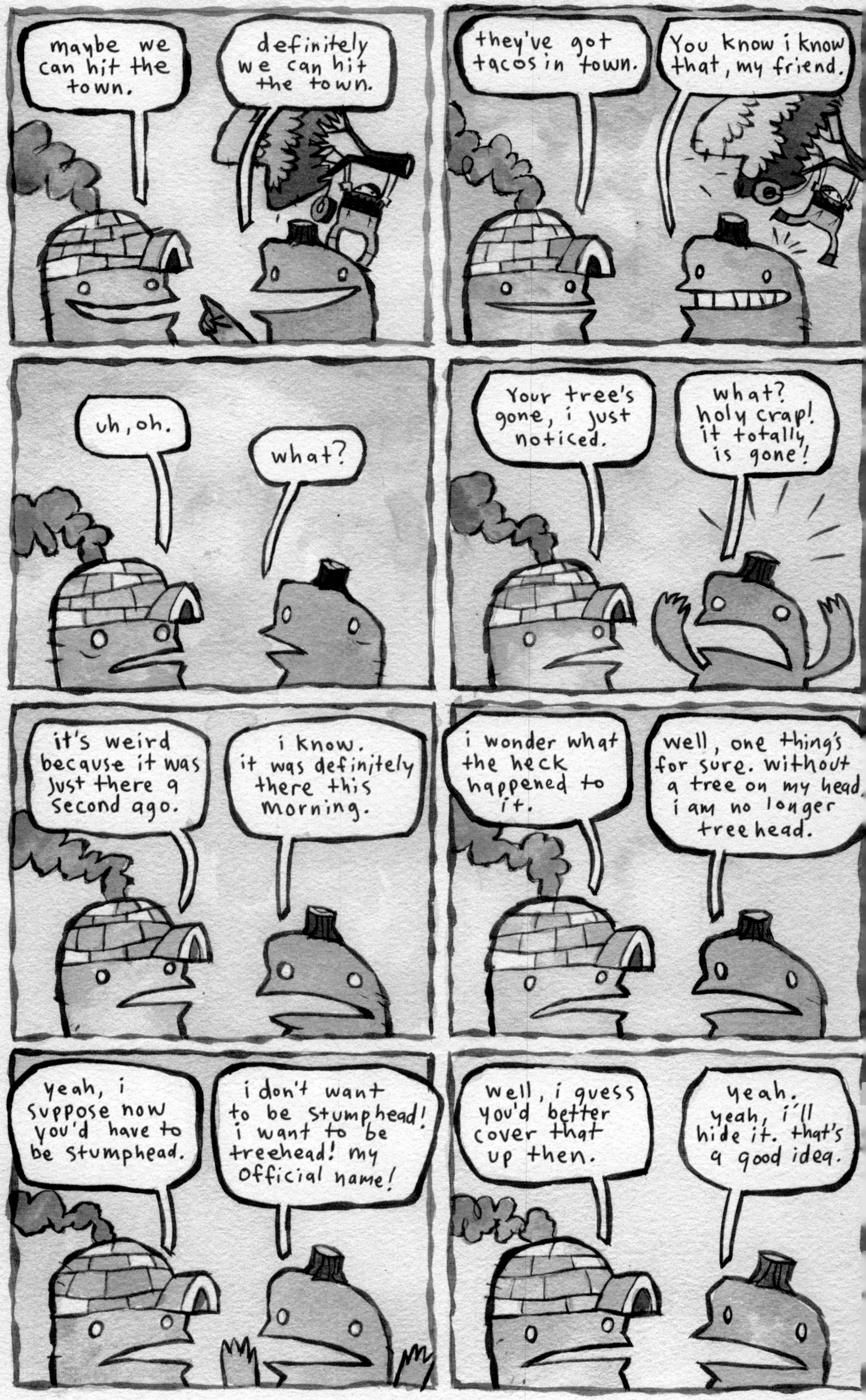
maybe we can hit the town.
definitely we can hit the town.
they've got tacos in town.
You know i know that, my friend.
uh, oh.
what?
Your tree's gone, i just noticed.
what? holy crap! it totally is gone!
it's weird because it was just there a second ago.
i know. it was definitely there this morning.
i wonder what the heck happened to it.
well, one thing's for sure. without a tree on my head i am no longer tree head.
yeah, i suppose now you'd have to be stumphead.
i don't want to be stumphead! i want to be treehead! my official name!
well, i guess you'd better cover that up then.
yeah. yeah, i'll hide it. that's a good idea.

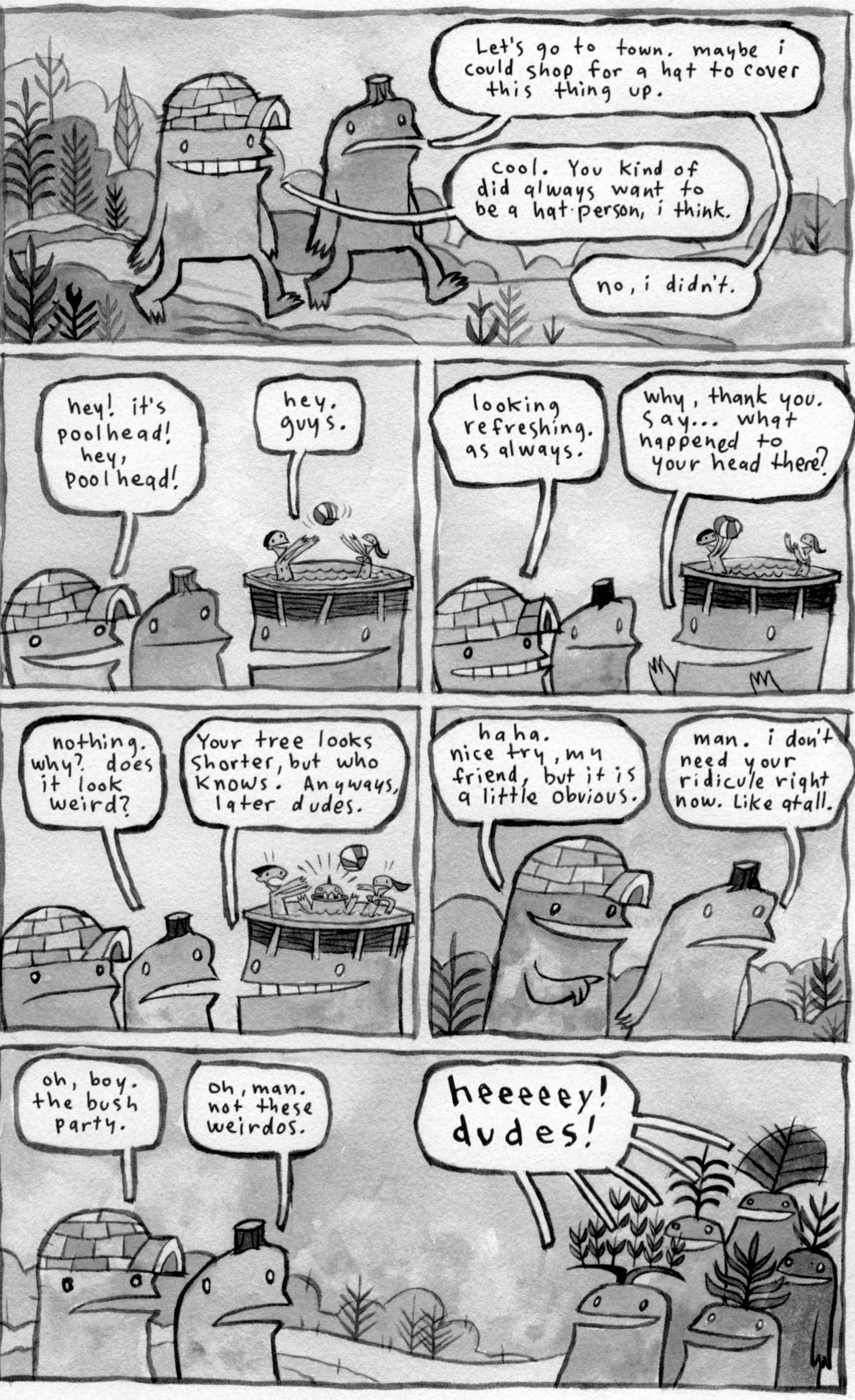
Let's go to town. maybe i could shop for a hat to cover this thing up.
cool. You kind of did always want to be a hat person, i think.
no, i didn't.
hey! it's poolhead! hey, Pool head!
hey. guys.
looking refreshing. as always.
why, thank you. Say... what happened to your head there?
nothing. why? does it look weird?
Your tree looks Shorter, but who Knows. Anyways, later dudes.
haha. nice try, my friend, but it is a little obvious.
man. i don't need your ridicule right now. Like atall.
oh, boy. the bush party.
oh, man. not these weirdos.
heeeeey! dudes!

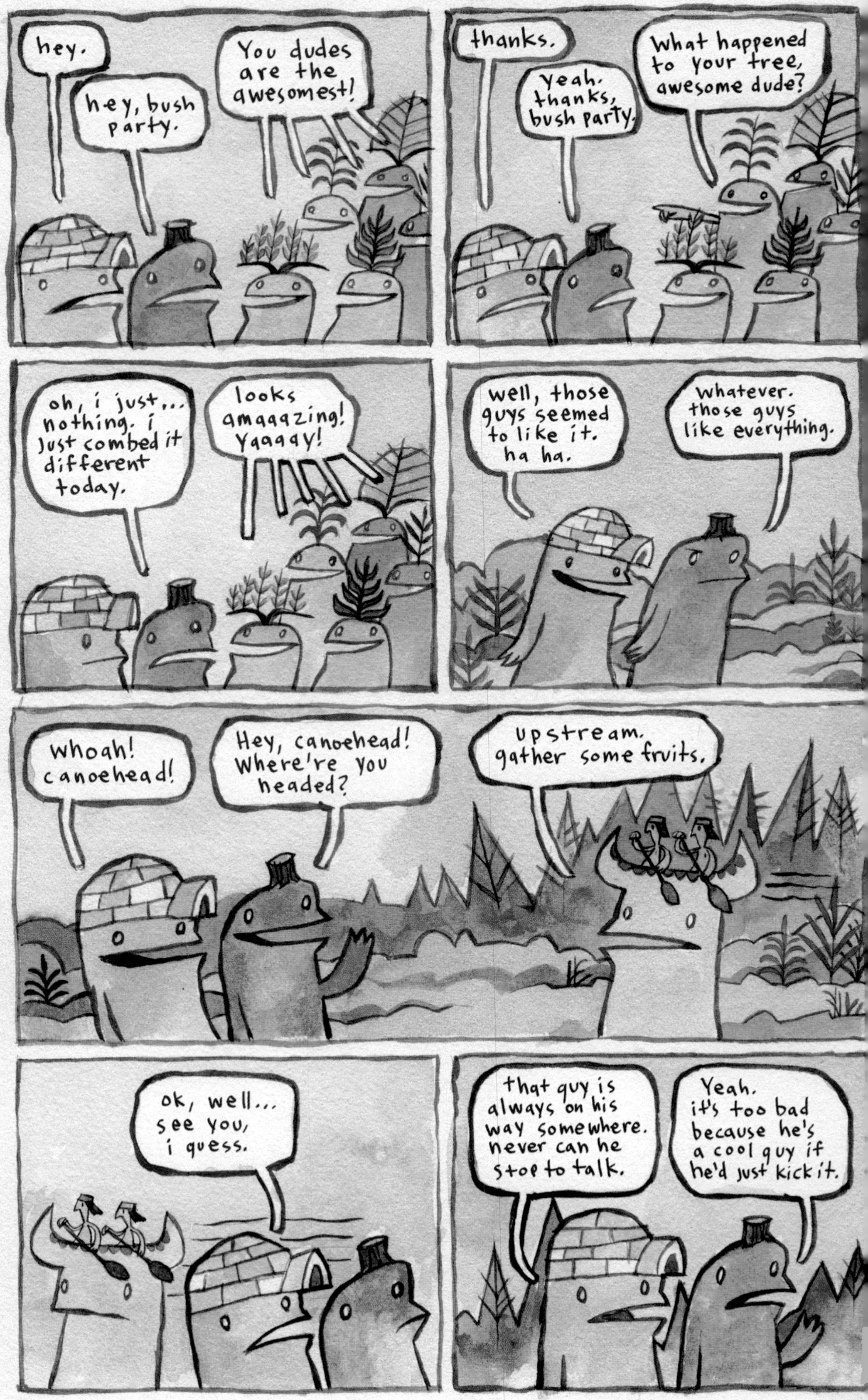
hey.
hey, bush party.
You dudes are the awesomest!
thanks.
Yeah. thanks, bush party.
What happened to your tree, awesome dude?
oh, i just... nothing. i just combed it different today.
looks amaaazing! Yaaaay!
well, those guys seemed to like it. ha ha.
whatever. those guys like everything.
Whoah! canoehead!
Hey, canoehead! Where're you headed?
upstream. gather some fruits.
ok, well... see you, i guess.
that guy is always on his way somewhere. never can he stop to talk.
Yeah. it's too bad because he's a cool guy if he'd just kick it.

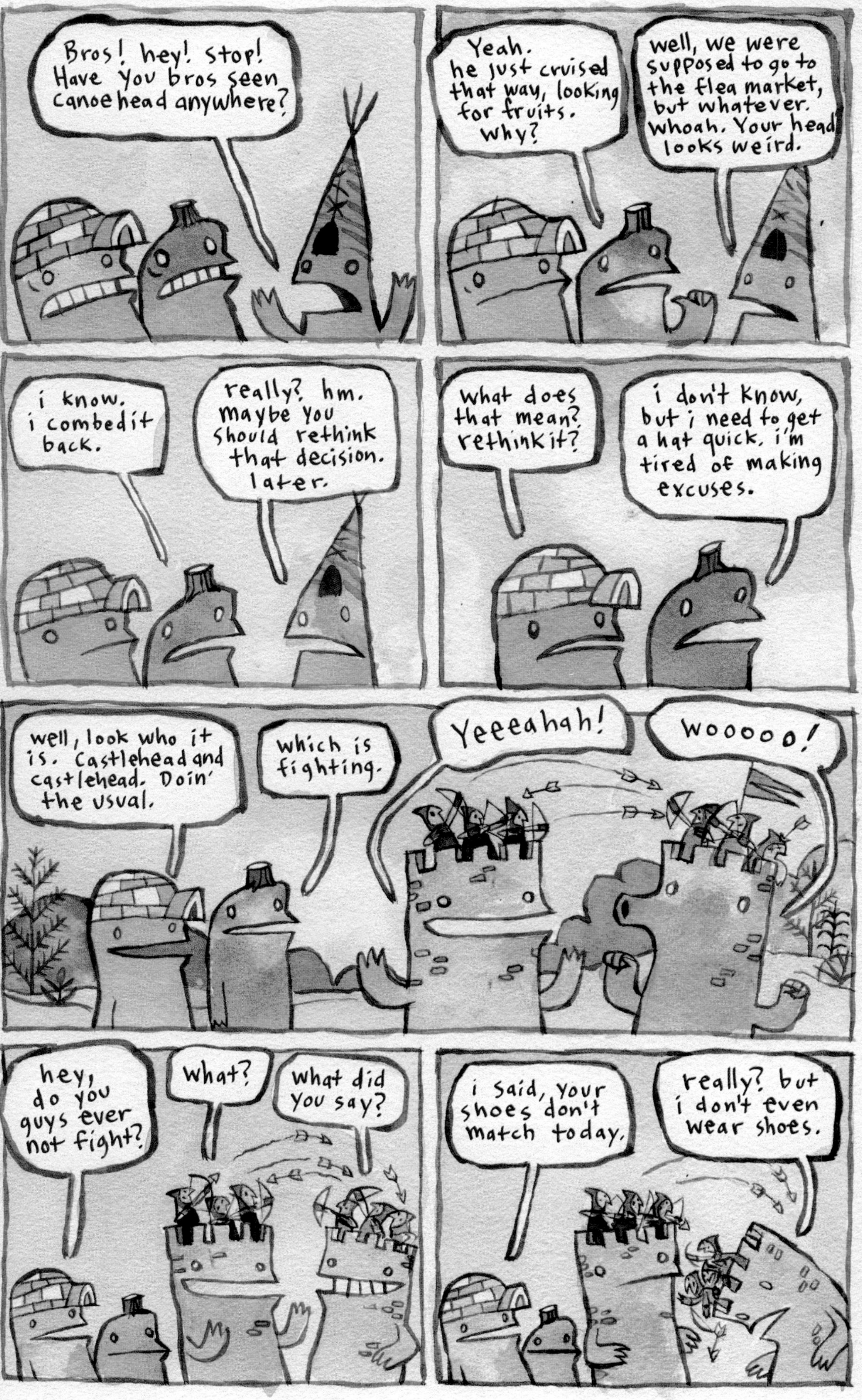
Bros! hey! Stop! Have you bros seen canoehead anywhere?
Yeah. he just cruised that way, looking for fruits. why?
well, we were supposed to go to the flea market, but whatever. whoah. Your head looks weird.
i know. i combed it back.
really? hm. maybe you should rethink that decision. later.
What does that mean? rethink it?
i don't know, but i need to get a hat quick. i'm tired of making excuses.
well, look who it is. Castlehead and castlehead. Doin' the usual.
which is fighting.
Yeeeahah!
Wooooo!
hey, do you guys ever not fight?
What?
What did you say?
i said, your shoes don't match today.
really? but i don't even wear shoes.

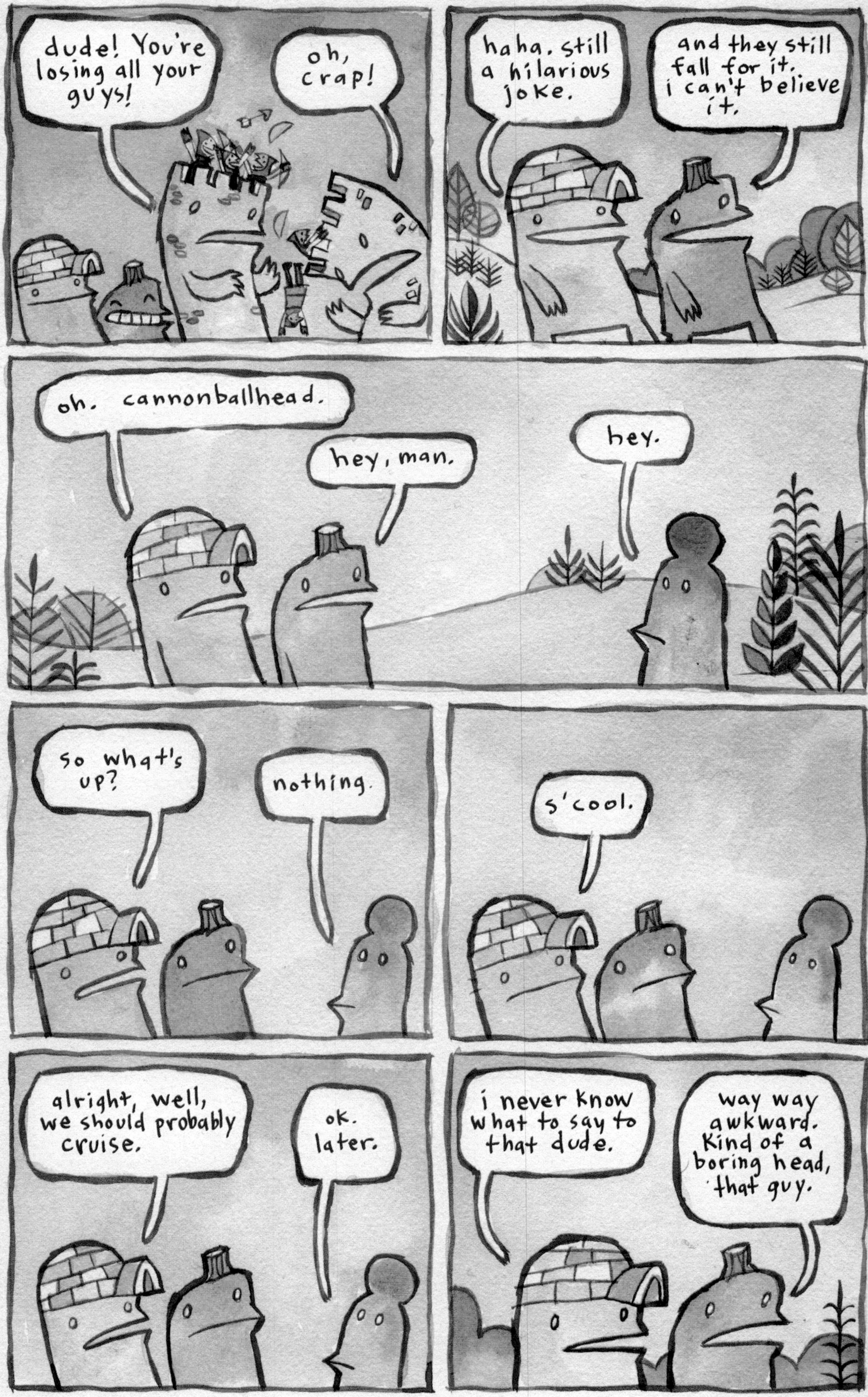
dude! You're losing all your guys!
oh, crap!
haha. still a hilarious joke.
and they still fall for it. i can't believe it.
oh. cannonballhead.
hey, man.
hey.
so what's up?
nothing.
s'cool.
alright, well, we should probably cruise.
ok. later.
i never know what to say to that dude.
way way awkward. Kind of a boring head, that guy.

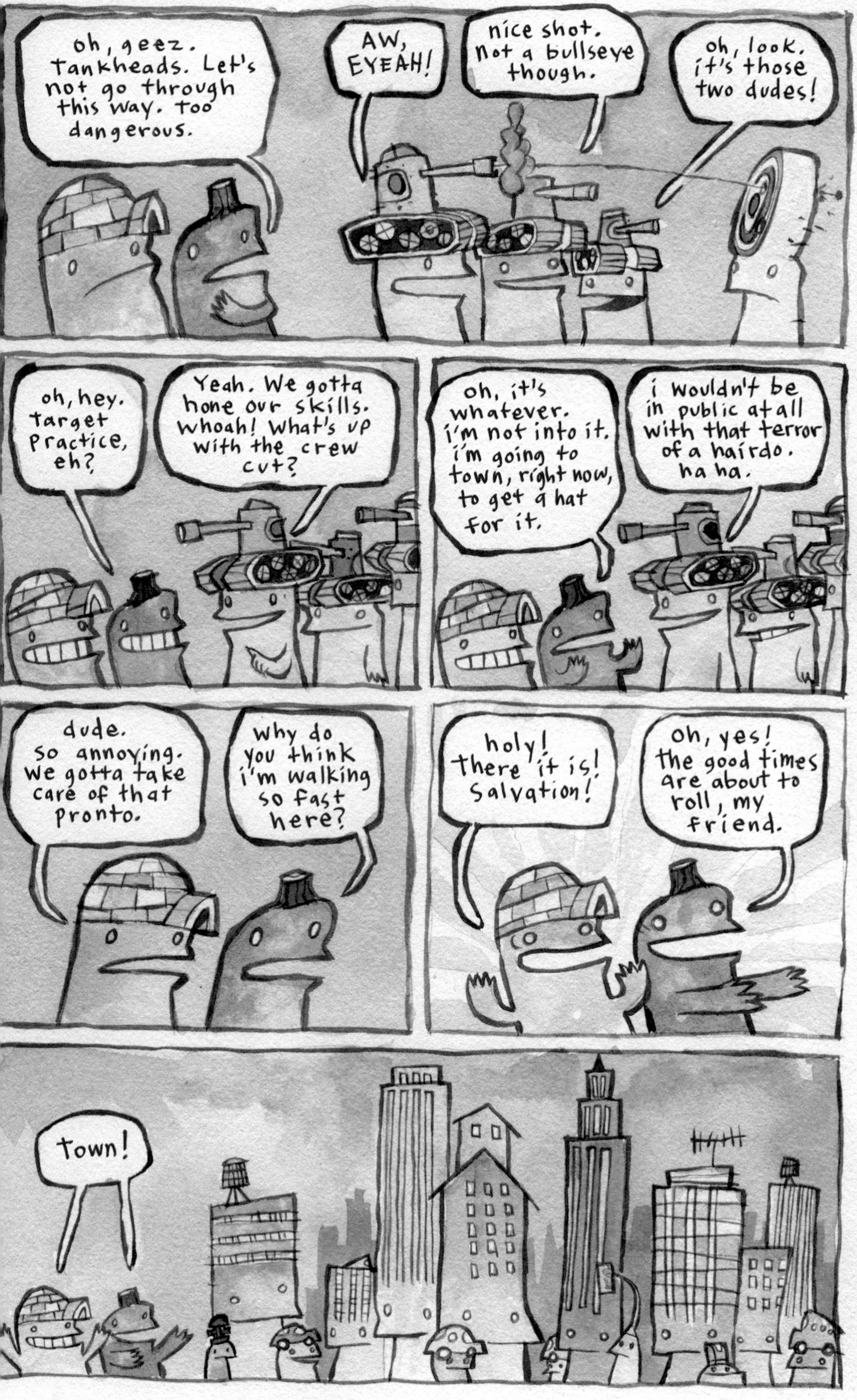
oh, geez. Tankheads. Let's not go through this way. too dangerous.
AW, EYEAH!
nice shot. Not a bullseye though.
oh, look. it's those two dudes!
oh, hey. target Practice, eh?
Yeah. We gotta hone our skills. whoah! What's up with the crew cut?
oh, it's whatever. i'm not into it. i'm going to town, right now, to get a hat for it.
i wouldn't be in public at all with that terror of a hairdo. ha ha.
dude. So annoying. We gotta take care of that Pronto.
Why do you think i'm walking so fast here?
holy! there it is! Salvation!
Oh, yes! the good times are about to roll, my friend.
Town!

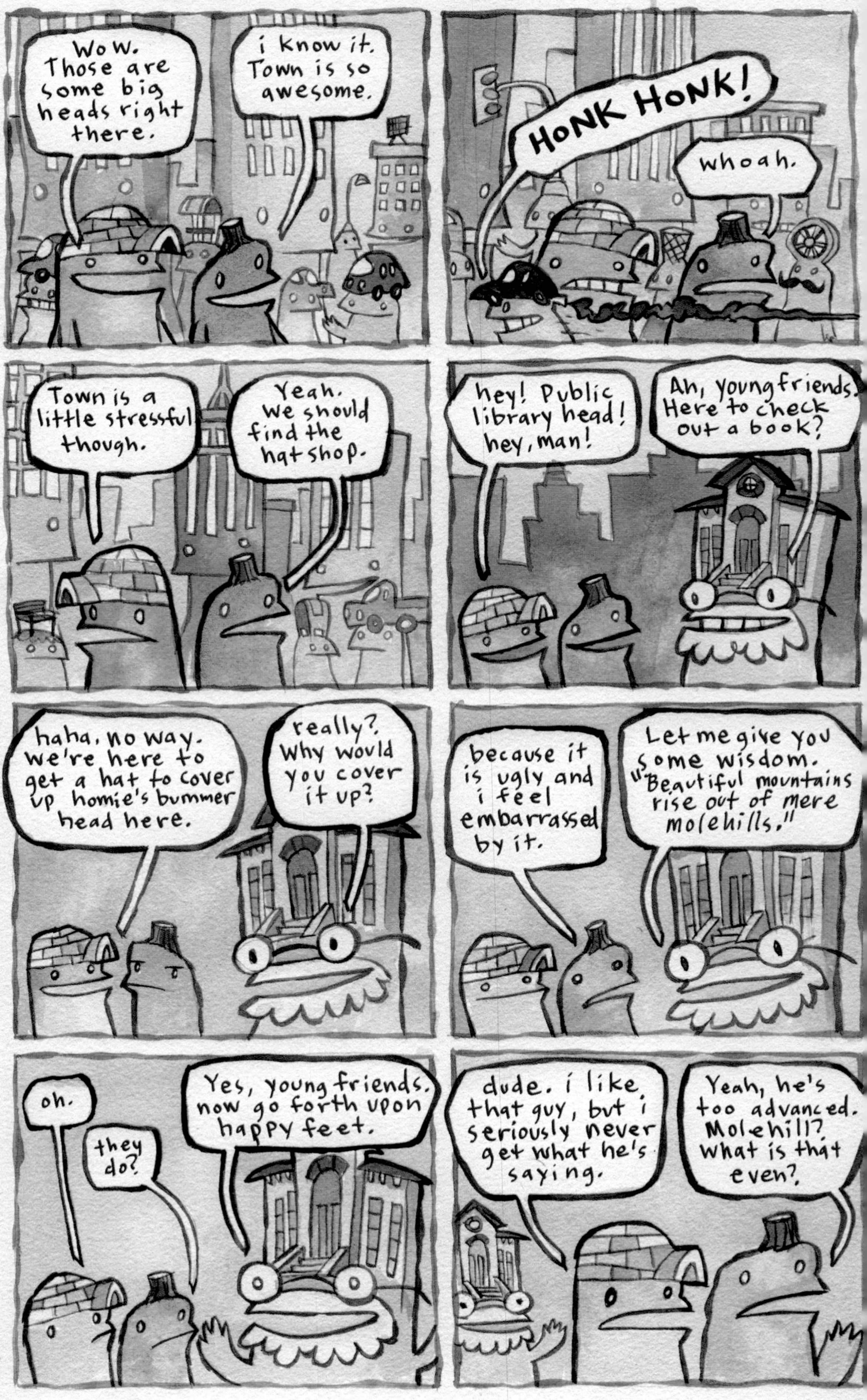
Wow. Those are some big heads right there.
i know it. Town is so awesome.
HONK HONK!
whoah.
Town is a little stressful though.
Yeah. We should find the hat shop.
hey! Public library head! hey, man!
Ah, young friends. Here to check out a book?
haha, no way. we're here to get a hat to cover up homie's bummer head here.
really? Why would you cover it up?
because it is ugly and i feel embarrassed by it.
Let me give you some wisdom. "Beautiful mountains rise out of mere molehills."
oh.
they do?
Yes, young friends. now go forth upon happy feet.
dude. i like that guy, but i seriously never get what he's saying.
Yeah, he's too advanced. Molehill? What is that even?

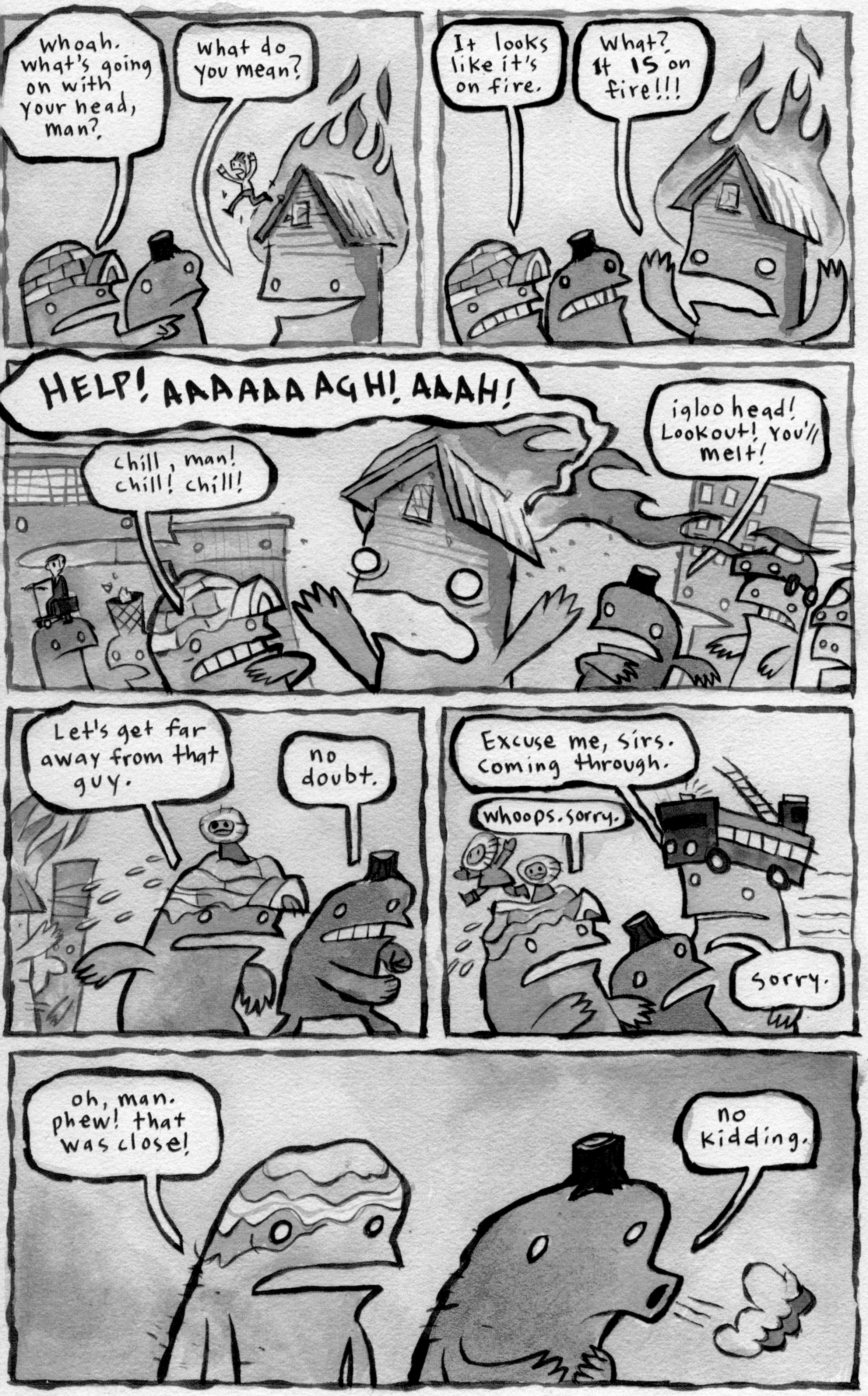
Whoah. what's going on with your head, man?
What do you mean?
It looks like it's on fire.
What? It IS on fire!!!
HELP! AAAAAAGH! AAAH!
chill, man! chill! chill!
igloo head! Lookout! You'll melt!
Let's get far away from that guy.
no doubt.
Excuse me, sirs. Coming through.
whoops. sorry.
sorry.
oh, man. phew! that was close!
no kidding.

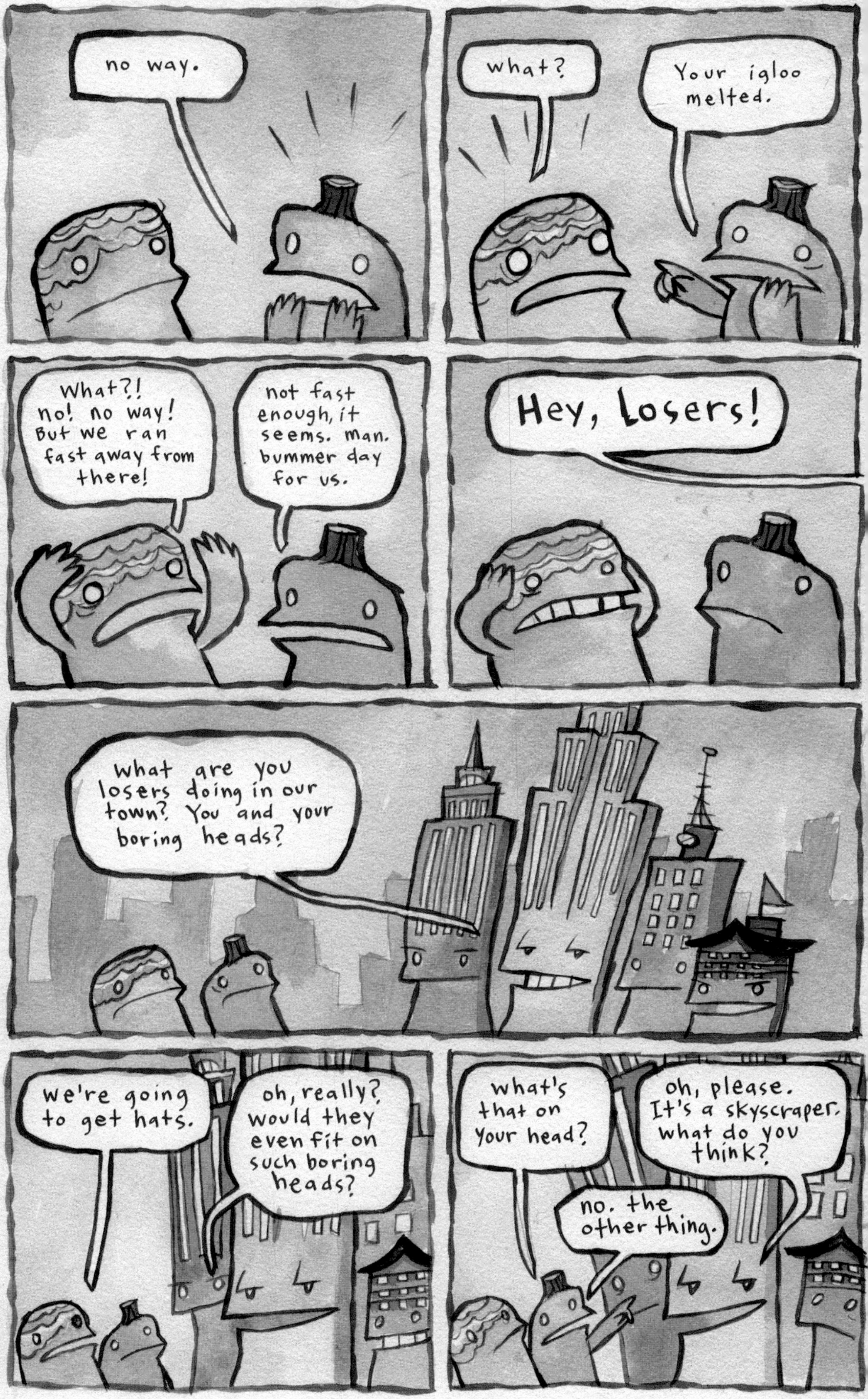
no way.
what?
Your igloo melted.
What?! no! no way! But we ran fast away from there!
not fast enough, it seems. man. bummer day for us.
Hey, Losers!
What are you losers doing in our town? You and your boring heads?
we're going to get hats.
oh, really? would they even fit on such boring heads?
what's that on your head?
oh, please. It's a skyscraper. what do you think?
no. the other thing.

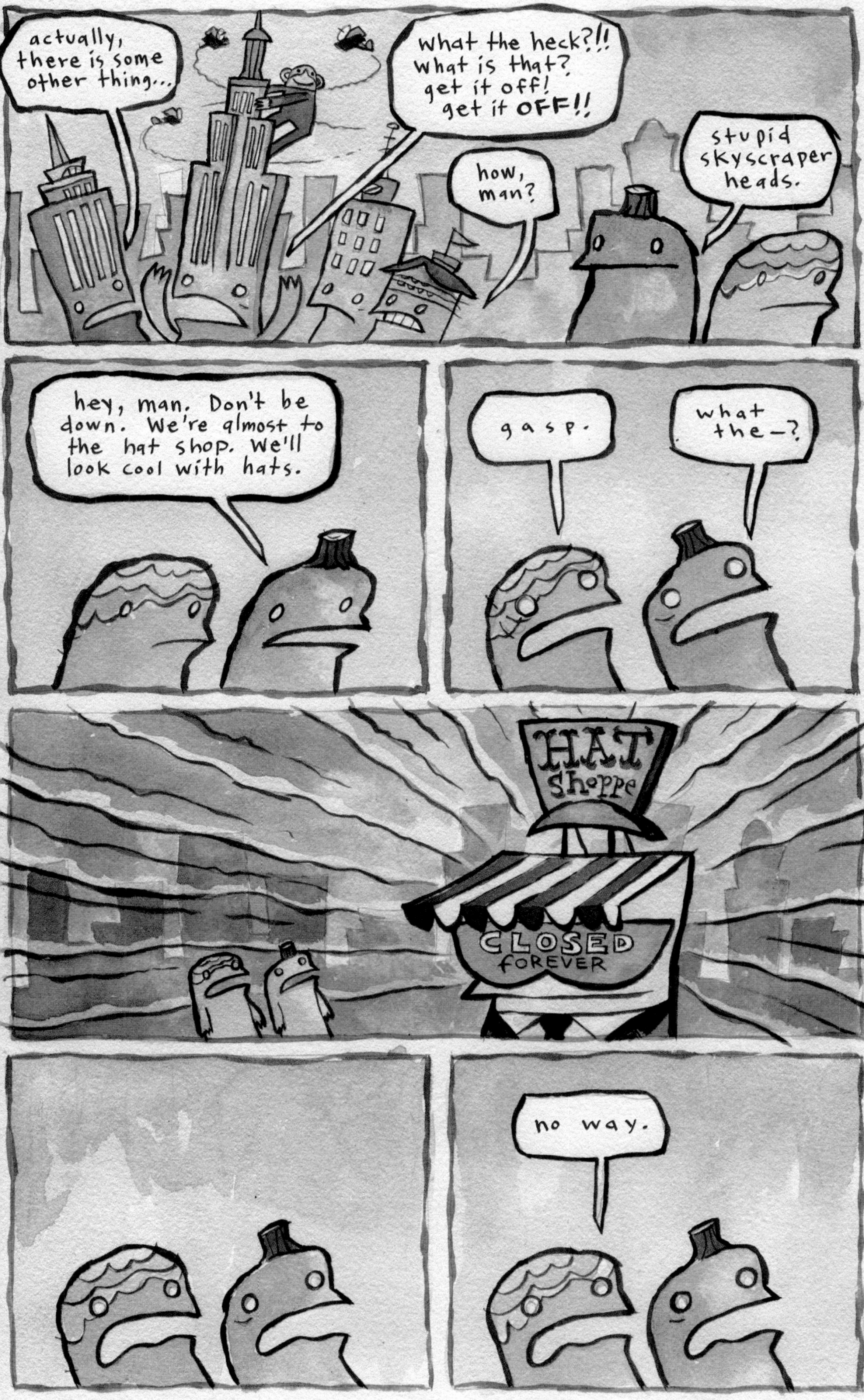
actually, there is some other thing...
what the heck?!! what is that? get it off! get it OFF!!
how, man?
stupid skyscraper heads.
hey, man. Don't be down. We're almost to the hat shop. We'll look cool with hats.
gasp.
what the—?
HAT Shoppe
CLOSED FOREVER
no way.

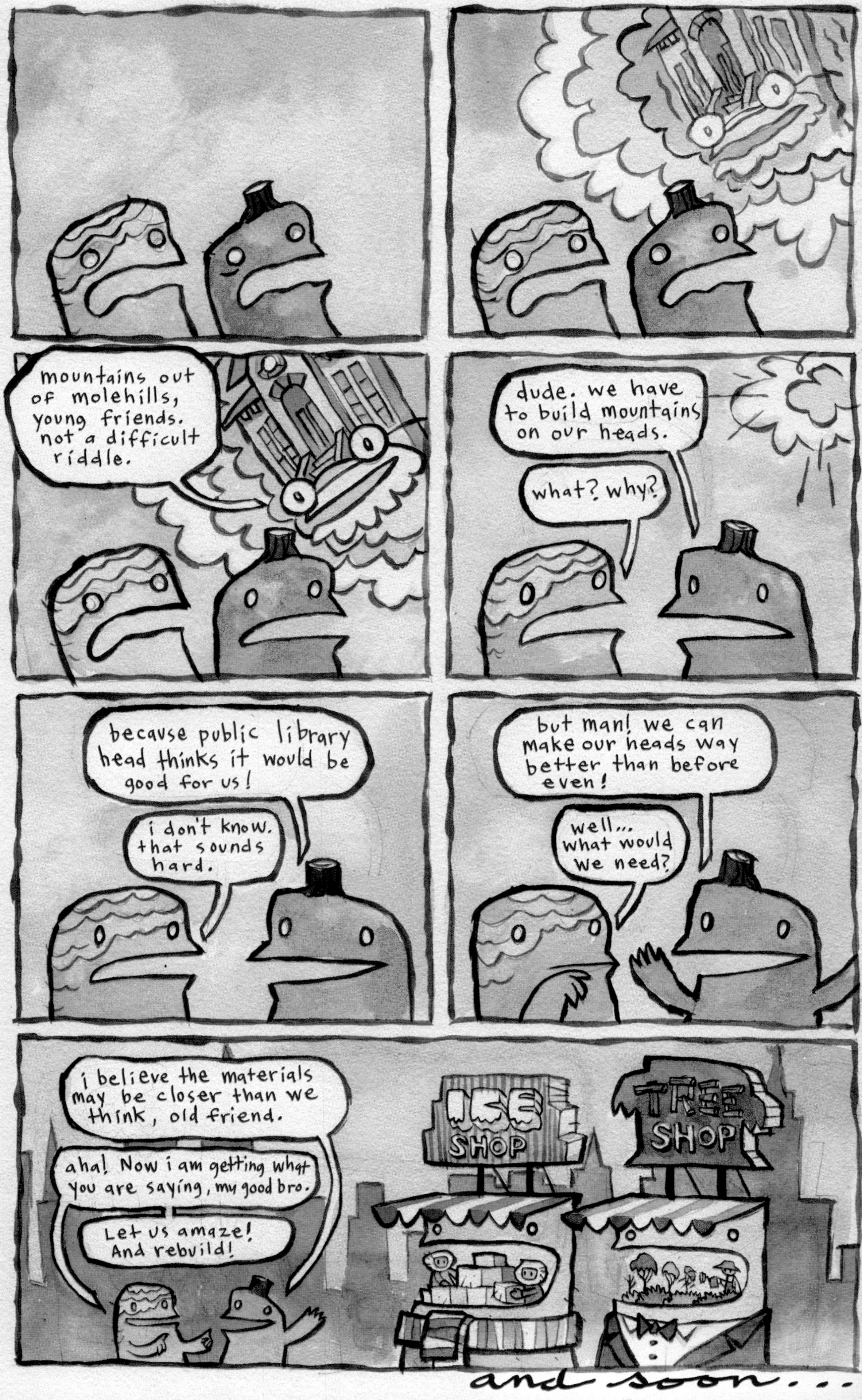
mountains out of molehills, young friends. not a difficult riddle.
dude. we have to build mountains on our heads.
what? why?
because public library head thinks it would be good for us!
i don't know. that sounds hard.
but man! we can make our heads way better than before even!
well... what would we need?
i believe the materials may be closer than we think, old friend.
aha! Now i am getting what you are saying, my good bro.
Let us amaze! And rebuild!
ICE SHOP
TREE SHOP
and soon...

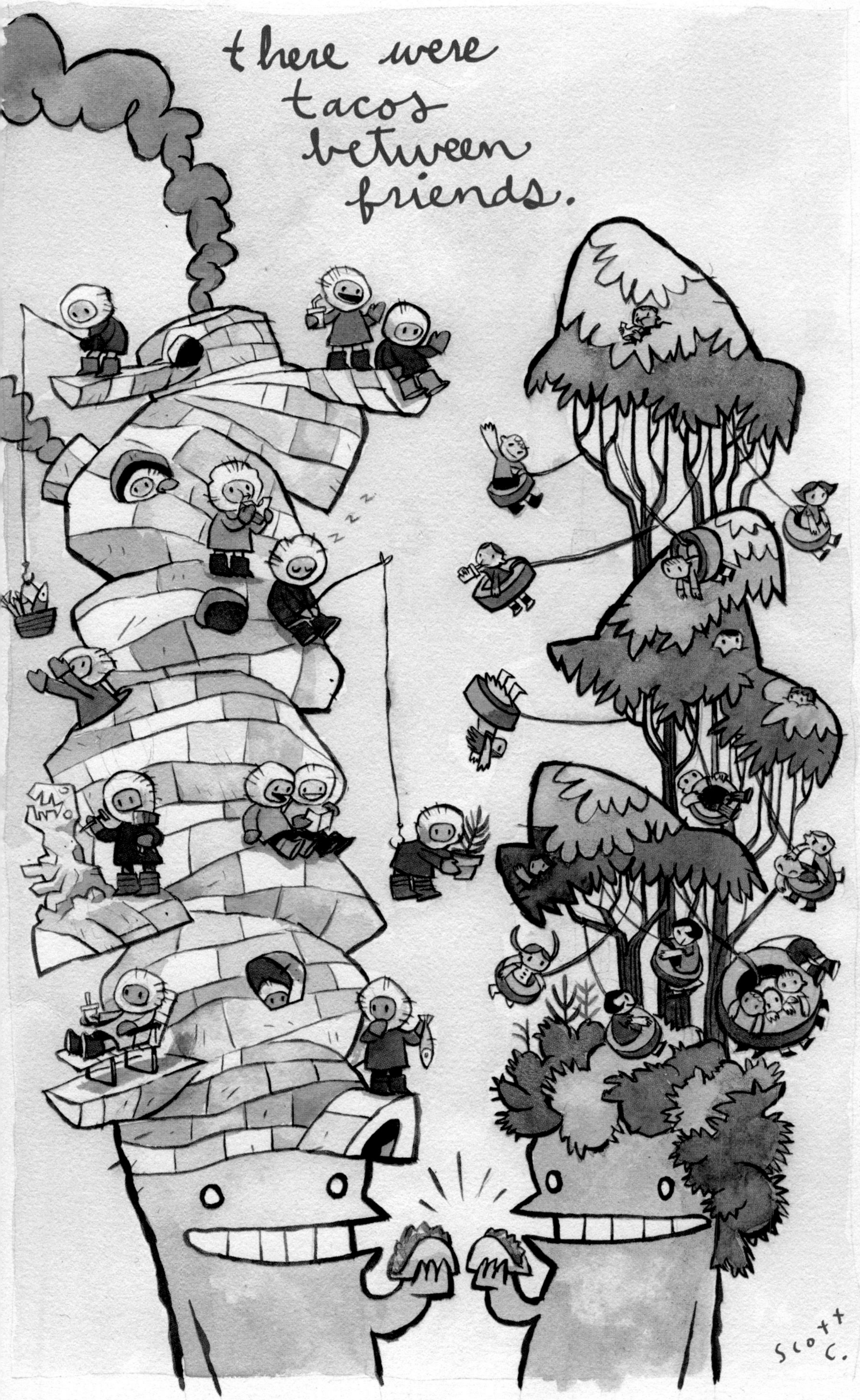
there were tacos between friends.
scott c.

THE RABBIT MAYOR

A Mayan Folk Tale

Illustrated by Jon Klassen

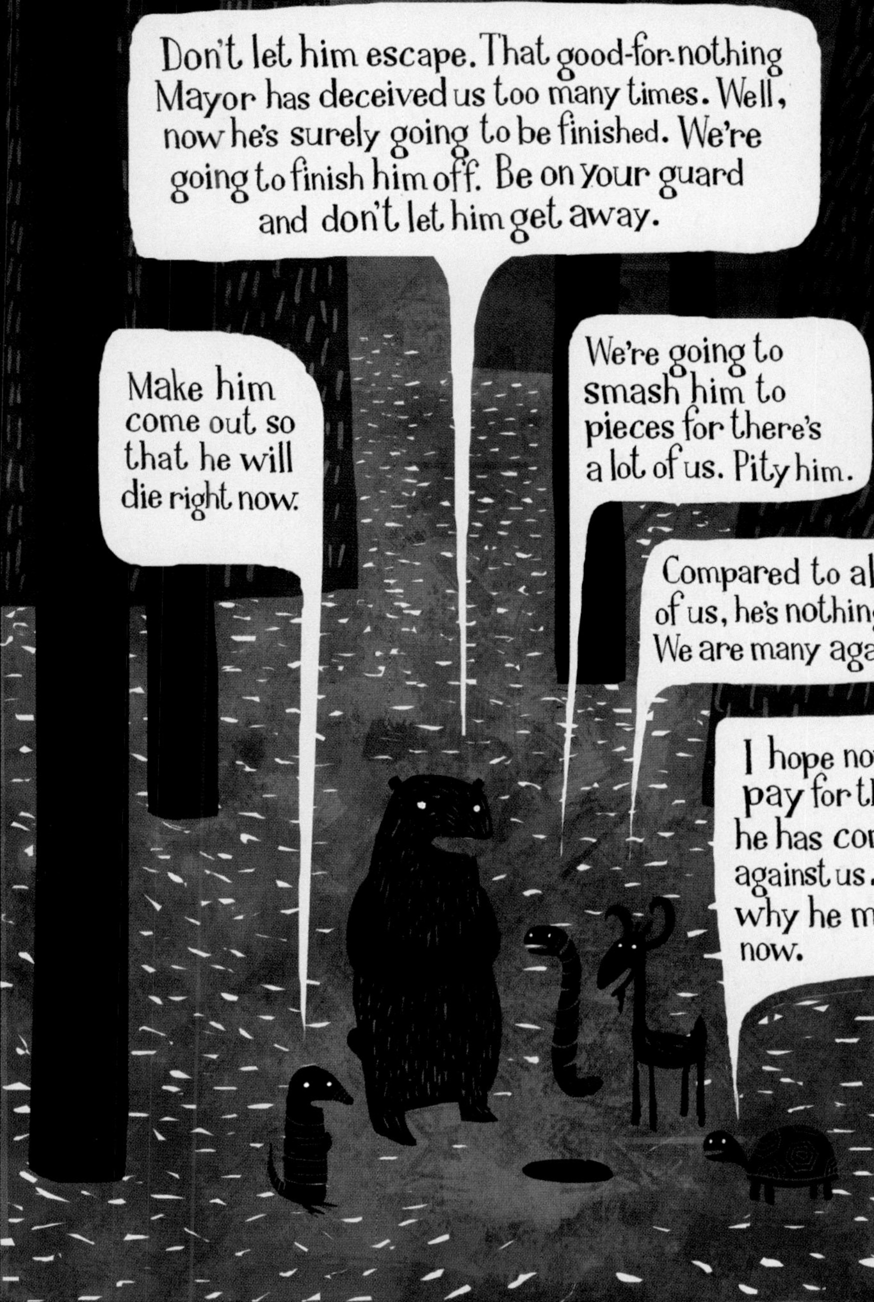

Don't let him escape. That good-for-nothing Mayor has deceived us too many times. Well, now he's surely going to be finished. We're going to finish him off. Be on your guard and don't let him get away.
Make him come out so that he will die right now.
We're going to smash him to pieces for there's a lot of us. Pity him.
Compared to al of us, he's nothin We are many aga
I hope no pay for th he has co against us why he m now.

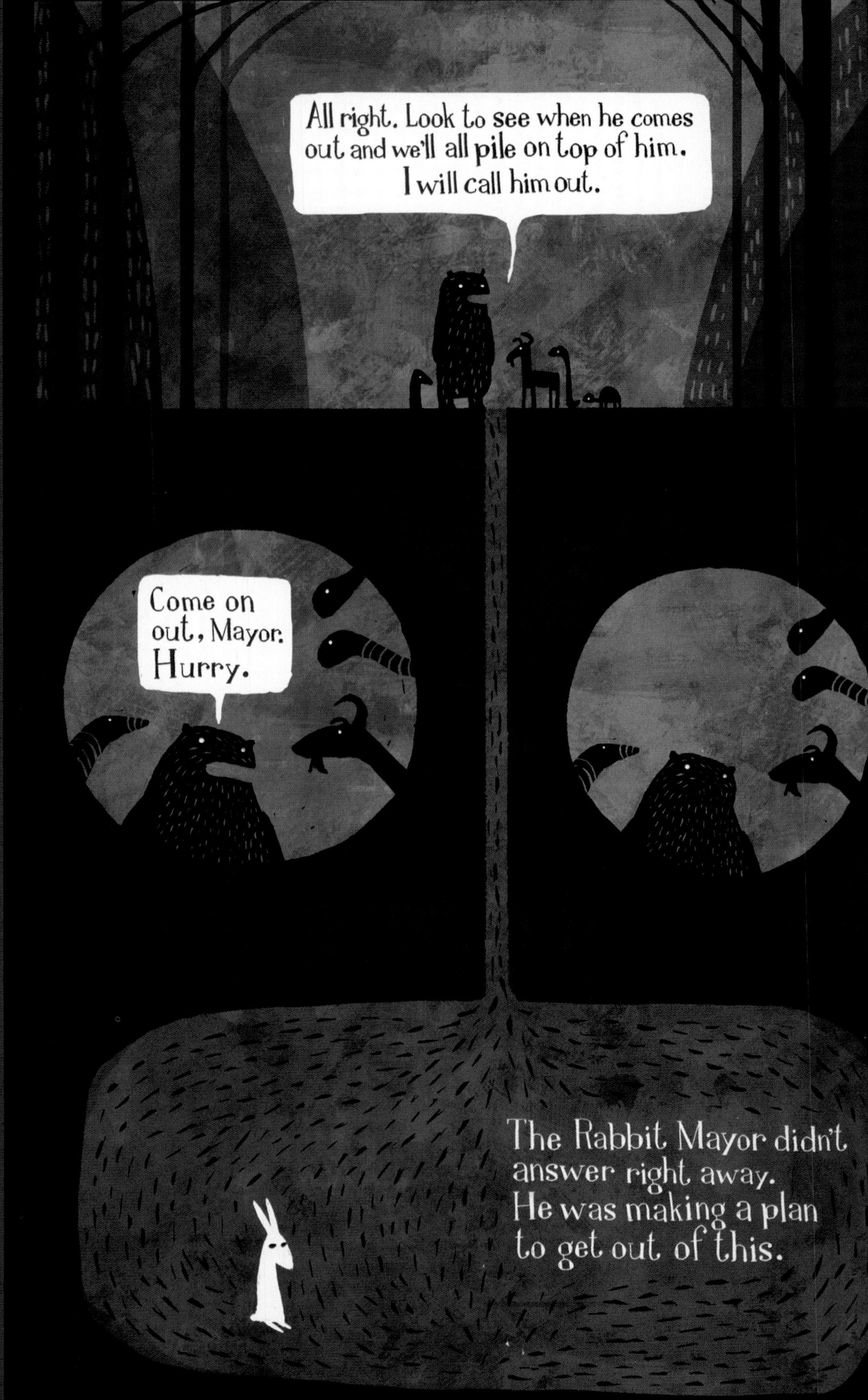
All right. Look to see when he comes out and we'll all pile on top of him. I will call him out.
Come on out, Mayor. Hurry.
The Rabbit Mayor didn't answer right away. He was making a plan to get out of this.

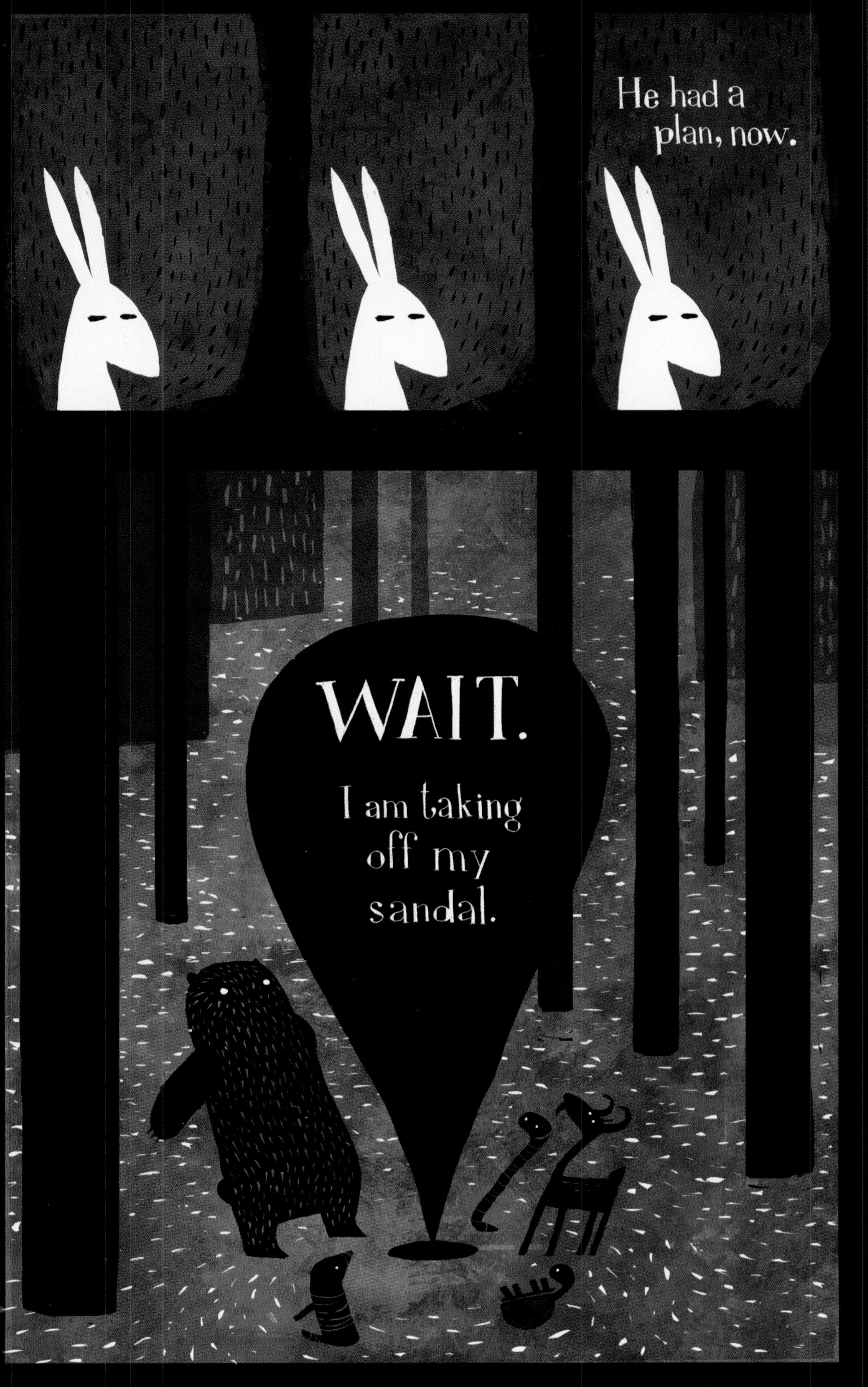
He had a plan, now.
WAIT.
I am taking off my sandal.

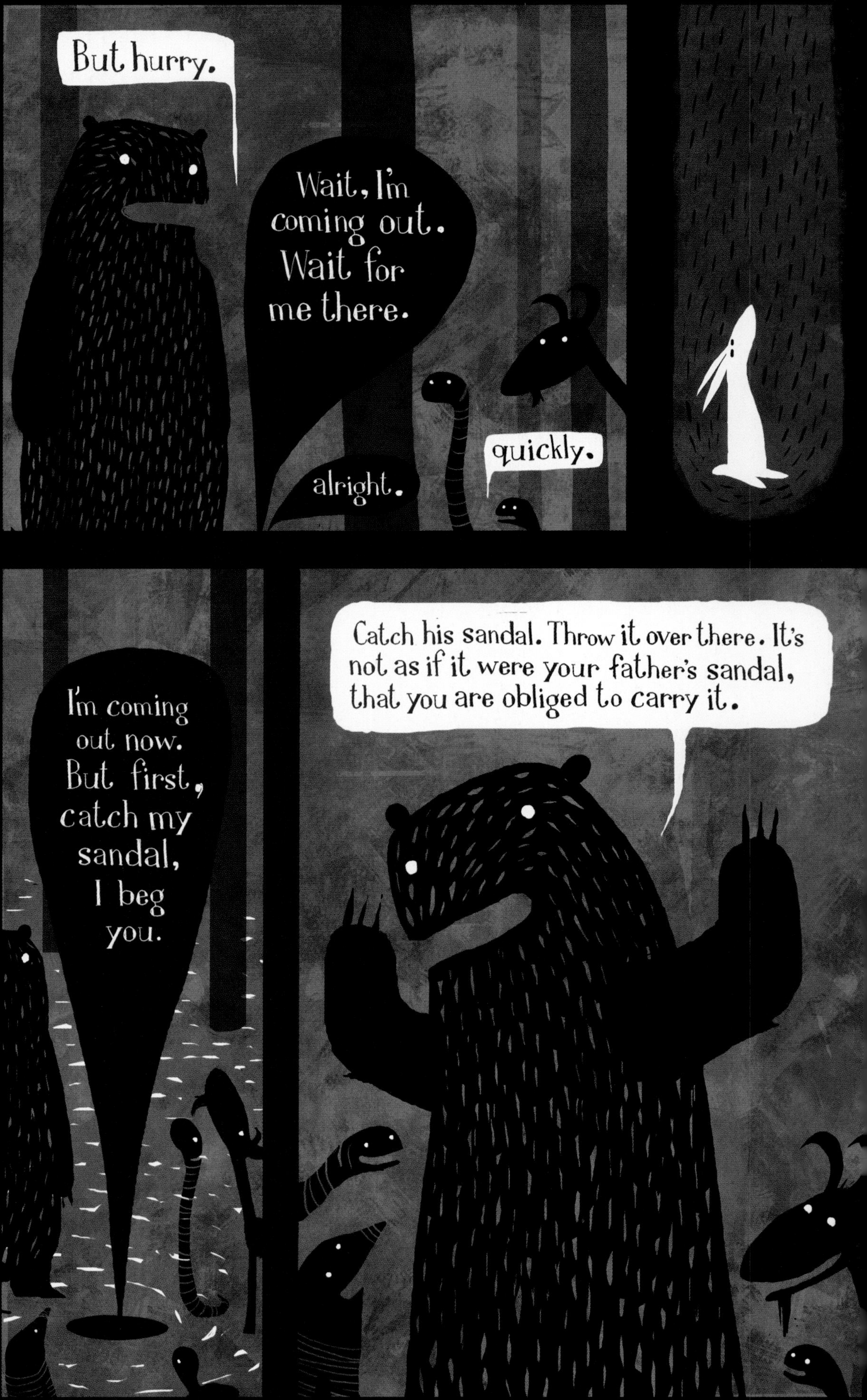
But hurry.
Wait, I'm coming out. Wait for me there.
alright.
quickly.
I'm coming out now. But first, catch my sandal, I beg you.
Catch his sandal. Throw it over there. It's not as if it were your father's sandal, that you are obliged to carry it.

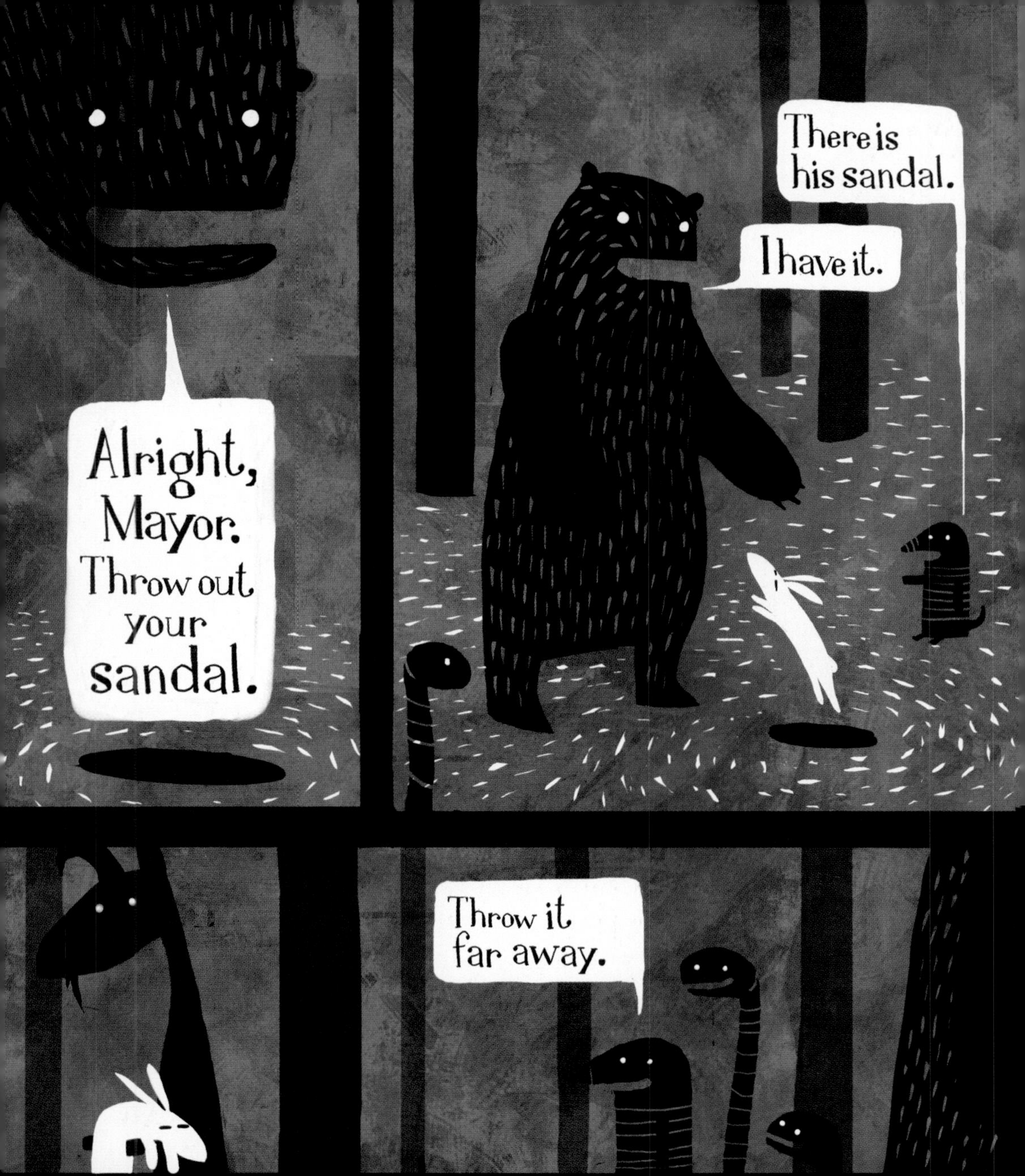
Alright, Mayor. Throw out your sandal.
There is his sandal.
I have it.
Throw it far away.

They gave it to the goat and he threw it away. They didn't know it was the Mayor they were throwing. They were all shouting into the hole.

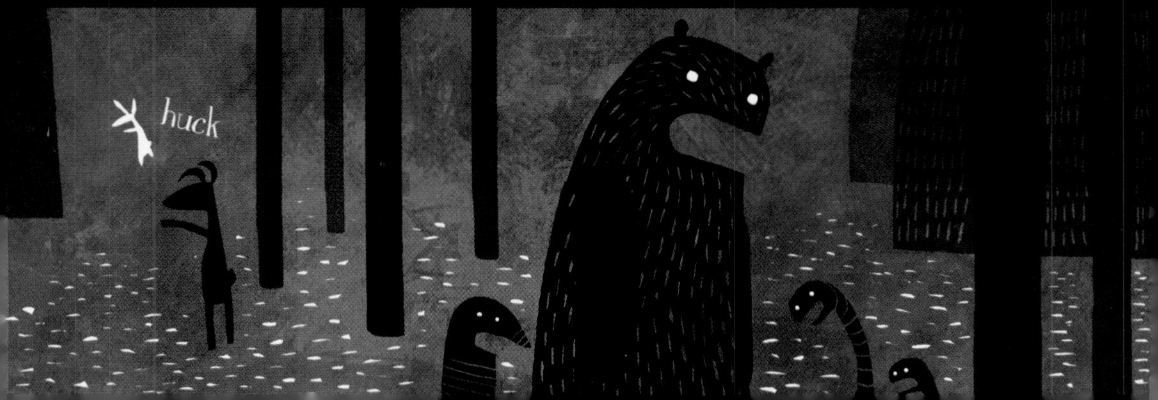
huck

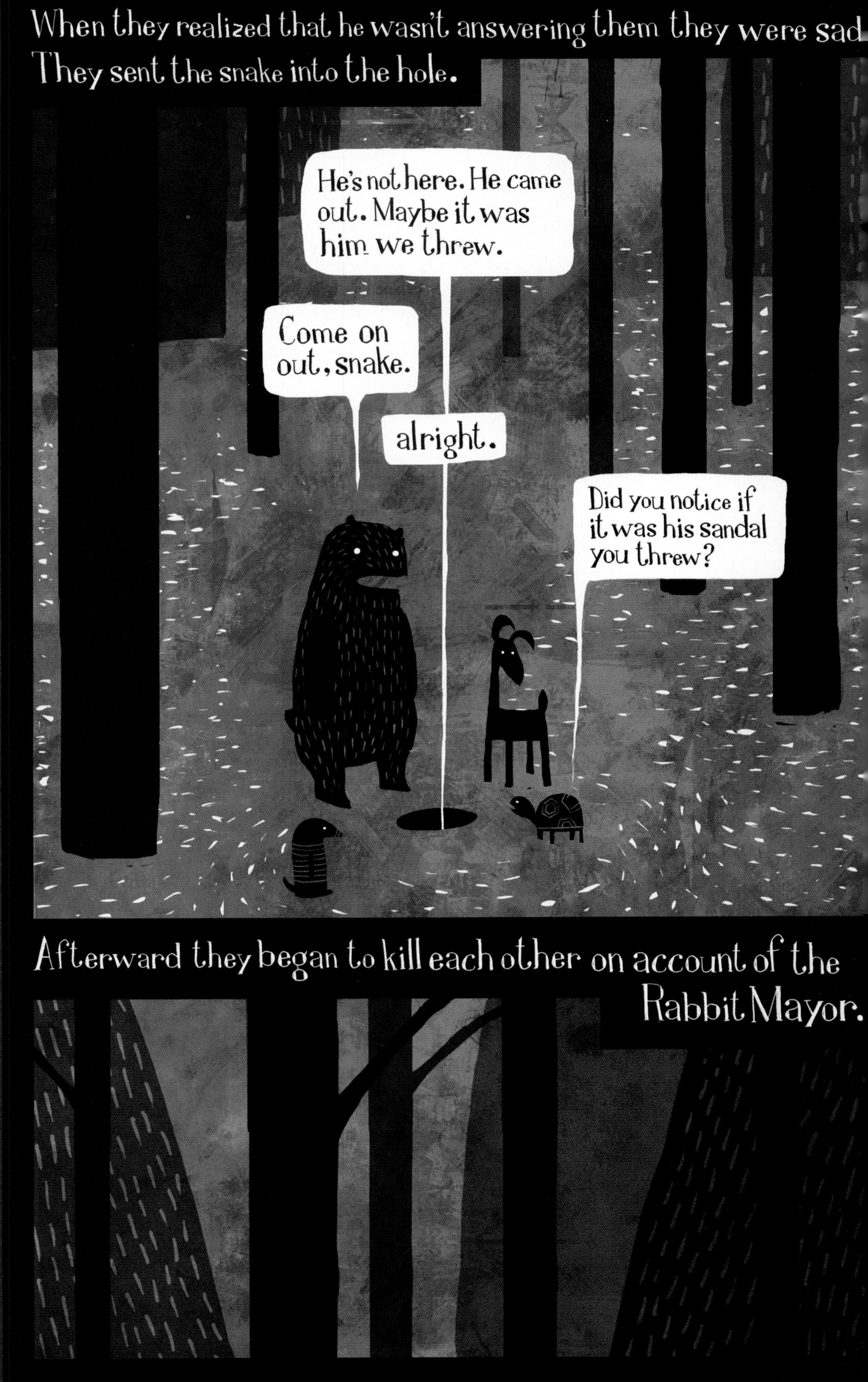
When they realized that he wasn't answering them they were sad
They sent the snake into the hole.
He's not here. He came out. Maybe it was him we threw.
Come on out, snake.
alright.
Did you notice if it was his sandal you threw?
Afterward they began to kill each other on account of the Rabbit Mayor.

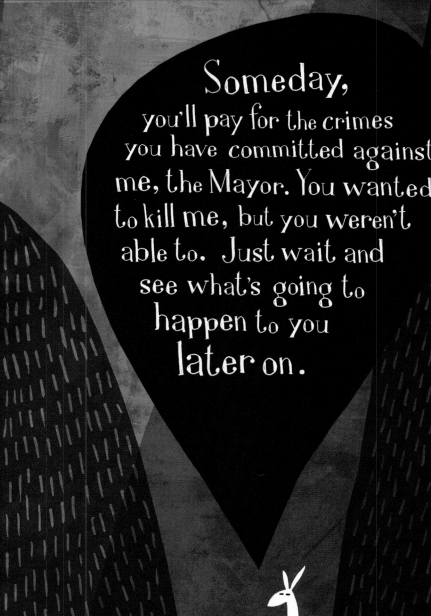

Someday, you'll pay for the crimes you have committed against me, the Mayor. You wanted to kill me, but you weren't able to. Just wait and see what's going to happen to you later on.

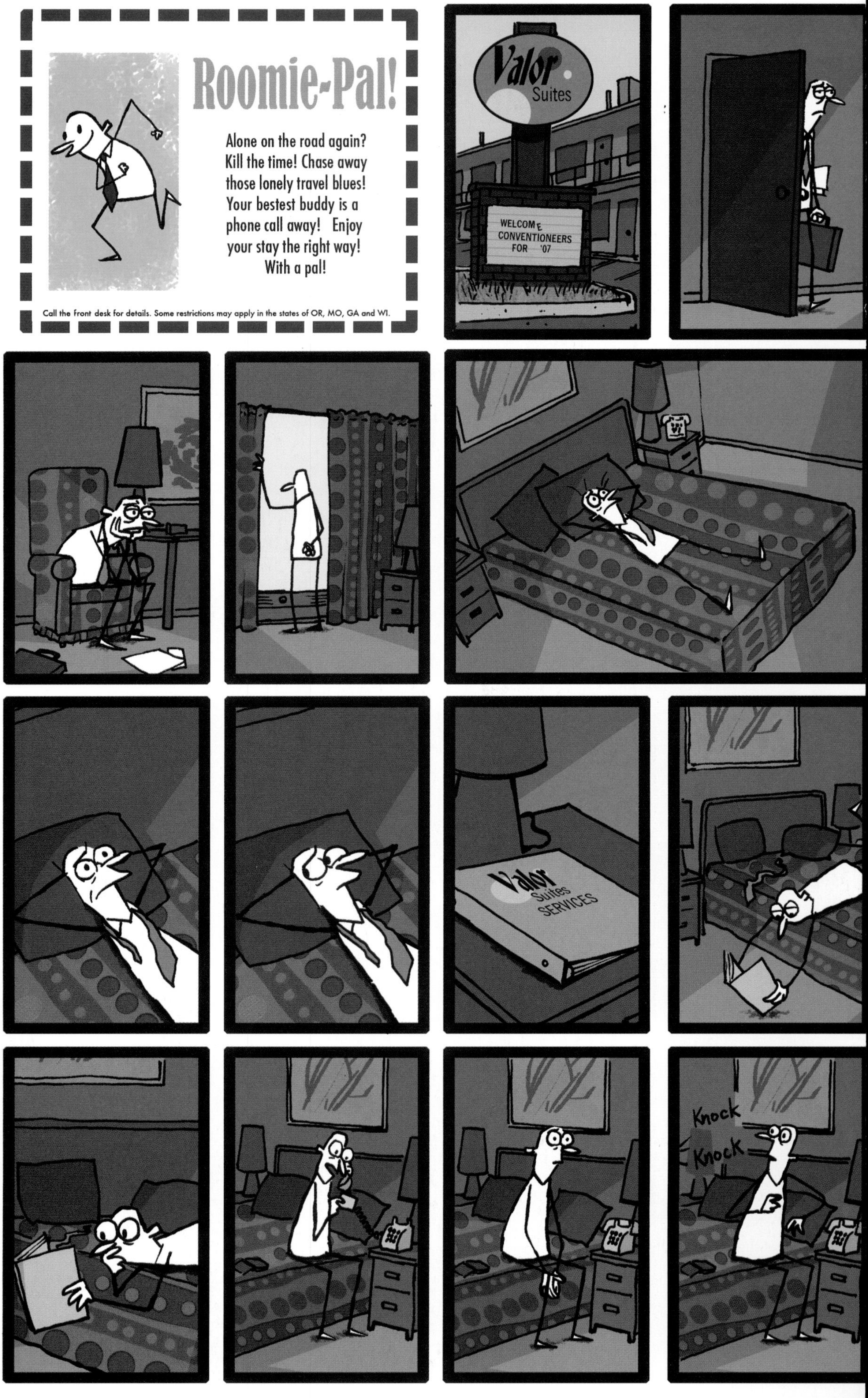
Roomie-Pal!
Alone on the road again? Kill the time! Chase away those lonely travel blues! Your bestest buddy is a phone call away! Enjoy your stay the right way! With a pal!
Call the front desk for details. Some restrictions may apply in the states of OR, MO, GA and WI.
Valor Suites
WELCOME CONVENTIONEERS FOR '07
Valor Suites SERVICES
Knock
Knock

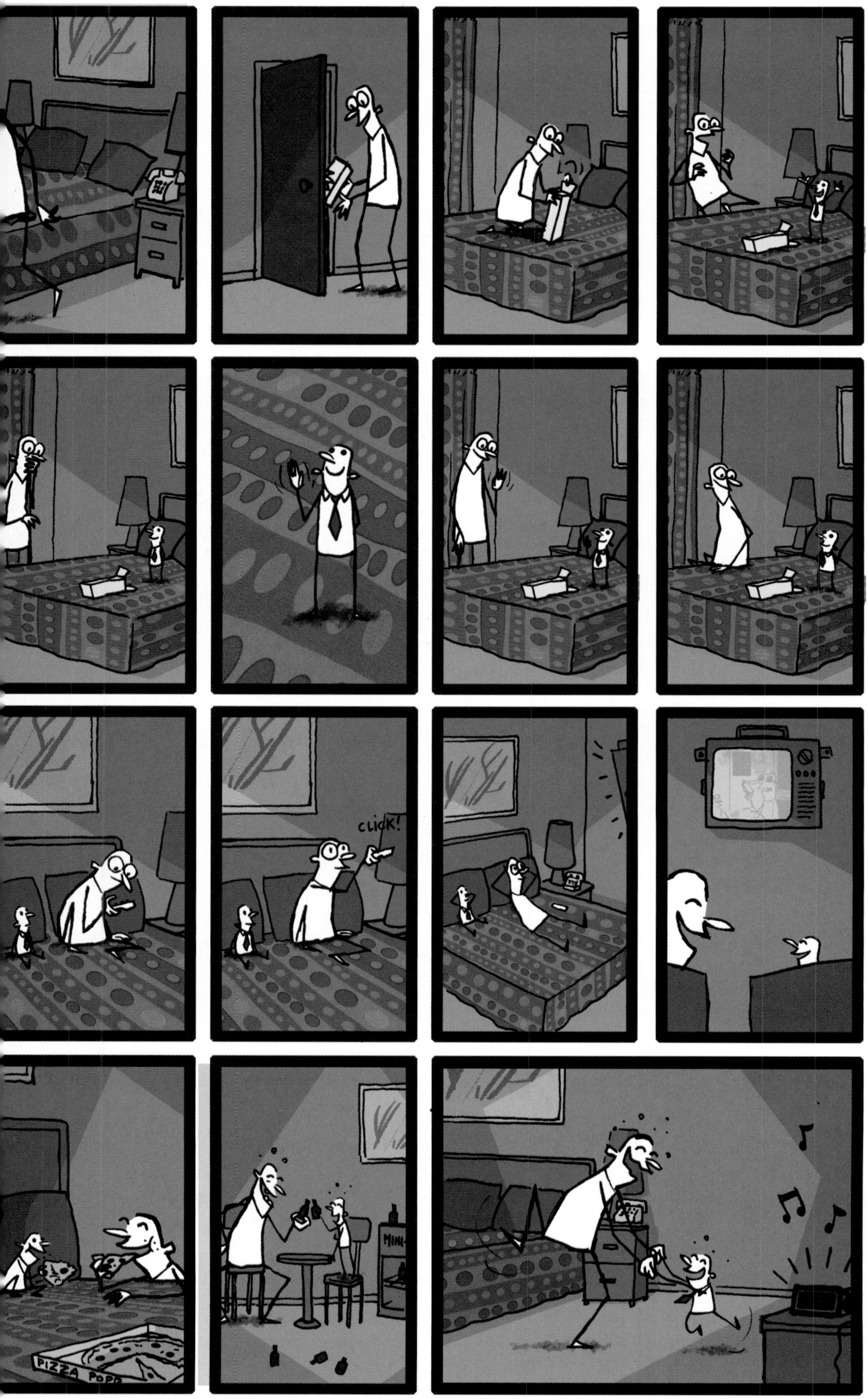
CLICK!
MINI-
PIZZA

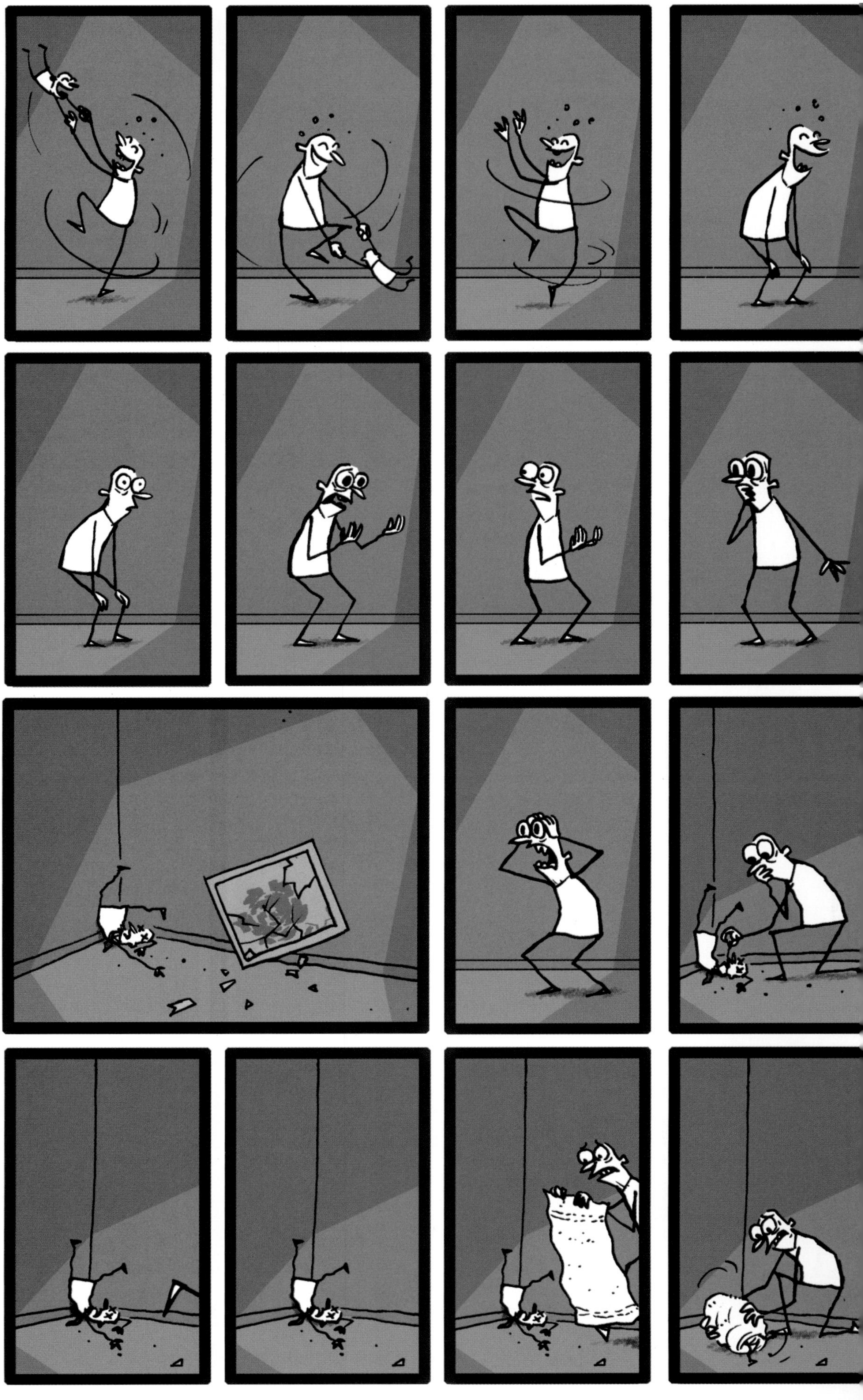

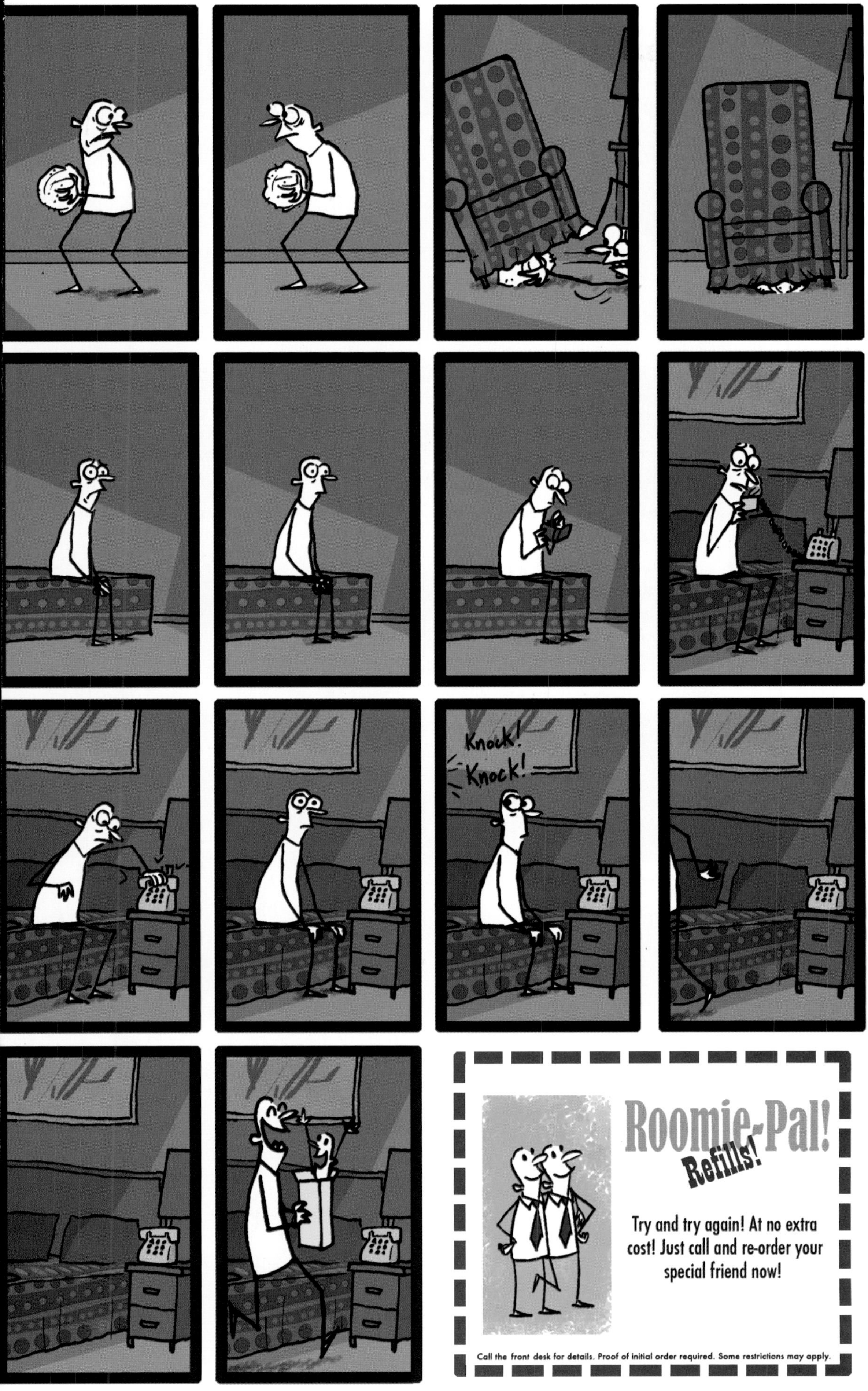
Knock!
Knock!
Roomie-Pal!
Refills!
Try and try again! At no extra cost! Just call and re-order your special friend now!
Call the front desk for details. Proof of initial order required. Some restrictions may apply.

from here to there . . .

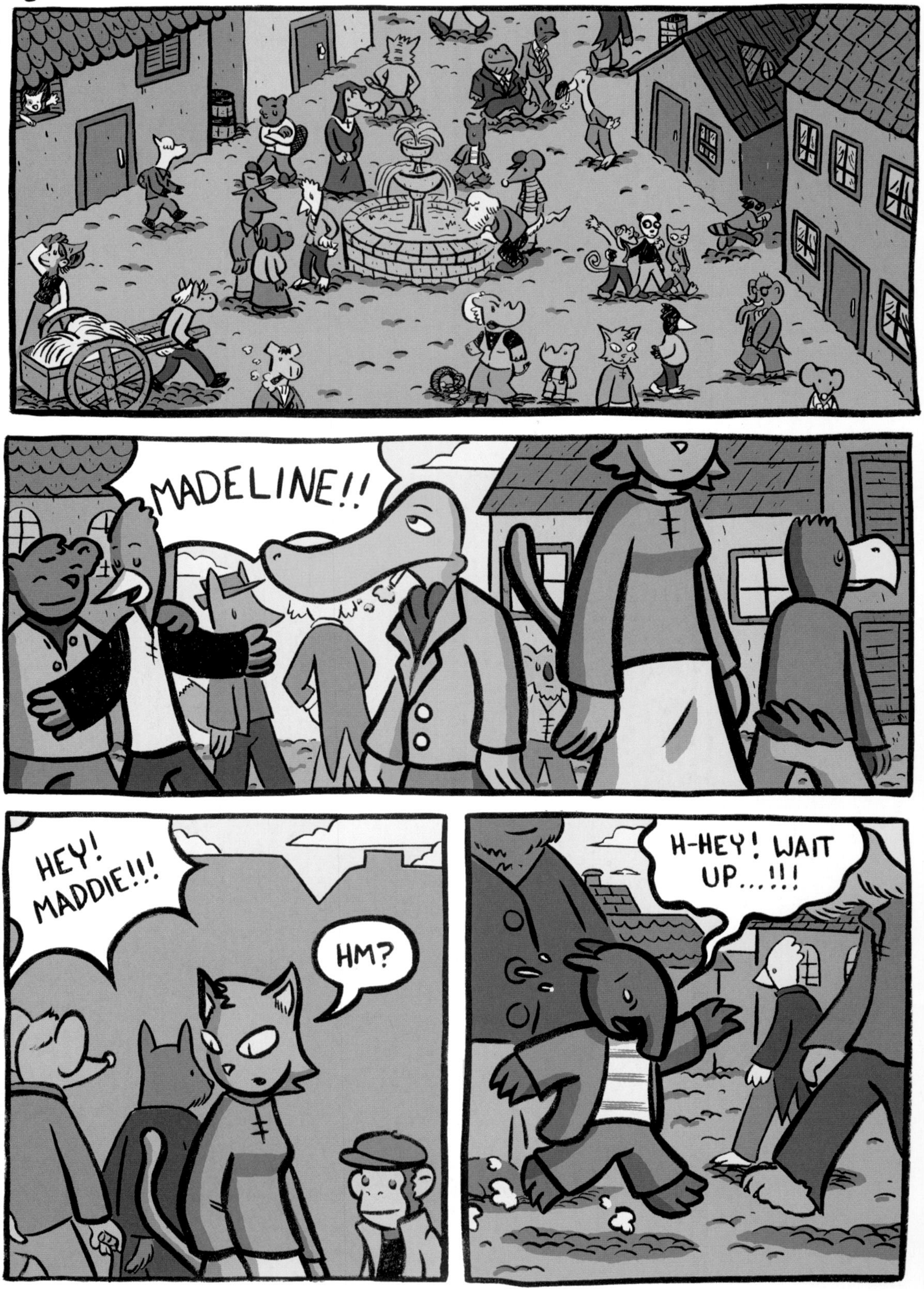
MADELINE!!
HEY! MADDIE!!!
HM?
H-HEY! WAIT UP...!!!

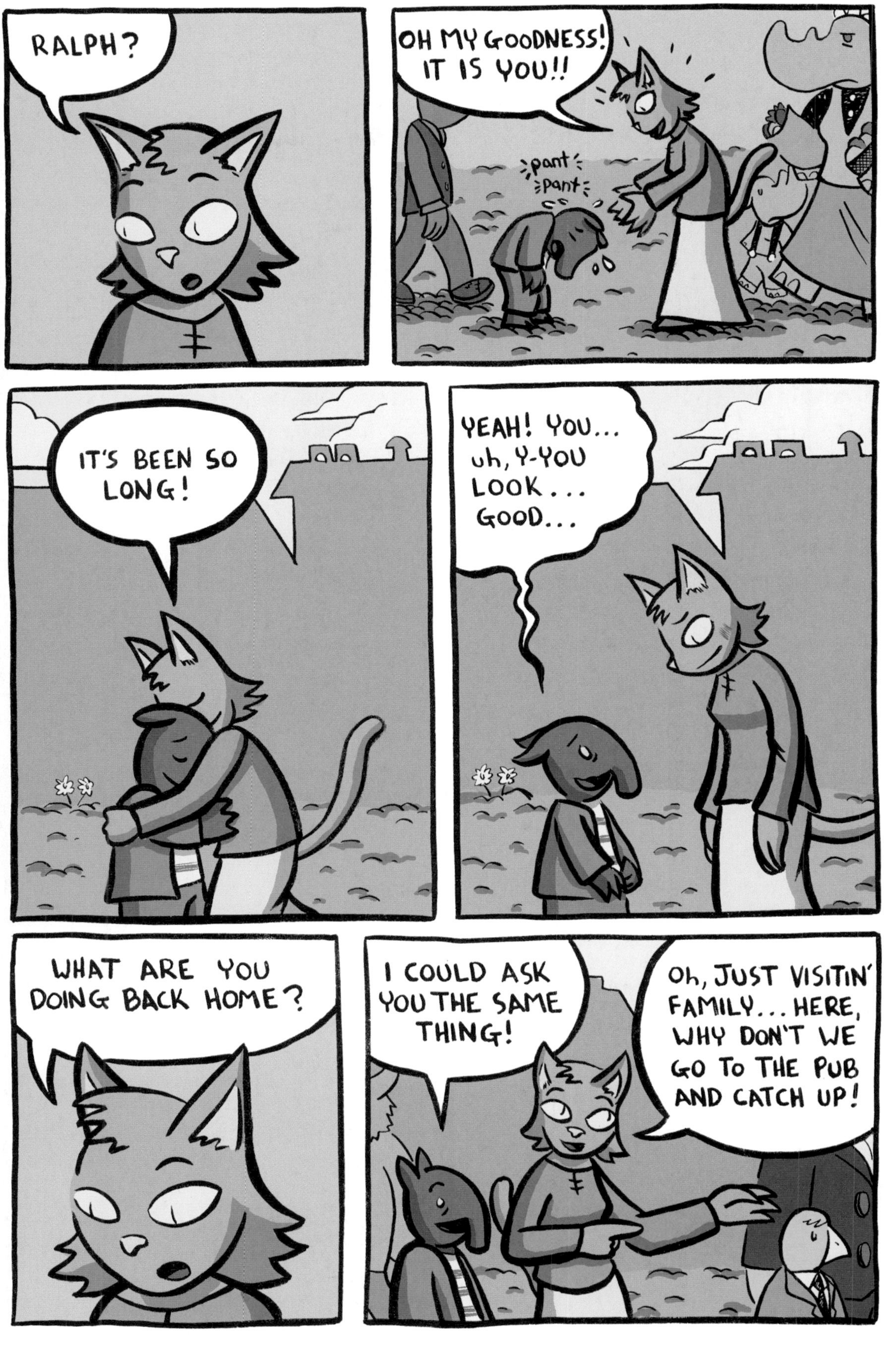
RALPH?
OH MY GOODNESS! IT IS YOU!!
pant pant
IT'S BEEN SO LONG!
YEAH! YOU... uh, Y-YOU LOOK... GOOD...
WHAT ARE YOU DOING BACK HOME?
I COULD ASK YOU THE SAME THING!
Oh, JUST VISITIN' FAMILY... HERE, WHY DON'T WE GO TO THE PUB AND CATCH UP!

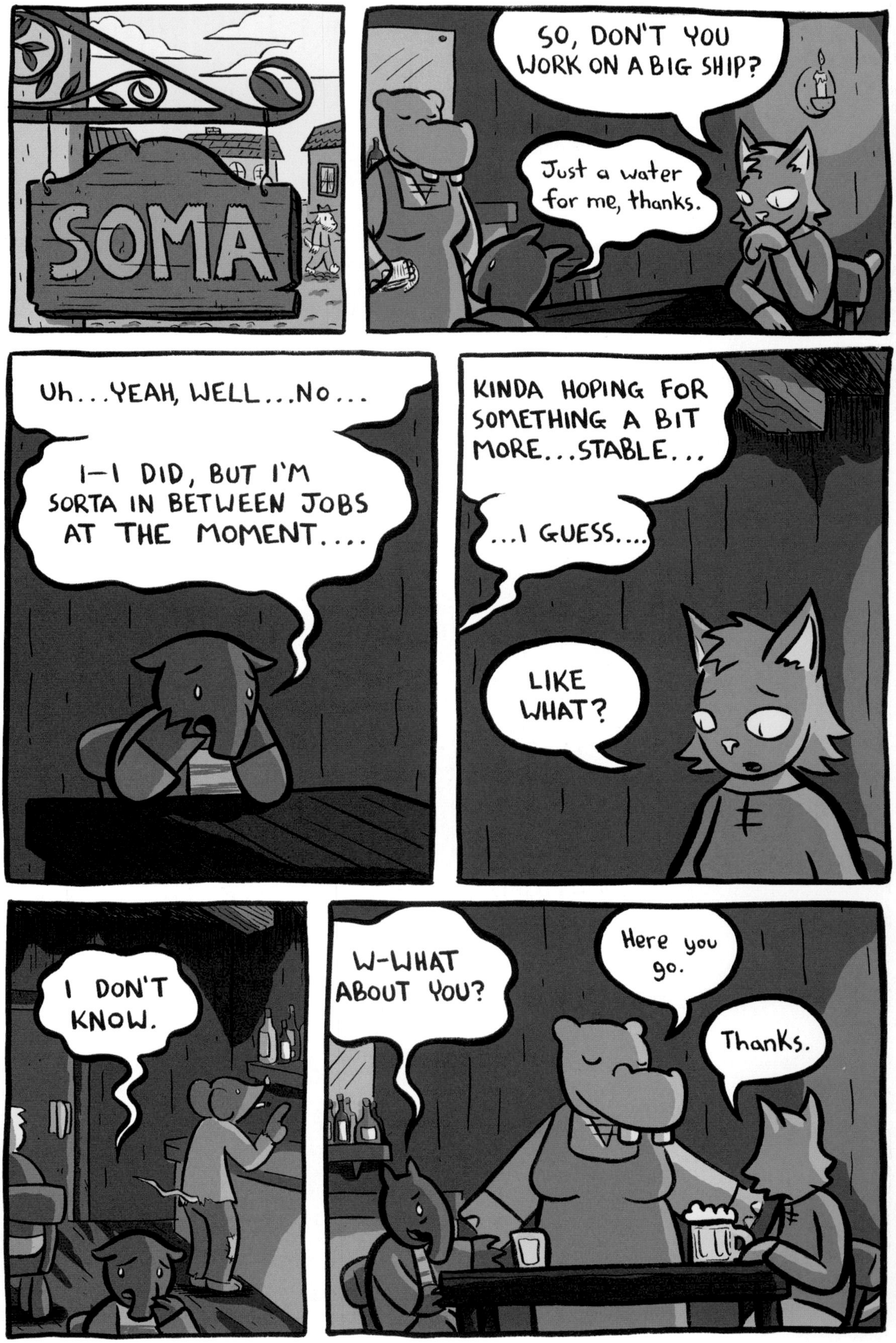
SOMA
SO, DON'T YOU WORK ON A BIG SHIP?
Just a water for me, thanks.
Uh...YEAH, WELL...No...
I-I DID, BUT I'M SORTA IN BETWEEN JOBS AT THE MOMENT....
KINDA HOPING FOR SOMETHING A BIT MORE...STABLE...
...I GUESS....
LIKE WHAT?
I DON'T KNOW.
W-WHAT ABOUT YOU?
Here you go.
Thanks.

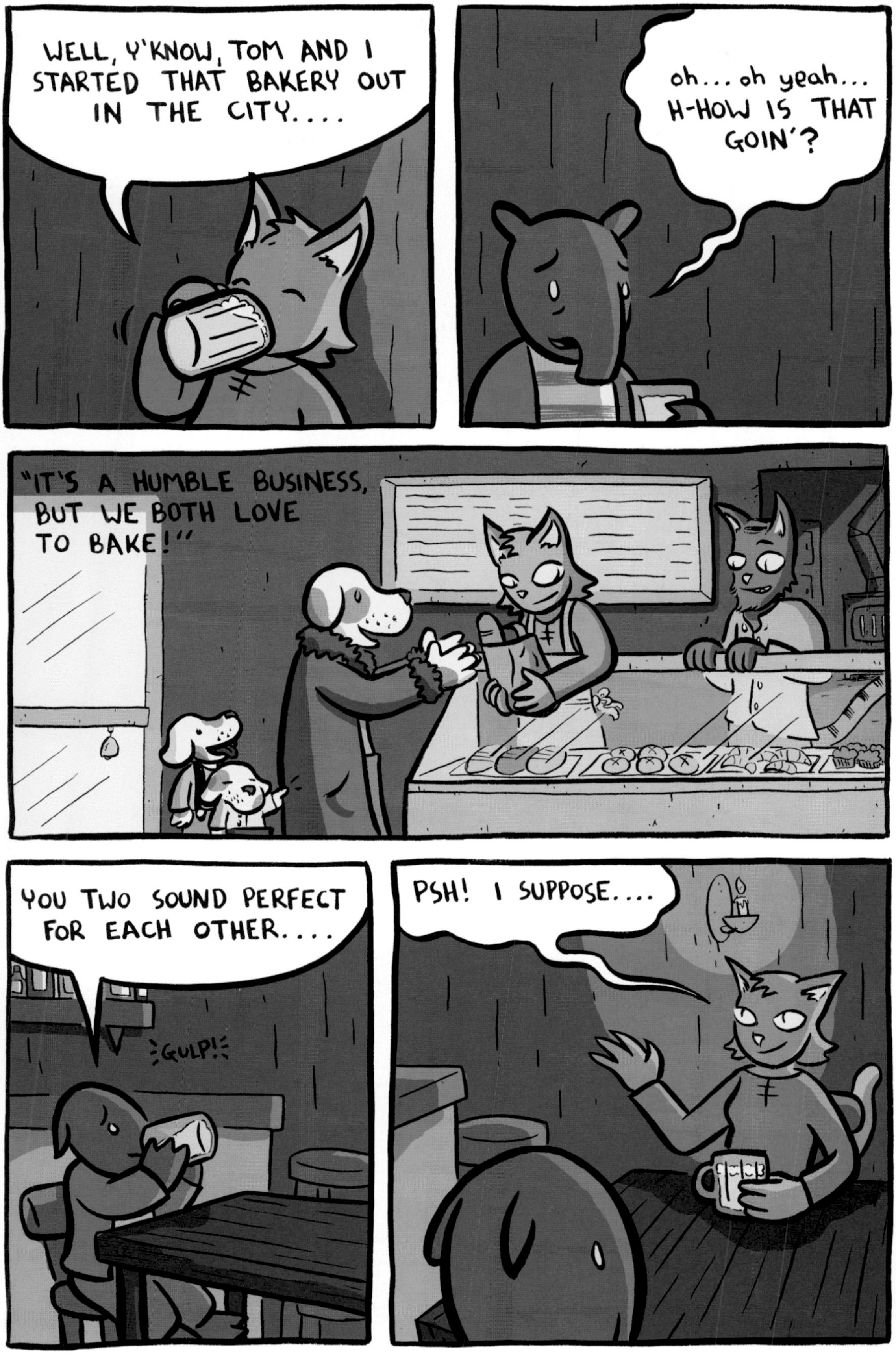
WELL, Y'KNOW, TOM AND I STARTED THAT BAKERY OUT IN THE CITY....
oh... oh yeah... H-HOW IS THAT GOIN'?
"IT'S A HUMBLE BUSINESS, BUT WE BOTH LOVE TO BAKE!"
YOU TWO SOUND PERFECT FOR EACH OTHER....
GULP!
PSH! I SUPPOSE....

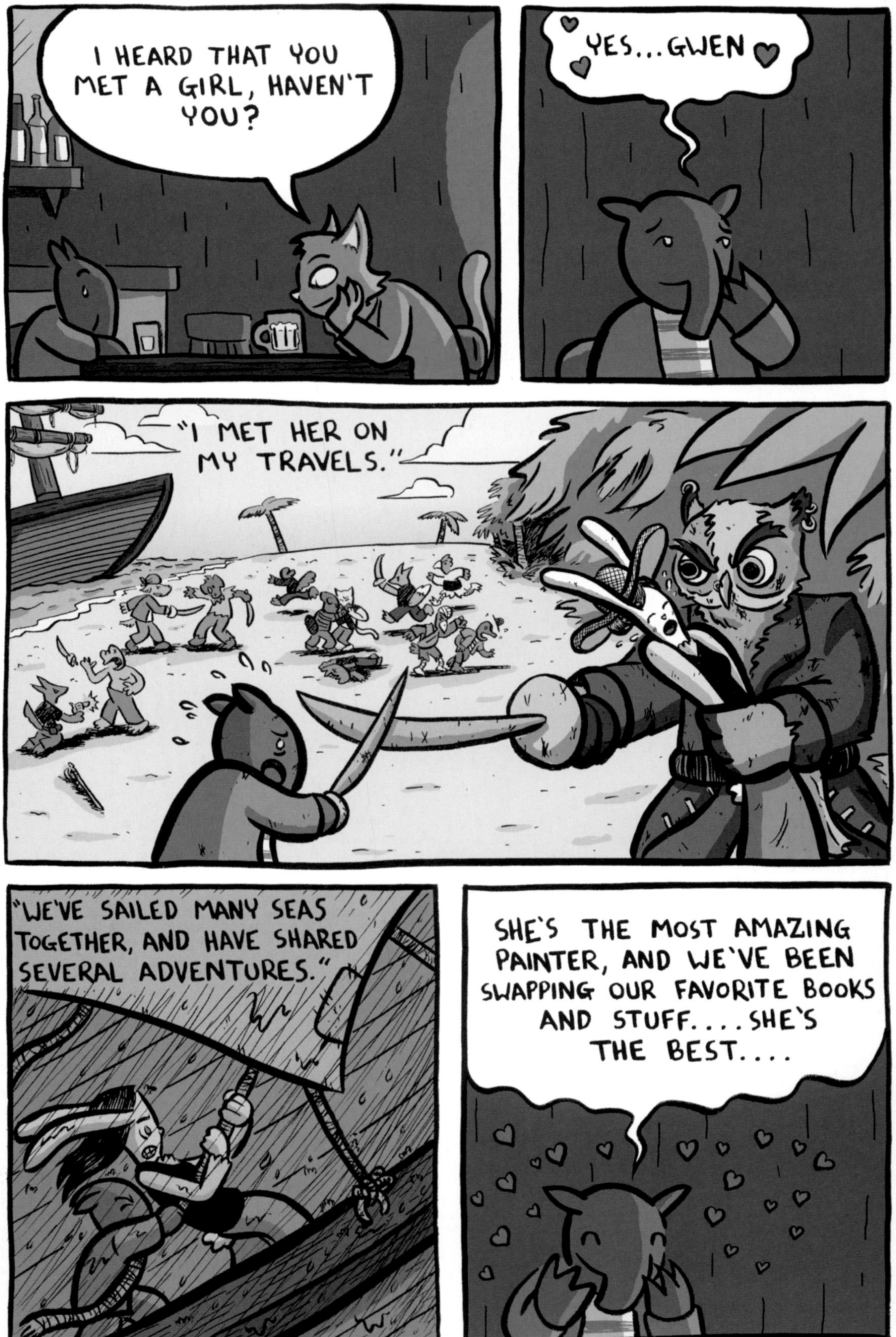
I HEARD THAT YOU MET A GIRL, HAVEN'T YOU?
YES...GWEN
"I MET HER ON MY TRAVELS."
"WE'VE SAILED MANY SEAS TOGETHER, AND HAVE SHARED SEVERAL ADVENTURES."
SHE'S THE MOST AMAZING PAINTER, AND WE'VE BEEN SWAPPING OUR FAVORITE BOOKS AND STUFF....SHE'S THE BEST....

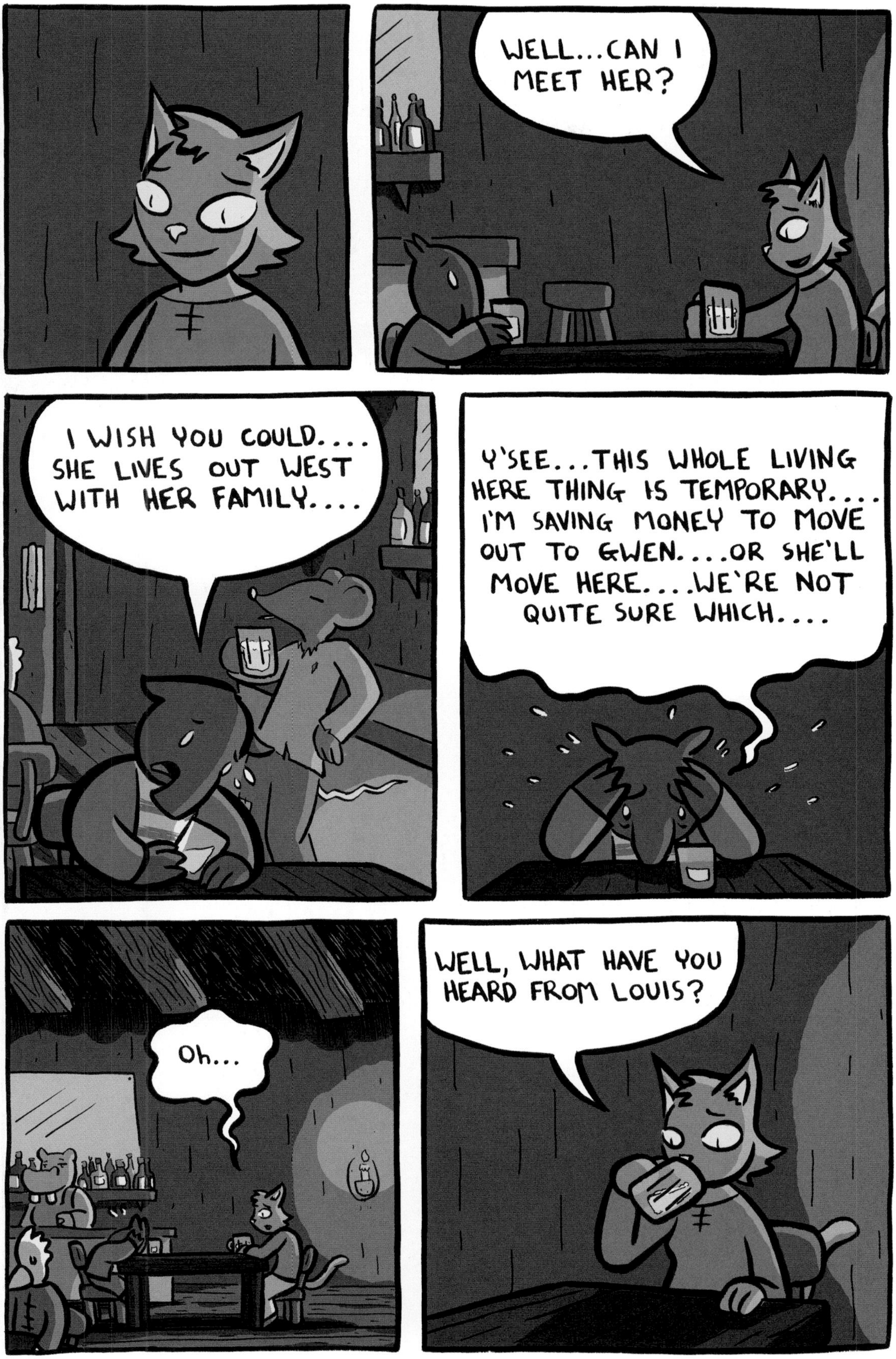
WELL...CAN I MEET HER?
I WISH YOU COULD.... SHE LIVES OUT WEST WITH HER FAMILY....
Y'SEE...THIS WHOLE LIVING HERE THING IS TEMPORARY.... I'M SAVING MONEY TO MOVE OUT TO GWEN....OR SHE'LL MOVE HERE....WE'RE NOT QUITE SURE WHICH....
Oh...
WELL, WHAT HAVE YOU HEARD FROM LOUIS?

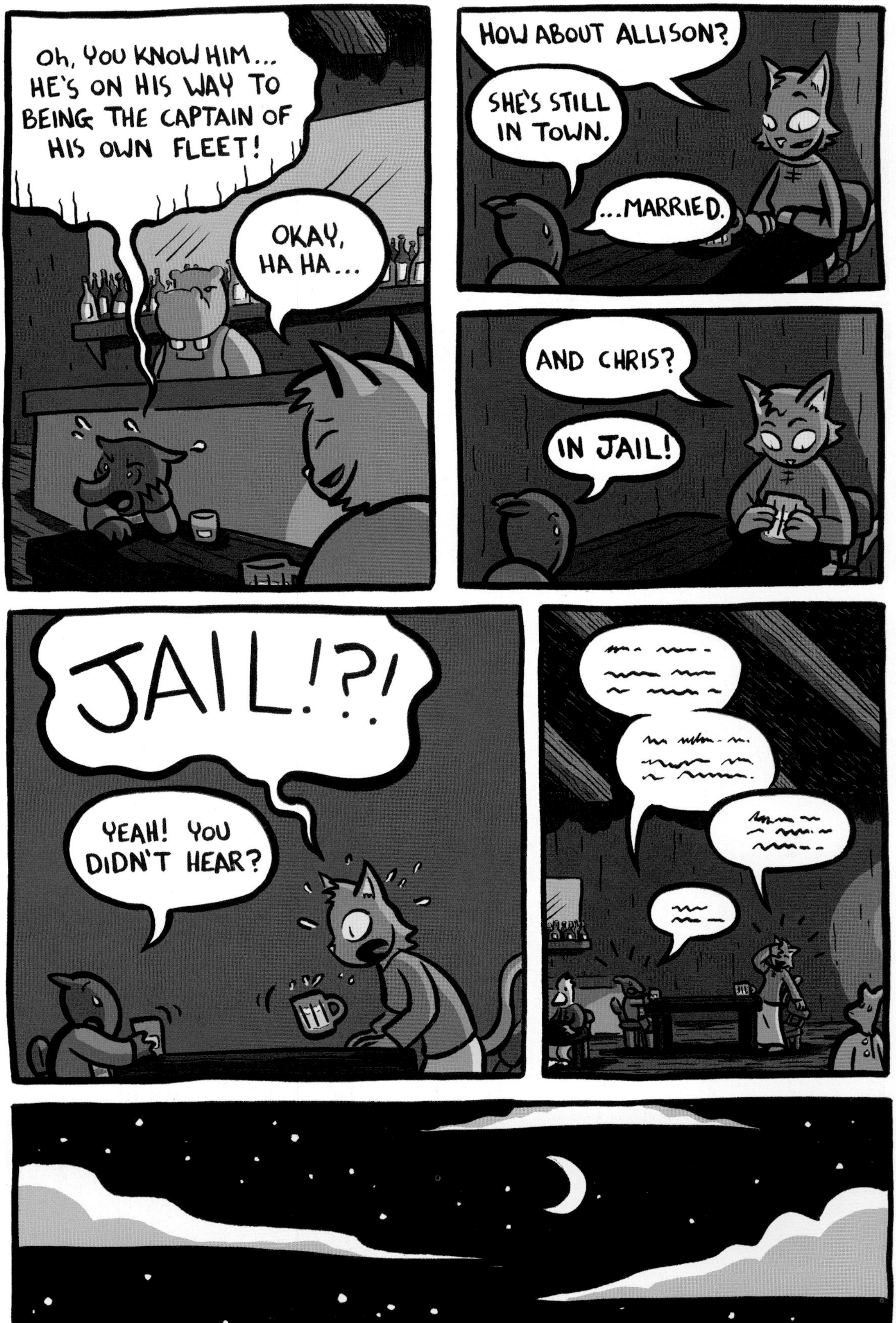

Oh, YOU KNOW HIM... HE'S ON HIS WAY TO BEING THE CAPTAIN OF HIS OWN FLEET!
OKAY, HA HA...
HOW ABOUT ALLISON?
SHE'S STILL IN TOWN.
...MARRIED.
AND CHRIS?
IN JAIL!
JAIL!?!
YEAH! YOU DIDN'T HEAR?

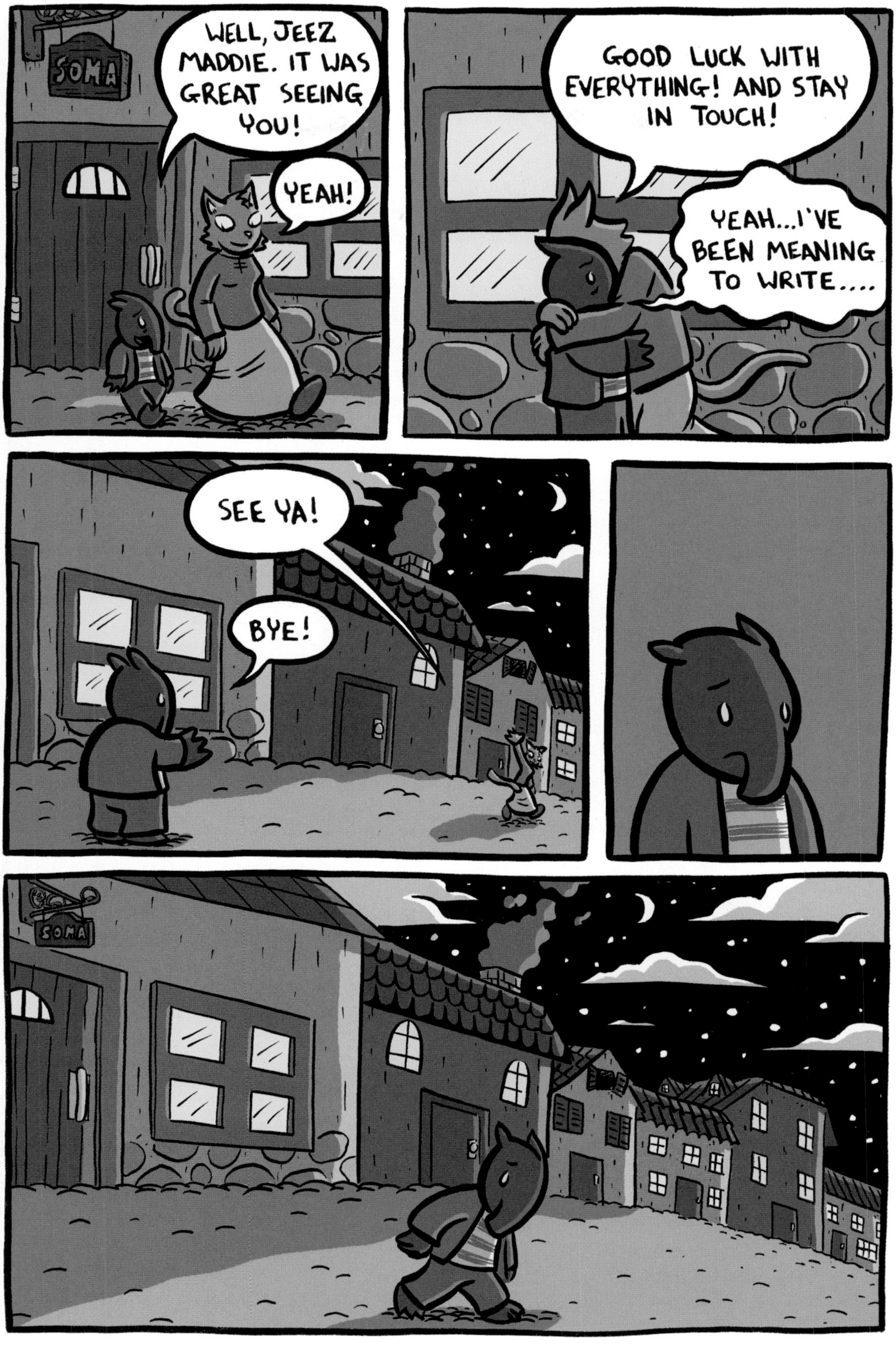
SOMA
WELL, JEEZ MADDIE. IT WAS GREAT SEEING YOU!
YEAH!
GOOD LUCK WITH EVERYTHING! AND STAY IN TOUCH!
YEAH...I'VE BEEN MEANING TO WRITE....
SEE YA!
BYE!
SOMA

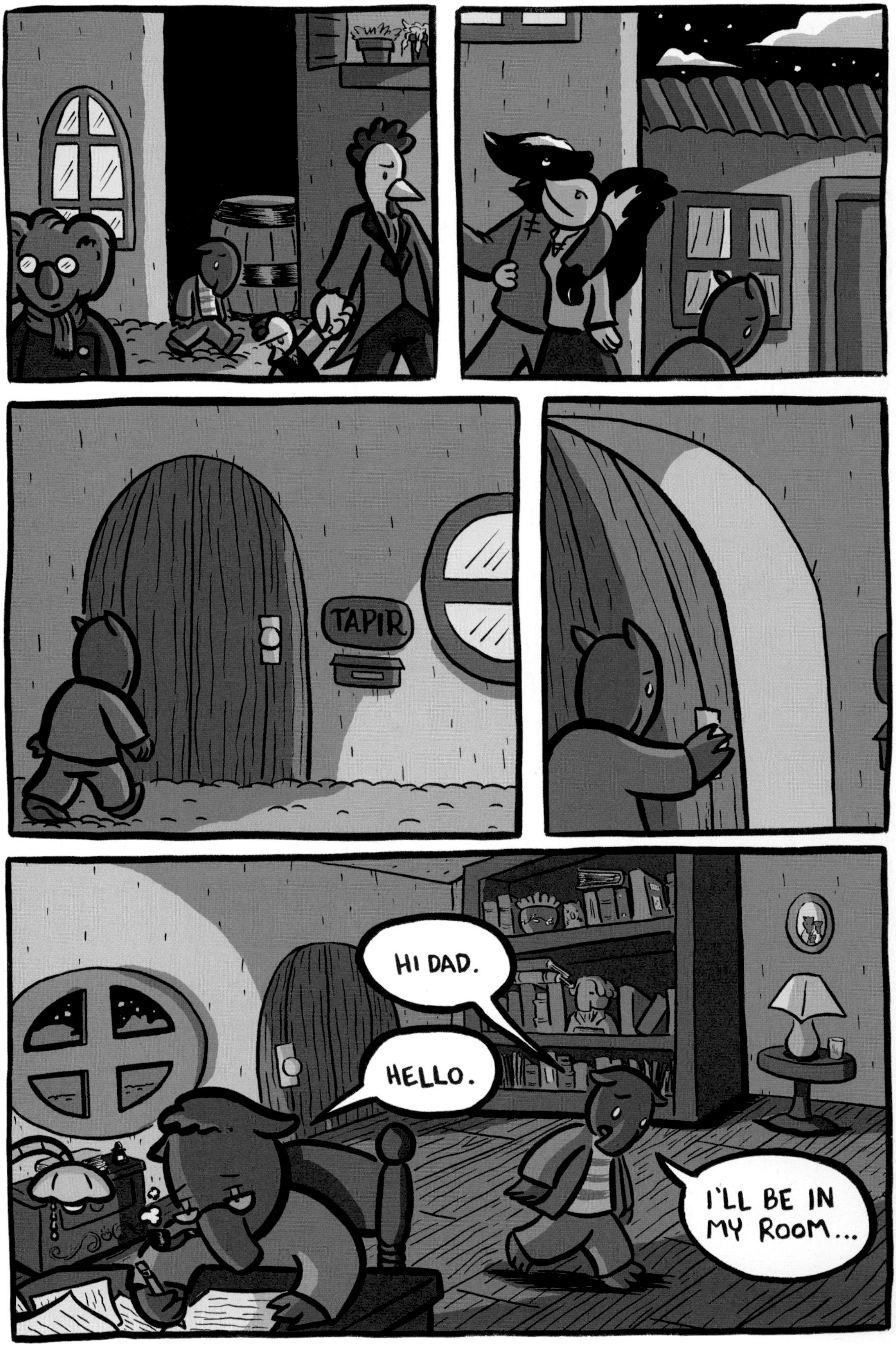
TAPIR
HI DAD.
HELLO.
I'LL BE IN MY ROOM...

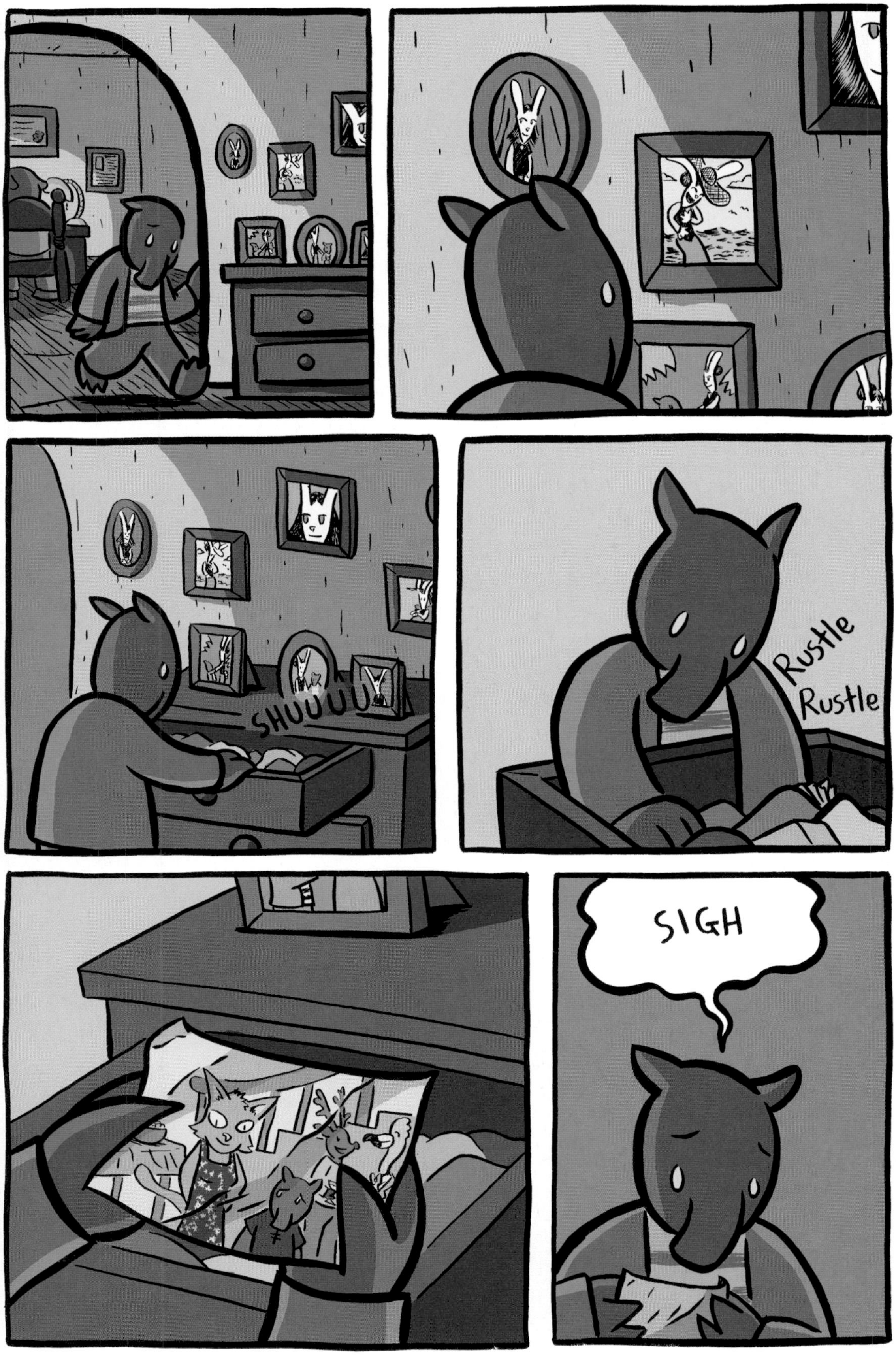
SHUUUU
Rustle
Rustle
SIGH

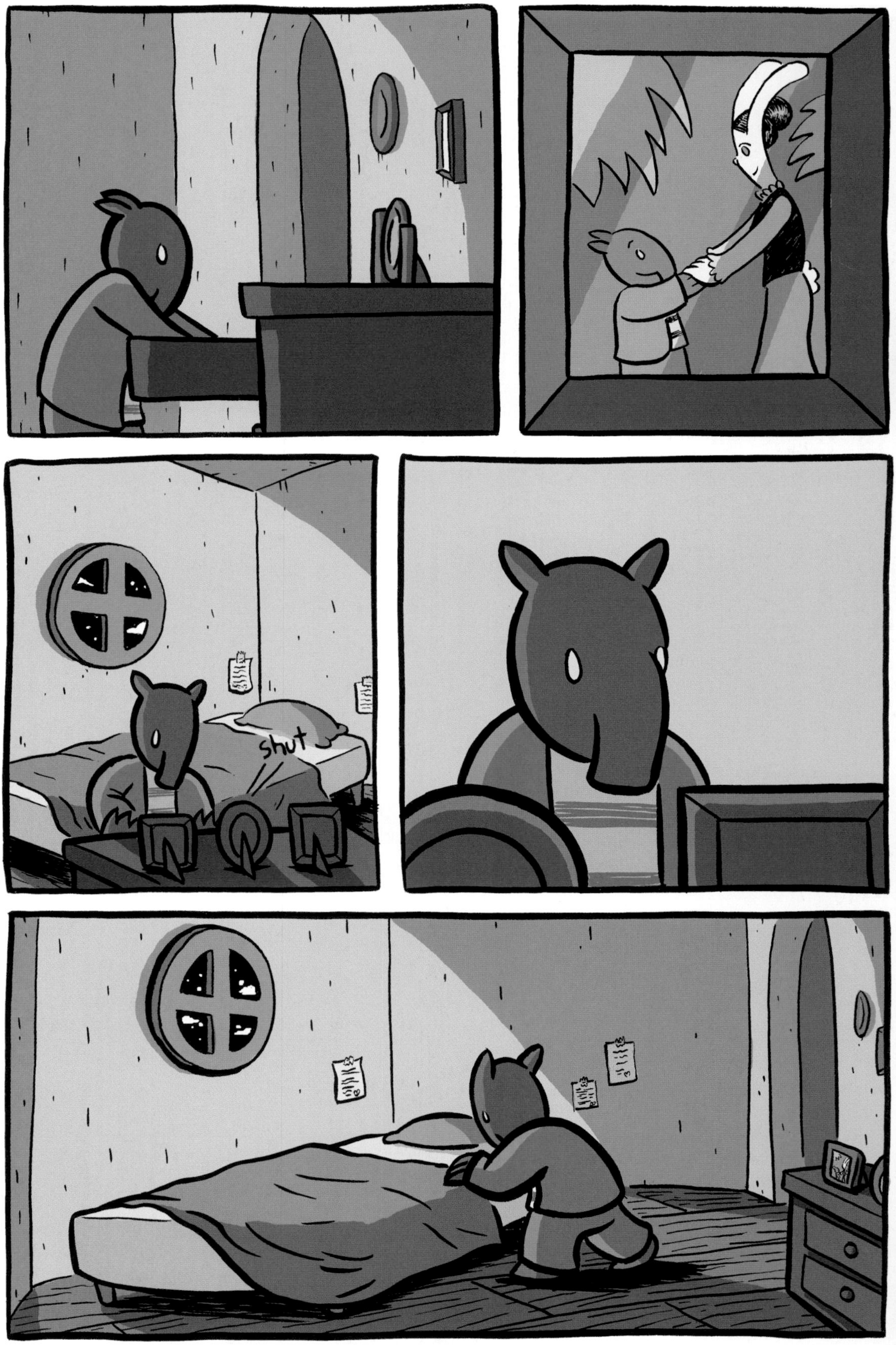
shut

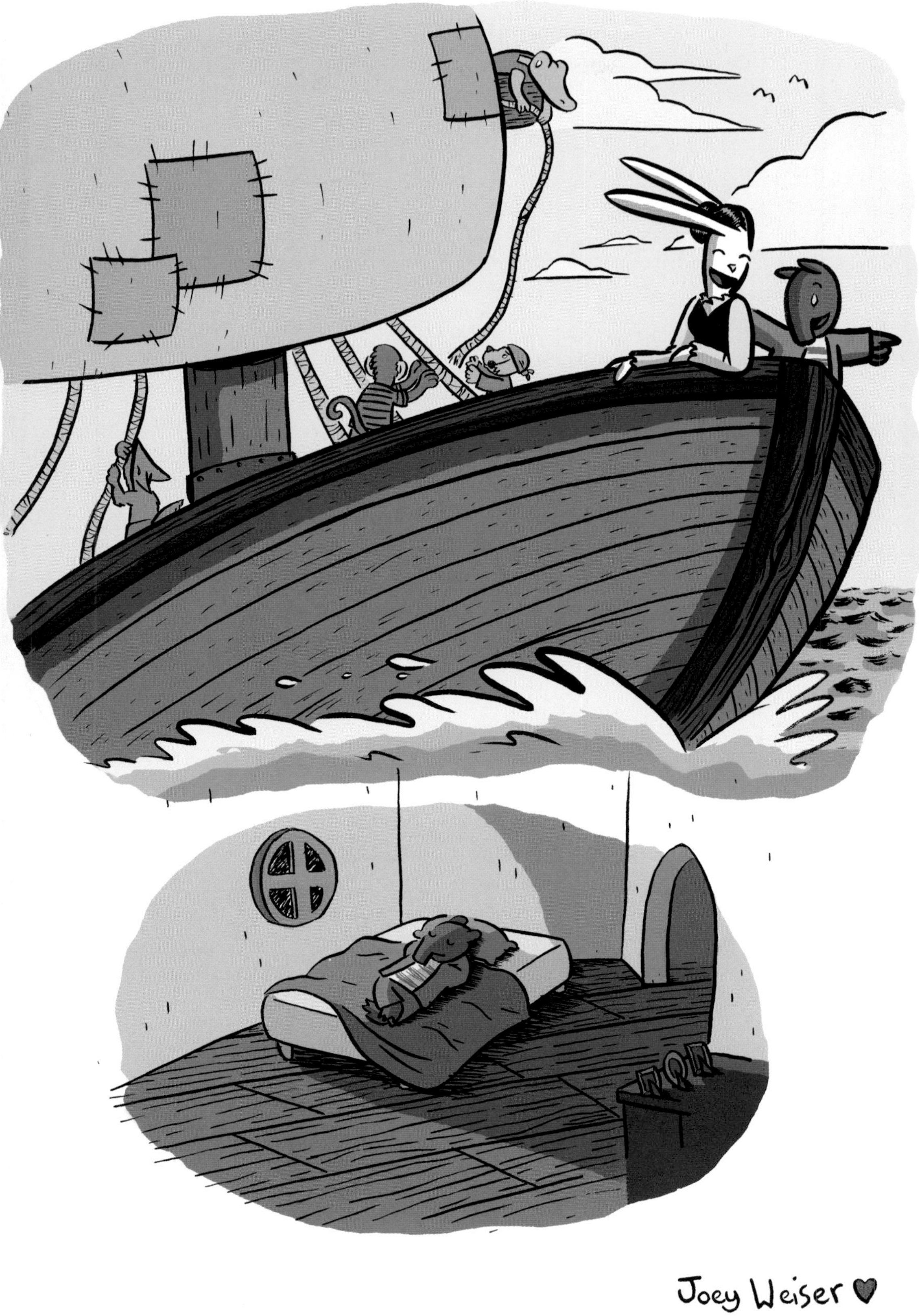

Joey Weiser ♥

Tripod

Story
Bannister

·

Art
Bannister & Joel Carroll

·

Colors
Corentin Jaffré

·

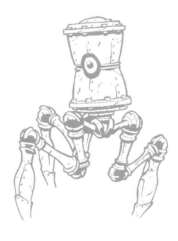

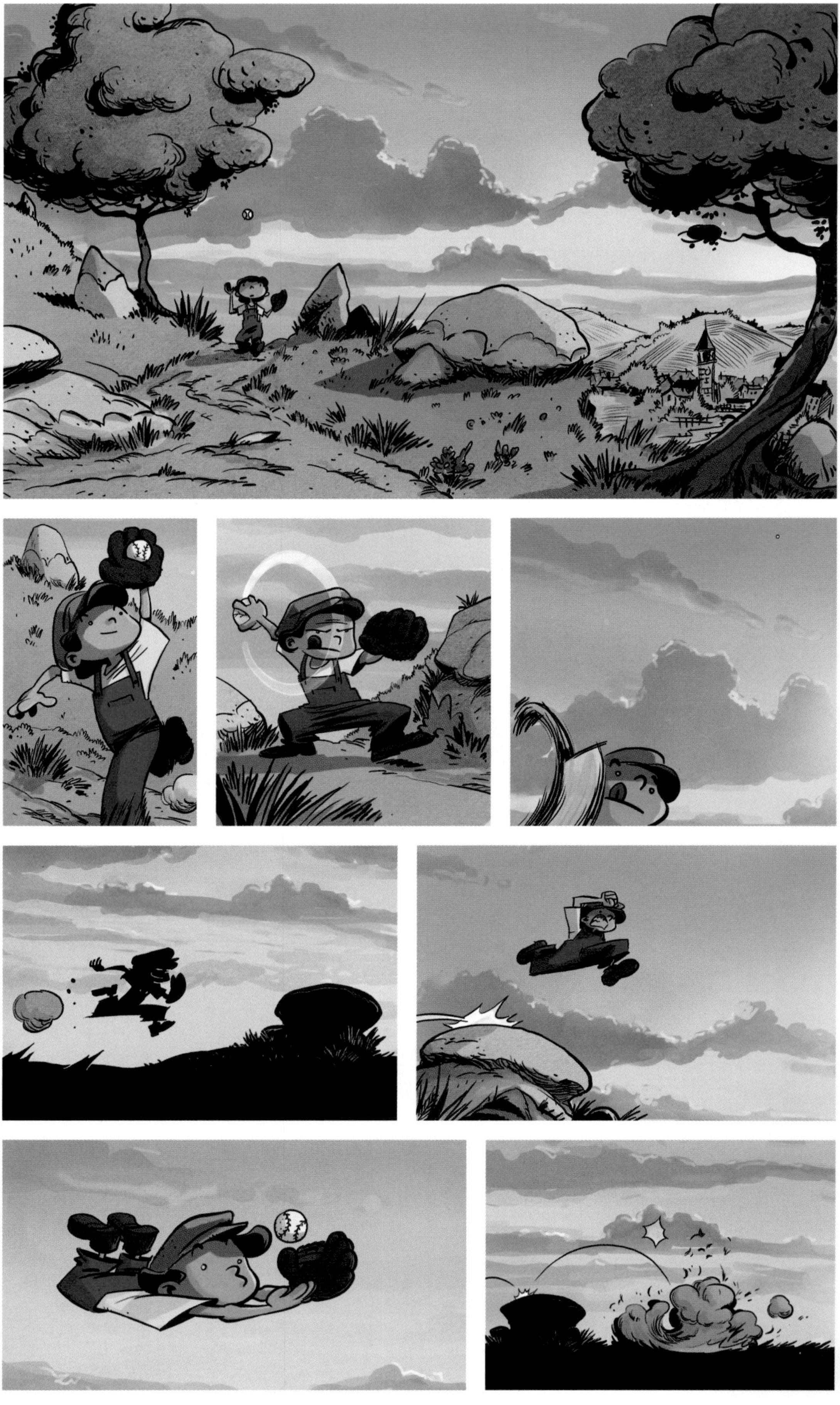

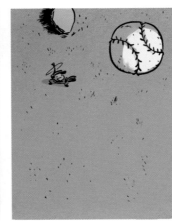

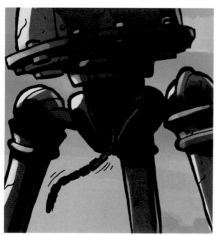

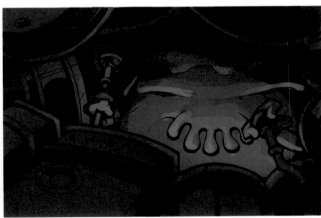

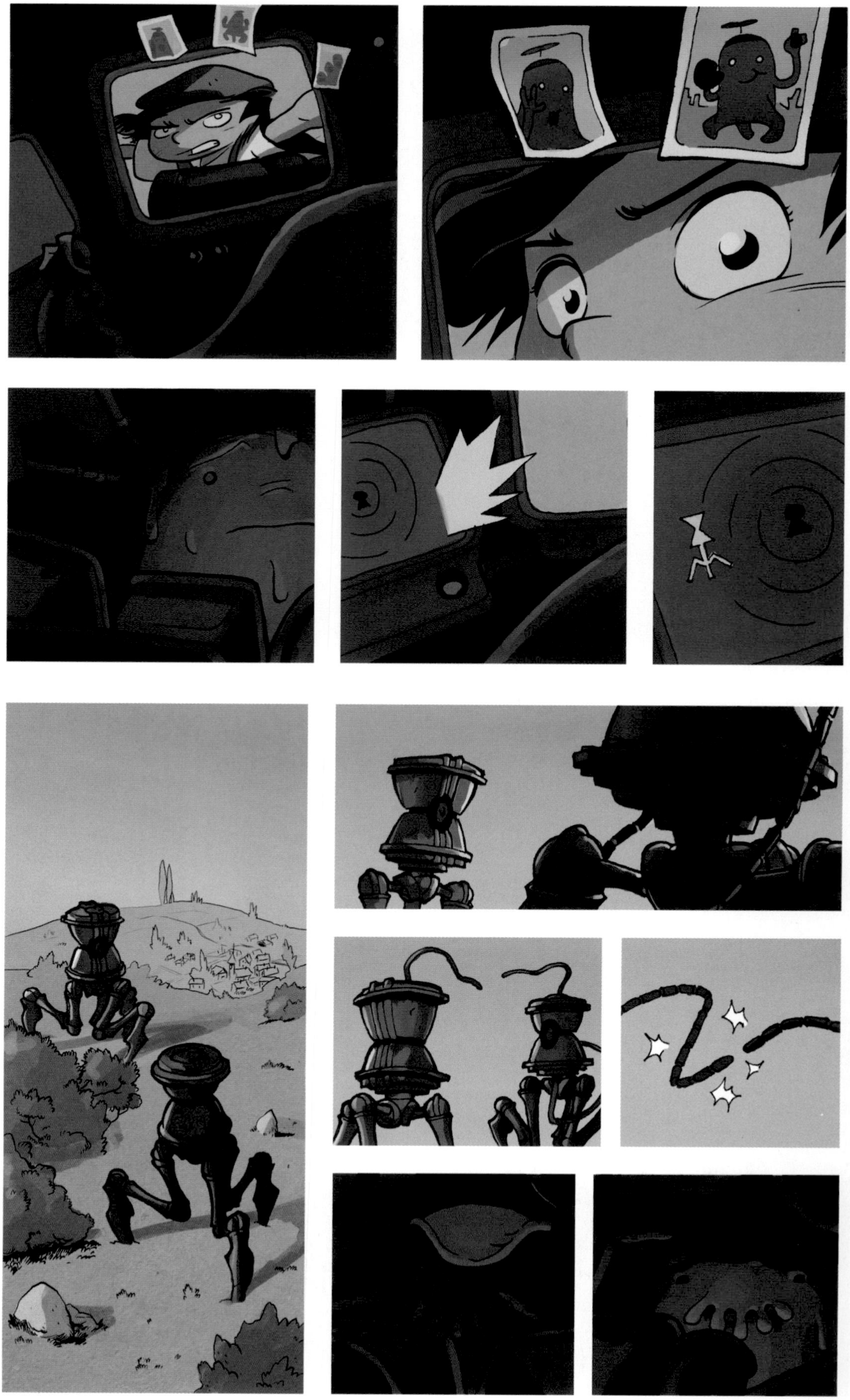

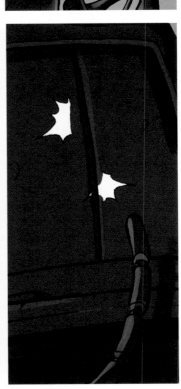
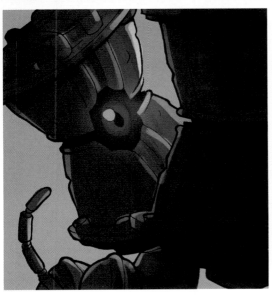

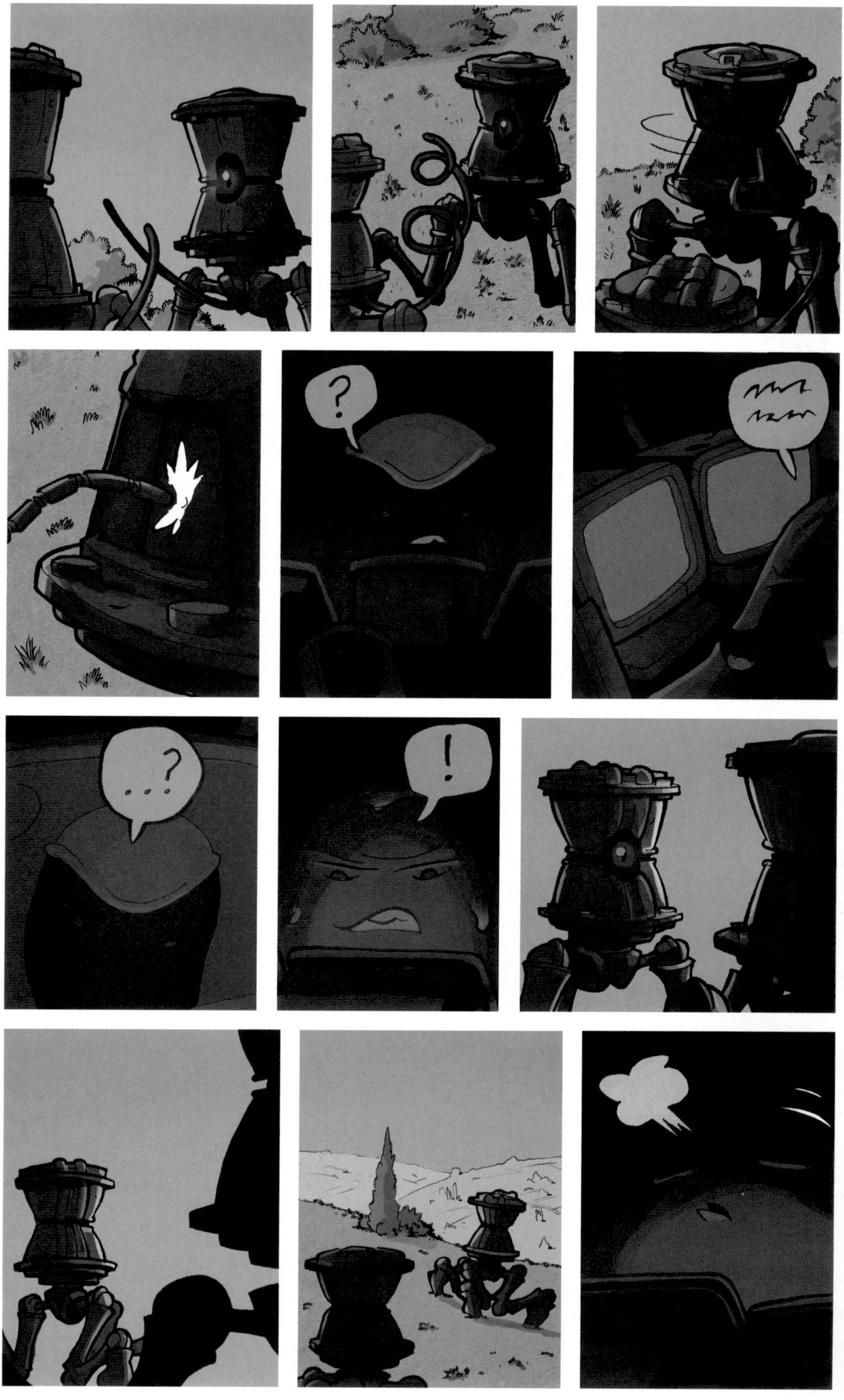
?
...?
!

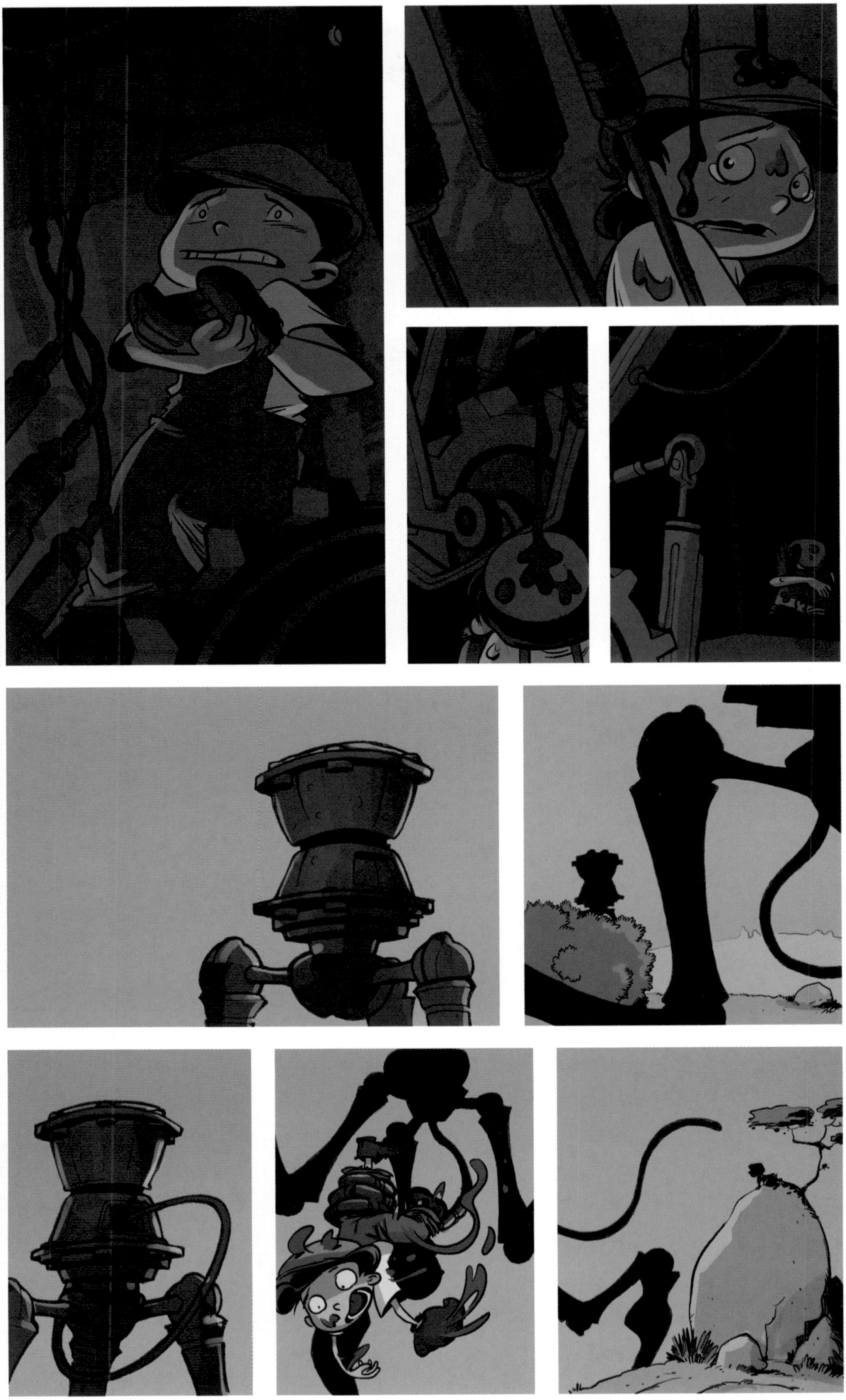

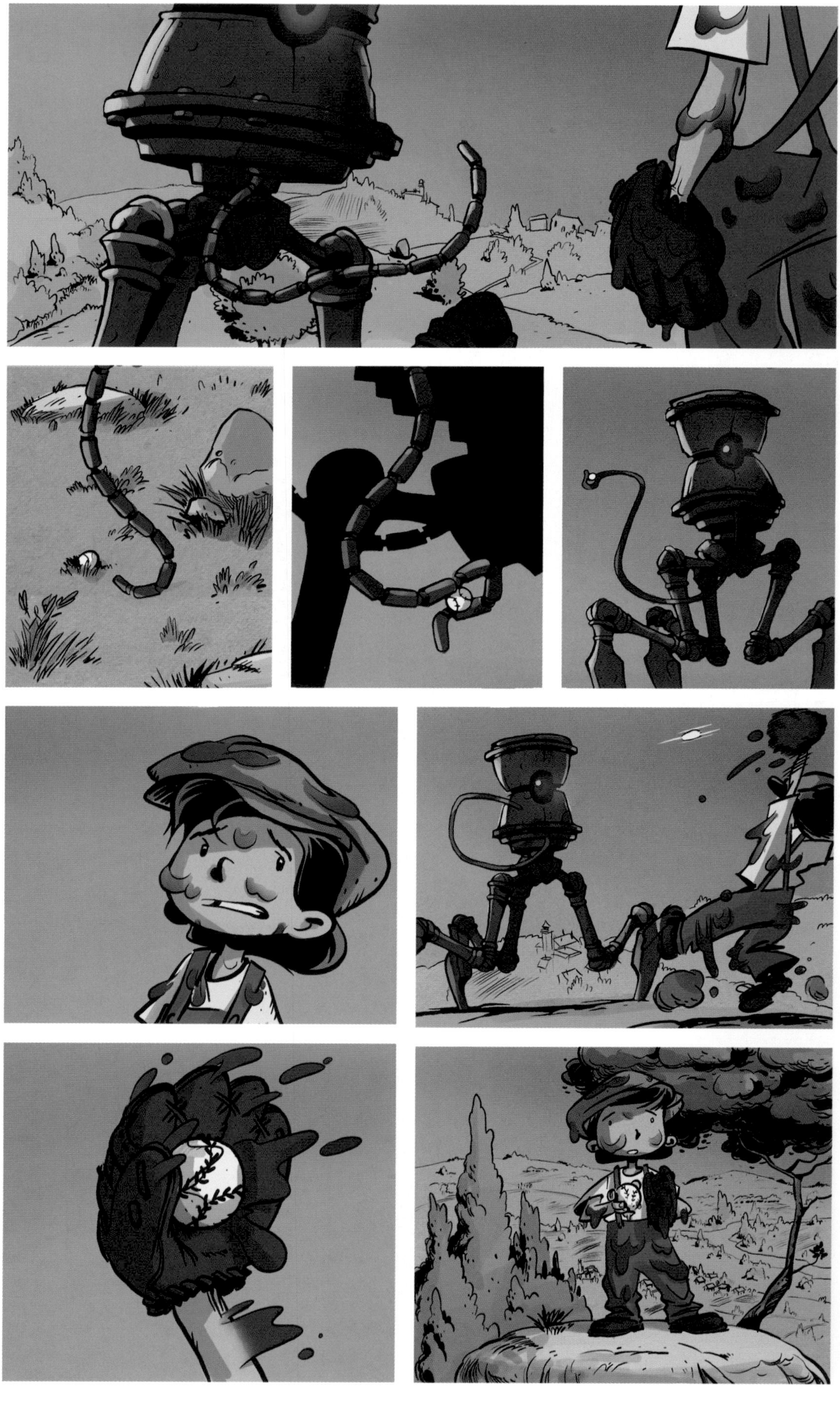

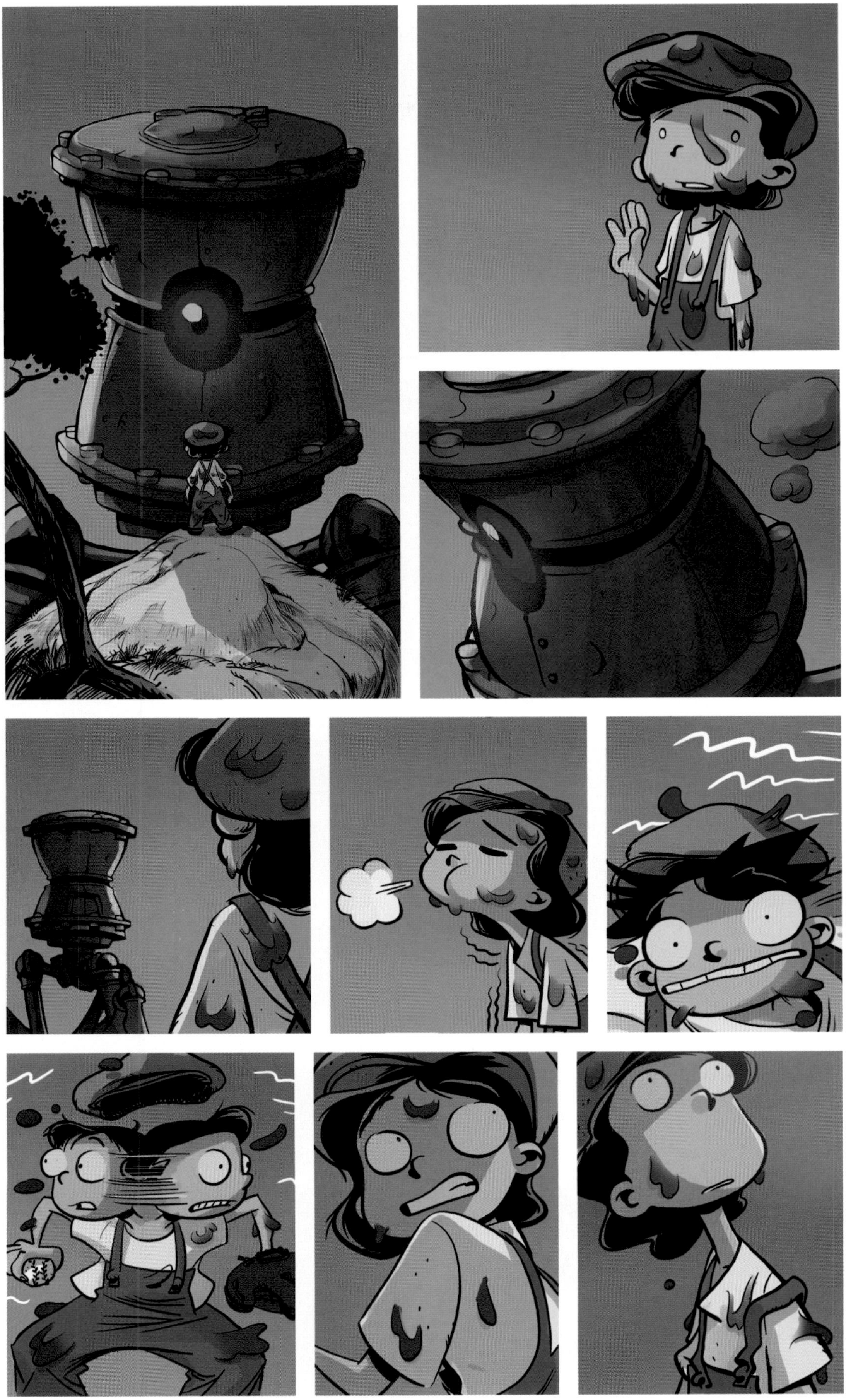

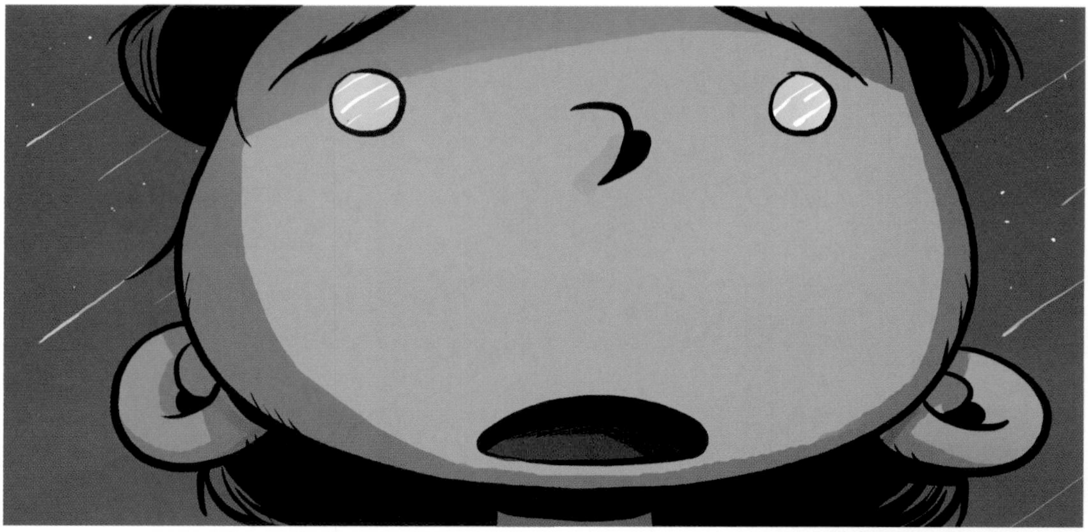

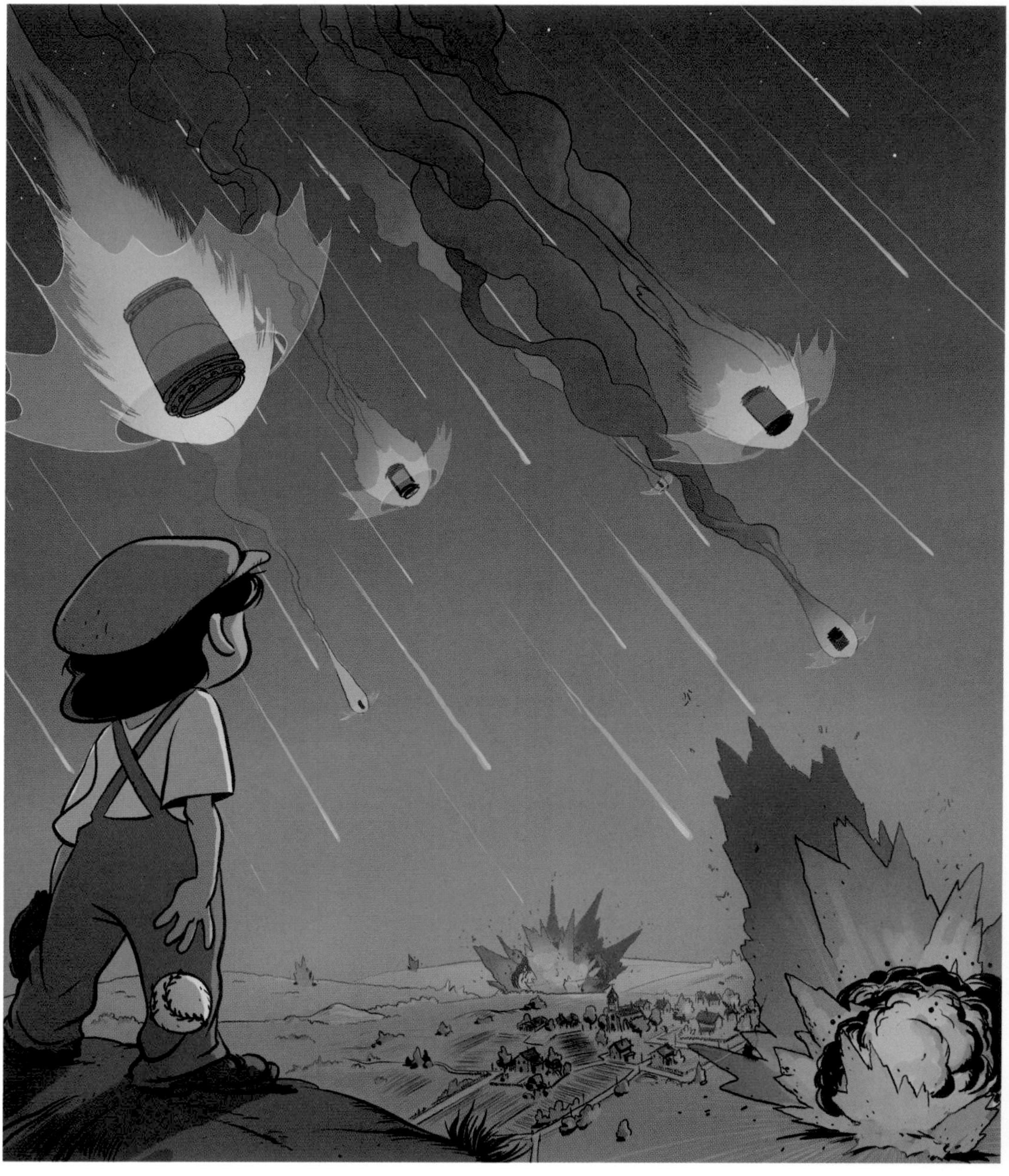

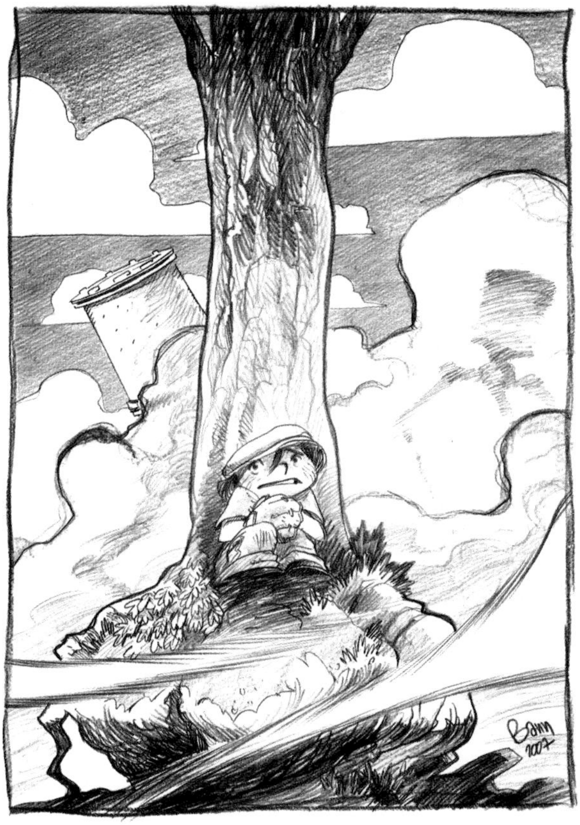
Bam
2007

The Vampyres of Salem

By Azad Injejikian

Although no one knows for certain why the plain, unremarkable
mining town of Salem was abandoned a century ago,
every account of its decline agrees on one point.

It began with the birth of
a child named Simon Webster.

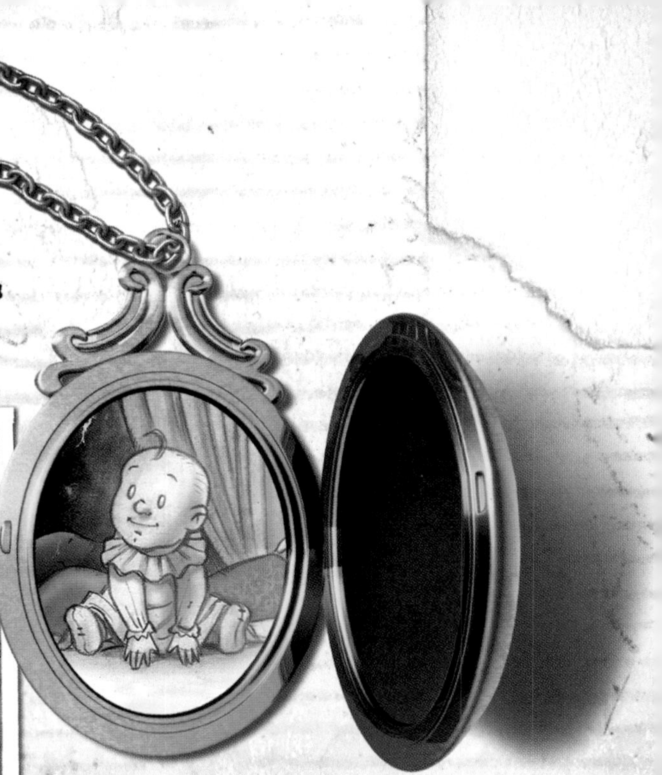

Simon was a striking baby whose eyes shone unlike the dull coal his father culled daily, but brilliant like finely polished diamonds.

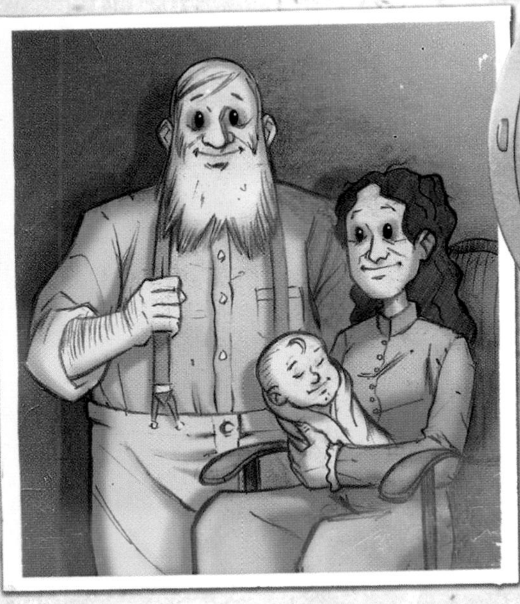

Word of Simon spread quickly throughout Salem and soon the happy parents' home was crowded with well-wishers hoping to catch a glimpse of little Simon and his pretty, shiny eyes.

Some reckoned that Simon could well be the prettiest son Salem had ever sired.

Old Joe even joked that Simon could well be prettier than not only the town's sons, but many of its daughters as well...

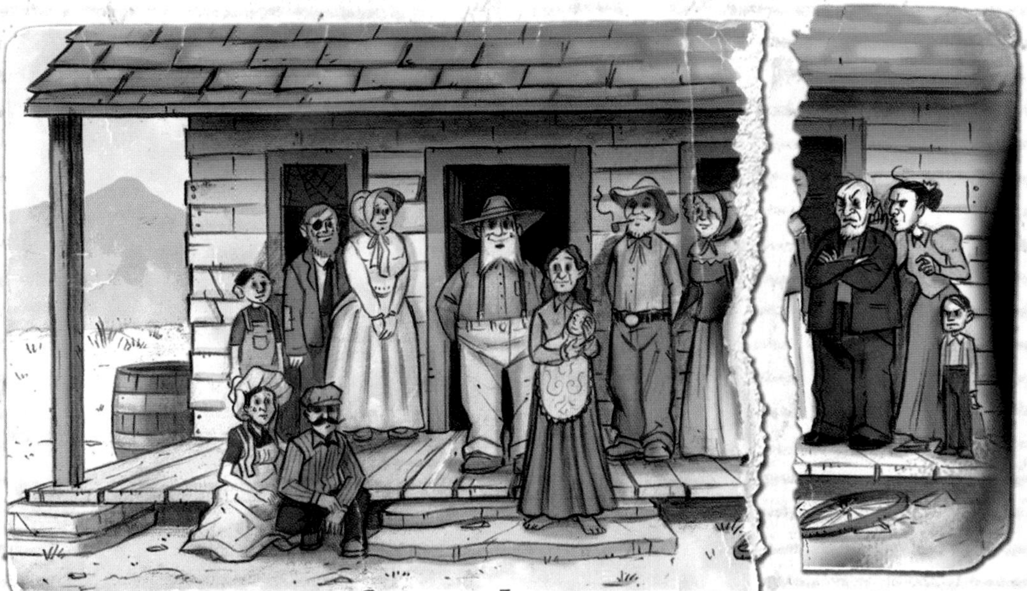

...but not all found Old Joe so funny.

Many envied Simon and his parents.

The people of Salem lived plain, unremarkable lives and the Websters were saddled with neither of those undesirable distinctions.

The worst were the expectant mothers who held high hopes that they too would be blessed with such adorable offspring that their neighbors would finally take interest in them.

But when nearly one year passed, and not a single child was born to the new mothers as special as Simon...

...their disappointment was more than they could bear.

Conversely, the Websters had long since grown tired of the unwanted attention, and moved far past the outskirts of town to preserve some sense of privacy.

But many mistook this as a sign of contempt.

One by one, resentment and jealousy infected the hearts of the town's folk until all but the happy couple were aware that something was not right.

So it came to pass that on the eve of Simon's first birthday, the fine people of Salem secured a special place in hell for themselves when they held a secret gathering to hatch a nasty plot.

The next morning, the daughters of Salem, dressed in their finest bonnets and frocks, were herded to Simon's home to offer gifts, well wishes, and most important,

birthday kisses.

"Kisses for Simon, tra la la,"
they sang as they stood line
waiting their turns.

"A kiss can be nice,
true and fair,
but the best ones
are served not in
singles, but pairs."

A kiss for each of Simon's
pretty, pretty eyes.

One after another,
every daughter took
their turn and
did their duty...

...one after another...
...after another...
...after another...
...after another...
...after another...
...after another...
...after another...
...after another...
...after another...
...after another...
...after another...

...Until their evil deed was done.

It wasn't until their guests had left that Simon's
parents made the gruesome discovery:

The acrid kisses of the town's daughters had rendered poor Simon's eyes lame. No longer did they shine like finely polished diamonds to be envied, but instead were unremarkable and dull,
not unlike the coal
his heartbroken father
begrudgingly culled
every
single day.

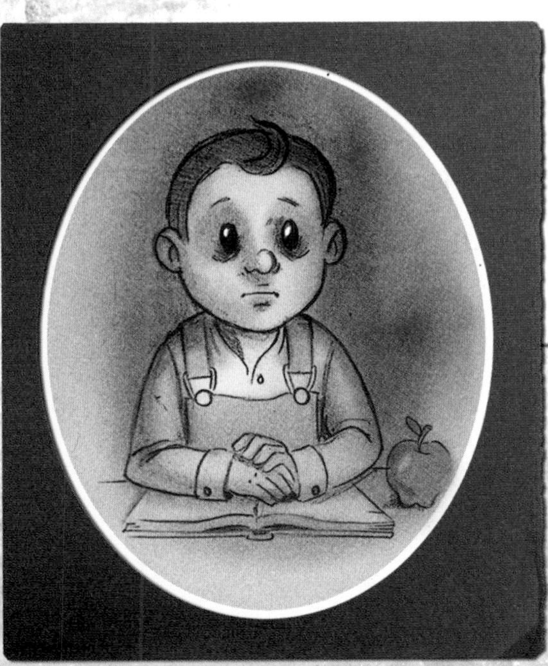

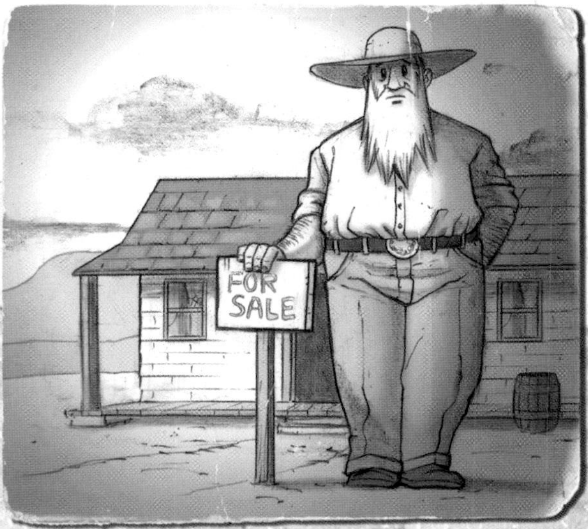
FOR SALE

Legend has it that it wasn't long after Simon and his family moved from Salem altogether that things took a turn for the worse, and the town was left to the elements.

Some say it was a drought.

Some say the mines went dry.

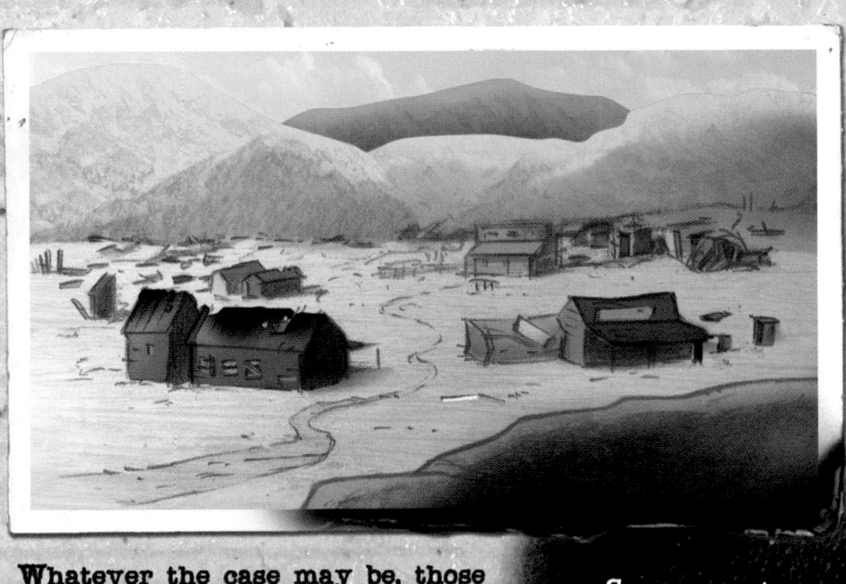

Whatever the case may be, those who were there thought better than to record it for posterity.

Some secrets are best left untold.

The Storm

by Pascal Campion

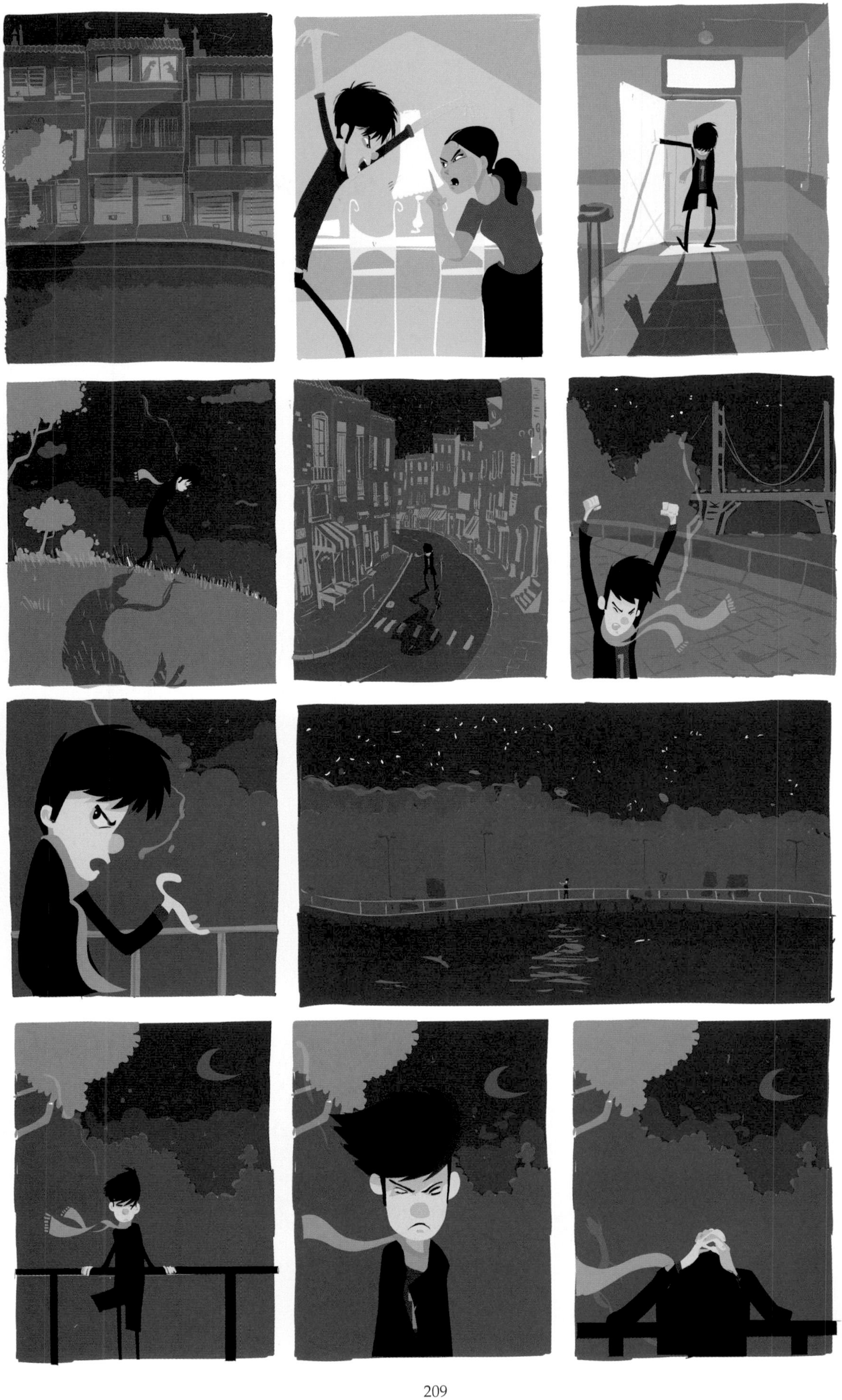

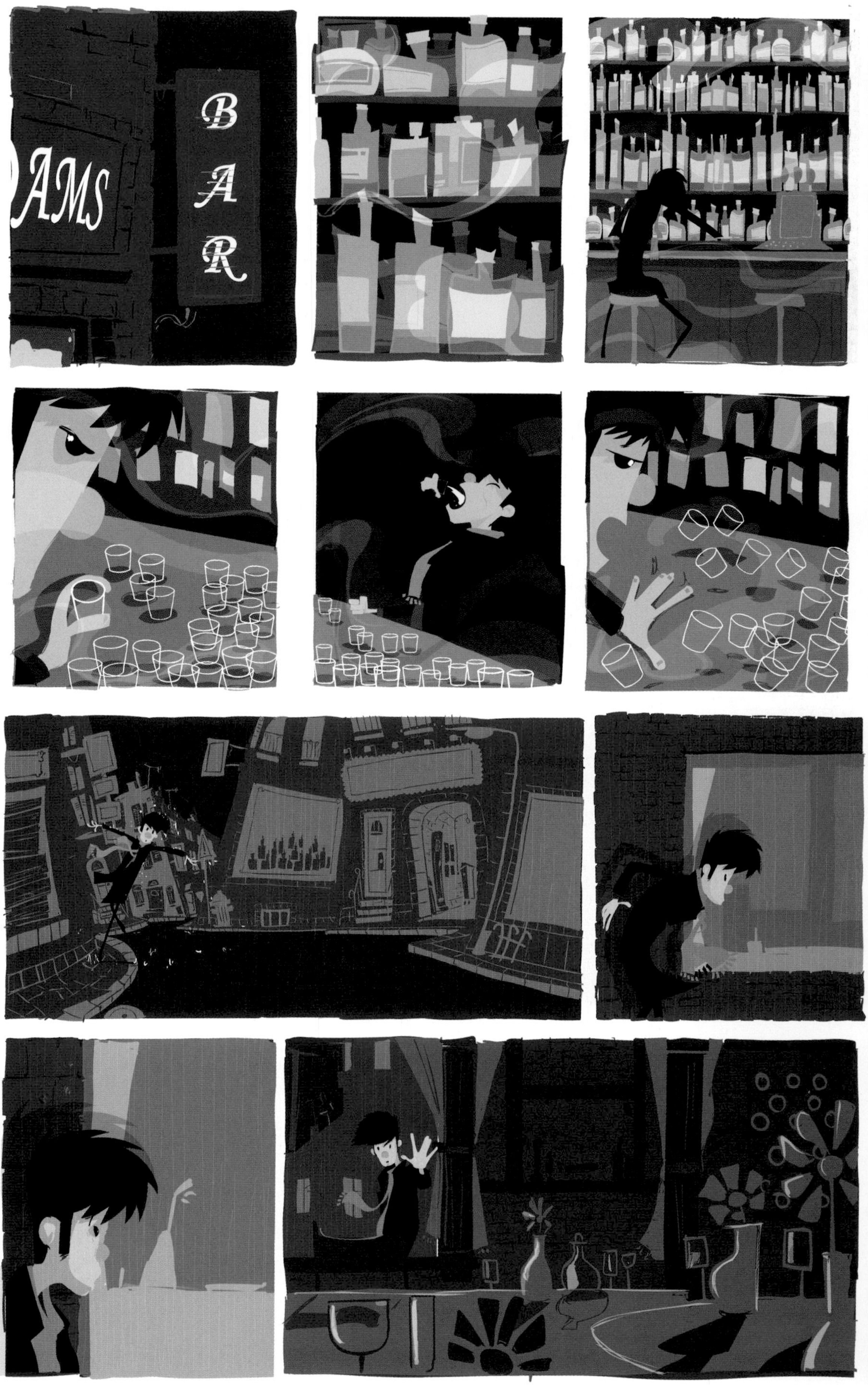
AMS
BAR

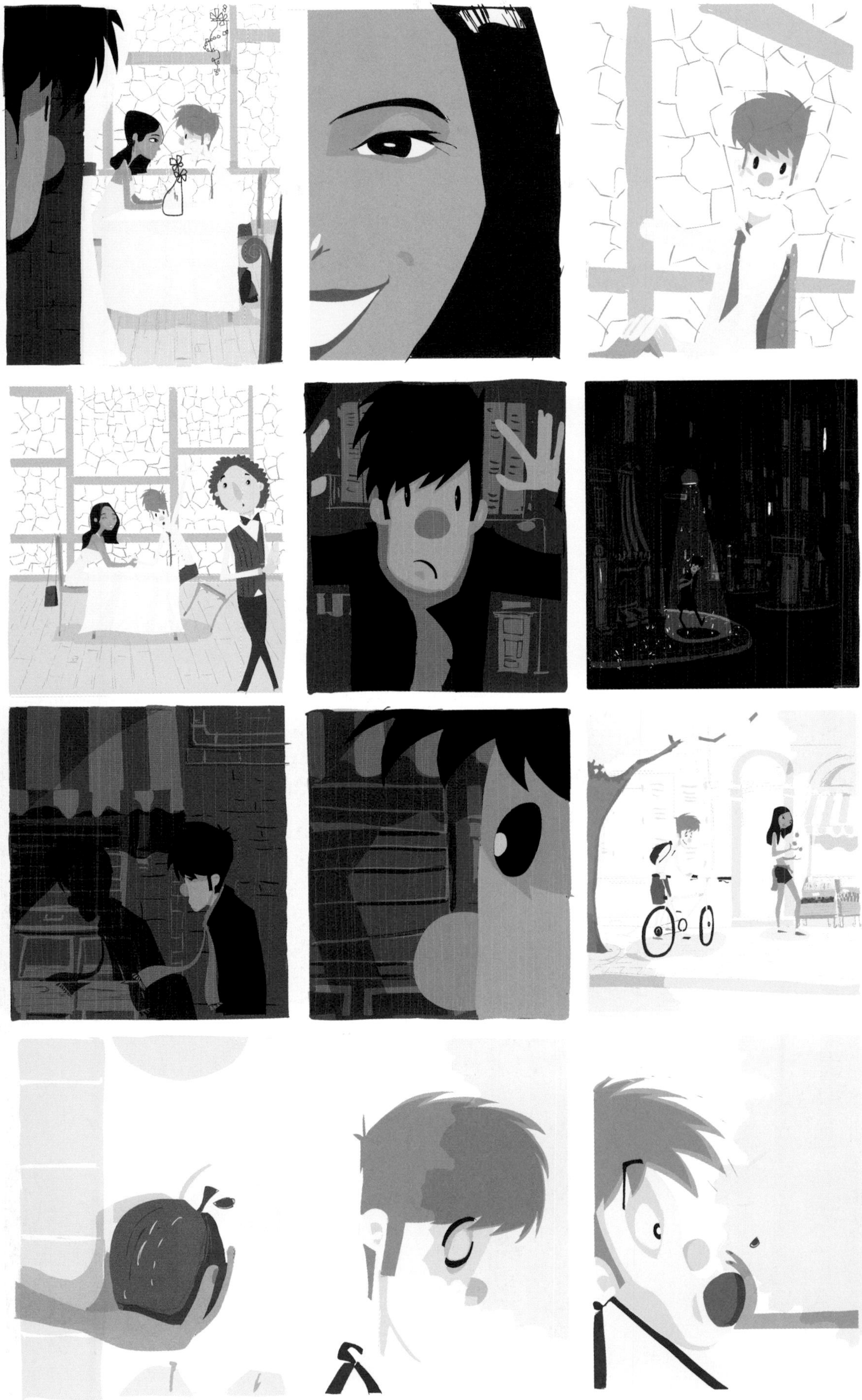

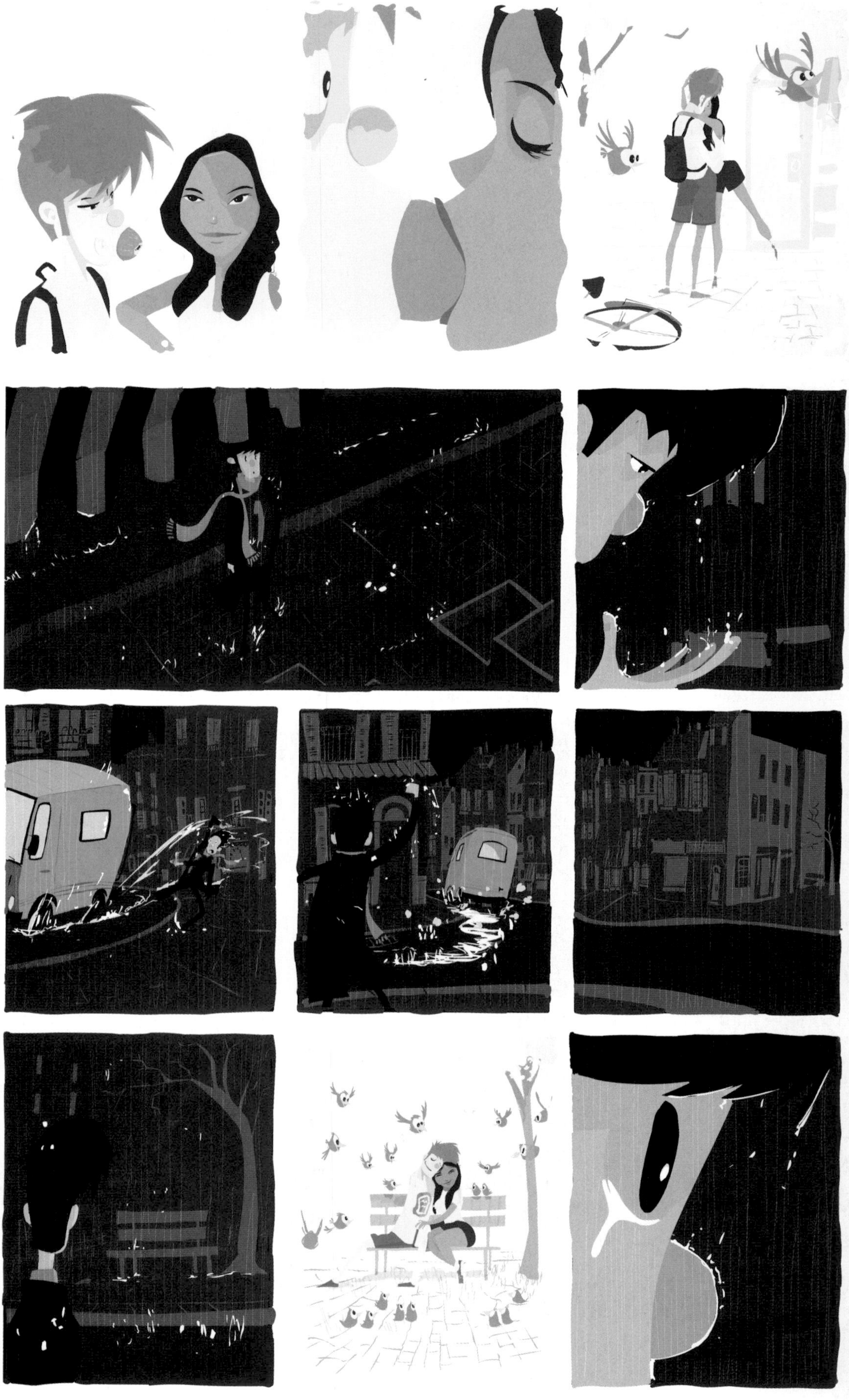

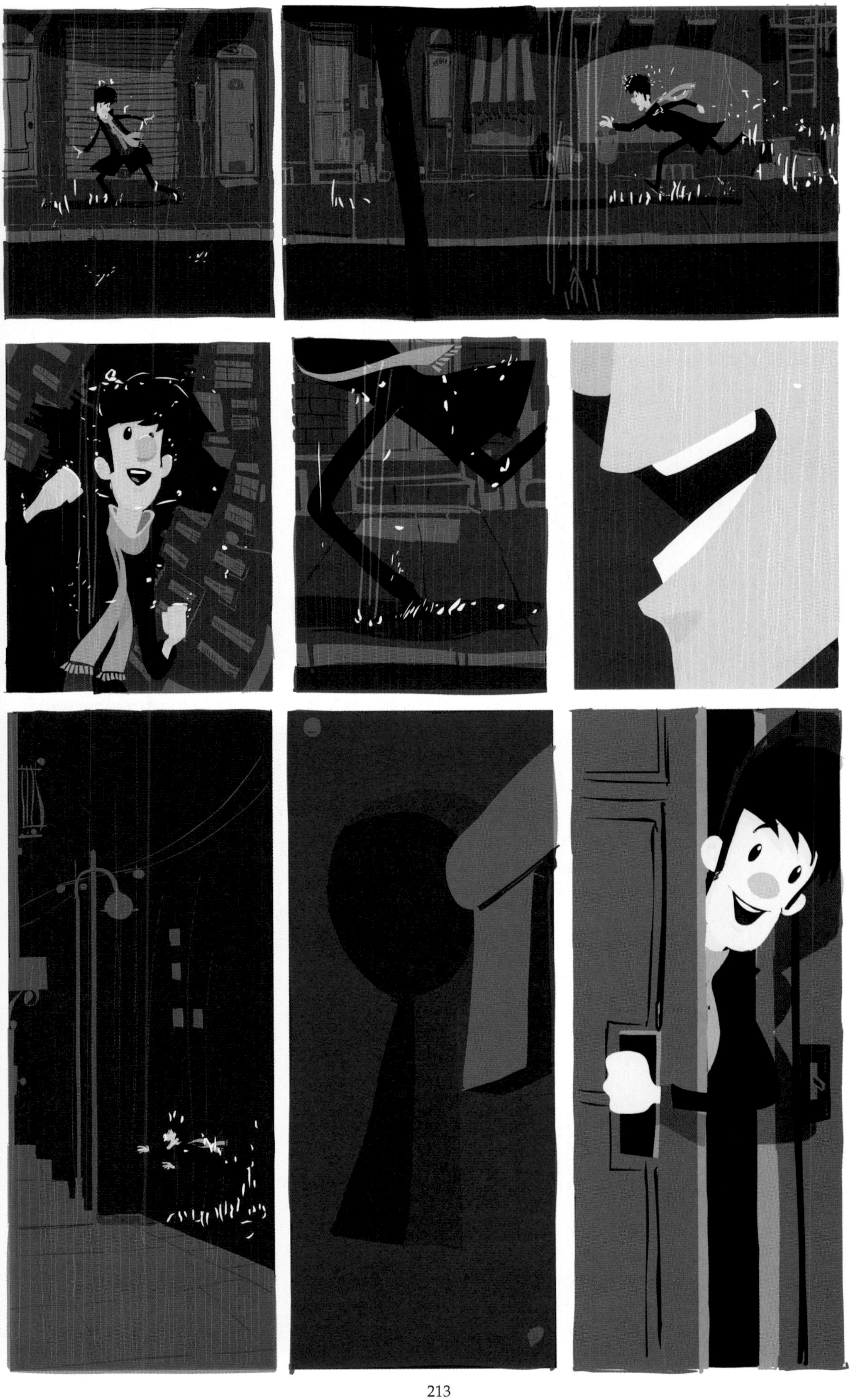

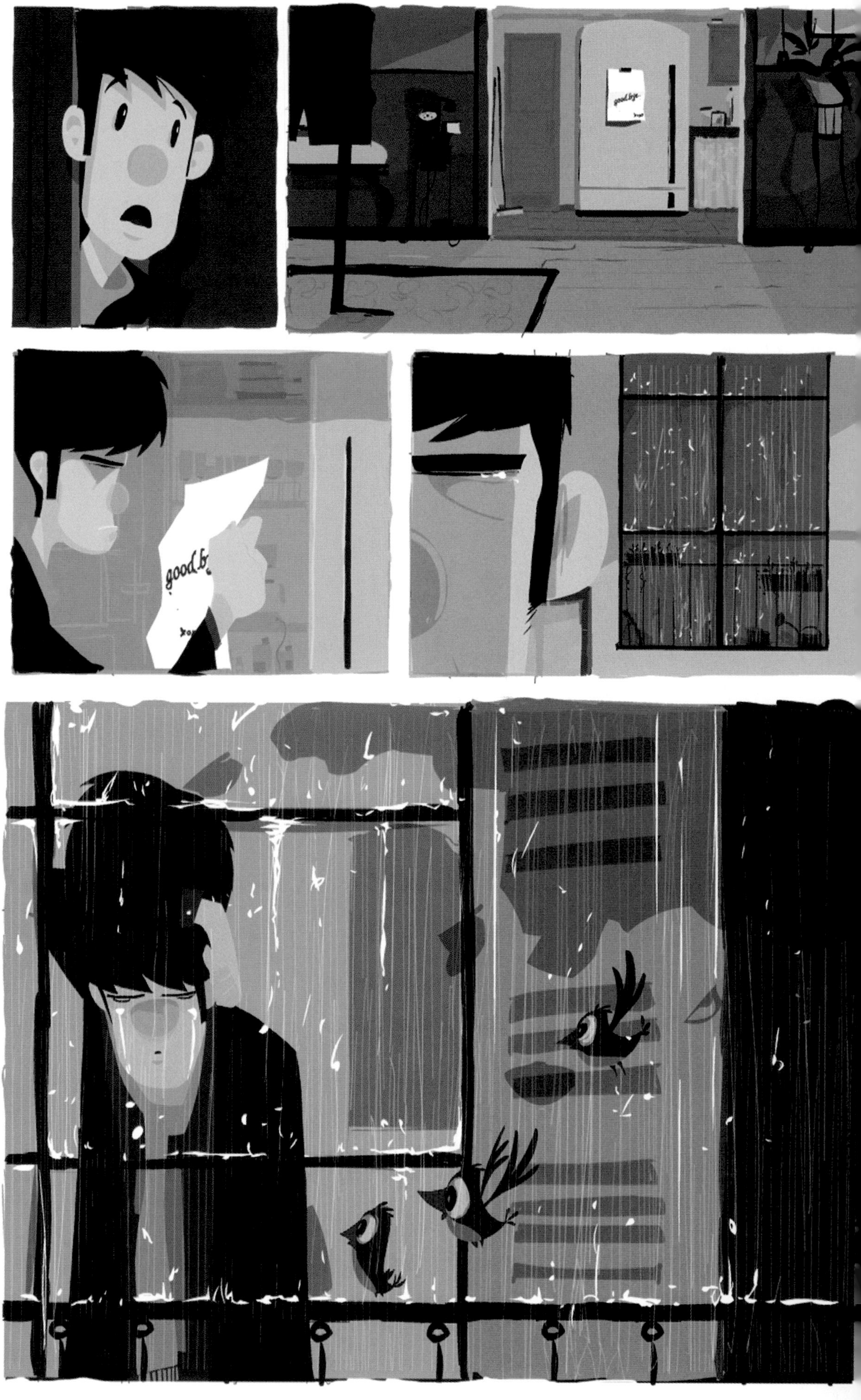
good bye

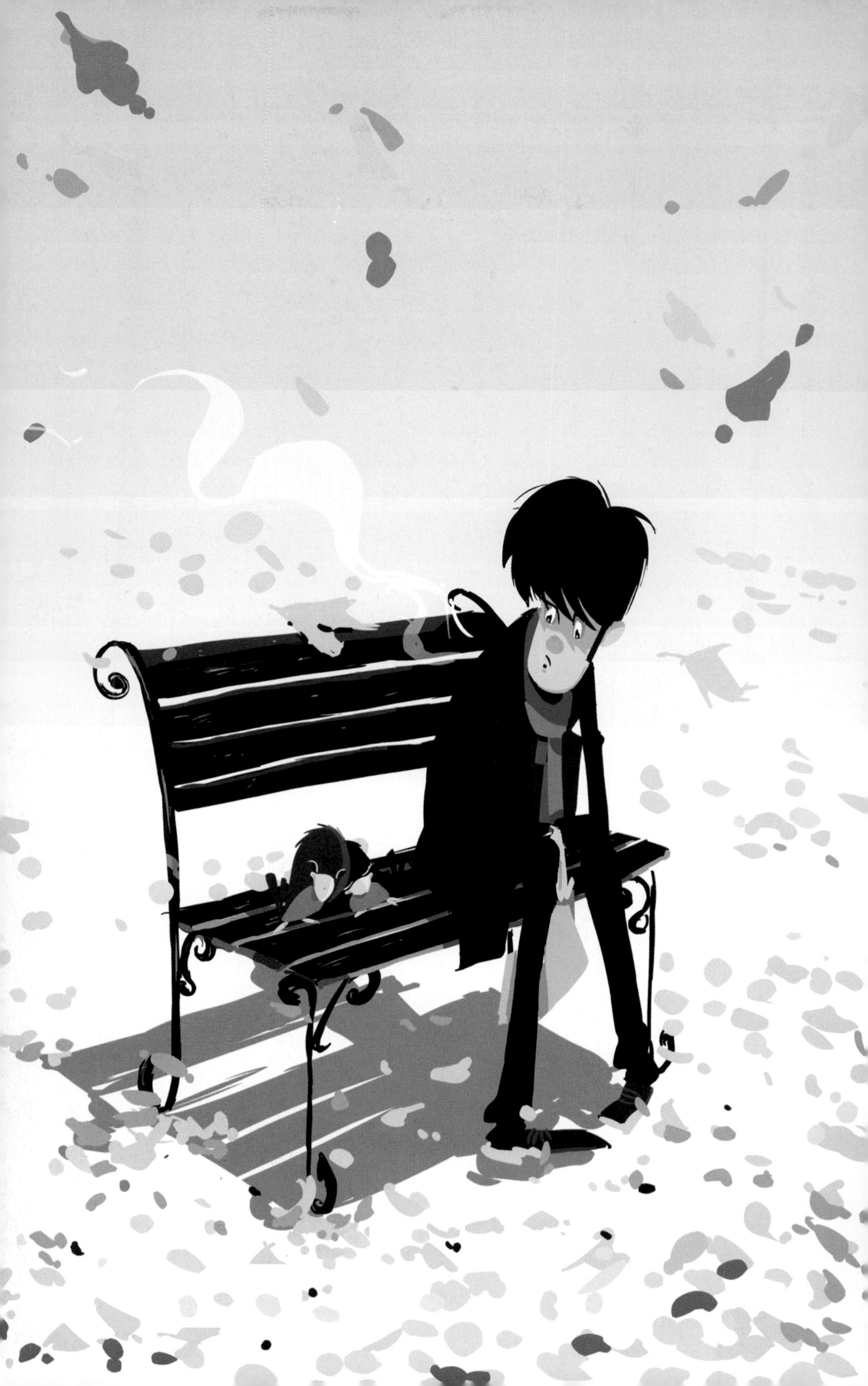

BIGWHEELS

BY:

OVI

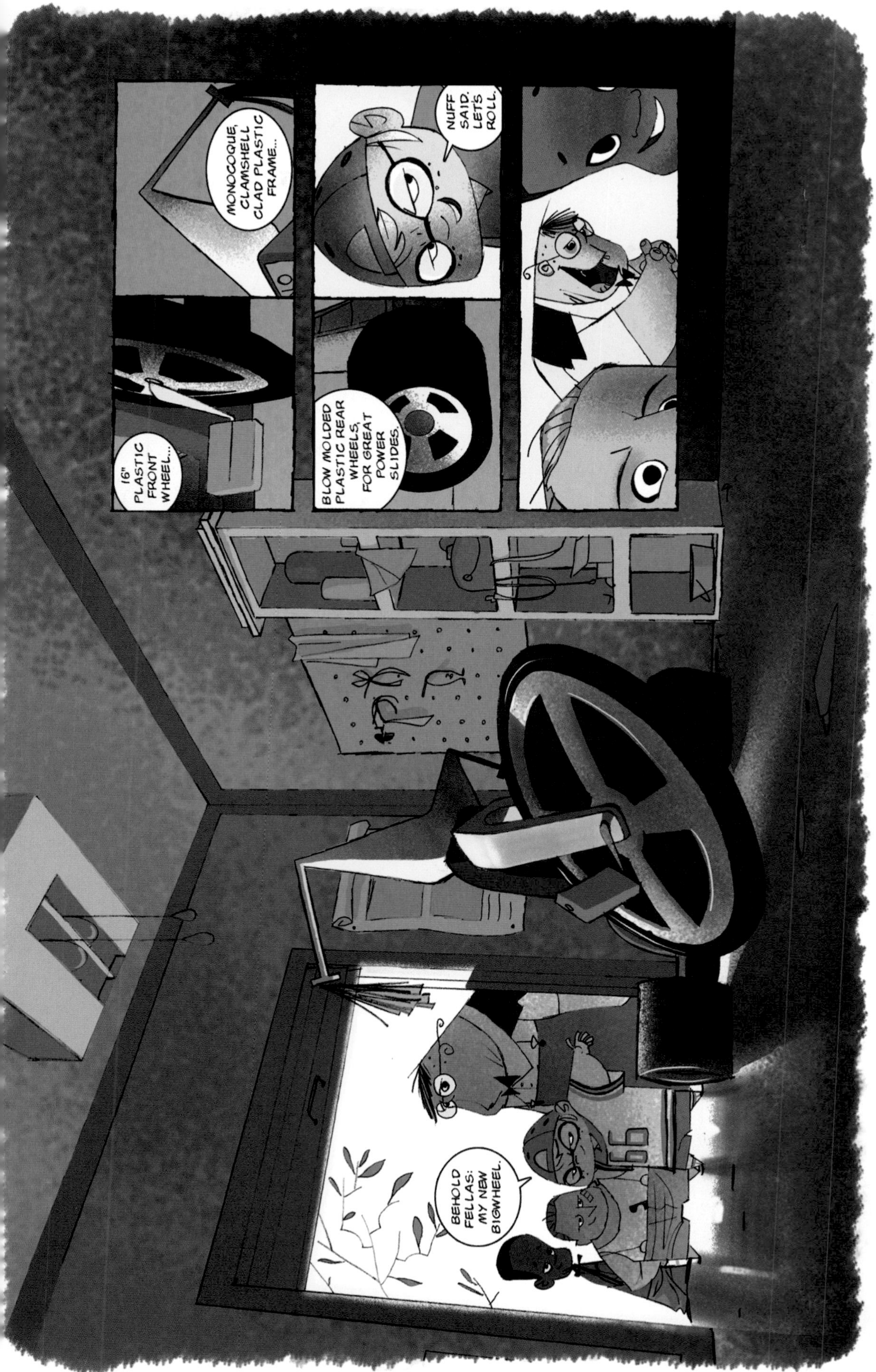
BEHOLD FELLAS: MY NEW BIGWHEEL.
16" PLASTIC FRONT WHEEL...
MONOCOQUE, CLAMSHELL CLAD PLASTIC FRAME...
BLOW MOLDED PLASTIC REAR WHEELS, FOR GREAT POWER SLIDES.
NUFF SAID. LETS ROLL.

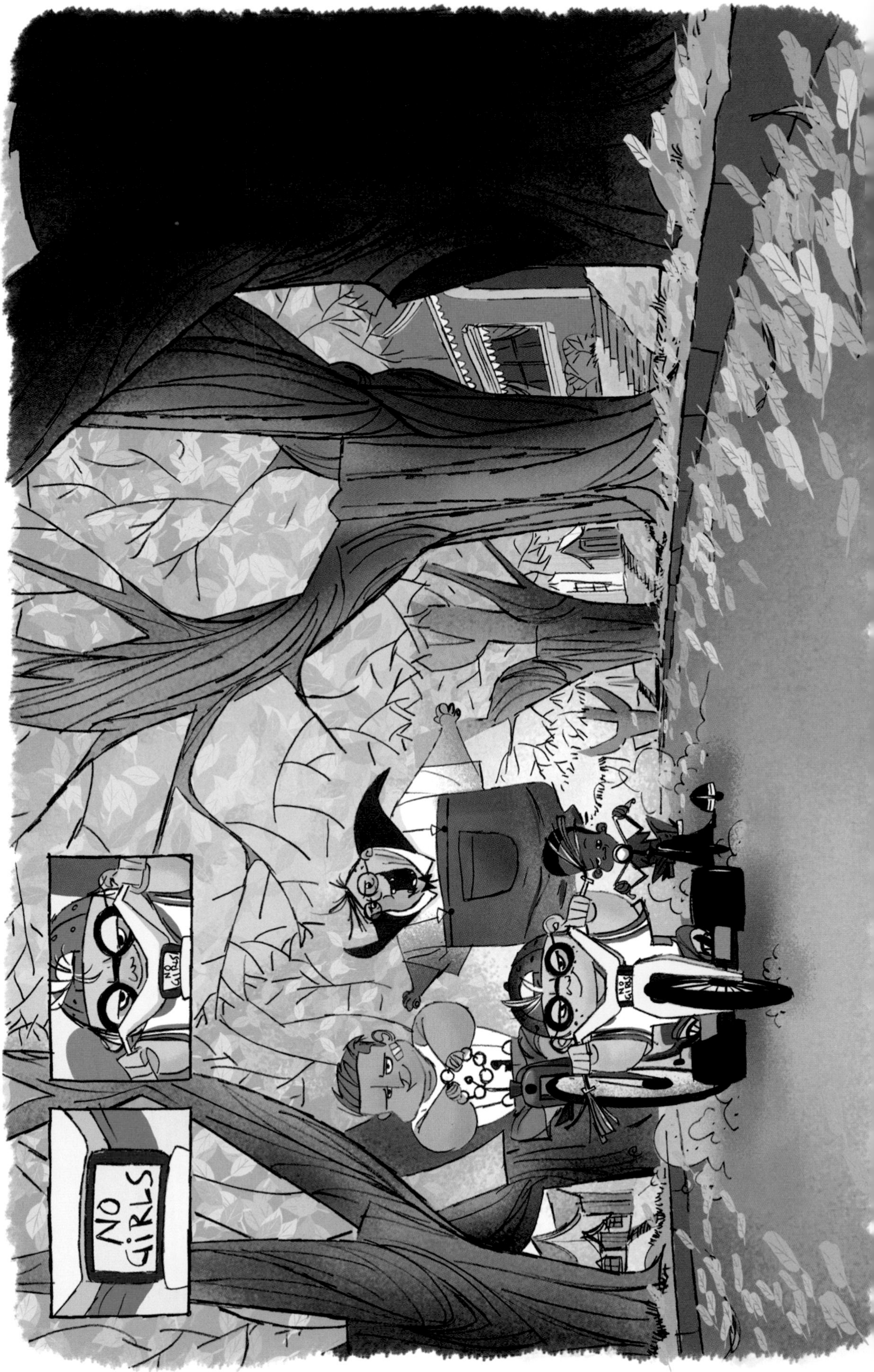
NO GIRLS
NO GIRLS
NO GIRLS

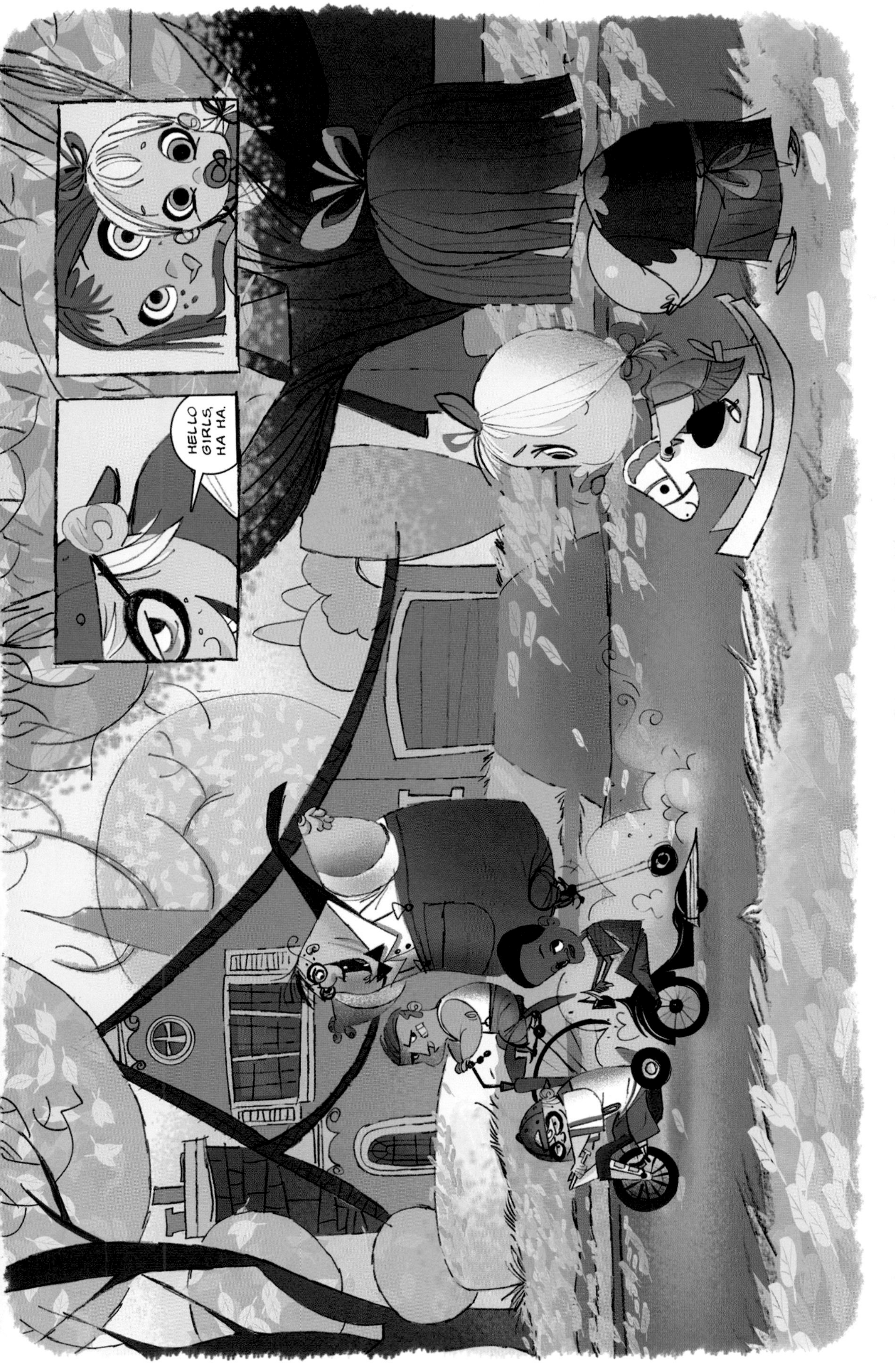
HELLO GIRLS, HA HA.

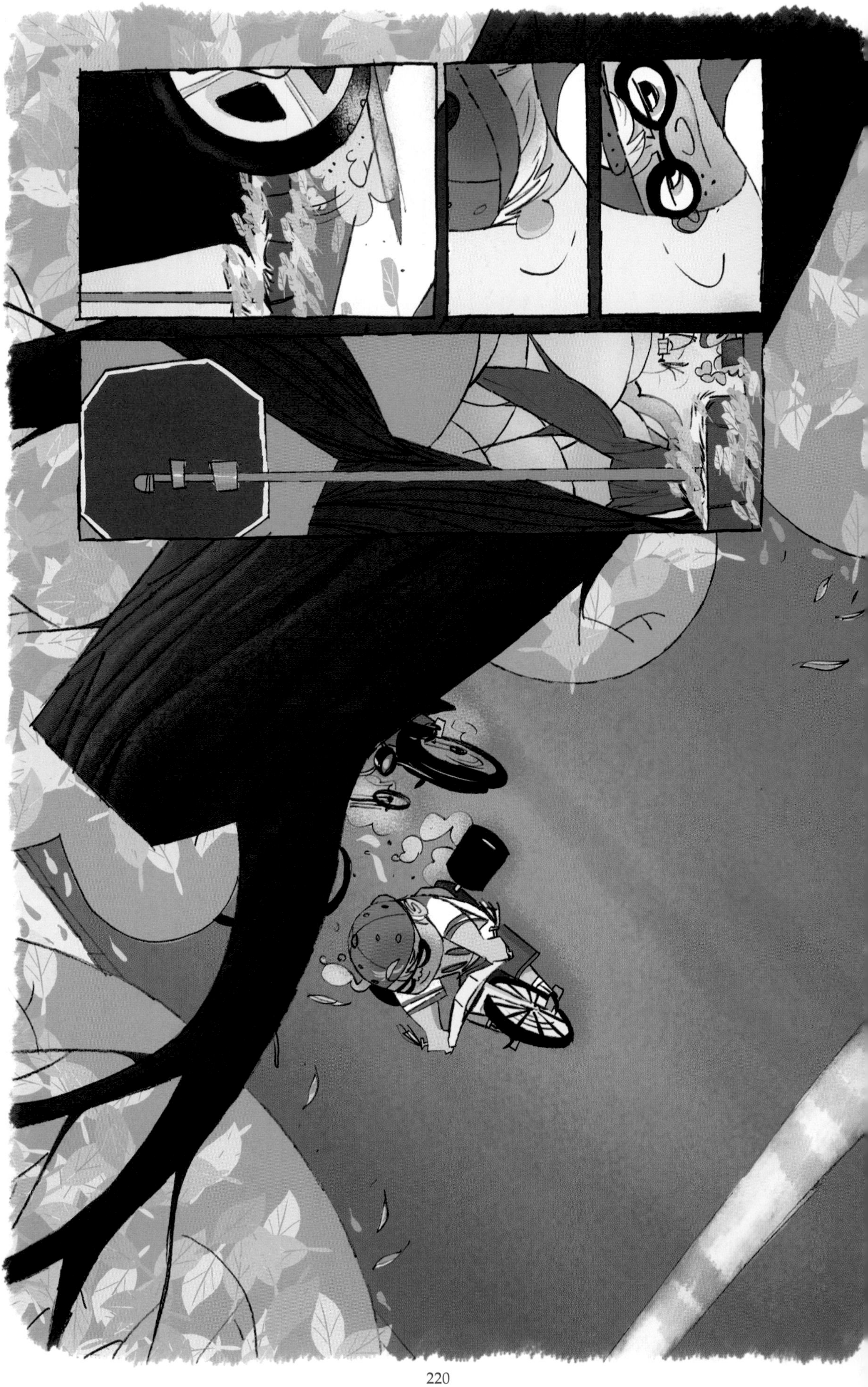

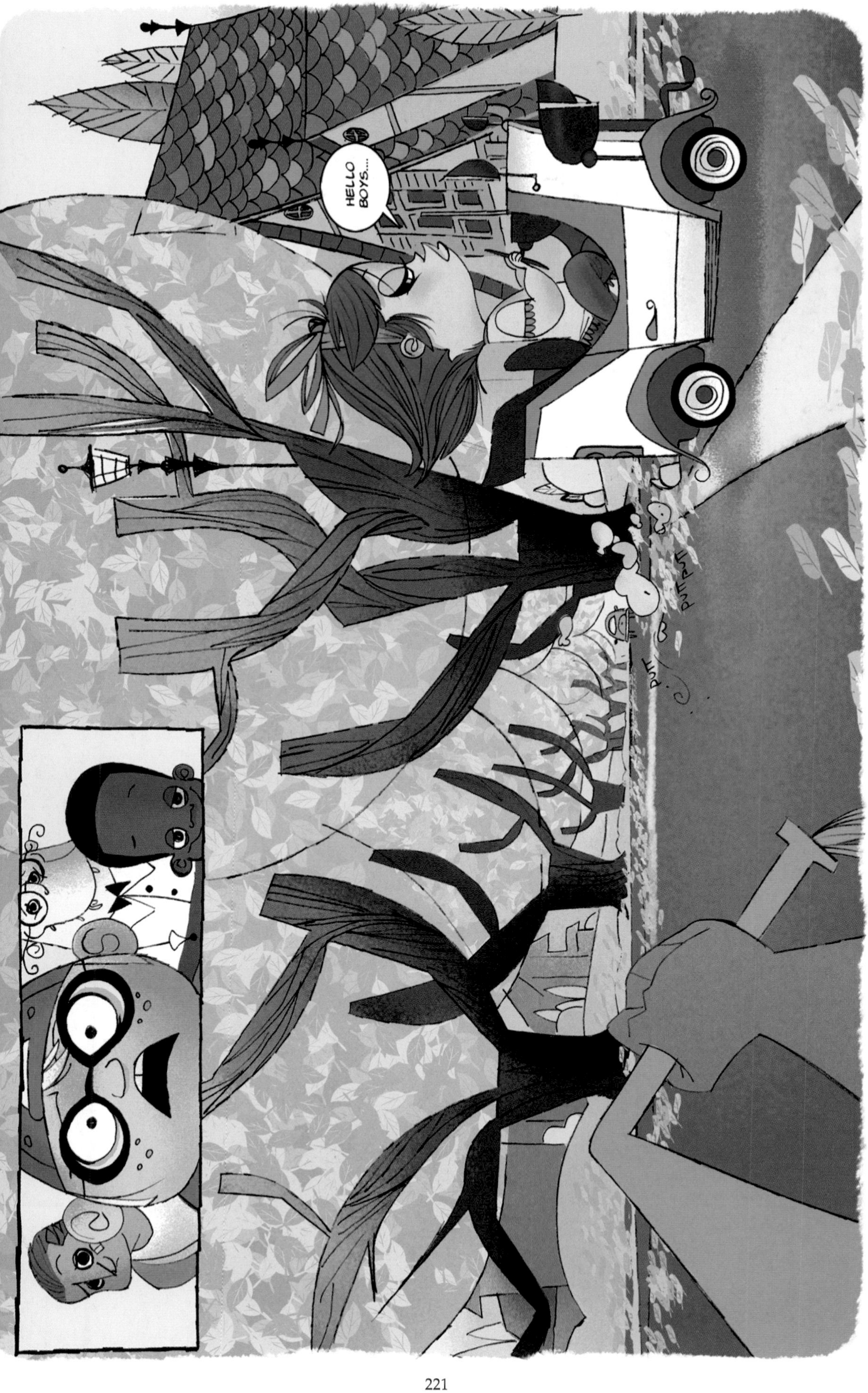
HELLO BOYS...
PUTT
PUTT PUTT

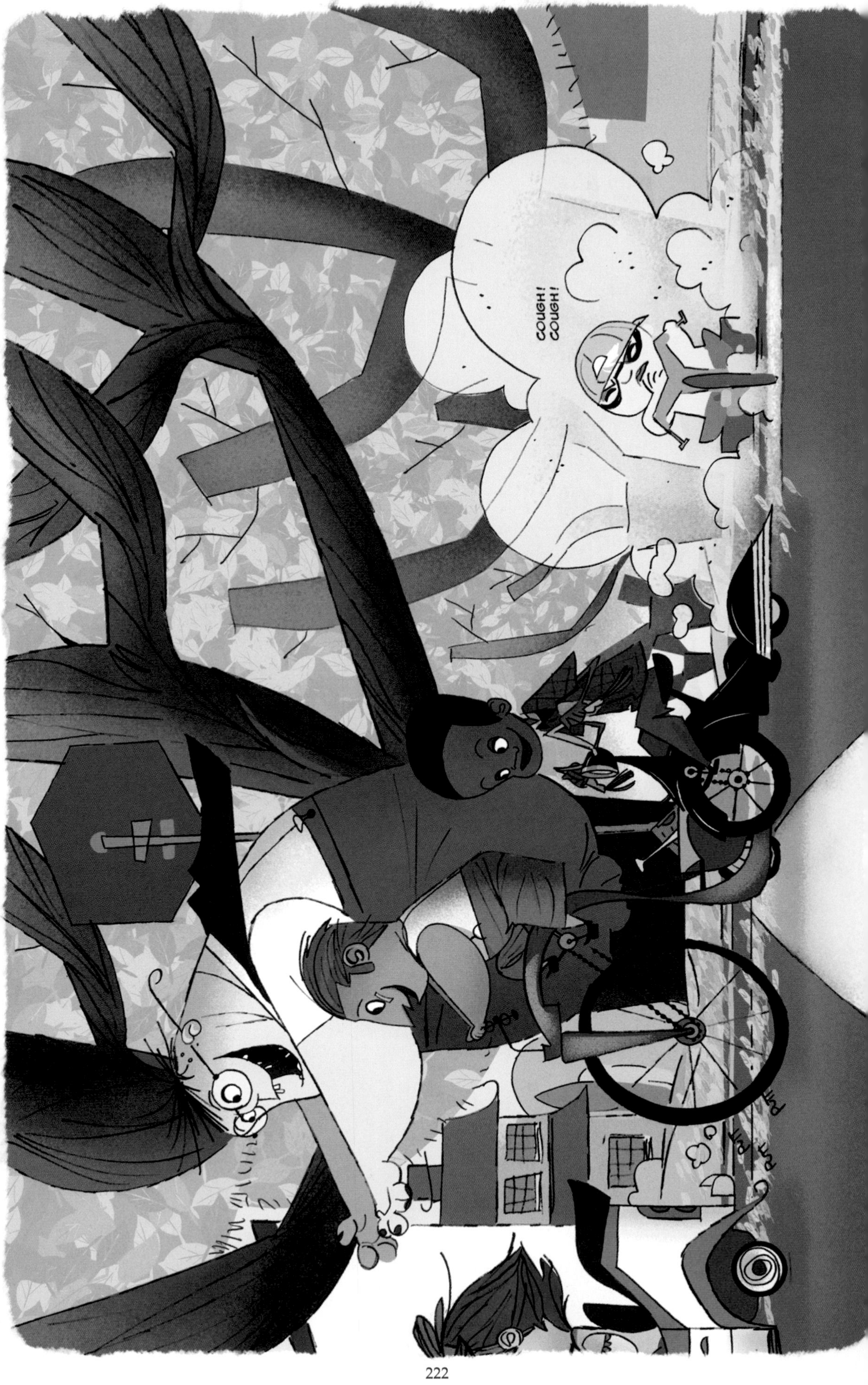
COUGH! COUGH!
PUTT
PUTT
PUTT

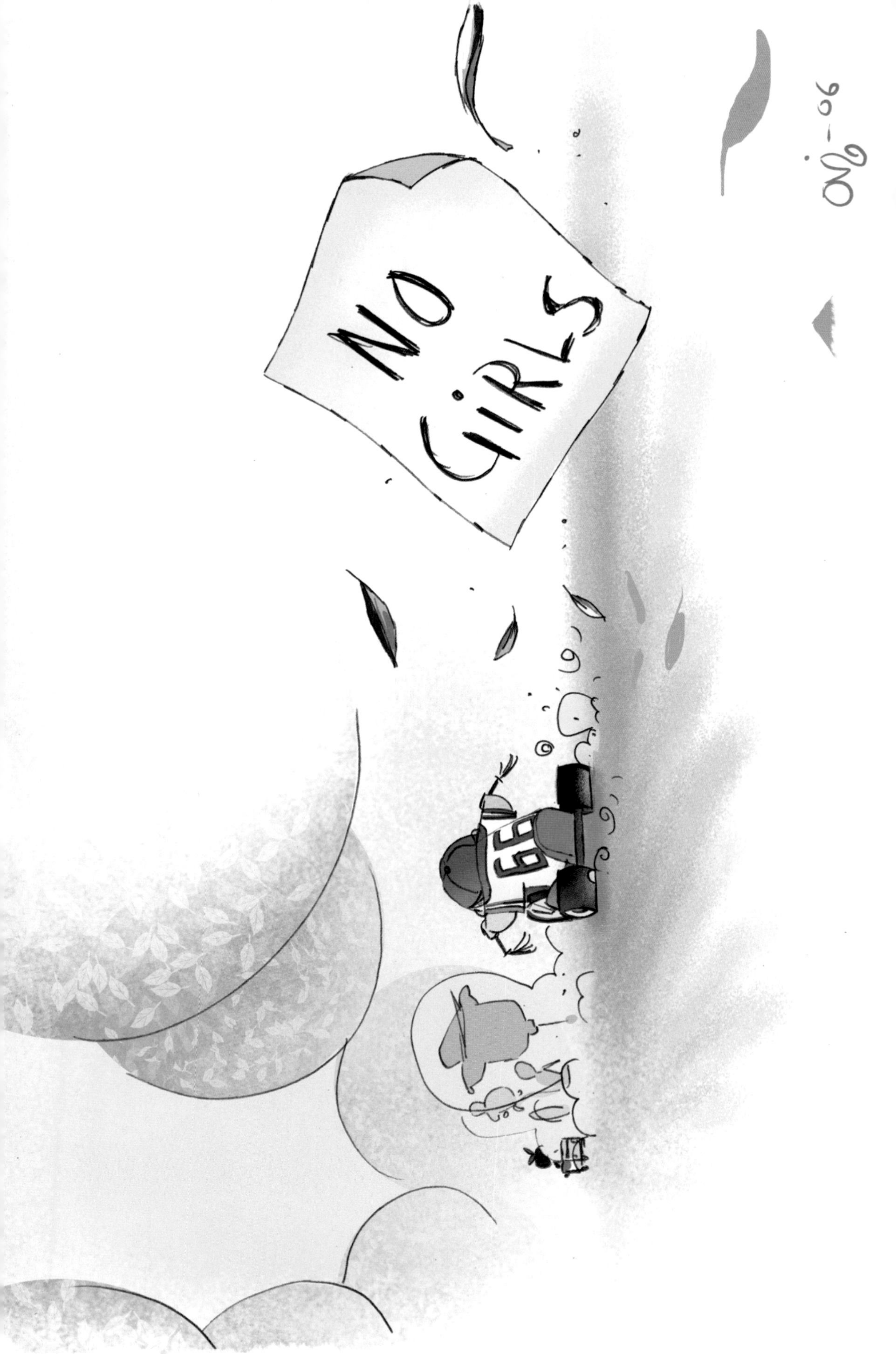
NO GIRLS

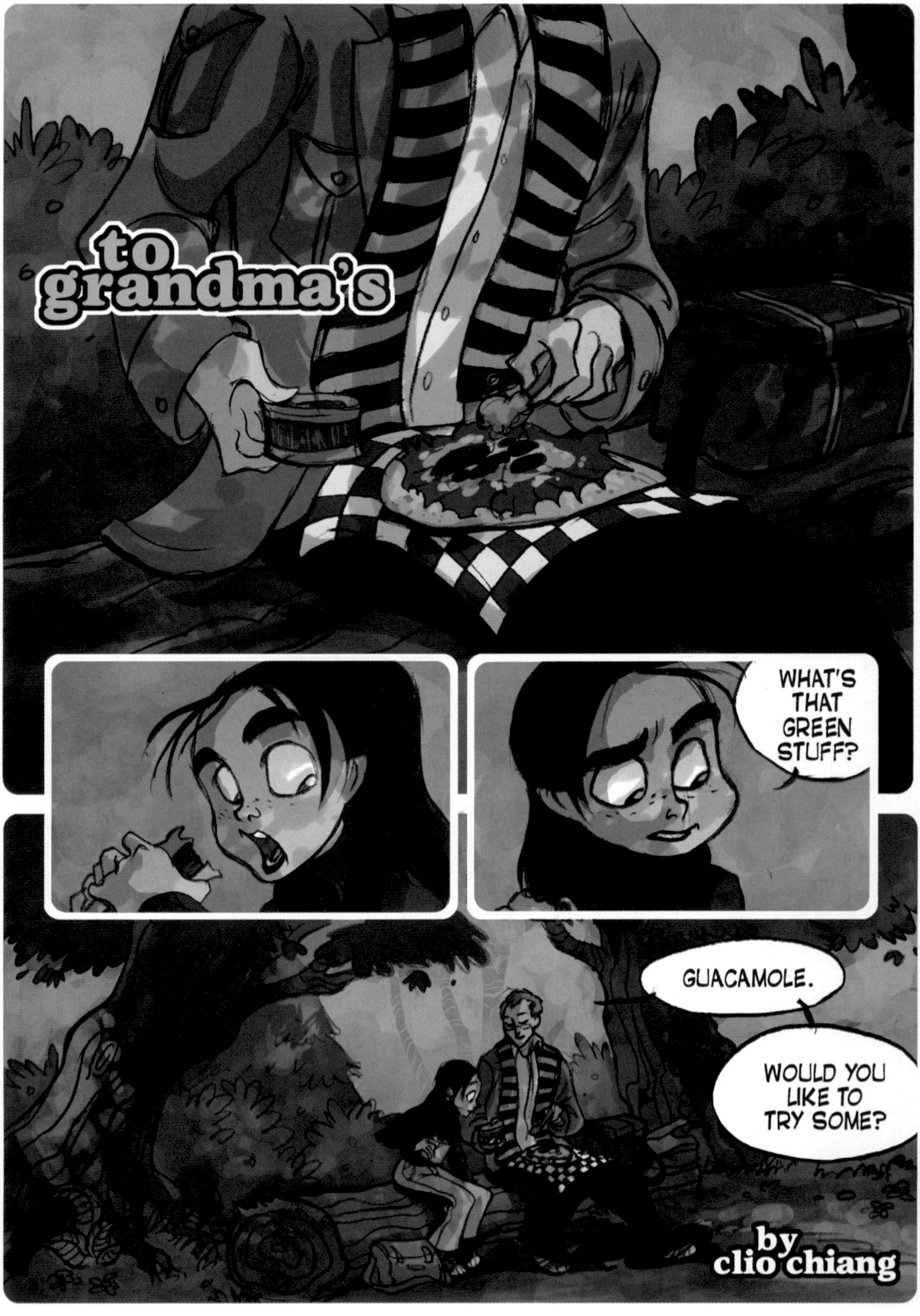
to grandma's
WHAT'S THAT GREEN STUFF?
GUACAMOLE.
WOULD YOU LIKE TO TRY SOME?
by clio chiang

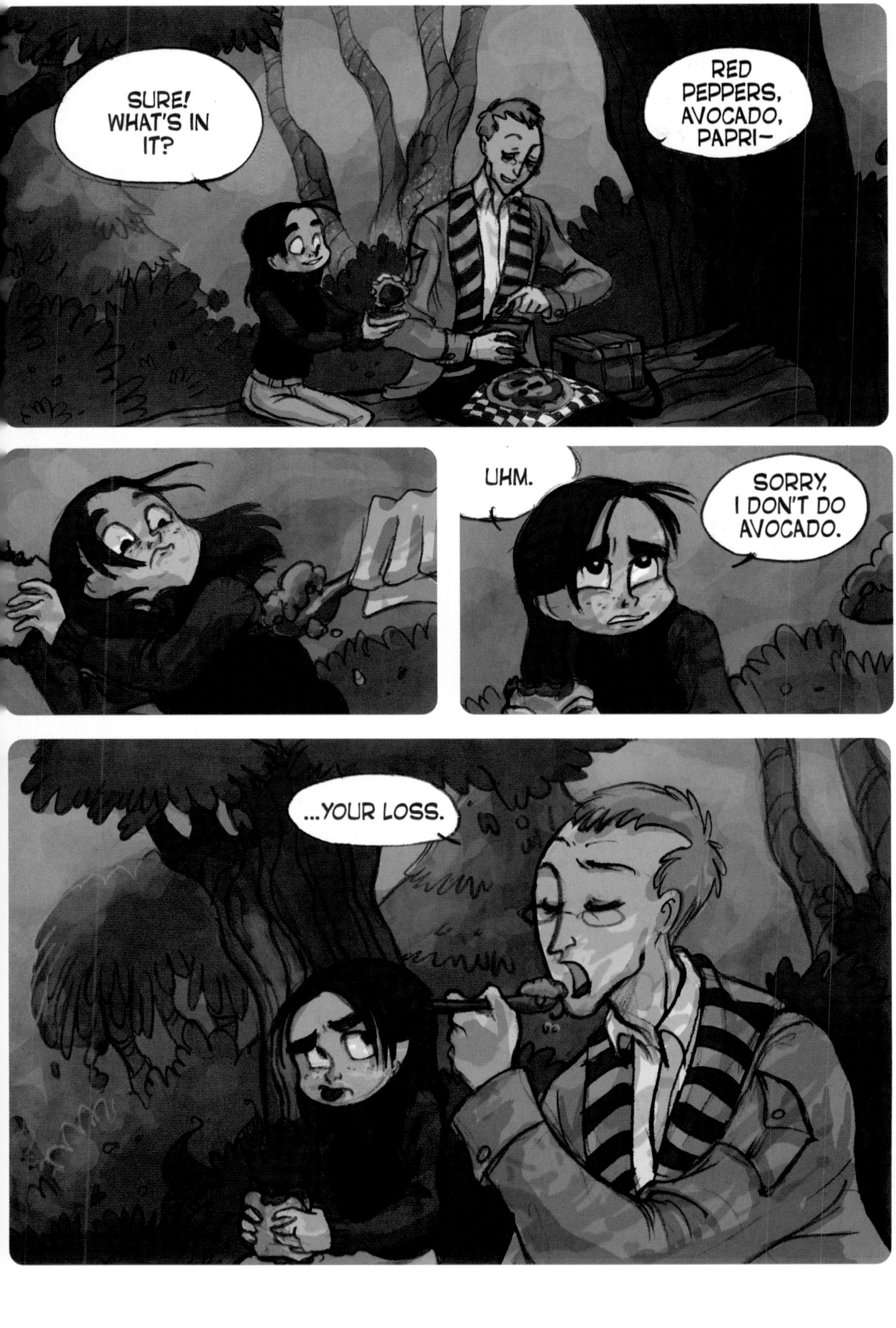
SURE! WHAT'S IN IT?
RED PEPPERS, AVOCADO, PAPRI–
UHM.
SORRY, I DON'T DO AVOCADO.
...YOUR LOSS.

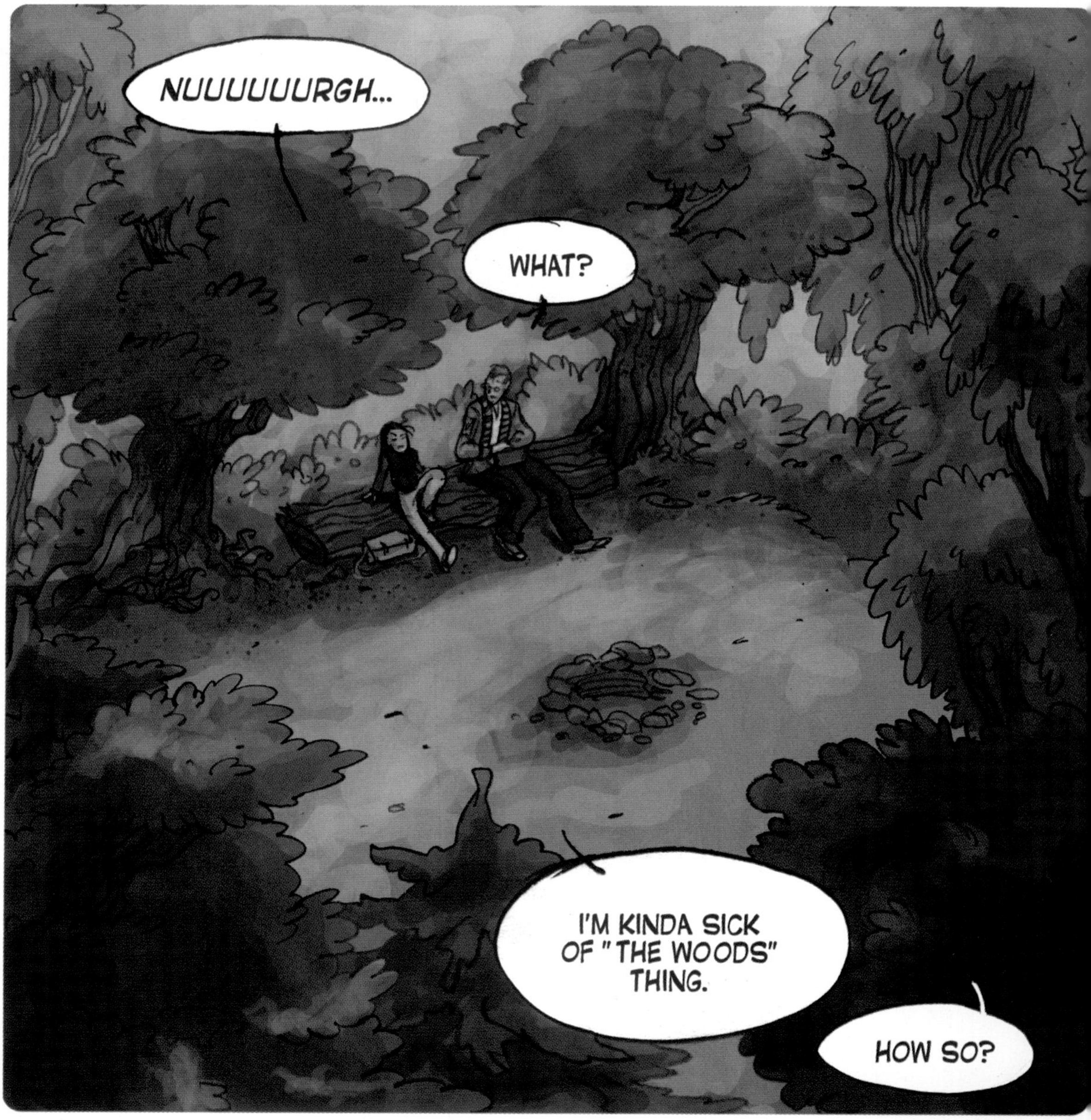
NUUUUUURGH...
WHAT?
I'M KINDA SICK OF "THE WOODS" THING.
HOW SO?

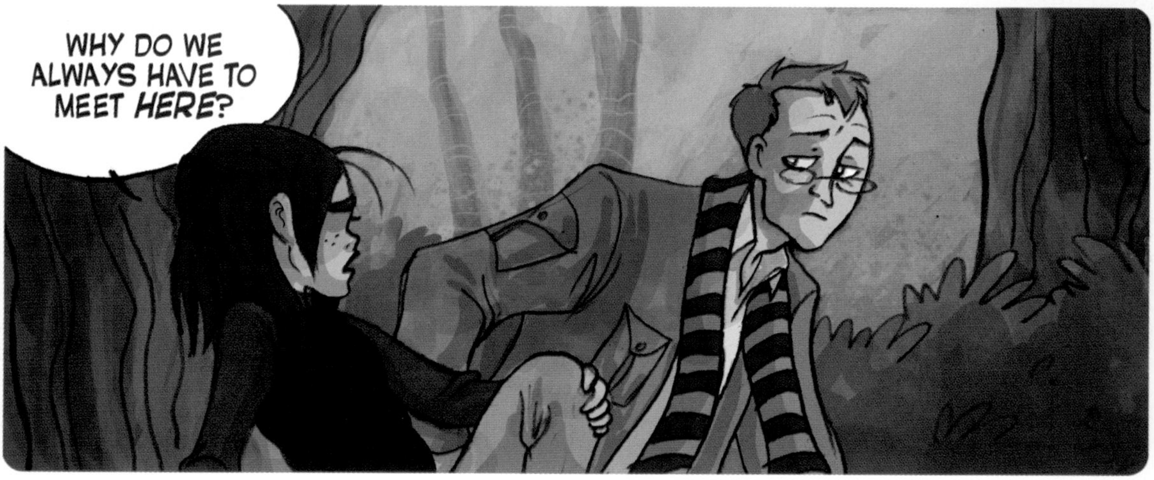
WHY DO WE ALWAYS HAVE TO MEET *HERE*?

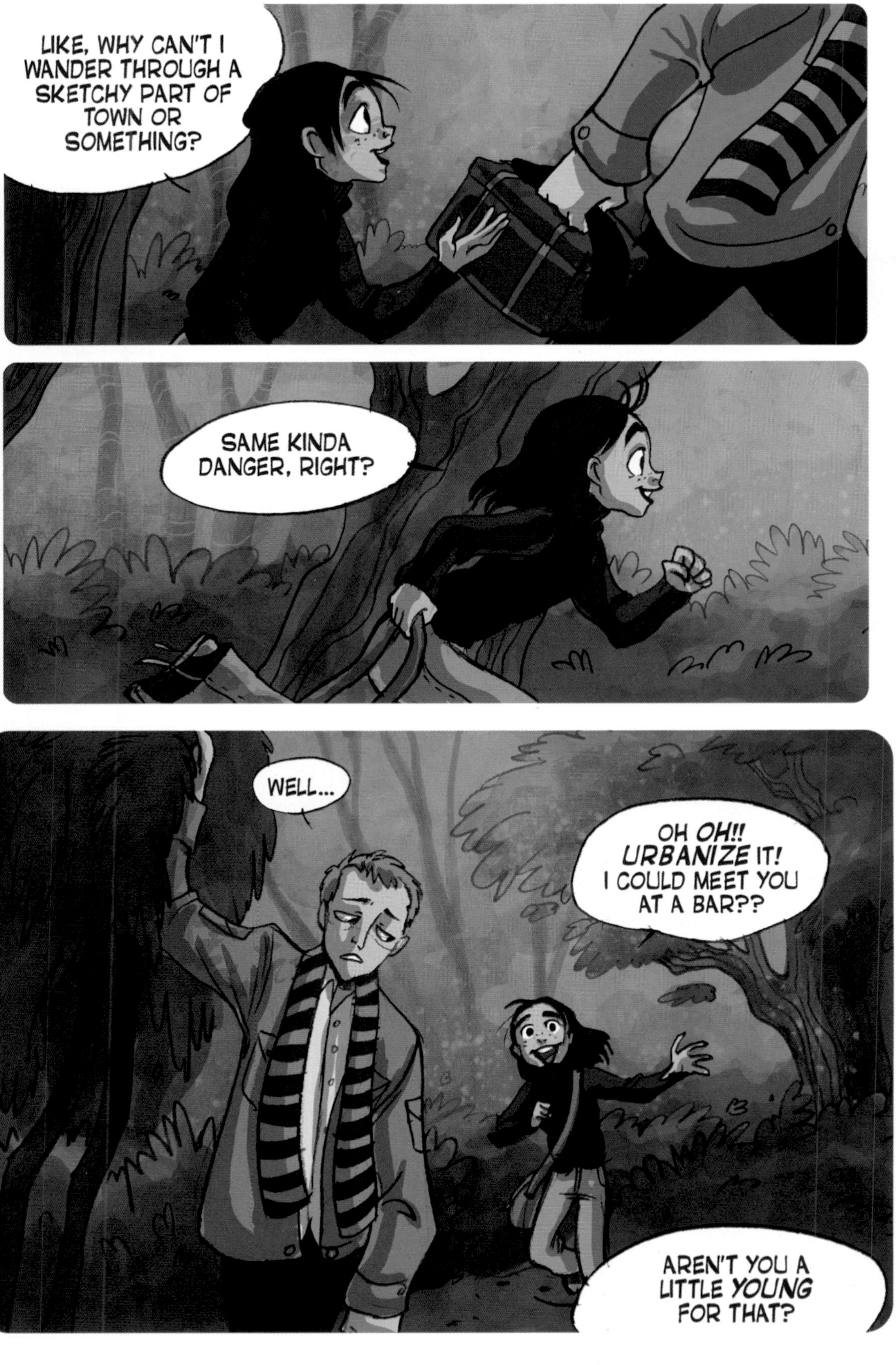
LIKE, WHY CAN'T I WANDER THROUGH A SKETCHY PART OF TOWN OR SOMETHING?
SAME KINDA DANGER, RIGHT?
WELL...
OH *OH!!* *URBANIZE* IT! I COULD MEET YOU AT A BAR??
AREN'T YOU A LITTLE *YOUNG* FOR THAT?

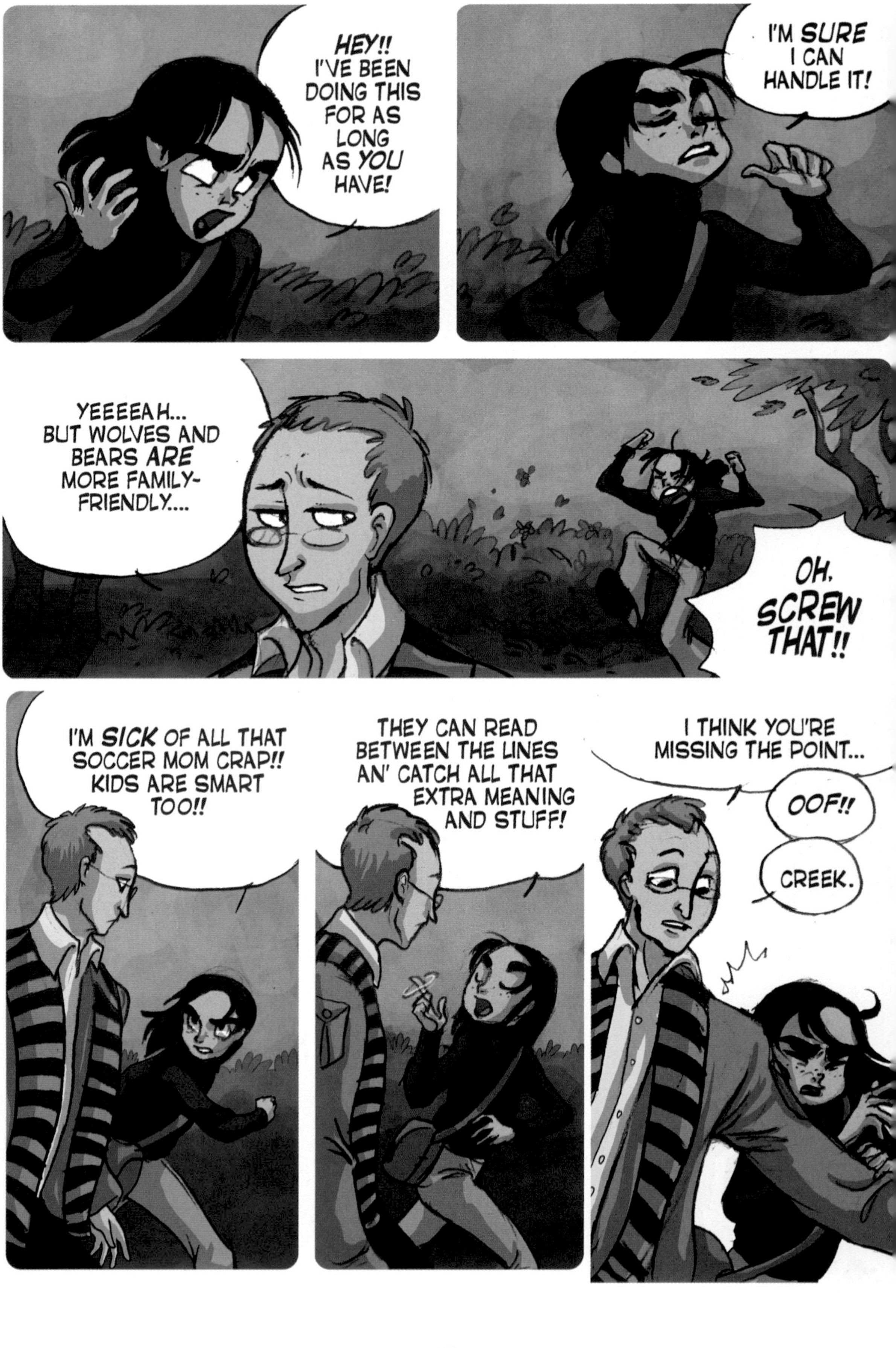
HEY!! I'VE BEEN DOING THIS FOR AS LONG AS YOU HAVE!
I'M SURE I CAN HANDLE IT!
YEEEEAH... BUT WOLVES AND BEARS ARE MORE FAMILY-FRIENDLY....
OH. SCREW THAT!!
I'M SICK OF ALL THAT SOCCER MOM CRAP!! KIDS ARE SMART TOO!!
THEY CAN READ BETWEEN THE LINES AN' CATCH ALL THAT EXTRA MEANING AND STUFF!
I THINK YOU'RE MISSING THE POINT...
OOF!!
CREEK.

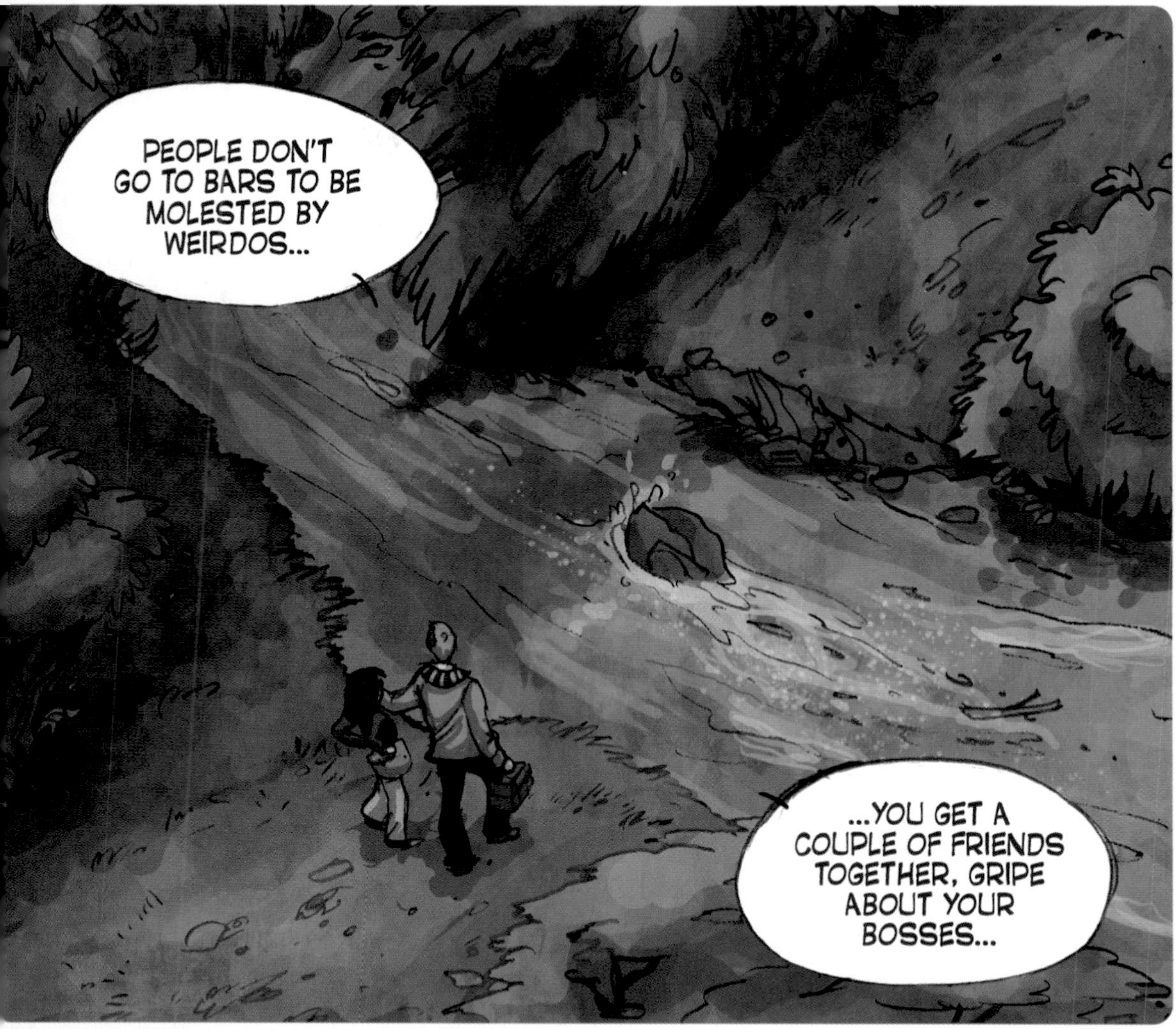
PEOPLE DON'T GO TO BARS TO BE MOLESTED BY WEIRDOS...
...YOU GET A COUPLE OF FRIENDS TOGETHER, GRIPE ABOUT YOUR BOSSES...

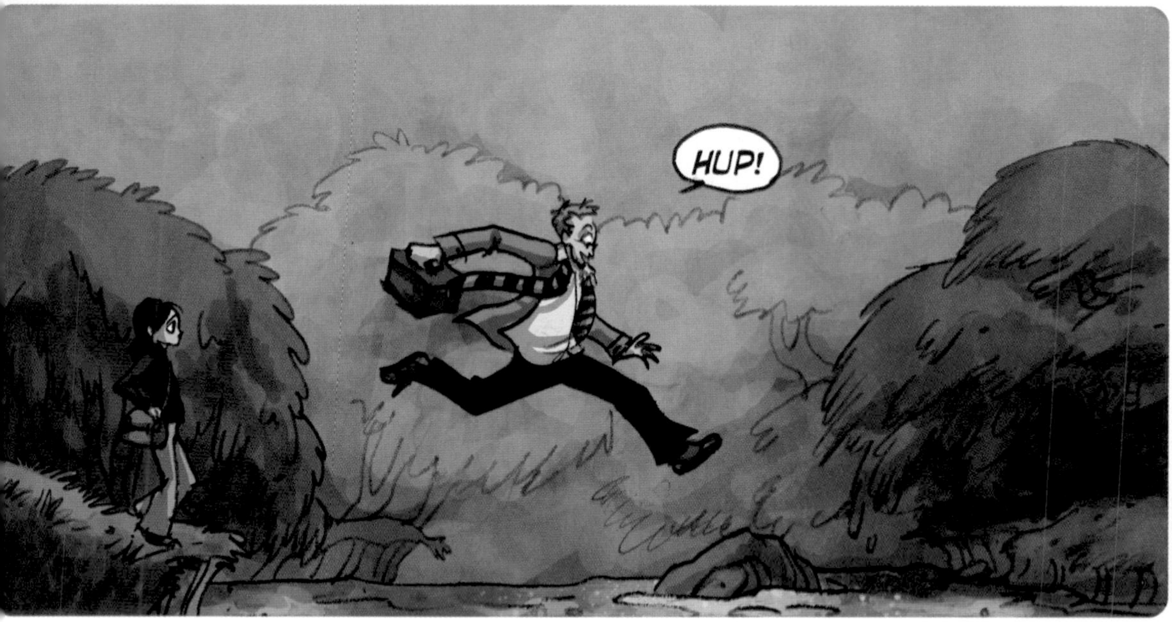
HUP!

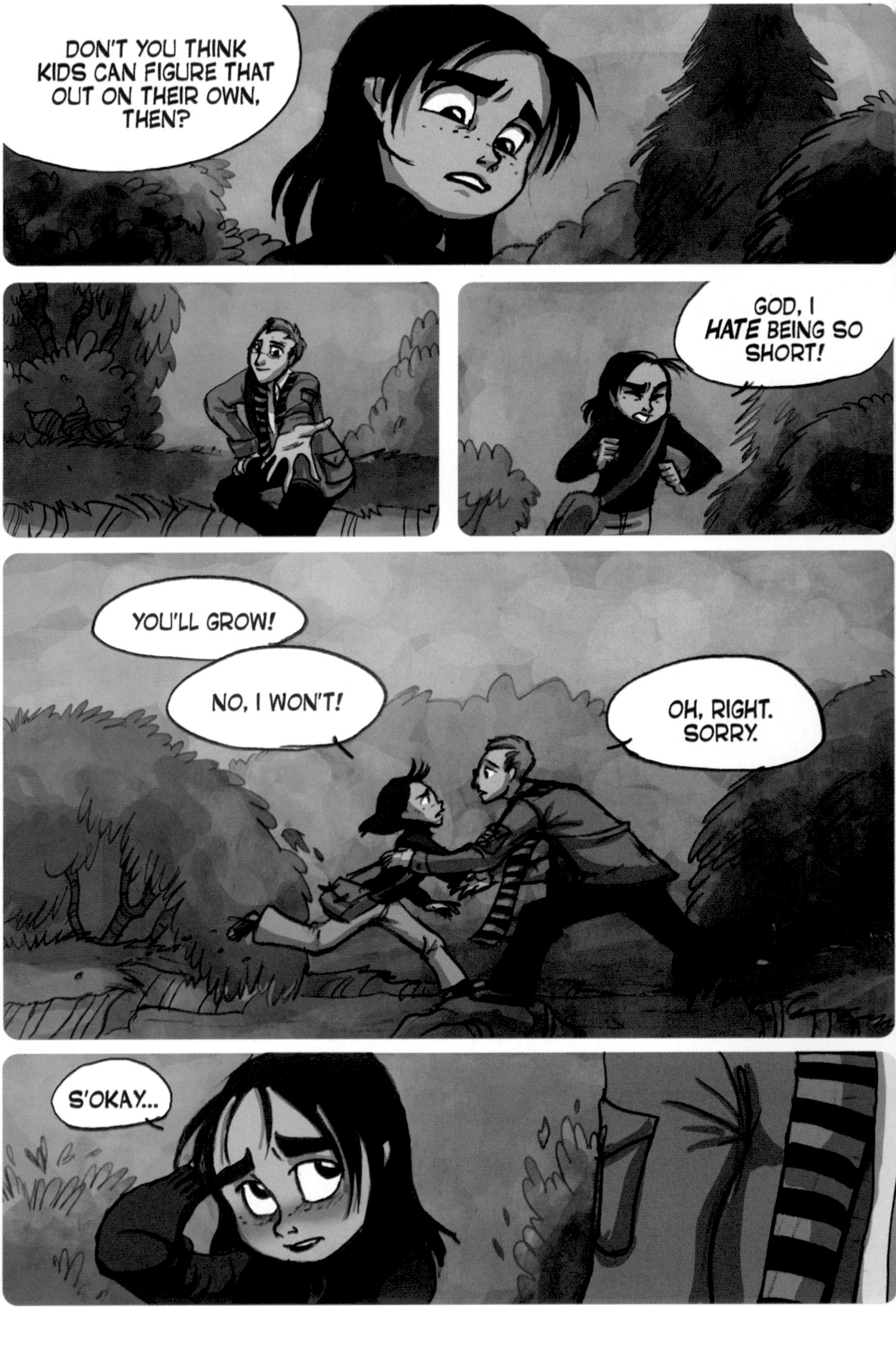
DON'T YOU THINK KIDS CAN FIGURE THAT OUT ON THEIR OWN, THEN?
GOD, I HATE BEING SO SHORT!
YOU'LL GROW!
NO, I WON'T!
OH, RIGHT. SORRY.
S'OKAY...

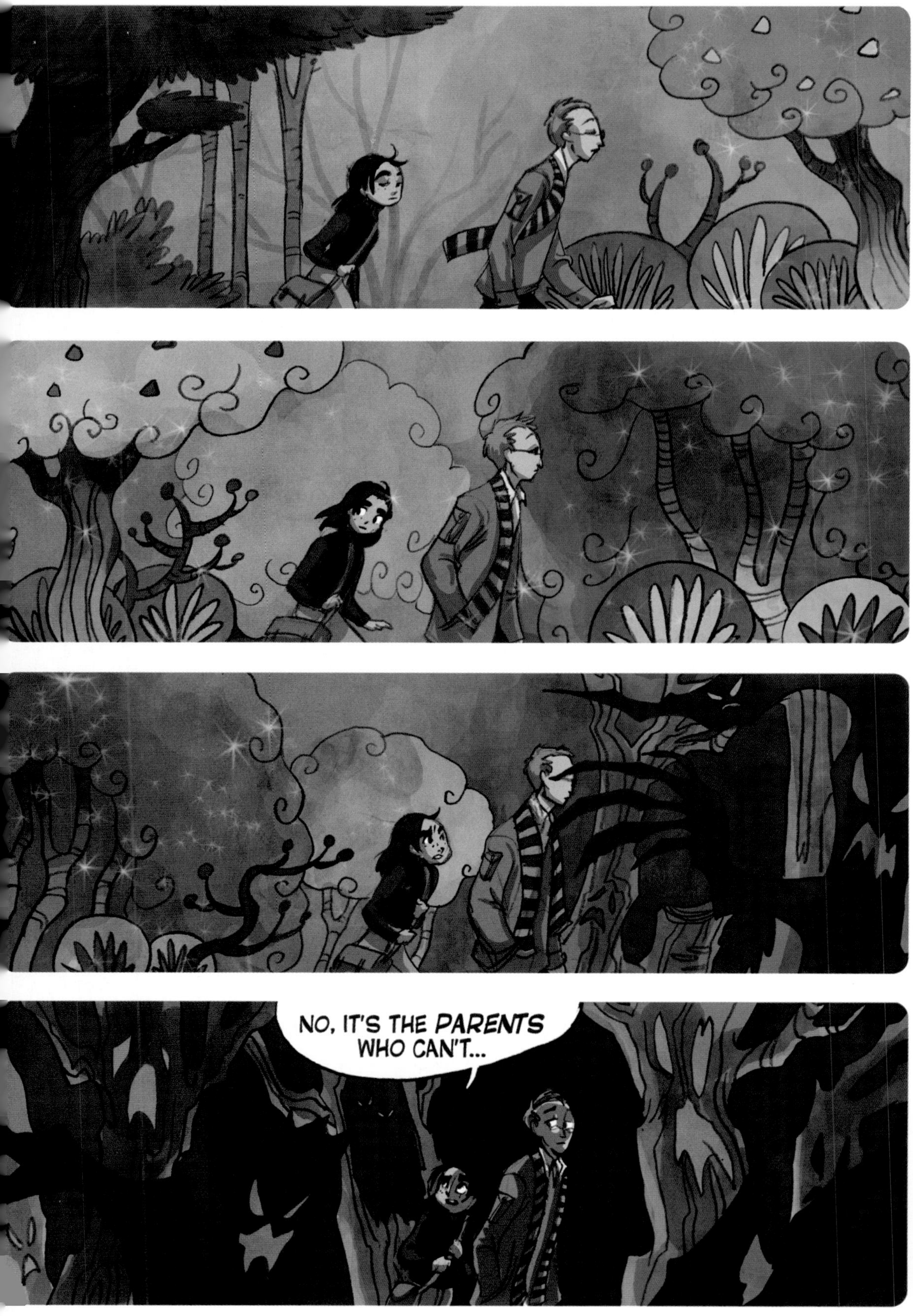
NO, IT'S THE PARENTS WHO CAN'T...

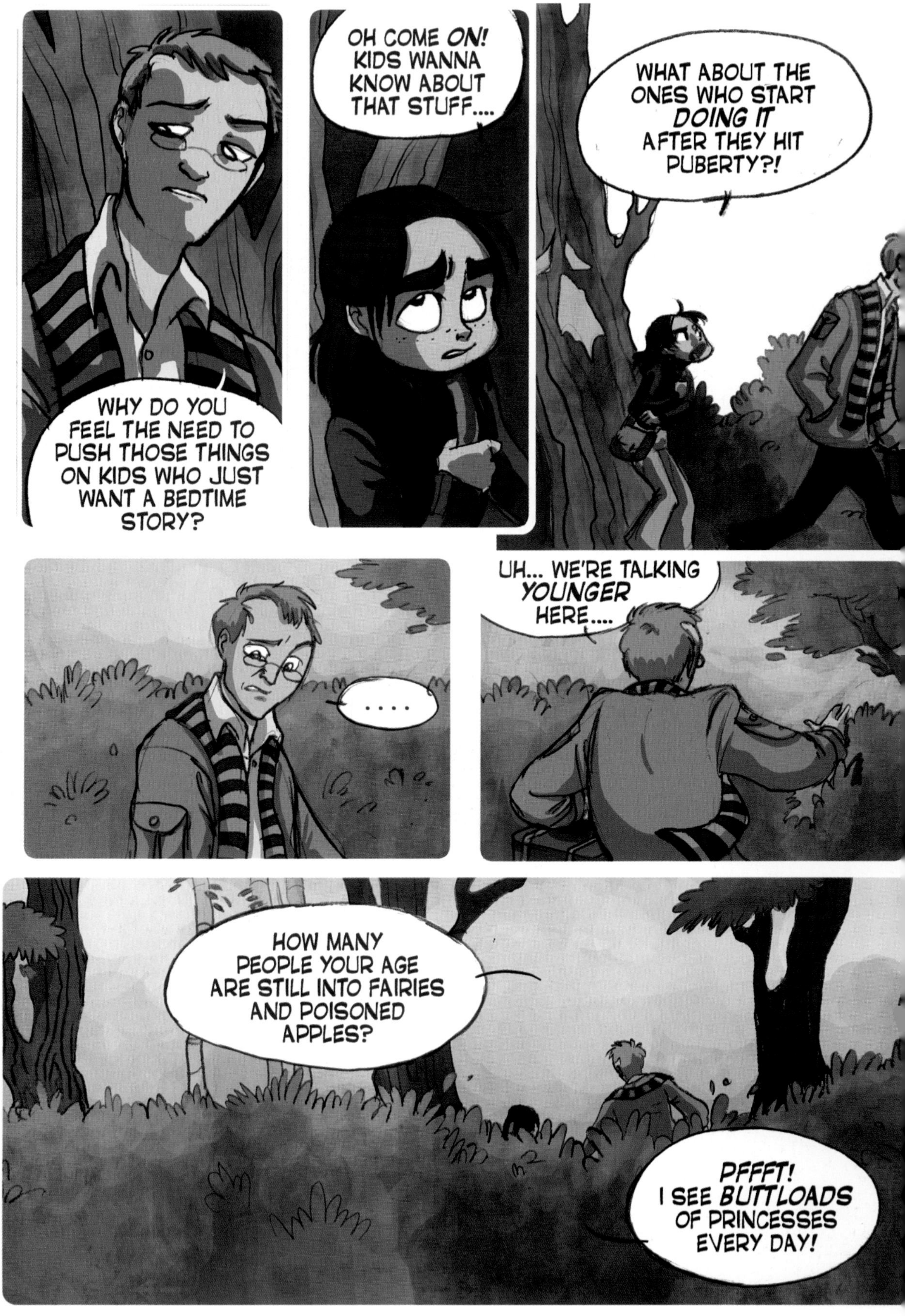
WHY DO YOU FEEL THE NEED TO PUSH THOSE THINGS ON KIDS WHO JUST WANT A BEDTIME STORY?
OH COME ON! KIDS WANNA KNOW ABOUT THAT STUFF....
WHAT ABOUT THE ONES WHO START DOING IT AFTER THEY HIT PUBERTY?!
....
UH... WE'RE TALKING YOUNGER HERE....
HOW MANY PEOPLE YOUR AGE ARE STILL INTO FAIRIES AND POISONED APPLES?
PFFFT! I SEE BUTTLOADS OF PRINCESSES EVERY DAY!

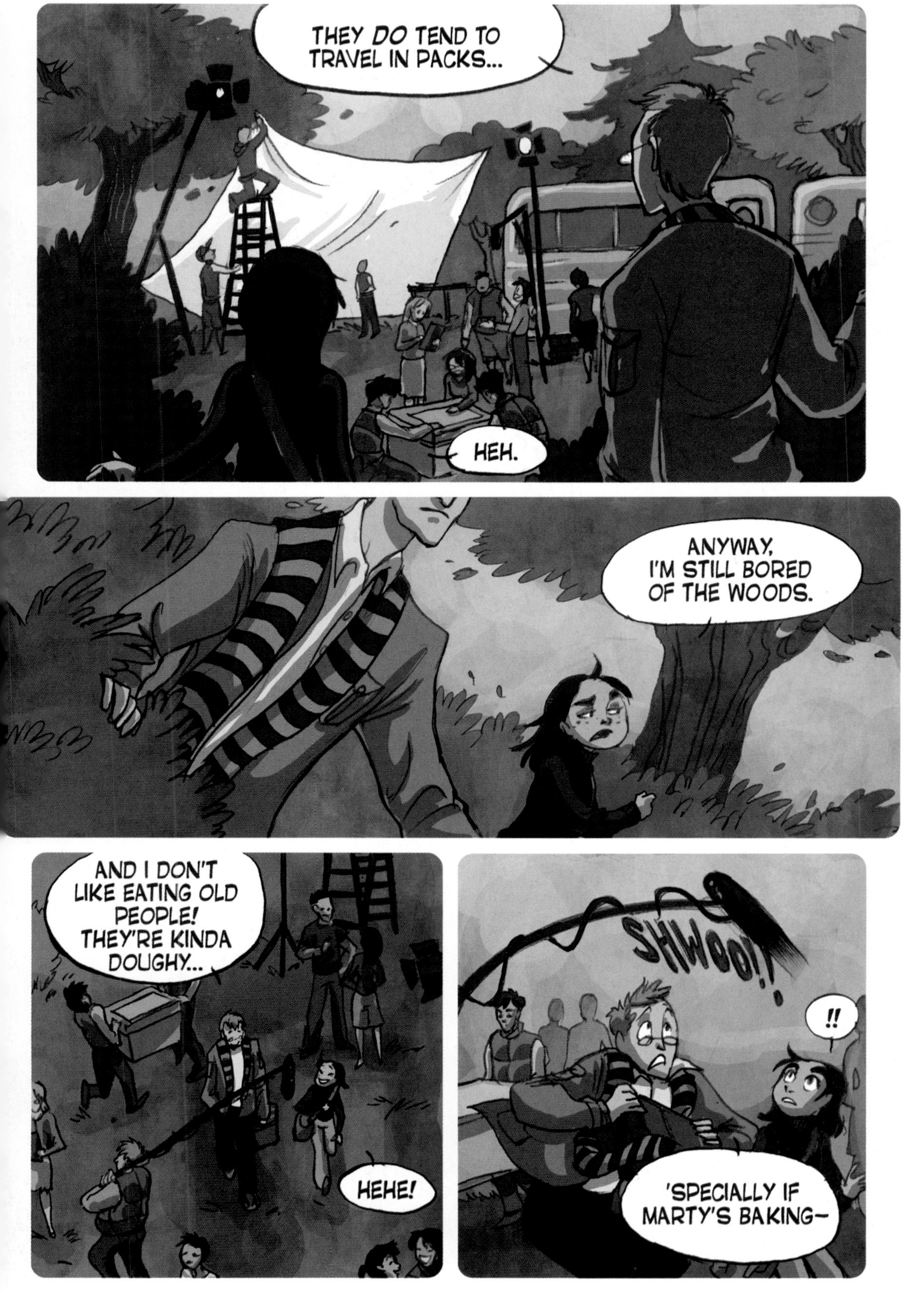
THEY DO TEND TO TRAVEL IN PACKS...
HEH.
ANYWAY, I'M STILL BORED OF THE WOODS.
AND I DON'T LIKE EATING OLD PEOPLE! THEY'RE KINDA DOUGHY...
HEHE!
SHWOOP!
!!
'SPECIALLY IF MARTY'S BAKING–

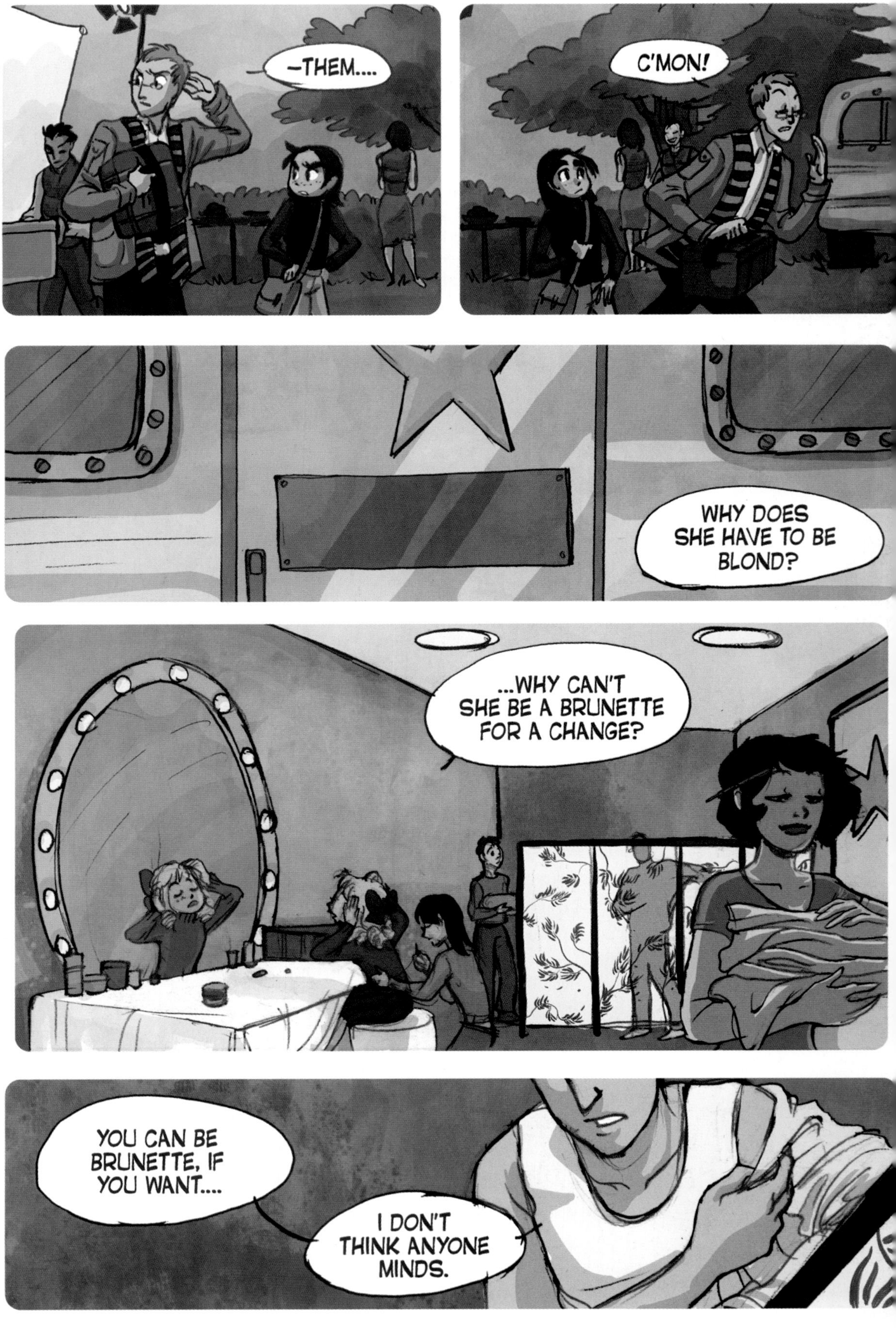
–THEM....
C'MON!
WHY DOES SHE HAVE TO BE BLOND?
...WHY CAN'T SHE BE A BRUNETTE FOR A CHANGE?
YOU CAN BE BRUNETTE, IF YOU WANT....
I DON'T THINK ANYONE MINDS.

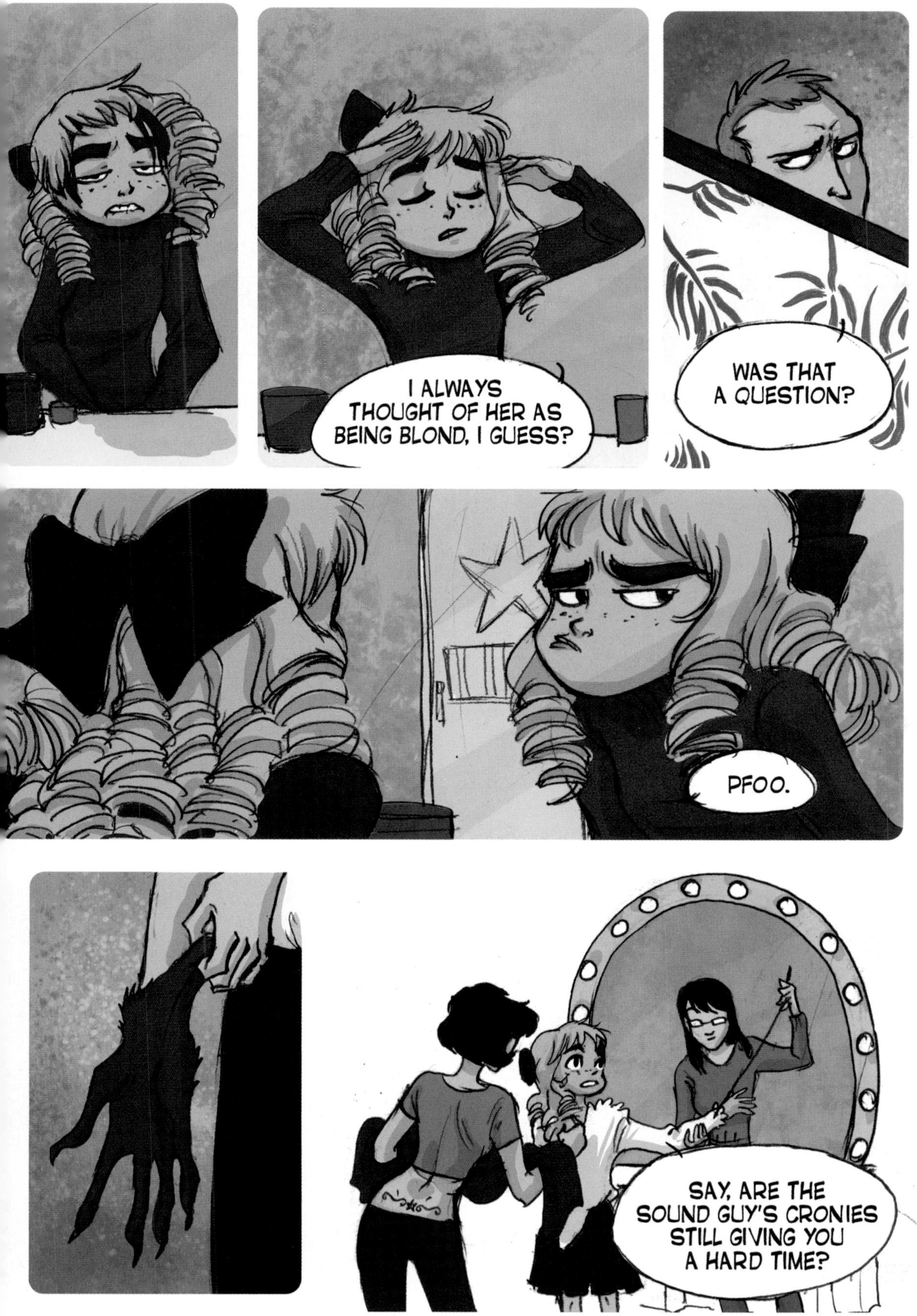
I ALWAYS THOUGHT OF HER AS BEING BLOND, I GUESS?
WAS THAT A QUESTION?
PFOO.
SAY, ARE THE SOUND GUY'S CRONIES STILL GIVING YOU A HARD TIME?

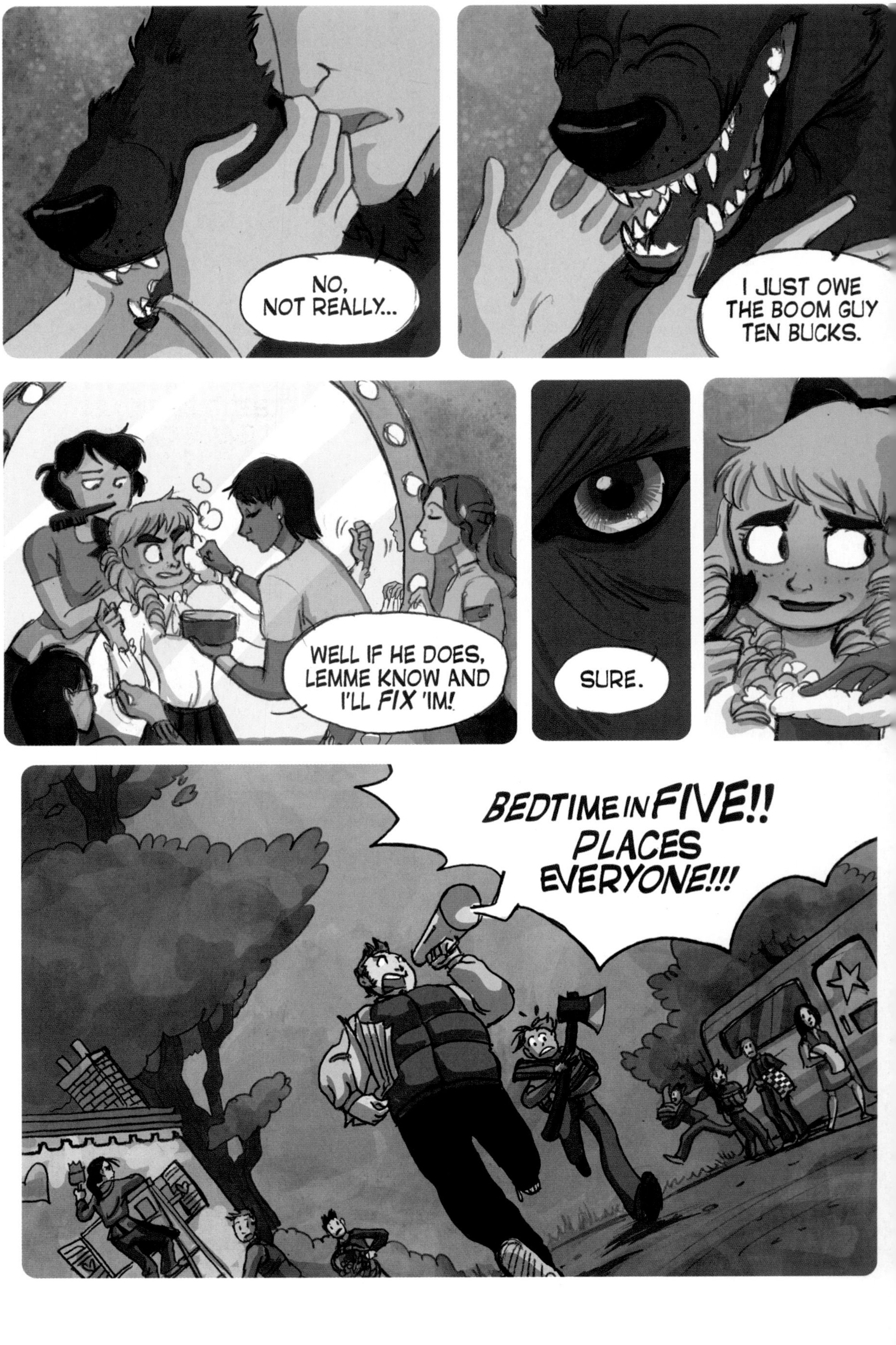
NO, NOT REALLY...
I JUST OWE THE BOOM GUY TEN BUCKS.
WELL IF HE DOES, LEMME KNOW AND I'LL FIX 'IM!
SURE.
BEDTIME IN FIVE!! PLACES EVERYONE!!!

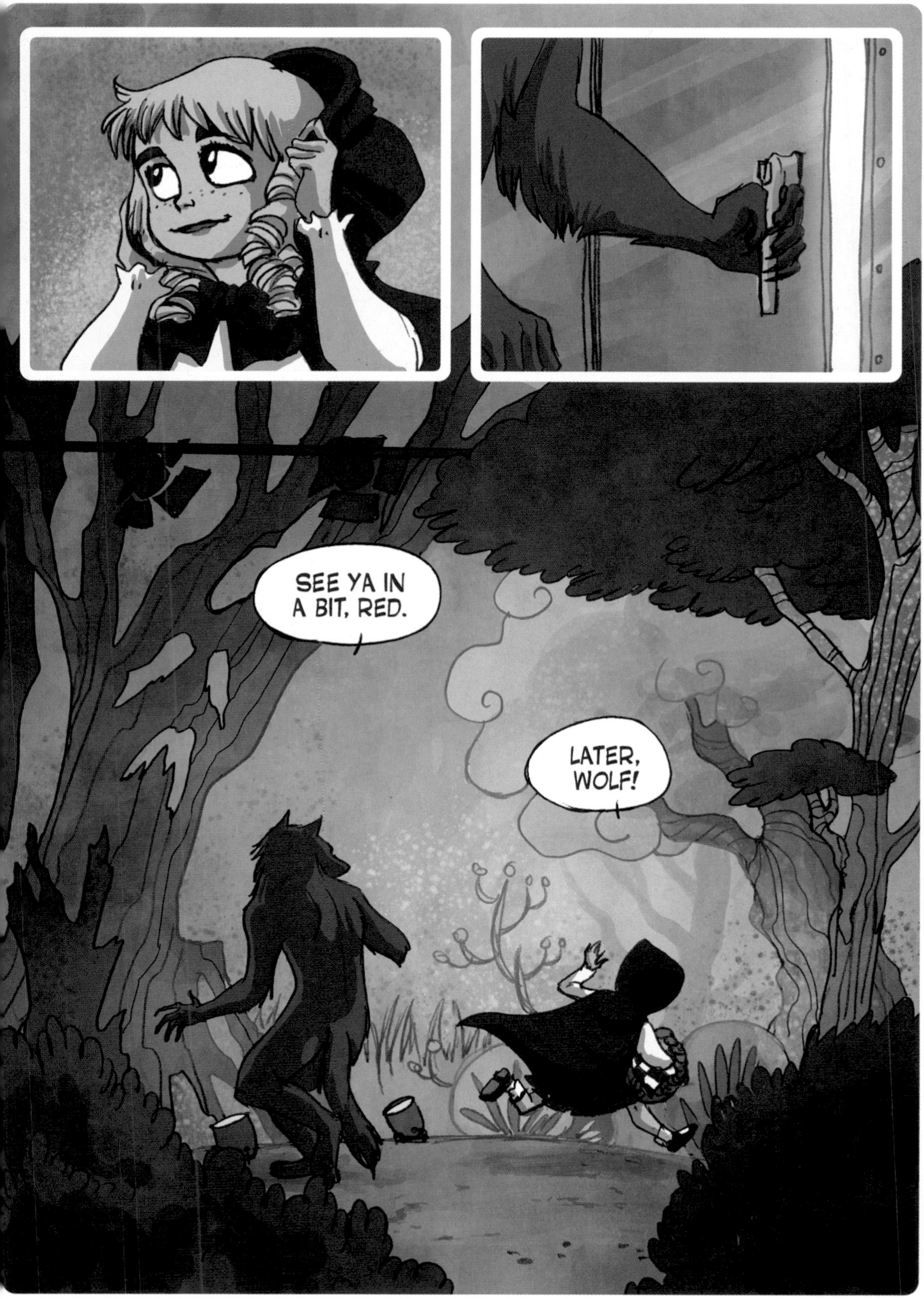
SEE YA IN A BIT, RED.
LATER, WOLF!

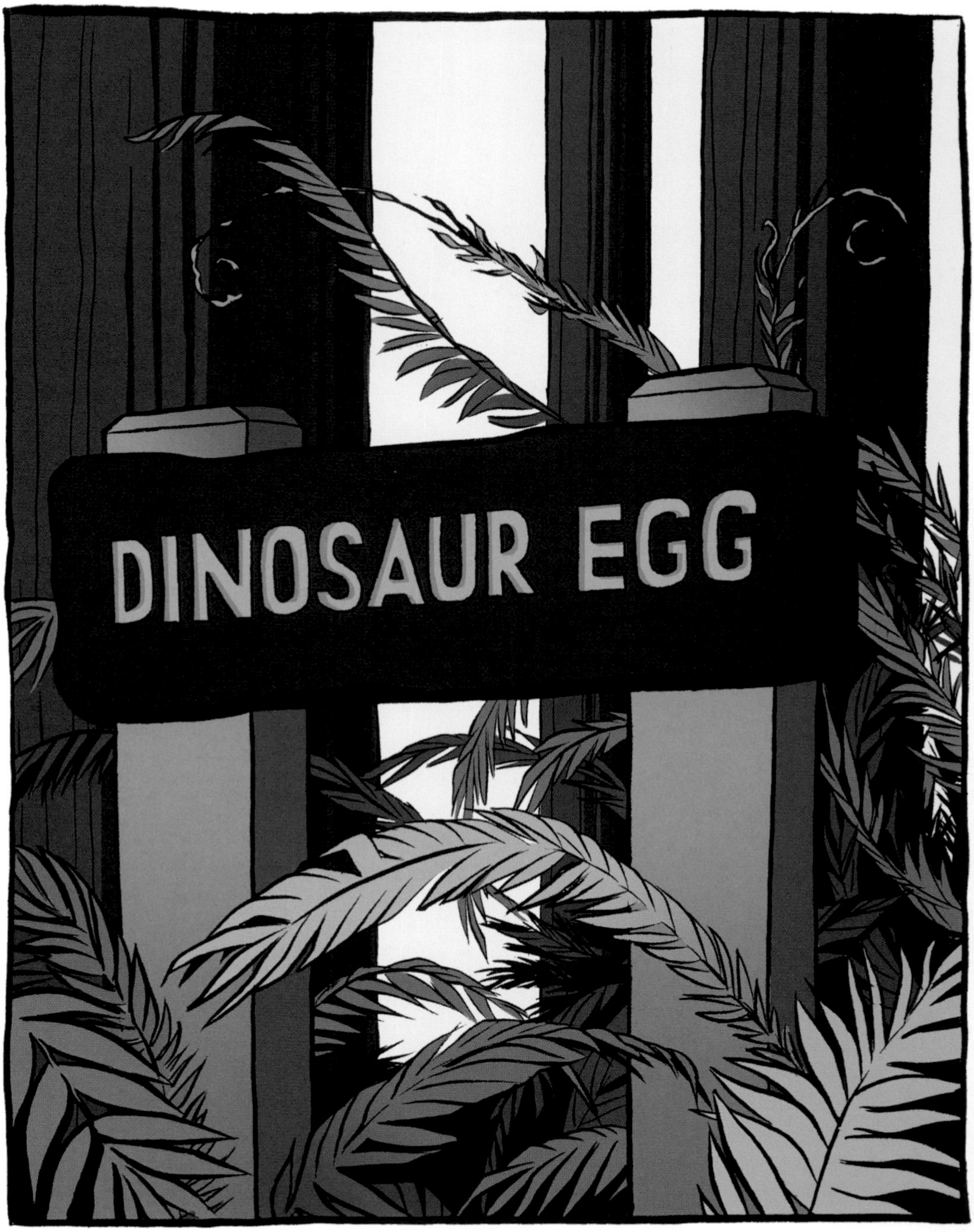
DINOSAUR EGG

by Raina Telgemeier

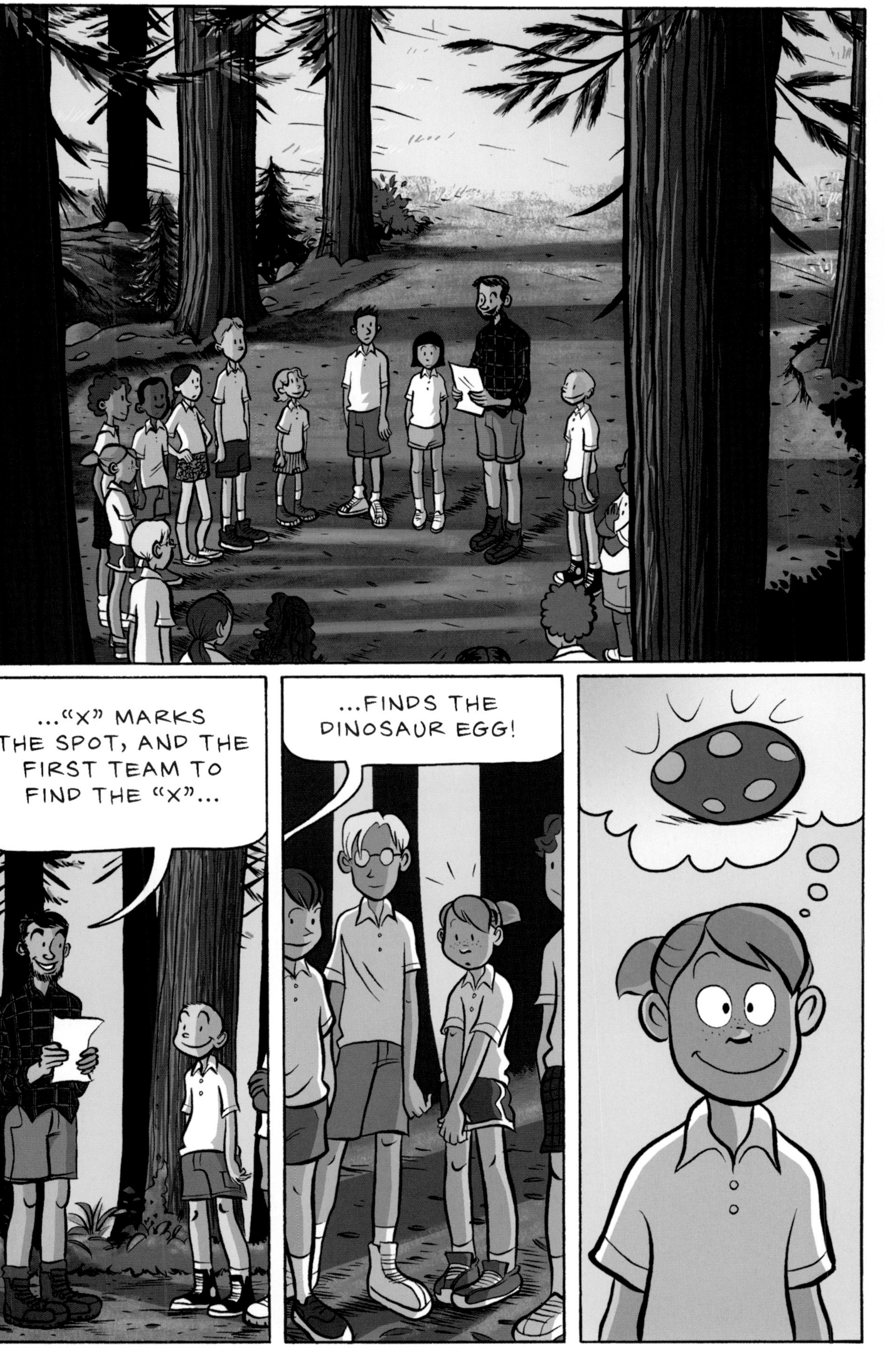
..."X" MARKS THE SPOT, AND THE FIRST TEAM TO FIND THE "X"...
...FINDS THE DINOSAUR EGG!

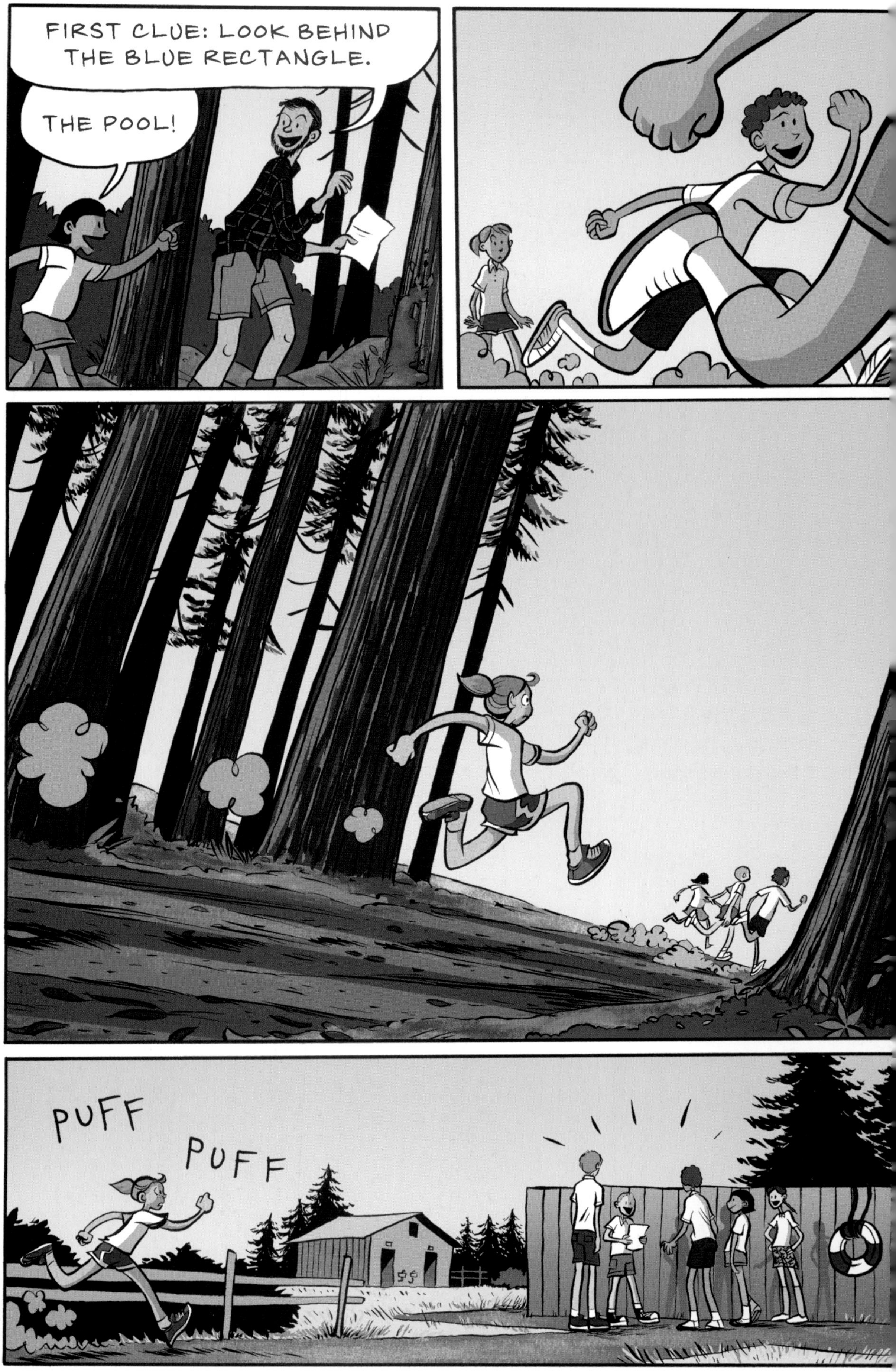
FIRST CLUE: LOOK BEHIND THE BLUE RECTANGLE.
THE POOL!
PUFF
PUFF

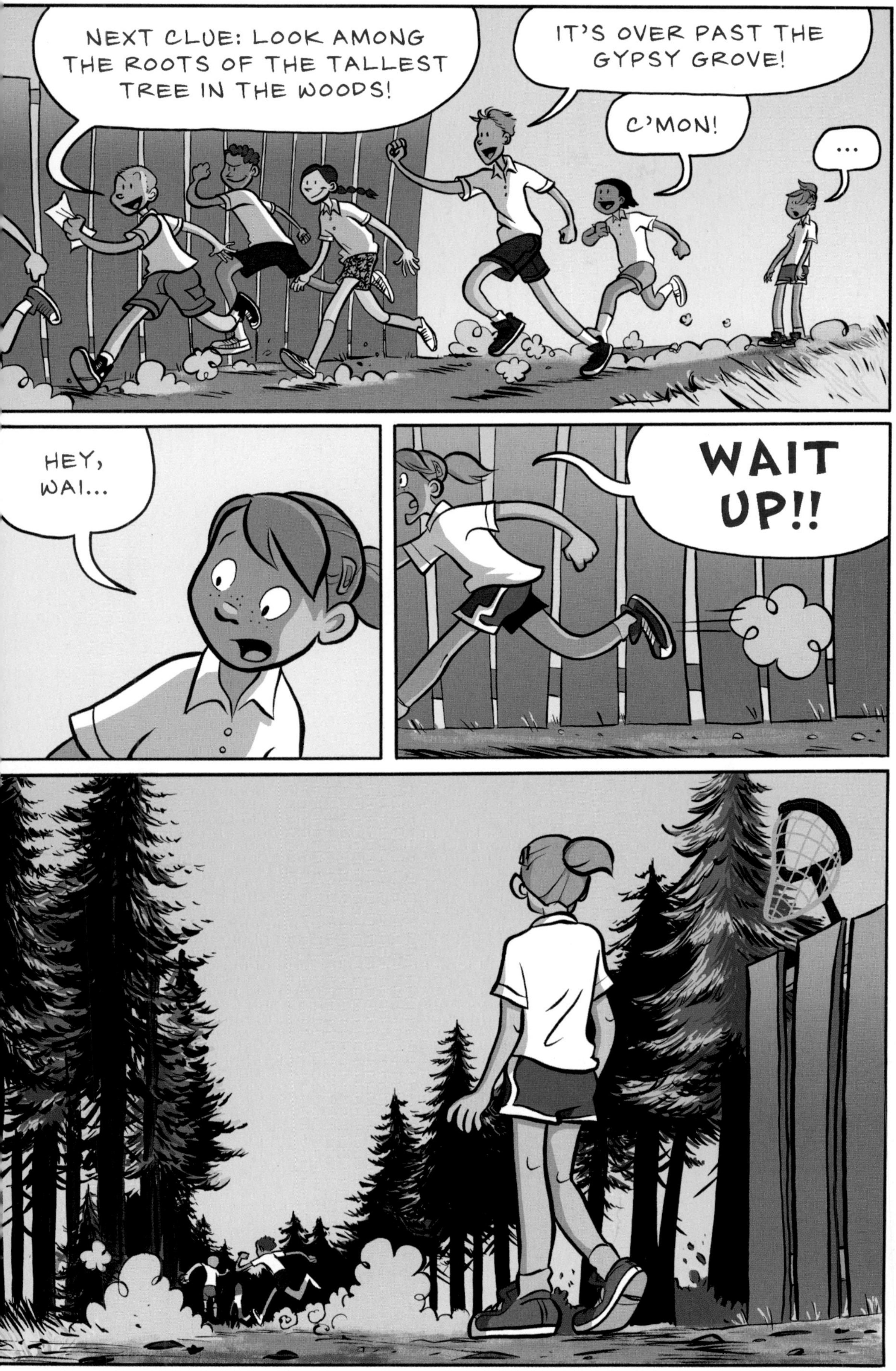
NEXT CLUE: LOOK AMONG THE ROOTS OF THE TALLEST TREE IN THE WOODS!
IT'S OVER PAST THE GYPSY GROVE!
C'MON!
...
HEY, WAI...
WAIT UP!!

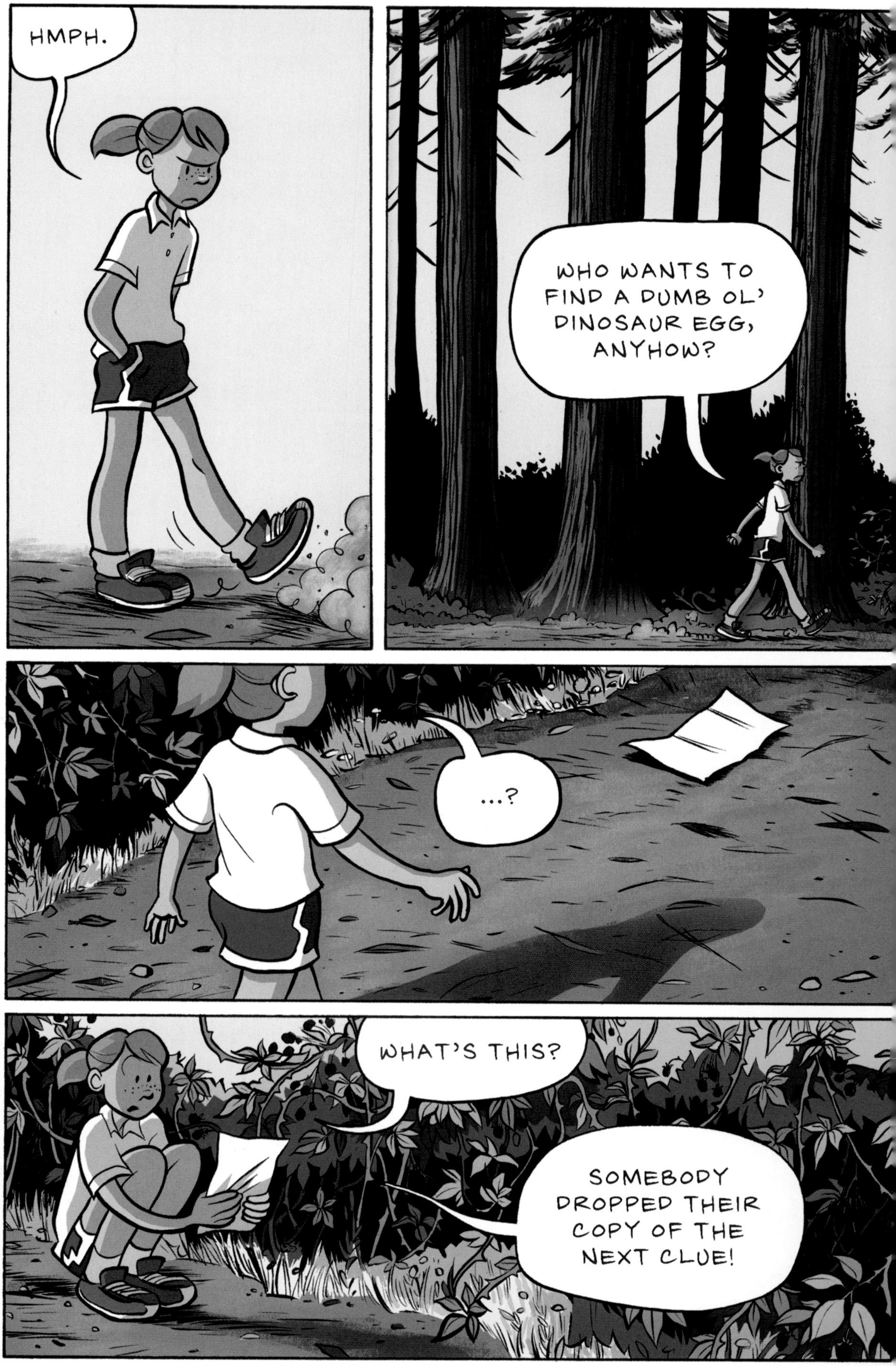
HMPH.
WHO WANTS TO FIND A DUMB OL' DINOSAUR EGG, ANYHOW?
...?
WHAT'S THIS?
SOMEBODY DROPPED THEIR COPY OF THE NEXT CLUE!

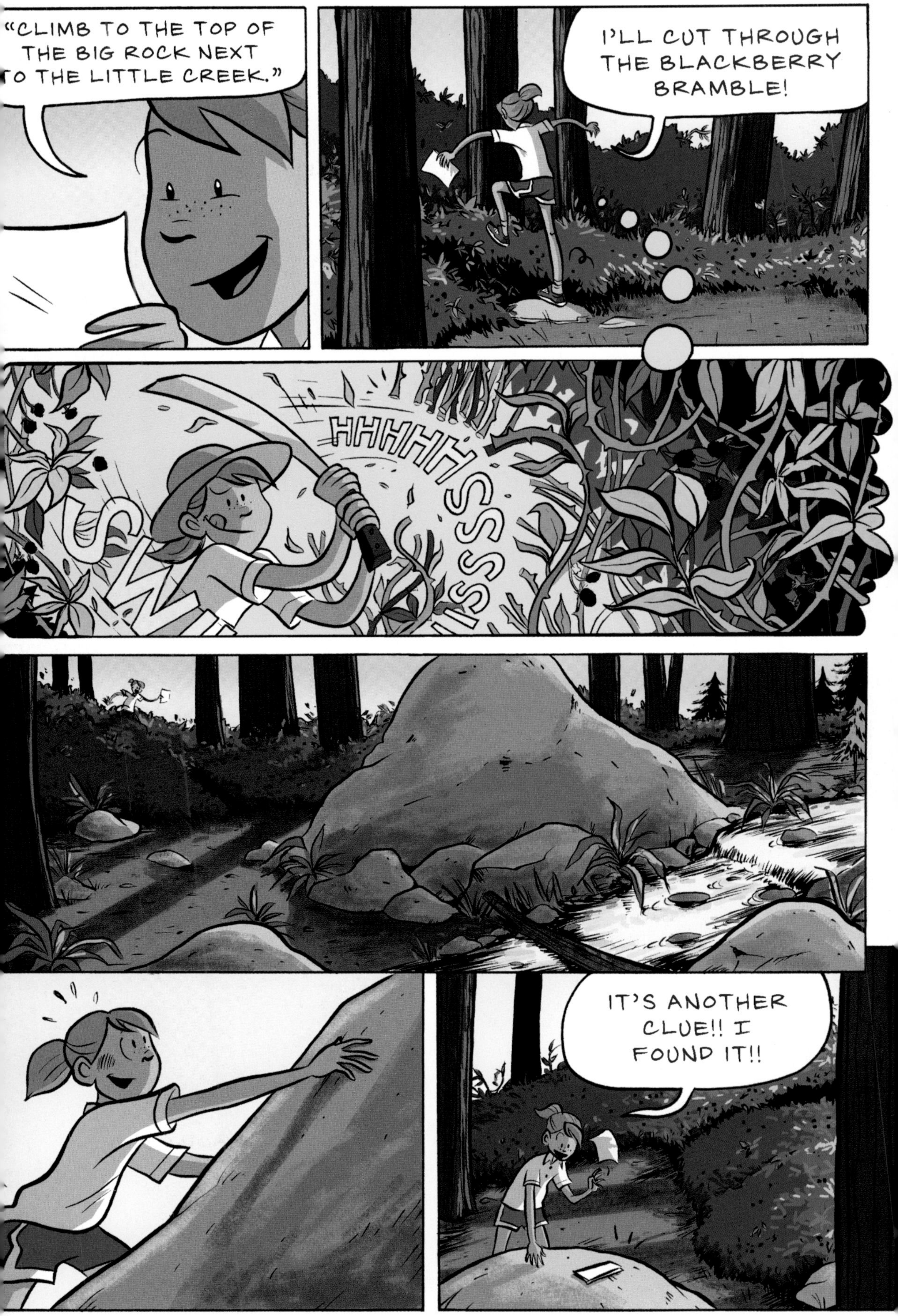
"CLIMB TO THE TOP OF THE BIG ROCK NEXT TO THE LITTLE CREEK."
I'LL CUT THROUGH THE BLACKBERRY BRAMBLE!
SWHHHHHSSSSS
IT'S ANOTHER CLUE!! I FOUND IT!!

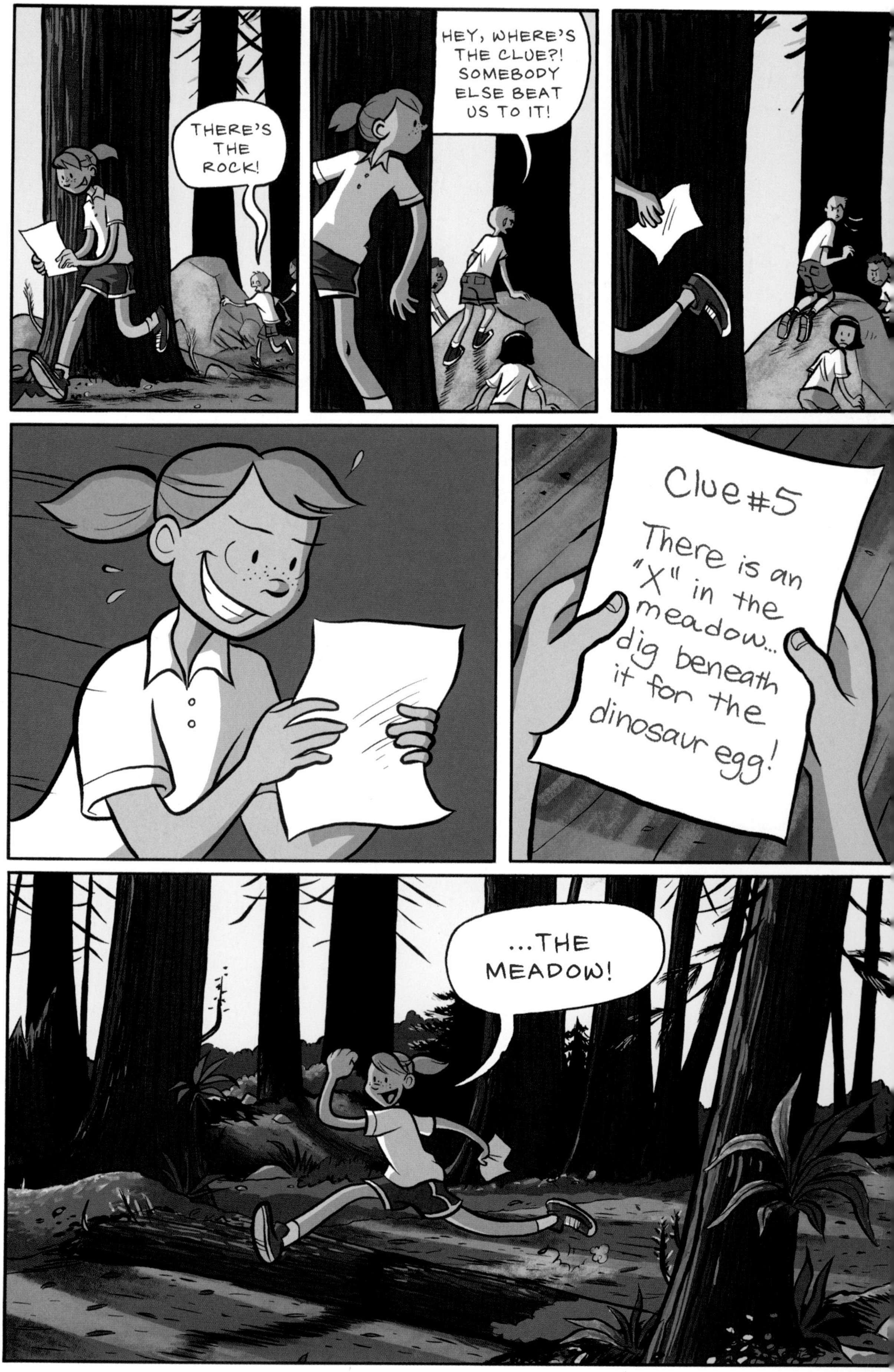
THERE'S THE ROCK!
HEY, WHERE'S THE CLUE?! SOMEBODY ELSE BEAT US TO IT!
Clue #5
There is an "X" in the meadow... dig beneath it for the dinosaur egg!
...THE MEADOW!

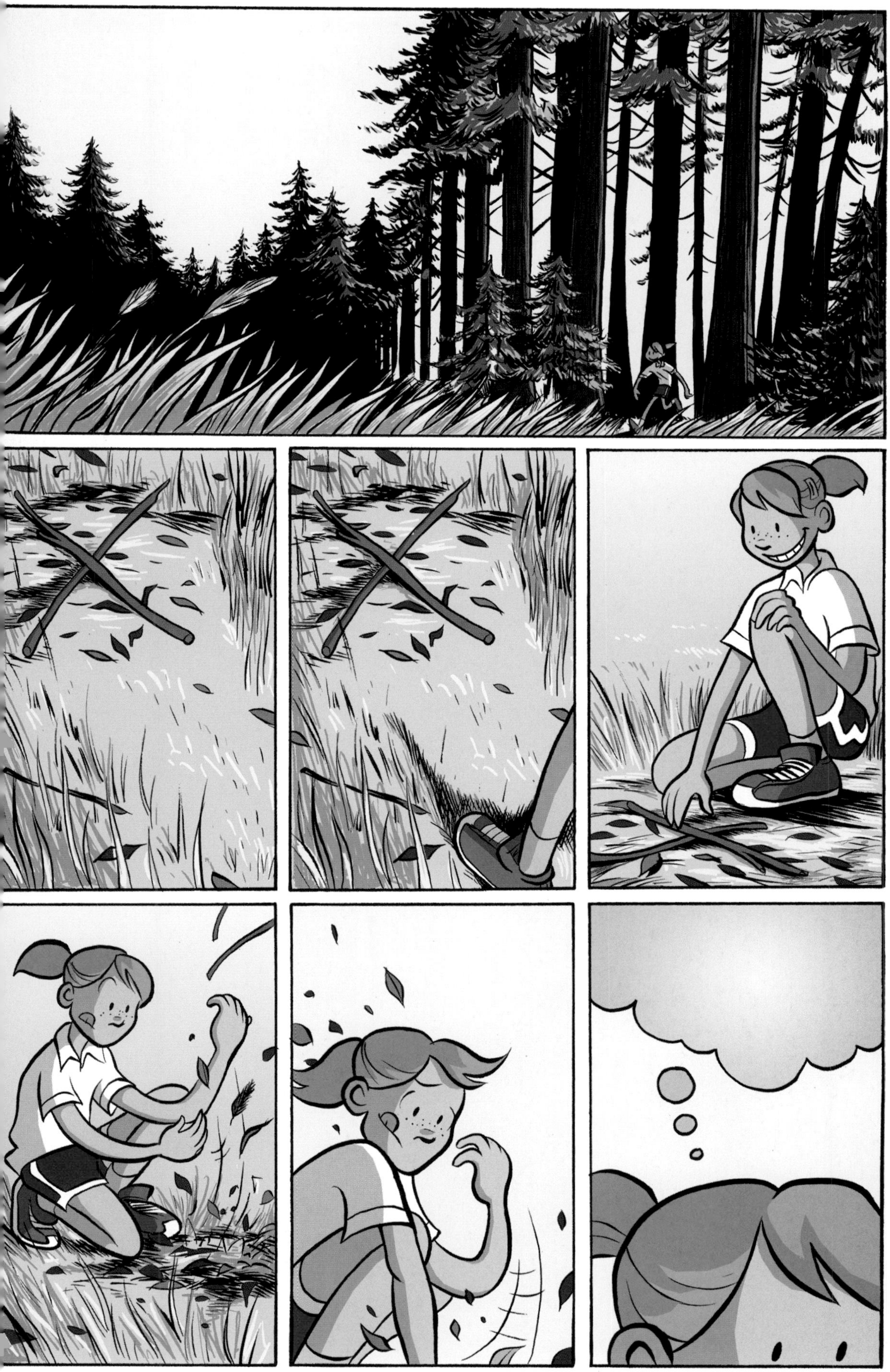

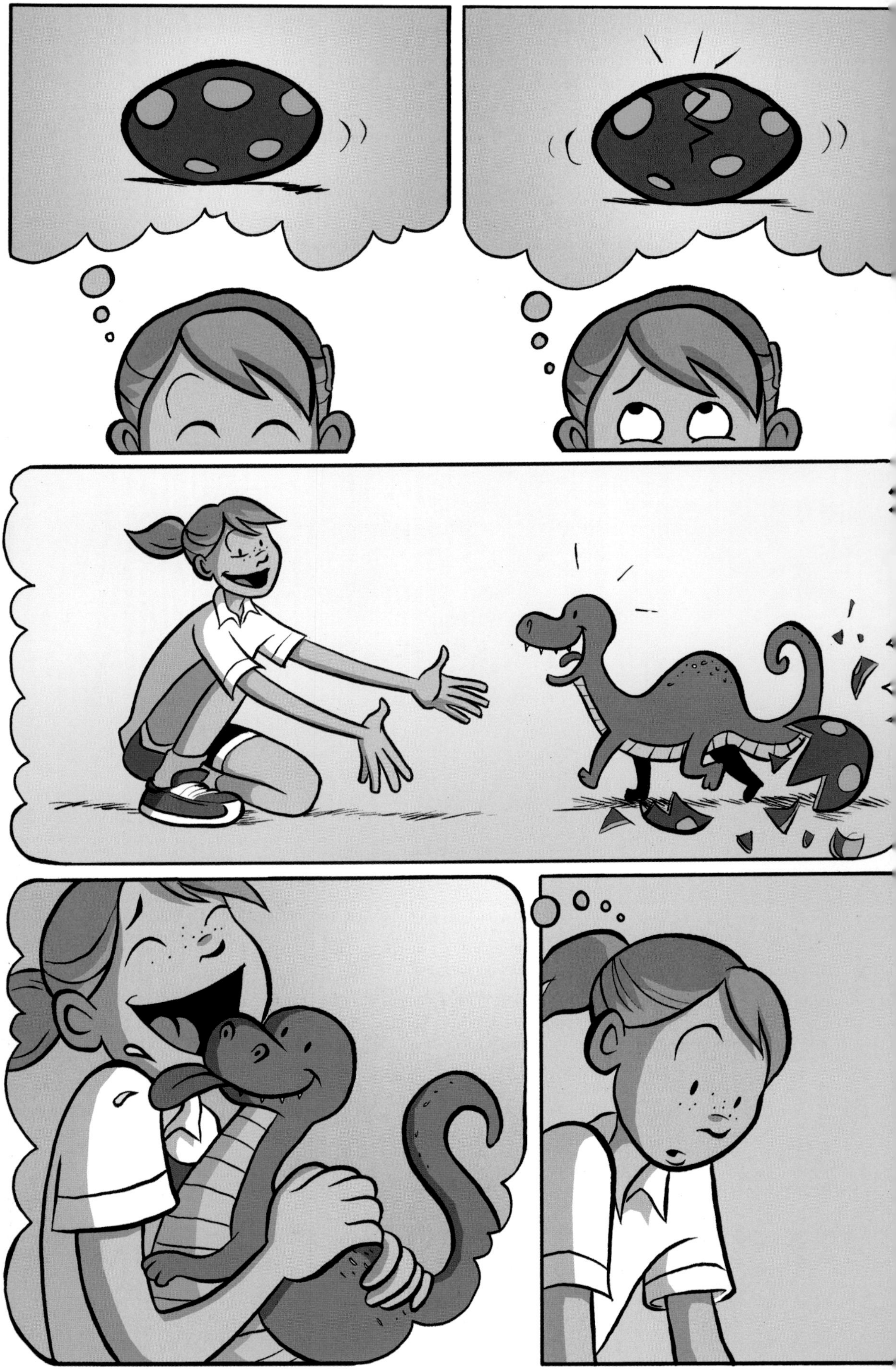

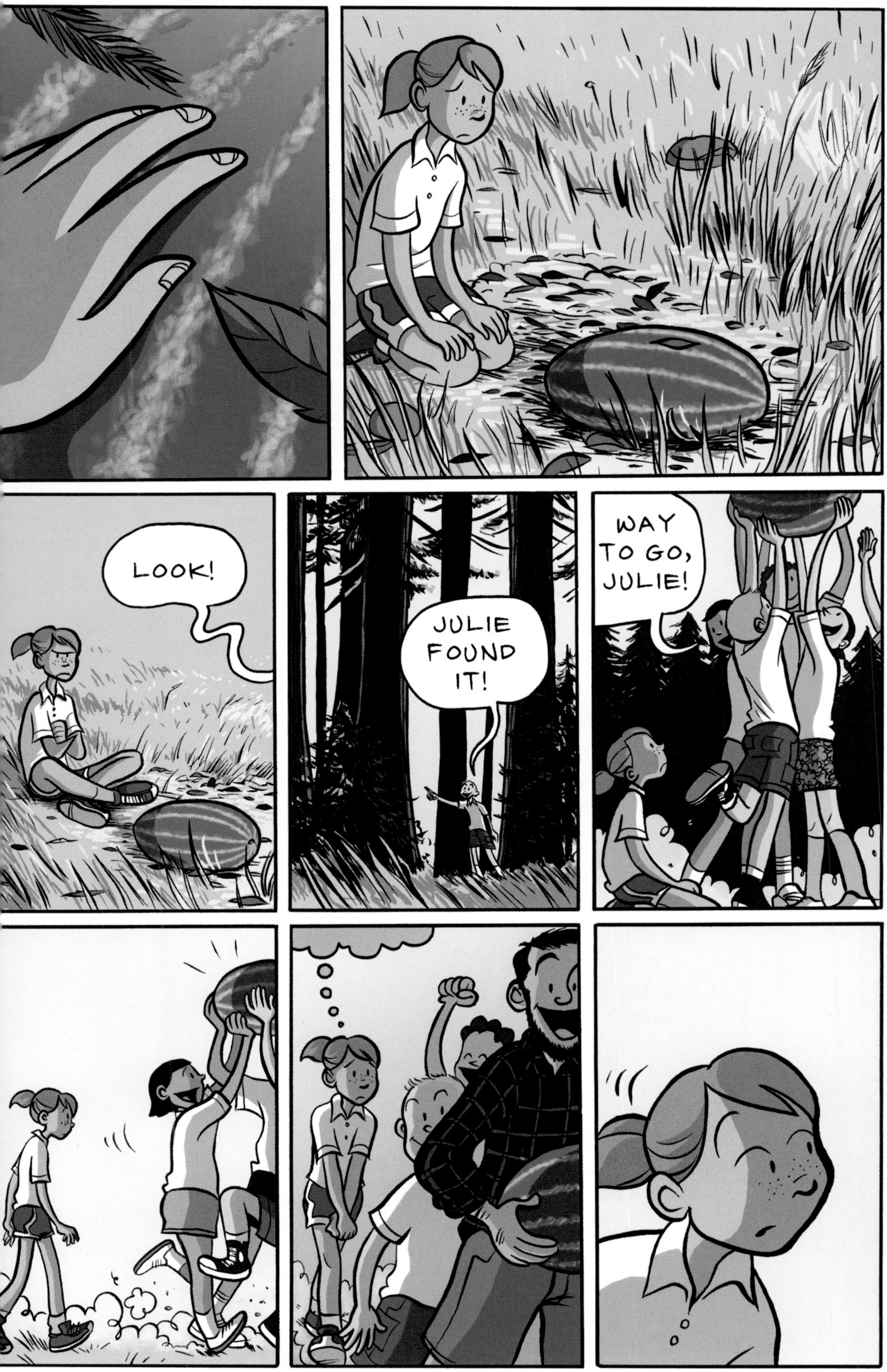
LOOK!
JULIE FOUND IT!
WAY TO GO, JULIE!

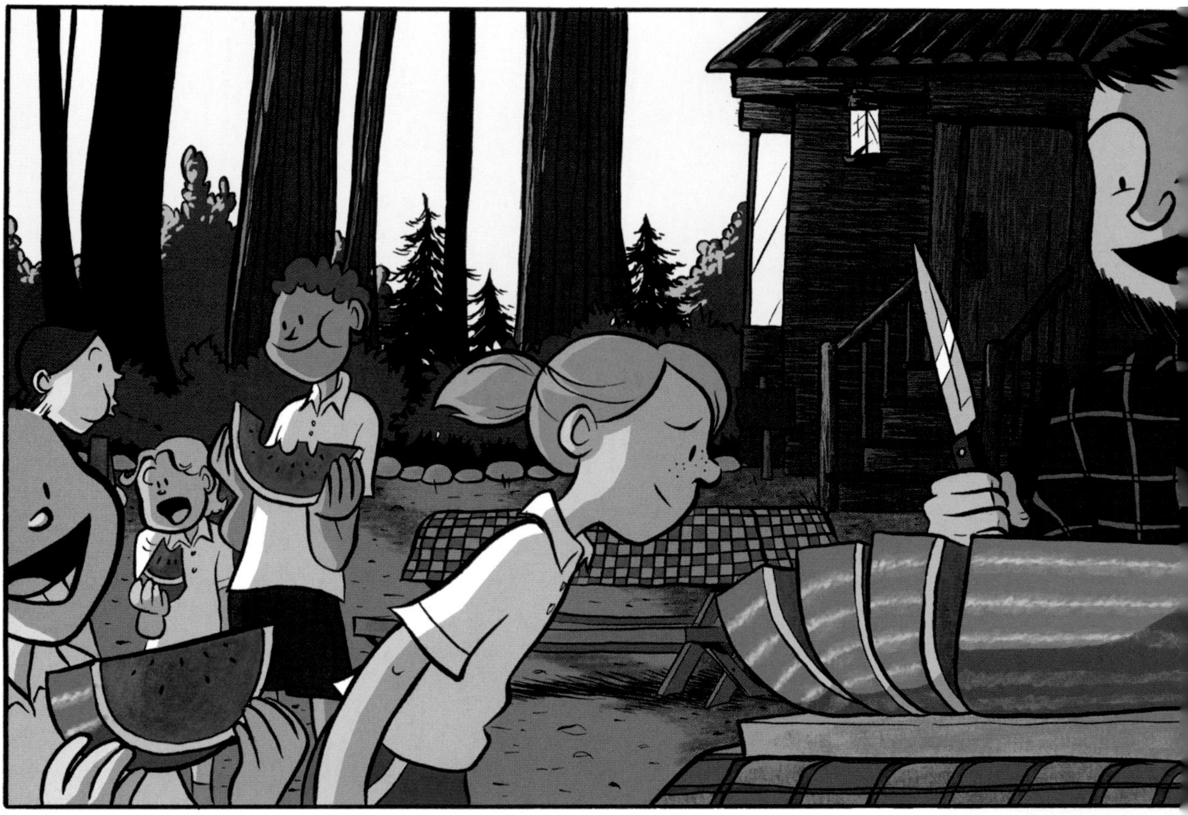

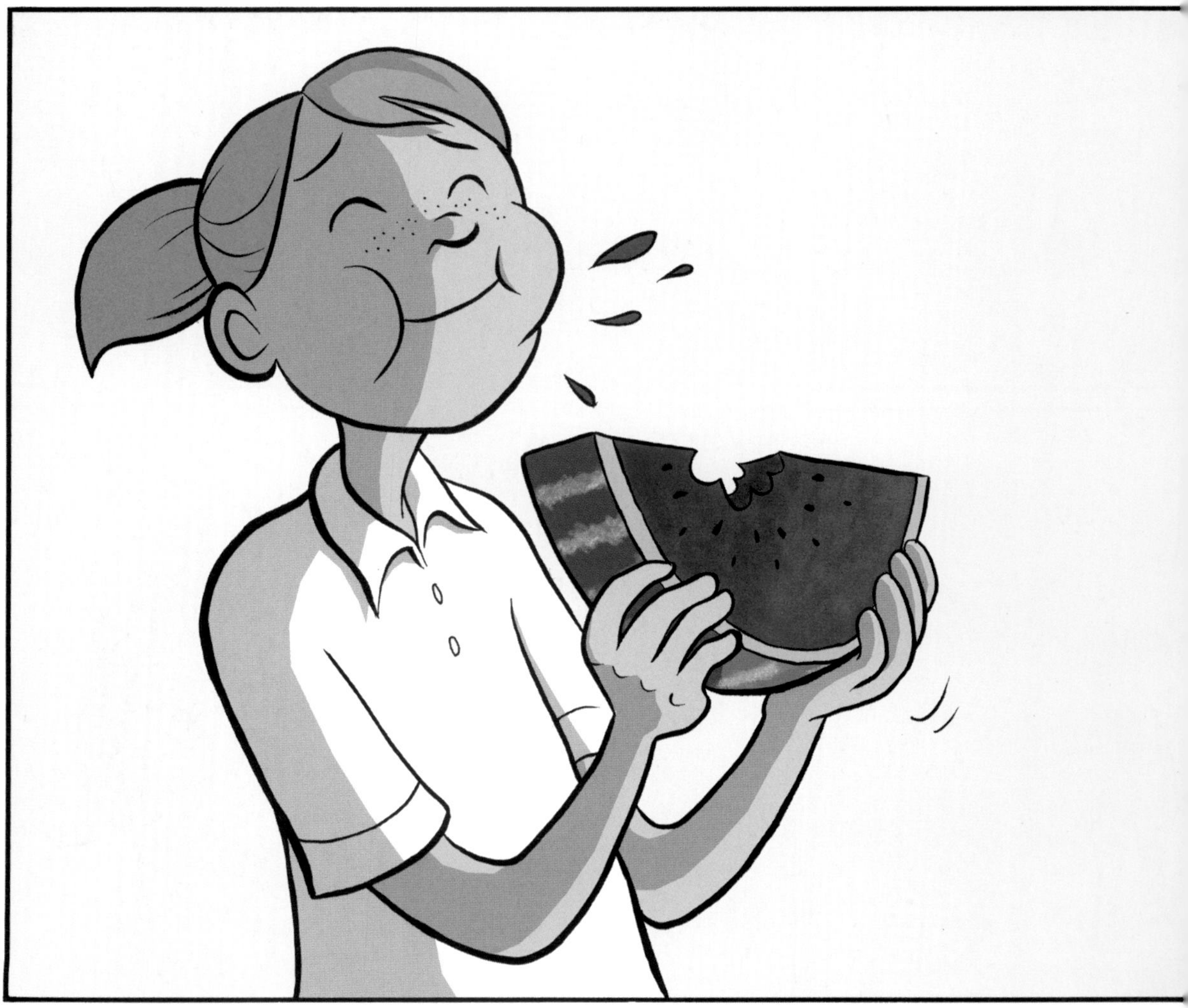

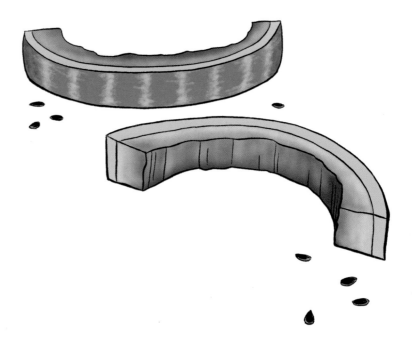

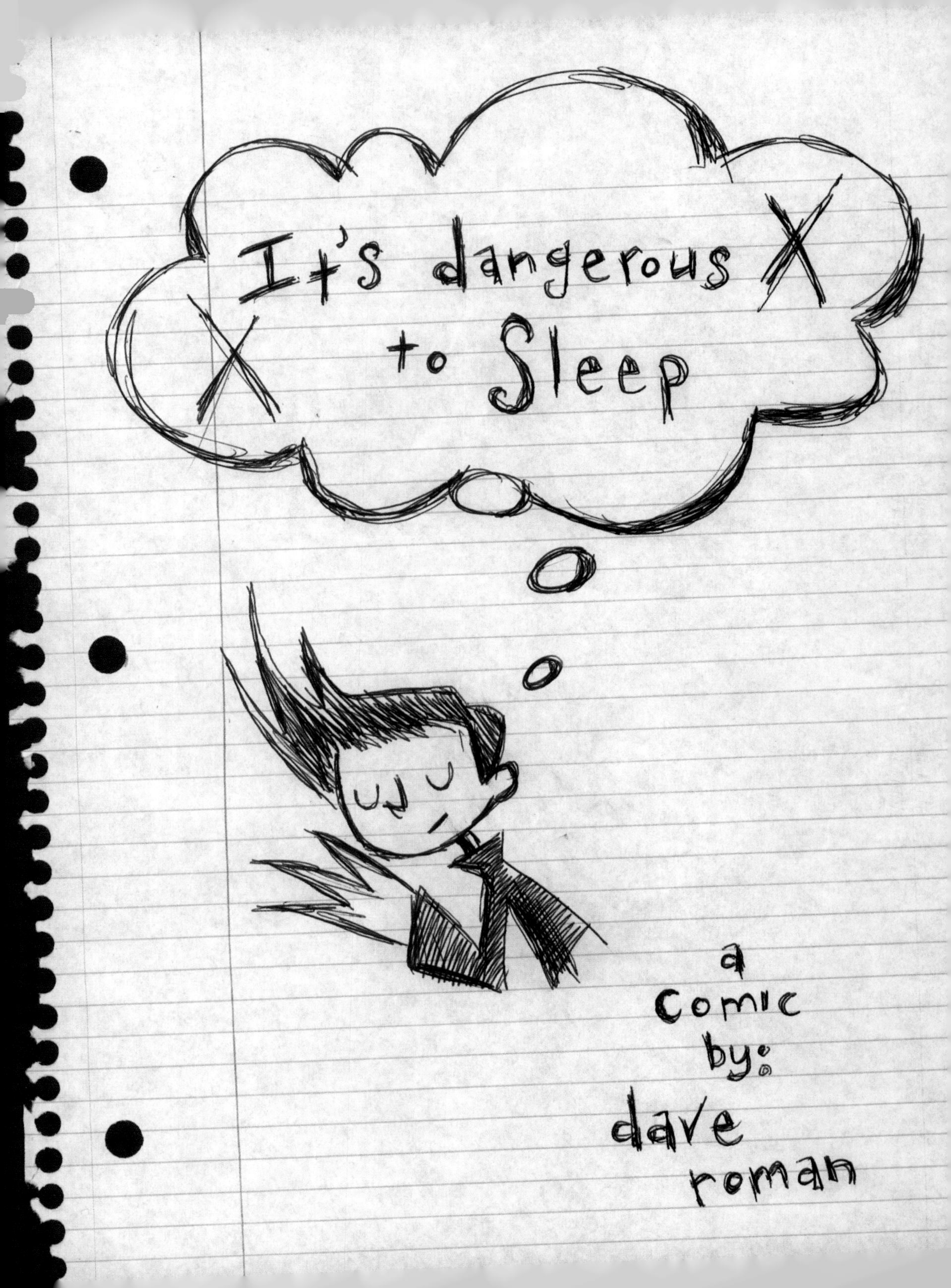
It's dangerous to Sleep
a comic by: dave roman

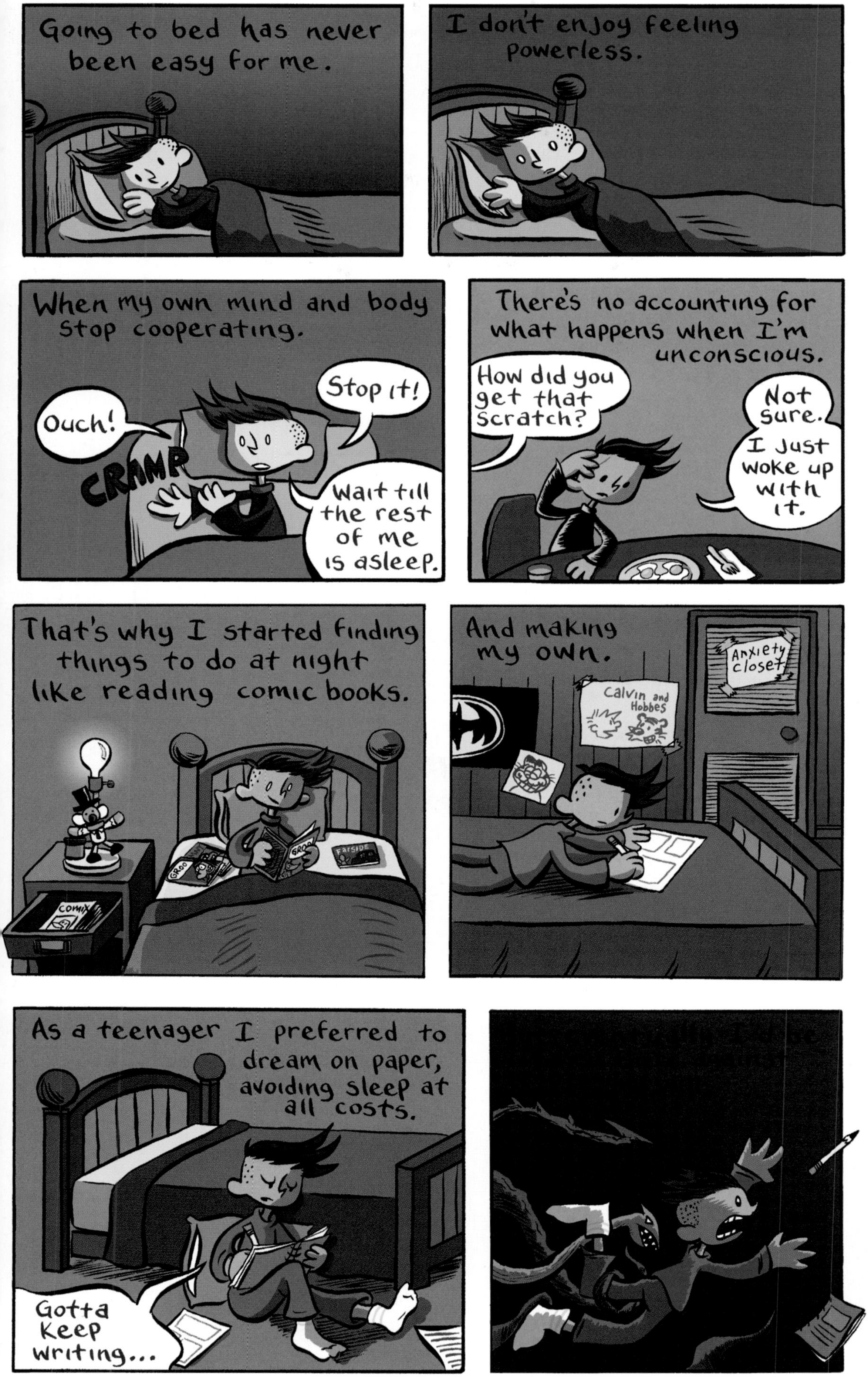
Going to bed has never been easy for me.
I don't enjoy feeling powerless.
When my own mind and body stop cooperating.
Ouch!
Stop it!
CRAMP
Wait till the rest of me is asleep.
There's no accounting for what happens when I'm unconscious.
How did you get that scratch?
Not sure.
I just woke up with it.
That's why I started finding things to do at night like reading comic books.
GROO
GROO
FARSIDE
COMIX
And making my own.
Anxiety closet
Calvin and Hobbes
As a teenager I preferred to dream on paper, avoiding sleep at all costs.
Gotta keep writing...

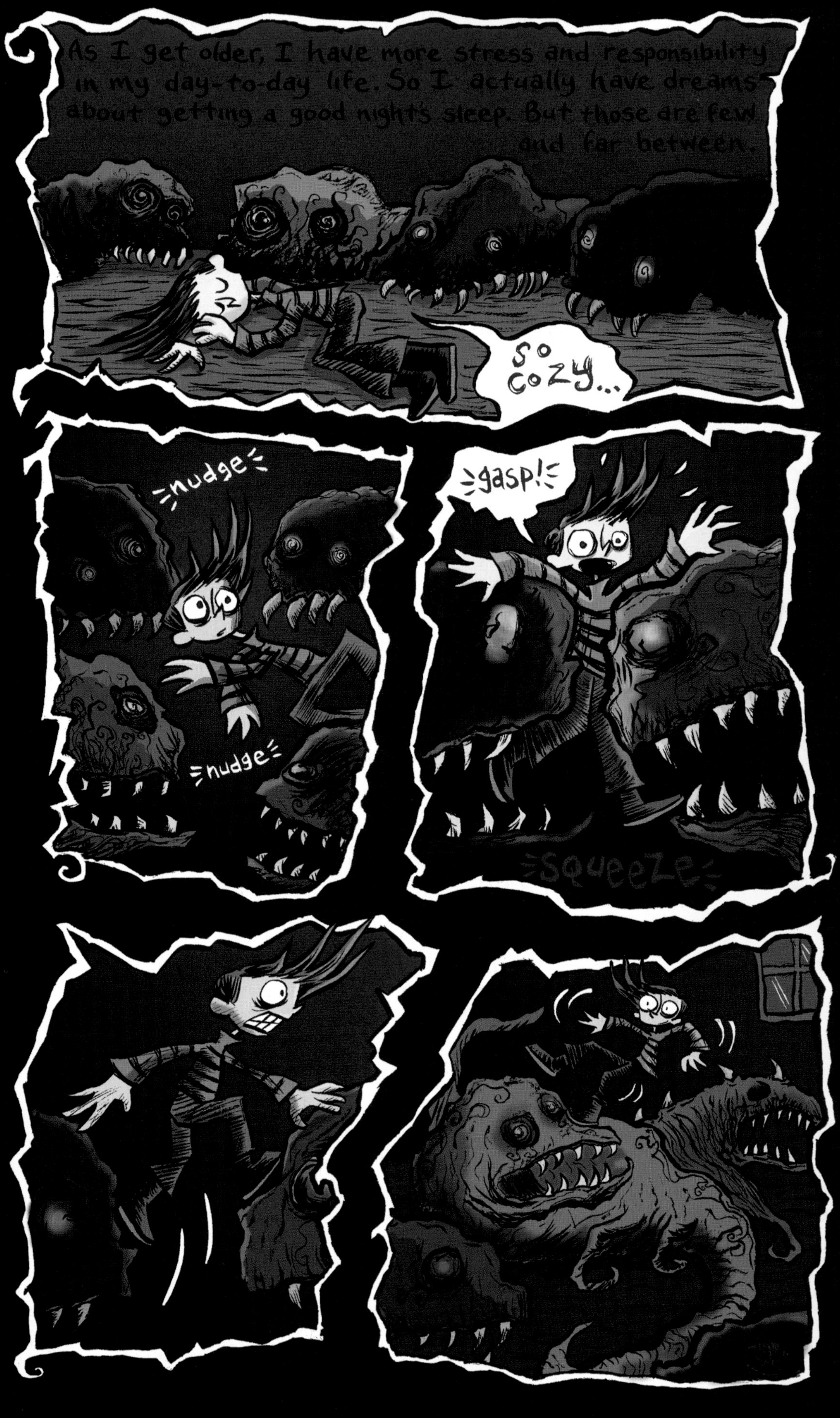

As I get older, I have more stress and responsibility in my day-to-day life. So I actually have dreams about getting a good night's sleep. But those are few and far between.
So cozy...
nudge
nudge
gasp!
squeeze

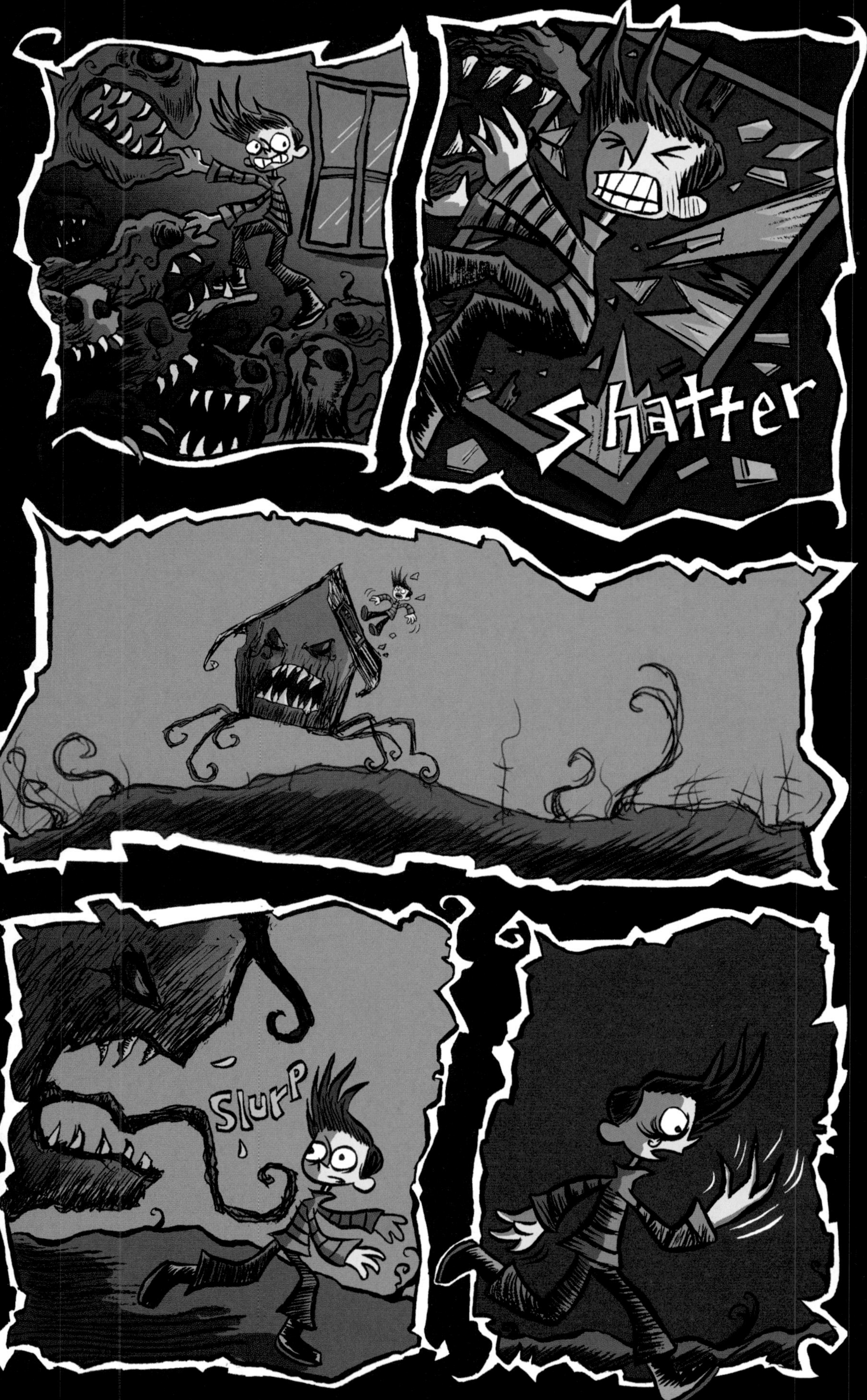
Shatter
Slurp

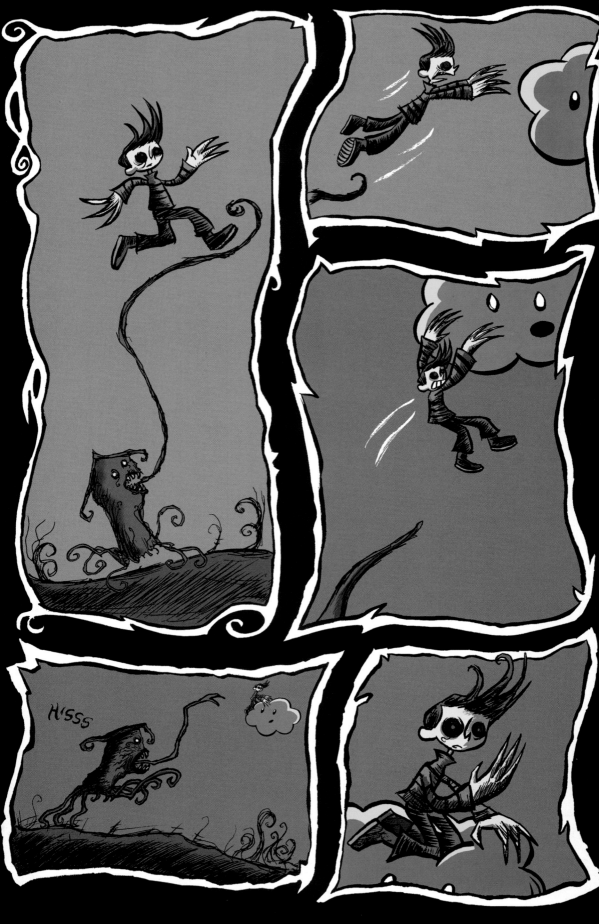

HISSS

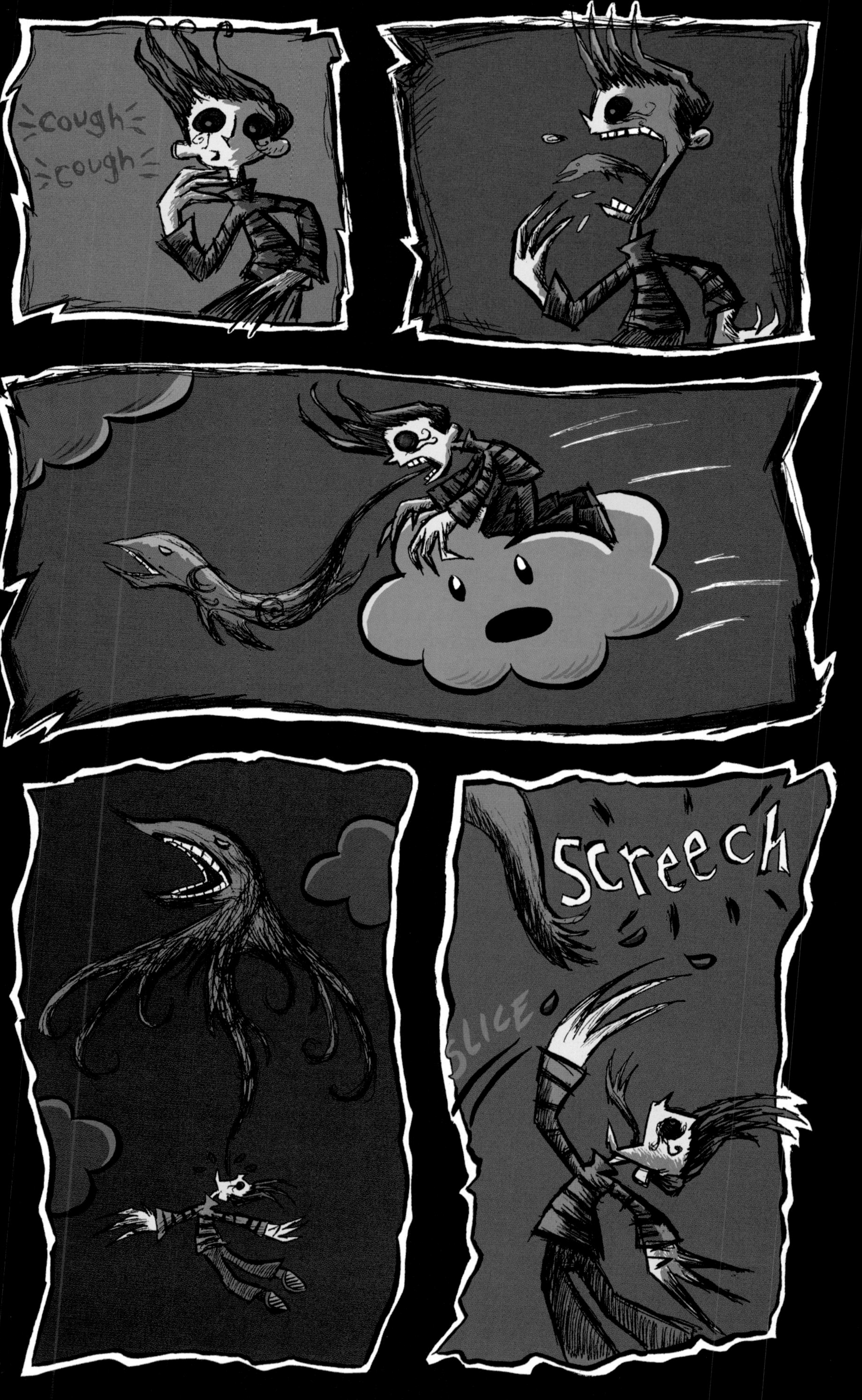
cough
cough
Screech
SLICE

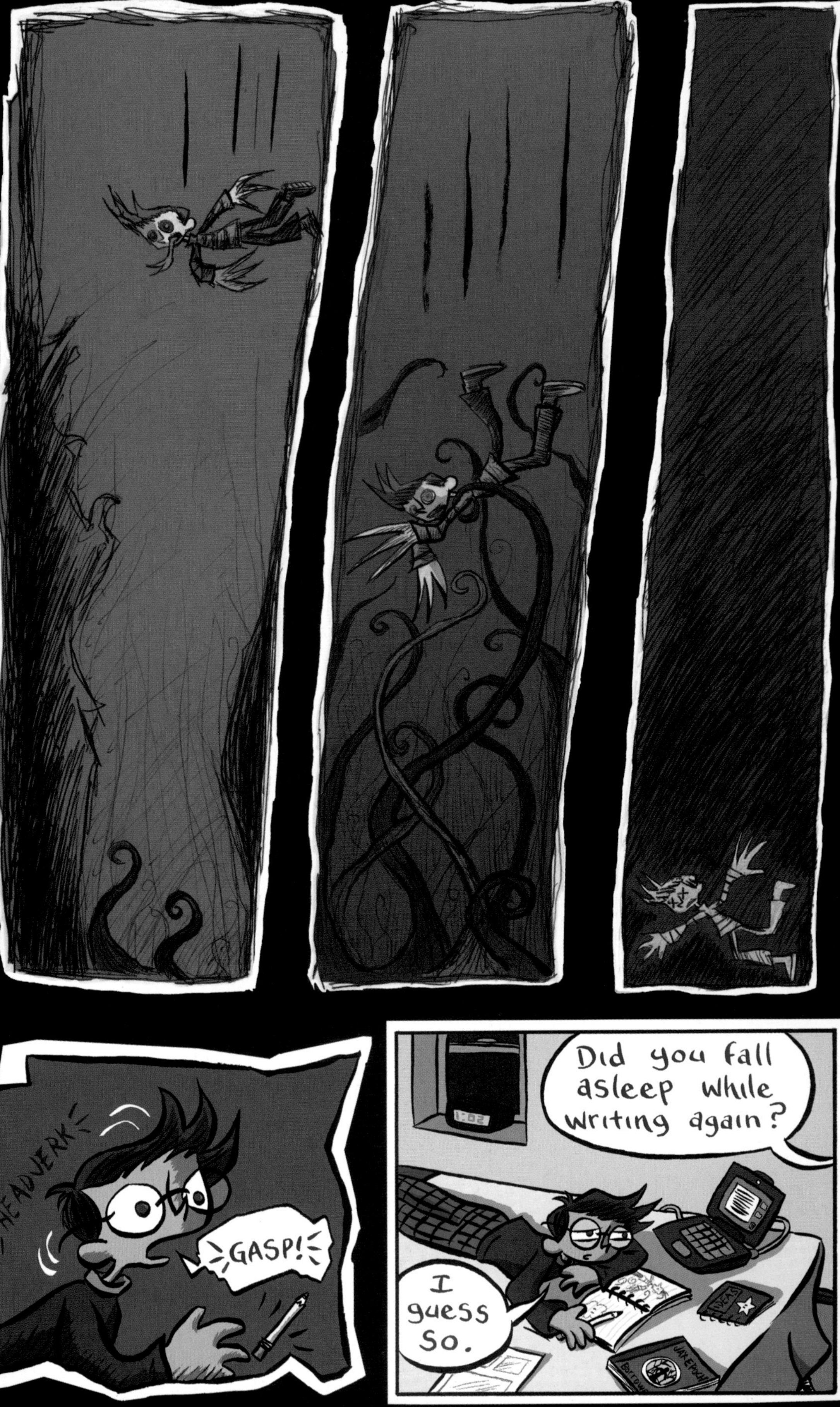
HEADJERK
GASP!
Did you fall asleep while writing again?
I guess so.

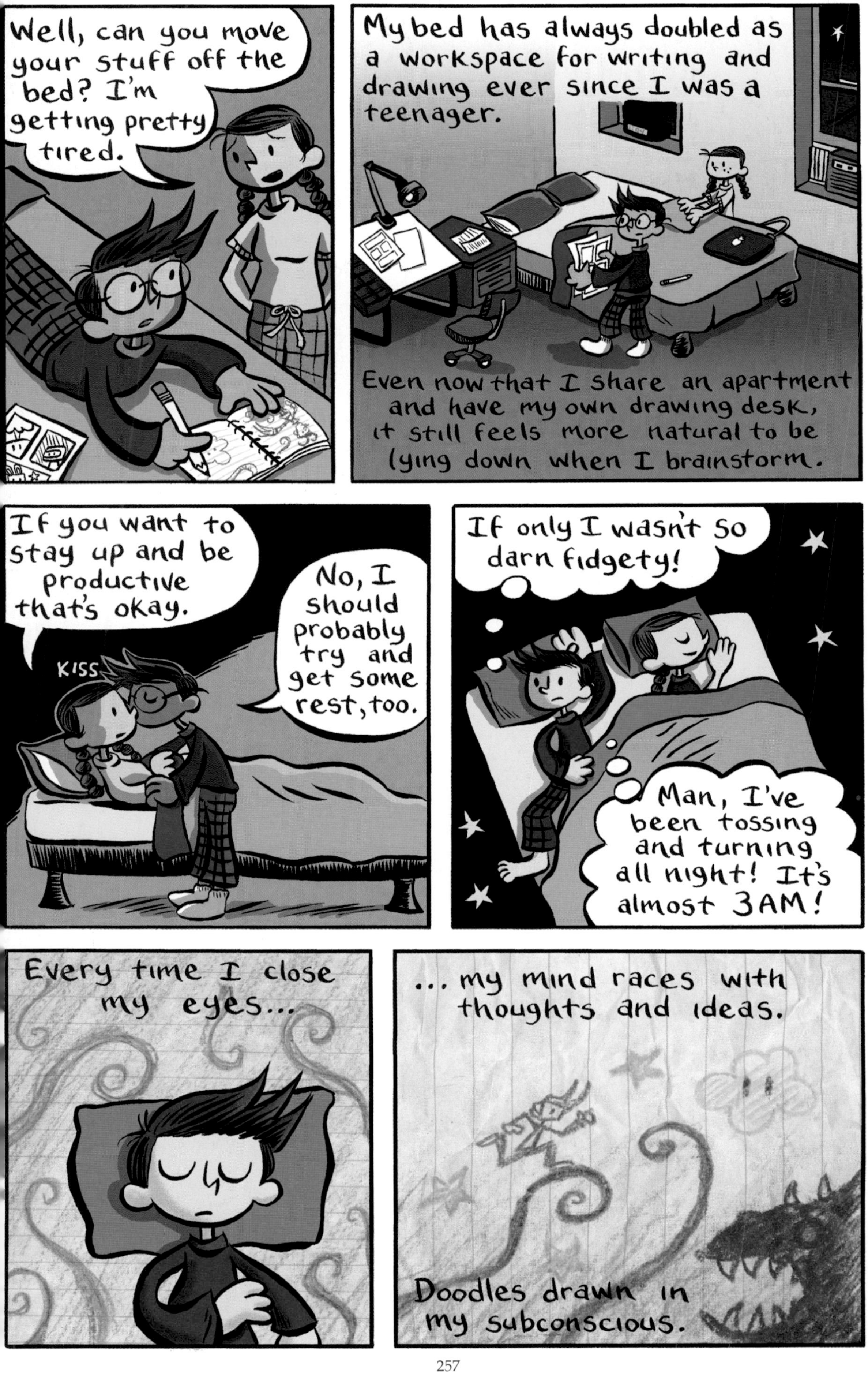
Well, can you move your stuff off the bed? I'm getting pretty tired.
My bed has always doubled as a workspace for writing and drawing ever since I was a teenager.
Even now that I share an apartment and have my own drawing desk, it still feels more natural to be lying down when I brainstorm.
If you want to stay up and be productive that's okay.
KISS
No, I should probably try and get some rest, too.
If only I wasn't so darn fidgety!
Man, I've been tossing and turning all night! It's almost 3AM!
Every time I close my eyes...
... my mind races with thoughts and ideas.
Doodles drawn in my subconscious.

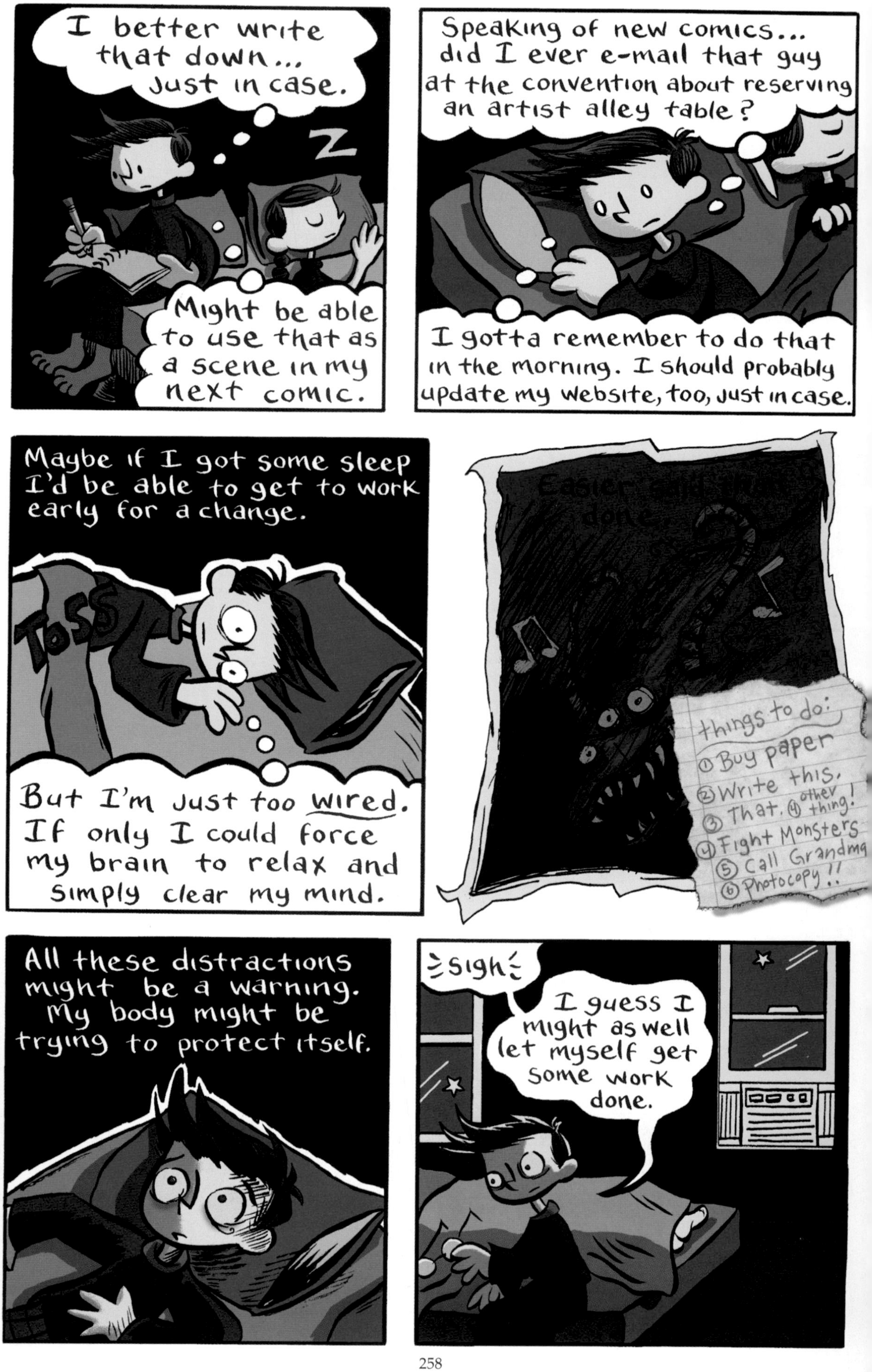
I better write that down... just in case.
Z
Might be able to use that as a scene in my next comic.
Speaking of new comics... did I ever e-mail that guy at the convention about reserving an artist alley table?
I gotta remember to do that in the morning. I should probably update my website, too, just in case.
Maybe if I got some sleep I'd be able to get to work early for a change.
TOSS
But I'm just too wired. If only I could force my brain to relax and simply clear my mind.
Easier said than done.
things to do:
① Buy paper
② Write this,
③ That, ④ other thing!
④ Fight Monsters
⑤ Call Grandma
⑥ Photocopy!!
All these distractions might be a warning. My body might be trying to protect itself.
Sigh
I guess I might as well let myself get some work done.

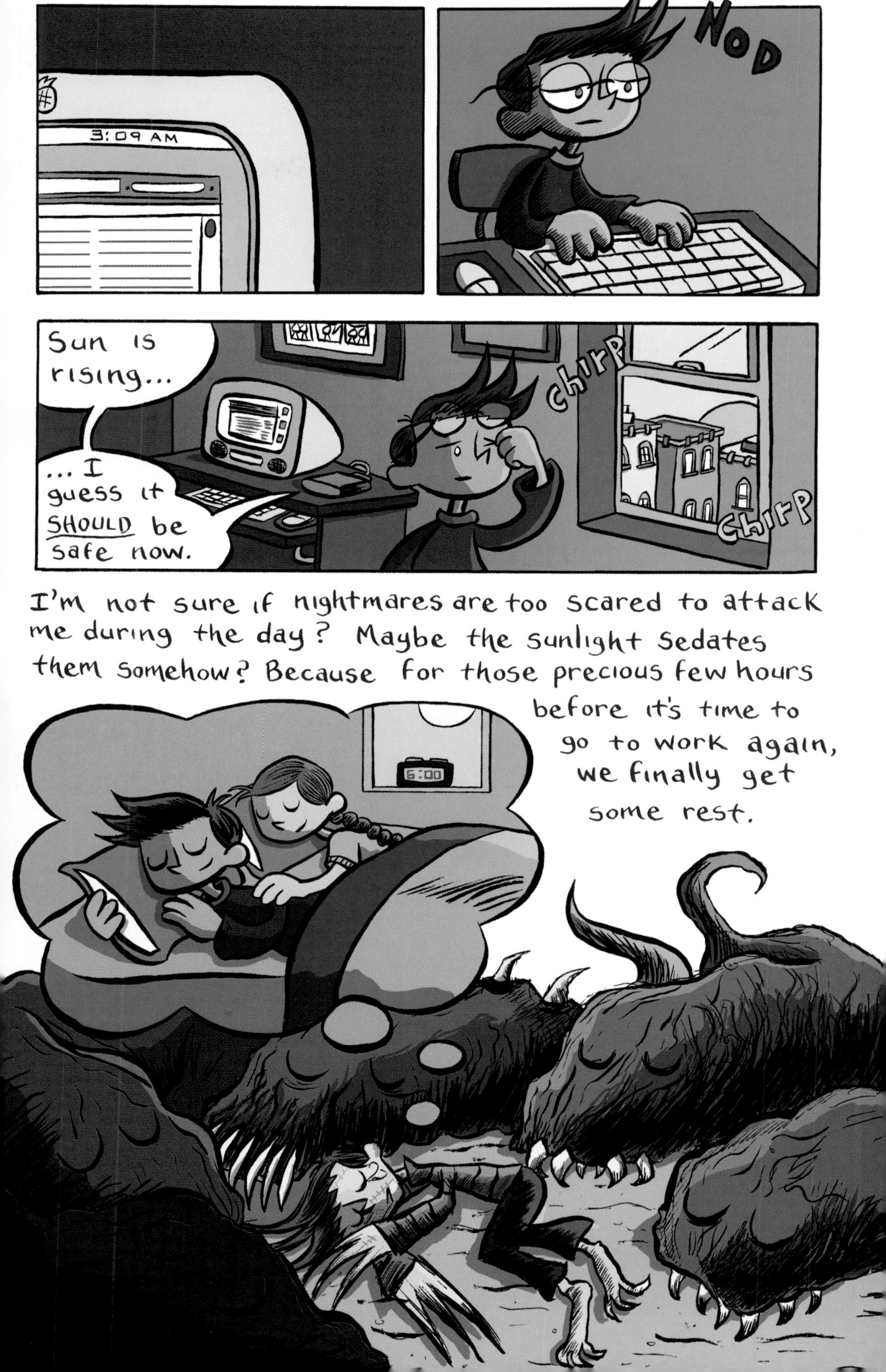
3:09 AM
NOD
Sun is rising...
... I guess it SHOULD be safe now.
CHIRP
CHIRP
I'm not sure if nightmares are too scared to attack me during the day? Maybe the sunlight sedates them somehow? Because for those precious few hours before it's time to go to work again, we finally get some rest.
6:00

MYSTICAL MONKEY

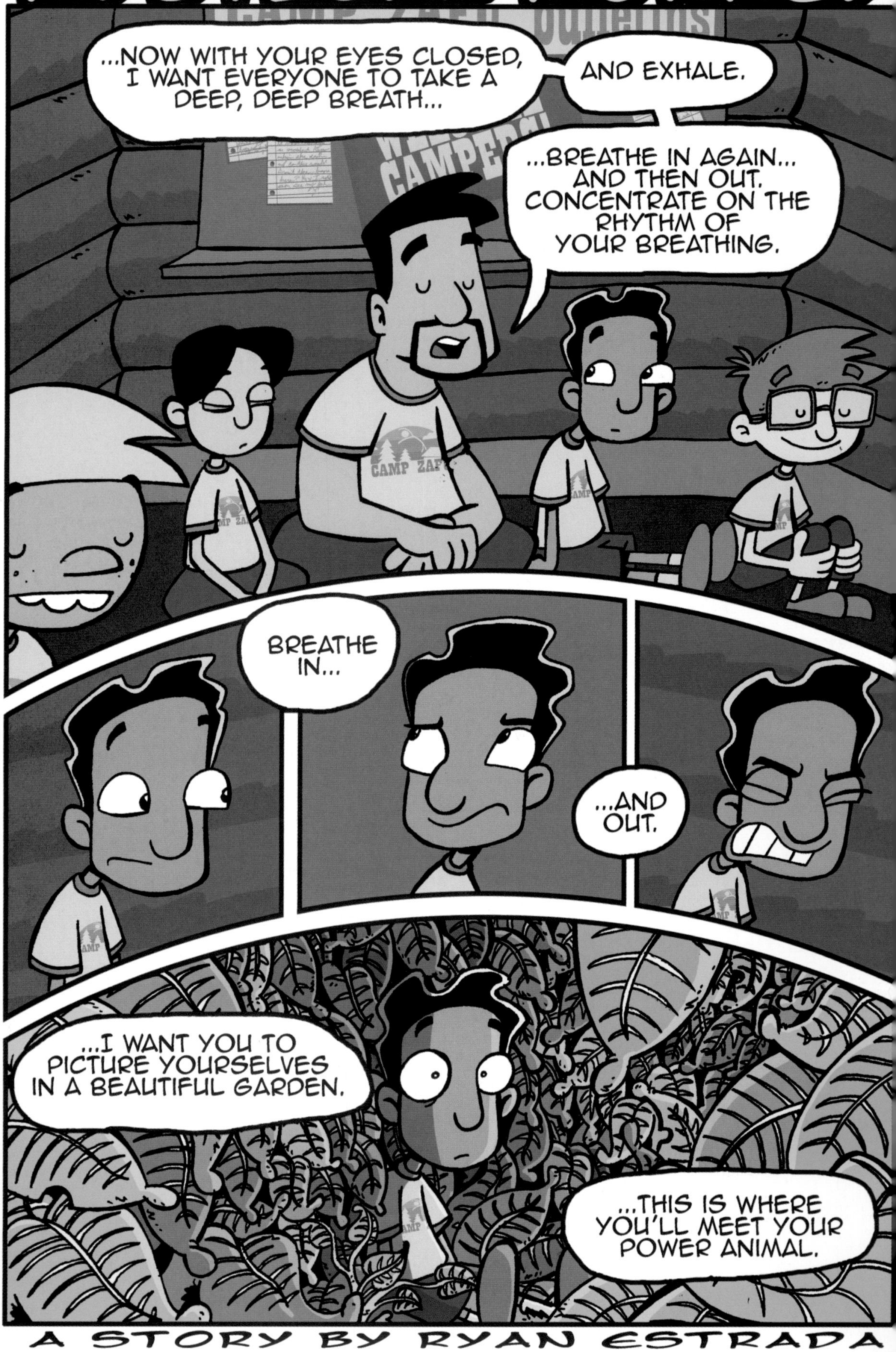
...NOW WITH YOUR EYES CLOSED, I WANT EVERYONE TO TAKE A DEEP, DEEP BREATH...
AND EXHALE.
...BREATHE IN AGAIN... AND THEN OUT. CONCENTRATE ON THE RHYTHM OF YOUR BREATHING.
CAMP ZAPP
BREATHE IN...
...AND OUT.
...I WANT YOU TO PICTURE YOURSELVES IN A BEAUTIFUL GARDEN.
...THIS IS WHERE YOU'LL MEET YOUR POWER ANIMAL.

A STORY BY RYAN ESTRADA

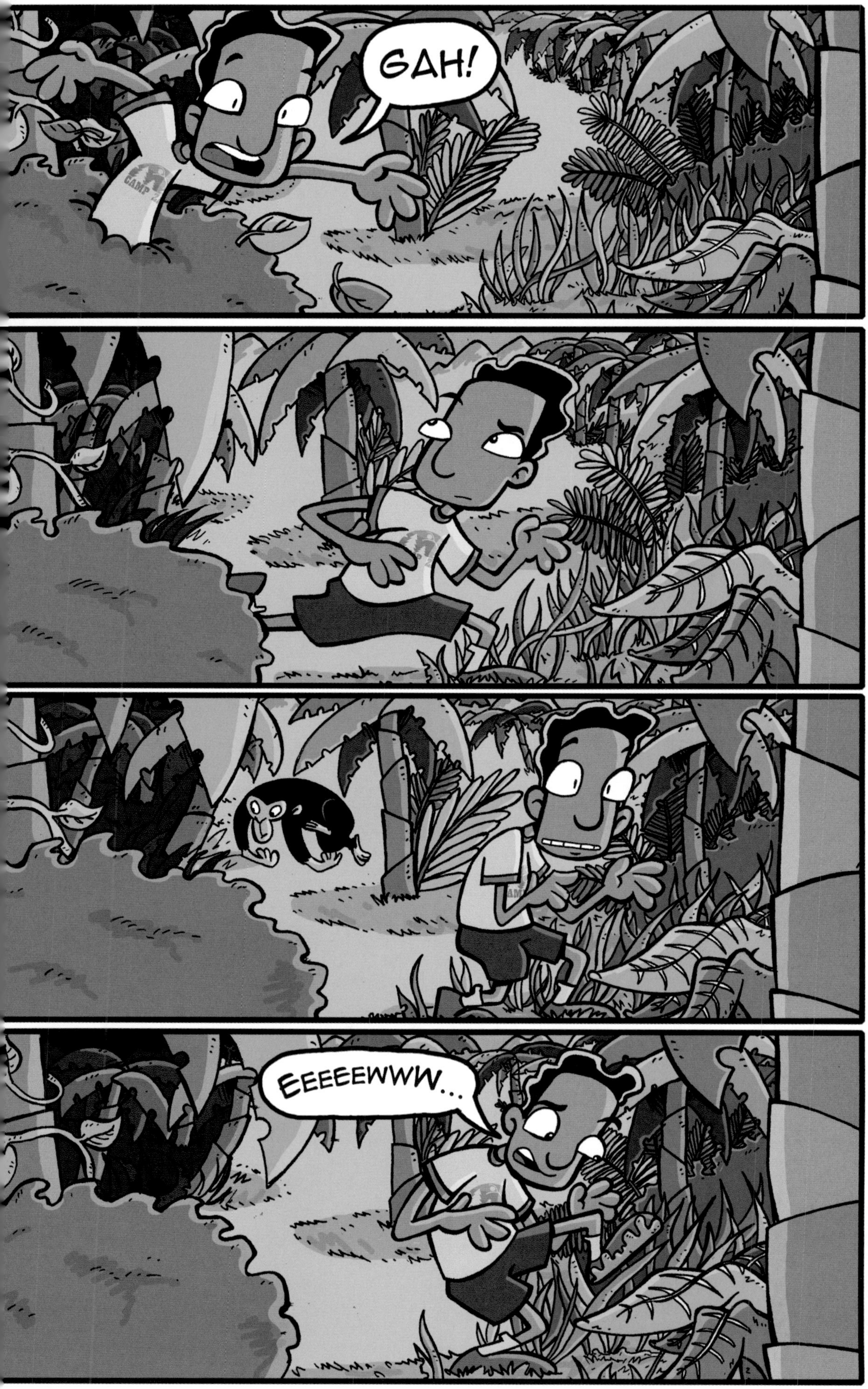
GAH!
EEEEEWWW...

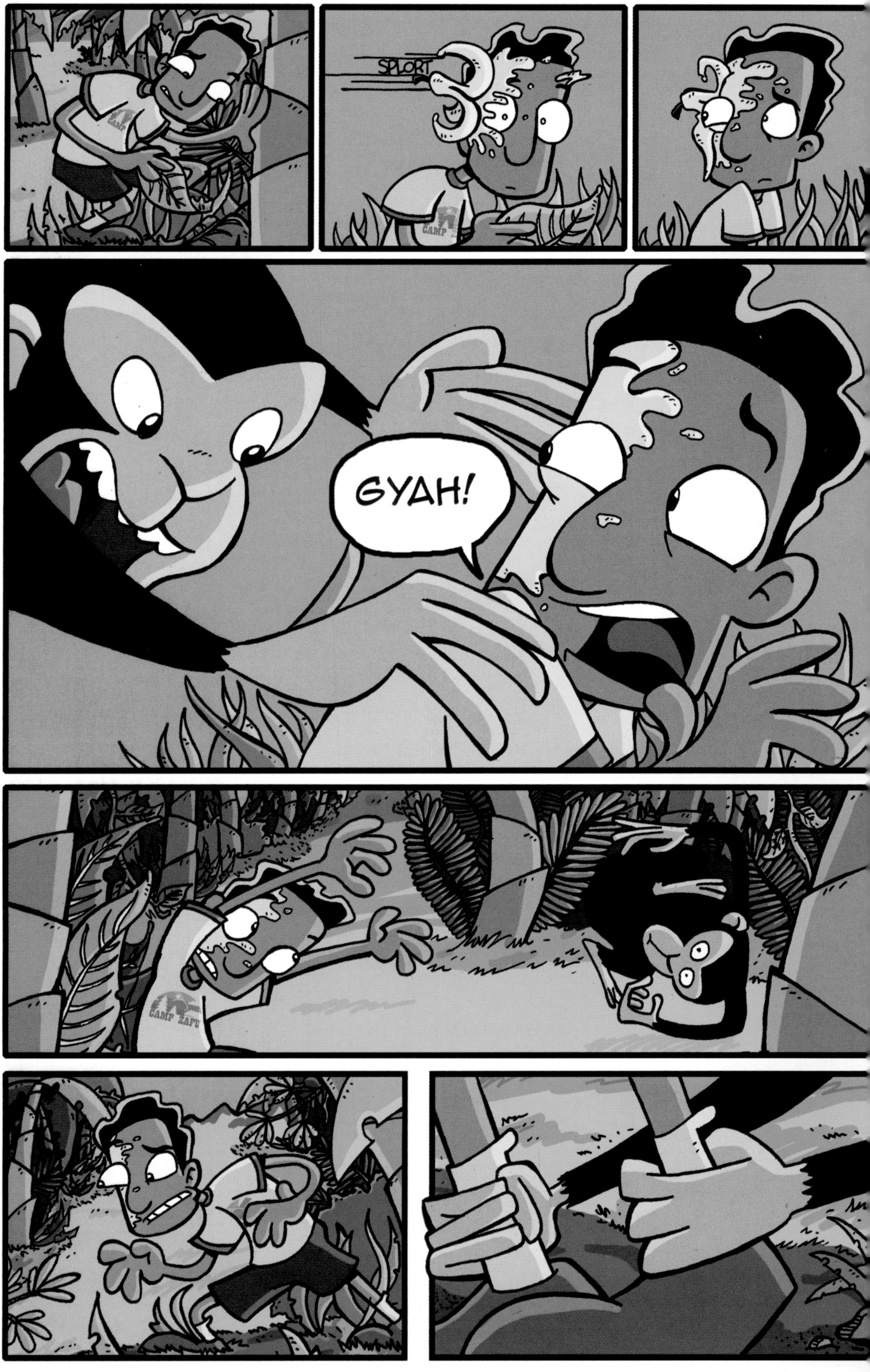
SPLORT
GYAH!

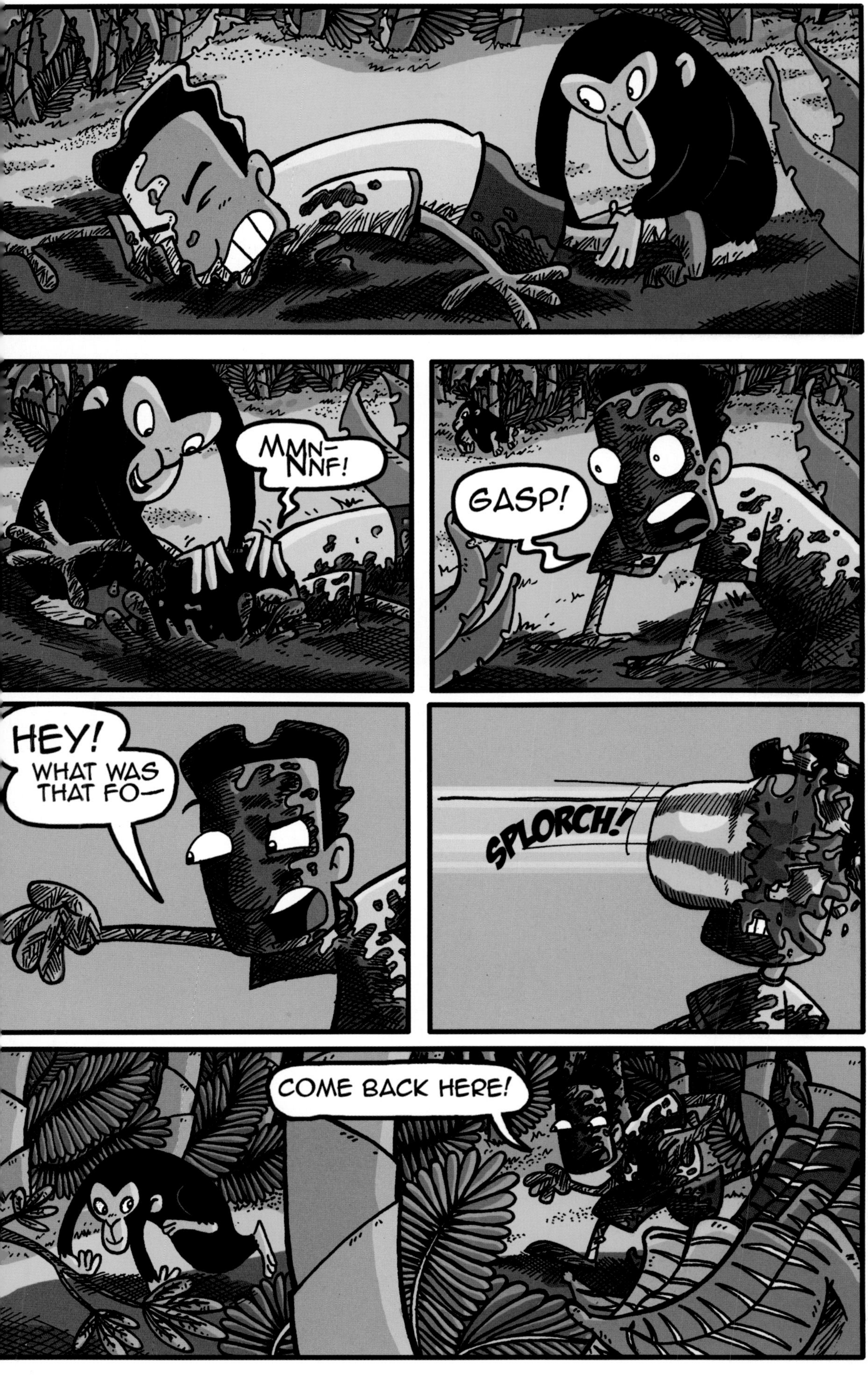
MMN-NNF!
GASP!
HEY! WHAT WAS THAT FO—
SPLORCH!
COME BACK HERE!

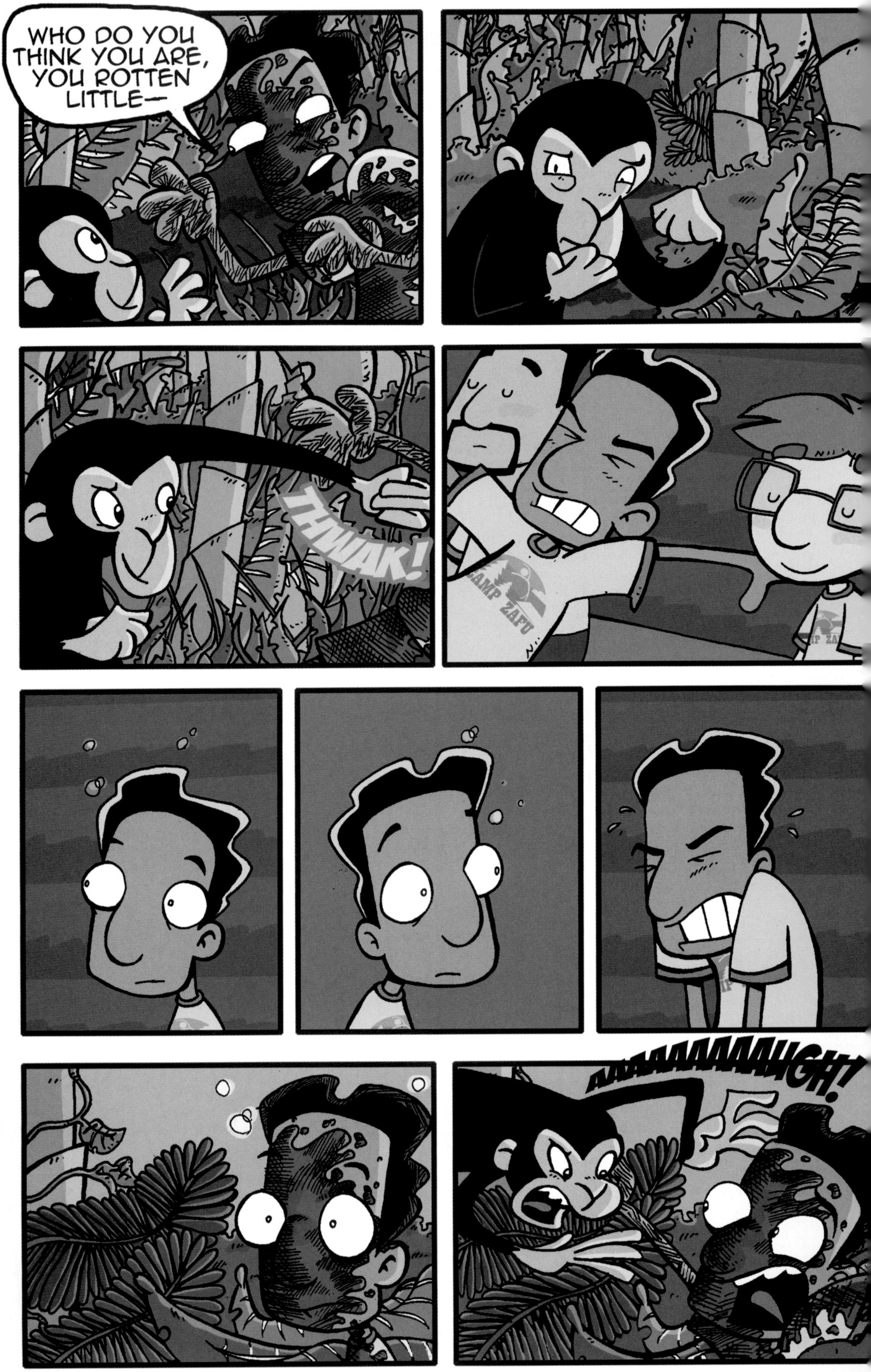
WHO DO YOU THINK YOU ARE, YOU ROTTEN LITTLE—
THWAK!
CAMP ZAFU
AAAAAAAAAAUGH!

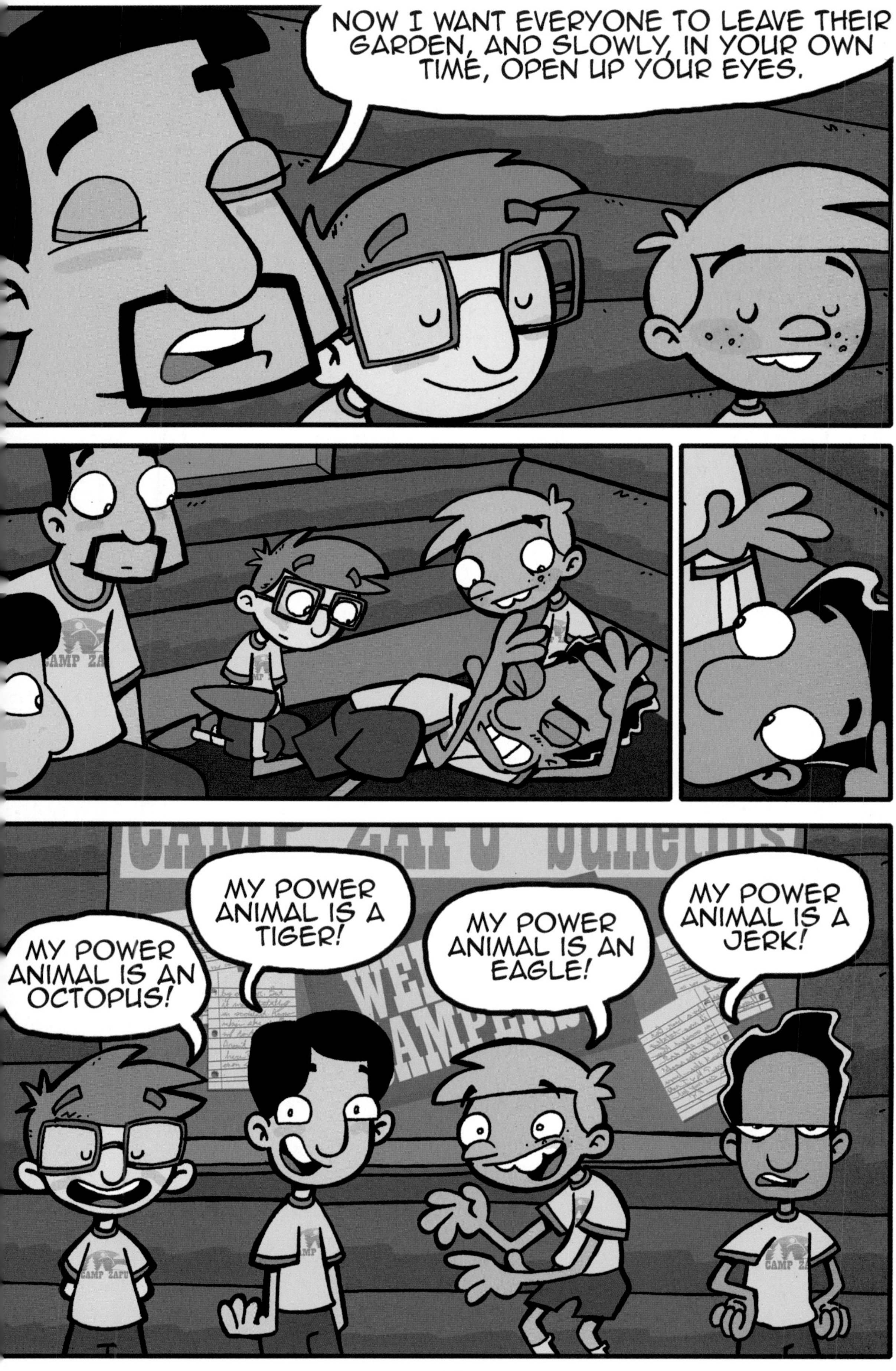
NOW I WANT EVERYONE TO LEAVE THEIR GARDEN, AND SLOWLY, IN YOUR OWN TIME, OPEN UP YOUR EYES.
CAMP ZAFO BULLETINS
MY POWER ANIMAL IS AN OCTOPUS!
MY POWER ANIMAL IS A TIGER!
MY POWER ANIMAL IS AN EAGLE!
MY POWER ANIMAL IS A JERK!

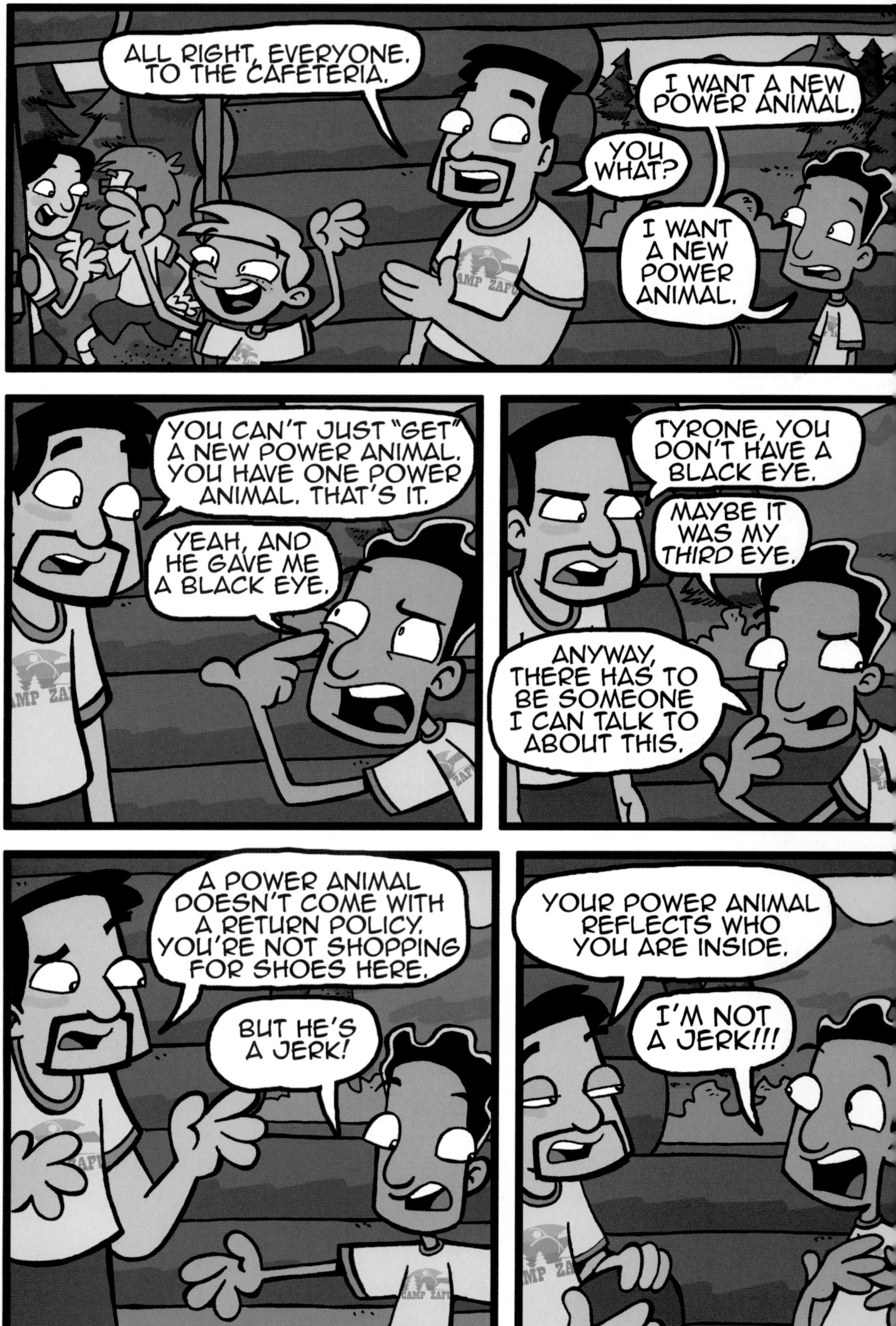
ALL RIGHT, EVERYONE. TO THE CAFETERIA.
I WANT A NEW POWER ANIMAL.
YOU WHAT?
I WANT A NEW POWER ANIMAL.
CAMP ZAFU
YOU CAN'T JUST "GET" A NEW POWER ANIMAL. YOU HAVE ONE POWER ANIMAL. THAT'S IT.
YEAH, AND HE GAVE ME A BLACK EYE.
TYRONE, YOU DON'T HAVE A BLACK EYE.
MAYBE IT WAS MY *THIRD* EYE.
ANYWAY, THERE HAS TO BE SOMEONE I CAN TALK TO ABOUT THIS.
A POWER ANIMAL DOESN'T COME WITH A RETURN POLICY. YOU'RE NOT SHOPPING FOR SHOES HERE.
BUT HE'S A JERK!
YOUR POWER ANIMAL REFLECTS WHO YOU ARE INSIDE.
I'M NOT A JERK!!!

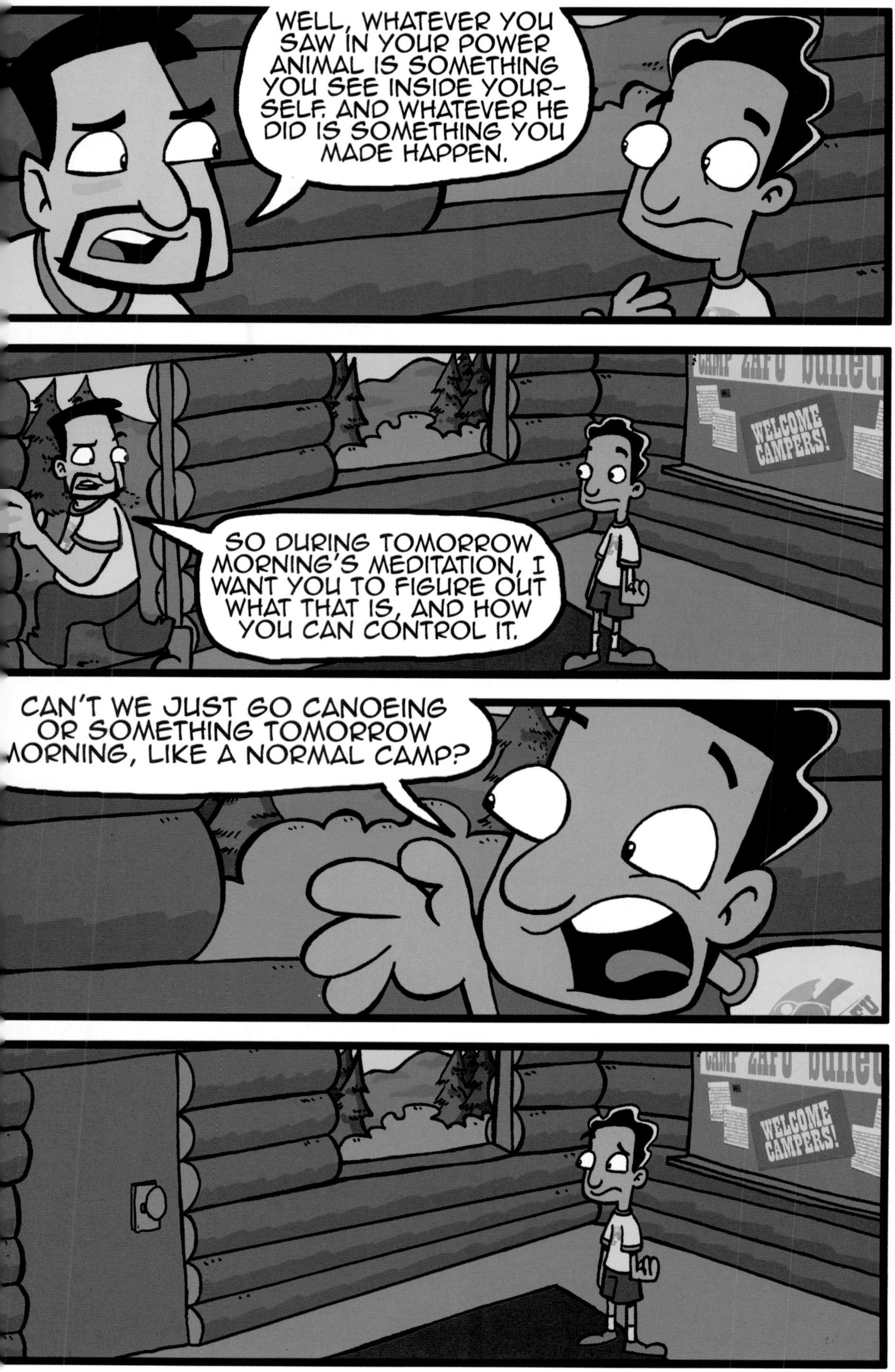
WELL, WHATEVER YOU SAW IN YOUR POWER ANIMAL IS SOMETHING YOU SEE INSIDE YOURSELF. AND WHATEVER HE DID IS SOMETHING YOU MADE HAPPEN.
WELCOME CAMPERS!
SO DURING TOMORROW MORNING'S MEDITATION, I WANT YOU TO FIGURE OUT WHAT THAT IS, AND HOW YOU CAN CONTROL IT.
CAN'T WE JUST GO CANOEING OR SOMETHING TOMORROW MORNING, LIKE A NORMAL CAMP?
WELCOME CAMPERS!

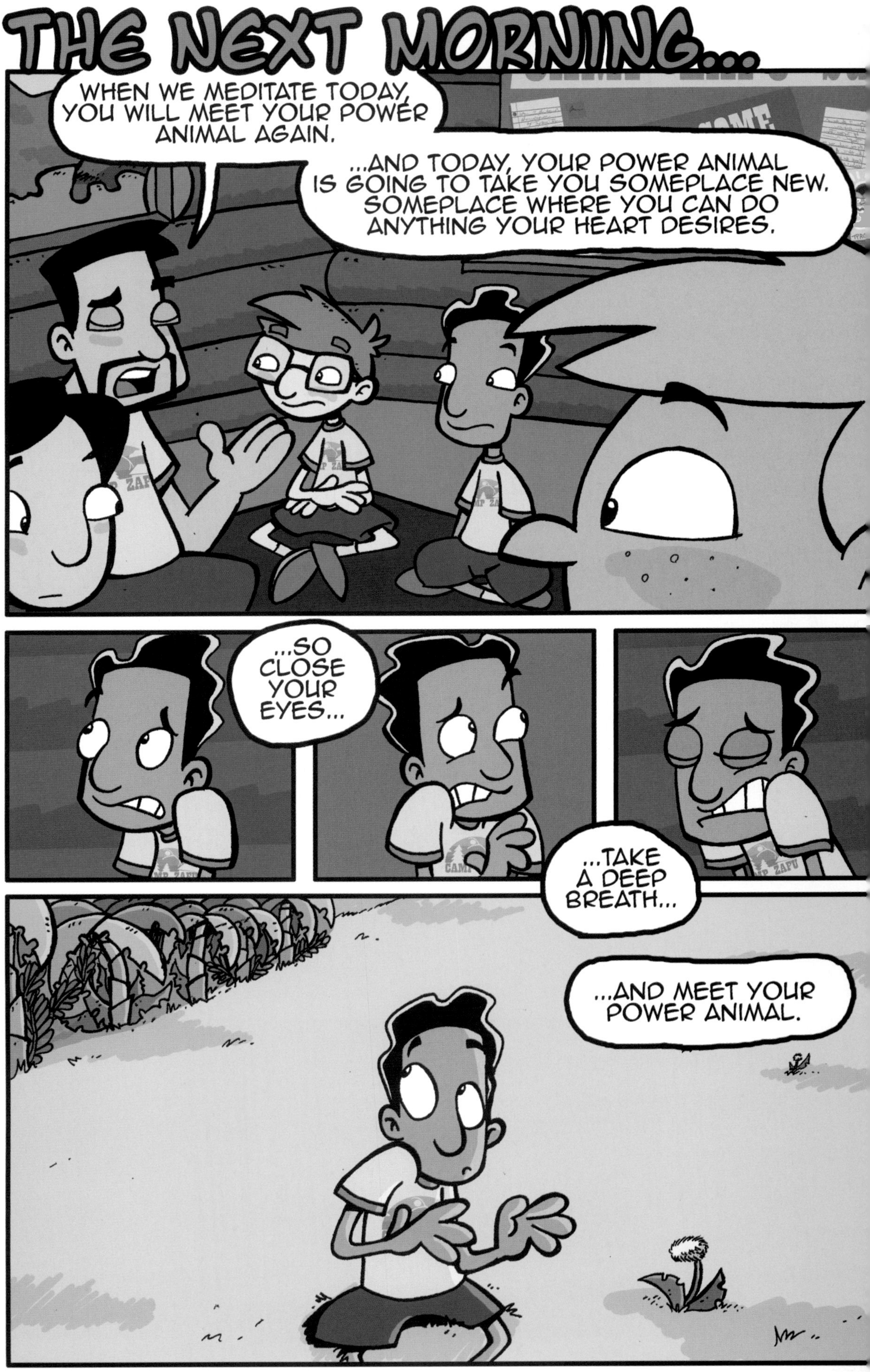
THE NEXT MORNING...
WHEN WE MEDITATE TODAY, YOU WILL MEET YOUR POWER ANIMAL AGAIN.
...AND TODAY, YOUR POWER ANIMAL IS GOING TO TAKE YOU SOMEPLACE NEW. SOMEPLACE WHERE YOU CAN DO ANYTHING YOUR HEART DESIRES.
CAMP ZAFU
...SO CLOSE YOUR EYES...
...TAKE A DEEP BREATH...
...AND MEET YOUR POWER ANIMAL.

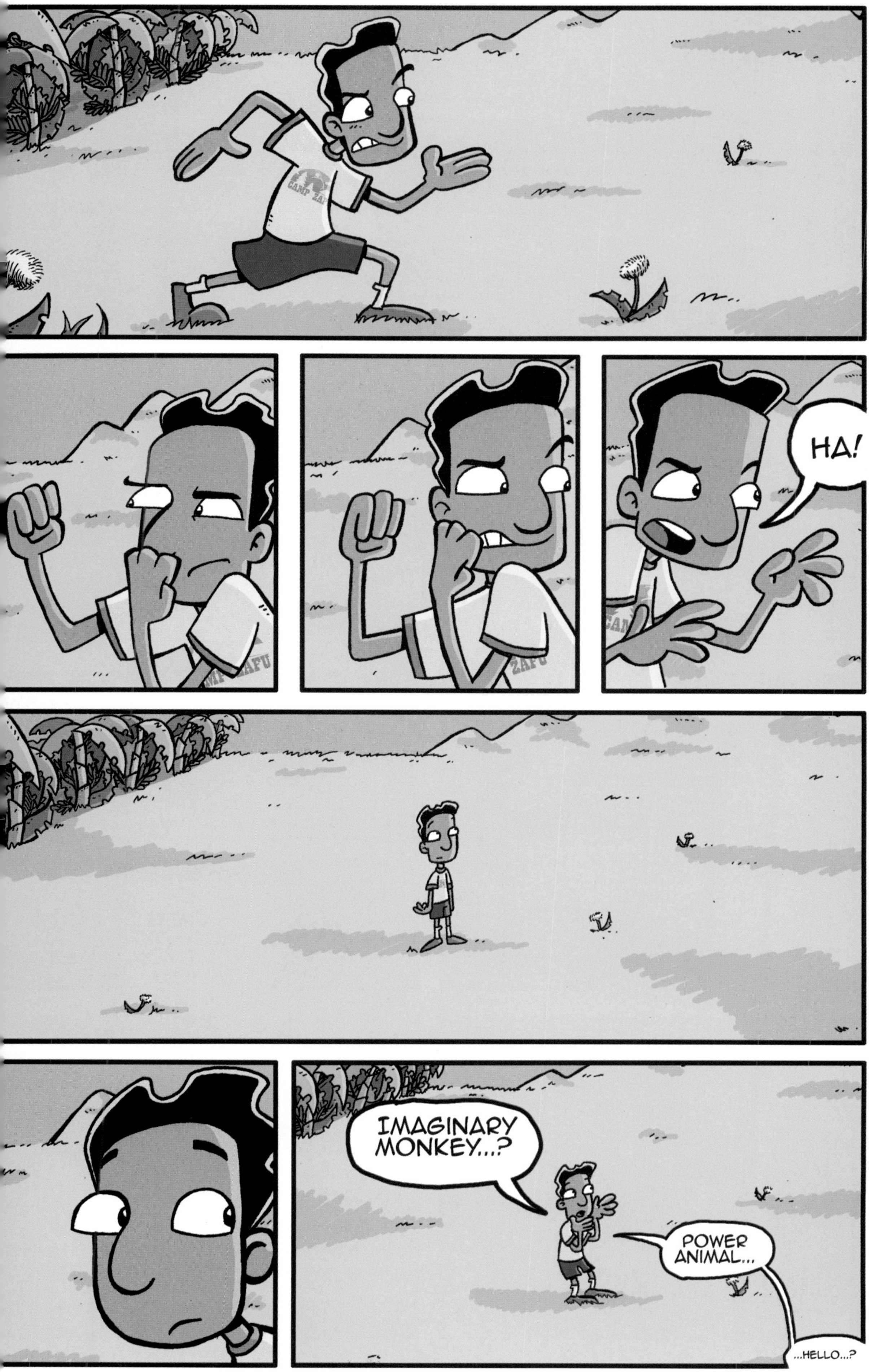
HA!
IMAGINARY MONKEY...?
POWER ANIMAL...
...HELLO...?

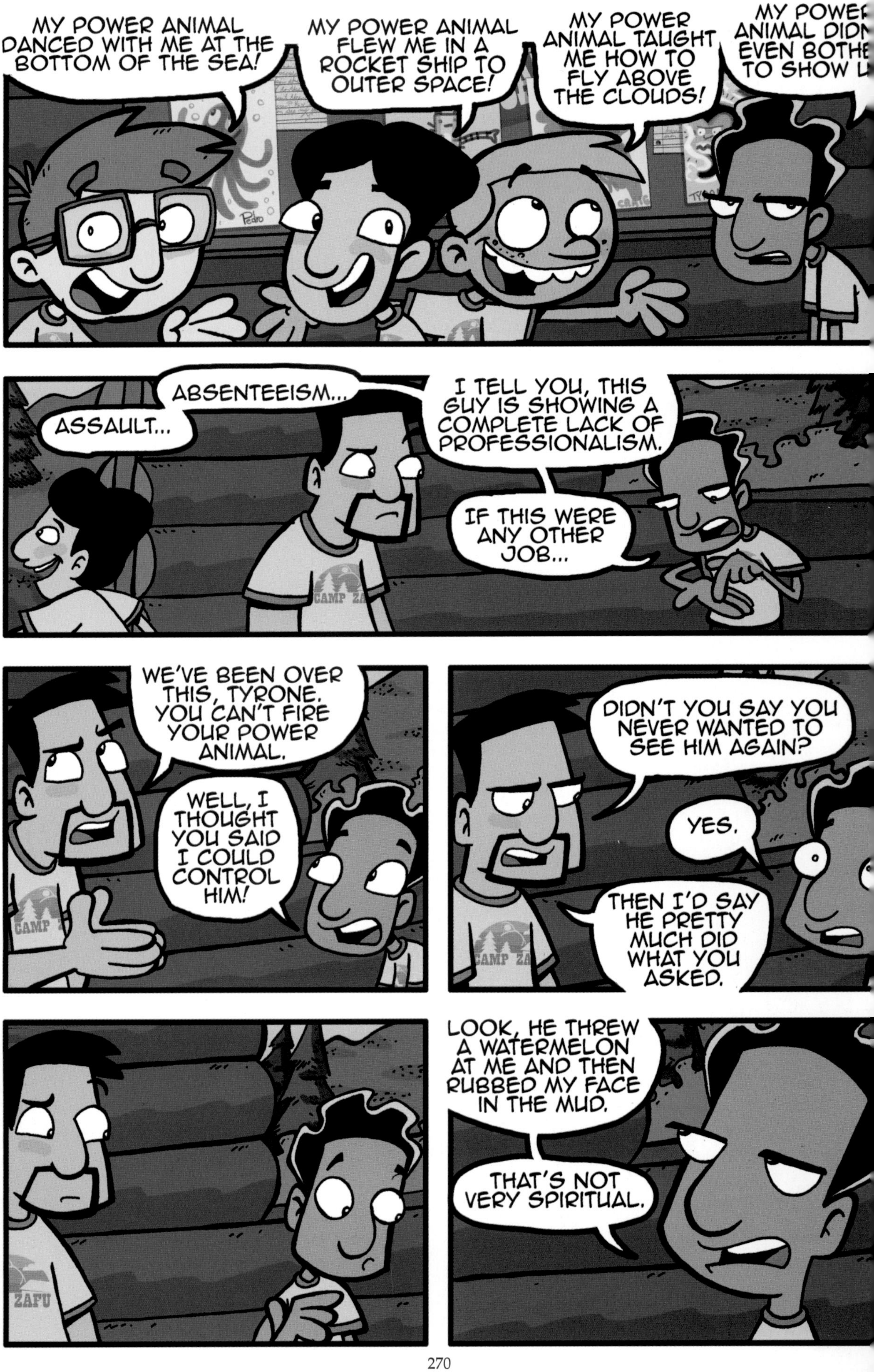
MY POWER ANIMAL DANCED WITH ME AT THE BOTTOM OF THE SEA!
MY POWER ANIMAL FLEW ME IN A ROCKET SHIP TO OUTER SPACE!
MY POWER ANIMAL TAUGHT ME HOW TO FLY ABOVE THE CLOUDS!
MY POWER ANIMAL DIDN EVEN BOTHE TO SHOW U
ASSAULT...
ABSENTEEISM...
I TELL YOU, THIS GUY IS SHOWING A COMPLETE LACK OF PROFESSIONALISM.
IF THIS WERE ANY OTHER JOB...
WE'VE BEEN OVER THIS, TYRONE. YOU CAN'T FIRE YOUR POWER ANIMAL.
WELL, I THOUGHT YOU SAID I COULD CONTROL HIM!
DIDN'T YOU SAY YOU NEVER WANTED TO SEE HIM AGAIN?
YES.
THEN I'D SAY HE PRETTY MUCH DID WHAT YOU ASKED.
LOOK, HE THREW A WATERMELON AT ME AND THEN RUBBED MY FACE IN THE MUD.
THAT'S NOT VERY SPIRITUAL.

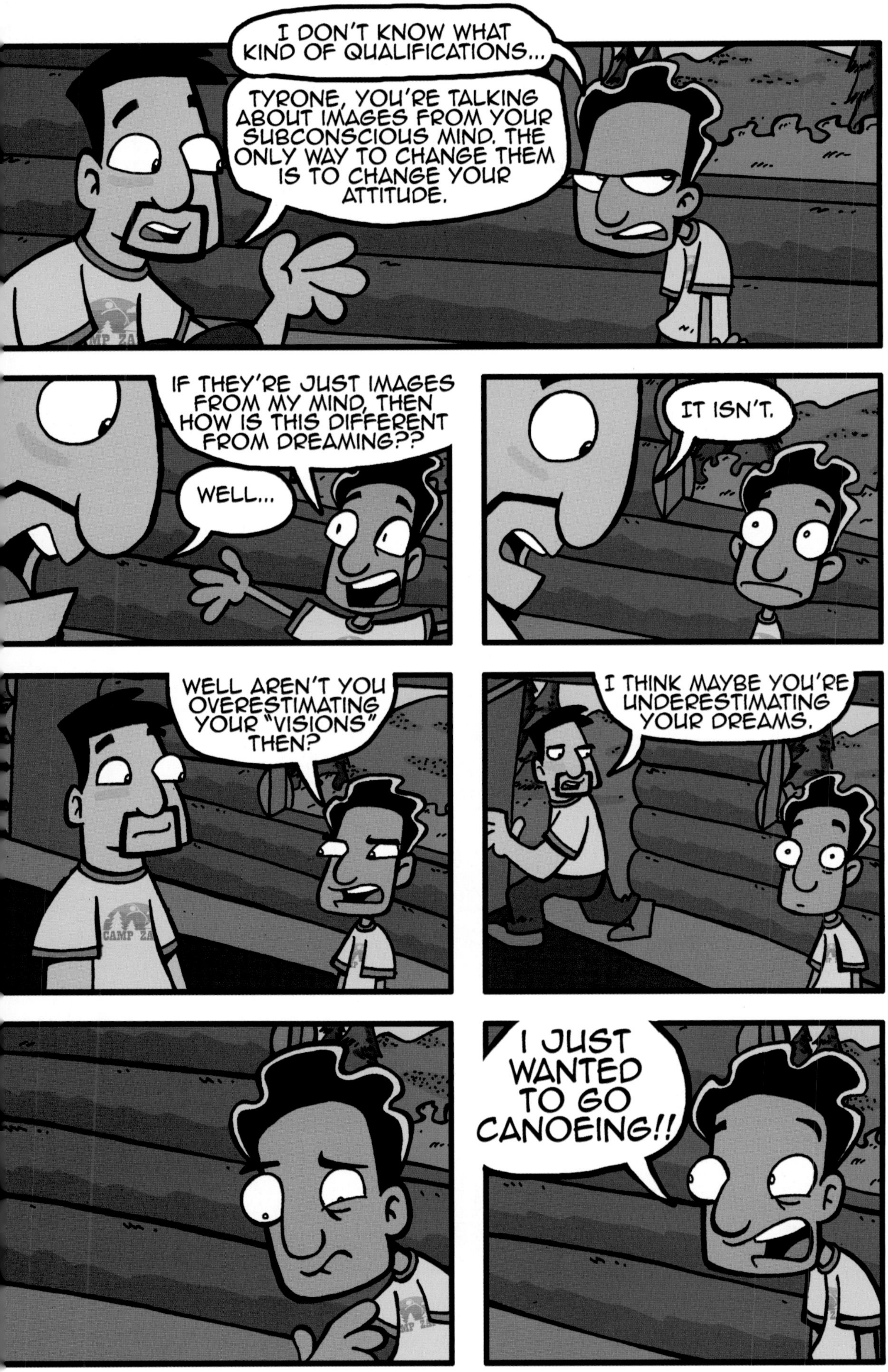
I DON'T KNOW WHAT KIND OF QUALIFICATIONS...
TYRONE, YOU'RE TALKING ABOUT IMAGES FROM YOUR SUBCONSCIOUS MIND. THE ONLY WAY TO CHANGE THEM IS TO CHANGE YOUR ATTITUDE.
IF THEY'RE JUST IMAGES FROM MY MIND, THEN HOW IS THIS DIFFERENT FROM DREAMING??
WELL...
IT ISN'T.
WELL AREN'T YOU OVERESTIMATING YOUR "VISIONS" THEN?
I THINK MAYBE YOU'RE UNDERESTIMATING YOUR DREAMS.
I JUST WANTED TO GO CANOEING!!

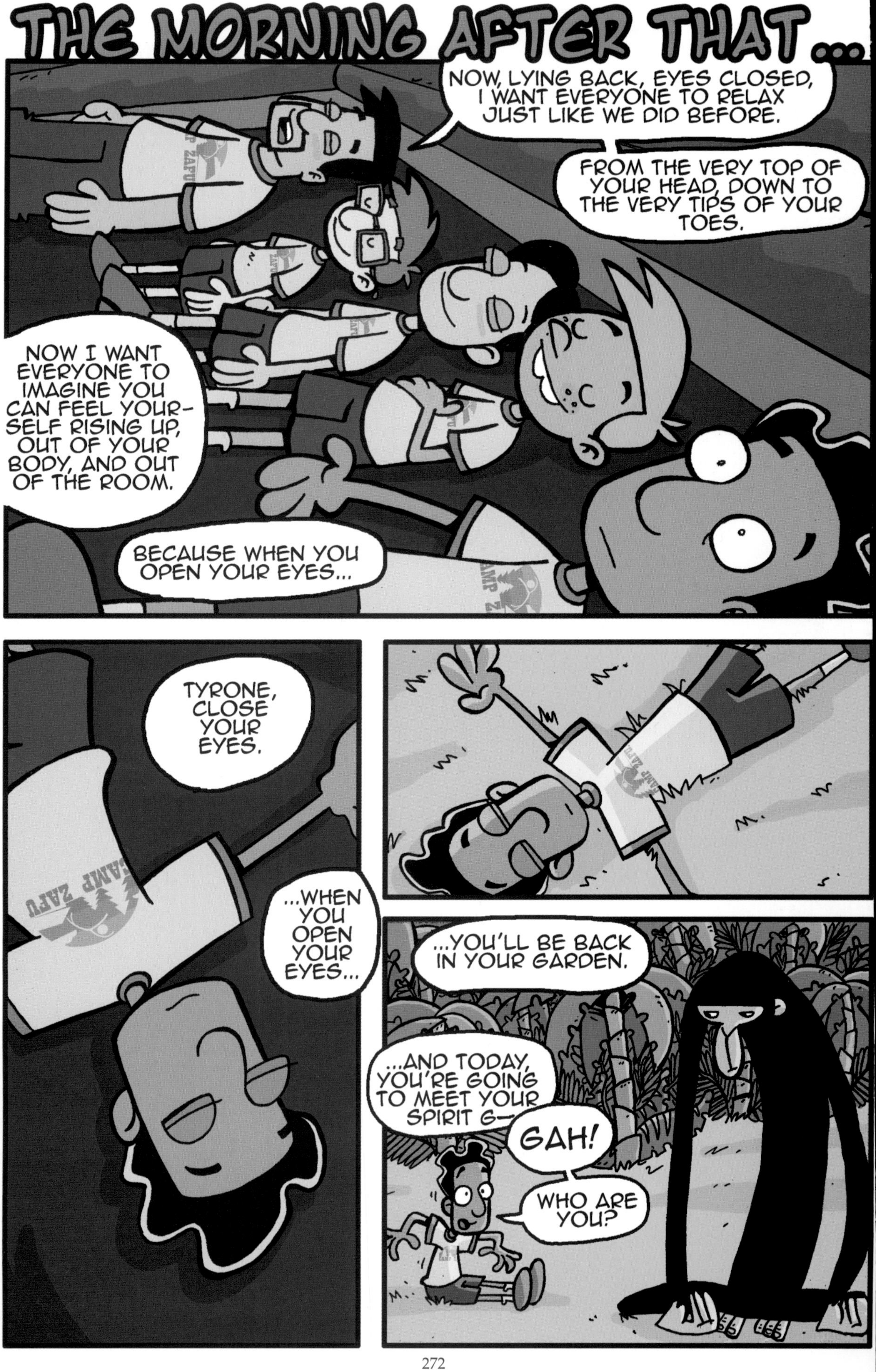
THE MORNING AFTER THAT...
NOW, LYING BACK, EYES CLOSED, I WANT EVERYONE TO RELAX JUST LIKE WE DID BEFORE.
FROM THE VERY TOP OF YOUR HEAD, DOWN TO THE VERY TIPS OF YOUR TOES.
NOW I WANT EVERYONE TO IMAGINE YOU CAN FEEL YOURSELF RISING UP, OUT OF YOUR BODY, AND OUT OF THE ROOM.
BECAUSE WHEN YOU OPEN YOUR EYES...
TYRONE, CLOSE YOUR EYES.
...WHEN YOU OPEN YOUR EYES...
...YOU'LL BE BACK IN YOUR GARDEN.
...AND TODAY, YOU'RE GOING TO MEET YOUR SPIRIT G—
GAH!
WHO ARE YOU?

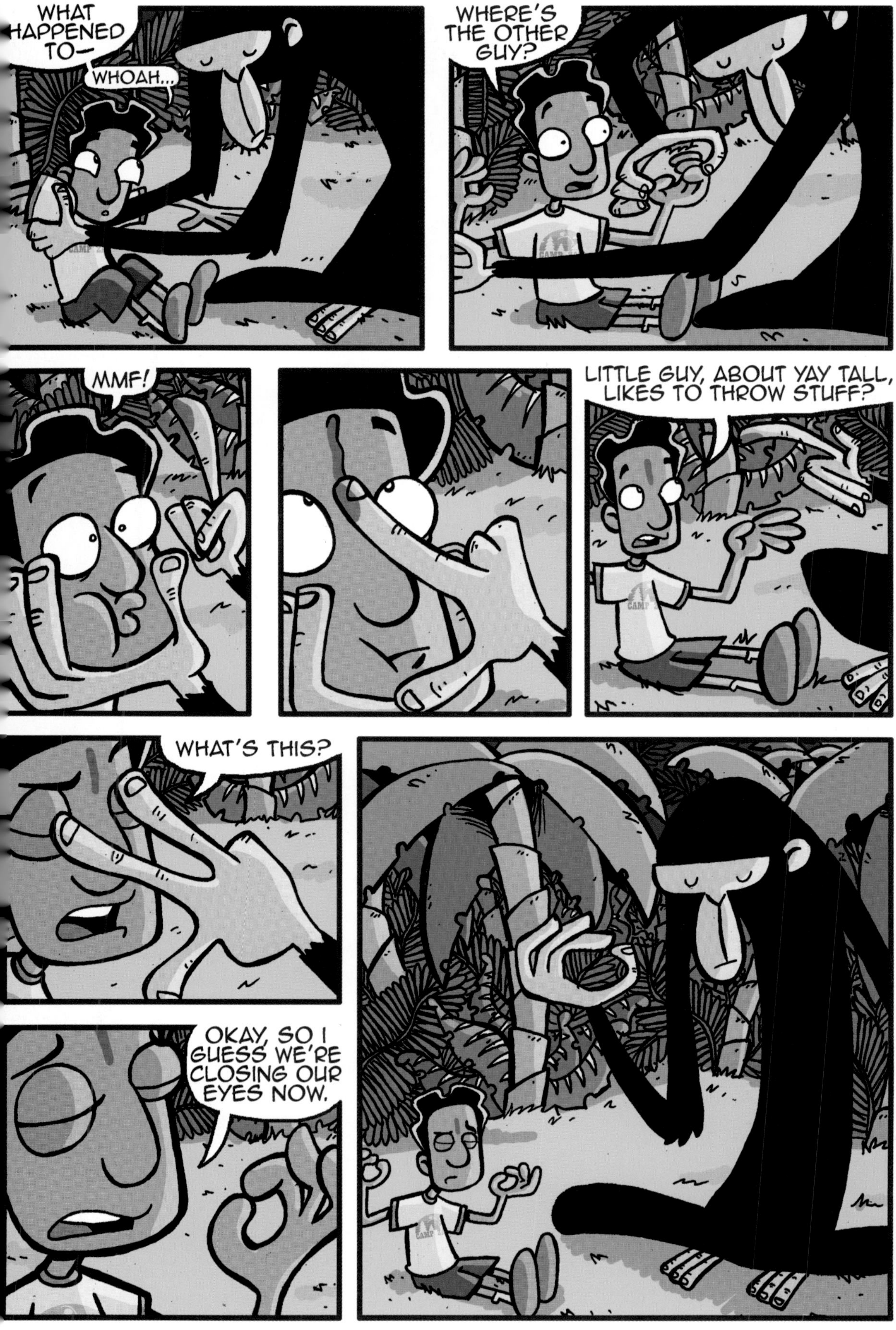
WHAT HAPPENED TO—
WHOAH...
WHERE'S THE OTHER GUY?
MMF!
LITTLE GUY, ABOUT YAY TALL, LIKES TO THROW STUFF?
WHAT'S THIS?
OKAY, SO I GUESS WE'RE CLOSING OUR EYES NOW.

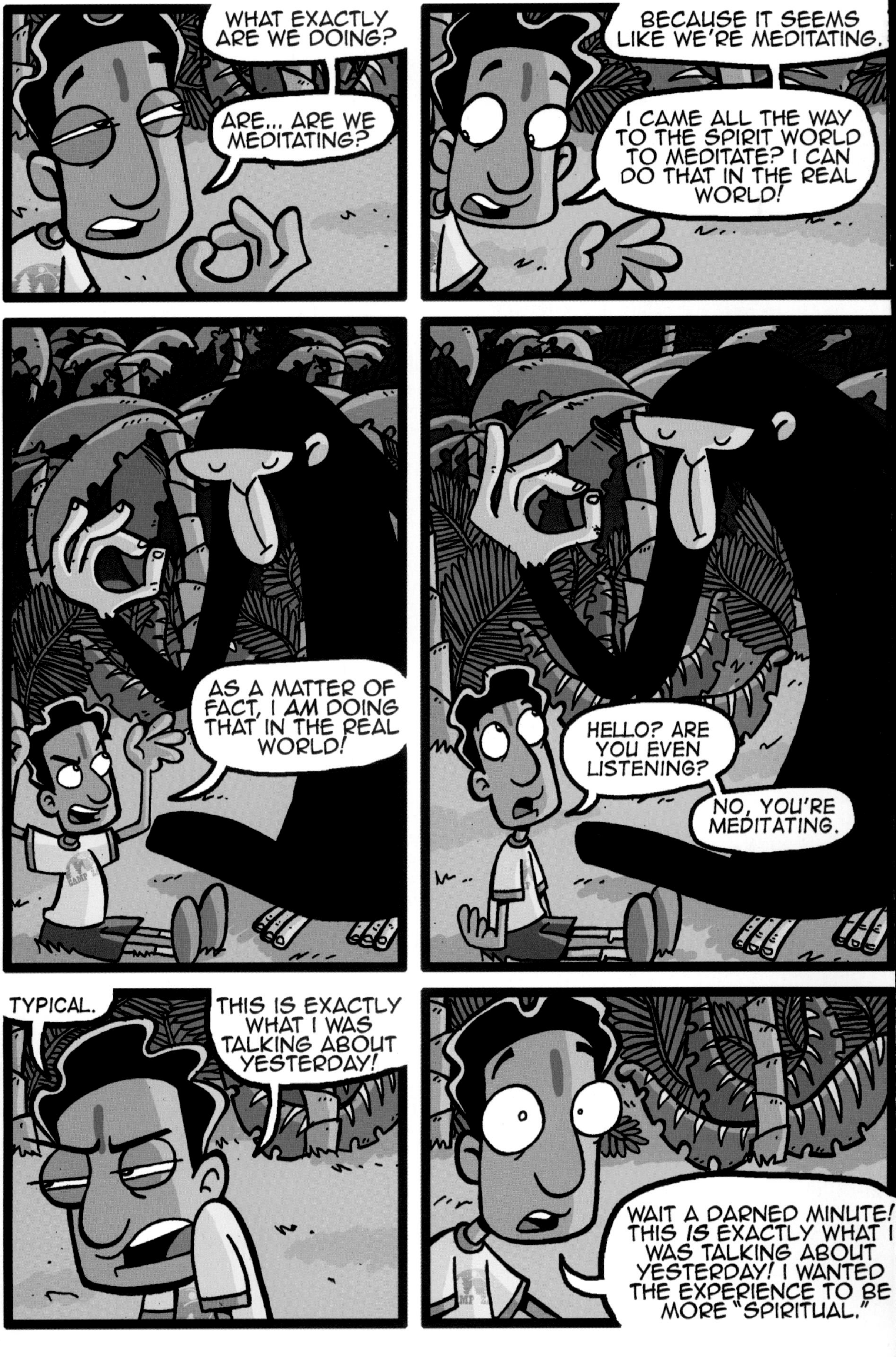
WHAT EXACTLY ARE WE DOING?
ARE... ARE WE MEDITATING?
BECAUSE IT SEEMS LIKE WE'RE MEDITATING.
I CAME ALL THE WAY TO THE SPIRIT WORLD TO MEDITATE? I CAN DO THAT IN THE REAL WORLD!
AS A MATTER OF FACT, I AM DOING THAT IN THE REAL WORLD!
HELLO? ARE YOU EVEN LISTENING?
NO, YOU'RE MEDITATING.
TYPICAL.
THIS IS EXACTLY WHAT I WAS TALKING ABOUT YESTERDAY!
WAIT A DARNED MINUTE! THIS *IS* EXACTLY WHAT I WAS TALKING ABOUT YESTERDAY! I WANTED THE EXPERIENCE TO BE MORE "SPIRITUAL."

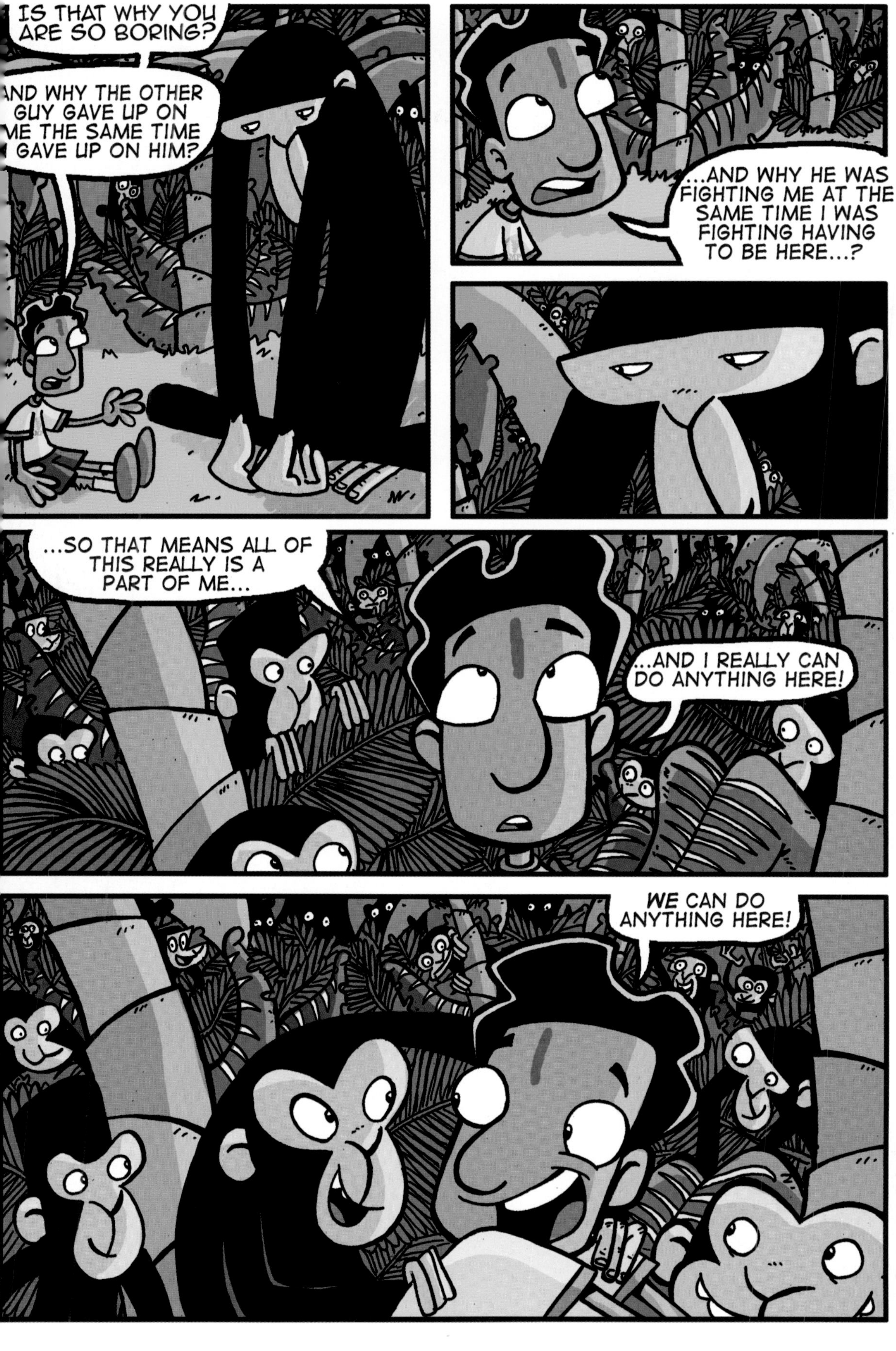
IS THAT WHY YOU ARE SO BORING?
AND WHY THE OTHER GUY GAVE UP ON ME THE SAME TIME I GAVE UP ON HIM?
...AND WHY HE WAS FIGHTING ME AT THE SAME TIME I WAS FIGHTING HAVING TO BE HERE...?
...SO THAT MEANS ALL OF THIS REALLY IS A PART OF ME...
...AND I REALLY CAN DO ANYTHING HERE!
WE CAN DO ANYTHING HERE!

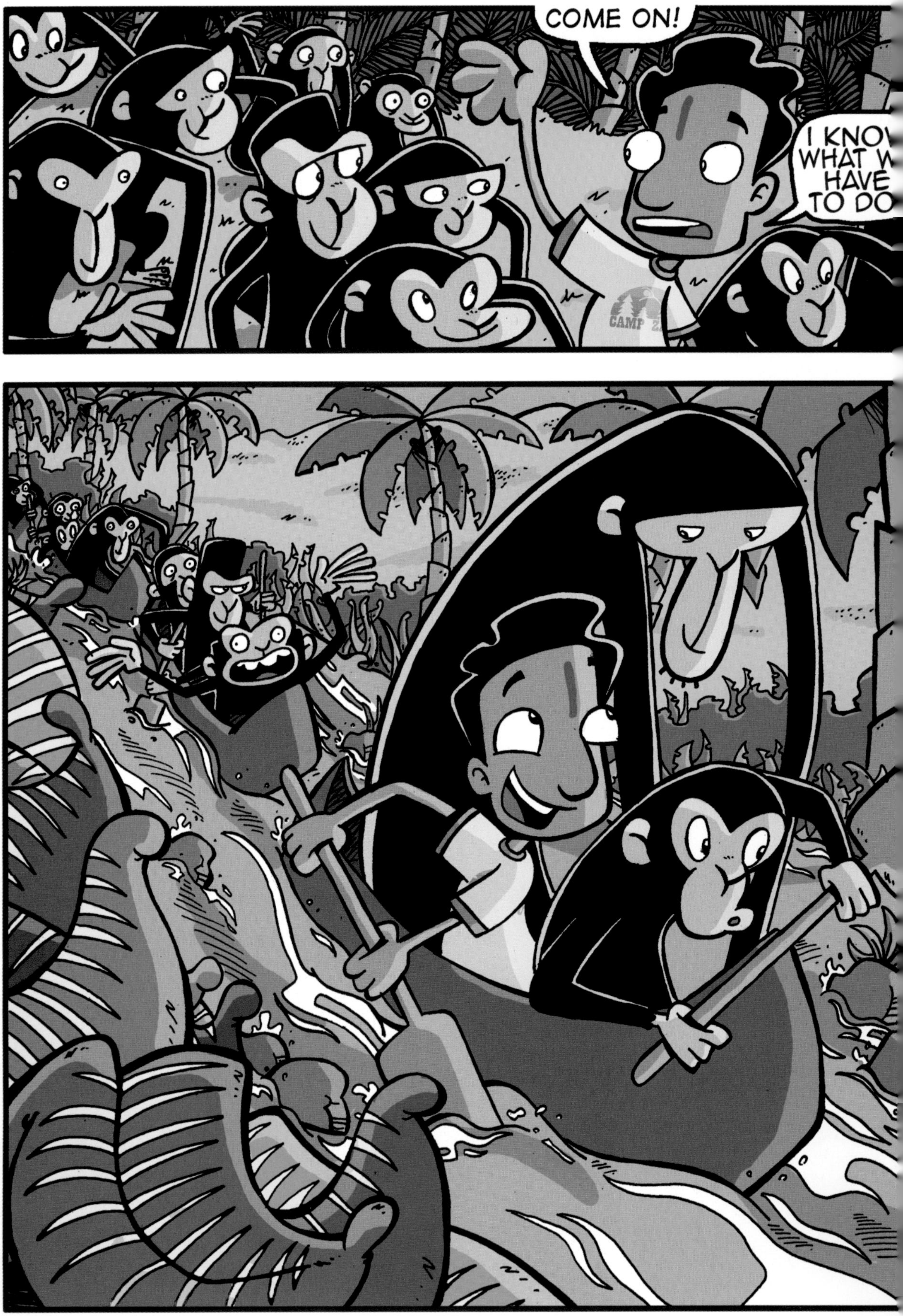
COME ON!
I KNOW WHAT W HAVE TO DO

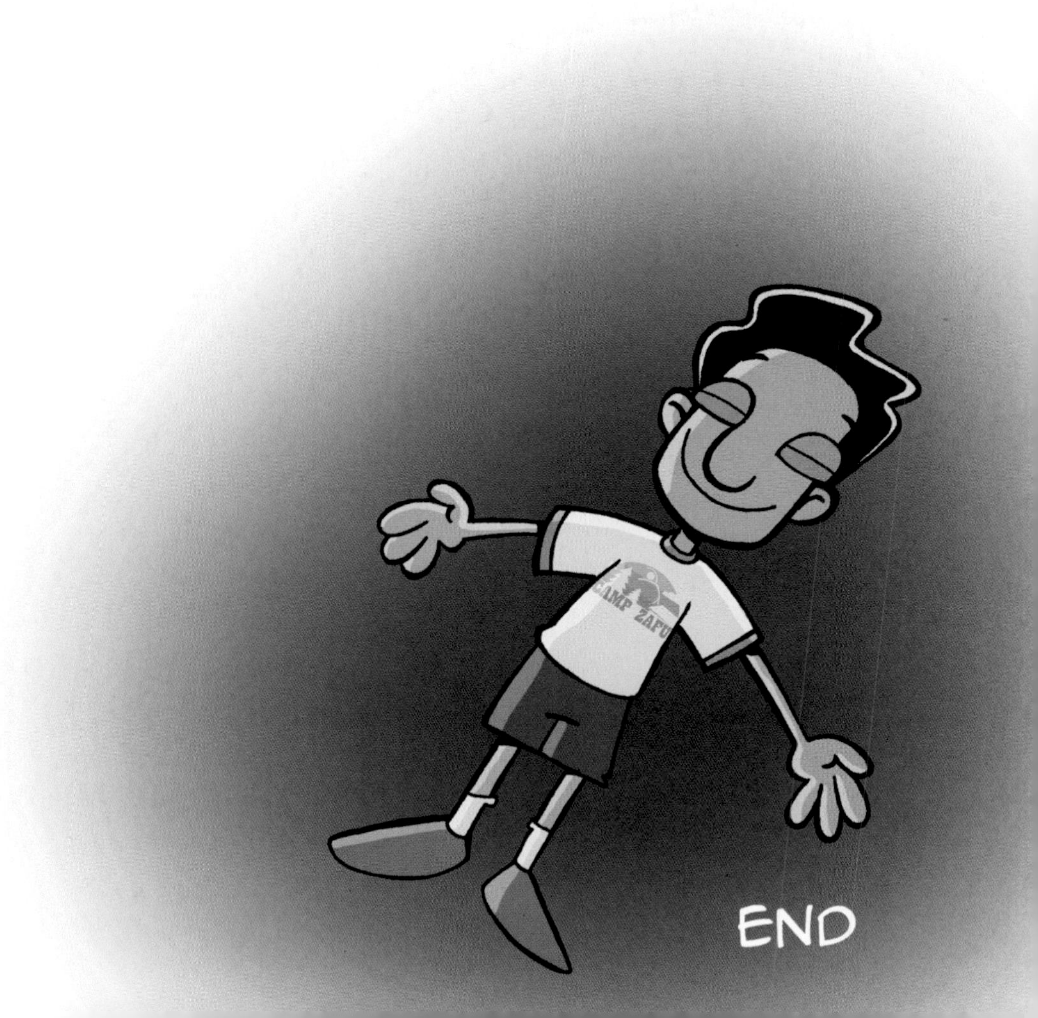
CAMP ZAFU
END

THE STORY

of

BINNY

by lark pien

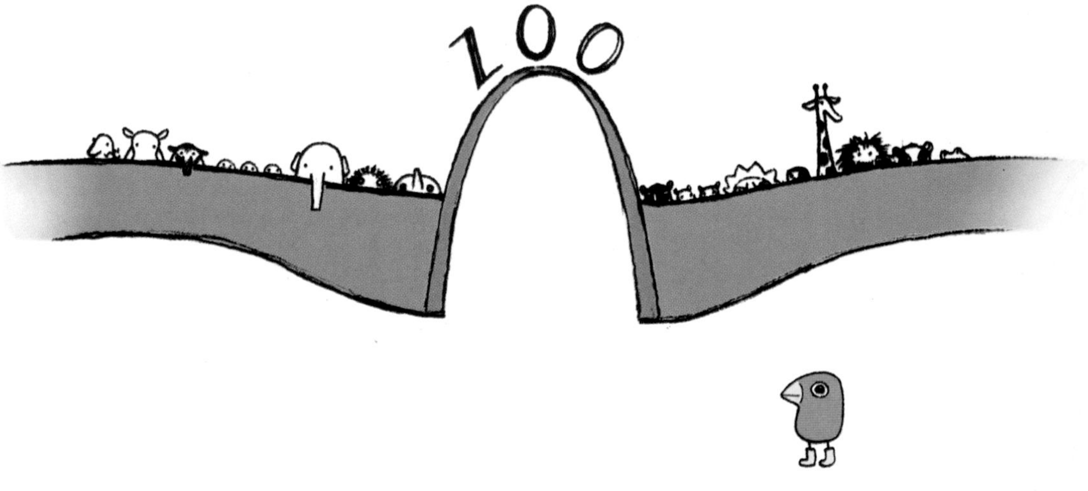
ZOO

CHAPTER 1

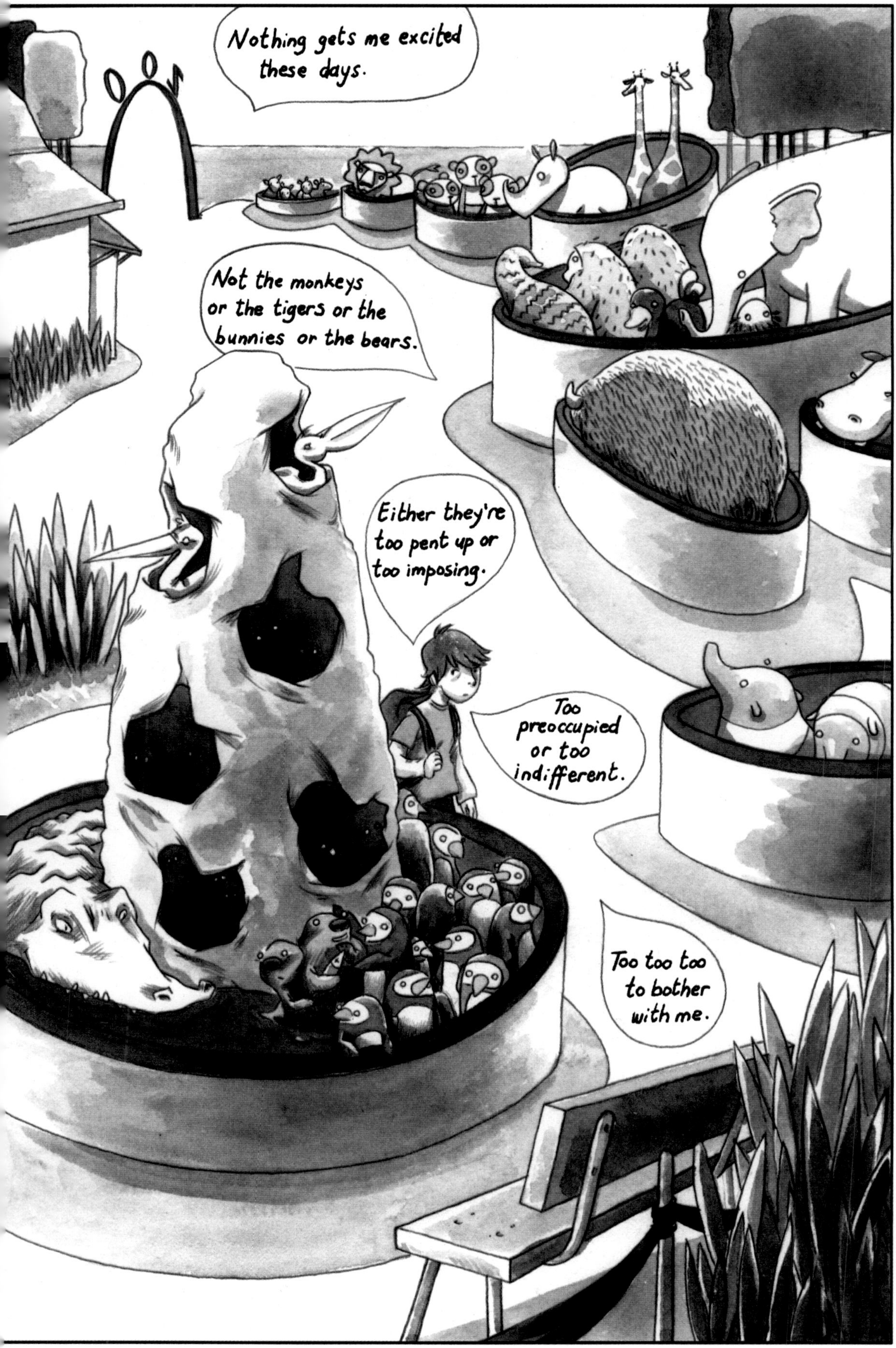
Nothing gets me excited these days.
Not the monkeys or the tigers or the bunnies or the bears.
Either they're too pent up or too imposing.
Too preoccupied or too indifferent.
Too too too to bother with me.

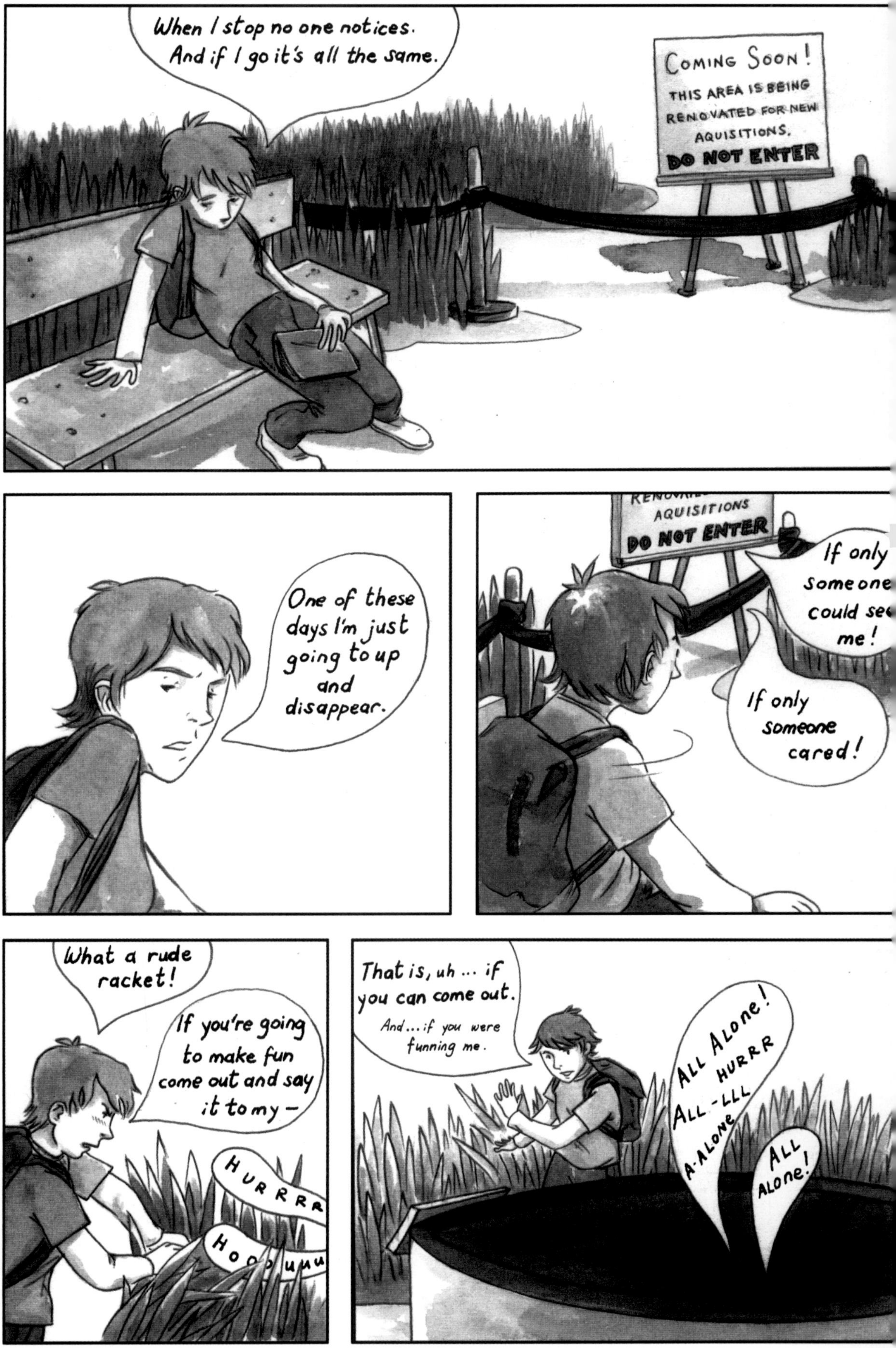
When I stop no one notices. And if I go it's all the same.
COMING SOON! THIS AREA IS BEING RENOVATED FOR NEW AQUISITIONS. DO NOT ENTER
One of these days I'm just going to up and disappear.
AQUISITIONS DO NOT ENTER
If only someone could se
me!
If only someone cared!
What a rude racket!
If you're going to make fun come out and say it to my—
HURRRR
HOOOUUU
That is, uh... if you can come out.
And... if you were funning me.
ALL ALONE! HURRR ALL-LLL A-ALONE
ALL ALONE!

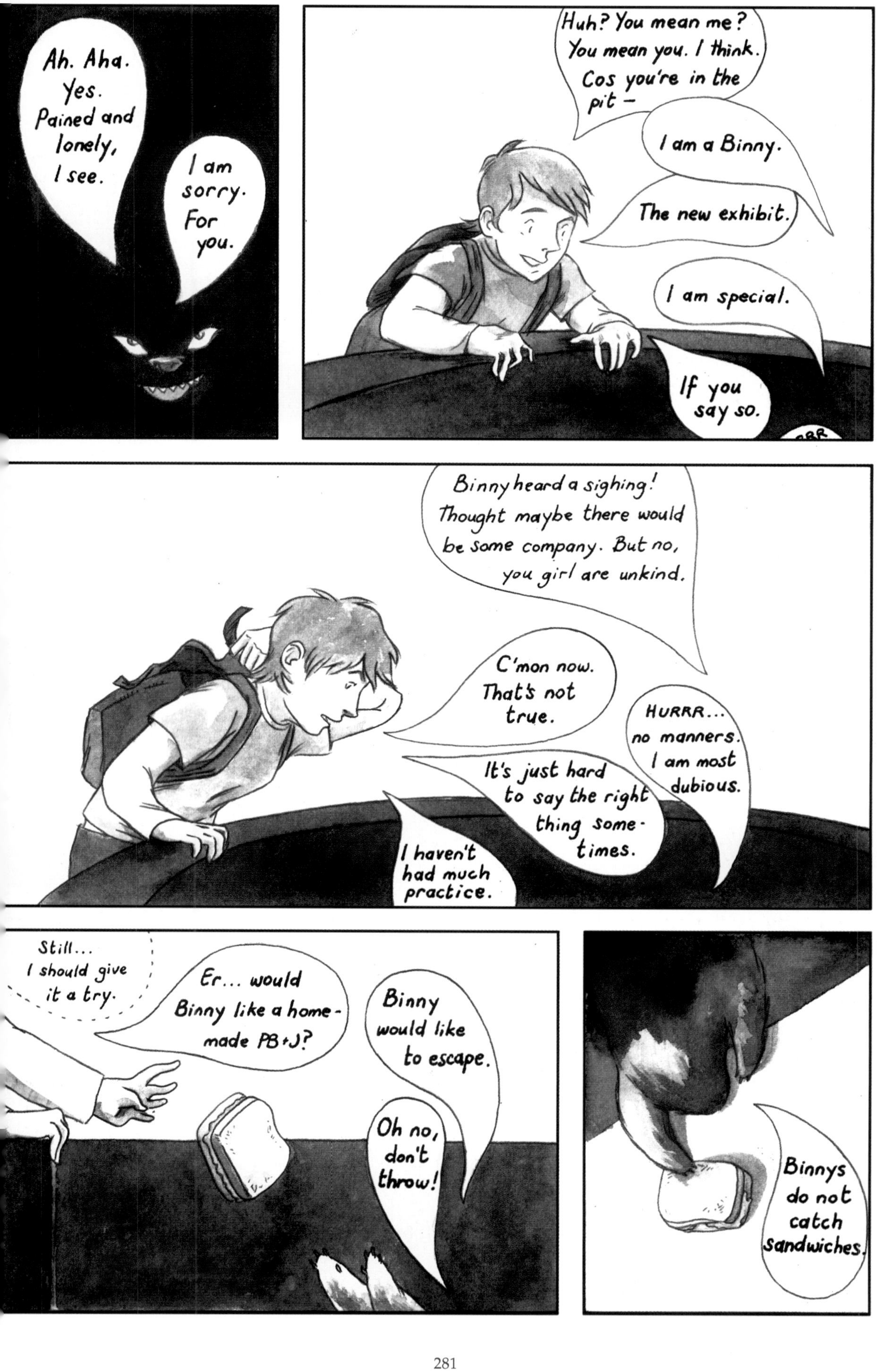
Ah. Aha. Yes. Pained and lonely, I see.
I am sorry. For you.
Huh? You mean me? You mean you. I think. Cos you're in the pit –
I am a Binny.
The new exhibit.
I am special.
If you say so.
Binny heard a sighing! Thought maybe there would be some company. But no, you girl are unkind.
C'mon now. That's not true.
HURRR... no manners. I am most dubious.
It's just hard to say the right thing some-times.
I haven't had much practice.
Still... I should give it a try.
Er... would Binny like a home-made PB+J?
Binny would like to escape.
Oh no, don't throw!
Binnys do not catch sandwiches.

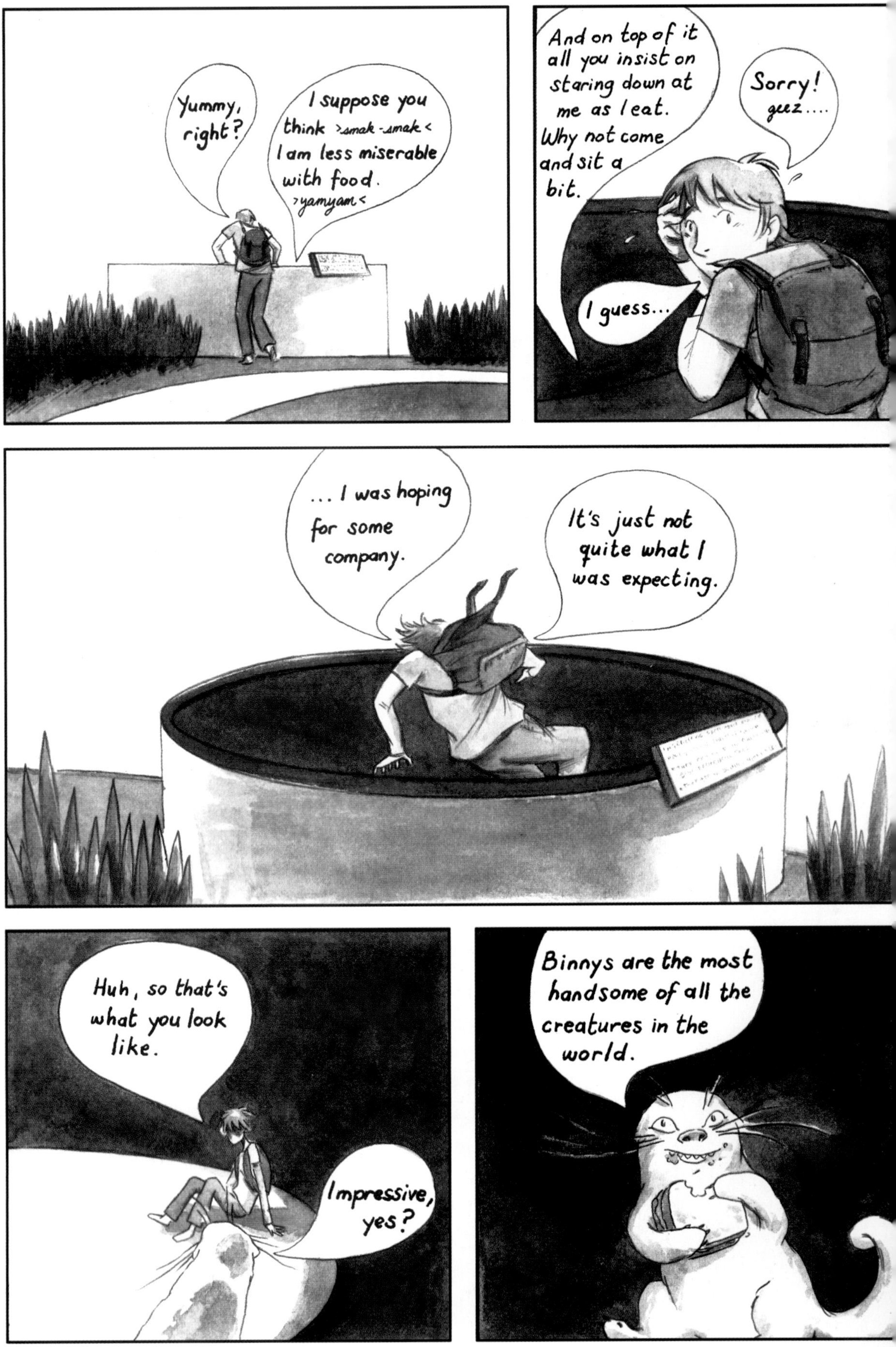
Yummy, right?
I suppose you think >smak-smak< I am less miserable with food. >yamyam<
And on top of it all you insist on staring down at me as I eat. Why not come and sit a bit.
Sorry! geez....
I guess...
... I was hoping for some company.
It's just not quite what I was expecting.
Huh, so that's what you look like.
Impressive, yes?
Binnys are the most handsome of all the creatures in the world.

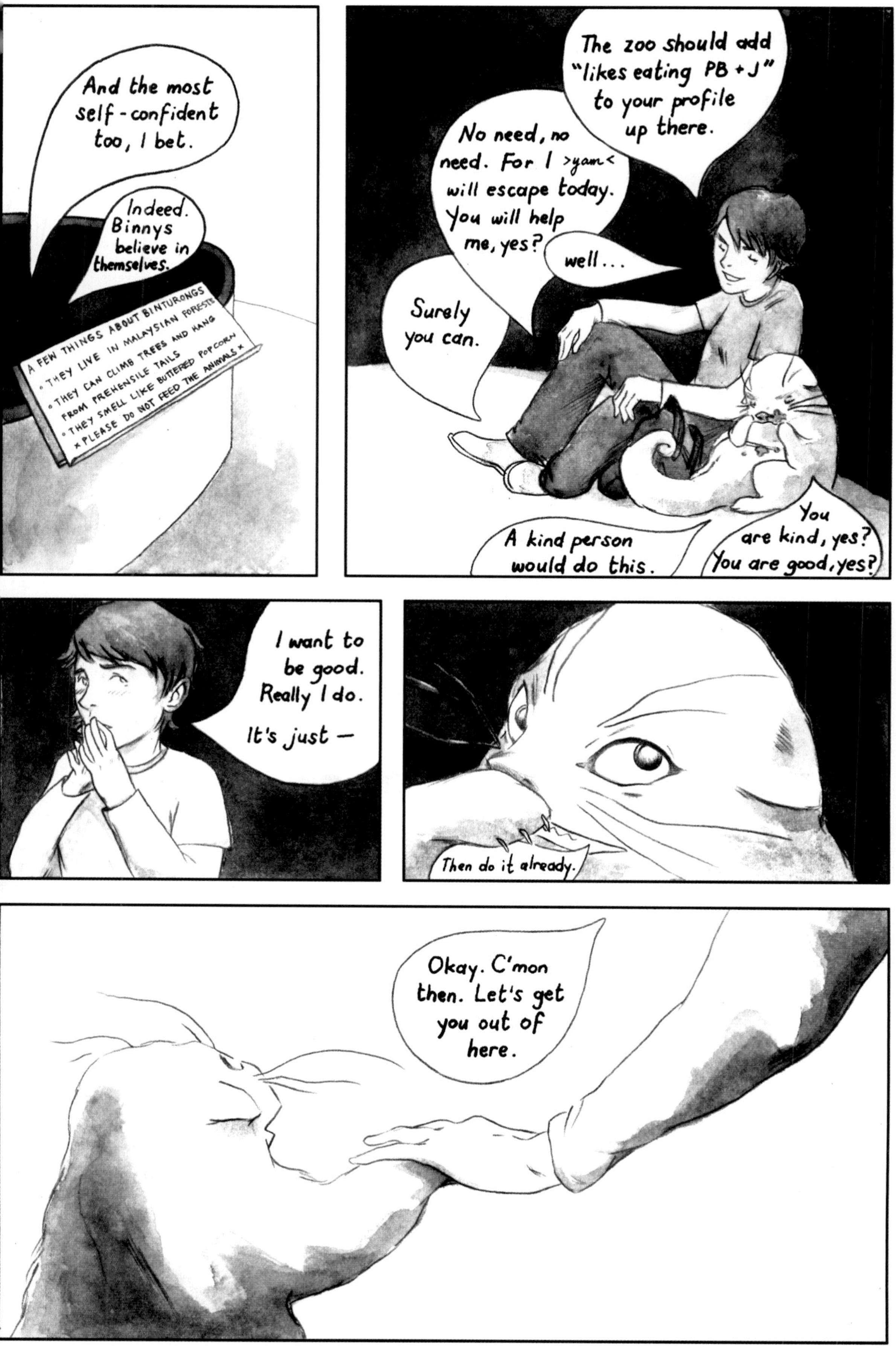
And the most self-confident too, I bet.
Indeed. Binnys believe in themselves.
A FEW THINGS ABOUT BINTURONGS
• THEY LIVE IN MALAYSIAN FORESTS
• THEY CAN CLIMB TREES AND HANG FROM PREHENSILE TAILS
• THEY SMELL LIKE BUTTERED POPCORN
× PLEASE DO NOT FEED THE ANIMALS ×
The zoo should add "likes eating PB + J" to your profile up there.
No need, no need. For I >yam< will escape today. You will help me, yes?
well...
Surely you can.
A kind person would do this.
You are kind, yes? You are good, yes?
I want to be good. Really I do.
It's just —
Then do it already.
Okay. C'mon then. Let's get you out of here.

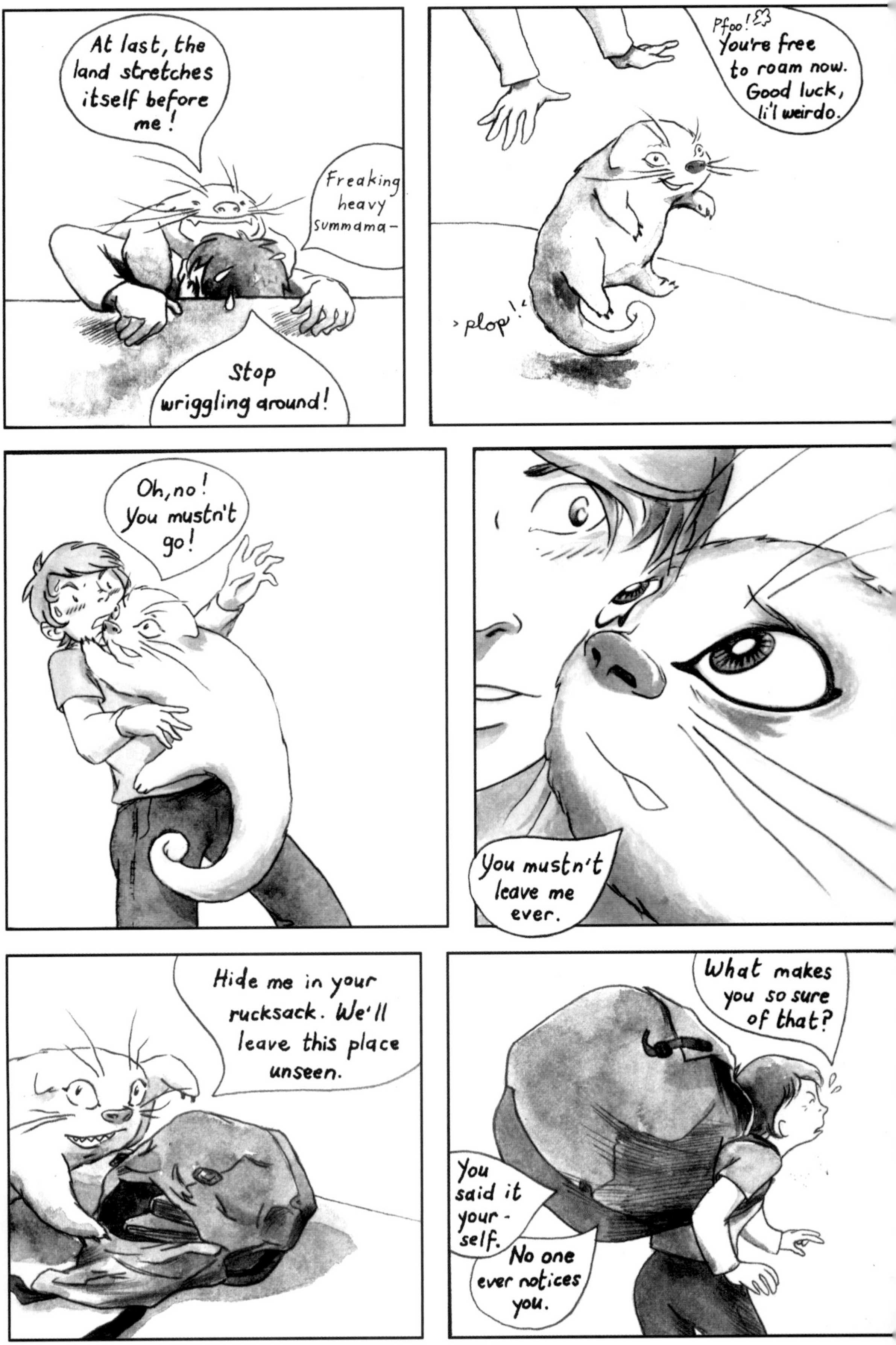
At last, the land stretches itself before me!
Freaking heavy summama-
Stop wriggling around!
Pfoo!
You're free to roam now. Good luck, li'l weirdo.
plop!
Oh, no! You mustn't go!
You mustn't leave me ever.
Hide me in your rucksack. We'll leave this place unseen.
What makes you so sure of that?
You said it yourself.
No one ever notices you.

CHAPTER 2

This is it!

Hurry, this bag is most uncomfortable.

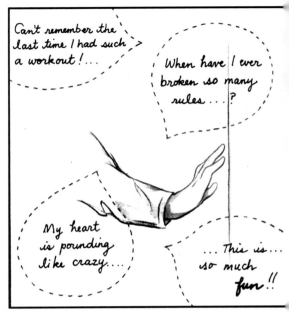

Can't remember the last time I had such a workout!...

When have I ever broken so many rules...?

My heart is pounding like crazy....

...This is.... so much *fun*!!

Welcome to your new home.

>plunk!<

So, just a few house rules to start with, okay?

We'll fine-tune things as we go.

We have to get you potty-trained, so stay on the linoleum, alright?

sniff

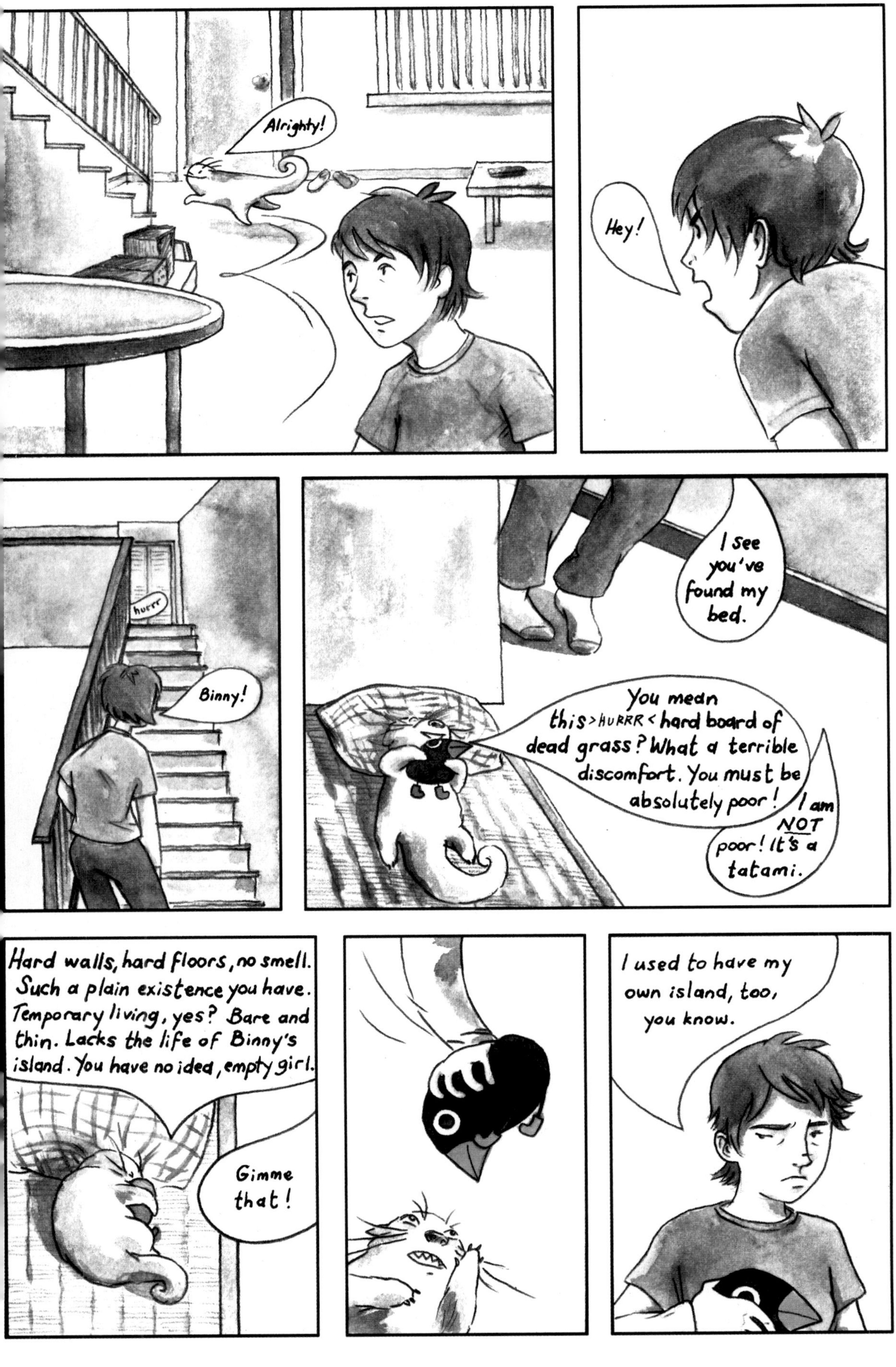
Alrighty!
Hey!
hurrr
Binny!
I see you've found my bed.
You mean this >HURRR< hard board of dead grass? What a terrible discomfort. You must be absolutely poor!
I am NOT poor! It's a tatami.
Hard walls, hard floors, no smell. Such a plain existence you have. Temporary living, yes? Bare and thin. Lacks the life of Binny's island. You have no idea, empty girl.
Gimme that!
I used to have my own island, too, you know.

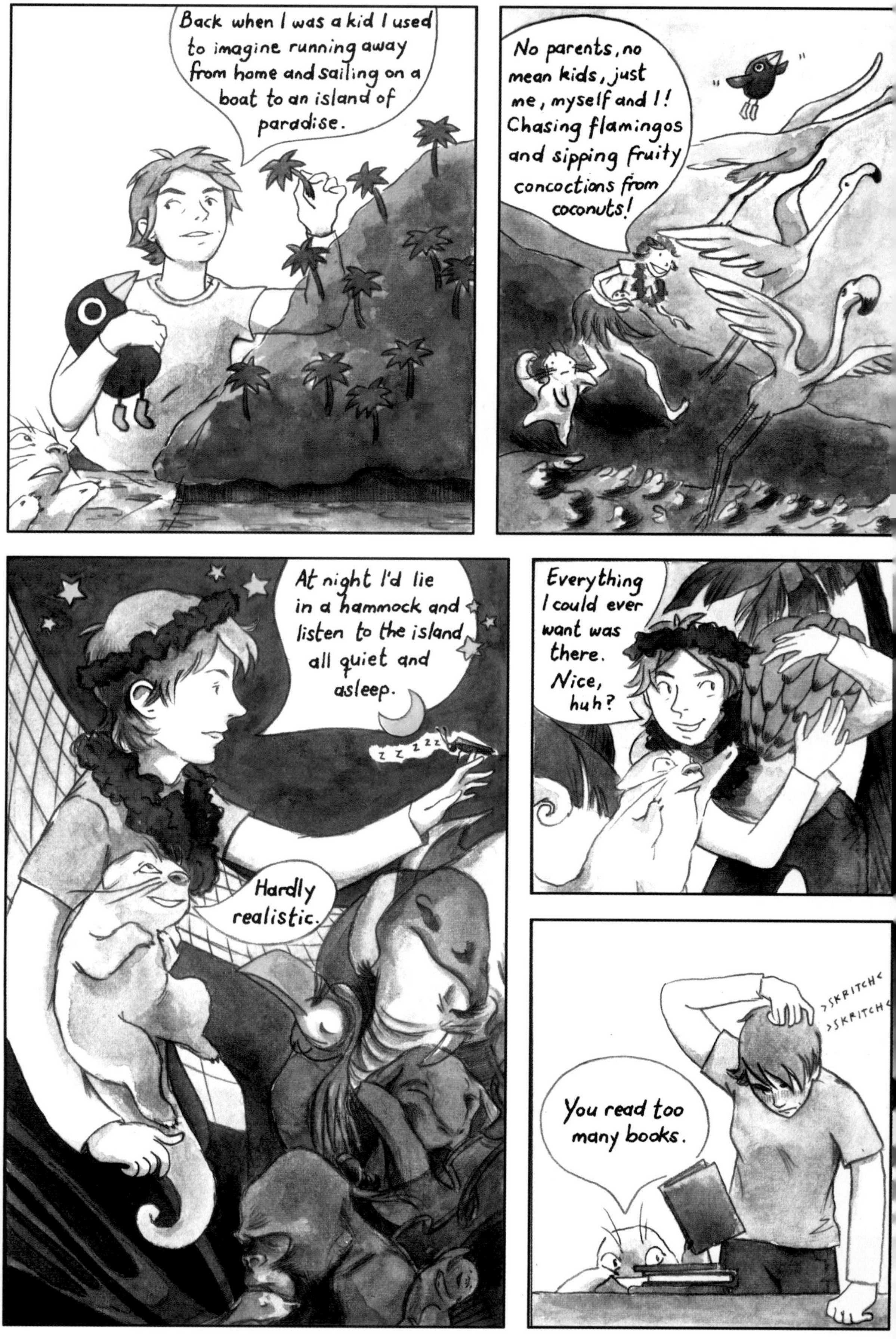
Back when I was a kid I used to imagine running away from home and sailing on a boat to an island of paradise.
No parents, no mean kids, just me, myself and I! Chasing flamingos and sipping fruity concoctions from coconuts!
At night I'd lie in a hammock and listen to the island all quiet and asleep.
Z Z Z Z Z
Hardly realistic.
Everything I could ever want was there. Nice, huh?
>SKRITCH<
>SKRITCH<
You read too many books.

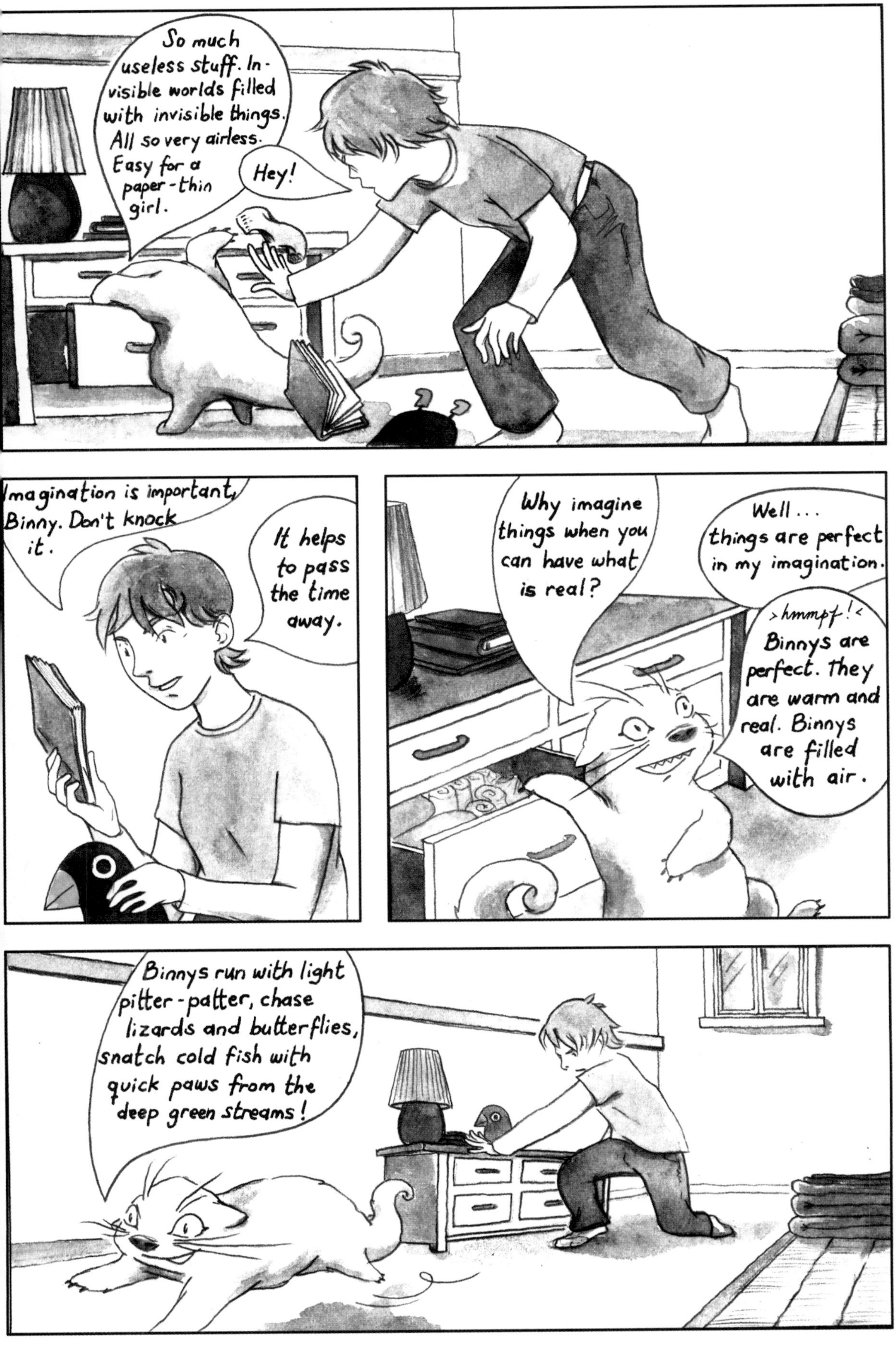

So much useless stuff. In-visible worlds filled with invisible things. All so very airless. Easy for a paper-thin girl.
Hey!
Imagination is important, Binny. Don't knock it.
It helps to pass the time away.
Why imagine things when you can have what is real?
Well... things are perfect in my imagination.
>hmmpf!<
Binnys are perfect. they are warm and real. Binnys are filled with air.
Binnys run with light pitter-patter, chase lizards and butterflies, snatch cold fish with quick paws from the deep green streams!

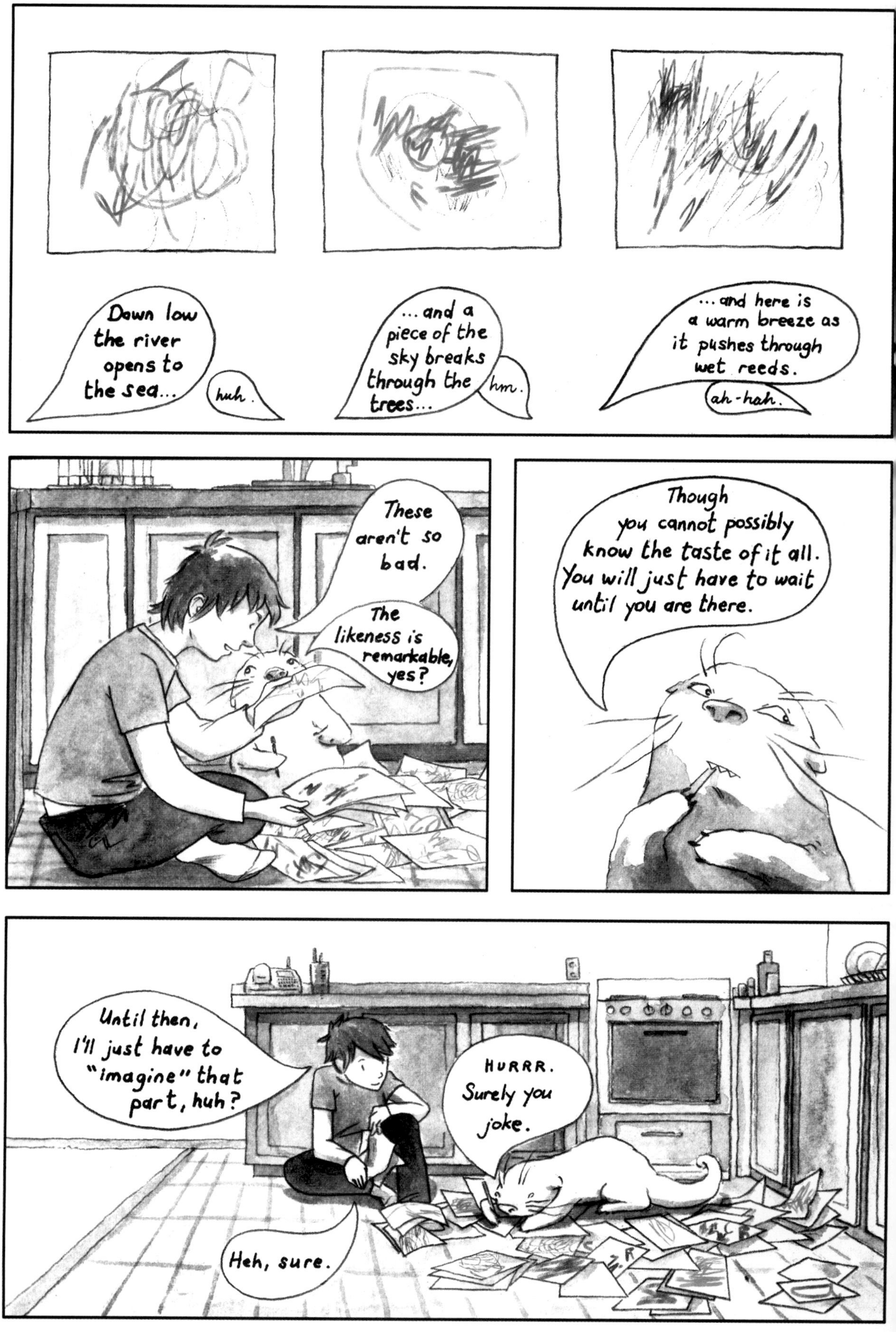
Down low the river opens to the sea...
huh.
... and a piece of the sky breaks through the trees...
hm.
... and here is a warm breeze as it pushes through wet reeds.
ah-hah.
These aren't so bad.
The likeness is remarkable, yes?
Though you cannot possibly know the taste of it all. You will just have to wait until you are there.
Until then, I'll just have to "imagine" that part, huh?
HURRR. Surely you joke.
Heh, sure.

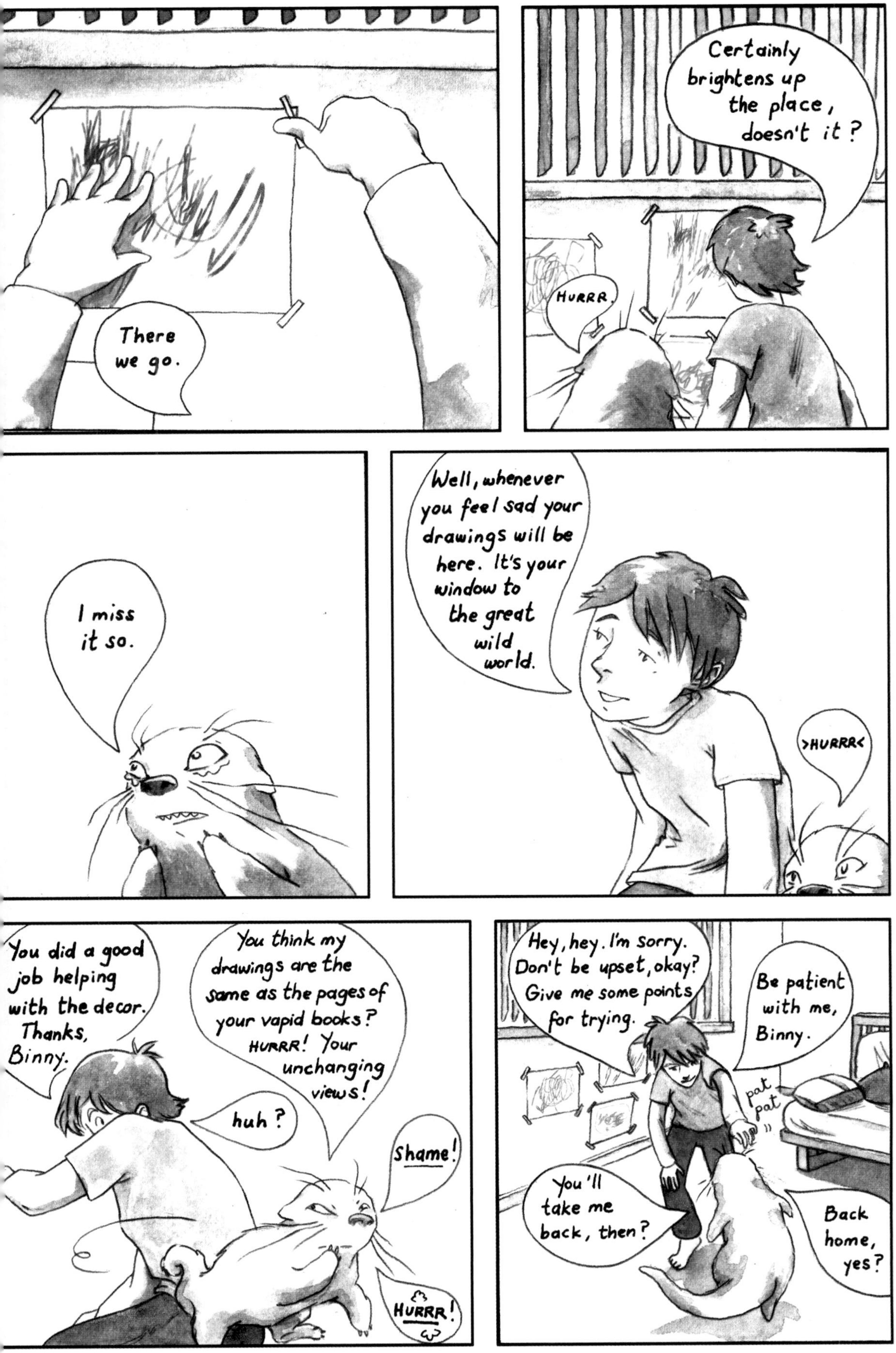
There we go.
Certainly brightens up the place, doesn't it?
HURRR.
I miss it so.
Well, whenever you feel sad your drawings will be here. It's your window to the great wild world.
>HURRR<
You did a good job helping with the decor. Thanks, Binny.
You think my drawings are the same as the pages of your vapid books? HURRR! Your unchanging views!
huh?
Shame!
HURRR!
Hey, hey. I'm sorry. Don't be upset, okay? Give me some points for trying.
Be patient with me, Binny.
pat pat
You'll take me back, then?
Back home, yes?

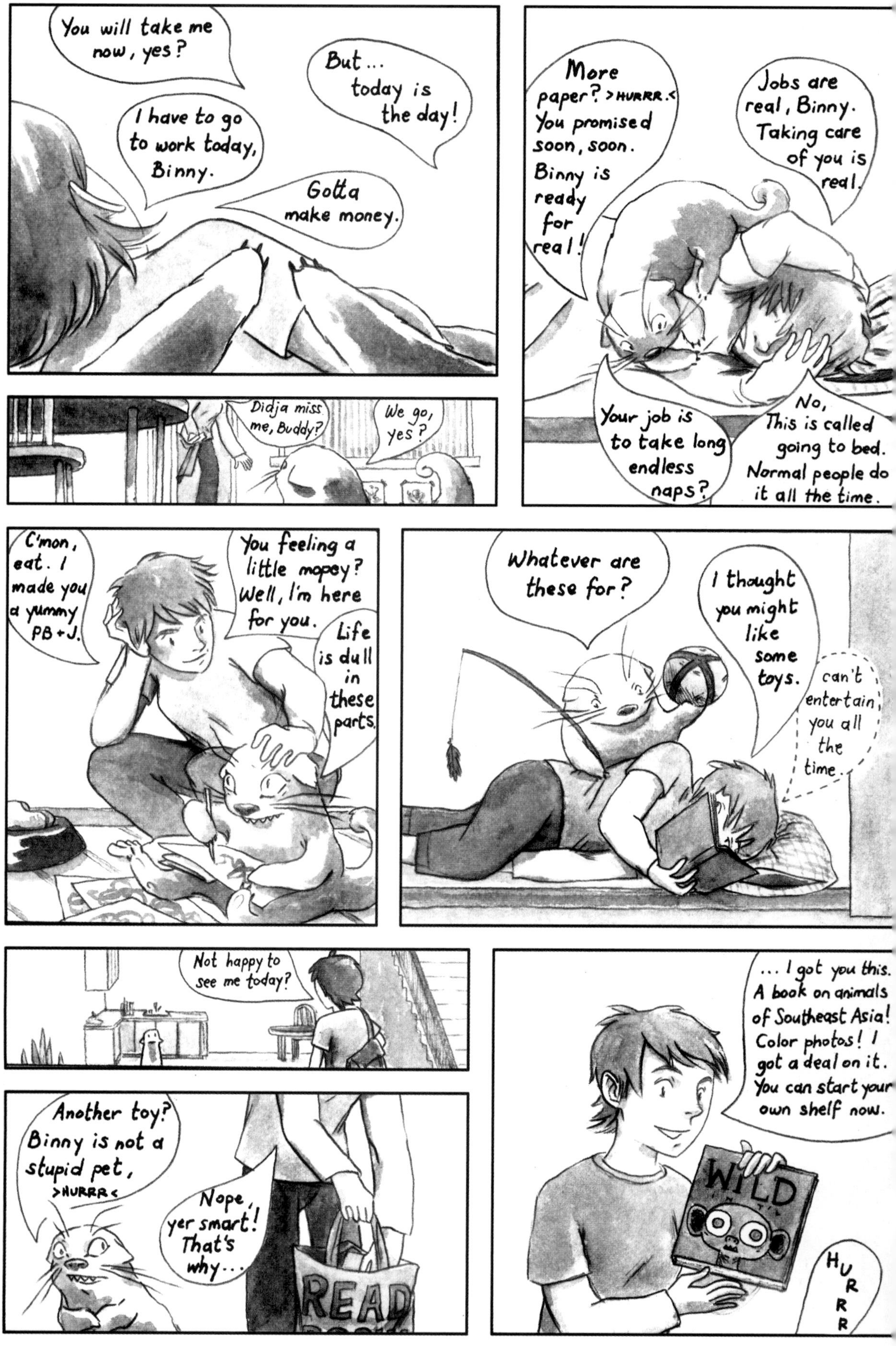
You will take me now, yes?
I have to go to work today, Binny.
But... today is the day!
Gotta make money.
More paper? >HURRR.< You promised soon, soon. Binny is ready for real!
Jobs are real, Binny. Taking care of you is real.
Your job is to take long endless naps?
No, This is called going to bed. Normal people do it all the time.
Didja miss me, Buddy?
We go, yes?
C'mon, eat. I made you a yummy PB+J.
You feeling a little mopey? Well, I'm here for you.
Life is dull in these parts.
Whatever are these for?
I thought you might like some toys.
can't entertain you all the time.
Not happy to see me today?
Another toy? Binny is not a stupid pet, >HURRR<
Nope, yer smart! That's why...
READ
... I got you this. A book on animals of Southeast Asia! Color photos! I got a deal on it. You can start your own shelf now.
WILD
HURRR

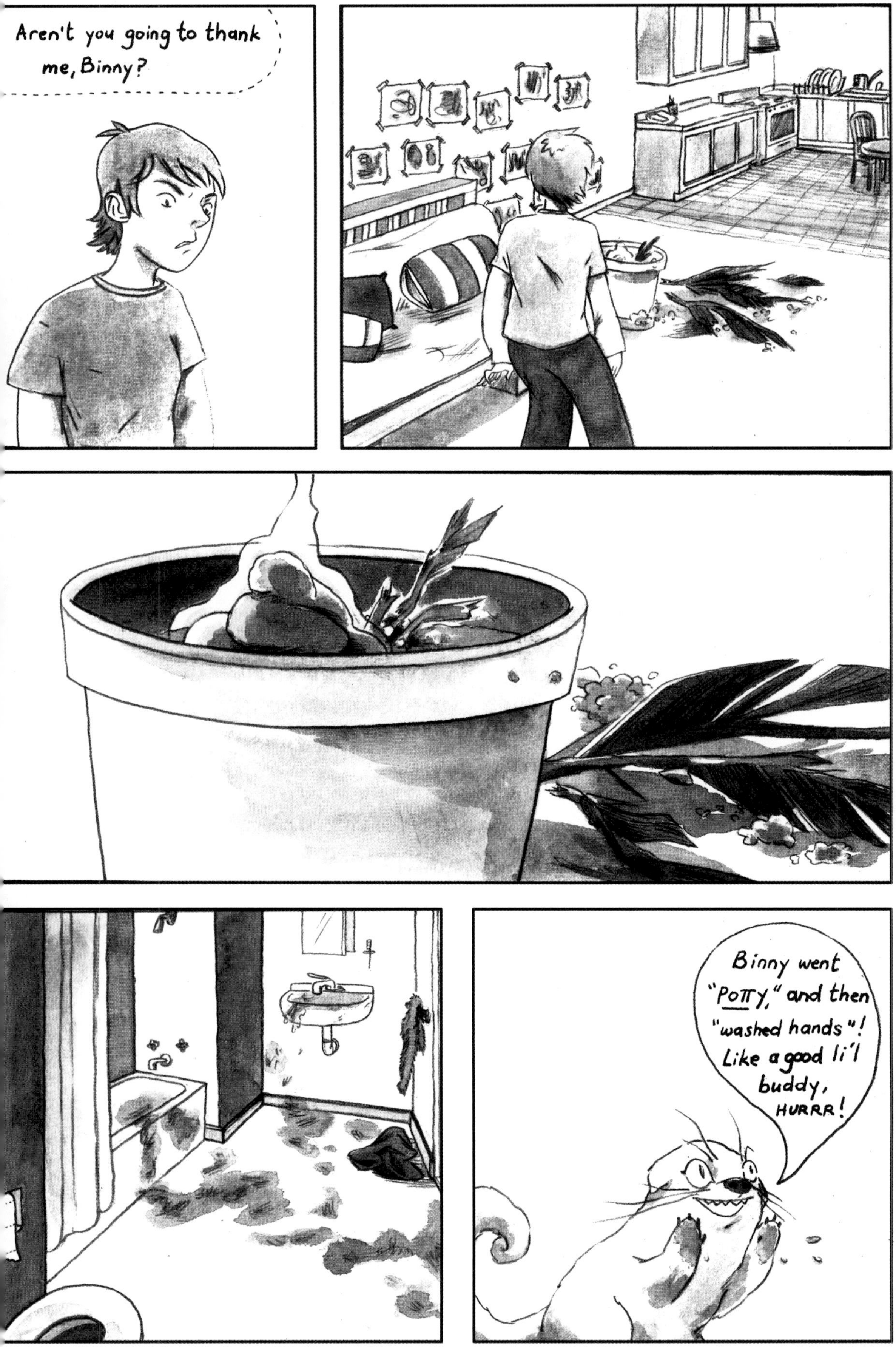
Aren't you going to thank me, Binny?
Binny went "POTTY," and then "washed hands"! Like a good li'l buddy, HURRR!

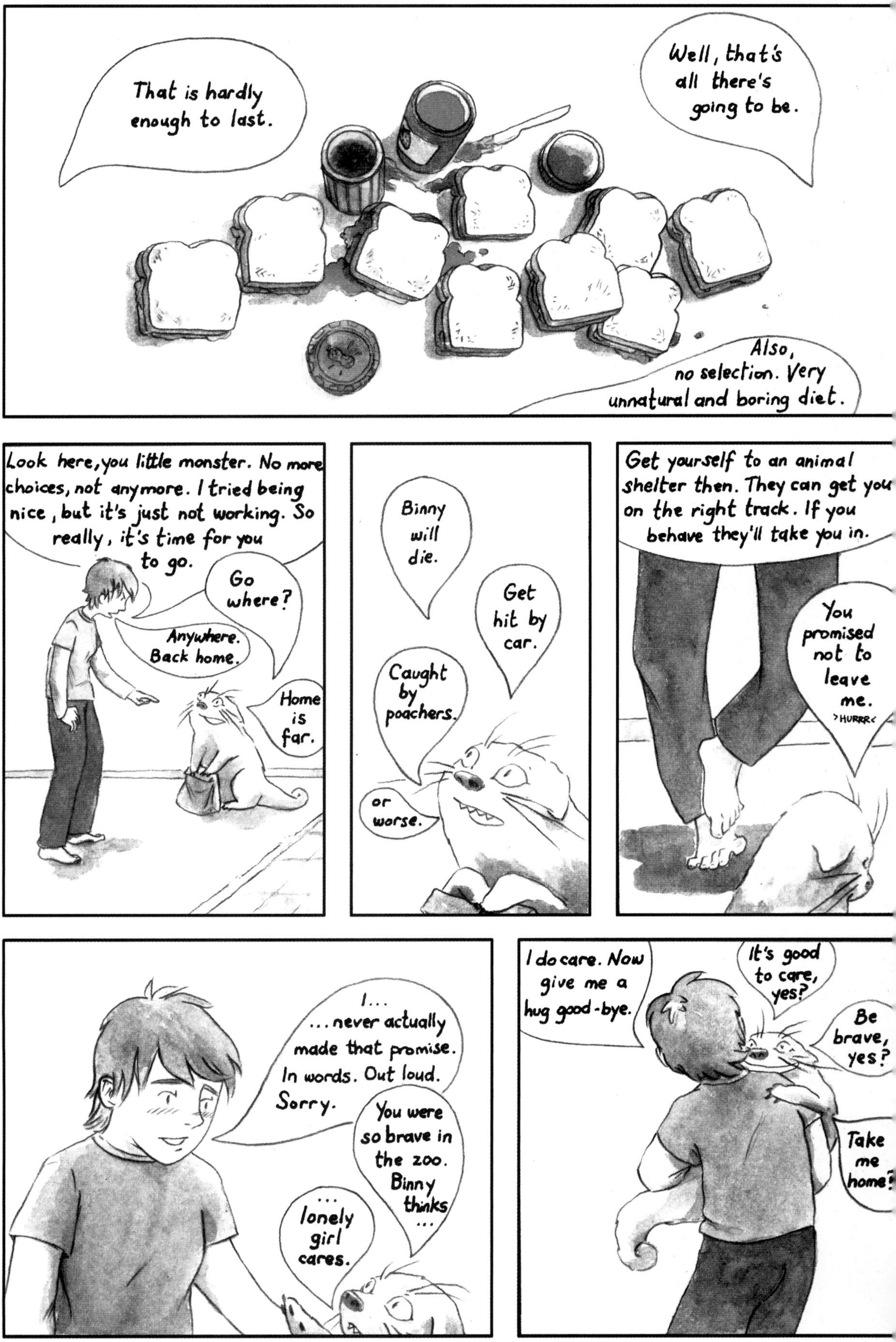
That is hardly enough to last.
Well, that's all there's going to be.
Also, no selection. Very unnatural and boring diet.
Look here, you little monster. No more choices, not anymore. I tried being nice, but it's just not working. So really, it's time for you to go.
Go where?
Anywhere. Back home.
Home is far.
Binny will die.
Get hit by car.
Caught by poachers.
or worse.
Get yourself to an animal shelter then. They can get you on the right track. If you behave they'll take you in.
You promised not to leave me.
>HURRR<
I... ...never actually made that promise. In words. Out loud. Sorry.
You were so brave in the zoo. Binny thinks ...
... lonely girl cares.
I do care. Now give me a hug good-bye.
It's good to care, yes?
Be brave, yes?
Take me home?

CHAPTER 3

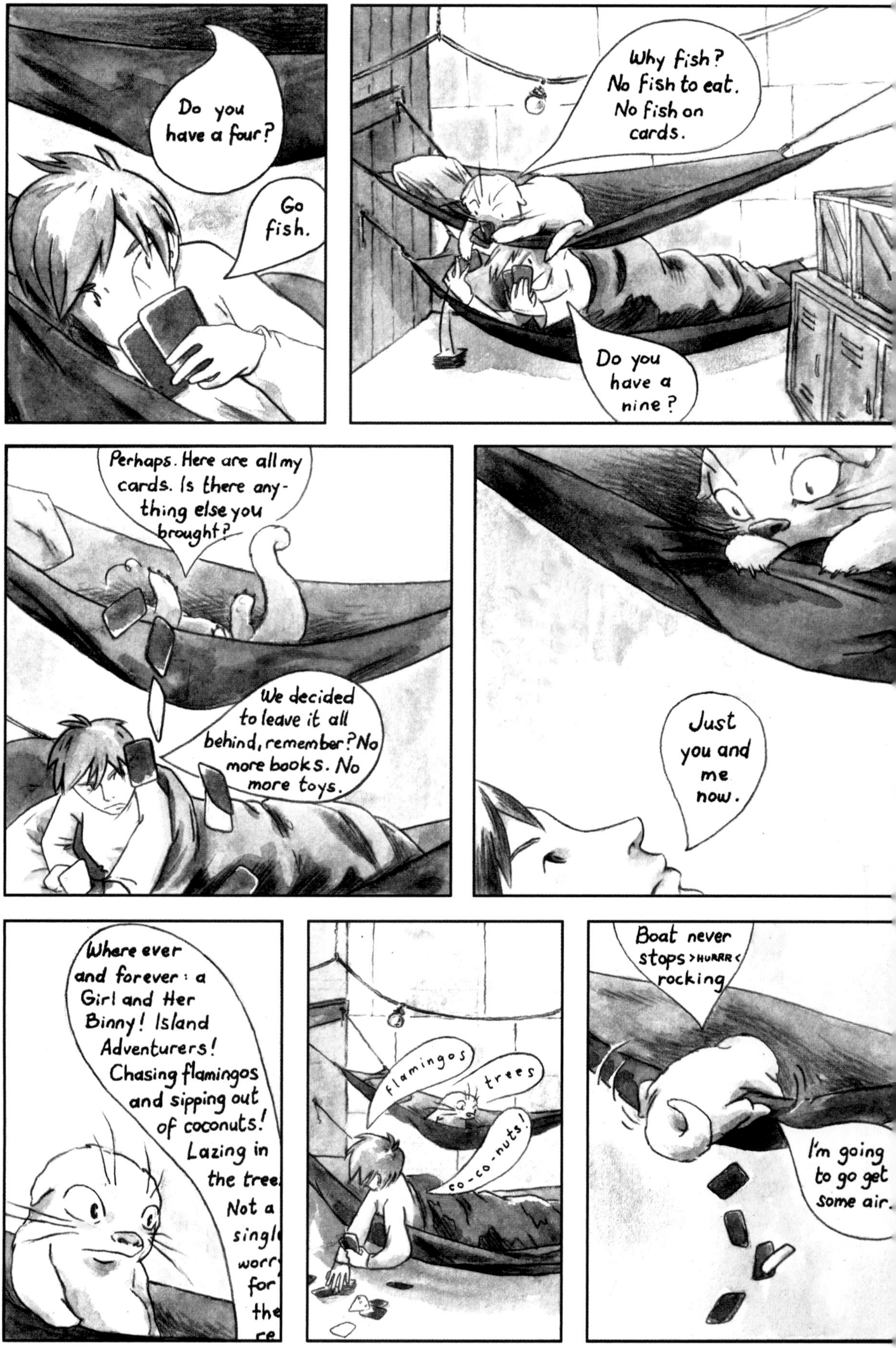
Do you have a four?
Go fish.
Why fish? No fish to eat. No fish on cards.
Do you have a nine?
Perhaps. Here are all my cards. Is there anything else you brought?
We decided to leave it all behind, remember? No more books. No more toys.
Just you and me now.
Where ever and forever: a Girl and Her Binny! Island Adventurers! Chasing flamingos and sipping out of coconuts! Lazing in the tree
flamingos
trees
co-co-nuts!
Boat never stops >HURRR< rocking
I'm going to go get some air.

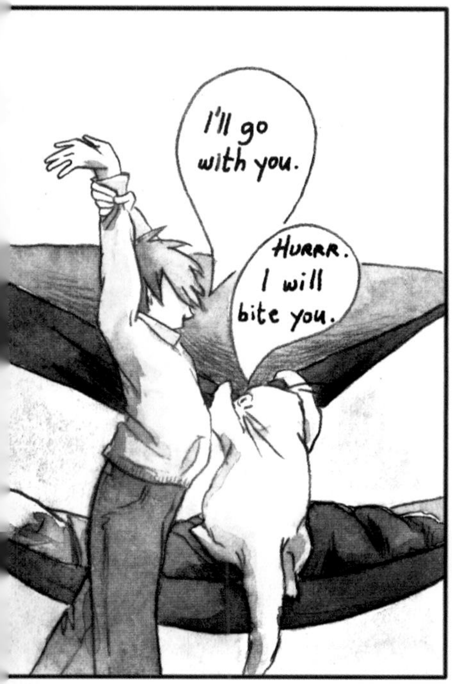
I'll go with you.
HURRR. I will bite you.

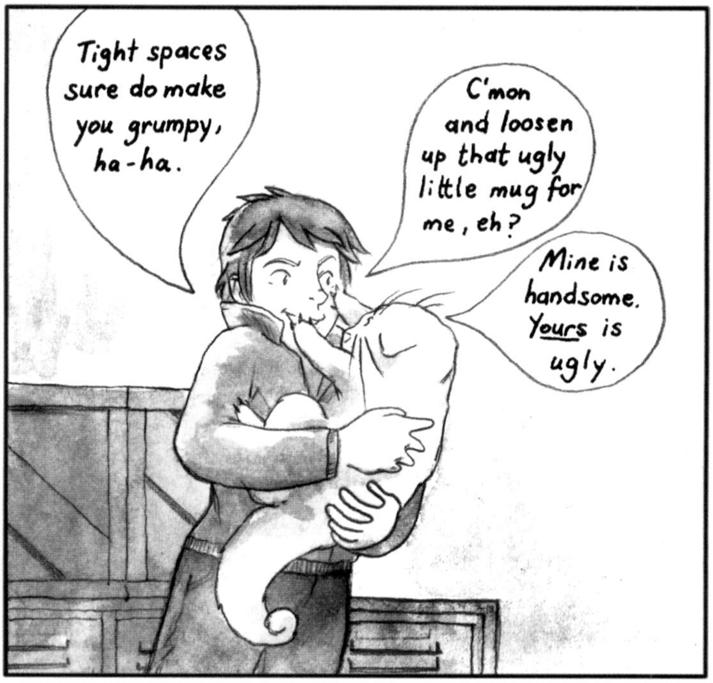
Tight spaces sure do make you grumpy, ha-ha.
C'mon and loosen up that ugly little mug for me, eh?
Mine is handsome. Yours is ugly.

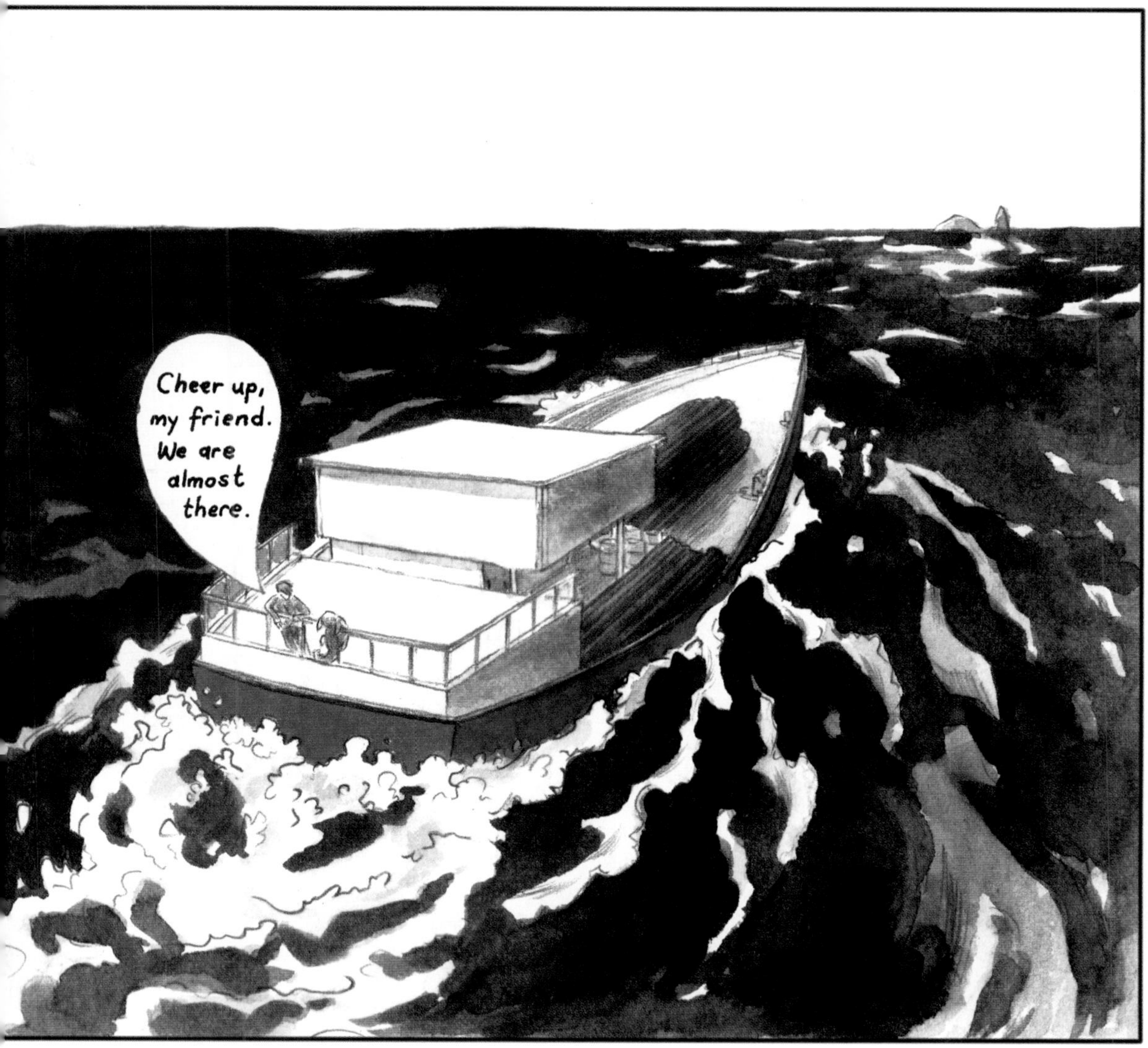
Cheer up, my friend. We are almost there.

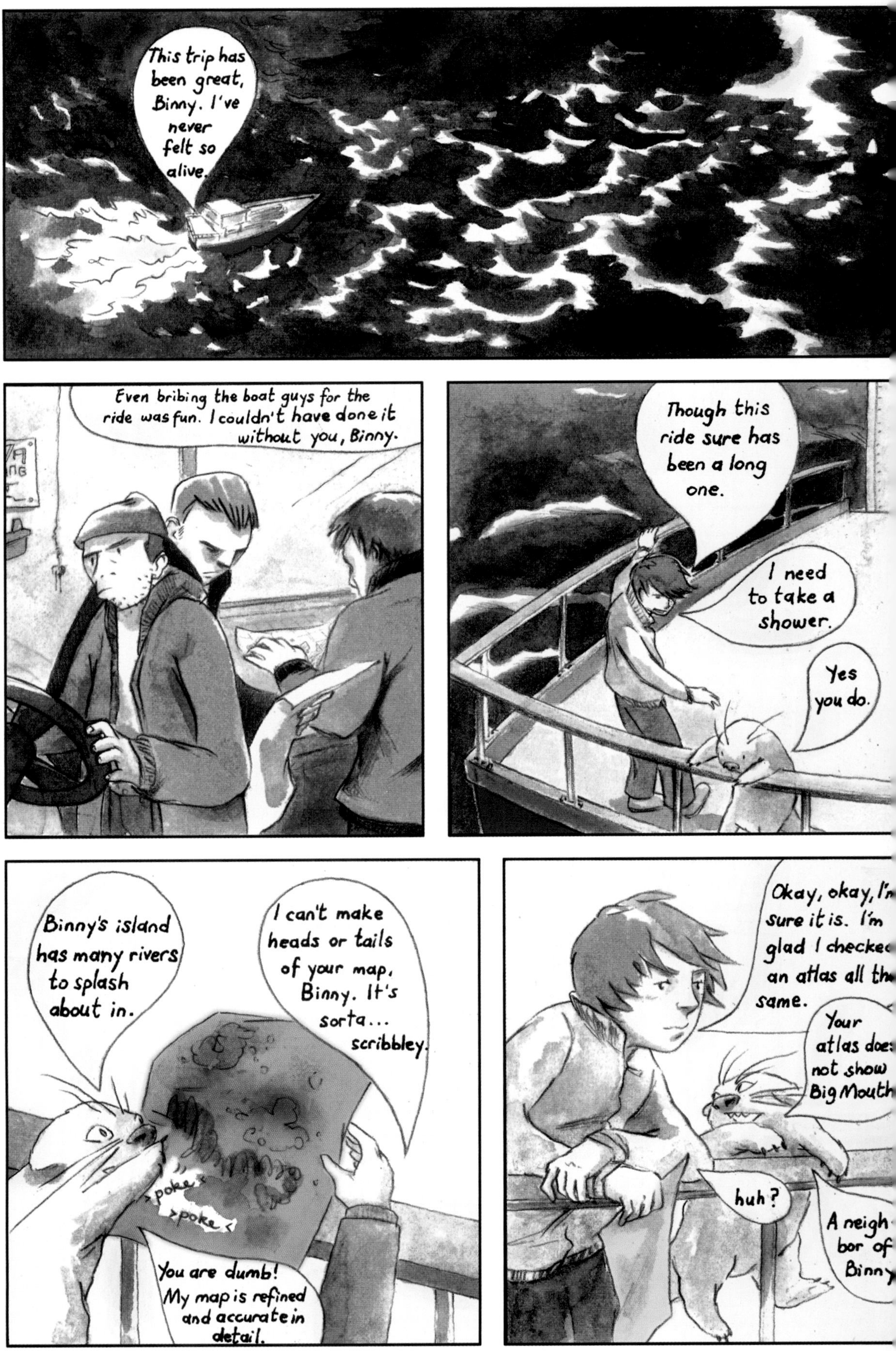
This trip has been great, Binny. I've never felt so alive.
Even bribing the boat guys for the ride was fun. I couldn't have done it without you, Binny.
Though this ride sure has been a long one.
I need to take a shower.
Yes you do.
Binny's island has many rivers to splash about in.
I can't make heads or tails of your map, Binny. It's sorta... scribbley.
>poke<
>poke<
You are dumb! My map is refined and accurate in detail.
Okay, okay, I'm sure it is. I'm glad I checked an atlas all the same.
Your atlas does not show Big Mouth
huh?
A neighbor of Binny

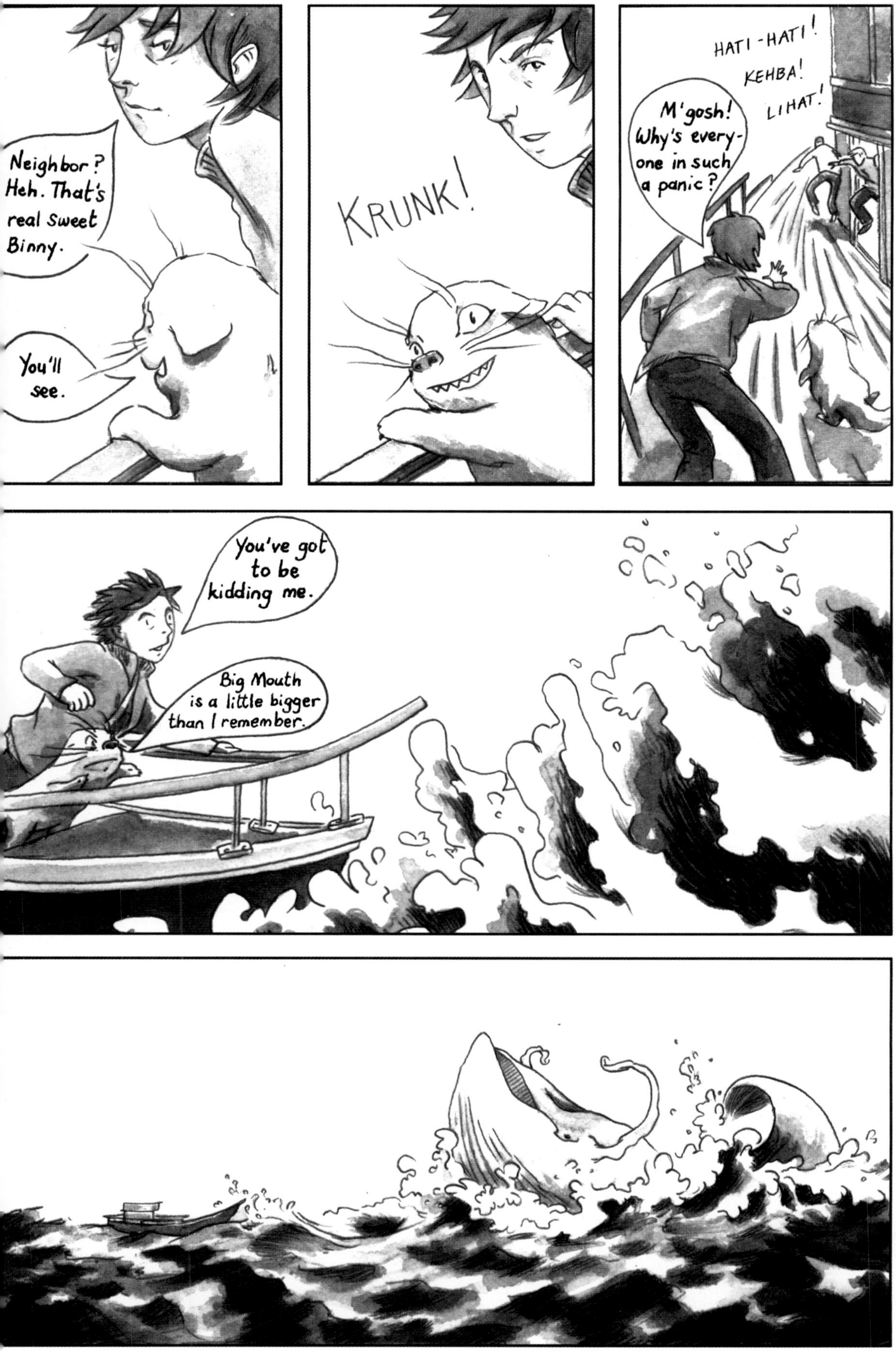
Neighbor? Heh. That's real sweet Binny.
You'll see.
KRUNK!
HATI-HATI!
KEHBA!
LIHAT!
M'gosh! Why's every-one in such a panic?
You've got to be kidding me.
Big Mouth is a little bigger than I remember.

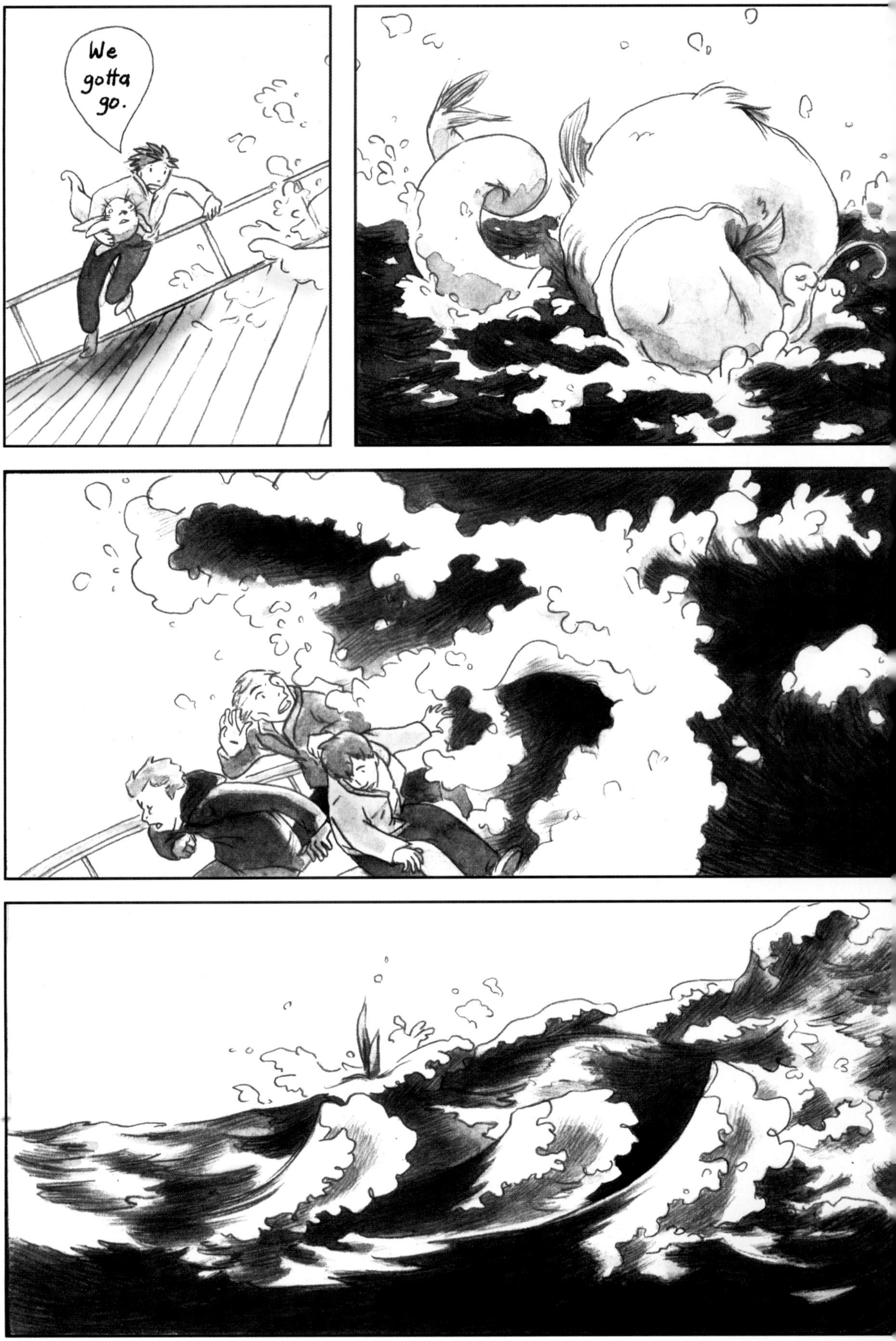
We gotta go.

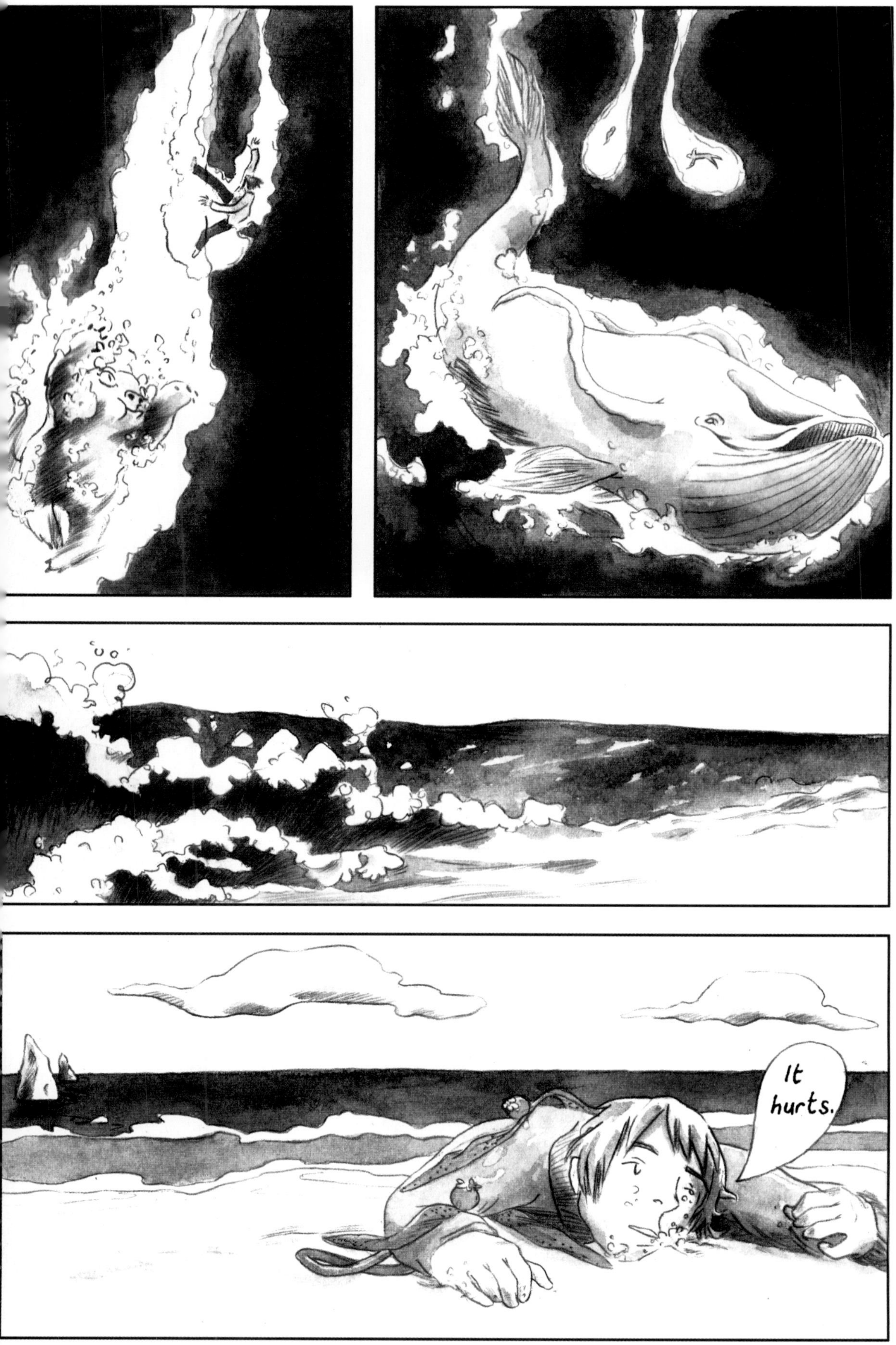
It hurts.

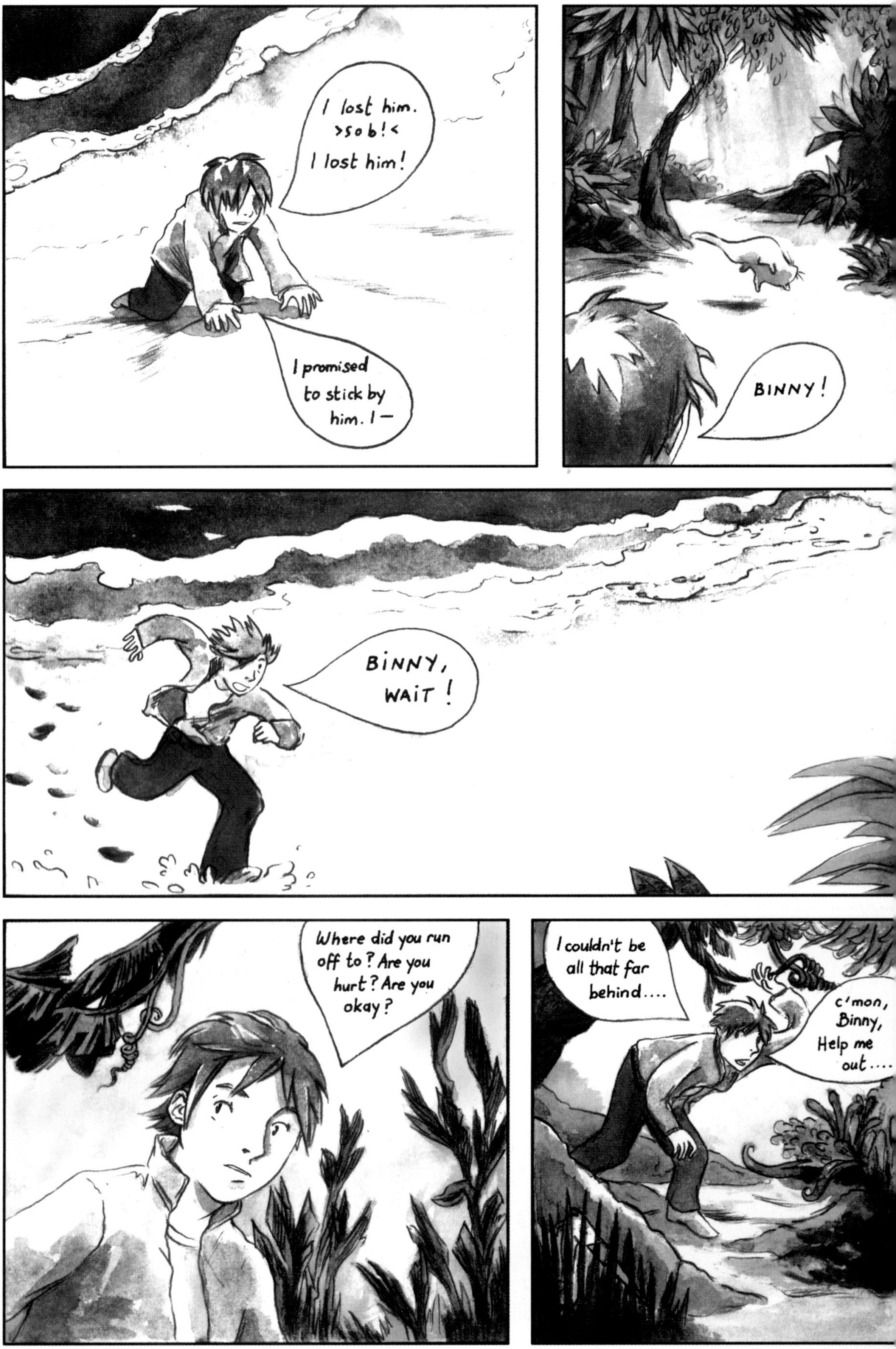

I lost him. >sob!< I lost him!
I promised to stick by him. I—
BINNY!
BINNY, WAIT!
Where did you run off to? Are you hurt? Are you okay?
I couldn't be all that far behind....
c'mon, Binny, Help me out....

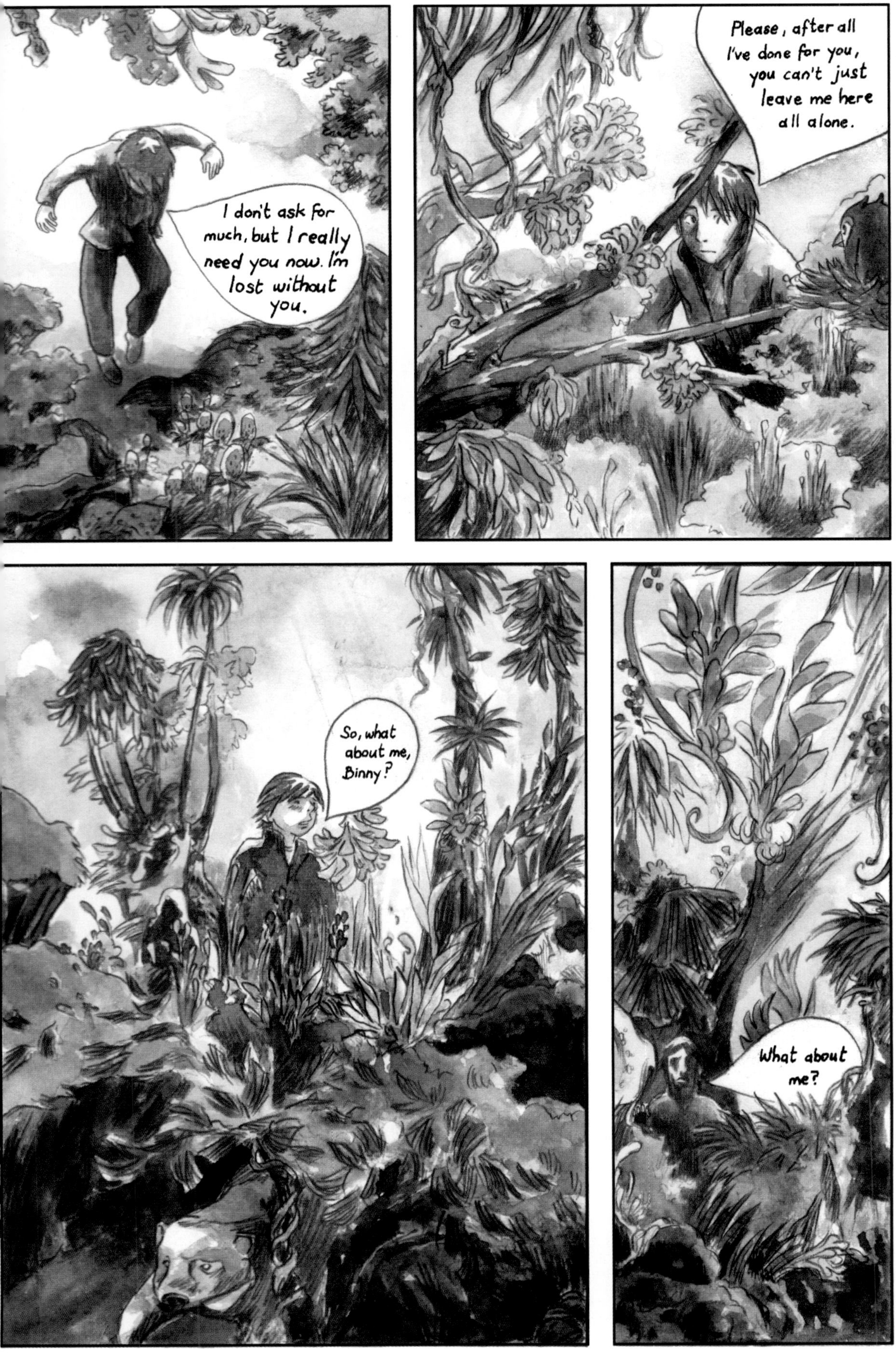
I don't ask for much, but I really need you now. I'm lost without you.
Please, after all I've done for you, you can't just leave me here all alone.
So, what about me, Binny?
What about me?

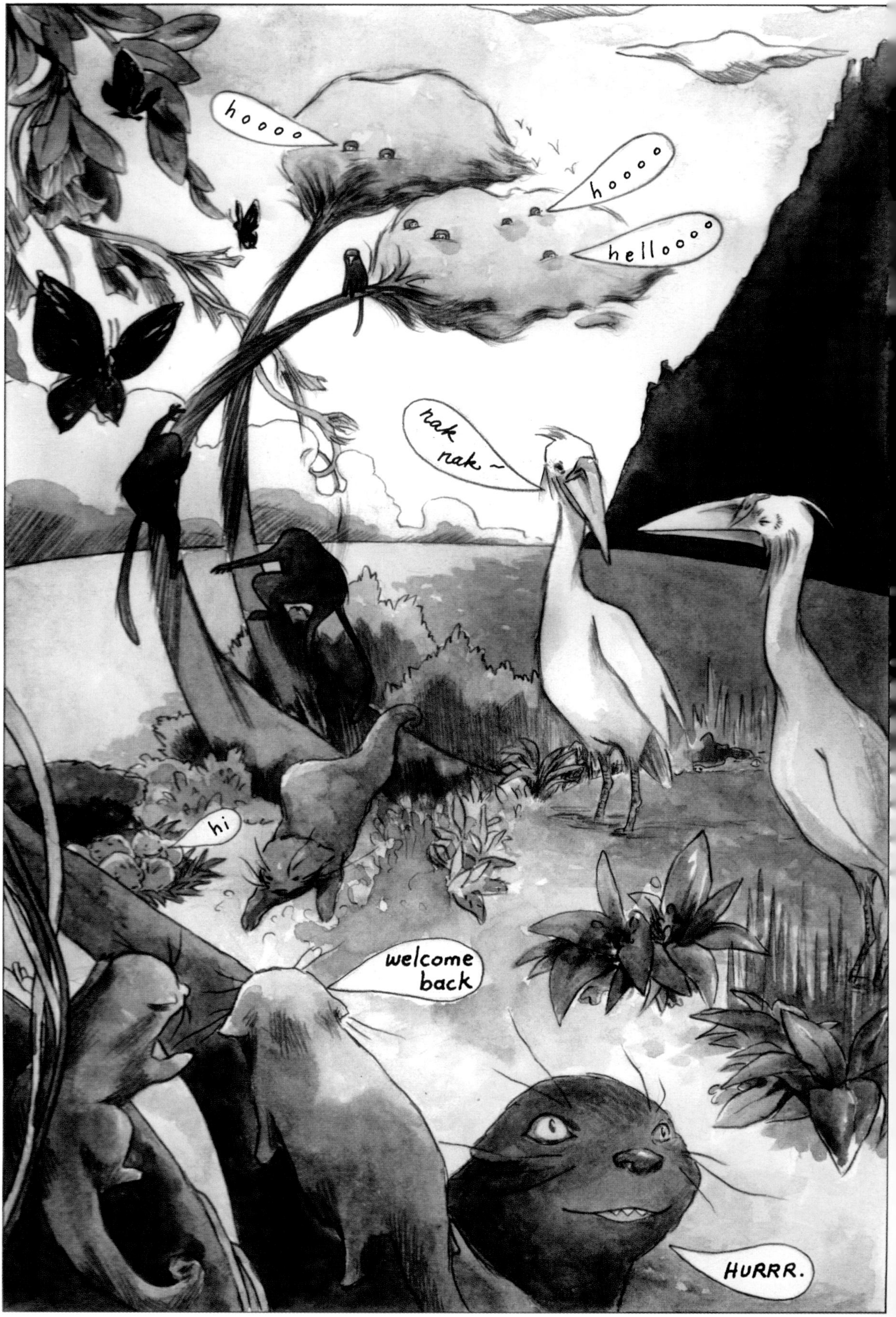
hoooo
hoooo
helloooo
rak rak ~
hi
welcome back
HURRR.

many thanks to those of FLIGHT
also thank you thien, anthony, & jae
a special thanks to jason shiga
and thank you for reading this story.

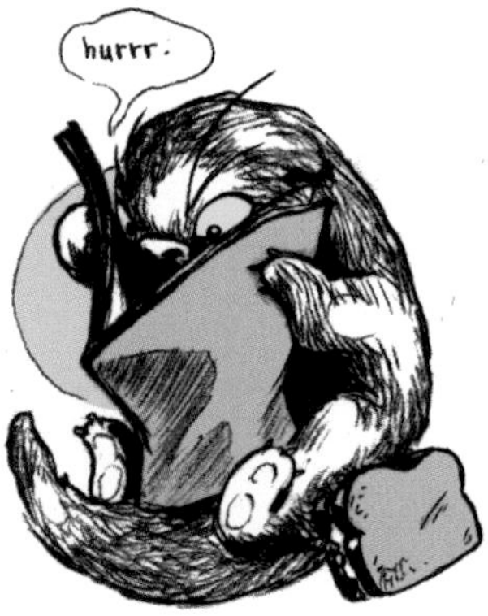
hurrr.

the end.

Cortina

By Fábio Moon

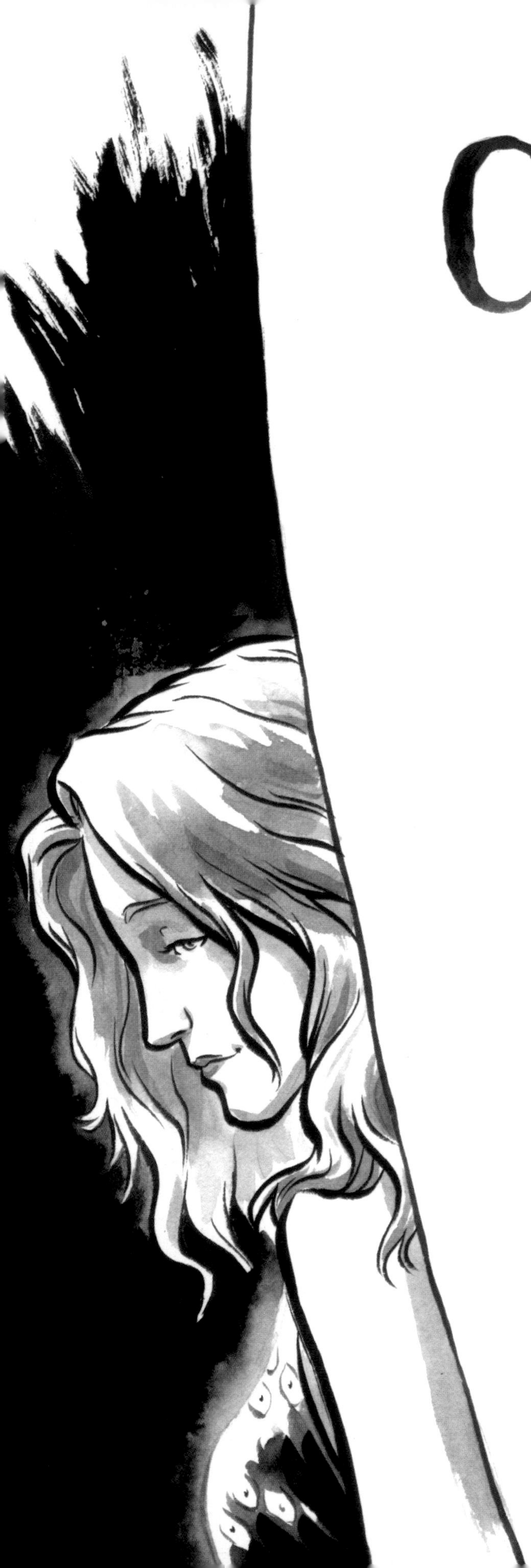

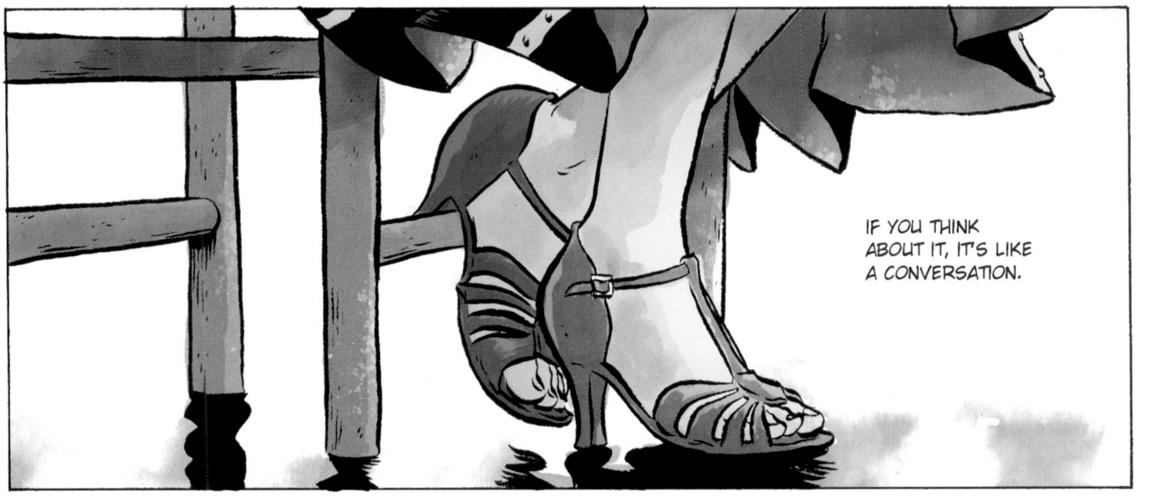
IF YOU THINK ABOUT IT, IT'S LIKE A CONVERSATION.

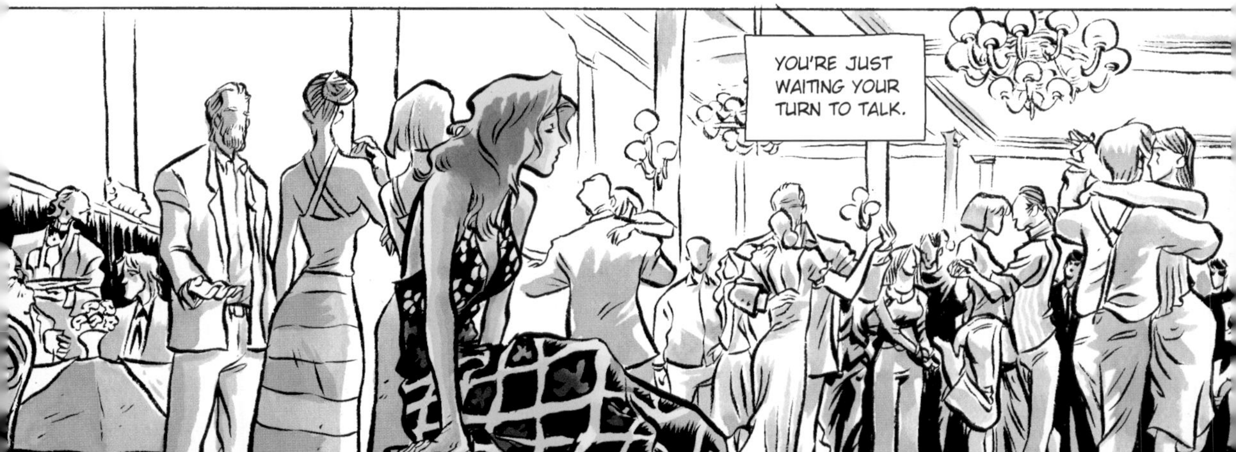
YOU'RE JUST WAITING YOUR TURN TO TALK.

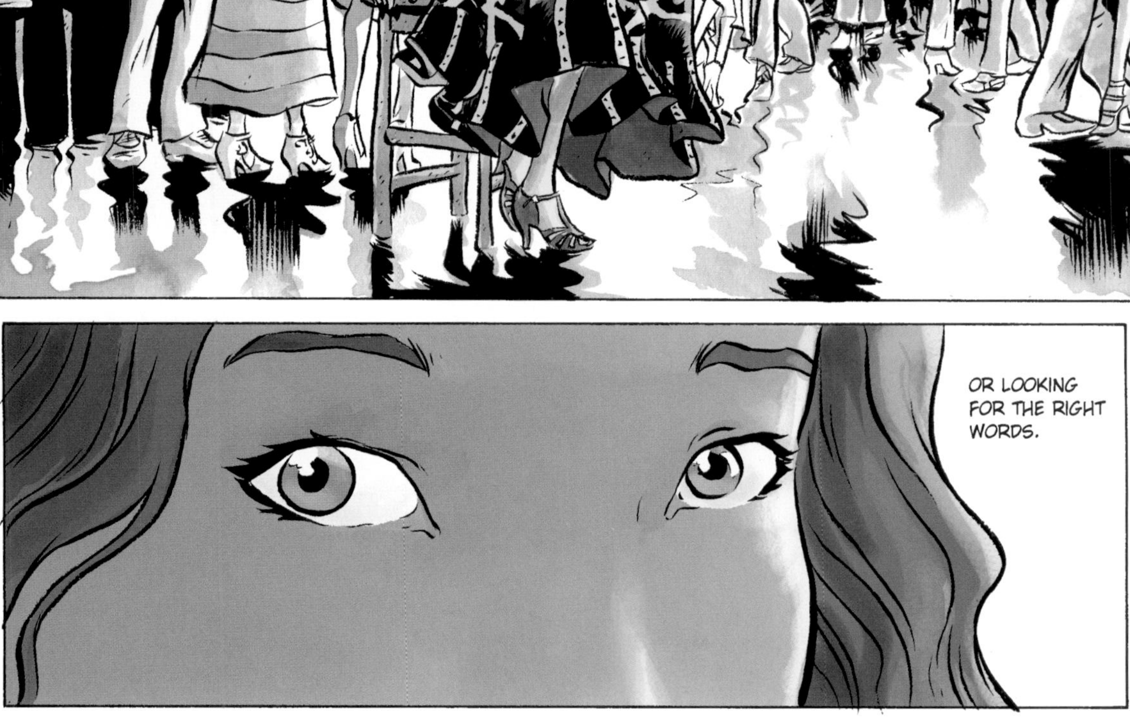
OR LOOKING FOR THE RIGHT WORDS.

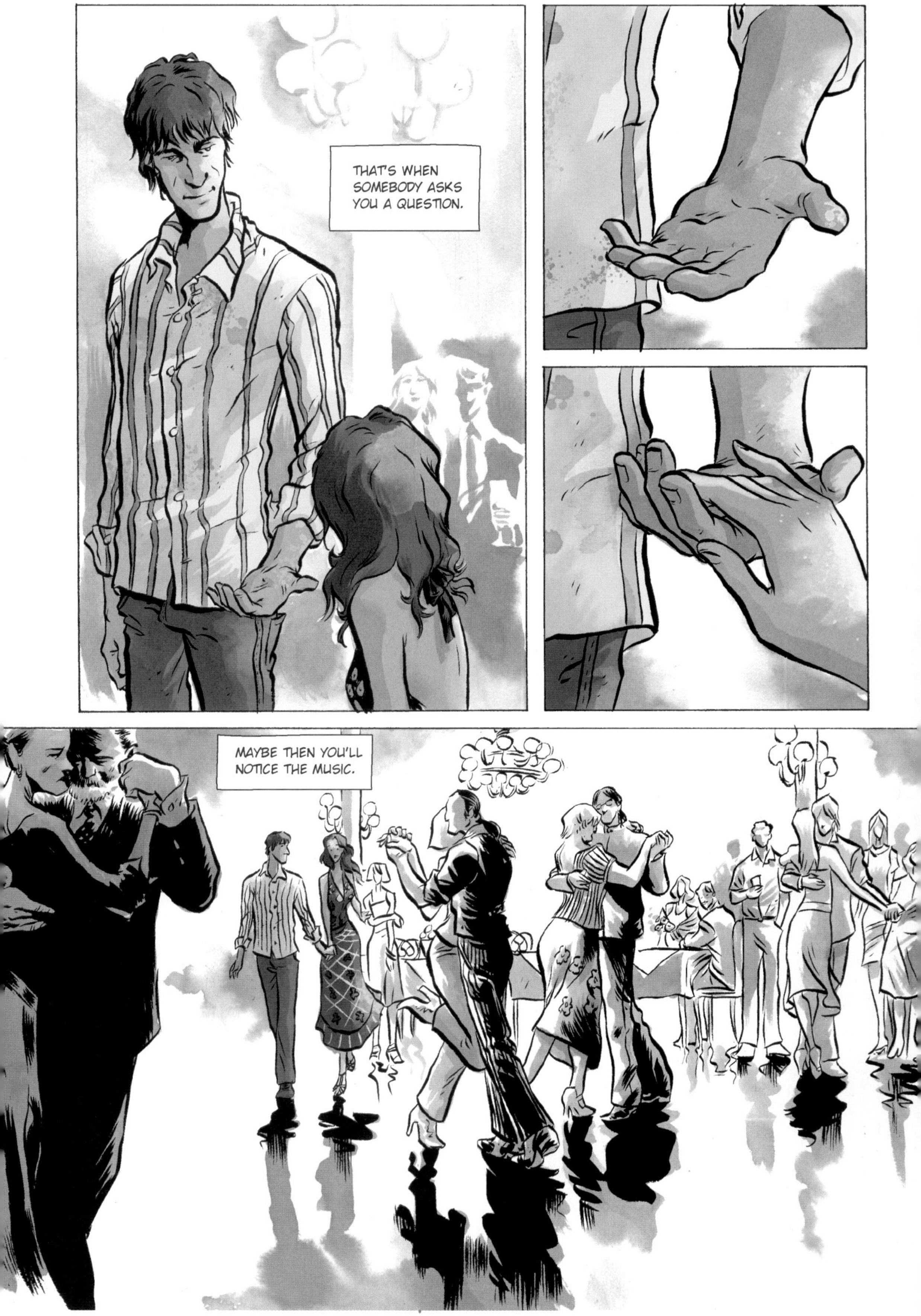
THAT'S WHEN SOMEBODY ASKS YOU A QUESTION.
MAYBE THEN YOU'LL NOTICE THE MUSIC.

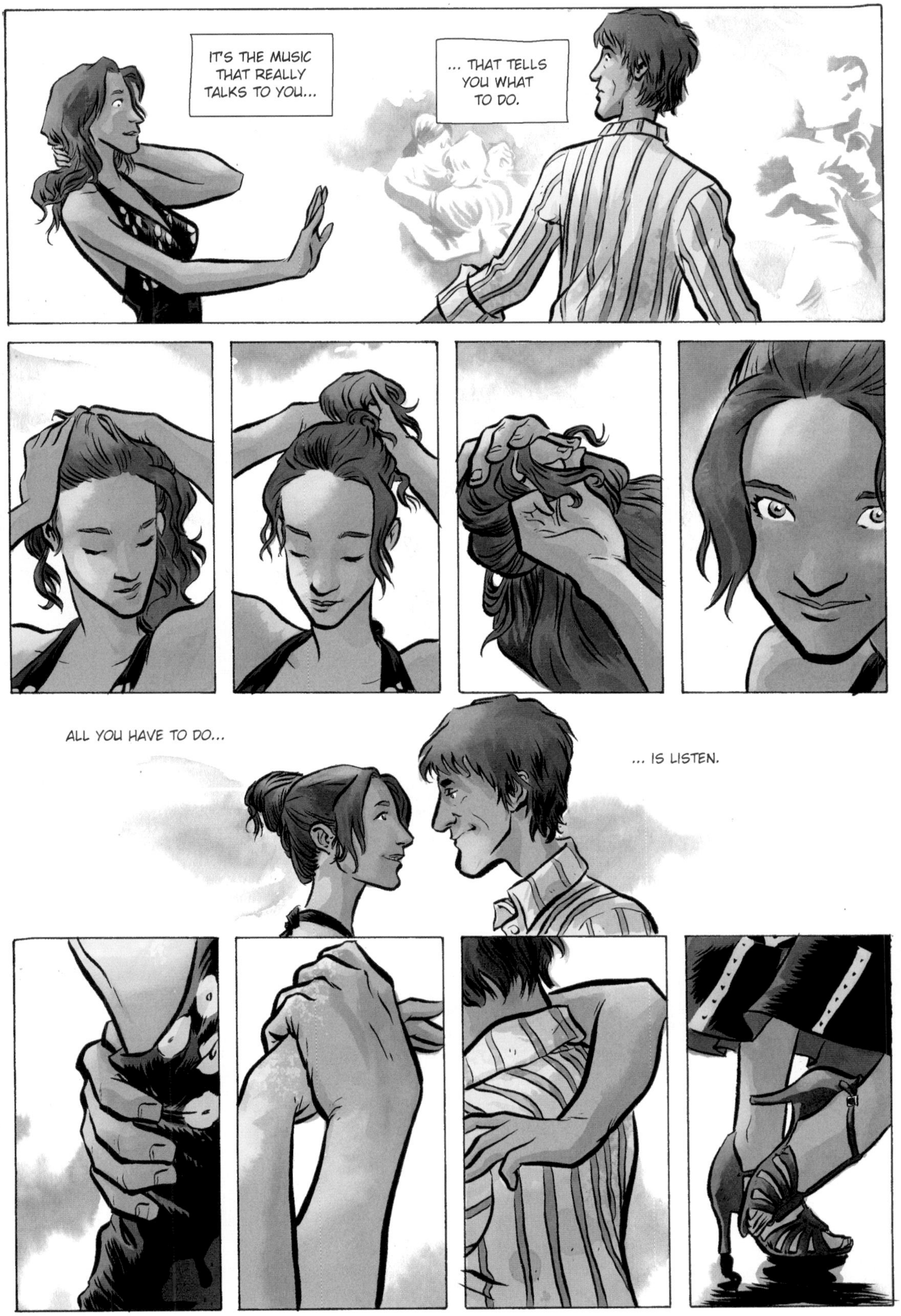
IT'S THE MUSIC THAT REALLY TALKS TO YOU...
... THAT TELLS YOU WHAT TO DO.
ALL YOU HAVE TO DO...
... IS LISTEN.

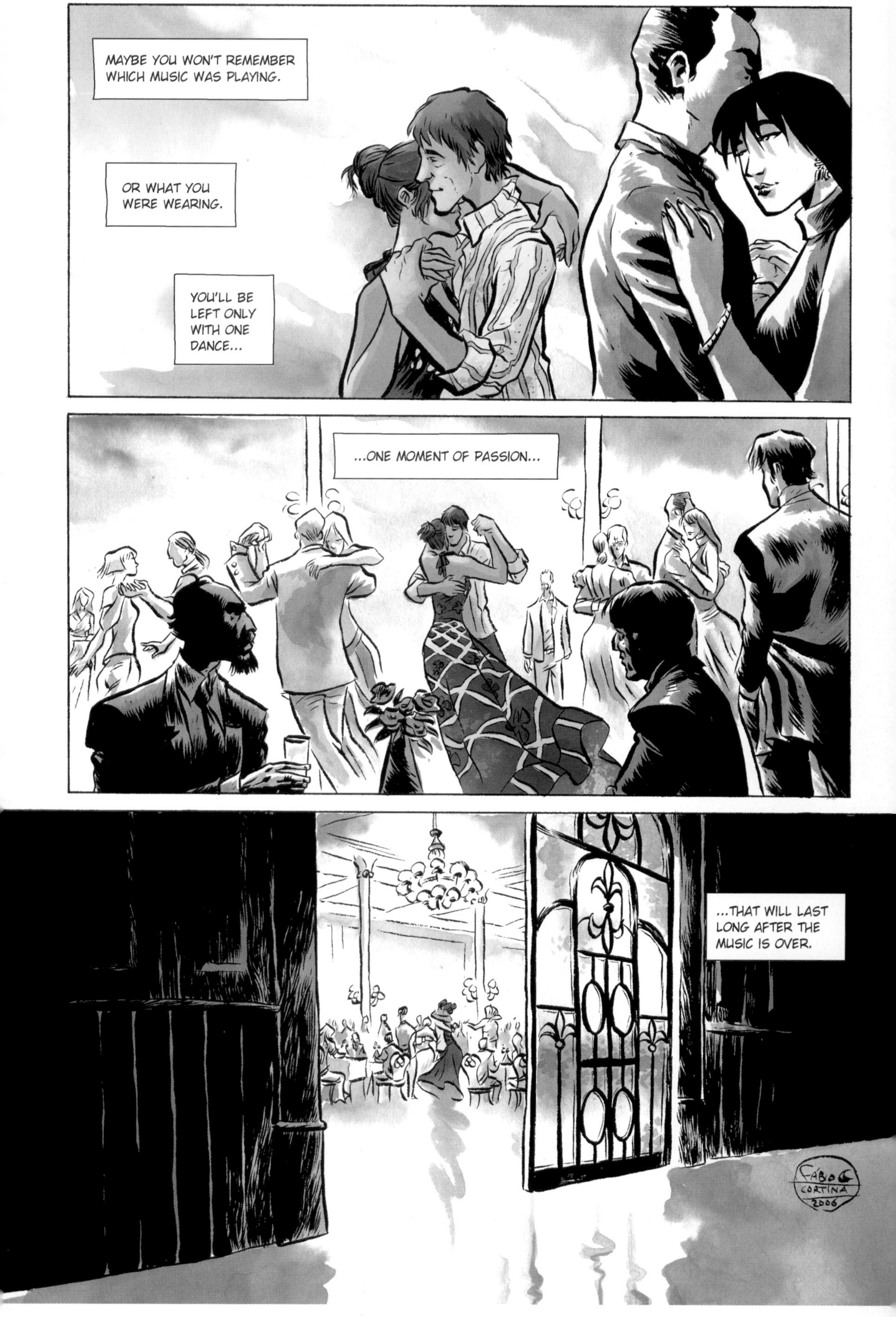
MAYBE YOU WON'T REMEMBER WHICH MUSIC WAS PLAYING.
OR WHAT YOU WERE WEARING.
YOU'LL BE LEFT ONLY WITH ONE DANCE...
...ONE MOMENT OF PASSION...
...THAT WILL LAST LONG AFTER THE MUSIC IS OVER.
FÁBIO CORTINA 2006

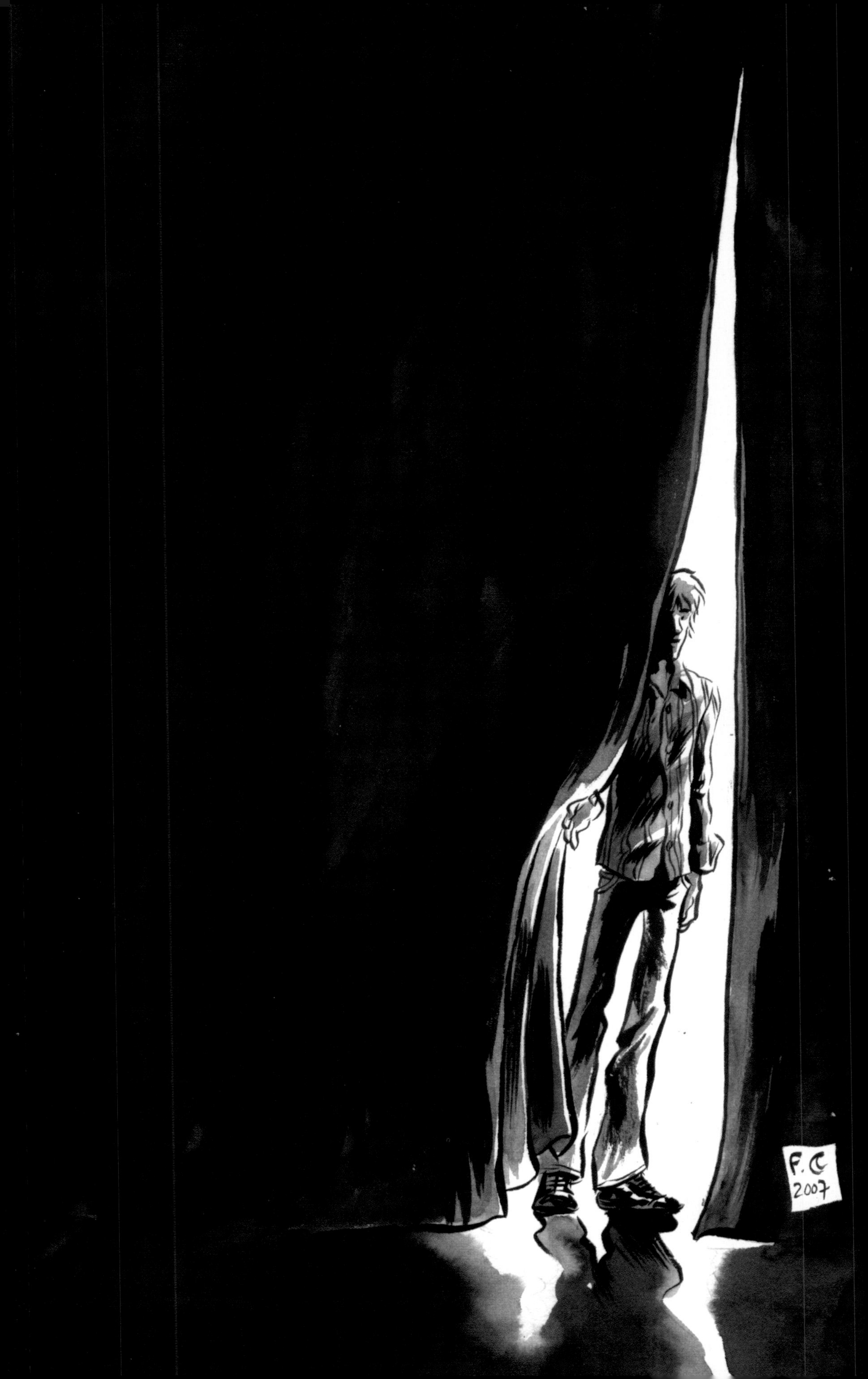
F. C
2007

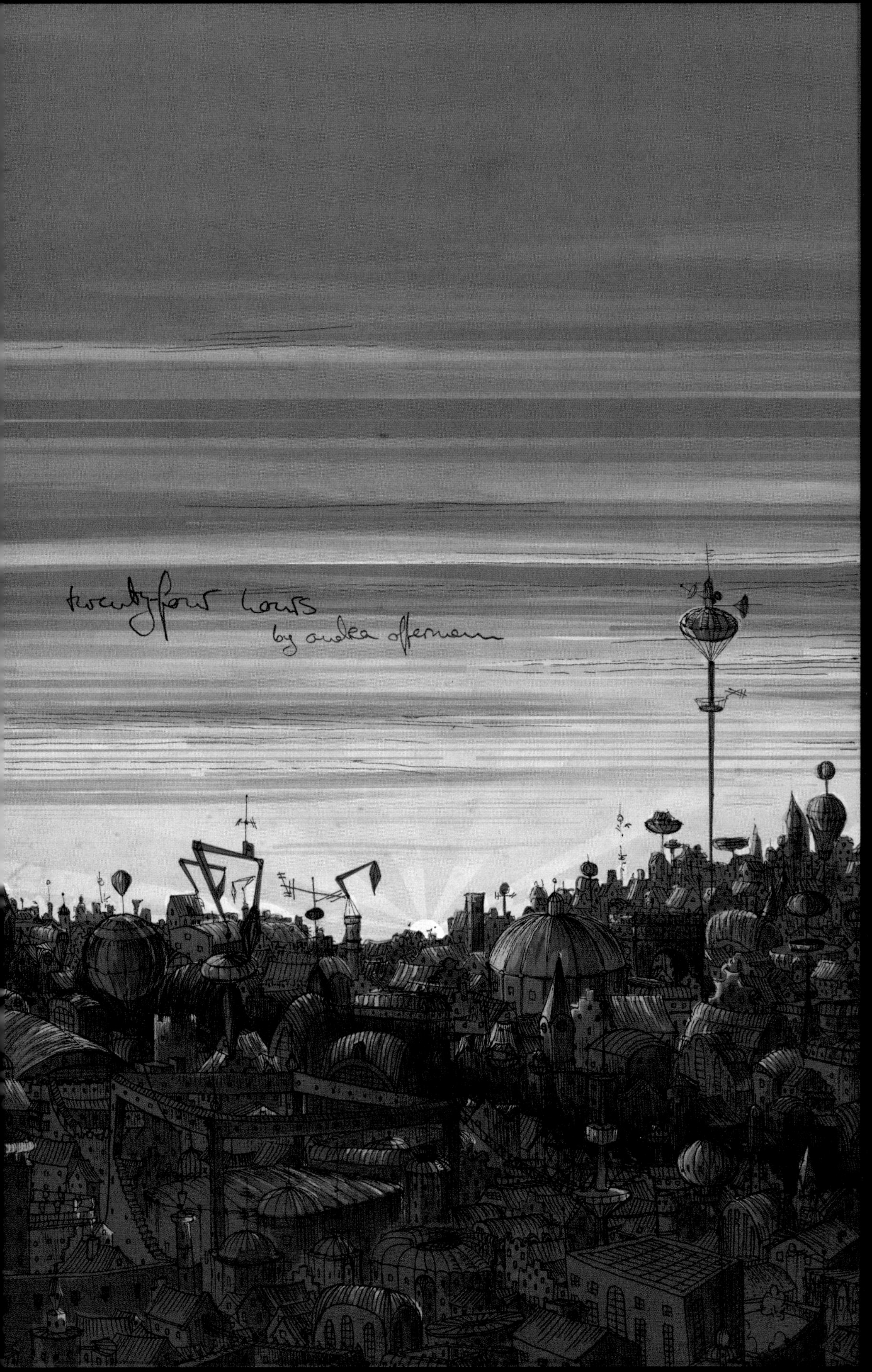
twentyfour hours
by andrea offermann

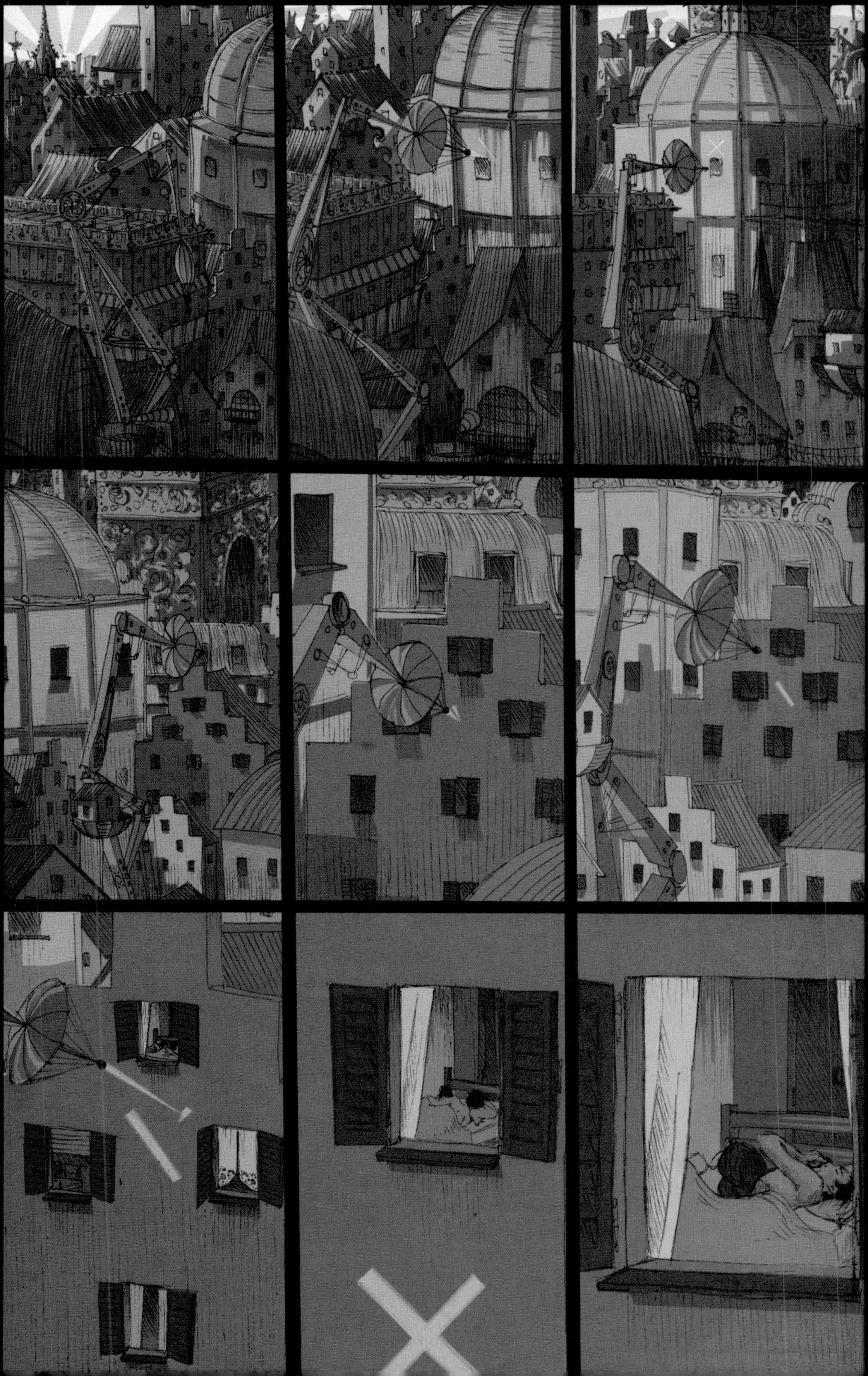

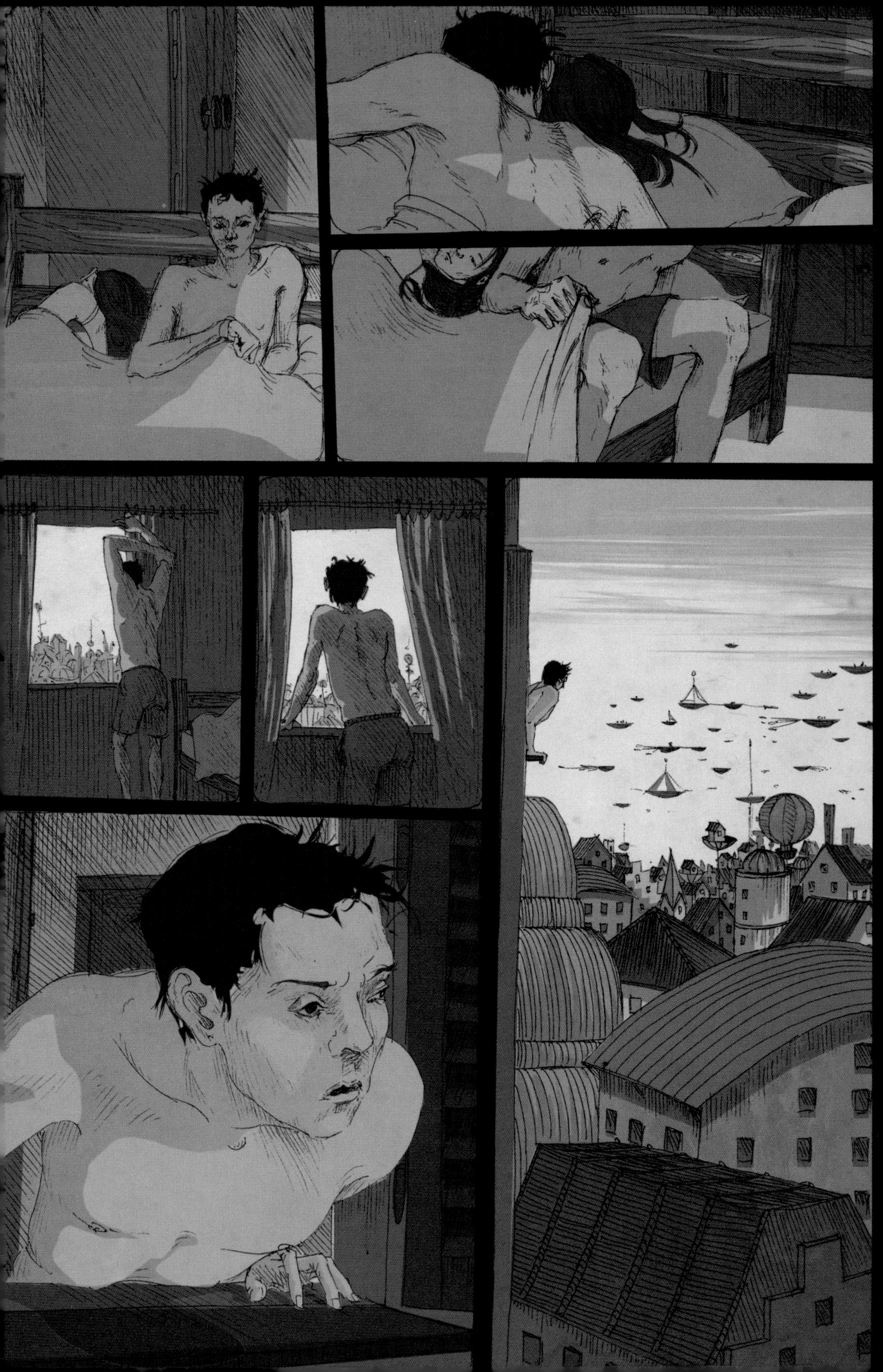

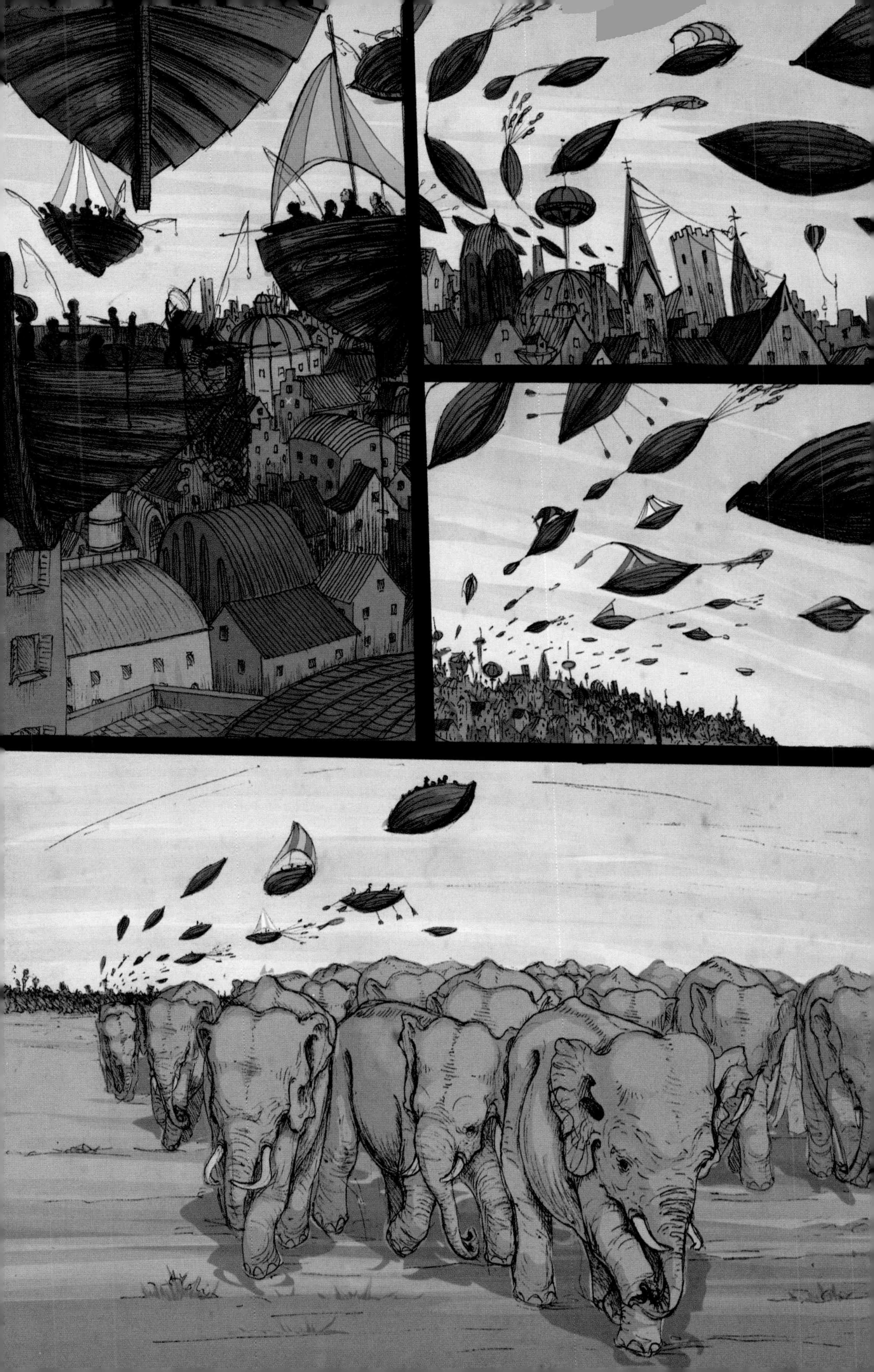

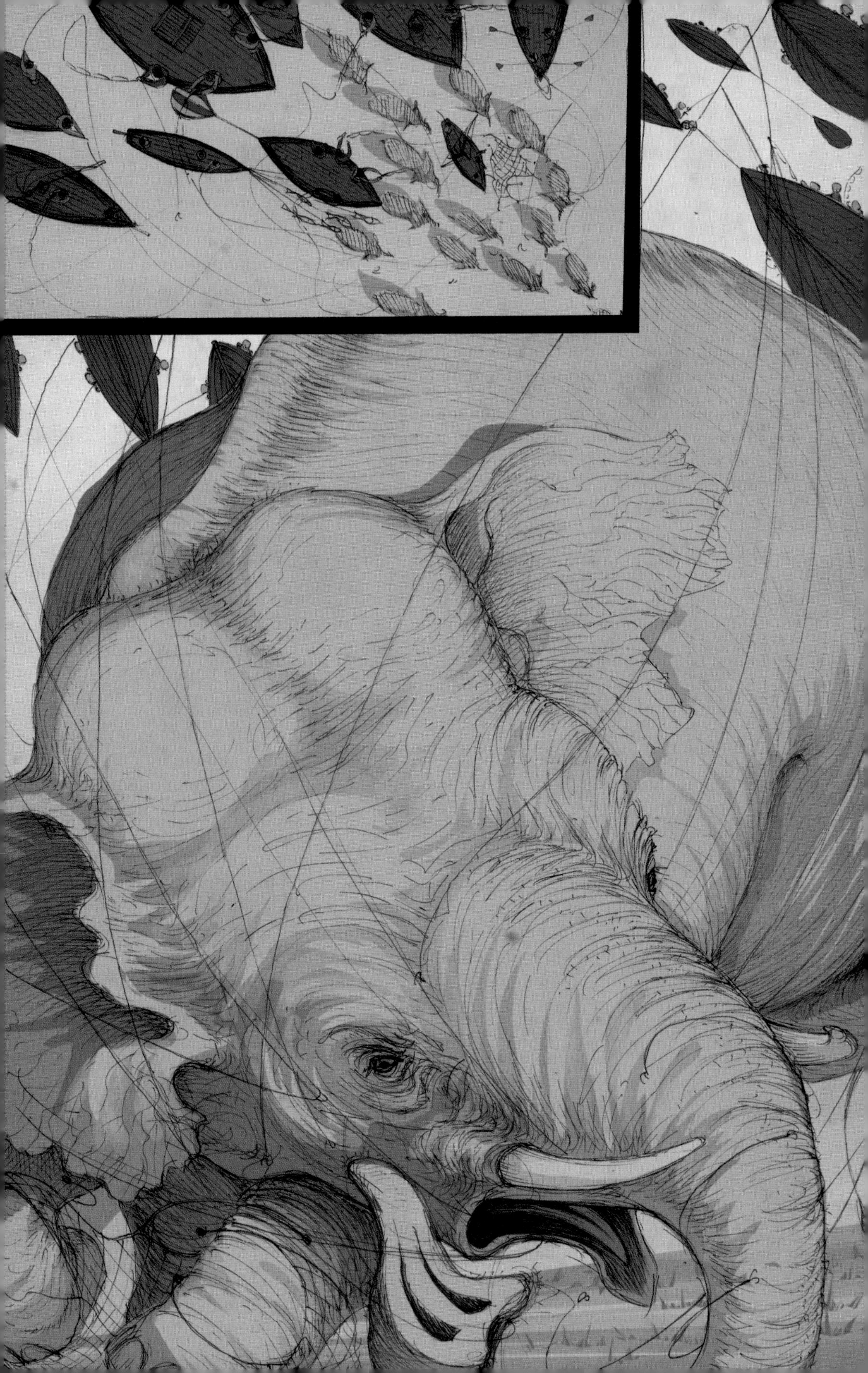

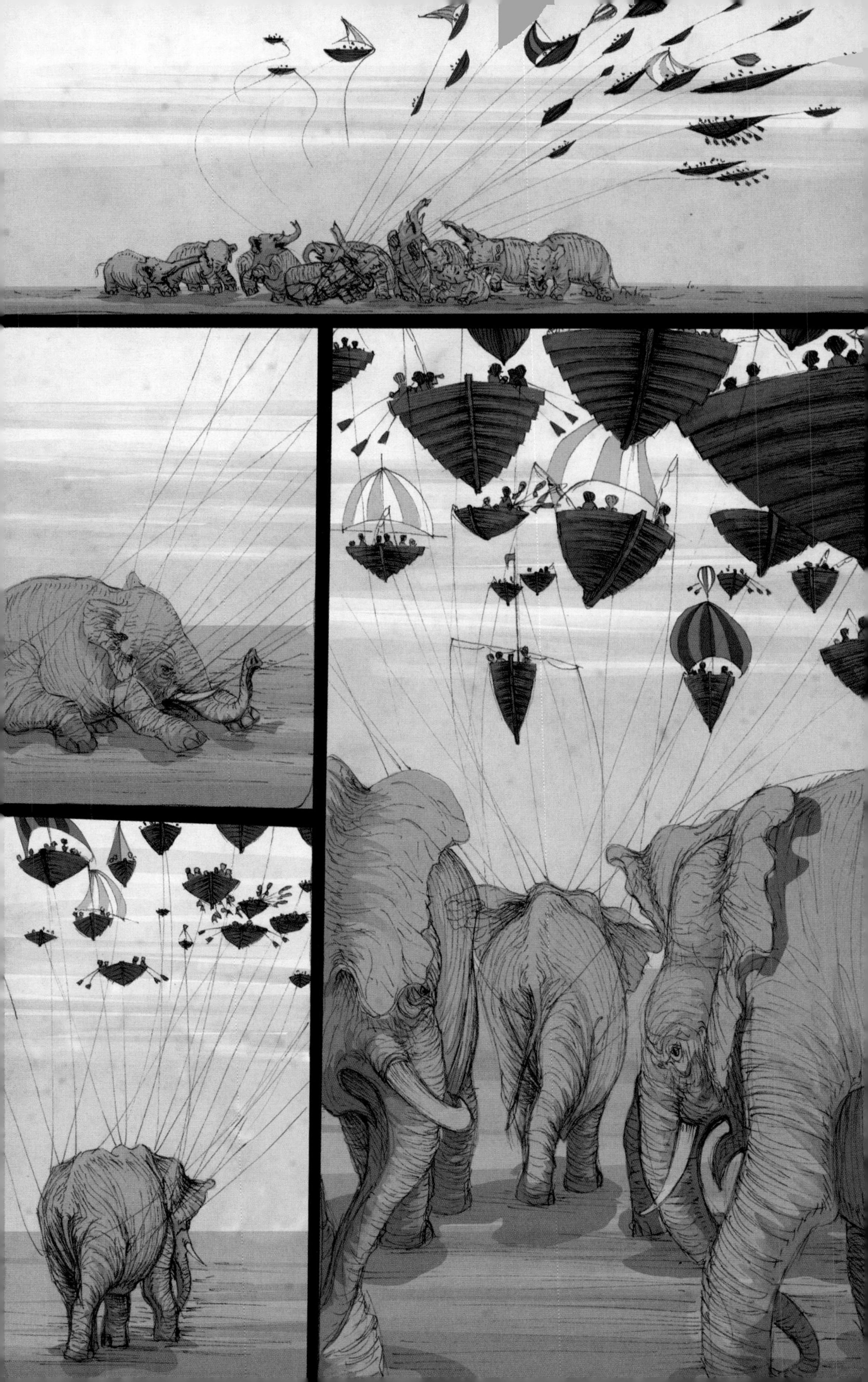

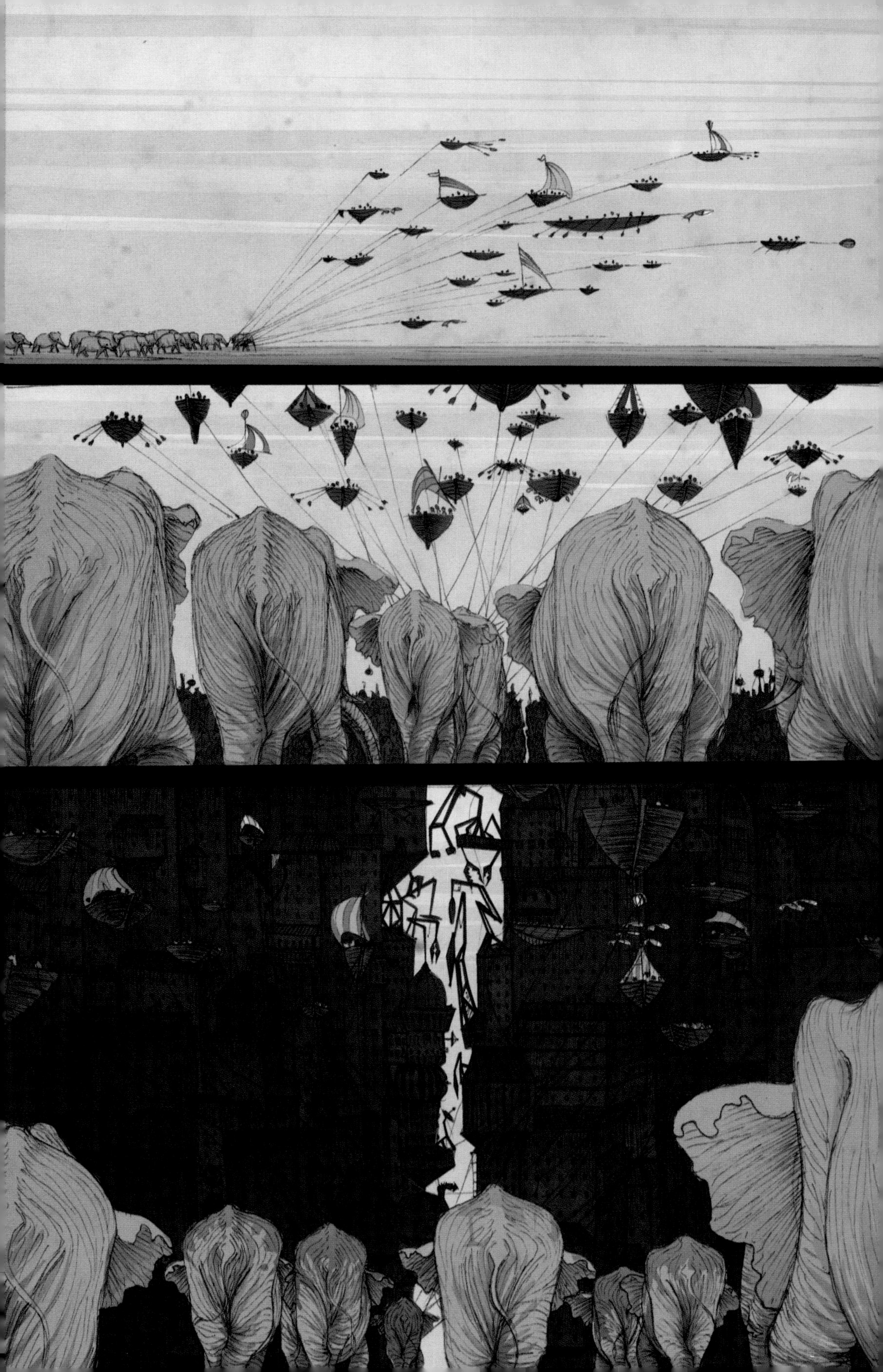

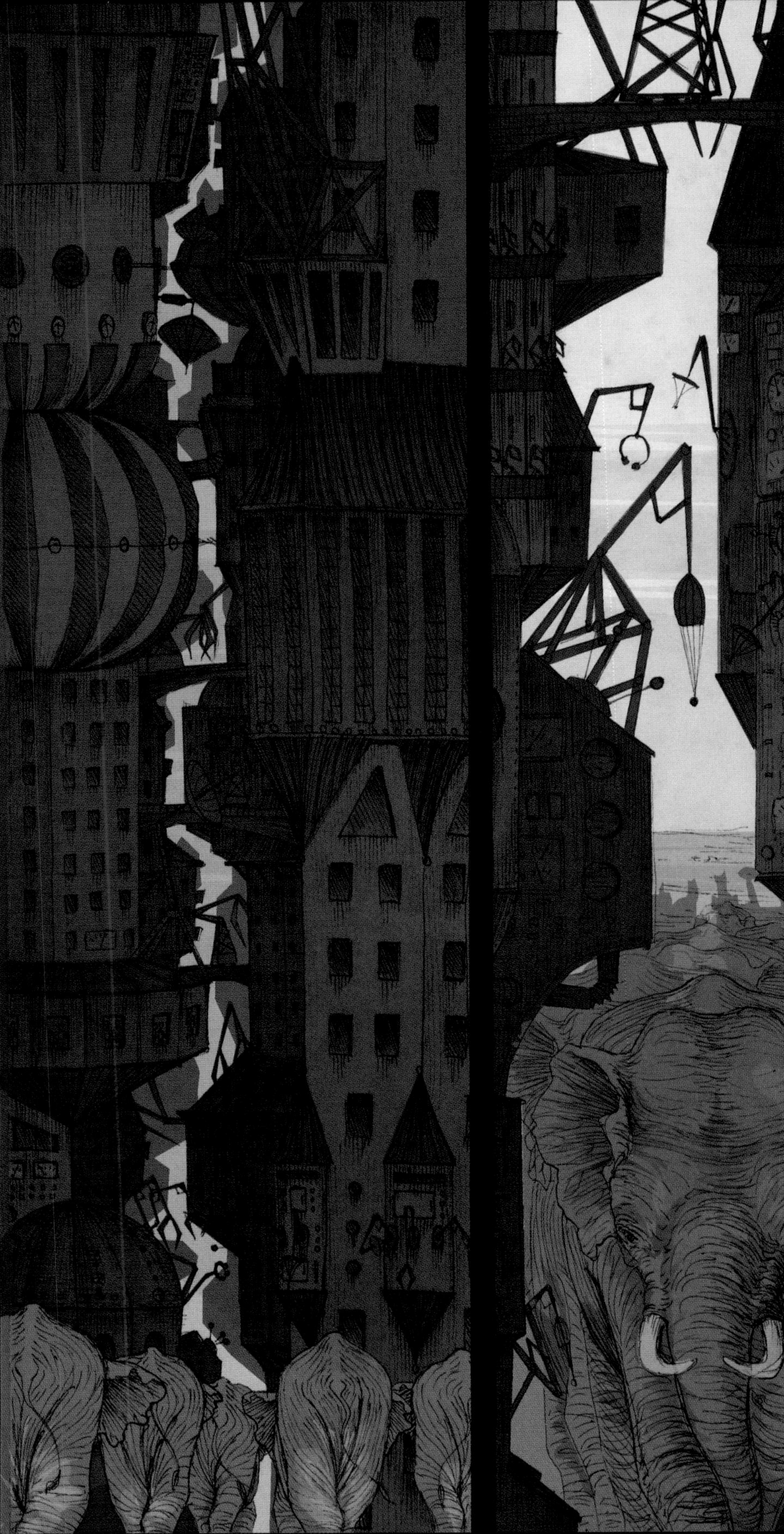

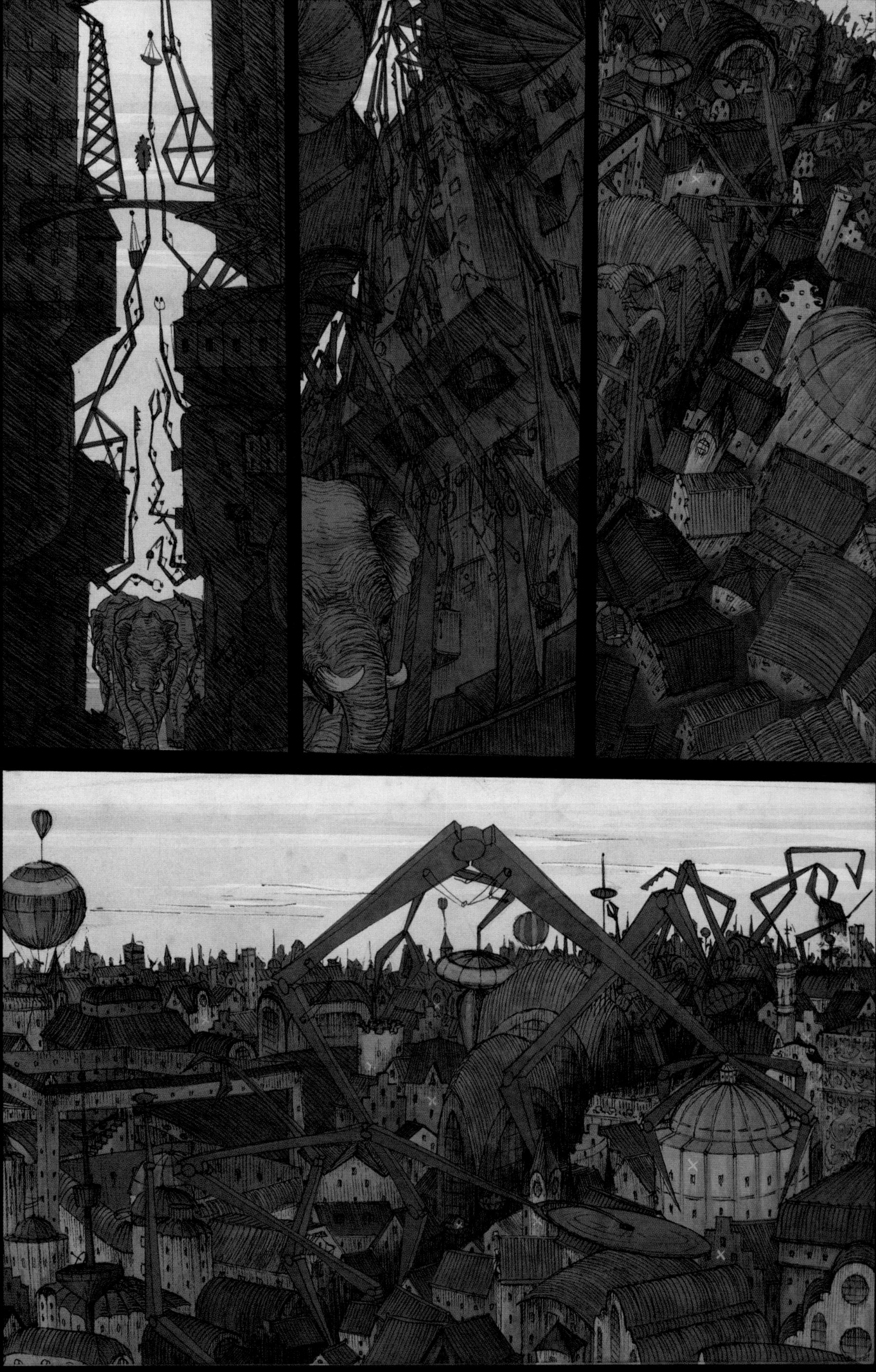

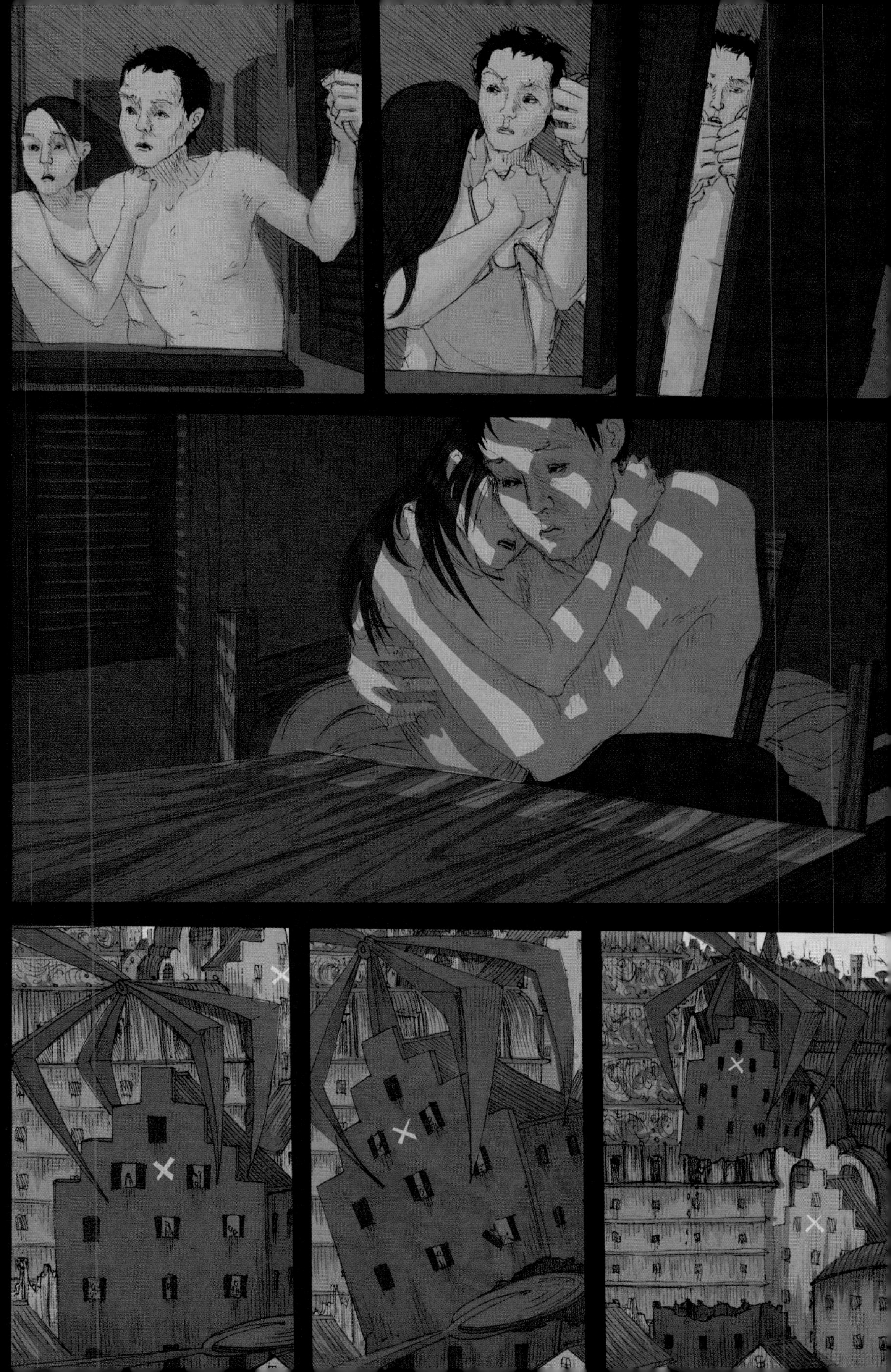

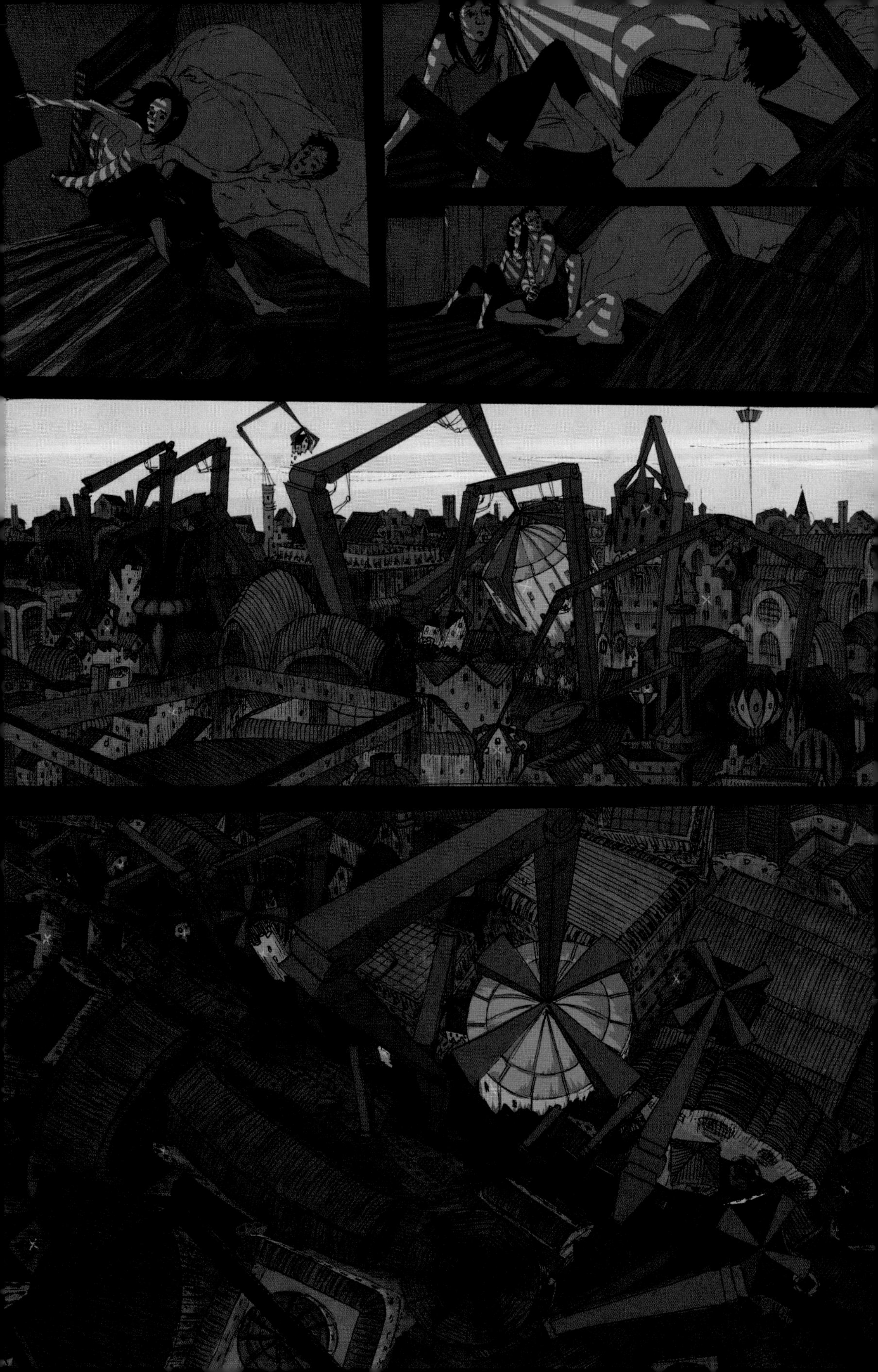

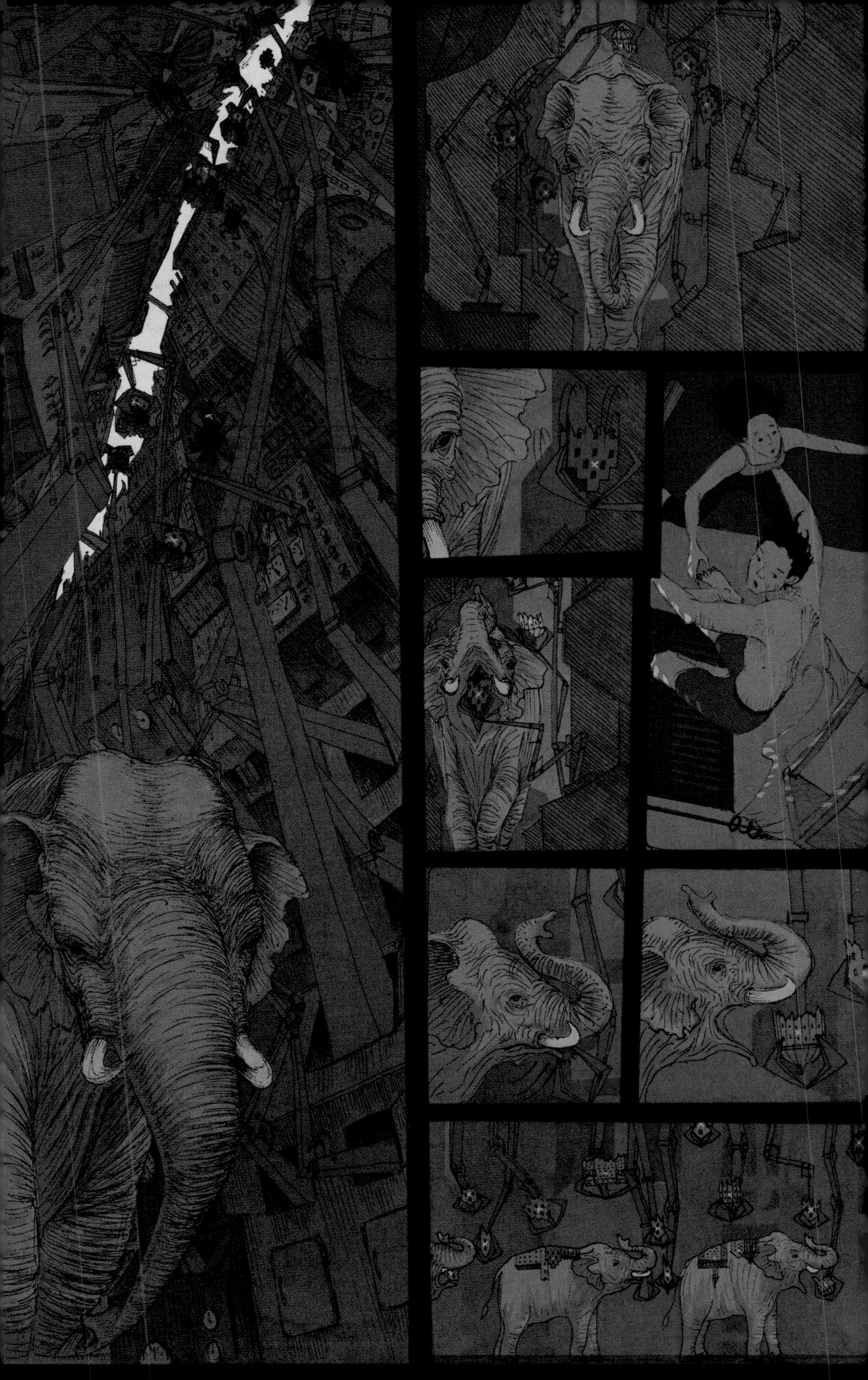

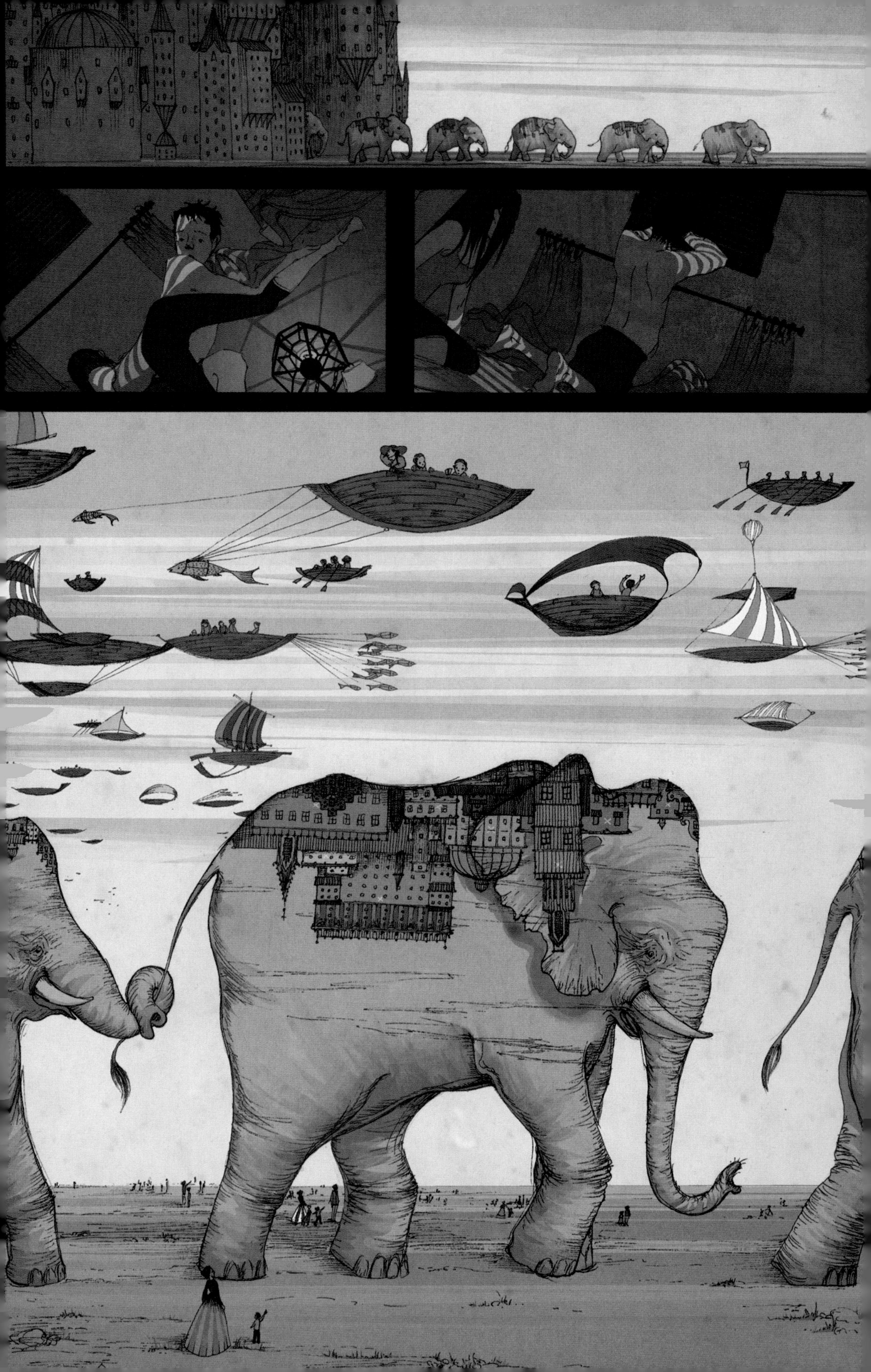

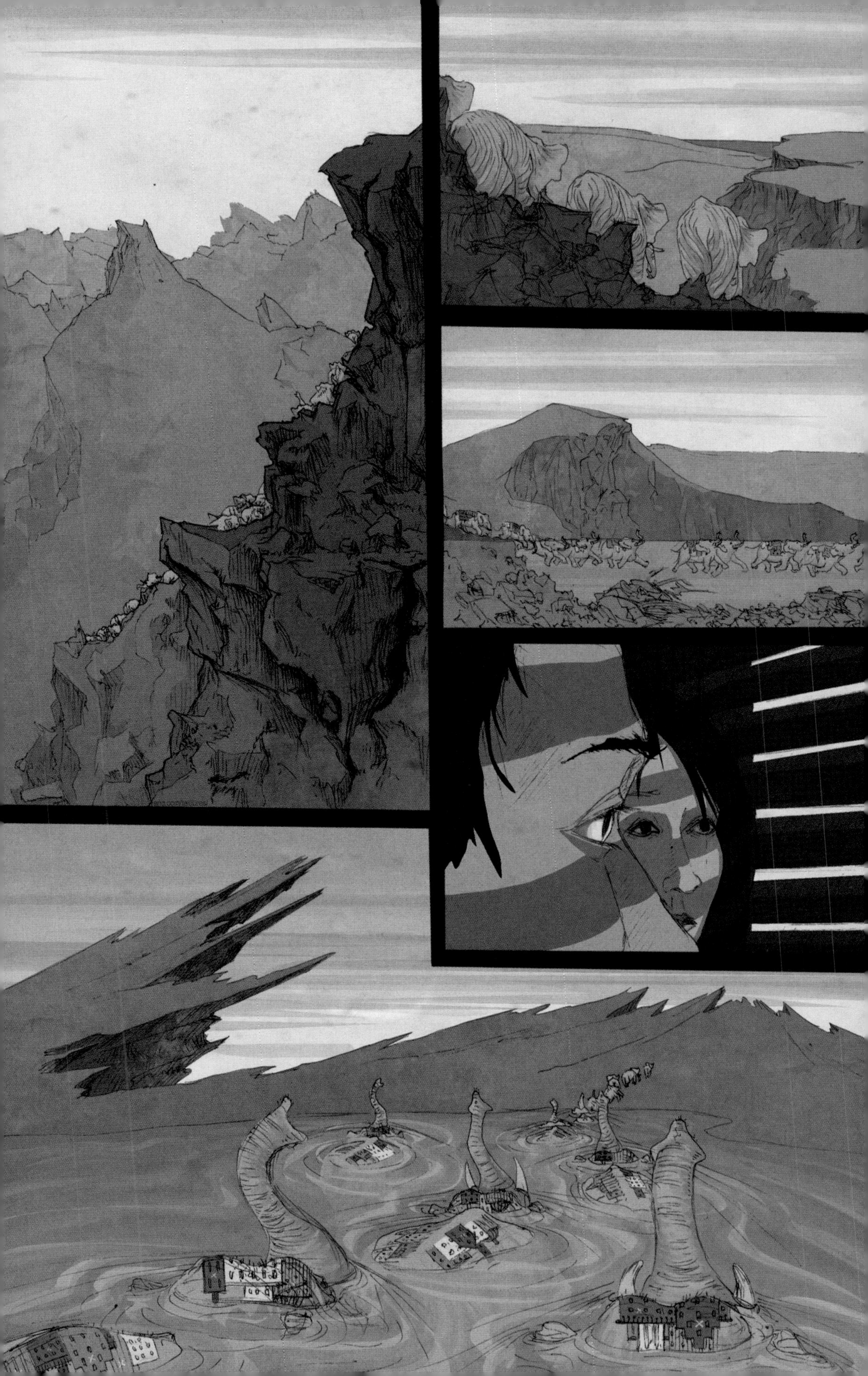

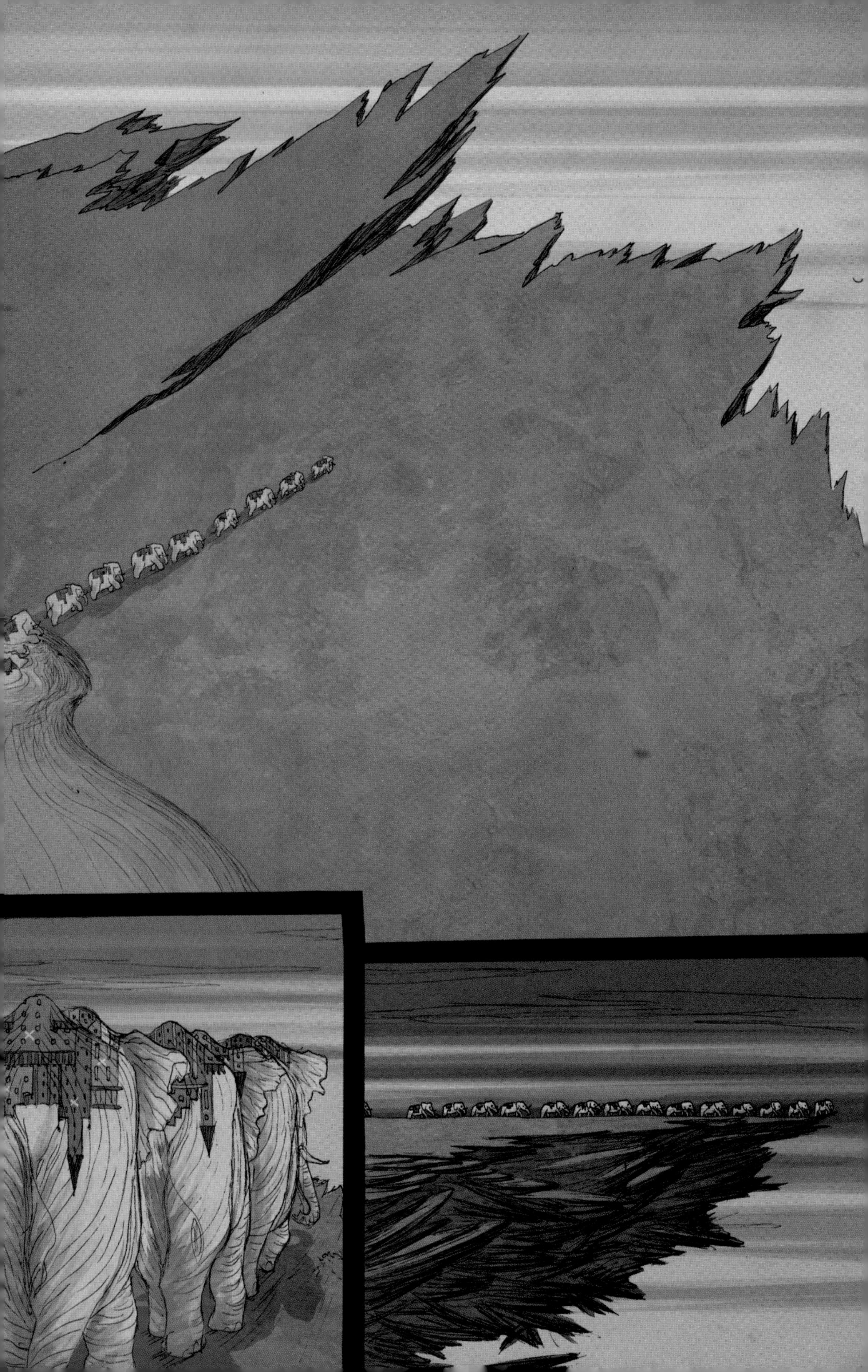

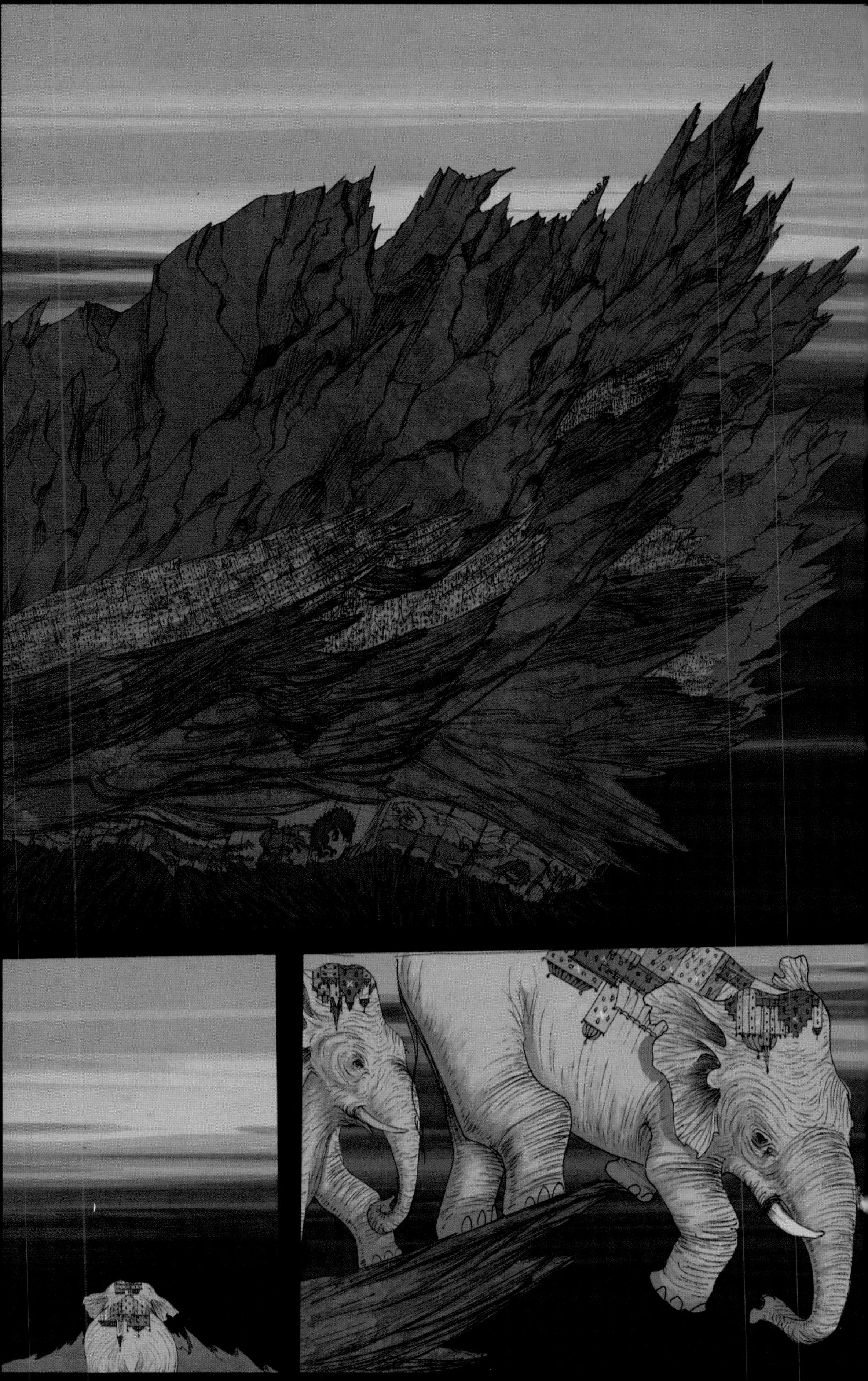

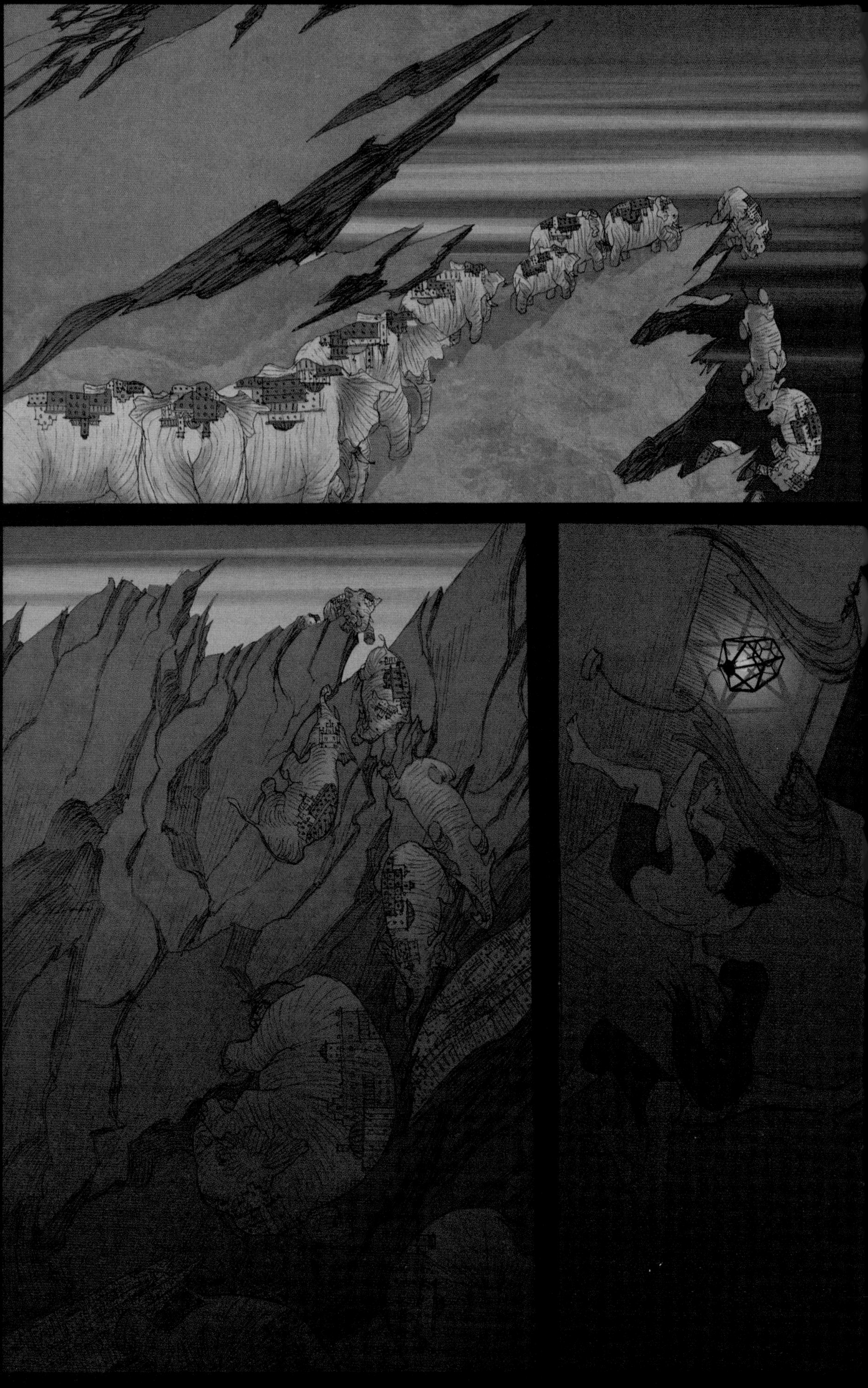

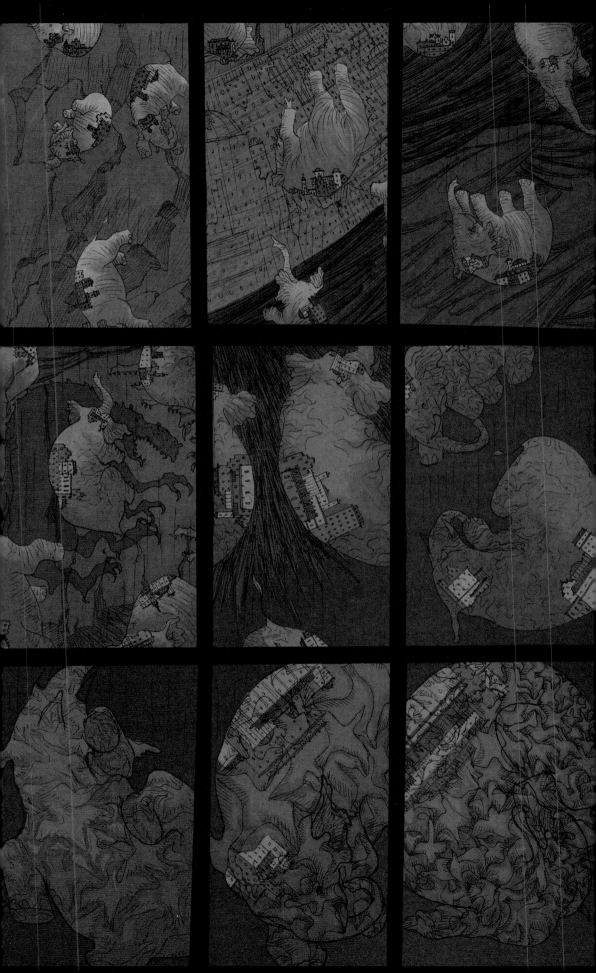

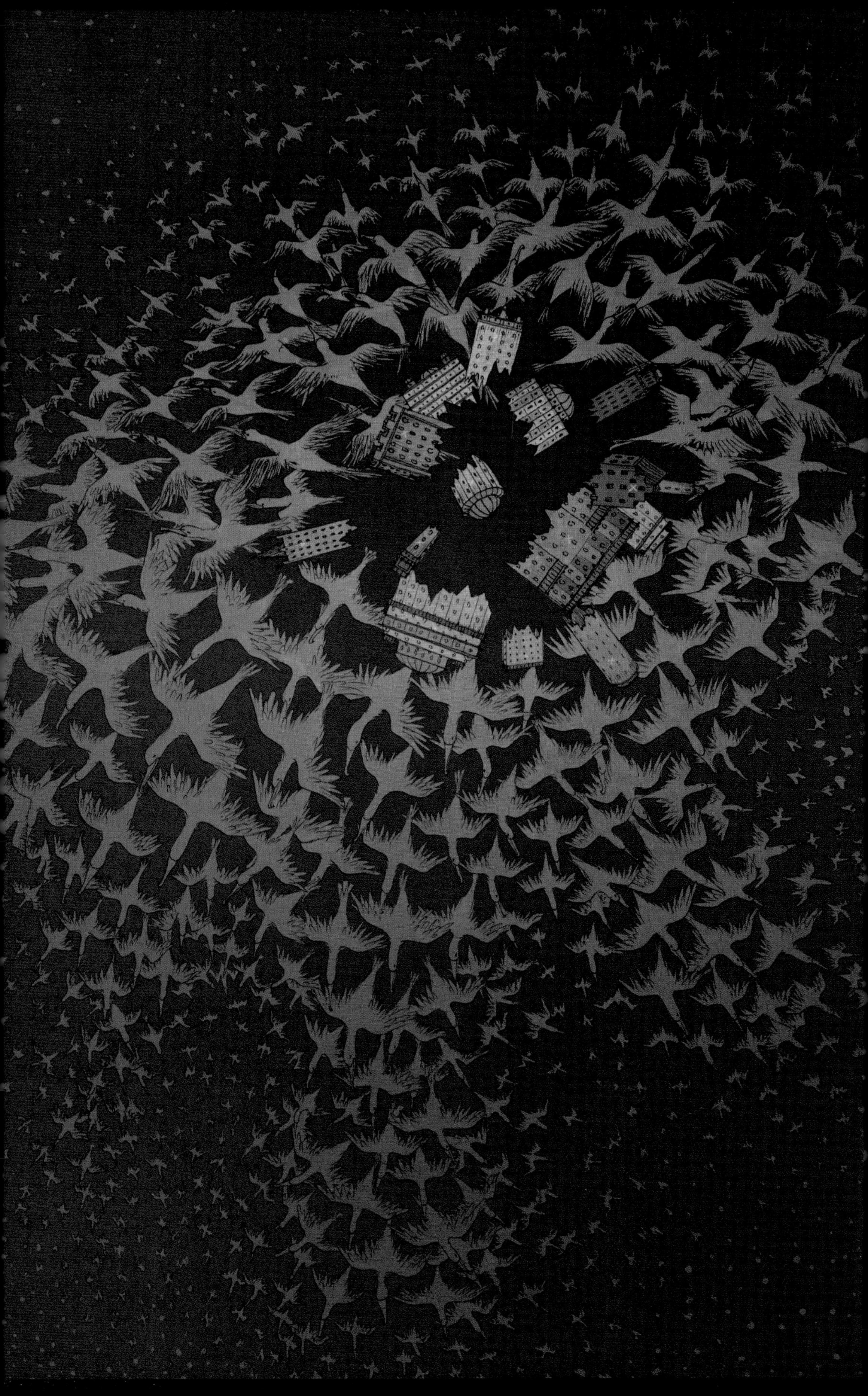

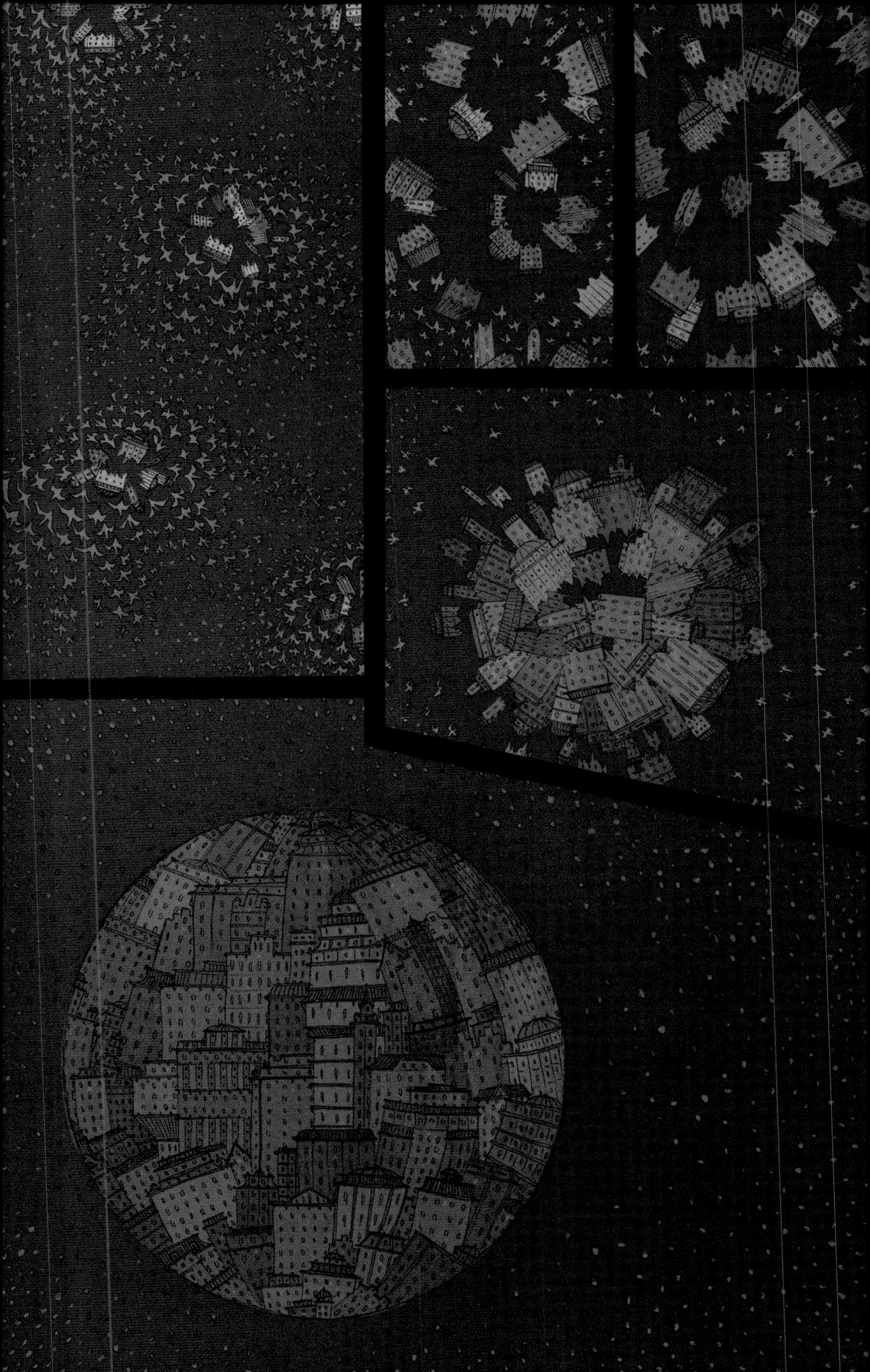

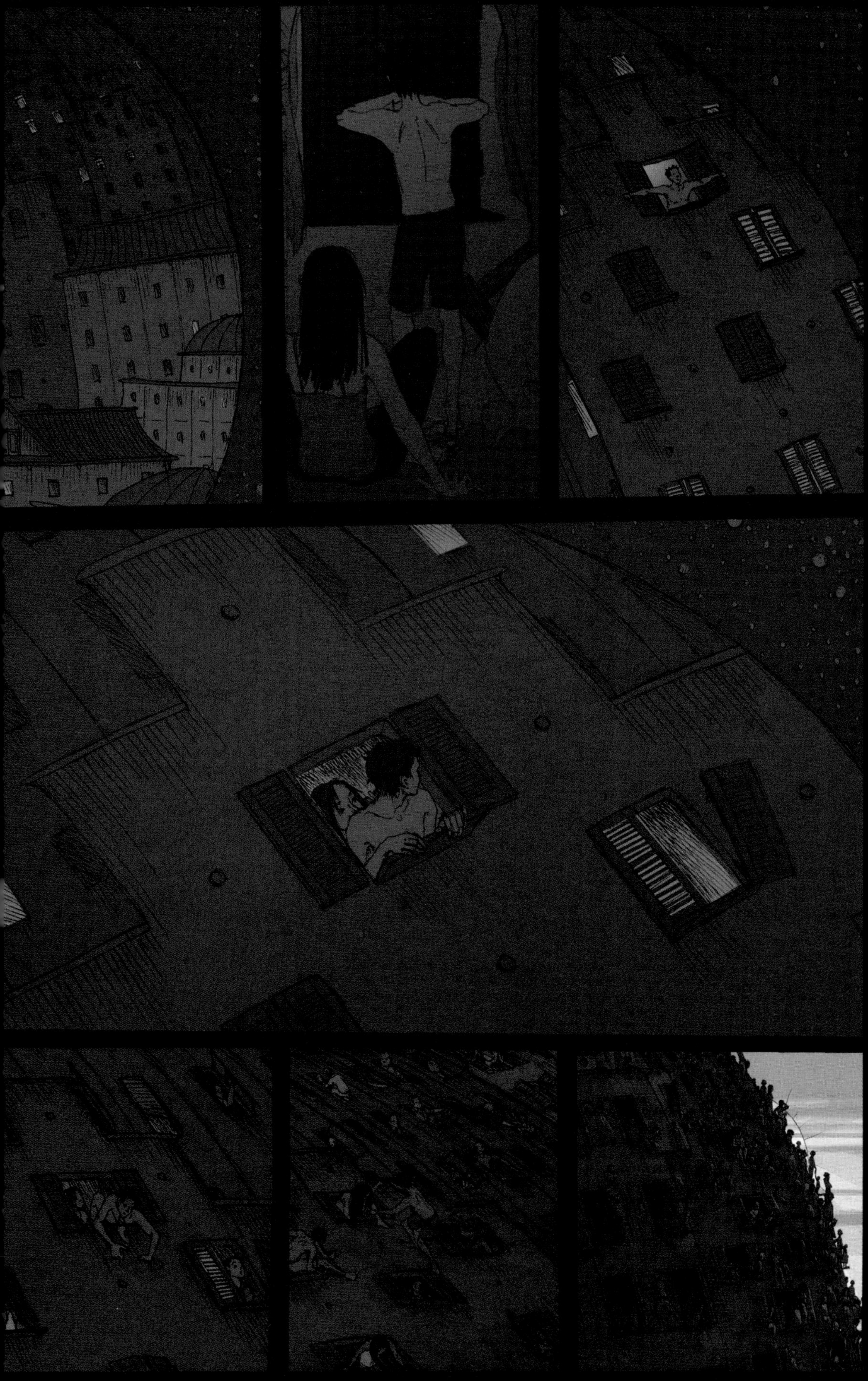

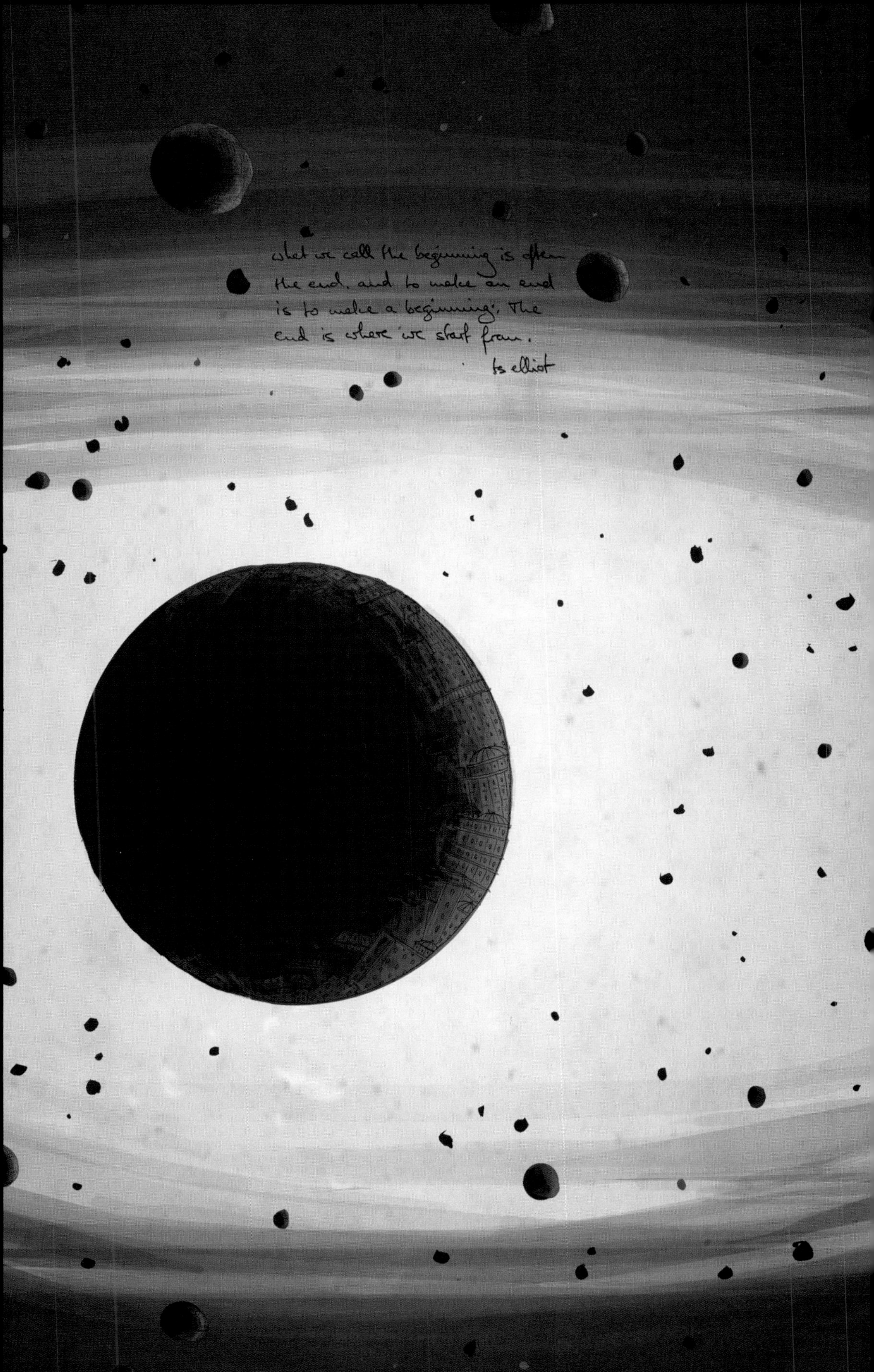
what we call the beginning is often
the end. and to make an end
is to make a beginning. The
end is where we start from.
ts elliot

the perfect spot

by Phil Craven

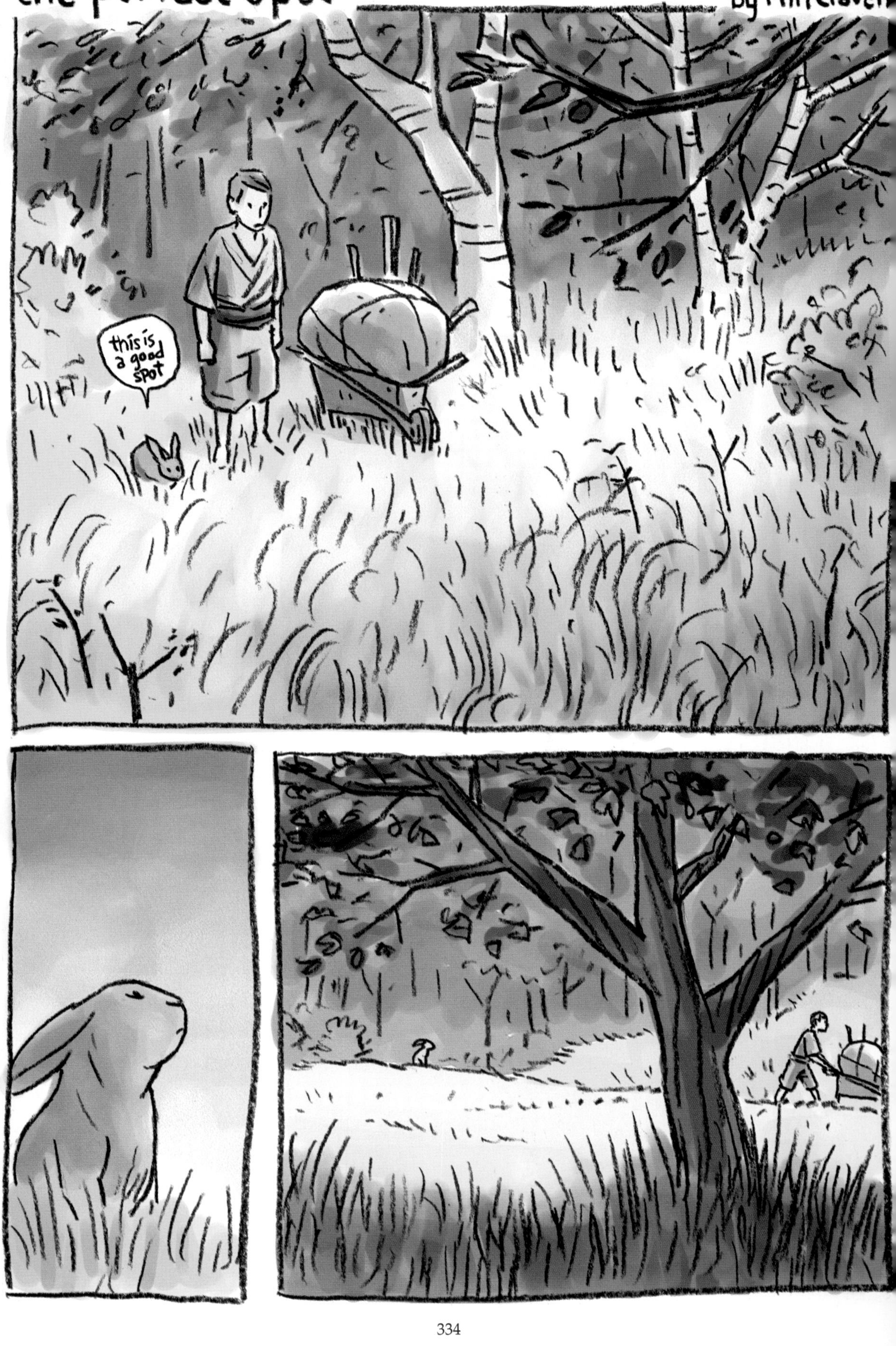
this is a good spot

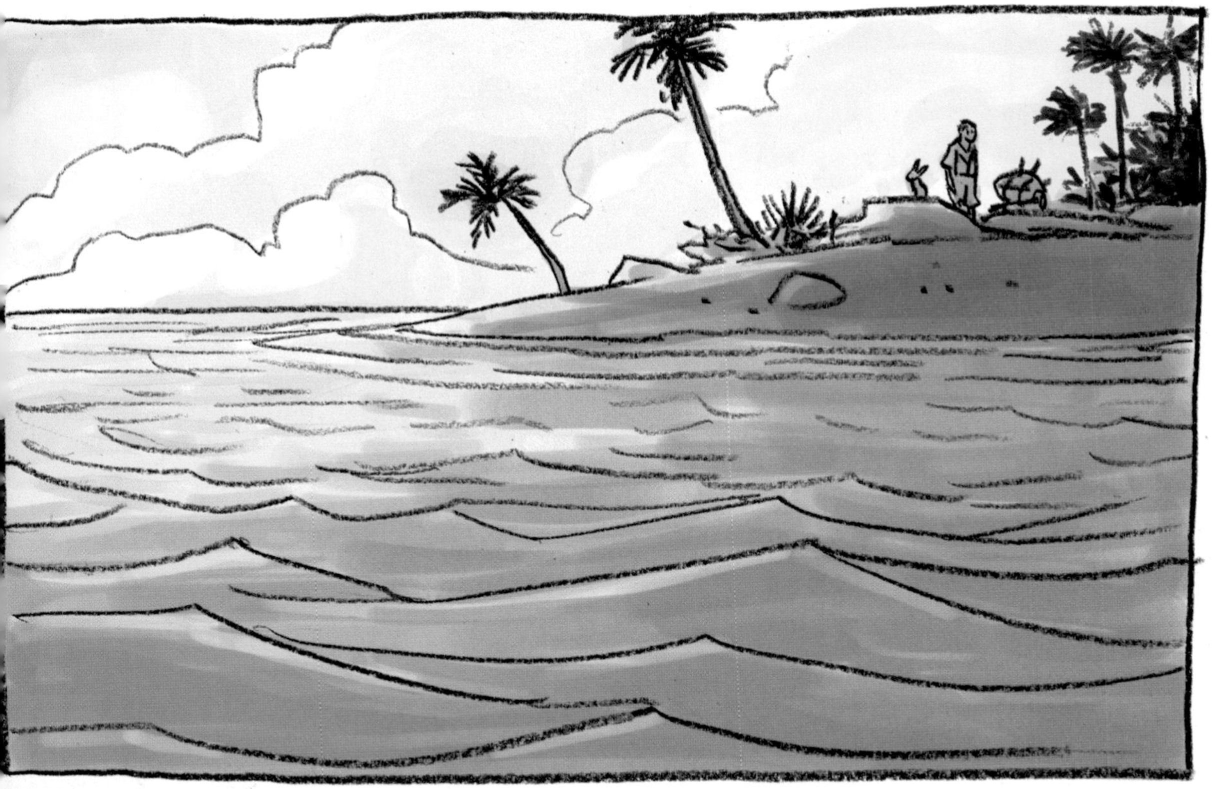

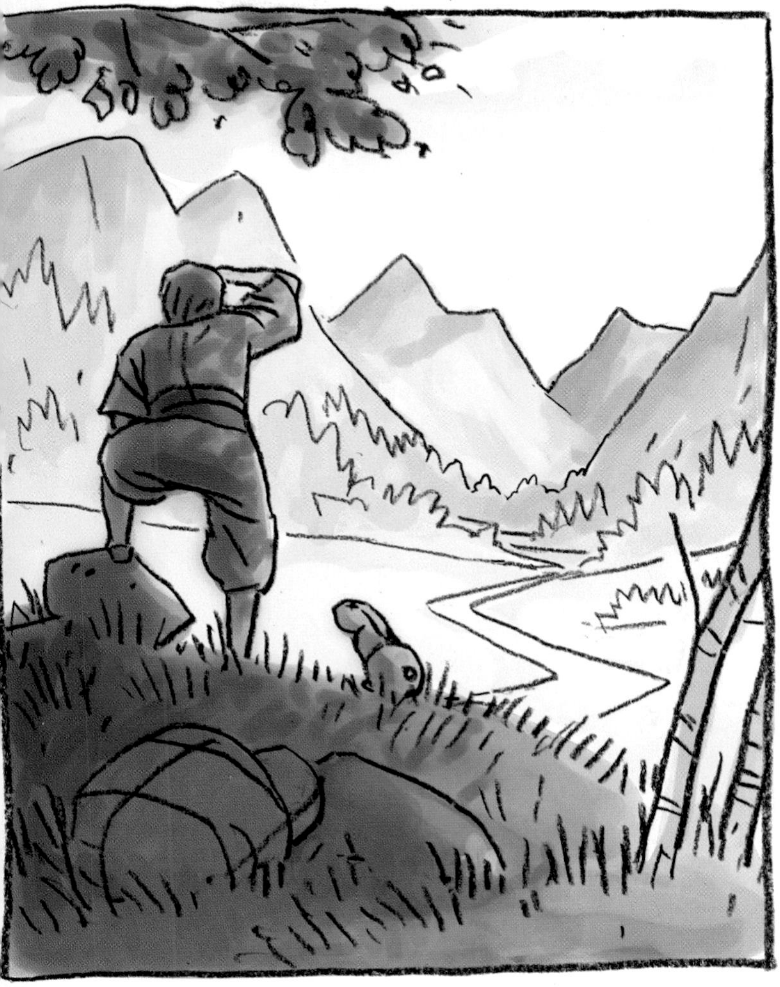

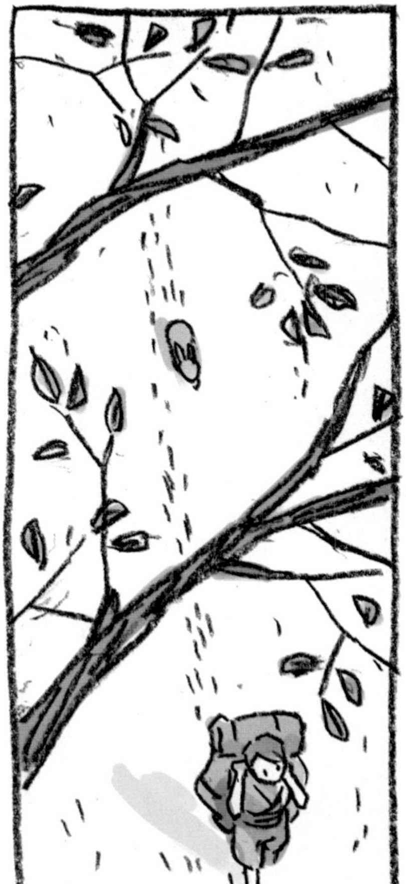

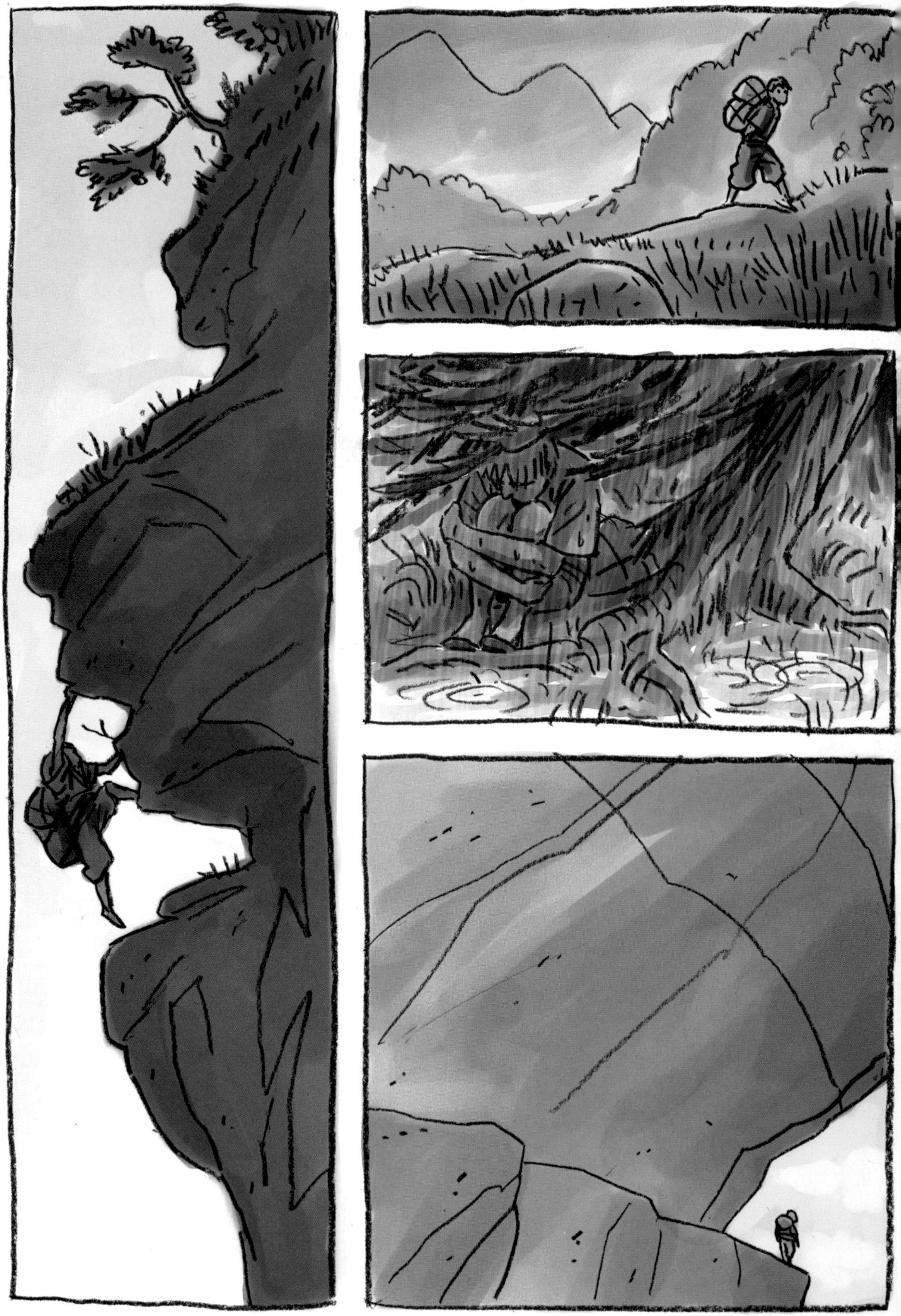

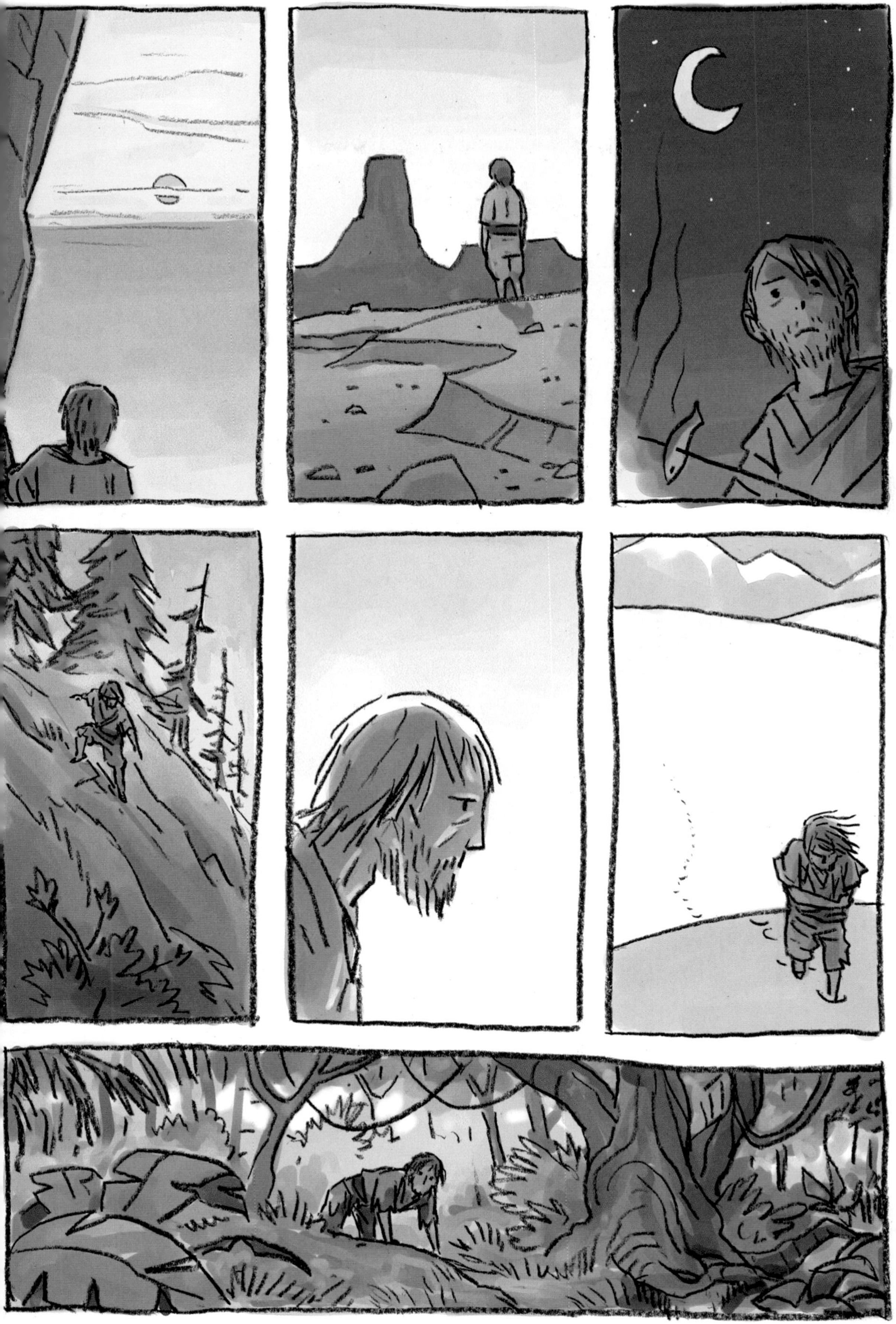

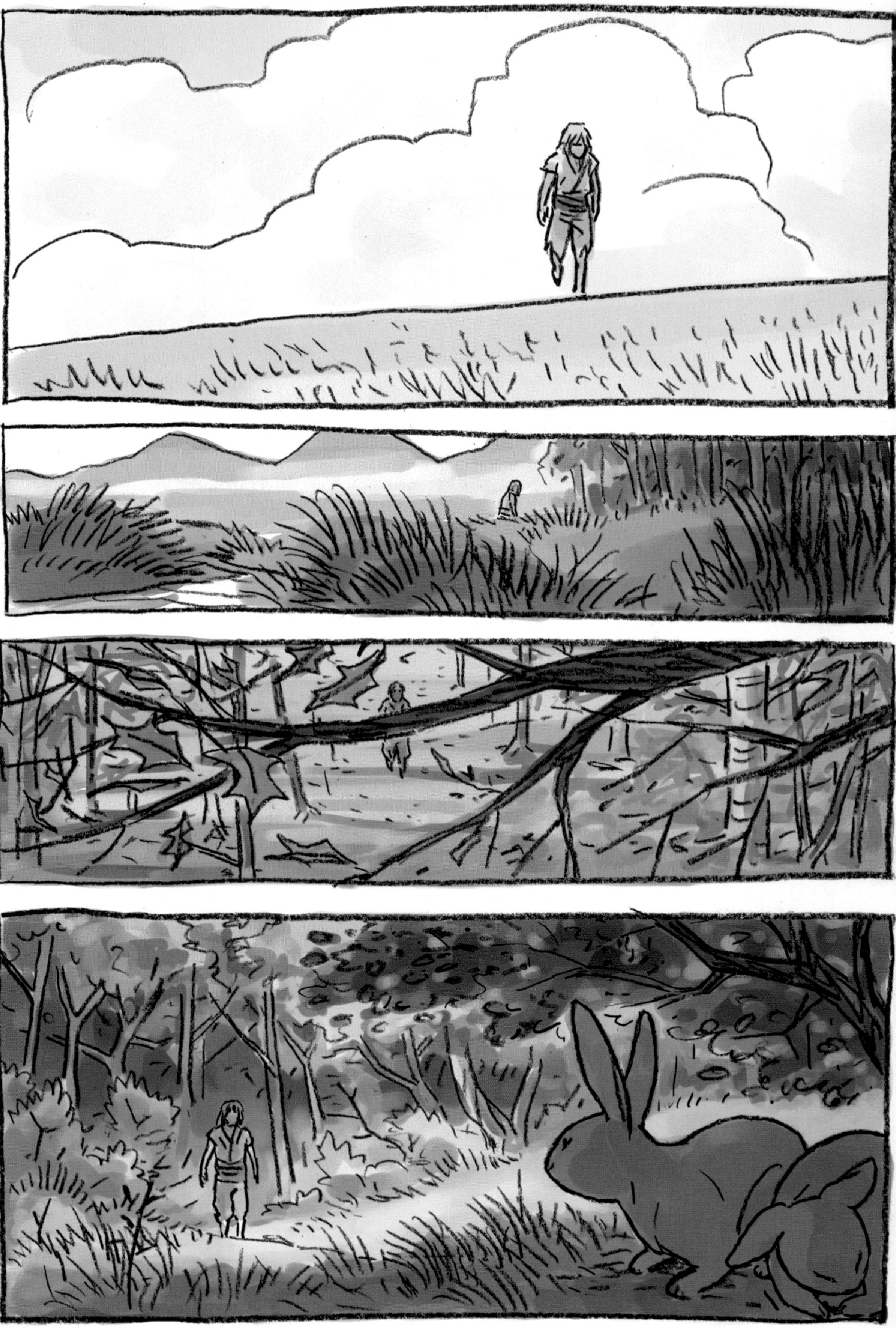

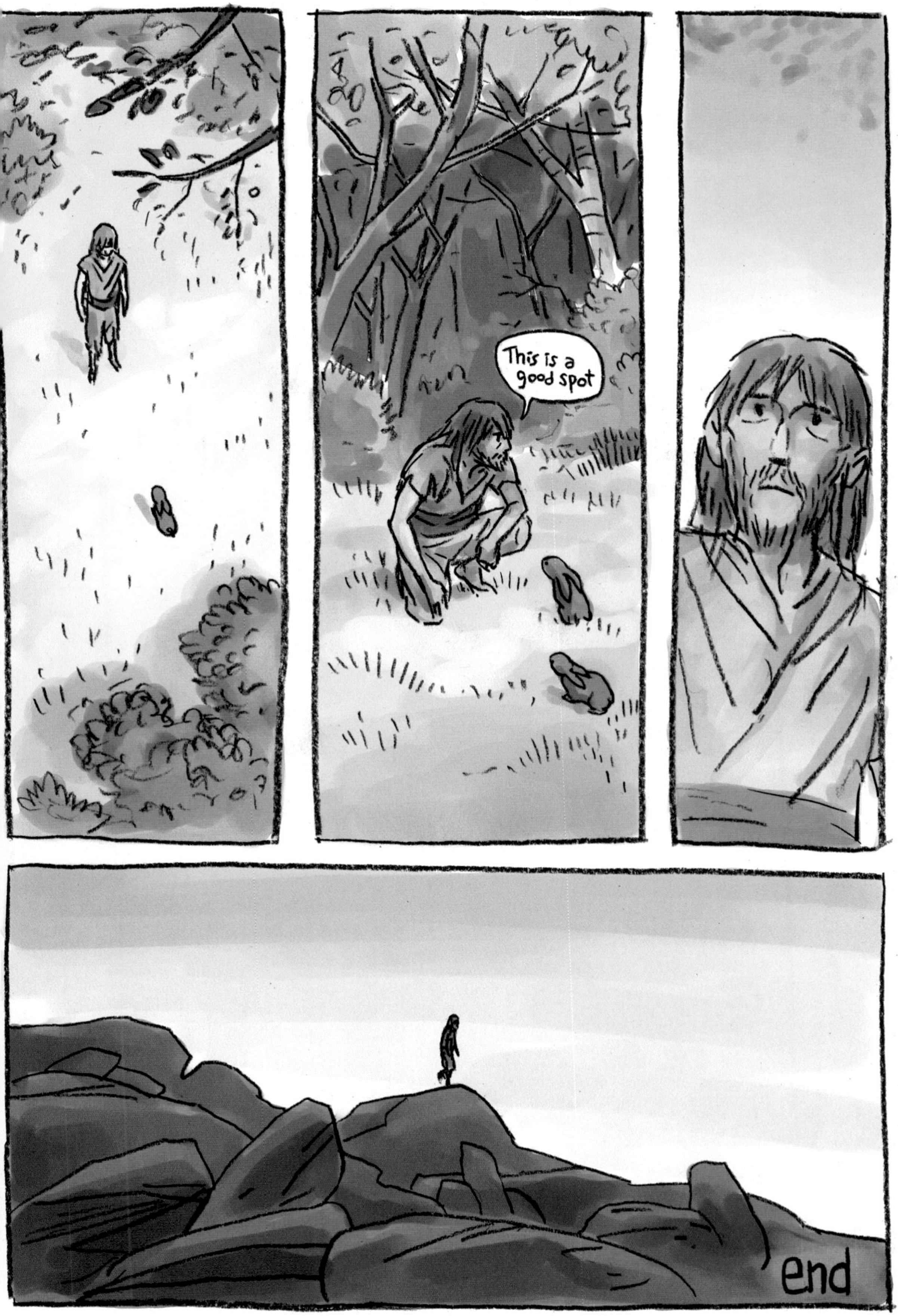
This is a good spot
end

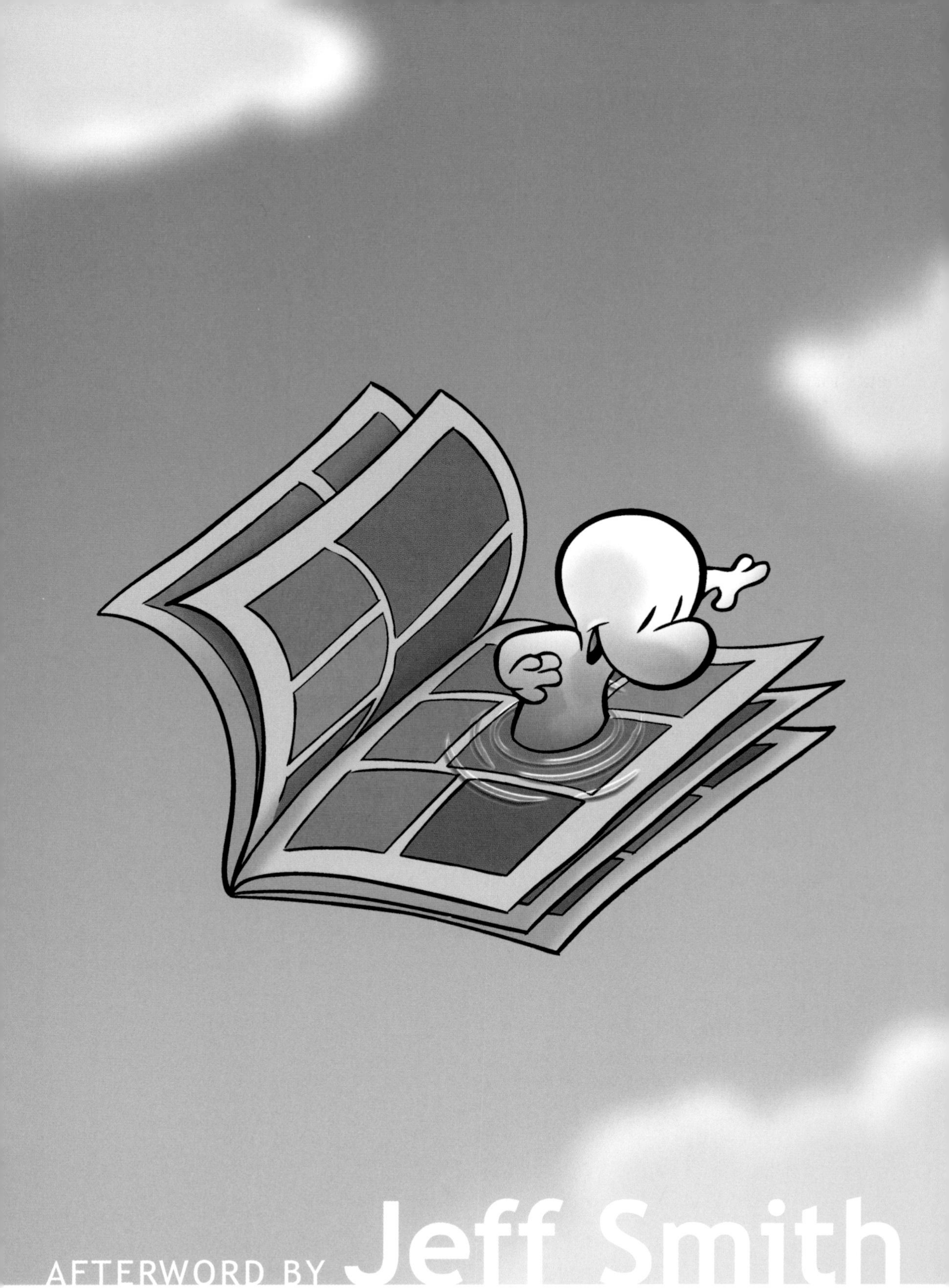

AFTERWORD BY Jeff Smith

the award-winning creator of ***Bone***

Here, at the end of the book, I find myself thinking this the best anthology of imagination since Moebius, Druillet, and Farkas launched *Métal Hurlant* (*Heavy Metal*) over thirty years ago.

These stories explore the human condition through the looking glass of fables, wonder, pathos, and humor. Graham Annable's "Roomie-Pal!," done with Harvey Kurtzman–like timing, is wide-eyed hilarious and not a little haunting. And if anyone saw the ending of Amy Kim Ganter's "Food from the Sea" coming, I'll eat my hat. . . . Hans Christian Andersen would have been proud. The simple and elegant metaphor that Thomas Herpich uses in "Farewell, Little Karla" is so insightful, I'm jealous I didn't think of it first.

This is a visually sophisticated group (it seems like half of them work in film), and they understand the tools of comics and storytelling. There is movement on these pages. The panels blur and merge into a visual slurry that lives and breathes.

A generation of cartoonists born on the Internet, the *Flight* crew has instant access to one another all over the globe. The field of comics has changed in the last twenty years, and along with the advent of graphic novels, the Web is the brightest factor in the expanding art form. Part of the secret is the online forums where they meet up and critique one another's work. I have watched as projects go from rough pencils to inks to fully rendered works of art; changing at each stage—bending, stretching, reaching for that right line or perfect piece of timing—all coached by one of the sharpest peer groups in the world.

In this fourth volume of *Flight,* the raw, highly talented young artists have matured. Go back and flip through to your favorite stories. They hold up on rereading.

Let your imagination soar.

Jeff Smith
February 21, 2007

FLIGHT: VOLUME FOUR CONTRIBUTORS

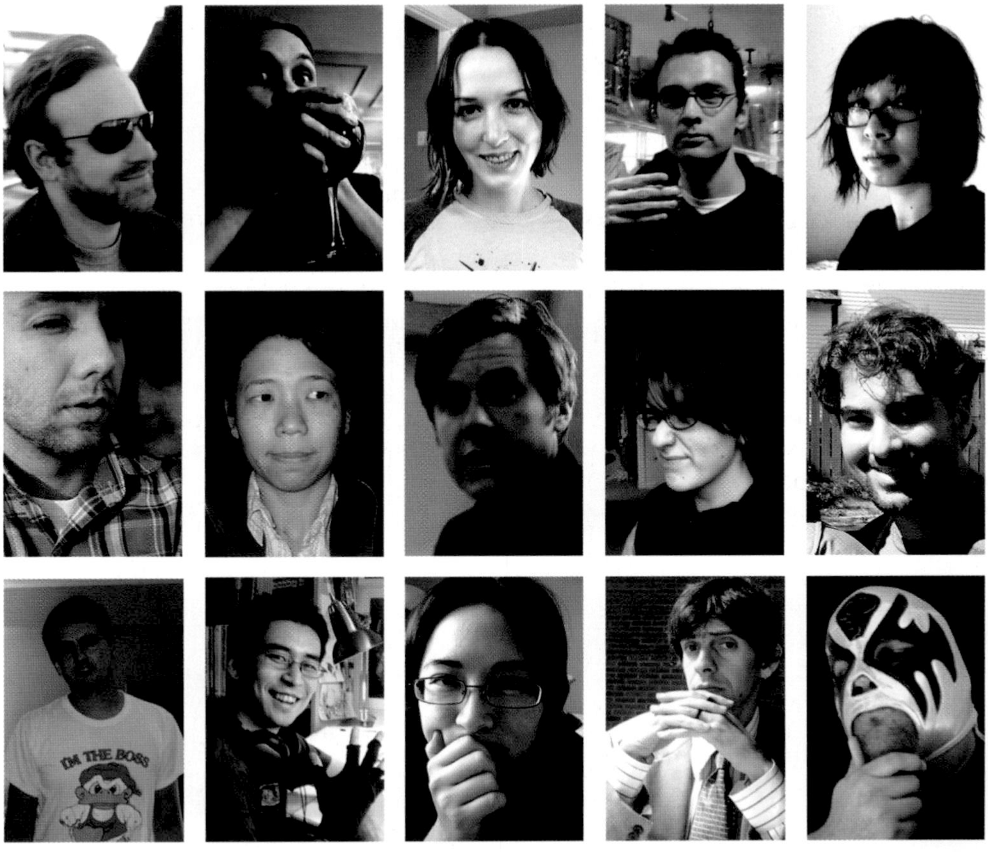
I'M THE BOSS

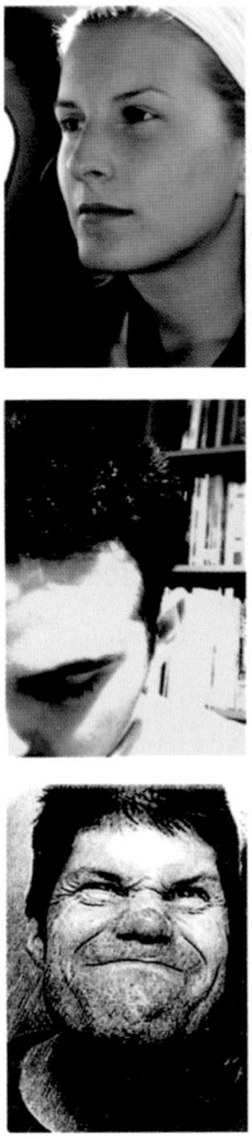

From left to right:

Top Row: Michel Gagné, JP Ahonen, Sarah Mensinga, Graham Annable, Clio Chiang
2nd Row: Jon Klassen, Lark Pien, Scott Campbell, Vera Brosgol, Azad Injejikian
3rd Row: Israel Sanchez, Kazu Kibuishi, Amy Kim Ganter, Fábio Moon, Joel Carroll
4th Row: Andrea Offermann, Joey Weiser, Dave Roman, Raina Telgemeier, Neil Babra
5th Row: Ovi Nedelcu, Ryan Estrada, Nicolas "Bannister" Seigneret, Phil Craven, Thomas Herpich
Bottom Row: Pascal Campion

After cutting his hair short, **JP Ahonen** suffered from a severe identity crisis. Word on the street is that he now resembles a hungover chimpanzee. What hasn't changed though, is JP's love for comics and storytelling. He continues to draw his *Northern Overexposure* comic strips and daydreams of publishing his *Druids* stories. [www.jpahonen.com]

Enjoying life with his wife in Portland, Oregon, **Graham Annable** is the creator behind the *Grickle* books and *Stickleback,* and editor and contributor of the *Hickee* anthology. [www.grickle.com]

Neil Babra currently resides in the San Francisco Bay Area and has created several comics and illustrations for various anthologies and children's magazines. He's working on a graphic novel adaptation for a large publisher as well as his own projects. You can find more of his work at www.neilcomics.com.

Bannister was born in 1973 in France. He currently lives near the Alps with his lovely girlfriend and no pets. His new story, *Les Enfants d'Ailleurs,* was published in January 2007 (Dupuis Publishing). He has collaborated on many projects both in Europe and overseas. [www.bannister.fr]

Vera Brosgol lives in Portland, Oregon, where she draws storyboards for animation. She enjoys painting, knitting, and buying shoes on the Internet. More of her work can be examined at www.verabee.com.

Scott Campbell, aka ScottC, is a regular contributor to *Hickee* comics and has appeared in a number of other comic anthologies over the years. *Pyramid Car* and *Advanced Talk* are sweet comics by ScottC. He does a comic every morning at work and puts it here: www.doublefine.com. At Double Fine he designs video games like Psychonauts. Other times, he paints. [www.scott-c.blogspot.com]

Pascal Campion comes from the south of France where he spent a good deal of his time riding his bike around. After going to art school in the northern part of France, he decided one day to try the United States to see what it would be like. He never went back. He now lives in beautiful San Francisco with his lovely wife and their dog, where he still enjoys riding his bike up and down the hills, and enjoys all the Indian food he can find.

Joel Carroll lives in Central Florida and designs video games, while teaching others to do the same. He likes to dabble in comics and promises to do more than that someday. [www.joelcarroll.com]

Clio Chiang is from Vancouver, British Columbia, where she is currently a working stiff in the animation industry on such shows as *Pucca* and *Ricky Sprocket.* She enjoys free time, green tea, and cooking. Occasionally she posts scribblings to www.cliochiang.com.

Phil Craven is from Georgia. He lives in California. He draws storyboards at DreamWorks Animation. He eats cereal and draws some more comics. [www.bluepillow.net]

Ryan Estrada has slept on a park bench during a typhoon in Japan (twice), and was involved in a coup at a South Korean publishing company, attacked by wild dogs in Thailand, an illegal immigrant to Burma, an ambassador to Australia, and forcibly ejected from Canada. He also makes comics which appear at www.ryanestrada.com.

Michel Gagné was born in Québec, Canada, and has had a highly successful career drawing characters and special effects for animated and live-action feature films such as *The Iron Giant* and *Osmosis Jones.* His independant short film, *Prelude to Eden,* is a favorite among animation students and teachers and has played in festivals throughout the world. Michel and his wife created Gagné International Press in 1998, and he has been writing, illustrating, and publishing books and comics ever since. [www.gagneint.com]

Amy Kim Ganter is the author and artist for the two-part romantic comedy *Sorcerers & Secretaries,* as well as the online comic *Reman Mythology.* She lives in California with her talented husband, Kazu, where they create comics and good times. Amy has a giant world map hanging on the wall above her drawing desk. [www.felaxx.com]

Thomas Herpich has been living in the mountains of North Carolina for the past two years. He spends his days drawing, tending to his chickens, and figuring out how to live without a job. [www.thomasherpich.com]

Azad Injejikian was born into a patrician family, the gens Julia, which claims descent from Iulus, son of the Trojan prince Aeneas, himself the son of the goddess Venus. Once he reached adulthood, he went on to write potty jokes on message boards and draw comics for the enjoyment of others. [www.guerrilla-comics.com]

Kazu Kibuishi is the editor and art director of *Flight:* Volume Four. He is also the creator of *Copper, Daisy Kutter,* and the upcoming graphic novel series *Amulet.* He lives and works in Alhambra, California, with his wife and fellow comic artist, Amy Kim Ganter. [www.boltcity.com]

Jon Klassen lives in Portland, Oregon, and works as an illustrator/procrastinator. He likes Airedales, paper cutouts, and digital watches. [www.burstofbeaden.com]

Originally from Toronto, **Sarah Mensinga** lives with her husband and two misbehaving cats in Texas. She has been an animator and concept designer and is now writing a graphic novel. In her free time she likes to write other stories, cook, and go dancing. [www.sarahmensinga.com]

Fábio Moon is the author, with his twin brother, of *Ursula* and *De:TALES,* and he makes comics and tells stories all day long. He also loves to dance. He reads less than he wants to and writes less than he should. [www.10paezinhos.com.br]

After two terrifying years at med school, **Andrea Offermann** found refuge at an art school and started by learning how to sharpen a pencil. Five years later she prefers pen and ink but is still in love with art of any kind. [www.andreaoffermann.com]

Ovi Nedelcu is the creator of *Pigtale* and currently works at Laika Studios. He balances working in print and animation. He lives in Portland, Oregon, with his wife and two kids. Ovi believes in three things: God, love, and human stupidity. [www.ovinedelcu.com and www.pigtalecomic.com]

Lark Pien draws the comics *Long Tail Kitty, Mr. Boombha,* and *Stories from the Ward.* When she is not drawing, she's painting. [www.larkpien.com and larkpien.blogspot.com]

Dave Roman lives in Astoria, New York, with his talented wife, Raina Telgemeier. He works at *Nickelodeon* magazine, draws a web comic called *Astronaut Elementary,* and is partially responsible for several comics projects including *Agnes Quill: An Anthology of Mystery* (Slave Labor Graphics), *Jax Epoch & the Quicken Forbidden* (AiT/PlanetLar), *Teen Boat* (Cryptic Press), and the video game art site LifeMeterComics.com. His story "The Great Bunny Migration" appeared in *Flight:* Volume Three. [www.yaytime.com]

Israel Sanchez studied art at Cal State Fullerton. He now works as a freelance illustrator in La Habra, California. [www.israelsanchez.com and www.thethoseguys.com]

Raina Telgemeier is best known for her graphic novel adaptations of the *Baby-sitters Club* series from Scholastic's Graphix imprint. She has been self-publishing her short comic stories as Take-Out Comics since 2001, and serializes her true dental adventures in her web comic, *Smile: A Dental Drama.* She has also done work for DC Comics, *Nickelodeon* magazine, and numerous other print publications. She lives in Astoria, New York, with her sleepy husband, Dave Roman. [www.goRaina.com]

After graduating from the Savannah College of Art and Design, **Joey Weiser** moved back to his hometown of Bloomington, Indiana. His work can be found in several anthologies—including *Flight:* Volume Three—and fall 2007 will see the publication of his first graphic novel, *The Ride Home,* by Adhouse Books. He's pretty nervous about everything, but it'll be all right. [www.tragic-planet.com]